Lecture Notes in Computer Sci

Commenced Publication in 1973
Founding and Former Series Editors:
Gerhard Goos, Juris Hartmanis, and Jan van Leeuwen

Editorial Board

Sehun Kim Moti Yung
Hyung-Woo Lee (Eds.)

Information
Security Applications

8th International Workshop, WISA 2007
Jeju Island, Korea, August 27-29, 2007
Revised Selected Papers

 Springer

Volume Editors

Sehun Kim
KAIST, Department of Industrial Engineering
373-1, Guseong-dong, Yuseong-gu, Daejeon, 305-701, Korea
E-mail: shkim@kaist.ac.kr

Moti Yung
Google Inc.
Columbia University, Computer Science Department
RSA Laboratories
S.W.Mudd Building, New York, NY10027, USA
E-mail: moti@cs.columbia.edu

Hyung-Woo Lee
Hanshin University
School of Computer Engineering
411, Yangsan-dong, Osan, Gyunggi, 447-791, Korea
E-mail: hwlee@hs.ac.kr

Library of Congress Control Number: 2007942182

CR Subject Classification (1998): E.3, D.4.6, F.2.1, C.2, J.1, C.3, K.6.5

LNCS Sublibrary: SL 4 – Security and Cryptology

ISSN	0302-9743
ISBN-10	3-540-77534-X Springer Berlin Heidelberg New York
ISBN-13	978-3-540-77534-8 Springer Berlin Heidelberg New York

Springer is a part of Springer Science+Business Media

springer.com

© Springer-Verlag Berlin Heidelberg 2007
Printed in Germany

Typesetting: Camera-ready by author, data conversion by Scientific Publishing Services, Chennai, India
Printed on acid-free paper   SPIN: 12210664   06/3180   5 4 3 2 1 0

Preface

The 8th International Workshop on Information Security Applications (WISA 2007) was held on Jeju Island, Korea during August 27–29, 2007. The workshop was sponsored by the Korea Institute of Information Security and Cryptology (KIISC), the Electronics and Telecommunications Research Institute (ETRI) and the Ministry of Information and Communication (MIC).

WISA aims at providing a forum for professionals from academia and industry to present their work and to exchange ideas. The workshop covers all technical aspects of security applications, including cryptographic and non-cryptographic techniques.

We were very pleased and honored to serve as the Program Committee Co-chairs of WISA 2007. The Program Committee received 95 papers from 20 countries, and accepted 27 papers for the full presentation track. The papers were selected after an extensive and careful refereeing process in which each paper was reviewed by at least three members of the Program Committee.

In addition to the contributed papers, the workshop had three special talks. Moti Yung gave a tutorial talk, entitled "Somebody You Know: The Fourth Factor of Authentication." Kihong Park and Nasir Memon gave invited talks, entitled "Reactive Zero-Day Attack Protection" and "Securing Biometric Templates," respectively.

Many people deserve our gratitude for their generous contributions to the success of the workshop. We would like to thank all the people involved in the technical program and in organizing the workshop. We are very grateful to the Program Committee members and the external referees for their time and efforts in reviewing the submissions and selecting the accepted papers. We also express our special thanks to the Organizing Committee members for their hard work in organizing the workshop.

Last but not least, on behalf of all those involved in organizing the workshop, we would like to thank all the authors who submitted papers to this workshop. Without their submissions and support, WISA could not have been a success.

December 2007

Sehun Kim
Moti Yung
Hyung-Woo Lee

Organization

Advisory Committee

Man-Young Rhee	Kyung Hee University, Korea
Hideki Imai	Tokyo University, Japan
Mun Kee Choi	ETRI, Korea
Bart Preneel	Katholieke Universiteit Leuven, Belgium
Kil-Hyun Nam	Korea National Defense University, Korea
Sang-Jae Moon	Kyungpook National University, Korea
Dong-Ho Won	Sungkyunkwan University, Korea
Pil-Joong Lee	POSTECH, Korea
Dae-Ho Kim	NSRI, Korea
Joo-Seok Song	Yonsei University, Korea

General Co-chairs

Min Surp Rhee	Dankook University, Korea
Sung-Won Sohn	ETRI, Korea

Steering Committee

Kyo-Il Chung	ETRI, Korea
TaeKyoung Kwon	Sejong University, Korea
Im-Yeong Lee	Soonchunhyang University, Korea
Dong-Il Seo	ETRI, Korea
OkYeon Yi	Kookmin University, Korea
Jae-Kwang Lee	Hannam University, Korea

Organizing Committee

Chair	Sang Choon Kim	Kangwon National University, Korea
Finance	Taenam Cho	Woosuk University, Korea
Publication	Ji-Young Lim	Korean Bible University, Korea
Publicity	Gang Shin Lee	KISA, Korea
	Heuisu Ryu	Gyeongin National University of Education, Korea
Registration	Yoonjeong Kim	Seoul Women's University, Korea
Treasurer	Jaehoon Nah	ETRI, Korea
Local Arrangements	Khi Jung Ahn	Cheju National University, Korea
	Dohoon Lee	NSRI, Korea

Program Committee

Co-chairs

Sehun Kim	KAIST, Korea
Moti Yung	Columbia University, USA
Hyung-Woo Lee	Hanshin University, Korea

Members

Gildas Avoine	MIT, CSAIL, USA
Lejla Batina	University of Leuven, Belgium
Mike Burmester	Florida State University, USA
Ki-Joon Chae	Ewha University, Korea
Myeonggil Choi	Inje University, Korea
Bruno Crispo	University of Trento, Italy
Sven Dietrich	CERT, CMU, USA
Helena Handschu	Spansion, France
Heng Swee Huay	Multimedia University, Malaysia
Maria Isabel Gonzalez Vasco	Universidad Rey Juan Carlos, Spain
Kil-Hyun Jeong	Jangan College, Korea
Gildas Avoine	MIT, CSAIL, USA
Soon-Won Jung	NITGEN, Korea
Stefan Katzenbeisser	Philips Research, Netherlands
Seungjoo Kim	Sungkyunkwan University, Korea
Seokwoo Kim	Hansei University, Korea
Brian King	Indiana University at Purdue, USA
Hong Seung Ko	Kyoto College of Graduate Studies for Informatics, Japan
Dong Hoon Lee	CIST, Korea University, Korea
Pil Joong Lee	POSTECH, Korea
Chae-Hun Lim	Sejong University, Korea
Dongdai Lin	SKLIS, Chinese Academy of Sciences, China
Mose Liskov	William and Mary College, USA
Michael Locasto	Columbia, USA
Havier Lopez	University of Malaga, Spain
Masahiro Mambo	Tsukuba, Japan
Jung Chan Na	ETRI, Korea
Shozo Naito	Kyoto College of Graduate Studies for Informatics, Japan
Yoram Ofek	University of Trento, Italy
Heekuck Oh	Hanyang University, Korea
Susan Pancho-Festin	University of the Philippines, Phillipines
In-Jae Park	Dream Security, Korea
Duong Hieu Phan,	University College London, UK
Raphael C.-W. Phan	EPFL, Switzerland
Vassilis Prevelakis	Drexel University, USA

Table of Contents

Secure Systems

Wireless and Mobile Security

Application Security/Secure Systems

Access Control/DB Security

Smart Cards/Secure Systems

Anonymity and P2P Security

Universal η_T Pairing Algorithm over Arbitrary Extension Degree

Masaaki Shirase[1], Yuto Kawahara[1], Tsuyoshi Takagi[1], and Eiji Okamoto[2]

[1] Future University-Hakodate, Japan
[2] University of Tsukuba, Japan

Abstract. The η_T pairing on supersingular is one of the most efficient algorithms for computing the bilinear pairing [3]. The η_T pairing defined over finite field $\mathbb{F}_{3^n}$ has embedding degree 6, so that it is particularly efficient for higher security with large extension degree n. Note that the explicit algorithm over $\mathbb{F}_{3^n}$ in [3] is designed just for $n \equiv 1 \pmod{12}$, and it is relatively complicated to construct an explicit algorithm for $n \not\equiv 1 \pmod{12}$. It is better that we can select many n's to implement the η_T pairing, since n corresponds to security level of the η_T pairing.

In this paper we construct an explicit algorithm for computing the η_T pairing with arbitrary extension degree n. However, the algorithm should contain many branch conditions depending on n and the curve parameters, that is undesirable for implementers of the η_T pairing. This paper then proposes the universal η_T pairing ($\widetilde{\eta_T}$ pairing), which satisfies the bilinearity of pairing (compatible with Tate pairing) without any branches in the program, and is as efficient as the original one. Therefore the proposed universal η_T pairing is suitable for the implementation of various extension degrees n with higher security.

Keywords: Tate pairing, η_T pairing, Duursma-Lee algorithm, efficient implementation.

1 Introduction

Recently, bilinear pairings defined on elliptic curves such as Tate pairing and the η_T pairing have been attracted to make new cryptographic protocols, for example, identity-based cryptosystem [5], short signature [7] and efficient broadcast cryptosystem [6], come true.

A standard algorithm for computing the Tate pairing is Miller algorithm [12]. The computational cost of Miller algorithm is generally larger than that of RSA or elliptic curve cryptosystems [2]. It is one of important research fields in cryptography to improve the computational cost of pairings. Supersingular curves with characteristic three has embedding degree 6, so that it is particularly efficient for higher security. Some efficient variations of Miller algorithm in base three have been proposed for computing Tate pairing on supersingular elliptic curves over characteristic three [2,10]. Duursma and Lee proposed a closed form generated by divisor $g_R = 3(R) + (-3R) - 4(\mathcal{O})$ for a point R, which

S. Kim, M. Yung, and H.-W. Lee (Eds.): WISA 2007, LNCS 4867, pp. 1–15, 2007.
© Springer-Verlag Berlin Heidelberg 2007

can efficiently compute Tate pairing [8]. Barreto *et. al.* then proposed the η_T pairing which can reduce the iteration number of the main loop of Duursma-Lee algorithm [3]. The computational cost of the η_T pairing is about half of the Duursma-Lee algorithm. The η_T pairing is currently one of the fastest algorithm for computing the bilinear pairing. It is easy to convert between Tate pairing and the η_T pairing (see [3] or [4] for details).

This paper focuses on the η_T pairing defined over finite field $\mathbb{F}_{3^n}$. Extension degree n of $\mathbb{F}_{3^n}$ has to satisfy the following conditions due to several attacks: n is an odd prime number, l is a large prime number with $l|(3^{6n}-1)$, where l is the order of the subgroup of the elliptic curve used in pairing. The extension degrees that satisfy these conditions are $n = 97, 163, 167, 193, 239, 313, 353, \ldots$. On the other hand the explicit algorithm for computing the η_T pairing in [3] deals only with $n \equiv 1 \pmod{12}$. Therefore, the previous researches on the η_T pairing have been implemented in the case of $n \equiv 1 \pmod{12}$ [3,4,14]. To our knowledge there is no literature that proposes the η_T pairing over $\mathbb{F}_{3^n}$ for general extension degree n.[1] Note that we should modify it if we try to construct an explicit algorithm for $n \not\equiv 1 \pmod{12}$, namely $n = 163, 167, 239, 353, \ldots$. It is relatively complicated to construct an explicit algorithm for $n \not\equiv 1 \pmod{12}$.

In this paper we present an explicit algorithm for arbitrary prime number n with $\gcd(n, 6) = 1$. The proposed explicit algorithm depends on the extension degree n and the coefficients of the underlying curves, which is not suitable for implementers of the η_T pairing. Therefore this paper proposes the universal η_T pairing whose algorithm does not depend on n and whose computational cost is same as the original η_T pairing. Moreover we present the explicit relationship between Tate pairing and the universal η_T pairing, which make the universal η_T pairing compatible with Tate pairing for arbitrary extension degree n.

The remainder of this paper is organized as follows: In Section 2 we explain about the known properties of the η_T pairing. In Section 3 we describe the proposed algorithms including an explicit algorithm for computing the η_T pairing over arbitrary degree n and the universal η_T pairing. Proposition 1 shows the relationship between Tate pairing and the universal η_T pairing. We then present some timings of the universal η_T pairing in C language. In Section 4 we present the proof of Proposition 1 and the correctness of algorithms appeared in Section 3. In Section 5 we conclude this paper.

2   Tate Pairing Over Supersingular Curve with Characteristic Three

Let $\mathbb{F}_{3^n}$ be an extension field over $\mathbb{F}_3$ of degree n. Let E^b be the supersingular elliptic curve defined by $y^2 = x^3 - x + b$ with $b \in \{1, -1\}$. All supersingular curves are isomorphic to this curve. The set of all points on E^b over $\mathbb{F}_{3^n}$ defined by

$$E^b(\mathbb{F}_{3^n}) = \{(x, y) \in \mathbb{F}_{3^n} \times \mathbb{F}_{3^n} : y^2 = x^3 - x + b\} \cup \{\mathcal{O}\},$$

---

[1] In the case of the η_T pairing over $\mathbb{F}_{2^n}$, MIRACL supports the general extension degree using 4 branches [13].

forms a group, where $\mathcal{O}$ is the point at infinity. Note that the extension degree n should be $gcd(n, 6) = 1$, it then satisfies $n \equiv 1, 5, 7, 11 \pmod{12}$ [3]. In this paper we deal with the arbitrary degree n with $gcd(n, 6) = 1$. We define b' as

$$b' = \begin{cases} b & \text{if } n \equiv 1, \ 11 \pmod{12}, \\ -b & \text{if } n \equiv 5, \ 7 \pmod{12}, \end{cases} \tag{1}$$

then it is known that

$$\#E^b(\mathbb{F}_{3^n}) = 3^n + 1 + b'3^{(n+1)/2}. \tag{2}$$

2.1 Tate Pairing

Let l be a large prime number, $l \mid \#E^b(\mathbb{F}_{3^n})$ and $l \mid (3^{6n} - 1)$. Let $P \in E^b(\mathbb{F}_{3^n})[l]$ and let $Q \in E^b(\mathbb{F}_{3^{6n}})/lE^b(\mathbb{F}_{3^{6n}})$. Then Tate pairing $e(P, Q)$ over $E^b(\mathbb{F}_{3^n})$ is a pairing, $e : E^b(\mathbb{F}_{3^n})[l] \times E^b(\mathbb{F}_{3^{6n}})/lE^b(\mathbb{F}_{3^{6n}}) \rightarrow \mathbb{F}_{3^{6n}}^*/(\mathbb{F}_{3^{6n}}^*)^l$, and defined as $e(P, Q) = f_{P,l}(Q)$, where $f_{P,N}$ is a function whose divisor is $(f_{P,N}) = (N - 1)(P) - ((N - 1)P) - (N - 2)(\mathcal{O})$ for any positive integer N.

Since $e(P, Q) \in \mathbb{F}_{3^{6n}}^*/(\mathbb{F}_{3^{6n}}^*)^l$, we require an arithmetic on $\mathbb{F}_{3^{6n}}$. A basis $\{1, \sigma, \rho, \sigma\rho, \rho^2, \sigma\rho^2\}$ of $\mathbb{F}_{3^{6n}}$ over $\mathbb{F}_{3^n}$ gives an efficient arithmetic on $\mathbb{F}_{3^{6n}}$, where σ and ρ satisfy $\sigma = -1$ and $\rho^3 = \rho + b$.

For a point $Q = (x, y) \in E^b(\mathbb{F}_{3^n})$ the distortion map ψ is one-to-one homomorphism defined by

$$\psi(x, y) = (\rho - x, y\sigma) \text{ in } E^b(\mathbb{F}_{3^{6n}}). \tag{3}$$

Then $e(P, \psi(Q))$ is defined for $P, Q \in E^b(\mathbb{F}_{3^n})$. Note that the representation of $e(P, \psi(Q))$ has ambiguity since $e(P, \psi(Q))$ is contained in a coset of the residue group $\mathbb{F}_{3^{6n}}^*/(\mathbb{F}_{3^{6n}}^*)^l$. In order to remove this ambiguity, the final exponentiation is required, which is a powering by $(3^{6n} - 1)/l$. Here we denote $e(P, \psi(Q))^{(3^{6n}-1)/l}$ by $\hat{e}(P, Q)$, then $\hat{e}(P, Q)$ has bilinearity, namely $\hat{e}(aP, Q) = \hat{e}(P, aQ) = \hat{e}(P, Q)^a$ for any non zero integer a. The bilinearity is used in many new cryptographic applications such as identity-based cryptosystem [5], short signature [7] and efficient broadcast cryptosystem [6].

Miller proposed an efficient algorithm for computing $f_{P,l}(\psi(Q))$ on arbitrary elliptic curve over arbitrary field [12]. Barreto $et. al.$ [2] and Galbraith $et. al.$ [10] proposed Miller algorithm in base three using the following calculation of function f at point $Q \in E^b(\mathbb{F}_{3^n})$, $f \leftarrow f^3 \cdot (l_1 l_2)(Q)$, where l_1, l_2 are a tangent line of E^b at Q and a line going through Q and $2Q$, respectively.

Miller algorithm in base three is suitable for pairing on $E^b(\mathbb{F}_{3^n})$ since cubing operation and a computation of $3Q$ are virtually for free. Note that $3Q$ for $Q = (x_q, y_q) \in E^b(\mathbb{F}_{3^n})$ is calculated as follows:

$$3Q = (x_q^9 - b, -y_q^9) = \phi\pi^2(Q), \tag{4}$$

where π is the 3rd-power Frobenius map on E^b, namely $\pi(Q) = (x_q^3, y_q^3)$, and ϕ is a map defined as

$$\phi(x_q, y_q) = (x_q - b, -y_q). \tag{5}$$

2.2 Duursma-Lee Algorithm

There is an important property of Tate pairing [10]. Let m be an integer such that $l \mid m$ and $m \mid (3^{6n} - 1)$. Then $f_{P,m}(\psi(Q))^{(3^{6n}-1)/m} = f_{P,l}(\psi(Q))^{(3^{6n}-1)/l} = \hat{e}(P, Q)$.

Duursma and Lee effectively used this property to propose a closed algorithm for computing Tate pairing on supersingular curves [8]. We know that $l \mid (3^{3n} + 1)$ and $(3^{3n} + 1) \mid (3^{6n} - 1)$ due to Eq.(2) and $l \mid \#E(\mathbb{F}_{3^n})$. In the algorithm $3^{3n} + 1$ is set to N, where the Hamming weight of N in base three is very sparse. Duursma and Lee then showed that the function $l_1 l_2$ of Miller algorithm in base three is equivalent to an explicit function

$$g_R(x, y) = y_r^3 y - (x_r^3 + x - b)^2, \tag{6}$$

whose divisor is $(g_R) = 3R + (-3R) - 4(\mathcal{O})$ for $R = (x_r, y_r)$.

The function g_R can be utilized to compute a function $f_{P,3^k+1}$ for any positive integer k [11],

$$f_{P,3^k+1} = g_P^{3^{k-1}} g_{3P}^{3^{k-2}} \cdots g_{3^{k-2}P}^3 g_{3^{k-1}P}. \tag{7}$$

Setting $k = 3n$ in Eq.(7), we see $f_{P,3^{3n}+1}(\psi(Q)) = \prod_{i=1}^{3n}(g_{3^{i-1}P}(\psi(Q)))^{3^{3n-i}}$. Therefore we obtain

$$f_{P,3^{3n}+1}(\psi(Q)) = \prod_{i=1}^{n} g_{\pi^i(P)}(\pi^{n+1-i}(\psi(-Q))) \tag{8}$$

due to $(g_{3^{i-1}P}(\psi(Q)))^{3^{3n-i}} = (g_{3^{i-n-1}P}(\psi(Q)))^{3^{2n-i}} = (g_{3^{i-2n-1}P}(\psi(Q)))^{3^{n-i}}$. The explicit description of Duursma-Lee algorithm is derived from Eq. (8) and thus it has n iterations in the main loop.

2.3 η_T Pairing

Barreto et. al. [3] proposed the η_T pairing to decrease the iteration number of Duursma-Lee algorithm. Here we describe the η_T pairing on supersingular curve over characteristic three. Let T be an integer such that

$$T = 3^{(n+1)/2} + b'. \tag{9}$$

Then the $\eta_T(P, Q)$ for $P, Q \in E^b(\mathbb{F}_{3^n})$ is defined as $\eta_T(P, Q) = f_{-P,T}(\psi(Q))$ if $b' = 1$ and $\eta_T(P, Q) = f_{P,T}(\psi(Q))$ otherwise.

Setting $k = (n + 1)/2$ in Eq.(7), we see $f_{P,3^{(n+1)/2}+1} = \prod_{i=1}^{(n+1)/2} g_{3^{i-1}}^{3^{(n+1)/2-i}}$. Barreto et. al. showed that the difference between $f_{\pm P,T}$ and $f_{P,3^{(n+1)/2}+1}$ is represented by a function of a line $l_{3P',b'P}$ going through $3P'$ and $b'P$, where $P' = 3^{(n-1)/2}P$. Then $\eta_T(P, Q) = l_{3P',b'P}(\psi(Q)) \prod_{j=0}^{(n-1)/2} g_{3^i P}(\psi(Q))^{3^{(n-1)/2-i}}$. Moreover it can be rewritten as

$$\eta_T(P, Q) = l_{3P',b'P}(\psi(Q)) \prod_{j=0}^{(n-1)/2} g_{3^{-j}P'}(\psi(Q))^{3^j}, \tag{10}$$

to remove the exponent $3^{(n-1)/2}$.

Eq.(10) is similar to Eq.(8), but only has $(n+1)/2$ iterations, which means the cost of η_T pairing is about half of Duursma-Lee algorithm. Note that $T = 3^{(n+1)/2} \pm 1$ is as large as $|\#E^b(\mathbb{F}_{3^n}) - 3^n - 1|$, which is the absolute value of the trace of $E^b(\mathbb{F}_{3^n})$.

$\eta_T(P,Q)$ itself is contained in a coset of the residue group $\mathbb{F}_{3^{6n}}^* / (\mathbb{F}_{3^{6n}}^*)^{\#E^b(\mathbb{F}_{3^n})}$. Therefore one cannot use $\eta_T(P,Q)$ in cryptographic protocols due to its ambiguity. $\eta_T(P,Q)$ requires the final exponentiation of powering by W to be a bilinear pairing, where W is an integer defined as

$$W = (3^{3n} - 1)(3^n + 1)(3^n + 1 - b'(3^{(n+1)})) \, (= (3^{6n} - 1)/\#E^b(\mathbb{F}_{3^n})). \quad (11)$$

There is an efficient algorithm for computing the final exponentiation in [15].

Let Z be an integer such that

$$Z = -b'3^{(n+3)/2}. \quad (12)$$

Then there is a relationship between the η_T pairing and Tate pairing,

$$(\eta_T(P,Q)^W)^{3T^2} = \hat{e}(P,Q)^Z. \quad (13)$$

It is essential to find an algorithm for computing $\hat{e}(P,Q)^X$ for some integer X that becomes a bilinear pairing. However, if we need to convert the η_T pairing to Tate pairing via Eq.(13), there is an efficient conversion algorithm, see [4].

Note that the original algorithm for computing the η_T pairing in [3] includes computations of cube root computations. In general it takes the cost of 0.8~2 multiplications [1], then we cannot neglect their costs. Beuchat $et.\,al.$ generated an algorithm (Algorithm 2 in [4]) that has no cube root and outputs $\eta_T(P,Q)^{3^{(n+1)/2}}$.

3   Proposed Explicit Algorithms

In this section we present an explicit algorithm for computing the η_T pairing with arbitrary extension degree n. We then propose the universal η_T pairing whose algorithm has no branch in the program.

3.1 η_T Pairing for Arbitrary n

An algorithm for computing the η_T pairing with arbitrary extension degree n can be constructed from Eq.(10). Since both $l_{3P',b'P}$ and $g_{3-jP'}$ depend on the extension degree n and the curve parameter b', the explicit description of η_T pairing has a complex form and causes many branches in the program. Lemma 5 of [3] explains about $l_{3P',b'P}$ in all cases, however $g_{3-jP'}$ is considered only for $n \equiv 1 \pmod{12}$. In this section we investigate $g_{3-jP'}$ in details.

Note that $g_{3-jP'}$ needs a computation of $P' = 3^{(n-1)/2}P$. In order to efficiently compute P' we use Eq.(4), then we see

$$P' = \phi^{(n-1)/2}\pi^{(n-1)}(P). \quad (14)$$

Algorithm 1.   Computation of $\eta_T(P,Q)^{3^{(n+1)/2}}$ for arbitrary n

input: $P = (x_p, y_p), Q = (x_q, y_q) \in E^b(\mathbb{F}_{3^n})$

output: $(\eta_T(P,Q))^{3^{(n+1)/2}} \in \mathbb{F}_{3^{6n}}^* / (\mathbb{F}_{3^{6n}}^*)^{\#E^b(\mathbb{F}_{3^n})}$

1. $b' \leftarrow \begin{cases} b & \text{if } n \equiv 1, 11 \pmod{12} \\ -b & \text{if } n \equiv 5, 7 \pmod{12} \end{cases}$

2. **if** $b' = 1$ **then** $y_p \leftarrow -y_p$

3. $R_0 \leftarrow \begin{cases} -y_p(x_p + x_q + b) + y_q\sigma + y_p\rho & \text{if } n \equiv 1 \pmod{12} \\ -y_p(x_p + x_q - b) + y_q\sigma + y_p\rho & \text{if } n \equiv 5 \pmod{12} \\ y_p(x_p + x_q + b) + y_q\sigma - y_p\rho & \text{if } n \equiv 7 \pmod{12} \\ y_p(x_p + x_q - b) + y_q\sigma - y_p\rho & \text{if } n \equiv 11 \pmod{12} \end{cases}$

4. $d \leftarrow \begin{cases} b & \text{if } n \equiv 1, 7 \pmod{12} \\ -b & \text{if } n \equiv 5, 11 \pmod{12} \end{cases}$

5. **for** $i \leftarrow 0$ **to** $(n-1)/2$ **do**

6. $\quad r_0 \leftarrow x_p + x_q + d$

7. $\quad R_1 \leftarrow \begin{cases} -r_0^2 + y_p y_q\sigma - r_0\rho - \rho^2 & \text{if } n \equiv 1, 5 \pmod{12} \\ -r_0^2 - y_p y_q\sigma - r_0\rho - \rho^2 & \text{if } n \equiv 7, 11 \pmod{12} \end{cases}$

8. $\quad R_0 \leftarrow R_0 R_1$

9. $\quad y_q \leftarrow -y_p$

10. $\quad x_q \leftarrow x_q^9, \; y_q \leftarrow y_q^9$

11. $\quad R_0 \leftarrow R_0^3$

12. $\quad d \leftarrow d - b \pmod 3$

13. **end for**

14. **return** R_0

The explicit description of P' depends on not only the extension degree n but also the curve parameter b arisen from ϕ in Eq. (5).

We present Algorithm 1 which is an explicit algorithm for computing the η_T pairing with arbitrary n. The proposed explicit algorithm is based on the variation of the η_T pairing discussed by Beuchat *et. al.* [4] which has no cube root computation for $n \equiv 1 \pmod{12}$. Refer Section 4.1 for a proof of the correctness of Algorithm 1.

The branches in Steps 1-4 and Step 7 are caused by $l_{3P',b'P}$ (Lemma 5 of [3]) and $g_{3-jP'}$, respectively.

3.2   Universal η_T Pairing

Algorithm 1 has many branches that depend on the value of $(n \bmod 12)$ and b'. If there is an algorithm without branches, then it becomes more implementor-friendly. Therefore Section 3.2 proposes the universal η_T pairing, $\widetilde{\eta_T}(P,Q)$, that has no branch and is as efficient as the original η_T pairing. The proposed algorithm is given by Algorithm 2.

The following proposition describes the difference between the η_T pairing (Algorithm 1) and the $\widetilde{\eta_T}$ pairing (Algorithm 2).

Algorithm 2. Computation of $\widetilde{\eta_T}(P,Q)$ for arbitrary n

---

input: $P = (x_p, y_p), Q = (x_q, y_q) \in E^b(\mathbb{F}_{3^n})$

output: $\widetilde{\eta_T}(P,Q) \in \mathbb{F}_{3^{6n}}^* / (\mathbb{F}_{3^{6n}}^*)^{\#E^b(\mathbb{F}_{3^n})}$

  1. $R_0 \leftarrow -y_p(x_p + x_q + b) + y_q \sigma + y_p \rho$

  2. $d \leftarrow b$

  3. **for** $i \leftarrow 0$ **to** $(n-1)/2$ **do**

  4. $r_0 \leftarrow x_p + x_q + d$

  5. $R_1 \leftarrow -r_0^2 + y_p y_q \sigma - r_0 \rho - \rho^2$

  6. $R_0 \leftarrow R_0 R_1$

  7. $y_q \leftarrow -y_p$

  8. $x_q \leftarrow x_q^9, y_q \leftarrow y_q^9$

  9. $R_0 \leftarrow R_0^3$

10. $d \leftarrow d - b \pmod{3}$

11. **end for**

12. **return** R_0

Proposition 1. *Let n be an odd prime with $\gcd(n, 6) = 1$, and let T, W and Z be integers defined as Eqs.(9), (11) and (12), respectively. Then we have the following properties of $\widetilde{\eta_T}(P,Q)$ for $P, Q \in E^b(\mathbb{F}_{3^n})$.*

(i) $\widetilde{\eta_T}(P,Q)^W$ with final exponentiation W is a non-degenerate and bilinear pairing.

(ii) $\widetilde{\eta_T}(P,Q)^W = \hat{e}(P,Q)^U$, where $U = (3^{(n-1)/2} \cdot VZT^{-2} \bmod \#E^b(\mathbb{F}_{3^n}))$ and V is defined by the following table.

	$b = 1$	$b = -1$
$n \equiv 1 \pmod{12}$	-1	1
$n \equiv 5 \pmod{12}$	$3^{(n+1)/2} - 2$	$3^{(n+1)/2} + 2$
$n \equiv 7 \pmod{12}$	-1	1
$n \equiv 11 \pmod{12}$	$-3^{(n+1)/2} - 2$	$-3^{(n+1)/2} + 2$

The proof of Proposition 1 is described in Section 4.2. The final exponentiation for $\widetilde{\eta_T}(P,Q)$ is same as that for the $\eta_T(P,Q)$ pairing, which is efficiently computed by the algorithm from [15]. Due to Proposition 1-(i) we can apply the $\widetilde{\eta_T}$ pairing to cryptographic applications with a bilinear pairing. If necessary, we can obtain Tate pairing $\hat{e}(P,Q)$ from $\widetilde{\eta_T}(P,Q)$ due to Proposition 1-(ii).

Note that $\widetilde{\eta_T}(P,Q)^W$ is included in the torus $T_2(\mathbb{F}_{3^{3n}})$. Therefore the conversion of $\widetilde{\eta_T}(P,Q)^W$ to $\hat{e}(P,Q)$, a powering by U^{-1}, can be efficiently performed with arithmetic in $T_2(\mathbb{F}_{3^{3n}})$, refer to [15].

Moreover, the proposed $\widetilde{\eta_T}$ pairing has good properties, namely it has no branch and no cube root computation unlike the original η_T pairing. The $\widetilde{\eta_T}$ pairing is as efficient as the variation of η_T pairing, which is one of the fastest implementations of a bilinear pairing [4].

3.3 Implementation Results

We implemented the $\widetilde{\eta_T}$ pairing (Algorithm 2) in C language. It is implemented on an AMD Opteron^{TM} Processor 275 at 2.2GHz using 8GByte RAM.

Table 1. Timing of operations on $\mathbb{F}_{3^n}$ and computation of the $\widetilde{\eta_T}$ pairing (μsec)

Extension degree (n)	97(SSE)	97	167	193	239	313
Addition	0.0083	0.0168	0.0210	0.0237	0.0265	0.0377
Cubing	0.0394	0.1610	0.2104	0.2694	0.3052	0.3943
Multiplication	0.5009	1.2056	2.9757	3.7164	5.3137	8.2219
Inversion	7.7111	12.0865	28.6980	39.7646	55.5295	95.9911
$\widetilde{\eta_T}^W$ (Alg.2+[15])	479.63	1164.16	4406.26	6267.99	10753.17	21796.96

We mainly follow the implementation described in [9]. The polynomial base representation is used for $\mathbb{F}_{3^n}$. Finite field $\mathbb{F}_3 = \{0, 1, 2\}$ is encoded by two bits, and an addition in $\mathbb{F}_3$ is programmed by 7 Boolean logic operations [9]. We implemented the multiplication by the right-to-left sfift-addition algorithm with the signed window method of width 3. The extended Euclidean algorithm is used for the inversion. We deploy the final exponentiation using the torus proposed by Shirase *et. al.* [15].

Table 1 presents the timing of the $\widetilde{\eta_T}$ pairing for different extension degrees $n = 97, 167, 193, 239, 313$. The timing is an average value for 1,000,000 randomly chosen elements on the base field $\mathbb{F}_{3^n}$ or elliptic curve $E^b(\mathbb{F}_{3^n})$. If we choose about twice larger extension degree, then the $\widetilde{\eta_T}$ pairing becomes about 5 times slower. The $\widetilde{\eta_T}$ pairing with $n = 313$ can be implemented in about 20 milliseconds. In case of $n = 97$ we optimized our programming suitable for the streaming SIMD extensions (SSE). The timing using SSE for the $\widetilde{\eta_T}$ pairing with $n = 97$ achieves under 0.5 milliseconds, which is more than twice as fast than the implementation without SSE. The embedded field of extension degree n is $\mathbb{F}_{3^{6n}}$, and their bit size are 923, 1589, 1836, 2273, 2977 for $n = 97, 167, 193, 239, 313$, respectively.

4   Proofs of Proposition and Algorithm

We prove the Proposition 1 and the correctness of Algorithm 1 described in this paper.

4.1   Proof of Algorithm 1

In order to prove the correctness of Algorithm 1 we introduce Algorithm 3 which is an extension of the original $\eta_T(P, Q)$ [3] to arbitrary extension degree n. Denote by $R_{0,j}^{(Alg.1)}$ and $R_{0,j}^{(Alg.3)}$ the value in register R_0 at the j-th loop of Algorithm 1 and Algorithm 3, respectively. They are related by equation $R_{0,j}^{(Alg.1)} = (R_{0,j}^{(Alg.3)})^{3^{j+1}}$ (see also Appendix II in [4]). Therefore we see that if Algorithm 3 outputs $\eta_T(P, Q)$ then Algorithm 1 outputs $\eta_T(P, Q)^{3^{(n+1)/2}}$. Then it is sufficient to prove the correctness of Algorithm 3.

Recall that $\eta_T(P, Q)$ for arbitrary n is defined using two values, $l_{3P', b'P}(\psi(Q))$ and $g_{3-jP'}(\phi(Q))^{3^j}$. We prove that $g_{3-jP'}(\phi(Q))^{3^j}$, which corresponds to the j-th loop of Step 5 and 6 in Algorithm 3, can be computed by Lemma 1.

Algorithm 3. Computation of $\eta_T(P,Q)$ for arbitrary n
(Including cube root version)

---

input: $P = (x_p, y_p), Q = (x_q, y_q) \in E^b(\mathbb{F}_{3^n})$

output: $\eta_T(P,Q) \in \mathbb{F}_{3^{6n}}^*/(\mathbb{F}_{3^{6n}}^*)^{\#E^b(\mathbb{F}_{3^n})}$

1. $b' \leftarrow \begin{cases} b & \text{if } n \equiv 1, 11 \pmod{12} \\ -b & \text{if } n \equiv 5, 7 \pmod{12} \end{cases}$

2. **if** $b' = 1$ **then** $y_p \leftarrow -y_p$

3. $R_0 \leftarrow \begin{cases} -y_p(x_p + x_q + b) + y_q\sigma + y_p\rho & \text{if } n \equiv 1 \pmod{12} \\ -y_p(x_p + x_q - b) + y_q\sigma + y_p\rho & \text{if } n \equiv 5 \pmod{12} \\ y_p(x_p + x_q + b) + y_q\sigma - y_p\rho & \text{if } n \equiv 7 \pmod{12} \\ y_p(x_p + x_q - b) + y_q\sigma - y_p\rho & \text{if } n \equiv 11 \pmod{12} \end{cases}$

4. **for** $i \leftarrow 0$ **to** $(n-1)/2$ **do**

5. $\qquad r_0 \leftarrow \begin{cases} x_p + x_q + b & \text{if } n \equiv 1, 7 \pmod{12} \\ x_p + x_q - b & \text{if } n \equiv 5, 11 \pmod{12} \end{cases}$

6. $\qquad R_1 \leftarrow \begin{cases} -r_0^2 + y_p y_q \sigma - r_0\rho - \rho^2 & \text{if } n \equiv 1, 5 \pmod{12} \\ -r_0^2 - y_p y_q \sigma - r_0\rho - \rho^2 & \text{if } n \equiv 7, 11 \pmod{12} \end{cases}$

7. $\qquad R_0 \leftarrow R_0 R_1$

8. $\qquad x_p \leftarrow x_p^{1/3}, \; y_p \leftarrow y_p^{1/3}$

9. $\qquad x_q \leftarrow x_q^3, \; y_q \leftarrow y_q^3$

10. **end for**

11. **return** R_0

Lemma 1. *Let n be an odd prime. Then*

$$g_{3^{-j}P'}(\phi(Q))^{3^j} = \begin{cases} -r_0^2 + y_p^{(-j)} y_q^{(j)}\sigma - r_0\rho - \rho^2 & \text{if } n \equiv 1 \pmod{4}, \\ -r_0^2 - y_p^{(-j)} y_q^{(j)}\sigma - r_0\rho - \rho^2 & \text{if } n \equiv 3 \pmod{4}, \end{cases}$$

for $P = (x_p, y_p)$, $Q = (x_q, y_q) \in E^b(\mathbb{F}_{3^n})$, where r_0 is defined as

$$r_0 = \begin{cases} x_p + x_q + b & \text{if } n \equiv 1 \pmod{6}, \\ x_p + x_q - b & \text{if } n \equiv 5 \pmod{6}. \end{cases}$$

Proof. See the appendix. □

Next we have

$$l_{3P', b'P}(x, y) = \begin{cases} y + y_p(x - x_p) - b'y_p & \text{if } n \equiv 1, 5 \pmod{12}, \\ y - y_p(x - x_p) - b'y_p & \text{if } n \equiv 7, 11 \pmod{12}. \end{cases} \quad (15)$$

from Lemma 5 of [3]. Therefore the formula for R_0 in Steps 1 and 3 can be obtained due to Eqs. (1) and (15). Therefore we prove the correctness of Algorithm 3.

4.2 Proof of Proposition 1

We first prove Proposition 1-(ii). Let $\widetilde{\eta_T}(P,Q)$ be the output of Algorithm 4. Denote by $R_{0,j}^{(Alg.2)}$ and $R_{0,j}^{(Alg.4)}$ the value in register R_0 at the j-th loop of Algorithm 2 and Algorithm 4, respectively. Then we see that

$$\widetilde{\eta_T}(P,Q) = \overline{\eta_T}(P,Q)^{3^{(n+1)/2}}, \quad (16)$$

Algorithm 4. Computation of $\overline{\eta_T}(P,Q)$ for arbitrary n

input: $P = (x_p, y_p), Q = (x_q, y_q) \in E^b(\mathbb{F}_{3^n})$

output: $\overline{\eta_T}(P,Q) \in \mathbb{F}_{3^{6n}}^*/(\mathbb{F}_{3^{6n}}^*)^{\#E^b(\mathbb{F}_{3^n})}$

1. $R_0 \leftarrow -y_p(x_p + x_q + b) + y_q\sigma + y_p\rho$
2. **for** $i \leftarrow 0$ **to** $(n-1)/2$ **do**
3. $r_0 \leftarrow x_p + x_q + b$
4. $R_1 \leftarrow -r_0^2 + y_p y_q \sigma - r_0\rho - \rho^2$
5. $R_0 \leftarrow R_0 R_1$
6. $x_p \leftarrow x_p^{1/3}, \; y_p \leftarrow y_p^{1/3}$
7. $x_q \leftarrow x_q^3, \; y_q \leftarrow y_q^3$
8. **end for**
9. **return** R_0

---

since $R_{0,j}^{(Alg.2)} = (R_{0,j}^{(Alg.4)})^{3^{j+1}}$. Due to Eqs.(13) and (16), it is enough to prove that $\overline{\eta_T}(P,Q)^W = \eta_T(P,Q)^{VW}$.

The difference between Algorithm 3 and 4 causes the corresponding difference between $\eta_T(P,Q)$ and $\overline{\eta_T}(P,Q)$. There are two differences, **the first difference** is that Algorithm 3 has the program

$$\text{`` if } b' = 1 \text{ then } y_p \leftarrow -y_p\text{''}, \tag{17}$$

and **the second difference** is that Algorithm 3 has the branches at Steps 1, 3, 5 and 6.

In order to investigate **the first difference**, we modify Algorithm 4 by appending the program (17) before Step 1. We call this modified algorithm as Algorithm 4', and denote by $\eta'_T(P,Q)$ the pairing value from Algorithm 4'. The relationship between $\overline{\eta_T}(P,Q)$ and $\eta'_T(P,Q)$ is obtained by Lemma 2.

Lemma 2. *We have*

$$\overline{\eta_T}(P,Q)^W = \begin{cases} (\eta'_T(P,Q)^W)^{-1} & \text{if } b' = 1 \\ \eta'_T(P,Q)^W & \text{if } b' = -1 \end{cases}$$

Proof. We see that $\overline{\eta_T}$ is identical to η'_T if $b = -1$. On the other hand, $\overline{\eta_T}$ is different from η'_T if $b = 1$. We obtain $\overline{\eta_T}(P,Q) = \eta'_T(-P,Q)$ since $-P = (x_p, -y_p)$ for $P = (x_p, y_p) \in E^b(\mathbb{F}_{3^n})$. Bilinearity of $\eta_T(P,Q)^W$ products a relationship $\overline{\eta_T}(P,Q)^W = \eta'_T(-P,Q)^W = (\eta'_T(P,Q)^W)^{-1}$. $\qquad\square$

Remark 1. $\overline{\eta_T}$ without the powering by W is not bilinear pairing. Then the powering by W is required in the statement of Lemma 2.

The second difference causes the difference between $\eta'_T(P,Q)$ and $\eta_T(P,Q)$. We soon see that $\eta'_T(P,Q) = \eta_T(P,Q)$ if $n \equiv 1 \pmod{12}$. When $n \equiv 5 \pmod{12}$, a converting $x_q \to x_q - b$, in other words $Q \to \phi^4(Q)$, in Algorithm 2 gives Algorithm 4. Then $\eta'_T(P,Q) = \eta_T(P,\phi^4(Q))$ if $n \equiv 5 \pmod{12}$. We easily see also that the relationship between $\eta'_T(P,Q)$ and $\eta_T(P,Q)$ for $n \equiv 7, 11 \pmod{12}$. Then we have

$$\eta_T'(P,Q) = \begin{cases} \eta_T(P,Q) & \text{if } n \equiv 1 \ (\mathrm{mod}\ 12) \\ \eta_T(P,\phi^4(Q))(= \eta_T(P,-\phi(Q))) & \text{if } n \equiv 5 \ (\mathrm{mod}\ 12) \\ \eta_T(P,-Q) & \text{if } n \equiv 7 \ (\mathrm{mod}\ 12) \\ \eta_T(P,\phi(Q)) & \text{if } n \equiv 11 \ (\mathrm{mod}\ 12) \end{cases} \tag{18}$$

Due to Lemma 2 and Eq.(18) we have the relationship $\overline{\eta_T}(P,Q)^W$ and $\eta_T(P,Q)^W$,

$$\overline{\eta_T}(P,Q)^W = \begin{cases} (\eta_T(P,Q)^W)^{-1} & \text{if } n \equiv 1 \ (\mathrm{mod}\ 12),\ b' = 1 \quad (b = 1) \\ \eta_T(P,Q)^W & \text{if } n \equiv 1 \ (\mathrm{mod}\ 12),\ b' = -1\ (b = -1) \\ (\eta_T(P,-\phi(Q))^W)^{-1} & \text{if } n \equiv 5 \ (\mathrm{mod}\ 12),\ b' = 1 \quad (b = -1) \\ \eta_T(P,-\phi(Q))^W & \text{if } n \equiv 5 \ (\mathrm{mod}\ 12),\ b' = -1\ (b = 1) \\ (\eta_T(P,-Q)^W)^{-1} & \text{if } n \equiv 7 \ (\mathrm{mod}\ 12),\ b' = 1 \quad (b = -1) \\ \eta_T(P,-Q)^W & \text{if } n \equiv 7 \ (\mathrm{mod}\ 12),\ b' = -1\ (b = 1) \\ (\eta_T(P,\phi(Q))^W)^{-1} & \text{if } n \equiv 11 \ (\mathrm{mod}\ 12),\ b' = 1 \quad (b = 1) \\ \eta_T(P,\phi(Q))^W & \text{if } n \equiv 11 \ (\mathrm{mod}\ 12),\ b' = -1\ (b = -1) \end{cases} \tag{19}$$

Lastly in order to show that ϕ is a homomorphism of $E^b(\mathbb{F}_{3^n})$, we show that ϕ is represented as a scalar multiplication.

Lemma 3. *For $P \in E^b(\mathbb{F}_{3^n})$, $\phi(P)$ is equal to a value in the following table.*

	$b = 1$	$b = -1$
$n \equiv 1$ *(mod 12)*	$3^n P$	$3^n P$
$n \equiv 5$ *(mod 12)*	$(-3^{(n+1)/2} + 2)P$	$(3^{(n+1)/2} + 2)P$
$n \equiv 7$ *(mod 12)*	$3^n P$	$3^n P$
$n \equiv 11$ *(mod 12)*	$(3^{(n+1)/2} + 2)P$	$(-3^{(n+1)/2} + 2)P$

Proof. See the appendix.   □

Here we go back to the proof of Proposition 1. Lemma 3, Eq.(19), and the bilinearity of $\eta_T(P,Q)^W$ yield Proposition 1-(ii). Finally we prove Proposition 1-(i) in the following. V and $3^{(n+1)/2}$ are coprime to $\#E^b(\mathbb{F}_{3^n})$ with $V = \pm 1, 3^{(n+1)} \pm 2, -3^{(n+1)} \pm 2$, which means that a powering by $3^{(n+1)/2} \cdot V$ is a group isomorphism in $\mathbb{F}_{3^{6n}}^*$. The η_T^W is a non-degenerate and bilinear pairing, then the $\overline{\eta_T}^W (= \eta_T^{W^{3^{(n+1)/2}}VW})$ is also a non-degenerate and bilinear pairing.

5   Conclusion

This paper provided an explicit algorithm for computing the η_T pairing with arbitrary degree n. It has many branches based on extension degree n and the curve parameter b. Therefore, this paper also proposed the universal η_T pairing ($\widetilde{\eta_T}$ pairing) which has no branch in the program and is suitable for the efficient implementation for arbitrary extension degree n. Moreover we proved the relationship between the $\widetilde{\eta_T}$ pairing and the Tate pairing for arbitrary n.

Finally we summarize the relationship of pairings appeared in this paper in the following table.

Pairing	Properties
$\hat{e}(P,Q)$	**no branch** and **no cube root** ([11])
$\uparrow$ Eq.(13) $\downarrow$	
$\eta_T(P,Q)^W$	branches and cube roots (Sec.3.1)
$\uparrow$ powering by V Proposition 1) $\downarrow$	
$\overline{\eta_T}(P,Q)^W$	**no branch** and cube roots (Sec.4.2)
$\uparrow$ powering by $3^{(n+1)/2}$ $\downarrow$	
$\widetilde{\eta_T}(P,Q)^W$	**no branch** and **no cube root** (Sec.3.2)

References

1. Barreto, P.: A note on efficient computation of cube roots in characteristic 3, Cryptology ePrint Archive, Report 2004/305 (2004)
2. Barreto, P., Kim, H., Lynn, B., Scott, M.: Efficient algorithms for pairing-based cryptosystems. In: Yung, M. (ed.) CRYPTO 2002. LNCS, vol. 2442, pp. 354–368. Springer, Heidelberg (2002)
3. Barreto, P., Galbraith, S., Ó hÉigeartaigh, C., Scott, M.: Efficient pairing computation on supersingular abelian varieties. In: Designs, Codes and Cryptography, vol. 42(3), pp. 239–271. Springer, Heidelberg (2007)
4. Beuchat, J.-L., Shirase, M., Takagi, T., Okamoto, E.: An algorithm for the η_T pairing calculation in characteristic three and its hardware implementation. In: 18th IEEE International Symposium on Computer Arithmetic, ARITH-18, pp. 97–104 (2007) full version, Cryptology ePrint Archive, Report 2006/327 (2006)
5. Boneh, D., Franklin, M.: Identity based encryption from the Weil pairing. SIAM Journal of Computing 32(3), 586–615 (2003)
6. Boneh, D., Gentry, C., Waters, B.: Collusion resistant broadcast encryption with short ciphertexts and private keys. In: Shoup, V. (ed.) CRYPTO 2005. LNCS, vol. 3621, pp. 258–275. Springer, Heidelberg (2005)
7. Boneh, D., Lynn, B., Shacham, H.: Short signature from the Weil pairing. Journal of Cryptology 17(4), 297–319 (2004)
8. Duursma, I., Lee, H.: Tate pairing implementation for hyperelliptic curves $y^2 = x^p - x + d$. In: Laih, C.-S. (ed.) ASIACRYPT 2003. LNCS, vol. 2894, pp. 111–123. Springer, Heidelberg (2003)
9. Granger, R., Page, D., Stam, M.: Hardware and software normal basis arithmetic for pairing-based cryptography in characteristic three. IEEE Transactions on Computers 54(7), 852–860 (2005)
10. Galbraith, S., Harrison, K., Soldera, D.: Implementing the Tate pairing. In: Fieker, C., Kohel, D.R. (eds.) Algorithmic Number Theory. LNCS, vol. 2369, pp. 324–337. Springer, Heidelberg (2002)
11. Kwon, S.: Efficient Tate pairing computation for supersingular elliptic curves over binary fields, Cryptology ePrint Archive, Report 2004/303 (2004)
12. Miller, V.: Short programs for functions on curves, Unpublished manuscript (1986), http://crypto.stanford.edu/miller/miller.pdf
13. MIRACL, ftp://ftp.computing.dcu.ie/pub/crypto/miracl.zip
14. Ronan, R., hÉigeartaigh, C.Ó., Murphy, C., Kerins, T., Barreto, P.: A reconfigurable processor for the cryptographic η_T pairing in characteristic 3. In: Information Technology: New Generations, ITNG 2007, pp. 11–16. IEEE Computer Society, Los Alamitos (2007)

15. Shirase, M., Takagi, T., Okamoto, E.: Some efficient algorithms for the final exponentiation of η_T pairing. In: ISPEC 2007. LNCS, vol. 4464, pp. 254–268. Springer,
Heidelberg (2007)
16. Silverman, J.: The arithmetic of elliptic curves. Springer, Heidelberg (1986)

A   Some Lemmas

In the appendix we prove two lemmas appeared in this paper.

Lemma 1. *Let n be an odd prime. Then*

$$g_{3^{-j}P'}(\phi(Q))^{3^j} = \begin{cases} -r_0^2 + y_p^{(-j)} y_q^{(j)} \sigma - r_0 \rho - \rho^2 & \text{if } n \equiv 1 \ (\text{mod } 4), \\ -r_0^2 - y_p^{(-j)} y_q^{(j)} \sigma - r_0 \rho - \rho^2 & \text{if } n \equiv 3 \ (\text{mod } 4), \end{cases}$$

for $P = (x_p, y_p)$, $Q = (x_q, y_q) \in E^b(\mathbb{F}_{3^n})$, where r_0 is defined as

$$r_0 = \begin{cases} x_p + x_q + b \text{ if } n \equiv 1 \ (\text{mod } 6), \\ x_p + x_q - b \text{ if } n \equiv 5 \ (\text{mod } 6). \end{cases}$$

Proof. First we inspect how $P' = 3^{(n-1)/2}P$ (Eq.(14)) is represented. We see
that

$$\phi^s(x, \ y) = \begin{cases} (x, \ y) & \text{if } s \equiv 0 \ (\text{mod } 6), \\ (x - b, \ -y) & \text{if } s \equiv 1 \ (\text{mod } 6), \\ (x + b, \ y) & \text{if } s \equiv 2 \ (\text{mod } 6), \\ (x, \ -y) & \text{if } s \equiv 3 \ (\text{mod } 6), \\ (x - b, \ y) & \text{if } s \equiv 4 \ (\text{mod } 6), \\ (x + b, \ -y) & \text{if } s \equiv 5 \ (\text{mod } 6), \end{cases} \tag{20}$$

for any $(x, y) \in E^b(\mathbb{F}_{3^n})$ and any integer s due to Eq.(5). Then we have

$$\phi^{(n-1)/2}(x, y) = \begin{cases} \phi^0(x, y) = (x, y) & \text{if } n \equiv 1 \ (\text{mod } 12), \\ \phi^2(x, y) = (x + b, y) & \text{if } n \equiv 5 \ (\text{mod } 12), \\ \phi^3(x, y) = (x, -y) & \text{if } n \equiv 7 \ (\text{mod } 12), \\ \phi^5(x, y) = (x + b, -y) & \text{if } n \equiv 11 \ (\text{mod } 12). \end{cases}$$

The notation of $a^{(i)}$ means a^{3^i}. We see that

$$\pi^n(x_p, y_p) = (x_p, y_p) \tag{21}$$

for $P = (x_p, y_p) \in E^b(\mathbb{F}_{3^n})$ since x_p and $y_p \in \mathbb{F}_{3^n}$. Then we have $\pi^{n-1}(x_p, y_p) = (x_p^{(-1)}, y_p^{(-1)})$. Therefore we see

$$P' = \begin{cases} (x_p^{(-1)}, \ y_p^{(-1)}) & \text{if } n \equiv 1 \ (\text{mod } 12), \\ (x_p^{(-1)} + b, \ y_p^{(-1)}) & \text{if } n \equiv 5 \ (\text{mod } 12), \\ (x_p^{(-1)}, \ -y_p^{(-1)}) & \text{if } n \equiv 7 \ (\text{mod } 12), \\ (x_p^{(-1)} + b, \ -y_p^{(-1)}) & \text{if } n \equiv 11 \ (\text{mod } 12). \end{cases}$$

Note that

$$\phi^3(x, y) = -(x, y), \tag{22}$$

due to $-(x, y) = (x, -y)$ and Eq.(20).

Next we use induction for j to prove Lemma 1. Definition equations of g_R and ψ, Eqs.(3) and (6), are utilized to prove Lemma 1 for $j = 0$.

Case of n $\equiv$ 1 (mod 12): By $P' = (x_p^{(-1)}, y_p^{(-1)})$,

$$g_{P'}(\psi(Q)) = (y_p^{(-1)})^3 y_q \sigma - ((x_p^{(-1)})^3 - (\rho - x_q) + b)^2$$
$$= y_p y_q \sigma - (x_p + x_q + b - \rho)^2 = -r_0^2 + y_p y_q \sigma - r_0 \rho - \rho^2,$$

where $r_0 = x_p + x_q + b$.

Case of n $\equiv$ 5 (mod 12): By $P' = (x_p^{(-1)} + b, y_p^{(-1)})$,

$$g_{P'}(\psi(Q)) = (y_p^{(-1)})^3 y_q \sigma - ((x_p^{(-1)} + b)^3 - (\rho - x_q) + b)^2$$
$$= y_p y_q \sigma - (x_p + x_q - b - \rho)^2 = -r_0^2 + y_p y_q \sigma - r_0 \rho - \rho^2,$$

where $r_0 = x_p + x_q - b$.

Case of n $\equiv$ 7 (mod 12): By $P' = (x_p^{(-1)}, -y_p^{(-1)})$,

$$g_{P'}(\psi(Q)) = (-y_p^{(-1)})^3 y_q \sigma - ((x_p^{(-1)})^3 - (\rho - x_q) + b)^2$$
$$= -y_p y_q \sigma - (x_p + x_q + b - \rho)^2 = -r_0^2 - y_p y_q \sigma - r_0 \rho - \rho^2,$$

where $r_0 = x_p + x_q + b$.

Case of n $\equiv$ 11 (mod 12): By $P' = (x_p^{(-1)} + b, -y_p^{(-1)})$,

$$g_{P'}(\psi(Q)) = (y_p^{(-1)})^3 y_q \sigma - ((x_p^{(-1)} + b)^3 - (\rho - x_q) + b)^2$$
$$= -y_p y_q \sigma - (x_p + x_q + b - \rho)^2 = -r_0^2 - y_p y_q \sigma - r_0 \rho - \rho^2,$$

where $r_0 = x_p + x_q - b$.

We complete proving Lemma 1 for $j = 0$.

We suppose that Lemma 1 is held for $j = j'$. Then we easily see that Lemma 1 is also held for $j = j' + 1$ with direct computations. □

Lemma 3. *For $P \in E^b(\mathbb{F}_{3^n})$, $\phi(P)$ is equal to a value in the following table.*

	$b = 1$	$b = -1$
$n \equiv 1$ *(mod 12)*	$3^n P$	$3^n P$
$n \equiv 5$ *(mod 12)*	$(-3^{(n+1)/2} + 2)P$	$(3^{(n+1)/2} + 2)P$
$n \equiv 7$ *(mod 12)*	$3^n P$	$3^n P$
$n \equiv 11$ *(mod 12)*	$(3^{(n+1)/2} + 2)P$	$(-3^{(n+1)/2} + 2)P$

Proof. Let $P = (x_p, y_p)$ be contained in $E^b(\mathbb{F}_{3^n})$. Then we can use addition and duplication formulae of elliptic curves (see [16] for details) to obtain equations

$$\begin{cases} \pi(P) + 2P = (x_p - 1, -y_p) & \text{if } b = 1, \\ -\pi(P) + 2P = (x_p + 1, -y_p) & \text{if } b = -1. \end{cases} \tag{23}$$

The following calculations complete the proof.

Case of n ≡ 1 (mod 12), b = 1:

$$3^n P = \phi^n \pi^{2n}(P) = \phi(P) \quad \text{by (4), (20), (21)}$$

Case of n ≡ 1 (mod 12), b = −1:

$$3^n P = \phi^n \pi^{2n}(P) = \phi(P) \quad \text{by(4), (20), (21)}$$

Case of n ≡ 5 (mod 12), b = 1:

$$
\begin{aligned}
(-3^{(n+1)/2} + 2)P &= -\phi^{(n+1)/2}\pi^{n+1}(P) + 2P && \text{by (4)} \\
&= -\phi^3 \pi(P) + 2P && \text{by (20), (21)} \\
&= \pi(P) + 2P && \text{by (22)} \\
&= \phi(P) && \text{by (23)}
\end{aligned}
$$

Case of n ≡ 5 (mod 12), b = −1:

$$
\begin{aligned}
(3^{(n+1)/2} + 2)P &= \phi^{(n+1)/2}\pi^{n+1}(P) + 2P && \text{by (4)} \\
&= \phi^3 \pi(P) + 2P && \text{by (20), (21)} \\
&= -\pi(P) + 2P && \text{by (22)} \\
&= \phi(P) && \text{by (23)}
\end{aligned}
$$

Case of n ≡ 7 (mod 12), b = 1:

$$3^n P = \phi^n \pi^{2n}(P) = \phi(P) \quad \text{by (4), (20), (21)}$$

Case of n ≡ 7 (mod 12), b = −1:

$$3^n P = \phi^n \pi^{2n}(P) = \phi(P) \text{ by } (4), (20), (21)$$

Case of n ≡ 11 (mod 12), b = 1:

$$
\begin{aligned}
(3^{(n+1)/2} + 2)P &= \phi^{(n+1)/2}\pi^{n+1}(P) + 2P && \text{by (4)} \\
&= \pi(P) + 2P && \text{by (20), (21)} \\
&= \phi(P) && \text{by (23)}
\end{aligned}
$$

Case of n ≡ 11 (mod 12), b = −1:

$$
\begin{aligned}
(-3^{(n+1)/2} + 2)P &= -\phi^{(n+1)/2}\pi^{n+1}(P) + 2P && \text{by (4)} \\
&= -\pi(P) + 2P && \text{by (20), (21)} \\
&= \phi(P) && \text{by (23)}
\end{aligned}
$$

We complete proving Lemma 3. □

Convertible Undeniable Proxy Signatures: Security Models and Efficient Construction*

Wei Wu, Yi Mu, Willy Susilo, and Xinyi Huang

Centre for Computer and Information Security Research
School of Computer Science & Software Engineering
University of Wollongong, Australia
{wei,ymu,wsusilo,xh068}@uow.edu.au

Abstract. In the undeniable signatures, the validity or invalidity can only be verified via the Confirmation/Disavowal protocol with the help of the signer. Convertible undeniable signatures provide the flexibility that a signer can convert an undeniable signature into publicly verifiable one. A proxy signature scheme allows an entity to delegate his/her signing capability to another entity in such a way that the latter can sign messages on behalf of the former when the former is not available. Proxy signatures have found numerous practical applications in ubiquitous computing, distributed systems, mobile agent applications, etc. In this paper, we propose the *first* convertible undeniable proxy signature scheme with rigorously proven security. The properties of Unforgeability, Invisibility and Soundness in the context of convertible undeniable proxy signatures are also clearly defined. The security of our construction is formally proven in the random oracle models, based on some natural complexity assumptions.

Keywords: Undeniable signatures, Proxy signatures, Convertible, Security models, Security proof.

1 Introduction

Undeniable signatures are like ordinary digital signatures, with the only difference that they are *not* universally verifiable and the validity or invalidity of an undeniable signature can only be verified via a Confirmation/Disavowal protocol with the help of the signer. Undeniable signatures have found various applications such as in licensing software, electronic voting and auctions. Since its introduction in Cypto'89 [5], there have been a number of schemes in the literature [1,6,7,8,9,11,19,20,21,23,24,25,31,32]. The concept of convertible undeniable signatures was introduced by Boyar, Chaum, Damgård and Pedersen [1] in Crypto'90. The new concept offers more flexibility than its original version in the sense that the signer has the ability to convert an undeniable signature into publicly verifiable one. Convertible undeniable signatures require two *convert* algorithms: *individually convert algorithm* and *universally convert*

---

* Supported by ARC Discovery Grant DP0557493 and DP0663306.

S. Kim, M. Yung, and H.-W. Lee (Eds.): WISA 2007, LNCS 4867, pp. 16–29, 2007.

algorithm. The individually convert algorithm allows the signer to convert an undeniable signature into a regular signature by releasing a piece of information at a later time. Moreover, the universally convert algorithm can help the signer to convert all the undeniable signatures into publicly verifiable ones. In this case, anyone can check the validity of any undeniable signature without any help of the signer.

The notion of proxy signature was introduced by Mambo, Usuda and Okamoto [22]. Based on the delegation type, there are three types of proxy signatures: *full delegation*, *partial delegation*, and *delegation by warrant*. In the full delegation system, Alice's secret key is given to Bob directly so that Bob can have the same signing capability as Alice. In practice, such schemes are obviously impractical and insecure. In a partial delegation proxy signature scheme, a proxy signer possesses a key, called private proxy key, which is different from Alice's private key. Hence, proxy signatures generated by using the private proxy key are different from Alice's signatures. However, in such schemes, the messages a proxy signer can sign are *not* limited. This weakness is eliminated in delegation by a warrant that specifies what kinds of messages are delegated. Here, the original signer uses the signing algorithm of a standard signature scheme and its secret key to sign a warrant and generate a signature on the warrant which is called as delegation. The proxy signer uses the delegation and his/her secret key to create a proxy signature on behalf of the original signer. According to whether the original signer can generate a valid proxy signature, proxy signatures can be further classified into *proxy-unprotected* and *proxy-protected* schemes. In a proxy-protected scheme only the proxy signer can generate proxy signatures, while in a proxy-unprotected scheme either the proxy signer or the original signer can generate proxy signatures. In many applications, proxy-protected schemes are required to avoid the potential disputes between the original signer and the proxy signer. Related works about proxy signature can be found in [4,12,13,16,17,18,28].

Our contribution

In this paper, we formalize the security models of the convertible undeniable proxy signatures. The properties Unforgeability, Invisibility and Soundness in the context of convertible undeniable proxy signatures are clearly defined. We then present a concrete construction of the convertible undeniable proxy signature. Our scheme is proxy-protected, even the original signer can not generate a valid convertible undeniable proxy signature. The validity or invalidity of a proxy signature can only be verified with the help of the proxy signer. The proxy signer can decide how to make his proxy signatures publicly verifiable, by releasing an individual proof or universal proof. The security of our construction is formally proved in the random oracle models, based on some natural complexity assumptions. To the best of our knowledge, our construction is the *first* convertible undeniable proxy signature scheme with rigorously proven security.

Paper Organization

The rest of this paper is organized as follows. In Section 2, we recall some fundamental backgrounds required throughout the paper. In Section 3, we propose the definition and security models of convertible undeniable proxy signatures. In Section 4, we provide our concrete convertible undeniable proxy signature scheme and its security analysis as well. Finally, we conclude our paper in Section 5.

2   Preliminaries

2.1   Bilinear Maps

Let $\mathbb{G}_1$ and $\mathbb{G}_T$ be two groups of prime order q and let g be a generator of $\mathbb{G}_1$. The map $e : \mathbb{G}_1 \times \mathbb{G}_1 \rightarrow \mathbb{G}_T$ is said to be an admissible bilinear map if the following three conditions hold true:

- e is bilinear, i.e. $e(g^a, g^b) = e(g, g)^{ab}$ for all $a, b \in \mathbb{Z}_q$.
- e is non-degenerate, i.e. $e(g, g) \neq 1_{\mathbb{G}_T}$.
- e is efficiently computable.

We say that $(\mathbb{G}_1, \mathbb{G}_T)$ are bilinear groups if there exists the bilinear map $e : \mathbb{G}_1 \times \mathbb{G}_1 \rightarrow \mathbb{G}_T$ as above, and e, and the group action in $\mathbb{G}_1$ and $\mathbb{G}_T$ can be computed efficiently. See [2] for more details on the construction of such pairings.

2.2   Complexity Assumptions

Discrete Logarithm Problem: Given $(g, g^a) \in \mathbb{G}$, find a.
Computational Diffie-Hellman Problem: Given a triple $\mathbb{G}$ elements (g, g^a, g^b), find the element $C = g^{ab}$.
3-Decisional Diffie-Hellman (3-DDH) Problem in $\mathbb{G}_1$: Given (g, g^a, g^b, g^c, h) $\in \mathbb{G}_1^5$ for some randomly chosen $a, b, c \in \mathbb{Z}_q$, decide whether $h \overset{?}{=} g^{abc}$.

3   Formal Definitions of Convertible Undeniable Proxy Signatures

3.1   Outline of Convertible Undeniable Proxy Signatures

The convertible undeniable proxy signature scheme consists of the following algorithms:

CPGen is a probabilistic algorithm, on input a security parameter k, outputs a string cp which denotes the common scheme parameters including the message space $\mathcal{M}$ and the signature space $\mathcal{S}$.
KGen is a probabilistic algorithm, on input a common parameter cp, outputs the secret/public key-pairs (sk, pk) for the user in the system.
SSign is a probabilistic (deterministic) algorithm, on input the common parameter cp, the signer's secret key sk and the message m to be signed, outputs the standard signature σ_s.

SVer is a deterministic algorithm, on input the common parameter cp, the signer's public key pk, the message-signature pair (m, σ_s), outputs 1 if it is a valid message-signature pair. Otherwise, outputs 0.

DGen is a probabilistic algorithm, on input system's parameter cp, the original signer's secret key sk_o and the warrant W to be signed, outputs the delegation σ_w.

DVer is a deterministic algorithm, on input the common parameter cp, the original signer's public key pk_o, the warrant-delegation pair (W, σ_w), outputs 1 if it is a valid warrant-delegation pair. Otherwise, outputs 0.

UPSign is a probabilistic algorithm, on input system's parameter cp, the warrant W, the delegation σ_w, the secret key sk_p of the proxy signer and the message M to be signed, outputs the undeniable proxy signature σ.

UPVer is a deterministic algorithm, on input the common parameter cp, original signer's public key pk_o and the proxy signer's secret/public key-pair (sk_p, pk_p), the warrant W, the signed message M and the signature σ, outputs 1 if it is a valid undeniable proxy signature. Otherwise, outputs 0.

CProtocol is an interactive (non-interactive) algorithm, on input the common parameter cp, the original signer's public key pk_o, the proxy signer's secret key sk_p, (possibly) the verifier V's public key pk_v, the warrant W, the message m and the signature σ, outputs a *non-transferable* transcript $Trans$ which can convince V about σ.

DProtocol is an interactive (non-interactive) algorithm, on input the common parameter cp, the original signer's public key pk_o, the proxy signer's secret key sk_p, (possibly) verifier's public key pk_v, the warrant W, the message m and the signature σ, outputs a *non-transferable* transcript $Trans$ which can deny σ to V.

ICon is a probabilistic (deterministic) algorithm, on input the common parameter cp, the proxy signer's secret key sk_p, the warrant W, the message m and the signature σ, outputs an individual proof $\Pi_{(pk_p, W)}^{(m, \sigma)}$ of this message.

IVer is a deterministic algorithm, on input the common parameter cp, the original signer's public key pk_o, the proxy signer's public key pk_p, the undeniable proxy signature tuple (m, W, σ) and the individual proof $\Pi_{(pk_p, W)}^{(m, \sigma)}$, outputs the verification decision $d \in \{Acc, Rej\}$.

UCon is a deterministic algorithm, on input the common parameter cp and the proxy signer's secret key sk_p, outputs the universal proof Π_{pk_p}.

UVer is a deterministic algorithm, on input the common parameter cp, the original signer's public key pk_o, the proxy signer's public key pk_p, *any* undeniable proxy signature tuple (m, W, σ) and the universal proof Π_{pk_p}, outputs the verification decision $d \in \{Acc, Rej\}$.

3.2 Adversaries and Oracles

We use a non-interactive designated verifier protocol as the CProtocol/DProtocol when we define the security of a convertible undeniable proxy signature scheme. Note that if the scheme employs the non-interactive confirmation and disavowal protocols, then it is not necessary to consider the active attack [27]. We allow the adversary to access the following oracles and submit their queries adaptively:

- KGen Oracle: On a key generation query for the ith user, this oracle runs the KGen algorithm to generate a secret/public key pair (sk_i, pk_i) of this user and the adversary receives the public key pk_i.
- SSign Oracle: On a standard sign query (m, pk), this oracle runs the SSign algorithm to obtain σ_S and returns it to the adversary.
- UPSign Oracle: On an undeniable proxy sign query (m, W, pk_o, pk_p), this oracle runs the UPSign algorithm to generate the undeniable proxy signature σ and returns it to the adversary.
- UPVer Oracle: On a verify query $(m, W, \sigma, pk_o, pk_p)$ (and possibly pk_v), this oracle first runs the UPVer algorithm to decide whether (m, W, σ) is a valid undeniable proxy signature tuple under the public keys pk_o and pk_p and outputs the decision result $d \in \{0, 1\}$. The adversary receives a transcript of CProtocol if $d = 1$. Otherwise, The adversary receives a transcript of DProtocol.
- ICon Oracle: On an individually convert query (m, W, σ, pk_p), this oracle runs the ICon algorithm to generate the individual proof $\Pi^{(m,\sigma)}_{(pk_p, W)}$ and returns it to the adversary.
- UCon Oracle: On a universally convert query pk_p, this oracle runs UCon algorithm to generate the universal proof Π_{pk_p} and returns it to the adversary.
- Corruption Oracle: On a corruption query pk, this oracle returns the corresponding secret key to the adversary.

3.3   Completeness

Essentially, completeness means that valid (invalid) signatures can always be proved valid (invalid). It can be described as following two cases:

1. If the UPVer algorithm outputs 1 for an undeniable proxy signature tuple (m, W, σ) under the public keys (pk_o, pk_p), then
    (a) (m, W, σ) can be confirmed by the CProtocol.
    (b) IVer algorithm will output Acc on input (m, W, σ) together with a valid individual proof $\Pi^{(m,\sigma)}_{(pk_p, W)}$.
    (c) UVer algorithm will output Acc, on input (m, W, σ) together with a valid universal proof Π_{pk_p}.
2. If the UPVer algorithm outputs 0 for a message-signature pair (m, W, σ) under the public keys (pk_o, pk_p), then
    (a) (m, W, σ) can be denied by the DProtocol.
    (b) IVer algorithm will output Rej on input (m, W, σ) together with a valid individual proof $\Pi^{(m,\sigma)}_{(pk_p, W)}$.
    (c) UVer algorithm will output Rej on input (m, W, σ) together with a valid universal proof Π_{pk_p}.

3.4   Non-transferability

The Non-Transferability requires that the transcript of the CProtocol/DProtocol with the designated verifier V can only convince V the validity or invalidity of an undeniable proxy signature tuple (m, W, σ). No one else could be convinced by this $Trans$ even if V shares all his secret information (including his secret key) with this party.

The CProtocol/DProtocol is non-transferable if there exists a probabilistic polynomial time algorithm $\mathcal{A}$ with input the verifier V's secret key sk_v such that for any other computationally unbounded verifier $\tilde{V}$, any tuple (m, W, σ), the transcript of the CProtocol/DProtocol generated by $\mathcal{A}$ is indistinguishable from that generated by the proxy signer.

3.5   Unforgeability

The standard notion of the security for digital signatures was defined by Goldwasser, Micali and Rivest [10]. In this paper, we use the same way to define the existential unforgeability of the convertible undeniable proxy signature scheme: adversary has access to all the oracles defined in Section 3.2. We say $\mathcal{F}$ wins if $\mathcal{F}$ outputs a valid undeniable proxy signature tuple (m^*, W_f, σ^{*f}) under the original signer's public keys pk_o and the proxy signer's public key pk_p, such that $\mathcal{F}$ has never issued (m^*, W_f, pk_o, pk_p) to the UPSign Oracle and one of the following two requirements is satisfied:

1. pk_p has never been submitted to the Corruption Oracle.
2. pk_o has never been submitted to the Corruption Oracle and (W_f, pk_o) has not been submitted to the SSign Oracle.

The success probability of an adaptively chosen message and chosen public key forger $\mathcal{F}$ wins the above game is defined as Succ $\mathcal{F}_{EUF,\ CUPS}^{CMA,\ CPKA}$.

Definition 1. *We say a convertible undeniable proxy signature scheme is unforgeable against a $(t, q_H, q_{KG}, q_{SS}, q_{UPS}, q_V, q_{IC}, q_{UC}, q_C)$ forger $\mathcal{F}_{EUF,\ CUPS}^{CMA,\ CPKA}$, if $\mathcal{F}_{EUF,\ CUPS}^{CMA,\ CPKA}$ runs in time at most t, makes at most q_H queries to the random oracles, q_{KG} queries to KGen Oracle, q_{SS} queries to SSign Oracle, q_{UPS} queries to UPSign Oracle, q_V queries to UPVer Oracle, q_{IC} queries to the ICon Oracle, q_{UC} queries to the UCon Oracle, q_C queries to the Corruption Oracle and Succ $\mathcal{F}_{EUF,\ CUPS}^{CMA,\ CPKA}$ is negligible.*

3.6   Invisibility

Given an undeniable proxy signature tuple (m, W, σ), the public keys pk_o of the original signer and pk_p of the proxy signer, the invisibility property requires that it is difficult to decide whether it is a valid undeniable proxy signature without the knowledge of the proxy signer's secret key, the individual proof $\Pi_{(pk_p, W)}^{(m,\sigma)}$ or universal proof Π_{pk_p}, even though the adversary knows the secret key sk_o of the original signer. It is defined using the games between the oracles defined in Section 3.2 and an adaptively chosen message attacker and chosen public key distinguisher $\mathcal{D}_{INV,\ CUPS}^{CMA,\ CPKA}$. The games are divided into two phases.

- Phase 1: In this phase, the distinguisher $\mathcal{D}$ can adaptively access all the Oracles.
- Challenge: When the distinguisher $\mathcal{D}$ decides the first phase is over, he submits (m^*, W_f, pk_o, pk_p) to UPSign Oracle as the challenge with the constraints that
  1. pk_p has never been submitted to the Corruption Oracle or UCon Oracle during Phase 1.
  2. (m^*, W_f, pk_o, pk_p) has never been submitted to the UPSign Oracle during Phase 1.

  As a response, the UPSign Oracle chooses a random bit $\gamma \in \{0, 1\}$. If $\gamma = 0$, this oracle will run UPSign algorithm to generate the undeniable signature σ and sets $\sigma^{*f} = \sigma$. Otherwise, this oracle chooses a random element σ^{*f} in the signature space $\mathcal{S}$. Then, this oracle returns the challenging signature σ^{*f} to $\mathcal{D}$.
- Phase 2: On receiving the challenging signature, the distinguisher $\mathcal{D}$ still can access the oracles adaptively except that
  1. pk_p can not be submitted to the Corruption Oracle or UCon Oracle.
  2. $(m^*, W_f, \sigma^*, pk_p)$ can not be submitted to the ICon Oracle.
  3. (m^*, W_f, pk_o, pk_p) cannot be submitted to the UPSign Oracle.
  4. $(m^*, W_f, \sigma^{*f}, pk_o, pk_p)$ cannot be submitted to the UPVer Oracle.
- Guessing: Finally, the distinguisher $\mathcal{D}$ outputs a guess γ'. The adversary wins the game if $\gamma = \gamma'$.

The advantage of an adaptively chosen message and chosen public key distinguisher $\mathcal{D}$ has in the above game is defined as $\mathsf{Adv}\ \mathcal{D}_{INV,\ CUPS}^{CMA,\ CPKA} = |\Pr[\gamma = \gamma'] - 1/2|$.

Definition 2. *We say a convertible undeniable proxy signature scheme is invisible against a $(t, q_H, q_{KG}, q_{SS}, q_{UPS}, q_V, q_{IC}, q_{UC}, q_C)$ distinguisher $\mathcal{D}_{INV,\ CUPS}^{CMA,\ CPKA}$, if $\mathcal{D}_{INV,\ CUPS}^{CMA,\ CPKA}$ runs in time at most t, makes at most q_H queries to the random oracles, q_{KG} queries to KGen Oracle, q_{SS} queries to SSign Oracle, q_{UPS} queries to UPSign Oracle, q_V queries to UPVer Oracle, q_{IC} queries to the ICon Oracle, q_{UC} queries to the UCon Oracle, q_C queries to the Corruption Oracle and $\mathsf{Adv}\ \mathcal{D}_{INV,\ CUPS}^{CMA,\ CPKA}$ is negligible.*

Remark: Anonymity is another security requirement of undeniable signatures. It has been shown in [14] that the property Invisibility and Anonymity are closely related in the notion of convertible undeniable signatures.

3.7   Soundness

Basically, soundness means that even the proxy signer himself can not convince a verifier V that a valid (invalid) signature is invalid (valid) without corrupting $V's$ secret key. It is defined by the games against an adversary $\widetilde{S}$ who can adaptively access to all the Oracles defined in Section 3.2. After all the queries, We say $\widetilde{S}$ wins the game if $\widetilde{S}$ can output $(m^*, W_f, \sigma^{*f}, Trans^*, pk_o, pk_p, pk_v)$ with the restrictions that

1. $\widetilde{S}$ has never queried pk_v to the Corruption Oracle.
2. σ^{*f} is not a valid undeniable proxy signature of message m^* under the warrant W and the public keys pk_o, pk_p and $Trans^*$ is a transcripts output by CProtocol. Or, σ^{*f} is a valid undeniable proxy signature of message m^* under the warrant W and the public keys pk_o, pk_p and $Trans^*$ is a transcript output by DProtocol.

The success probability of an adaptively chosen message and chosen public key adversary $\widetilde{S}$ wins the above game is defined as $\mathsf{Succ}\ \widetilde{S}_{Sound,\ CUPS}^{CMA,\ CPKA}$.

Definition 3. *We say a convertible undeniable proxy signature scheme satisfies the property of soundness against a $(t, q_H, q_{KG}, q_{SS}, q_{UPS}, q_V, q_{IC}, q_{UC}, q_C)$ adversary $\widetilde{S}_{Sound,\ CUPS}^{CMA,\ CPKA}$, if $\widetilde{S}_{Sound,\ CUPS}^{CMA,\ CPKA}$ runs in time at most t, makes at most q_H queries to the random oracles, q_{KG} queries to KGen Oracle, q_{SS} queries to the SSign Oracle, q_{UPS} queries to UPSign Oracle, q_V queries to UPVer Oracle, q_{IC} queries to the ICon Oracle, q_{UC} to the UCon Oracle, q_C queries to the Corruption Oracle and $\mathsf{Succ}\ \widetilde{S}_{Sound,\ CUPS}^{CMA,\ CPKA}$ is negligible.*

4 Our Proposed Scheme

In this section we will describe our convertible undeniable proxy signature scheme with security analysis.

4.1 Concrete Scheme

CPGen: Let $(\mathbb{G}_1, \mathbb{G}_T)$ be bilinear groups where $|\mathbb{G}_1| = |\mathbb{G}_T| = q$, for some prime number $q \geq 2^k$, k be the system security number and g be the generator of $\mathbb{G}_1$. e denotes the bilinear map $\mathbb{G}_1 \times \mathbb{G}_1 \rightarrow \mathbb{G}_T$. Let $h_0, h_1, h_2, h_3 : \{0,1\}^* \rightarrow \mathbb{G}_1^*, h_4 : \{0,1\}^* \rightarrow \mathbb{Z}_q$ be five secure cryptographic hash functions.

KGen: The original signer O picks $x_o, y_o \in_R \mathbb{Z}_q^*$ and sets the secret key $sk_o = (x_o, y_o)$. Then O computes the public key $pk_o = (X_o, Y_o) = (g^{x_o}, g^{y_o})$. The proxy signer P picks $x_p, y_p \in_R \mathbb{Z}_q^*$ and sets the secret key $sk_p = (x_p, y_p)$. Then P computes the public key $pk_p = (X_p, Y_p) = (g^{x_p}, g^{y_p})$. Similarly, the verifier V's secret/public key-pair is $(sk_v, pk_v) = (x_v, y_v, X_v, Y_v)$ where x_v, y_v are randomly chosen in $\mathbb{Z}_q^*$.

SSign: Let m be the message to be signed by the signer whose secret/public key pair is $(x, y, X, Y) = (x, y, g^x, g^y)$. The standard signature is generated as: $\sigma_s = h_0(m)^x$.

SVer: Given the message m and the standard signature σ_s, anyone can verify whether $e(\sigma_s, g) \overset{?}{=} e(h_0(m), X)$. If the equality holds, outputs 1. Otherwise, the result is 0.

DGen: Let W be the warrant to be signed by the original signer O who wants to delegate his signing rights to the proxy signer P. O runs the algorithm SSign to generate the delegation $\sigma_w = h_0(W)^{x_o}$. Then O sends the warrant W and the delegation σ_w to P.

DPVer: Given the warrant W and the delegation σ_w, the proxy signer P runs the algorithm SVer to check its validity.

UPSign: For a message m to be signed, let $\vartheta = m\|pk_o\|pk_p\|W$. P chooses a random number t in $\mathbb{Z}_q^*$ and computes $\sigma_1 = \sigma_w h_1(\vartheta)^{x_p y_p} h_2(\vartheta)^{y_p} h_3(m\|W\|\sigma_2)^t = h_0(W)^{x_o} h_1(\vartheta)^{x_p y_p} h_2(\vartheta)^{y_p} h_3(m\|W\|\sigma_2)^t$ and $\sigma_2 = g^t$. The signature is generated as $\sigma = (\sigma_1, \sigma_2)$.

UPVer: For a signature $\sigma = (\sigma_1, \sigma_2)$ on the message m and warrant W, let $\vartheta = m\|pk_o\|pk_p\|W$. The proxy signer uses his secret key x_p, y_p to check if $e(\sigma_1, g) \stackrel{?}{=} e(h_0(W), X_o)e(h_1(\vartheta), g^{x_p y_p})e(h_2(\vartheta), Y_p)e(h_3(m\|W\|\sigma_2), \sigma_2)$. If the equality holds, output 1. Otherwise, outputs 0.

CProtocol: Given the verifier V's public key $pk_v = (X_v, Y_v)$, a warrant $W \in \{0,1\}^*$, a message $m \in \{0,1\}^*$, and a valid signature $\sigma = (\sigma_1, \sigma_2)$ to be confirmed, let $\vartheta = m\|pk_o\|pk_p\|W$. The proxy signer P will use the designated verifier techniques [15] to prove its validity.

- The proxy signer P chooses $c_v, d_v, r \in_R \mathbb{Z}_q^*$ and computes:
  1. $A = g^r$, $B = e(h_1(\vartheta), X_p)^r$, $C = g^{d_v} Y_v^{c_v}$.
  2. $h = h_4(m\|W\|\sigma\|pk_v\|A\|B\|C)$, $c_s = h - c_v \pmod q$ and $d_s = r - c_s y_p \pmod q$.

  P then sends (c_s, c_v, d_s, d_v) to the verifier V.
- On receiving (c_s, c_v, d_s, d_v), the verifier V computes $A' = g^{d_s} Y_p^{c_s}$, $B' = e(h_1(\vartheta), X_p)^{d_s}[e(\sigma_1, g)/(e(h_0(W), X_o)e(h_2(\vartheta), Y_p)e(h_3(m\|W\|\sigma_2), \sigma_2))]^{c_s}$, $C' = g^{d_v} Y_v^{c_v}$. Then, V checks whether $c_s + c_v \stackrel{?}{=} h_4(m\|W\|\sigma\|pk_v\|A'\|B'\|C')$. If the equality holds, V will accept σ as a valid undeniable proxy signature.

DProtocol: Given the verifier V's public key $pk_v = (X_v, Y_v)$, a warrant $W \in \{0,1\}^*$, a message $m \in \{0,1\}^*$, and a signature $\sigma = (\sigma_1, \sigma_2)$ to be disavowed, let $\vartheta = m\|pk_o\|pk_p\|W$. The proxy signer P will use the designated verifier techniques [15] to prove its invalidity.

- The proxy signer P chooses $c_v, d_v, r, \alpha, \beta \in_R \mathbb{Z}_q^*$ and computes:
  1. $Z = e(\sigma_1, g)/(e(h_0(W), X_o)e(h_2(\vartheta), Y_p)e(h_3(m\|W\|\sigma_2), \sigma_2))$.
  2. $A = [e(h_1(\vartheta), X_p)^{y_p}/Z]^r$, $B = e(h_1(\vartheta), X_p)^{\alpha}/Z^{\beta}$, $C = g^{\alpha}/Y_p^{\beta}$, $D = g^{d_v} Y_v^{c_v}$.
  3. $h = h_4(m\|W\|\sigma\|pk_v\|A\|B\|C\|D)$ and $c_s = h - c_v \pmod q$.
  4. $d_s = \alpha + c_s y_p r \pmod q$ and $\widehat{d_s} = \beta + c_s r \pmod q$.

  The proxy signer P then sends $(A, c_s, c_v, d_s, \widehat{d_s}, d_v)$ to the verifier V.
- On receiving $(A, c_s, c_v, d_s, \widehat{d_s}, d_v)$, V computes
  1. $Z = e(\sigma_1, g)/(e(h_0(W), X_o)e(h_2(\vartheta), Y_p)e(h_3(m\|W\|\sigma_2), \sigma_2))$.
  2. $B' = e(h_1(\vartheta), X_p)^{d_s}/(Z^{\widehat{d_s}} \cdot A^{c_s})$, $C' = g^{d_s}/Y_p^{\widehat{d_s}}$, $D' = g^{d_v} Y_v^{c_v}$.

  If $A \neq 1$ and $c_s + c_v = h_4(m\|W\|\sigma\|pk_v\|A\|B'\|C'\|D')$, V will believe σ is not a valid undeniable proxy signature.

ICon: When the proxy signer wants to make his undeniable proxy signature tuple (m, W, σ) publicly verifiable, he first runs the algorithm UPVer:

- If the algorithm UPVer outputs 1, the proxy signer generates the individual proof $\Pi^{(m,\sigma)}_{(pk_p,W)}$ as follows: it first chooses $r \in_R \mathbb{Z}^*_q$ and computes $A = g^r$, $B = e(h_1(\vartheta), X_p)^r$, where $\vartheta = m\|pk_o\|pk_p\|W$, $c_s = h_4(m\|W\|\sigma\|A\|B)$, $d_s = r - c_s y_p \pmod{q}$. Then, the proxy signer sets $\Pi^{(m,\sigma)}_{(pk_p,W)} = (c_s, d_s)$.

- Otherwise, the algorithm UPVer outputs 0. The proxy signer P chooses $r, \alpha, \beta \in_R \mathbb{Z}^*_q$ and computes:

$$Z = e(\sigma_1, g)/(e(h_0(W), X_o)e(h_2(\vartheta), Y_p)e(h_3(m\|W\|\sigma_2), \sigma_2)),$$

$A = [e(h_1(\vartheta), X_p)^{y_p}/Z]^r$, $B = e(h_1(\vartheta), X_p)^\alpha/Z^\beta$, $C = g^\alpha/Y_p^\beta$, $c_s = h_4(m\|W\|\sigma\|pk_v\|A\|B\|C)$, $d_s = \alpha + c_s y_p r \pmod{q}$ and $\widehat{d_s} = \beta + c_s r \pmod{q}$. P then sets $\Pi^{(m,\sigma)}_{(pk_p,W)} = (A, c_s, d_s, \widehat{d_s})$.

IVer: For an undeniable proxy signature tuple (m, W, σ) and the individual proof $\Pi^{(m,\sigma)}_{(pk_p,W)}$,

- If $\Pi^{(m,\sigma)}_{(pk_p,W)}$ has the form (c_s, d_s), the verifier V computes $A' = g^{d_s} Y_p^{c_s}$, $B' = e(h_1(\vartheta), X_p)^{d_s}[e(\sigma_1, g)/(e(h_0(W), X_o)e(h_2(\vartheta), Y_p)e(h_3(m\|W\|\sigma_2), \sigma_2))]^{c_s}$. Then, V checks whether $c_s \stackrel{?}{=} h_4(m\|W\|\sigma\|pk_v\|A'\|B')$. If the equality holds, V will accept σ as a valid undeniable proxy signature.

- Otherwise, $\Pi^{(m,\sigma)}_{(pk_p,W)} = (A, c_s, d_s, \widehat{d_s})$. V computes

$$Z = e(\sigma_1, g)/(e(h_0(W), X_o)e(h_2(\vartheta), Y_p)e(h_3(m\|W\|\sigma_2), \sigma_2)),$$

$B' = e(h_1(\vartheta), X_p)^{d_s}/(Z^{\widehat{d_s}} \cdot A^{c_s})$, $C' = g^{d_s}/Y_p^{\widehat{d_s}}$. If $A \neq 1$ and $c_s = h_4(m\|W\|\sigma\|pk_v\|A\|B'\|C')$, V will believe σ is not a valid undeniable proxy signature.

UCon: When the proxy signer wants to make all his undeniable proxy signatures publicly verifiable, he computes $\Pi_{pk_p} = g^{x_p y_p}$ and publishes Π_{pk_p}.

UVer: For any undeniable proxy signature tuple (m, W, σ) and the universal proof Π_{pk_p}, let $\vartheta = m\|pk_o\|pk_p\|W$.

- anyone can check whether $e(g, \Pi_{pk_p}) \stackrel{?}{=} e(X_p, Y_p)$. If this equality holds, one continues to compute

- $Z = e(\sigma_1, g)/(e(h_0(W), X_o)e(h_2(\vartheta), Y_p)e(h_3(m\|W\|\sigma_2), \sigma_2))$ and check $Z \stackrel{?}{=} e(h_1(\vartheta), \Pi_{pk_p})$. If this equality holds as well, one can accept σ as a valid undeniable proxy signature. Otherwise, it is invalid.

4.2   Security Analysis of the Proposed Scheme

In this section, we will give a formal security analysis of our proposed schemes.

Theorem 1. *The proposed scheme satisfies the property* **Completeness** *and* **Non-Transferability**.

Proof. It is easy to check our scheme satisfies the definition of the Completeness in Section 3.3. We will show our protocols satisfy the property of **Non-Transferability**. Given any undeniable proxy signature tuple (m, W, σ) (either valid or invalid) and two public keys pk_o, pk_p, the verifier's secret key $sk_v = (x_v, y_v)$, let $\vartheta = m \| pk_o \| pk_p \| W$. The algorithm $\mathcal{A}$ can output the transcripts of the CProtocol and DProtocol as follows.

1. To simulate a transcript of the confirmation protocol which is designated to V, $\mathcal{A}$ randomly chooses $c_s, d_s \in \mathbb{Z}_q, r \in \mathbb{Z}_q^*$ and computes

$$Z = e(\sigma_1, g)/(e(h_2(\vartheta), Y_p)e(h_0(W), X_o)e(h_3(m \| W \| \sigma_2), \sigma_2)),$$

$A = g^{d_s} Y_p^{c_s}$, $B = e(h_1(\vartheta), X_p)^{d_s} Z^{c_s}$ and $C = g^r$. Then $\mathcal{A}$ computes $c_v = h_4(m \| W \| \sigma \| pk_v \| A \| B \| C) - c_s \pmod{q}$ and $d_v = r - c_v y_v \pmod{q}$. At last, $\mathcal{A}$ outputs (c_s, c_v, d_s, d_v) as the transcript of the confirmation protocol.

2. To simulate a transcript of the disavowal protocol which is designated to V, $\mathcal{A}$ chooses a random element $A \in \mathbb{G}_T$ such that $A \neq 1$. $\mathcal{A}$ continues to choose four random elements $c_s, d_s, \widehat{d_s} \in \mathbb{Z}_q, r \in \mathbb{Z}_q^*$ and computes

$$Z = e(\sigma_1, g)/(e(h_2(\vartheta), Y_p)e(h_0(W), X_o)e(h_3(m \| W \| \sigma_2), \sigma_2)),$$

$B = e(h_1(\vartheta), X_p)^{d_s}/(Z^{\widehat{d_s}} \cdot A^{c_s})$, $C = g^{d_s}/Y_p^{\widehat{d_s}}$ and $D = g^r$. Then V computes $c_v = h_4(m \| W \| \sigma \| pk_v \| A \| B \| C \| D) - c_s \pmod{q}$ and $d_v = r - c_v y_v \pmod{q}$. At last, $\mathcal{A}$ outputs $(A, c_s, c_v, d_s, \widehat{d_s}, d_v)$ as the transcript of the disavowal protocol.

Due to the random numbers chosen by $\mathcal{A}$, the transcripts generated by $\mathcal{A}$ are indistinguishable from those generated by the proxy signer P.

Theorem 2. *If there exists a $(t, q_H, q_{KG}, q_{SS}, q_{UPS}, q_V, q_{IC}, q_{UC}, q_C)$ forger $\mathcal{F}_{EUF, CUPS}^{CMA, CPKA}$ can win the game defined in Section 3.5 with non-negligible success probability* $\mathsf{Succ}\, \mathcal{F}_{EUF, CUPS}^{CMA, CPKA}$, *then there exists an algorithm $\mathcal{A}$ who can use $\mathcal{F}$ to solve a random instance of Computational Diffie-Hellman problem with probability* $\mathsf{Succ}_{\mathcal{A}, \mathbb{G}_1}^{CDH} \geq \frac{4}{(q_{SS} + q_{UPS})^2}(1 - \frac{2}{q_{UPS} + q_{SS} + 2})^{q_{SS} + q_{UPS} + 2} \frac{2}{q_{KG}}(1 - \frac{1}{q_{KG}})^{q_C} \mathsf{Succ}\, \mathcal{F}_{EUF, CUPS}^{CMA, CPKA}$ *in polynomial time.*

Proof. Due to the page limitation, please refer to the full version of this paper.

Theorem 3. *If there exists a $(t, q_H, q_{KG}, q_{SS}, q_{UPS}, q_V, q_{IC}, q_{UC}, q_C)$ distinguisher $\mathcal{D}_{INV, CUPS}^{CMA, CPKA}$ who can have non-negligible advantage* $\mathsf{Adv}\, \mathcal{D}_{INV, CUPS}^{CMA, CPKA}$ *in the game defined in Section 3.6, then there exists an algorithm $\mathcal{A}$ who can use $\mathcal{D}$ to solve a random instance of 3-Diffie-Hellman problem with advantage* $\mathsf{Adv}\, \mathcal{A}_{\mathbb{G}_1}^{3-DDH} = \frac{1}{q_{KG}(q_{UPS})^2}(1 - \frac{1}{q_{UPS} + 1})^{2(q_{UPS} + 1)}(1 - \frac{1}{q_{KG}})^{q_{UC} + q_C} \mathsf{Adv}\, \mathcal{D}_{INV, CUPS}^{CMA, CPKA}$ *in polynomial time.*

Proof. Due to the page limitation, please refer to the full version of this paper.

Theorem 4. *If there exists a* $(t, q_H, q_{KG}, q_{SS}, q_{UPS}, q_V, q_{IC}, q_{UC}, q_C)$ *adversary* $\widetilde{S}_{Sound, \ CUPS}^{CMA, \ CPKA}$ *can win the game defined in Section 3.7 with non-negligible success probability* $\mathsf{Succ} \ \widetilde{S}_{Sound, \ CUPS}^{CMA, \ CPKA}$, *then there exists an algorithm* $\mathcal{A}$ *who can use* $\widetilde{S}$ *to solve a random instance of Discrete Logarithm problem with probability* $Succ_{\mathcal{A}, \mathbb{G}_1}^{DL} \geq \frac{1}{q_{KG}}(1 - \frac{1}{q_{KG}})^{q_C} \mathsf{Succ} \ \widetilde{S}_{Sound, \ CUPS}^{CMA, CPKA}$ *in polynomial time.*

Proof. Due to the page limitation, please refer to the full version of this paper.

5   Conclusion

In this paper, we proposed the first convertible undeniable proxy signature scheme with formal security analysis. The signature for a message consists of two elements in the group $\mathbb{G}_1$, which is only around 340 bits when appropriate elliptic curve is used. We provided a formal security analysis to show that our scheme satisfies the properties of Unforgeability, Invisibility and Soundness in the random oracle models.

Acknowledgement

The authors would like to thank the anonymous referees of the 8th International Workshop on Information Security Applications (WISA 2007) for the suggestions to improve this paper.

References

1. Boyar, J., Chaum, D., Damgård, I.B., Pedersen, T.P.: Convertible Undeniable Signatures. In: Menezes, A.J., Vanstone, S.A. (eds.) CRYPTO 1990. LNCS, vol. 537, pp. 189–205. Springer, Heidelberg (1991)
2. Boneh, D., Lynn, B., Shacham, H.: Short Signatures from the Weil Pairing. In: Boyd, C. (ed.) ASIACRYPT 2001. LNCS, vol. 2248, pp. 514–532. Springer, Heidelberg (2001)
3. Boyar, J., Chaum, D., Damgard, I.B., Pedersen, T.P.: Convertible Undeniable Signatures. In: Menezes, A.J., Vanstone, S.A. (eds.) CRYPTO 1990. LNCS, vol. 537, pp. 189–205. Springer, Heidelberg (1991)
4. Boldyreva, A., Palacio, A., Warinschi, B.: Secure Proxy Signature Schemes for Delegation of Digning Rights, http://eprint.iacr.org/2003/096
5. Chaum, D., Antwerpen, H.v.: Undeniable Signatures. In: Brassard, G. (ed.) CRYPTO 1989. LNCS, vol. 435, pp. 212–216. Springer, Heidelberg (1990)
6. Damgård, I.B., Pedersen, T.P.: New Convertible Undeniable Signature Schemes. In: Maurer, U.M. (ed.) EUROCRYPT 1996. LNCS, vol. 1070, pp. 372–386. Springer, Heidelberg (1996)
7. Galbraith, S.D., Mao, W., Paterson, K.G.: RSA-Based Undeniable Signatures for General Moduli. In: Preneel, B. (ed.) CT-RSA 2002. LNCS, vol. 2271, pp. 200–217. Springer, Heidelberg (2002)

8. Galbraith, S.D., Mao, W.: Invisibility and Anonymity of Undeniable and Confirmer Signatures. In: Joye, M. (ed.) CT-RSA 2003. LNCS, vol. 2612, pp. 80–97. Springer, Heidelberg (2003)

9. Gennaro, R., Krawczyk, H., Rabin, T.: RSA-Based Undeniable Signatures. In: Kaliski Jr., B.S. (ed.) CRYPTO 1997. LNCS, vol. 1294, pp. 132–149. Springer, Heidelberg (1997)

10. Goldwasser, S., Micali, S., Rivest, R.: A Digital signature scheme secure against adaptively chosen message attacks. SIAM Journal on Computing 17(2), 281–308 (1988)

11. Gennaro, R., Rabin, T., Krawczyk, H.: RSA-Based Undeniable Signatures. Journal of Cryptology 13(4), 397–416 (2000)

12. Huang, X., Mu, Y., Susilo, W., Zhang, F., Chen, X.: A short proxy signature scheme: Efficient authentication in the ubiquitous world. In: Enokido, T., Yan, L., Xiao, B., Kim, D., Dai, Y., Yang, L.T. (eds.) Embedded and Ubiquitous Computing – EUC 2005 Workshops. LNCS, vol. 3823, pp. 480–489. Springer, Heidelberg (2005)

13. Huang, X., Susilo, W., Mu, Y., Wu, W.: Proxy Signature without Random Oracles. In: Cao, J., Stojmenovic, I., Jia, X., Das, S.K. (eds.) MSN 2006. LNCS, vol. 4325, pp. 473–484. Springer, Heidelberg (2006)

14. Huang, X., Mu, Y., Susilo, W., Wu, W.: Provably Secure Pairing-based Convertible Undeniable Signature with Short Signature Length. In: International Conference on Pairing-based Cryptography (Pairing 2007), Tokyo, Japan, July 2-4, 2007. LNCS, Springer, Heidelberg (to appear, 2007)

15. Jakobsson, M., Sako, K., Impagliazzo, R.: Designated Verifier Proofs and Their Applications. In: Maurer, U.M. (ed.) EUROCRYPT 1996. LNCS, vol. 1070, pp. 143–154. Springer, Heidelberg (1996)

16. Kim, S., Park, S., Won, D.: Proxy Signatures, Revisited. In: Han, Y., Quing, S. (eds.) ICICS 1997. LNCS, vol. 1334, pp. 223–232. Springer, Heidelberg (1997)

17. Lee, J.-Y., Cheon, J.H., Kim, S.: An analysis of proxy signatures: Is a secure channel necessary? In: Joye, M. (ed.) CT-RSA 2003. LNCS, vol. 2612, pp. 68–79. Springer, Heidelberg (2003)

18. Lee, B., Kim, H., Kim, K.: Secure mobile agent using strong nondesignated proxy signature. In: Varadharajan, V., Mu, Y. (eds.) ACISP 2001. LNCS, vol. 2119, pp. 474–486. Springer, Heidelberg (2001)

19. Libert, B.: Jean-Jacques Quisquater. In: Okamoto, T. (ed.) CT-RSA 2004. LNCS, vol. 2964, pp. 112–125. Springer, Heidelberg (2004)

20. Lyuu, Y.-D., Wu, M.-L.: Convertible Group Undeniable Signatures. In: Lee, P.J., Lim, C.H. (eds.) ICISC 2002. LNCS, vol. 2587, pp. 48–61. Springer, Heidelberg (2003)

21. Laguillaumie, F., Vergnaud, D.: Time-Selective Convertible Undeniable Signatures. In: Menezes, A.J. (ed.) CT-RSA 2005. LNCS, vol. 3376, pp. 154–171. Springer, Heidelberg (2005)

22. Mambo, M., Usuda, K., Okamoto, E.: Proxy signature: Delegation of the power to sign messages. IEICE Trans. Fundamentals E79-A(9), 1338–1353 (1996)

23. Miyazaki, T.: An Improved Scheme of the Gennaro-Krawczyk-Rabin Undeniable Signature System Based on RSA. In: Won, D. (ed.) ICISC 2000. LNCS, vol. 2015, pp. 135–149. Springer, Heidelberg (2001)

24. Michels, M., Petersen, H., Horster, P.: Breaking and Repairing a Convertible Undeniable Signature Scheme. In: Third ACM Conference on Computer and Communications Security, pp. 148–152. ACM Press, New York (1996)

25. Monnerat, J., Vaudenay, S.: Undeniable Signatures Based on Characters: How to Sign with One Bit. In: Bao, F., Deng, R., Zhou, J. (eds.) PKC 2004. LNCS, vol. 2947, pp. 69–85. Springer, Heidelberg (2004)
26. Monnerat, J., Vaudenay, S.: Short 2-Move Undeniable Signatures. In: International Conference on Cryptology in Vietnam 2006. LNCS, Springer, Heidelberg (to appear)
27. Ogata, W., Kurosawa, K., Heng, S.-H.: The Security of the FDH Variant of Chaums Undeniable Signature Scheme. In: Vaudenay, S. (ed.) PKC 2005. LNCS, vol. 3386, pp. 328–345. Springer, Heidelberg (2005)
28. Park, H.-U., Lee, I.-Y.: A digital nominative proxy signature scheme for mobile communications. In: Qing, S., Okamoto, T., Zhou, J. (eds.) ICICS 2001. LNCS, vol. 2229, pp. 451–455. Springer, Heidelberg (2001)
29. Pointcheval, D., Stern, J.: Security arguments for digital signatures and blind signatures. Journal of Cryptology 13(3), 361–396 (2000)
30. Shamir, A.: Identity-based Cryptosystems and Signature Schemes. In: Blakely, G.R., Chaum, D. (eds.) CRYPTO 1984. LNCS, vol. 196, pp. 47–53. Springer, Heidelberg (1985)
31. Wang, G., Qing, S., Wang, M., Zhou, Z.: Threshold Undeniable RSA Signature Scheme. In: Qing, S., Okamoto, T., Zhou, J. (eds.) ICICS 2001. LNCS, vol. 2229, pp. 221–232. Springer, Heidelberg (2001)
32. Zhang, F., Safavi-Naini, R., Susilo, W.: Attack on Han et al.'s ID-based Confirmer (Undeniable) Signature at ACM-EC 2003, http://eprint.iacr.org/2003/129

Secret Signatures: How to Achieve Business Privacy Efficiently?

Byoungcheon Lee[1,*], Kim-Kwang Raymond Choo[2,**], Jeongmo Yang[1], and Seungjae Yoo[1]

[1] Department of Information Security, Joongbu University
101 Daehak-Ro, Chubu-Myeon, Geumsan-Gun, Chungnam, 312-702, Korea
{sultan,jmyang,sjyoog}@joongbu.ac.kr
[2] Australian Institute of Criminology
GPO Box 2944, Canberra ACT 2601, Australia
raymond.choo@aic.gov.au

Abstract. Digital signatures provide authentication and non-repudiation in a public way in the sense that anyone can verify the validity of a digital signature using the corresponding public key. In this paper, we consider the issues of (1) signature privacy and (2) the corresponding public provability of signature. We propose a new digital signature variant, *secret signature*, which provides authentication and non-repudiation to the designated receiver only. If required, the correctness of the secret signature can be proven to the public either by the signer or the receiver. We conclude with a discussion to demonstrate the usefulness of the proposed cryptographic primitive (e.g., achieving signature privacy in an efficient manner).

Keywords: Secret signature, signature privacy, public provability, key agreement, anonymity, public auction.

1 Introduction

Digital signature, first proposed by Diffie and Hellman in 1976 [11], is an electronic version of handwritten signatures for digital documents. A digital signature on some message, m, is generated by a signer, A, using a secret signing key, sk_A. The correctness of the generated signature is verified using the corresponding public key, pk_A. It provides authentication and non-repudiation in a public way, in the sense that anyone can verify the validity of the digital signature, since pk_A is public information.

* This work was supported by Korea Research Foundation Grant funded by Korea Government (MOEHRD, Basic Research Promotion Fund), grant No. KRF-2005-003-D00375.
** The views and opinions expressed in this paper are those of the author and do not reflect those of the Australian Government or the Australian Institute of Criminology. This research was not undertaken as part of the author's work at the Australian Institute of Criminology.

S. Kim, M. Yung, and H.-W. Lee (Eds.): WISA 2007, LNCS 4867, pp. 30–47, 2007.

Signature Privacy. In this paper, we consider a business scenario where both the sender (signer) and the receiver (verifier) wish to keep their exchanged signatures private – we term this *signature privacy*. Such a (signature privacy) property does not appear to be easily achieved using general digital signature schemes. A 'straightforward' approach would be to encrypt a digital signature with the receiver's public key (or with an agreed key) so that only the legitimate receiver can decrypt and retrieve the original signature. This is the so-called *sign-then-encrypt* approach, which is widely adopted in the real world. In order to implement the signature and encryption operations in a more efficient manner, signcryption [26] was proposed in 1997 by Zheng. Alternative solutions to achieve signature privacy include using special signature schemes that limit the verifiability of the signature only to a designated entity (e.g., the designated verifier signature (DVS) [6,15] and the limited verifier signature (LVS) [1,9]).

Public Provability of Signature. Assume that we use a signature scheme designed to provide *signature privacy*. In the event that a dispute arises between a signer and a receiver during a business transaction, any chosen third party (e.g., a judge or the public) should be able to prove the correctness of the digital signature. We term such a property the *public provability* of a signature. This property can be easily achieved using either general digital signature schemes (i.e., by verifying the signature using the signer's public key) or the sign-then-encrypt schemes (i.e., by decrypting the encrypted signature and verifying the retrieved signature in a standard way). In the latter sign-then-encrypt approach, proving the correctness of decryption is a computationally expensive operation (e.g., include zero-knowledge proofs).

If we use signature schemes designed to provide signature privacy, then the public provability of generated signatures becomes an important requirement to ensure the fairness of business transactions. Although signcryption schemes appear to provide such a public provability feature, the original authors have not specified (this feature) explicitly. DVS and LVS schemes. DVS and LVS schemes, on the other hand, are unable to provide the public provability feature, since the designated verifier cannot transfer his conviction to others as the designated verifier is able to open the signature in any way of his choice using the knowledge of his/her private key.

OUR APPROACH. In this paper, we introduce a new digital signature variant, *secret signature (SS)*, designed to provide signature privacy. Advantages of our proposed SS scheme include providing all the following properties efficiently:

1. Authenticity and non-repudiation;
2. Signature privacy; and
3. Public provability of signature.

More specifically, in our proposed SS scheme:

– A signer, A, computes a signature using A's private key together with the public key of a receiver, B.
– B can then verify the signature using B's private key and A's public key.

- Given a (signed) message, no one other than the designated receiver can identify the message's authorship (e.g., what message is signed by whom and addressed to whom).
- If required, either A or B can provide a proof of validity of the signature. Given the proof of validity, any third party will be able to verify the validity of the associated signature.

To obtain the above-mentioned functionalities, we combine a secure signature scheme with a non-interactive one-way key agreement scheme between a signer and a receiver. In other words, our proposed SS can be viewed as a signature on a message and a secret agreed key. The designated receiver can recover the secret agreed key and verify the signature, but no third party can identify what message is signed by whom and addressed to whom.

Secret signature is useful in many real-world applications where

1. the privacy of the generated signature needs to be maintained, but the authorship of the signature can be publicly proven at a later stage,
2. message confidentiality is not required, and
3. efficiency is critical.

A main distinction between our proposed SS scheme and general signcryption schemes[1] is that SS scheme provides signature privacy without using encryption. Thus it is more efficient than signcryption in many applications where message confidentiality is not required. We describe some application examples in Section 7.

OUTLINE. We define the proposed SS scheme and provide security definitions in Section 2. In the following section, a concrete construction example of SS in discrete logarithm (DL)-based cryptosystems and the security proofs in the random oracle model are presented. We then present a brief discussion on how to prove the validity of SS in Section 4. We compare the features of SS with previously published signature privacy-related schemes in Section 5 and compare the efficiency of SS with signcryption in Section 6. Several possible applications are presented in Section 7. Section 8 concludes this paper.

2   Definitions

2.1   Definition of Secret Signature Scheme

There are two entities in the SS scheme, namely, a signer (sender), A, and a verifier (receiver), B. The formal definition of SS scheme is as follows.

Definition 1 (Secret Signature Scheme). *A secret signature (SS) scheme consists of the following six algorithms.*

---

[1] In this paper, we do not consider various features provided by different variants of the signcryption scheme (e.g., [10] and [17]).

1. **Setup** : params $\leftarrow SS.SetUp(1^k)$.

   A probabilistic algorithm, SS.SetUp, which takes a security parameter, k, as input and outputs the public parameters, params.

2. **Key Generation** : $(pk, sk) \leftarrow SS.KeyGen($params$)$.

   A probabilistic algorithm, SS.KeyGen, which takes the public parameters, params, *as input and outputs a pair (pk, sk) of matching public and private keys. For example, the public/private key pairs of the signer and receiver, (pk_S, sk_S) and (pk_R, sk_R), are generated using SS.KeyGen.*

3. **Signing** : $(V,$ seed$) \leftarrow SS.Sign($params$, m, sk_S, pk_R)$.

   A probabilistic algorithm, SS.Sign, run by the signer, which takes as input the public parameters, params, *a plaintext message, $m \in \{0, 1\}^*$, signer's private key, sk_S, and receiver's public key, pk_R; and outputs a secret signature, V and the random* seed *which was used to compute the signature. Signer has to keep* seed *secretly by himself.*

4. **Verification** : result $\leftarrow SS.Verify($params$, V, m, pk_S, sk_R)$.

   A deterministic algorithm, SS.Verify, run by the receiver, which takes as input the public parameters, params, *a secret signature, V, a plaintext message, m, the signer's public key, pk_S, and receiver's private key, sk_R, and outputs* result. *If V is a valid secret signature, then* result $= valid$, *otherwise,* result $= invalid$. *If correct signature $V = SS.Sign($params$, m, sk_S, pk_R)$ is tested, the verification result SS.Verify($params$, V, m, pk_S, sk_R) \mapsto$* result *should be valid.*

5. **Public Proving**

   A probabilistic algorithm that is run by either the signer or the receiver to prove the validity of the secret signature to public.

   Run by the signer : proof$_S \leftarrow SS.Proof.Signer($params$, V,$ seed$)$.

   SS.Proof.Signer which takes as input required parameters, params, *the signer's random* seed *used to compute the secret signature, and the secret signature, V, and outputs a proof,* proof$_S$.

   Run by the receiver : proof$_R \leftarrow SS.Proof.Receiver($params$, V, sk_R)$.

   SS.Proof.Receiver which takes as input required parameters, params, *the secret signature, V, and the receiver's private key, sk_R, and outputs a proof,* proof$_R$.

6. **Public Verification** : result $\leftarrow SS.PubVerify($params$, m, V, pk_S, pk_R,$ proof$)$.

   A deterministic algorithm, SS.PubVerify, which takes as input the public parameters, params, *a message m, a secret signature, V, the public keys of the signer and the intended receiver, and the validity proof* proof *(either* proof$_S$ *or* proof$_R$ *), and outputs a verification result,* result *(either valid or invalid).*

2.2 Security Definitions

Informally we consider the following security requirements for the proposed SS scheme described in Definition 1.

Correctness. If a secret signature is generated by following the protocol correctly, then the result of the verification always return *valid*.

Unforgeability. Anyone except the signer can have a non-negligible advantage
  in forging a secret signature.

Non-Repudiation. The signer is unable to repudiate the generation of a secret signature that the signer has previously generated. If unforgeability is
  provided, then non-repudiation is obtained consequently.

Signature Privacy. The secret signature generated by the signer is verifiable
  only by the designated receiver. No other entity except the signer and the
  receiver is able to have a non-negligible advantage in distinguishing the secret
  signature. Signature privacy is defined in terms of invisibility.

Public Provability. The validity of the signature can be proven to public by
  the signer or the verifier, if the need arises.

  To define the unforgeability and non-repudiation more formally, we recall the
widely accepted security notions on digital signatures, unforgeability against
chosen-message attacks. In order to provide non-repudiation, we would like to
prevent the forgery of A's signature without knowledge of A's signing key, except
with negligible probability. As shown in the seminal paper of Diffie and Hellman
[11], the security of such a scheme in the public key setting typically depends on
the existence of a one-way function. A formalized and widely accepted security
notion for digital signature was introduced by Goldwasser, Micali, and Rivest
[14], which they term *existential unforgeability under adaptive chosen-message
attack* (EF-ACMA).

  However, in our proposed SS scheme, there are two inputs: the message to be
signed and the intended recipient's public key. Hence, we extend the standard
security definition to the *existential unforgeability under the adaptive chosen-
message chosen-receiver attack* (EF-ACMCRA) in which the attacker is allowed
to query secret signatures to the signing oracle for any chosen message and
receiver's public key adaptively. An unforgeability of secret signature can be
defined in terms of the following unforgeability game.

Game Unforgeability: Let $\mathcal{F}$ be a forger and k be a security parameter.

1. (Initialization) First, params $\leftarrow SS.SetUp(1^k)$ is executed and the signer's
   key pair $(pk_S, sk_S) \leftarrow SS.KeyGen(\text{params})$ is computed. pk_S is given to $\mathcal{F}$.
2. (Training) $\mathcal{F}$ is allowed to ask a series of $SS.Sign$ queries for any combination
   of message m and receiver's public key, pk_R, chosen by $\mathcal{F}$ to the signing
   oracle. To do this, $\mathcal{F}$ computes $(pk_R, sk_R) \leftarrow SS.KeyGen(\text{params})$, and asks
   secret signature to the signing oracle by sending (m, pk_R, sk_R). Then the
   signing oracle provides valid secret signatures V.
3. (Output) $\mathcal{F}$ outputs a pair (m', pk'_R, sk'_R, V') as a forgery of a secret signature
   on message m' from the signer S to a receiver R'.

  $\mathcal{F}$ wins the game if valid $\leftarrow SS.Verify(\text{params}, V', m', pk_S, sk'_R)$ and the tuple (m', pk'_R, sk'_R, V') has never been queried to $SS.Sign$. In this definition of
unforgeability we assume that receiver's key pair is known to $\mathcal{F}$ and the signing
oracle. Without the knowledge of receiver's private key the signing oracle cannot

simulate secret signature and $\mathcal{F}$ cannot verify the validity of received secret signature. Since the main concern of the unforgeability game is the unforgeability of signer's signature, this assumption is reasonable.

Definition 2. *(Unforgeability)* *A secret signature scheme is said to be secure in the sense of existential unforgeability under the adaptive chosen-message chosen-receiver attack (EF-ACMCRA), if no probabilistic, polynomial-time (PPT) forger, $\mathcal{F}$, can have a non-negligible advantage in Game Unforgeability.*

Signature privacy requires that a given secret signature is a private information between the signer and the receiver. Any other entity cannot distinguish a secret signature from a random string in a signature space. Signature privacy can be defined in terms of the following invisibility game.

Game Invisibility: Let $\mathcal{D}$ be a distinguisher. First, params $\leftarrow$ $SS.SetUp(1^k)$ is executed and the signer's key pair $(pk_S, sk_S) \leftarrow SS.KeyGen(\text{params})$ is computed. pk_S is given to $\mathcal{D}$. Let $(pk_R, sk_R) \leftarrow SS.KeyGen(\text{params})$ be the receiver's key pair. pk_R is given to $\mathcal{D}$. At some point $\mathcal{D}$ outputs a message m' and requests for a challenge secret signature V' to the challenger $\mathcal{C}$. The challenge V' is generated by $\mathcal{C}$ based on the outcome of a hidden coin toss b. If $b = 1$, V' is generated by running $SS.Sign$. If $b = 0$, V' is chosen randomly in the signature space. At the end of the game, $\mathcal{D}$ outputs a guess b'. $\mathcal{D}$ wins if $b = b'$ and the tuple (m', V') has never been queried to $SS.Sign$.

In this invisibility game, receiver's private key sk_R is hidden from $\mathcal{D}$, since $\mathcal{D}$ is not the designated receiver. The designated receiver can distinguish the secret signature using his private key.

Definition 3. *(Invisibility)* *A secret signature scheme is said to provide invisibility, if no probabilistic, polynomial-time distinguisher, $\mathcal{D}$, can have a non-negligible advantage in Game Invisibility.*

2.3   General Implementation

The underlying intuition behind the general implementation of the proposed SS schemes is to combine a secure signature scheme and a non-interactive one-way key agreement. We denote the signer as A and the intended receiver as B.

Key agreement. Assume that A wants to send a secret signature for a message m to B. Using a non-interactive one-way key agreement scheme A generates an agreed secret (session) key, K, using B's public key, pk_B. For example, in DL-based cryptosystems, A chooses a random seed r_A and computes an agreed key $K = pk_B^{r_A} = g^{x_B r_A} = (g^{r_A})^{x_B}$.

Signing. A generates a signature, V, by signing $m\|K$ with A's signing key, sk_A. We can interpret V as a secret signature for the message m that is privately shared between A and B, since no one else should be able to verify V without knowledge of K.

Verification. B is able to compute the shared key using his private key and, hence, verify the secret signature. Any entity other than the signer and intended receiver cannot compute K, thus cannot determine the validity of the signature, even cannot tell what message was signed by whom to which receiver.

Note that signatures on the same message generated by the same signer for the same receiver will differ from one session to another due to the additional session key component in the generation of the secret signature. Also the session key K provides a binding between the signature and the recipient, thus the same signature cannot be used for other recipient.

We remark that we mainly focus on the signature privacy, rather than the message confidentiality. Depending on the requirement of the applications, the nature in which the actual message is exchanged can be sent in clear, sent in ciphertext, or does not need to be sent (implicitly known to the receiver).

3   DL-Based Implementation of Secret Signature Scheme

The proposed SS scheme can be implemented using different public key cryptosystems (e.g., identity-based cryptosystems). In this section, we present an implementation example of the SS scheme in the discrete logarithm-based setting.

1: Setup
>   We assume common system parameters (p, q, g) where p and q are large primes satisfying $q|p - 1$ and g is an element of order q in $\mathbb{Z}_q^*$. We then require a secure cryptographic hash function, $\mathcal{H} : \{0, 1\} \mapsto \mathbb{Z}_q$, which we will model as a random oracle [4]. For readability, we will omit the modulo p in our subsequent equations, if it is clear. Let $\in_R$ denote uniform random selection.

2: Key Generation
>   A signer A has a long-term certified key pair (x_A, y_A), where $x_A \in_R \mathbb{Z}_q^*$ and $y_A = g^{x_A}$. A receiver B has a long-term certified key pair (x_B, y_B), where $x_B \in_R \mathbb{Z}_q^*$ and $y_B = g^{x_B}$.

3: Signing
>   Let m denote the message to be signed. The signer, A, selects a random seeds $r_A \in_R \mathbb{Z}_q^*$. Using r_A, A now computes $U = g^{r_A}$ and the key to be shared with the verifier, $W = y_B^{r_A}$. A computes $V = r_A + x_A \mathcal{H}(m, U, W)$. A sends the secret signature, $\langle m, U, V \rangle$, to the intended receiver, B.

4: Verification
>   The receiver, B, uses his private key, x_B, to compute the exchanged key chosen by the signer, $W = U^{x_B}$. B then verifies V by $g^V \overset{?}{=} U \cdot y_A^{\mathcal{H}(m, U, W)}$. If V verifies correctly, then B knows that the message is indeed signed by A.

5: Public Proving
>   The validity of secret signature $\langle m, U, V \rangle$ is proven to public either by the signer or the receiver. In this stage we consider the following two cases according to the information revealed.

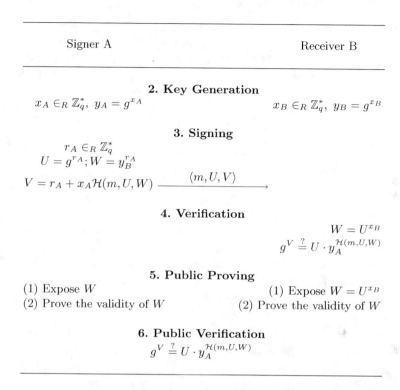

Signer A	Receiver B

2. Key Generation

$x_A \in_R \mathbb{Z}_q^*, \; y_A = g^{x_A}$ $\qquad\qquad$ $x_B \in_R \mathbb{Z}_q^*, \; y_B = g^{x_B}$

3. Signing

$r_A \in_R \mathbb{Z}_q^*$
$U = g^{r_A}; W = y_B^{r_A}$
$V = r_A + x_A \mathcal{H}(m, U, W) \xrightarrow{\quad \langle m, U, V \rangle \quad}$

4. Verification

$W = U^{x_B}$
$g^V \overset{?}{=} U \cdot y_A^{\mathcal{H}(m,U,W)}$

5. Public Proving

(1) Expose W $\qquad\qquad\qquad$ (1) Expose $W = U^{x_B}$
(2) Prove the validity of W $\qquad$ (2) Prove the validity of W

6. Public Verification

$g^V \overset{?}{=} U \cdot y_A^{\mathcal{H}(m,U,W)}$

Fig. 1. DL-based implementation

(1) **Message proving.** If the receiver information needs not be exposed, just reveal W. With the additional information, W, anyone can verify that (U, V) is a correct signature of the signer A for the message m and W. If only message proving is required, it is very efficient.

(2) **Receiver proving.** If the receiver information needs to be proven, reveal W and prove its correctness with respect to the receiver's public key. Its validity can be proven by the signer or the receiver either non-anonymously (using the general proof) or anonymously (using the anonymous proof) which will be described in Section 4.

6: Public Verification

Given W which is proven to be correct, anyone can verify the validity of the secret signature by checking $g^V \overset{?}{=} U \cdot y_A^{\mathcal{H}(m,U,W)}$.

We prove the security of our scheme assuming the intractability of the discrete log problem and also in the random oracle model (ROM).

Theorem 1. *The proposed SS scheme is EF-ACMCRA secure (in the sense of Definition 2) in the random oracle model under the assumption that the discrete logarithm problem is intractable.*

Proof Sketch. Since the proposed SS scheme is a ElGamal family signature scheme, Forking lemma [21,20] can be applied. We assume that there exists a forger $\mathcal{F}$ (described in Definition 2) that can forge a secret signature in time $t(k)$ with a non-negligible advantage $\epsilon(k)$. In the training stage $\mathcal{F}$ can ask signing queries for any combination of message and receiver pair to the signing oracle and receive correct secret signatures from the signing oracle. The challenger $\mathcal{C}$ controls all communication of $\mathcal{F}$ and simulate the signing queries.

The signing algorithm uses a hash function which is modeled by an random oracle under the random oracle model. For each signing query (M, y_R, x_R) given by $\mathcal{F}$, $\mathcal{C}$ picks random integers $a, b \in_R Z_q^*$ and computes

$$U \leftarrow g^a y_A^b, \quad W \leftarrow U^{x_R}, \quad h \leftarrow -b, \quad V = a.$$

$\mathcal{C}$ gives h as a random oracle answer to the $\mathcal{H}(m, U, W)$ query and (U, V) as the signature for (M, y_R, x_R) signing query. Then this simulated signatures can pass $\mathcal{F}$'s signature verification and are indistinguishable from the real signatures.

The remaining proof is the same as the case for the original Schnorr signature. The discrete logarithm problem can be solved in time $t'(k)$ with advantage $\epsilon'(k)$ where

$$t'(k) \approx \{2(t(k) + q_H \tau) + O_B(q_S k^3)\}/\epsilon(k), \quad \epsilon'(k) \approx q_H^{-0.5}$$

where q_S and q_H are the numbers of signing queries and hash oracle queries, respectively, and τ is time for answering a hash query. If a successful forking is found, signer's private key x_A can be computed, which contradicts the discrete logarithm assumption. □

Theorem 2. *The proposed SS scheme provides signature privacy (invisibility) in the sense of Definitions 3 under the random oracle model, if the decisional Diffie-Hellman (DDH) problem is intractable.*

The proof for Theorem 2 generally follows that of Galbraith and Mao [13]. We assumes that there exist an adversary $\mathcal{D}$, who can gain a non-negligible advantage in distinguishing the signatures in the game outlined in Definition 3. We now construct another algorithm, $\mathcal{D}_{DDH}$, to break the decisional Diffie–Hellman (DDH) problem using $\mathcal{D}$.

4   Proving the Validity of Secret Signature

In the public proving stage, the signer or the receiver prove the validity of secret signature to a judge or public. Once the proof is given, anyone can verify the validity of secret signature and non-repudiation is provided. Here we consider the following two cases.

General Proof. In this protocol, the identity of the entity (signer or receiver) who proves the validity of the SS is revealed, since the signer's proof and the receiver's proof are distinguishable.

Anonymous Proof. As the name suggests, the identity of the entity who proves the validity of the SS is not revealed, since the signer's proof and the receiver's proof are indistinguishable. However, this proof is computationally more expensive than that of the general proof.

4.1   General Proof Protocol

In this protocol, either the signer, A, or the receiver, B, reveals the shared key W and proves its validity using the proof outlined in Appendix A.

- The signer A proves $ZKP(r_A) : (\log_g U = \log_{y_B} W = r_A)$ using his knowledge of r_A.
- The receiver B proves $ZKP(x_B) : (\log_g y_B = \log_U W = x_B)$ using his knowledge of x_B.

It is easy to see that the proofs initiated by the signer and the receiver are distinguishable, hence the identity of the entity who had exposed the secret signature is revealed.

4.2   Anonymous Proof Protocol

There might exist situations where we are unable to reveal the identity of the entity who exposed the secret signature, perhaps, due to privacy or legal restrictions. In such cases, we cannot employ the general proof protocol presented above. Here we show how the signer or the receiver can prove the validity of secret signature anonymously without revealing their identity.

Note that the tuple $\langle g, U, y_B, W \rangle$ has the special relations depicted in Figure 2. The signer knows $r_A (= \log_g U = \log_{y_B} W)$ and the receiver knows $x_B (= \log_g y_B = \log_U W)$.

The anonymous proof protocol can be initiated either by A or by B. They expose the shared key $W = y_B^{r_A} = U^{x_B} = g^{r_A x_B}$ and demonstrate their knowledge of the corresponding secret information as follows.

$$ZKP(r_A \vee x_B) : (\log_g U = \log_{y_B} W = r_A) \vee (\log_g y_B = \log_U W = x_B).$$

It is a OR combination of two zero-knowledge proofs of the equality of two discrete logarithms described in Appendix B. A or B is able to prove the validity of W by using their knowledge of r_A or x_B.

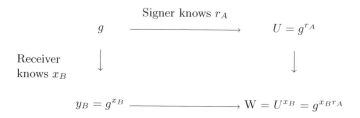

Fig. 2. Special relations of the tuple $\langle g, U, y_B, W \rangle$

Although these two proofs by the signer and the receiver are computed differently, any public verifier is unable to distinguish whether the proof is provided by the signer or the receiver. If one of the party opens the secret signature anonymously, the other partner know that no one other than the partnering entity has opened the secret signature. However, the party is unable to prove that the other partnering entity has opened the secret signature. From the public's perspective, the identity remains anonymous.

5   Comparison of Features

Several signature variants found in the literature also provide signature-privacy-related functionalities. We now compare these schemes with our proposed SS scheme.

Sign-then-encrypt approach: Although this approach provides signature privacy property, it has the following disadvantage. Once the receiver decrypt the encrypted signature and obtain the corresponding publicly verifiable signature, the message is no longer linkable to the receiver. Thus the receiver or any third party can use it for malicious purposes. On the other hand, this is not the case in our SS scheme as the (special) signature generated by a signer is given to a specific receiver.

Undeniable signature [8] and designated confirmer signature [5]: In the former scheme, the recipient has to interact with the signer to be convinced of its validity whilst in the latter scheme, the signatures has to be verified by interacting with an entity, the confirmer, designated by the signer. Both signature schemes require an interactive protocol to carry out signature verification. In our proposed SS scheme only a simple and computationally cheap algorithm is required to carry out the signature verification.

Nominative signature [16] scheme: This scheme allows a nominator (signer) and a nominee (verifier) to jointly generate and publish the signature in such a way that only the nominee can verify the signature and if necessary, only the nominee can prove to a third party that the signature is valid. Although signature privacy can be achieved using this scheme, it requires an interactive protocol for the signing stage. In our proposed SS scheme, a signer is able to generate the signature on his/her own.

Designated Verifier Signature (DVS) scheme: This scheme, independently proposed by Jakobsson, Sako, and Impagliazzo [15][2] and Chaum [6] in 1996, provides signature privacy. Although the designated verifier can be convinced of the validity of the signature in the DVS scheme, the verifier is unable to transfer the conviction to any other entity. A major difference between our proposed SS scheme and the DVS scheme is that the latter is unable to provide public provability of the signature.

Limited Verifier Signature (LVS) scheme: This scheme, first proposed by Araki, Uehara, and Imamura in 1999 [1], differs from the DVS scheme in that

---

[2] Lipmaa, Wang, and Bao [19] pointed out a weakness in this DVS scheme [15].

the limited verifier is able to transfer the proof to convince another entity (e.g., a judge) if the signer has violated some rule non-cryptographically. Such a proof is, however, not transferrable to a third entity. In 2004, Chen *et. al.* proposed a convertible limited verifier signature scheme in a pairing-based setting [9]. Their scheme allows the limited verifier signature to be transformed into a publicly verifiable signature. This converted limited verifier signature, however, is rather loosely related to the limited verifier any more since the limited verifier is unable to prove that he is the intended recipient of the converted signature. On the other hand in our proposed SS scheme, any receiver can prove publicly that he is the legitimate receiver of the corresponding signature.

Anonymous signature scheme: First proposed by Yang *et al.* [25], this scheme appears to have similar property. However, the anonymous signature scheme provides signer anonymity and does not have an intended receiver when the signature is generated. We will provide an example in Section 7 to better explain this difference.

Signcryption scheme [26]: This scheme, first proposed by Zheng in 1997, is perhaps most similar to our proposed SS scheme. The signcryption scheme is built from a clever combination of a secure encryption scheme and a secure signature scheme, providing both confidentiality and non-repudiation. Many extensions of the signcryption scheme have also been proposed (e.g., [2,3,18,22,23][3]). Signcryption provides signature privacy by encrypting the message. However, this is computationally expensive particularly for applications that do not require message confidentiality. SS is a new approach to provide signature privacy without encryption.

At first read, our proposed SS scheme might be confused with other previously published signature privacy-related signature schemes. However, if we refer to the definition of SS scheme given in Definition 1, it is clear that:

- The undeniable signature scheme differs from the SS scheme since interactive protocol between the signer and the verifier is required in the signature verification algorithm.
- DVS and LVS schemes differ from the SS scheme since public provability cannot be achieved.
- Convertible LVS scheme differs from the SS scheme since the converted signature is not related with the receiver in any way.
- The anonymous signature scheme differs from the SS scheme since the signature does not have an intended receiver when the signature is generated whilst in our proposed SS scheme, an intended receiver is required at the time of signature generation.

On the other hand, the signcryption scheme is most similar to our proposed SS scheme if the public proving/verification algorithms are further defined.

---

[3] The signcryption scheme of Libert and Quisquater [18] is shown to be insecure [24].

6 Comparison of Efficiency

Since the signature-privacy-related signature schemes presented in Section 5 – with the exception of the signcryption scheme – have rather different functionalities, we will restrict our comparison only to the signcryption scheme. Since public proving/verification protocols were not defined in the original signcryption scheme, we assume that similar zero-knowledge proof techniques are applied in order to facilitate our comparison. Note that both the general and anonymous proofs are also possible in the signcryption scheme.

For completeness, we now describe briefly how the general and anonymous proofs are possible in Zheng's signcryption scheme. To prove the correctness of signcryption, either the signer or the receiver has to compute and reveal the following information (we use the same notation as the original paper).

- The signer, A, has to keep the random number, x, used in the signcryption secret. A has to compute and reveal y_b^x and g^x (requires 1 extra E). In this case, the public verifier has to check whether $g^x \stackrel{?}{=} g^{rs} y_a^s$ holds (requires $2E$).
- The receiver, B, has to compute and reveal $g^x = g^{rs} y_a^s$ and $y_b^x = (g^x)^{x_b}$ (requires $3E$).

Now, using the general proof protocol, the signer can then prove $ZKP(x)$: $(\log_g g^x = \log_{y_b} y_b^x = x)$ and the receiver can prove $ZKP(x_b)$: $(\log_g y_b = \log_{g^x} y_b^x = x_b)$, which requires $2E$ for proof and $4E$ for verification. Anonymous proof is also possible for the $\langle g, g^x, y_b, y_b^x \rangle$ tuple, which requires $6E$ for proof and $8E$ for verification.

Some of the computations required by the signer in our scheme can be performed offline (i.e., before the message to be sent and the receiver are known), such as $U = g^{r_A}$, and hence, provides efficiency. In Table 1, we compare the efficiency of our scheme with Zheng's signcryption scheme. The notation used in Table 1 is as follows: E and E_{off} denotes online and offline modular exponentiations, respectively; and ED denotes the cost for symmetric encryption or

Table 1. Summary of efficiency analysis

		Signcryption [26]	Proposed SS scheme
Signing		$1E + 1ED$	$1E + 1E_{off}$
Verification		$2E + 1ED$	$3E$
General proof	Proof	$3E$	$2E$
by signer	Verification	$6E$	$4E$
General proof	Proof	$5E$	$2E$
by receiver	Verification	$4E$	$4E$
Anonymous proof	Proof	$7E$	$6E$
by signer	Verification	$10E$	$8E$
Anonymous proof	Proof	$9E$	$6E$
by receiver	Verification	$8E$	$8E$
Public verification		$1ED$	$2E$

decryption. For simplicity, we ignore modulo multiplication/division operations and hash operations in our comparison.

Compared with Zheng's signcryption, our proposed SS scheme is more efficient both in the actual signature scheme and the public proving. Since the SS scheme does not use symmetric encryption, it is more efficient than signcryption, especially with long message when message confidentiality is not required. In public proving, the same zero-knowledge proofs can be used. In signcryption, however, both the signer and receiver have to compute and reveal additional information. All required information is already included in the generated signature in the SS scheme. Therefore, the SS scheme is more efficient than signcryption when used in business transactions that do not require confidentiality of messages.

7 Applications of Secret Signatures

The proposed SS scheme can be used as an important cryptographic primitive to achieve business privacy, providing both signature privacy and public provability of signature efficiently.

Secret signature is useful in many applications where (1) the privacy of generated signature needs to be maintained, but the authorship of the signature can be publicly proven at a later stage, (2) message confidentiality is not very important, and (3) efficiency is critical.

We now describe some possible application examples.

Application 1: Private Business Transaction

Let's assume that two business entities, A and B, wanting to exchange some not-so-confidential contract document, m (e.g., m can be constructed using open source information). Although the contents of m do not need to be confidential, both A and B do not want to reveal to other entities that they had signed m. By using the proposed SS scheme, both A and B are assured that no third party is aware that m has been signed. In the event that one of the entities violates a non-cryptographic business rule, the other entity can prove the validity of their private contract to a third party by opening the generated secret signature. The public provability property guarantees the fairness of private business.

Application 2: Public Auction

We consider an application is a public auction (or English auction) setting where bidding prices are published and the bidders are allowed to bid prices anonymously as frequently as desired. When the winner is finally decided, the anonymity of the winning bid is revealed and the correctness of the winning bid should be proven publicly (to provide public verifiability). This is a typical example where message confidentiality is not required, but signature privacy and public provability are required.

To provide the anonymity of bid with public provability, we can use the proposed SS scheme. In the bidding stage, bidders bid their prices using a secret signature with the auctioneer as a receiver. For example, let A be the auctioneer, B_i be bidders, and p_j be the bidding prices. Bidder B_i computes

$$s_{i,j} = SS.Sign(\text{params}, p_j, sk_{B_i}, pk_A), \quad k_{i,j} = E_{pk_A}(B_i),$$

and posts $\langle p_j, s_{i,j}, k_{i,j} \rangle$ on the bulletin board, where $k_{i,j}$ is an encrypted ID information of the bidder (can be decrypted only by the auctioneer). In the winner announcement stage, the auctioneer opens the highest price bid and proves the correctness of secret signature. Any misbehavior of the auctioneer or bidders can be proven publicly. Note that bidder anonymity was achieved easily without using any encryption. Also note that threshold cryptography can be used by the auctioneer such that pk_A is distributed to multiple auctioneers and bidder information of the losing bids is kept secret.

Application 3: Paper Submission System

Consider a paper submission system for a conference. In this case submitted papers should be anonymous while they need not be encrypted. Authors need to commit the following facts to the program chair with a signature; (1) the submitted paper is their authentic work, (2) the submitted paper is not submitted in parallel to another conference or journal, (3) the authors will present the paper if accepted, and etc. Upon receiving the submission, the program chair has to issue a receipt for the submitted paper to the author.

In such an application, the authors and the conference program chair can exchange secret signatures with the other entity as a receiver (or publish the secret signature on the bulletin board as a public commitment). If general signatures are exchanged, anonymity will be broken (since anyone can verify the authorship of the submitted paper using the respective public keys). In the unlikely event of a dispute between the program chair and an author at a later stage, it can be resolved easily by using the public proving feature of secret signature.

One may note that the generated secret signature is tightly bound to the recipient, the program chair of the conference. Hence, the same signature cannot be submitted to another recipient, the program chair of another conference. Therefore, if it was subsequently discovered that the same paper with two different signatures was submitted to two different conferences in parallel, the author cannot repudiate his misbehavior. However, this is not the case for Yang et $al.$'s [25] anonymous signature scheme; the generated signature is not bound to any recipient. The signer is able to repudiate that someone other than the signer has forwarded the signature and the paper to the program chair of another conference without the signer's knowledge.

8   Conclusion

We had discussed the signature privacy issue and introduced a new signature variant, which we termed secret signature (SS). The SS scheme provides signature privacy and public provability of signature in an efficient manner by combining secure signature schemes and non-interactive one-way key agreement schemes. Although this is a very simple concept, it is a useful and efficient cryptographic tool to achieve business privacy.

We then presented a concrete implementation example of secret signature in discrete logarithm-based cryptosystems. Future extension of this work includes implementing the SS scheme in other cryptosystems such as RSA-based and pairing-based cryptosystems.

Acknowledgement

The second author would like to thank Sherman SM Chow for pointing out references [10] and [17].

References

1. Araki, S., Uehara, S., Imamura, K.: The Limited Verifier Signature and its Applications. IEICE Transactions E82-A(1), 63–68 (1999)
2. Baek, J., Steinfeld, R., Zheng, Y.: One-time Verifier-based Encrypted Key Exchange. In: Naccache, D., Paillier, P. (eds.) PKC 2002. LNCS, vol. 2274, pp. 80–98. Springer, Heidelberg (2002)
3. Bao, F., Deng, R.H.: A Signcryption Scheme with Signature Directly Verifiable by Public Key. In: Imai, H., Zheng, Y. (eds.) PKC 1998. LNCS, vol. 1431, pp. 55–59. Springer, Heidelberg (1998)
4. Bellare, M., Rogaway, P.: Random Oracles Are Practical: A Paradigm For Designing Efficient Protocols. In: ACM CCS 1993, pp. 62–73. ACM Press, New York (1993)
5. Chaum, D.: Undeniable Signatures. In: De Santis, A. (ed.) EUROCRYPT 1994. LNCS, vol. 950, pp. 86–91. Springer, Heidelberg (1995)
6. Chaum, D.: Private Signature and Proof Systems. United States Patent 5,493,614 (1996)
7. Chaum, D., Pedersen, T.P.: Wallet Databases with Observers. In: Brickell, E.F. (ed.) CRYPTO 1992. LNCS, vol. 740, pp. 89–105. Springer, Heidelberg (1993)
8. Chaum, D., van Antwerpen, H.: Undeniable Signatures. In: Brassard, G. (ed.) CRYPTO 1989. LNCS, vol. 435, pp. 212–216. Springer, Heidelberg (1990)
9. Chen, X., Zhang, F., Kim, K.: Limited Verifier Signature Scheme from Bilinear Pairings. In: Jakobsson, M., Yung, M., Zhou, J. (eds.) ACNS 2004. LNCS, vol. 3089, pp. 135–148. Springer, Heidelberg (2004)
10. Chow, S.S.M., Yiu, S.M., Hui, L.C.K., Chow, K.P.: Efficient Forward and Provably Secure ID-Based Signcryption Scheme with Public Verifiability and Public Ciphertext Authenticity. In: Lim, J.-I., Lee, D.-H. (eds.) ICISC 2003. LNCS, vol. 2971, pp. 352–369. Springer, Heidelberg (2004)
11. Diffie, W., Hellman, M.: Multiuser Cryptographic Techniques. In: AFIPS 1976 National Computer Conference, pp. 109–112. AFIPS Press (1976)
12. Fiat, A., Shamir, A.: How to Prove Yourself: Practical Solutions to Identification and Signature Problems. In: Odlyzko, A.M. (ed.) CRYPTO 1986. LNCS, vol. 263, pp. 186–194. Springer, Heidelberg (1987)
13. Galbraith, S.D., Mao, W.: Invisibility and Anonymity of Undeniable and Confirmer Signatures. In: Joye, M. (ed.) CT-RSA 2003. LNCS, vol. 2612, pp. 80–97. Springer, Heidelberg (2003)

14. Goldwasser, S., Micali, S., Rivest, R.L.: A Digital Signature Scheme Secure Against Adaptive Chosen-Message Attacks. SIAM Journal on Computing 17(2), 281–308 (1988)
15. Jakobsson, M., Sako, K., Impagliazzo, R.: Designated Verifier Proofs and Their Applications. In: Maurer, U.M. (ed.) EUROCRYPT 1996. LNCS, vol. 1070, pp. 321–331. Springer, Heidelberg (1996)
16. Kim, S.J., Park, S.J., Won, D.H.: Zero-Knowledge Nominative Signatures, pp. 380–392 (1996)
17. Li, C.K., Yang, G., Wong, D.S., Deng, X., Chow, S.S.M.: An Efficient Signcryption Scheme with Key Privacy. In: EuroPKI 2007. LNCS, vol. 4582, pp. 78–93. Springer, Heidelberg (2007)
18. Libert, B., Quisquater, J.-J.: Efficient Signcryption with Key Privacy from Gap Diffie-Hellman Groups. In: Bao, F., Deng, R., Zhou, J. (eds.) PKC 2004. LNCS, vol. 2947, pp. 187–200. Springer, Heidelberg (2004)
19. Lipmaa, H., Wang, G., Bao, F.: Designated Verifier Signature Schemes- Attacks, New Security Notions and a New Construction. In: Welzl, E., Montanari, U., Rolim, J.D.P. (eds.) ICALP 2000. LNCS, vol. 1853, pp. 459–471. Springer, Heidelberg (2000)
20. Mao, W.: Modern Cryptography: Theory and Practice. Prentice-Hall, Englewood Cliffs (2003)
21. Pointcheval, D., Stern, J.: Security Arguments for Digital Signatures and Blind Signatures. Journal of Cryptology 13, 361–396 (2000)
22. Shin, J.-B., Lee, K., Shim, K.: New DSA-Verifiable Signcryption Schemes. In: Deng, R.H., Qing, S., Bao, F., Zhou, J. (eds.) ICICS 2002. LNCS, vol. 2513, pp. 35–47. Springer, Heidelberg (2002)
23. Steinfeld, R., Zheng, Y.: A Signcryption Scheme Based on Integer Factorization. In: Okamoto, E., Pieprzyk, J.P., Seberry, J. (eds.) ISW 2000. LNCS, vol. 1975, pp. 308–322. Springer, Heidelberg (2000)
24. Yang, G., Wong, D.S., Deng, X.: Analysis and Improvement of a Signcryption Scheme with Key Privacy. In: Zhou, J., Lopez, J., Deng, R.H., Bao, F. (eds.) ISC 2005. LNCS, vol. 3650, pp. 218–232. Springer, Heidelberg (2005)
25. Yang, G., Wong, D.S., Deng, X., Wang, H.: Anonymous Signature Schemes. In: Yung, M., Dodis, Y., Kiayias, A., Malkin, T.G. (eds.) PKC 2006. LNCS, vol. 3958, Springer, Heidelberg (2006)
26. Zheng, Y.: Digital Signcryption or How to Achieve Cost (Signature & Encryption) << Cost (Signature) + Cost (Encryption). In: Kaliski Jr., B.S. (ed.) CRYPTO 1997. LNCS, vol. 1294, pp. 1165–1793. Springer, Heidelberg (1997)

A   Proving the Equality of Two Discrete Logarithms

Let α and β be two independent generators of order q in modular p. A prover P tries to prove to a verifier V that two numbers $a = \alpha^x$ and $b = \beta^x$ have the same exponent without exposing x. We denote this proof as

$$ZKP(x) : (\log_\alpha a = \log_\beta b = x).$$

Based on the scheme by Chaum and Pedersen [7] and Fiat-Shamir's heuristics [12] the non-interactive proof can be done as follows.

$ZKP(x) : (\log_\alpha a = \log_\beta b = x)$

- Proof: Prover P randomly chooses t from $\mathbb{Z}_q^*$ and computes $c = \alpha^t$ and $d = \beta^t$. He computes $h = \mathcal{H}(\alpha, \beta, a, b, c, d)$ and $s = t + hx$, then sends (c, d, s) to the verifier. Proof requires two exponentiation operations.
- Verification: Verifier V first computes $h = \mathcal{H}(\alpha, \beta, a, b, c, d)$. Then he checks $\alpha^s \overset{?}{=} ca^h$ and $\beta^s \overset{?}{=} db^h$. Verification requires four exponentiation operations.

B   OR Proving the Equality of Two Discrete Logarithms

Let α_1, β_1, α_2, β_2 be four independent generators of order q in modular p.

A prover P tries to prove to a verifier V that either $\log_{\alpha_1} a_1 = \log_{\beta_1} b_1 (= x_1)$ or $\log_{\alpha_2} a_2 = \log_{\beta_2} b_2 (= x_2)$ holds using his knowledge of x_1 or x_2 without exposing it. It is an OR combination of two proofs for the equality of two discrete logarithms. We denote this proof as

$$ZKP(x_1 \lor x_2) : (\log_{\alpha_1} a_1 = \log_{\beta_1} b_1 = x_1) \lor (\log_{\alpha_2} a_2 = \log_{\beta_2} b_2 = x_2).$$

The prover knows either x_1 or x_2, but does not know them all. This proof can be done as follows.

$ZKP(x_1 \lor x_2) : (\log_{\alpha_1} a_1 = \log_{\beta_1} b_1 = x_1) \lor (\log_{\alpha_2} a_2 = \log_{\beta_2} b_2 = x_2)$

- Proof: Assume that the prover P knows x_b and does not know $x_{b'}$.
  - Randomly chooses $r_b, s_{b'}, t_{b'}$ from $\mathbb{Z}_q^*$.
  - Computes $c_b = \alpha_b^{r_b}, d_b = \beta_b^{r_b}, c_{b'} = \alpha_{b'}^{s_{b'}} a_{b'}^{t_{b'}}, d_{b'} = \beta_{b'}^{s_{b'}} b_{b'}^{t_{b'}}$ (incurring six exponentiation operations).
  - Computes $t = \mathcal{H}(\alpha_1, \beta_1, \alpha_2, \beta_2, a_1, b_1, a_2, b_2, c_1, d_1, c_2, d_2)$.
  - Computes $t_b = t - t_{b'}$ and $s_b = r_b - t_b x_b$, then sends $(c_1, d_1, c_2, d_2, s_1, t_1, s_2, t_2)$.
- Verification: Verifier V checks
  - $c_1 \overset{?}{=} \alpha_1^{s_1} a_1^{t_1}, \ d_1 \overset{?}{=} \beta_1^{s_1} b_1^{t_1}, \ c_2 \overset{?}{=} \alpha_2^{s_2} a_2^{t_2}, \ d_2 \overset{?}{=} \beta_2^{s_2} b_2^{t_2}$ and
  - $t_1 + t_2 \overset{?}{=} \mathcal{H}(\alpha_1, \beta_1, \alpha_2, \beta_2, a_1, b_1, a_2, b_2, c_1, d_1, c_2, d_2)$.

Implementation of BioAPI Conformance Test Suite Using BSP Testing Model

Jihyeon Jang[1], Stephen J. Elliott[2], and Hakil Kim[1]

[1] School of Information & Communication Engineering, Inha University
jhjang@vision.inha.ac.kr, hikim@inha.ac.kr
[2] Department of Industrial Technology, Purdue University
elliott@purdue.edu

Abstract. The purpose of this paper is to design a Conformance Test Suite(CTS) for BSPs(Biometric Service Provider) based upon the BioAPI (Biometric Application Programming Interface) v2.0, an international standard by ISO/IEC JTC1/SC37. The proposed BioAPI CTS enables users to test BSPs without depending on various frameworks. In this paper, a test scheduling tool has been embodied in order to use Test Assertion with XML. In order to demonstrate the performance of the CTS, the experiment was performed using both commercial fingerprint verification and identification BSPs. The developed CTS will be installed at Korean National Biometrics Test Center and used to test whether commercial biometrics products are compliant to BioAPI.

Keywords: BioAPI, Conformance Test Suite, Biometric Service Provider.

1 Introduction

Biometrics recognition technology is rapidly developing with numerous biometrics products entering the marketplace, and are becoming pervasive in some areas. Each vendor develops biometrics products in different technical schemes, and the market suffers from the problem of 'One-Vendor Solution,' which means that end user's system becomes dependent on a particular vendor's solution and nearly impossible to upgrade by other vendor's solution. This problem is caused by the lack of standards in biometrics technology. Numerous studies have been conducted to overcome the problem of 'One-Vendor Solution', thus, the need for a standardized interface of biometrics products has increased.

Since the establishment of ISO/IEC JTC1/SC37 in 2002, the standardization of biometrics technology has been actively progressed. One of the most important standards for biometrics is ISO 19784-1, BioAPI Specification (Biometric Application Programming Interface - Part 1: Specification). This standard defines the Application Programming Interface and Service Provider Interface (SPI) for standard interfaces within a biometric system consisting of components from multiple vendors. Commercial products are required to be compliant to this standard, hence, need to be tested for conformance.

S. Kim, M. Yung, and H.-W. Lee (Eds.): WISA 2007, LNCS 4867, pp. 48–60, 2007.

The Conformance Test Suite (CTS) is a means of identifying whether a product satisfies a corresponding standard. Once certified by the CTS, the product is deemed interoperable with standard-compliant devices manufactured by other vendors. The previous versions of BioAPI CTS initially developed by Korea Information Security Agency (KISA) in 2003 [1-3] and by NIST in 2006[4], were based on BioAPI v1.1 proposed by the Biometrics Consortium [5]. These versions indirectly tested whether BSPs (Biometric Service Provider) were compliant to the standard, using the consortium's BioAPI framework which is a middleware infrastructure between BioAPI compliant applications and BSPs. The problem with these previous versions is that when an error occurs, the CTS cannot find whether it originated from the BSP under test or from the framework.

In order to resolve the problem stated above, this study develops a new BioAPI CTS in the following technical aspects. Firstly, the new CTS which is based on BioAPI v2.0 standards [6] is able to test BSPs without the BioAPI framework. Secondly, it can load various test procedures arbitrarily designed depending on the purpose of the test. Thirdly, the new CTS report the test results in XML format. Finally, it is implemented to test each BSP differently, depending on the purpose of the BSP.

The following section introduces the conformance test methods and models. The third section describes the design and implementation of the proposed CTS. The forth section concludes this paper and discusses further works.

2   Conformance Test Suite for BioAPI: Methods and Models [7]

Conformance test is defined as an evaluation of whether a developed product meets standard requirements. That is, it must provide a message to inform the vendor that the usage form of a product is incorrect or it is omitted items of standards specifications. Accordingly, the CTS must be composed so that it can evaluate whether a product appropriately applies the standard.

2.1   Conformance Testing Methods

As presented in Fig. 1, the conformance test of BioAPI is divided into a Function Test, to evaluate BioAPI functions, and a Scenario Test, to evaluate whether the BSP functions perform correctly. The function test evaluates whether mandatory and optional functions conform to the standard. If a function subject to be tested is called, function mapping proceeds in the framework and the BSP function is implemented through the relevant SPI (Service Provider Interface) function. The return values on each function implemented in the BSP are delivered to an application, and the result is output through test log after the performance process is finished. All BSPs support basic component management, handle, event and utility operations. The callback, database and BioAPI unit operations are optional. Second, the scenario test is a method of evaluating whether the BSP is capable of calling successive functions prescribed by the standard. The processes of the three types of scenario test are defined as the following.

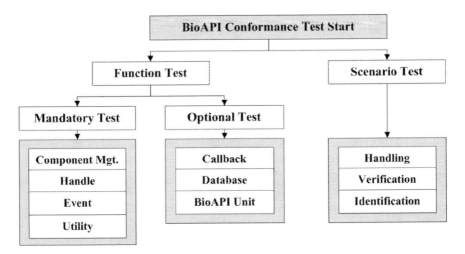

Fig. 1. Test method structure for conformance test

Handling Scenario

When a BSP creates a new BIR (Biometric Information Record), it returns a "handle" to it. The majority of local operations can be performed without moving the BIR out of the BSP. However, if the application is required to manage the BIR, it can acquire the BIR using the handle. In order to test the BIR creation function, it is mandatory to run BioAPI_Capture prior to running other BIR functions because it needs the biometric image. After the image is captured using BioAPI_Capture, the handling process is carried out by the BIR handle function.

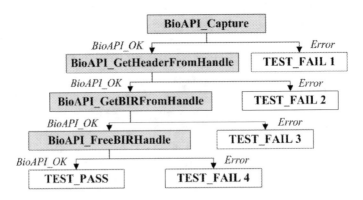

Fig. 2. Test scenario for BIR handling

Verification Scenario

he verification process matches the biometric template with an input image, where it compares the similarity. For verification, first the BSP or application should capture, and then determine the match/non-match with a stored template.

The Enrollment process should be tested before the Verification process. The verification process addresses the testing of whether BioAPI_Verify and BioAPI_Identify are called and BioAPI_Enroll is called. Using BioAPI_Caputer, an image is captured, the image process is carried out by the BioAPI_Process. Identification work is achieved with BioAPI_IdentifyMatching. This step is descried in Fig. 3.

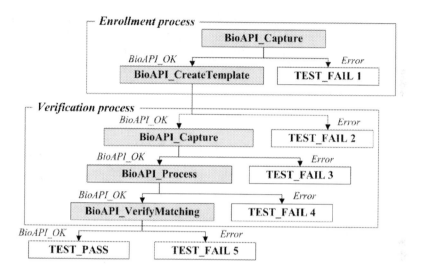

Fig. 3. Test scenario for verification process

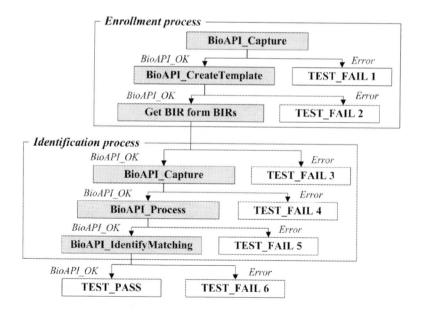

Fig. 4. Test scenario for identification process

Identification Scenario

The identification process matches the entire stored template with input image, where it determines the best match. To verify the identification function, the following functions are required. For identification, first the BSP or application should capture, and then determine the match/non-match.

The Enrollment process is tested before the Identification process. The Identification process addresses the testing of whether BioAPI_Verify and BioAPI _Identify are called after BioAPI_Enroll is called. After the image is captured using BioAPI_Capture, the image process is carried out with BioAPI_Process. Identification work is conducted by BioAPI_IdentifyMatching.

2.2   Conformance Testing Models

The conformance testing model is based on a variation of the basic BioAPI architecture. The basic BioAPI architecture is described as being comprised of a normal BioAPI application, BioAPI framework, and one or more normal BioAPI BSPs. The conformance testing methodology specified in the BioAPI specification, addresses each of the standard components of the BioAPI architecture separately. Three conformance testing models are defined the methodology, for the testing of each standard component.

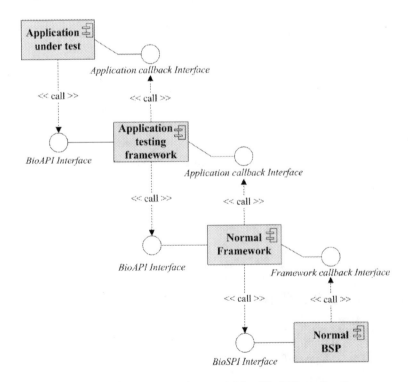

Fig. 5. Conformance testing model for BioAPI application

Applications Testing Component Model

As presented in Fig. 5, in the conformance testing model for BioAPI applications, the application-testing framework is inserted between the application under test and a normal framework. This testing component shall implement the BioAPI standard interface on one side and the application callback interface on the other side. As a result, it shall appear to the application as a framework, and to a framework as an application. This testing component shall have the ability to relay application calls to the normal framework. The framework calls the application during testing, and the ability to observe, analyze, log the flow of incoming calls, and generate extra calls are tested.

Framework Testing Component Model

Fig. 6 presents the conformance testing model for BioAPI frameworks, the framework-testing application replaces the normal application, and framework-testing BSP shall replace the normal BSP. These two testing components lie in the framework for testing. The framework-testing application shall implement the application callback interface, and the framework-testing BSP shall implement the BioSPI interface. Therefore, the framework being tested cannot distinguish between these interfaces and the corresponding components. In addition, each testing component contains a special testing interface, enabling them to interact with each other for the purpose of performing tests.

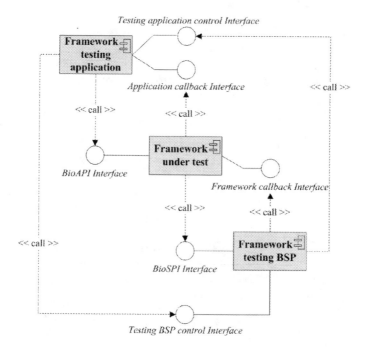

Fig. 6. Conformance testing model for BioAPI frameworks

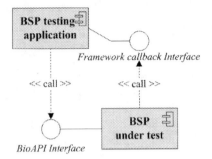

Fig. 7. Conformance testing model for BioAPI BSPs

BSP Testing Component Model

As presented in Fig. 7, in the conformance testing model for BioAPI BSPs, the BSP-testing application shall replace the normal application and the normal framework. This testing component shall act both as a BioAPI application and BioAPI framework, and shall implement the framework callback interface. As a result, it appears as a framework to the BSP being tested. The testing component shall be able to make calls to the BioSPI interface of the BSP under testing.

3   Implementation of CTS for BioAPI BSP

The previous CTS indirectly tested whether BSPs were compliant to the standard, using the Biometrics Consortium's BioAPI framework. However, when the CTS discovers an error, it does not distinguish whether they originate from the BSP under test or the BioAPI framework. Therefore, the new version of the CTS developed in this paper implements the BSP testing component model as shown in Fig. 7. The testing mechanism of the new CTS based on BioAPI v2.0 is illustrated in Fig. 8.

In order to resolve the above problem, the following four functions are newly implemented in the comparison with the previous versions of CTS. Firstly, the

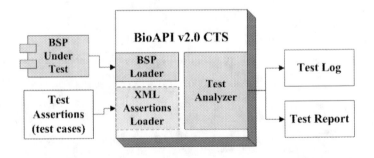

Fig. 8. Mechanism of the BioAPI v2.0 CTS

Table 1. Summary of BioAPI conformant BSPs

Conformant Type	Comments
Verification BSP	Perform 1:1 matching
Identification BSP	Perform both 1:N identification matching as well as 1:1 matching
Capture	Provide an interface to one or more biometric sensors and return intermediate BIRs that can be used by other BSPs
Verification Engine	Contain biometric processing and 1:1 matching algorithms, but do not perform biometric capture.
Identification Engine	Contain biometric processing and 1:N matching algorithms, but do not perform biometric capture.

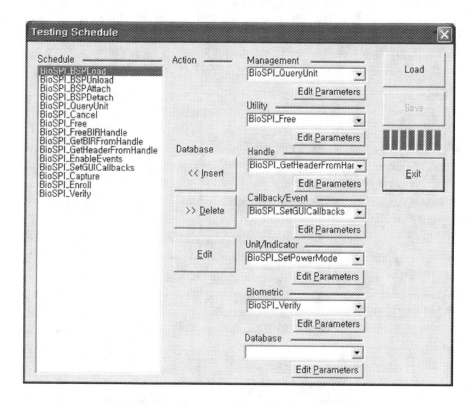

Fig. 9. Testing scheduling of BioAPI v2.0 CTS

new CTS is capable of testing a BSP which does not abide by the framework on the basis of the BioAPI v2.0 standards.Secondly, it can load arbitrarily designed test procedures by the test scheduler. The test scheduler will be replaced by a test assertion loader in the next version of the BioAPI CTS when ISO 24709-2, BioAPI Conformance Testing - Part 2: Test Assertions for BSPs [8] becomes an international standard. Fig. 9 depicts the implementation of the test scheduler. Thirdly, the new CTS produces the test results in XML format which is the standard format for both the input and the output to the BioAPI CTS in ISO 24709-2. Finally, it is implemented to test each BSP differently, depending on the purpose of the BSP, for example, verification or identification. The following Table 1 is a summary of BioAPI conformant BSPs.

4   Experimental Results

In order to evaluate the operation of implemented BioAPI CTS, this paper tested BioAPI v2.0 with three commercial fingerprint recognition BSPs. Two tests of the BSPs were modules for verification [9, 10], and the others were for identification [11]. The BioAPI function and the associated BSPs are shown in Table 2.

Fig. 10 presents the process of performing the BSP conformance test for fingerprint recognition. When the test is completed, the result is found in an XML

Table 2. Conformance of test BSPs

	BioSPI Function	**Company A**	**Company B**	**Company C**
Component Management Functions	BioSPI_BSPLoad	○	○	○
	BioSPI_BSPUnload	○	○	○
	BioSPI_BSPAttach	○	○	○
	BioSPI_BSPDetach	○	○	○
	BioSPI_QueryUnits	○	○	○
Handle Functions	BioSPI_FreeBIRHandle	○	○	○
	BioSPI_GetBIRFromHandle	○	○	○
	BioSPI_GetHeaderFromHandle	○	○	○
Callback and Event Functions	BioSPI_EnabelEvents	○	○	○
	BioSPI_SetGUICallbacks	-	○	-
Biometric Functions	BioSPI_Capture	-	○	○
	BioSPI_CreateTemplate	-	○	○
	BioSPI_Process	-	○	○
	BioSPI_ProcessWithAuxBIR	-	○	○
	BioSPI_VerifyMatch	-	○	○
	BioSPI_IdentifyMatch	-	○	○
	BioSPI_Enroll	○	○	○
	BioSPI_Verify	○	○	○
	BioSPI_Identify	-	-	○
	BioSPI_Import	-	○	○
	BioSPI_PresetIdentifyPupulation	-	-	○
Utility Functions	BioSPI_Cancel	○	○	○
	BioSPI_Free	○	○	○

(*Note*) ○ : supported function, - : function not supported

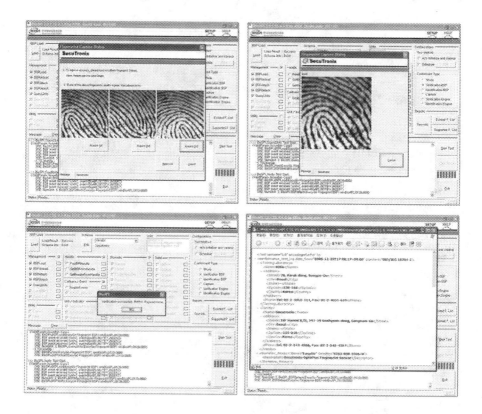

Fig. 10. Process of performing the BSP conformance test

test result, as shown in Table 3. If a BioAPI function exists in the BSP, the message of BioAPI_OK is returned, while if it does not exist or is not performed normally, an error code is returned [6].

The result of BSP conformance test is provided in XML format, as shown in Table 3. However, BSPs tested in this paper only provided functions necessary for verification and identification, so it could not be confirmed whether the implemented CTS would operate properly with a BSP which provides all the functions defined in BioAPI v2.0. Thus, a sample BSP was developed, and all the functions of BioAPI were tested to simulate a full CTS experiment. Table 4 contains the results of two experiments, firstly, over three commercial BSPs for fingerprint recognition, and secondly, a test BSP developed in this study in order to test all the BioAPI functions. These experiments demonstrate that the BioAPI CTS performs properly over the BSPs supplied by manufactures. At the same time, it is recognized that the BSPs under test are compliant to BioAPI v2.0 standards.

Table 3. Test Log of sample BSP

```
<?xml version="1.0" encoding="utf-8" ?>
  -    <conformance_test_log    date_time="2007-5-23T17:15:56+09:00"
standard="ISO/IEC 19784-1">
 - <TestingLaboratory>
  <Name>KISA</Name>
 - <Address>
  <Street>78, Karak dong, Songpa-Gu</Street>
  <City>Seoul</City>
  <State>-</State>
  <ZipCode>138-160</ZipCode>
  <Country>Korea</Country>
  </Address>
  <Phone>Tel: 82-2-4055-114, Fax: 82-2-4055-619</Phone>
  </TestingLaboratory>
 - <Vendor>
  <Name>Secutronix</Name>
 - <Address>
  <Street>10F    Hanmi    B/D,    192-19    Nonhyeon-dong,    Gangnam-
Gu</Street>
  <City>Seoul</City>
  <State>-</State>
  <ZipCode>135-010</ZipCode>
  <Country>Korea</Country>
  </Address>
  <Phone>Tel: 82-2-543-4366, Fax: 82-2-543-4367</Phone>
  </Vendor>
 - <Biometric_Product Name="EasyGo" SerialNo="ST03-000-10367A">
  <Description>Secutronix          OptoPlus          Fingerprint
Sensor</Description>
  </Biometric_Product>
  <CtsId>BioAPI 2.0 CTS</CtsId>
 - <test_assertion>
  <package_name>d9adf620-d88b-11d8-9669-
0800200c9a66</package_name>
  <assertion_name>BioSPI_BSPLoad_ValidParam</assertion_name>
  <input name="_moduleUuid" value="???" />
  <input name="_BioAPINotifyCallback" value="???" />
  <input name="_BioAPINotifyCallbackCtx" value="???" />
 - <inline_response>
  <conformance>pass</conformance>
  </inline_response>
  </test_assertion>
 - <test_assertion>
  <package_name>3ca56130-d997-11d8-9669-
0800200c9a66</package_name>
  <assertion_name>BioSPI_BSPLoad_InvalidUUID</assertion_name>
  <input name="_moduleUuid" value="???" />
  <input name="_BioAPINotifyCallback" value="???" />
  <input name="_BioAPINotifyCallbackCtx" value="???" />
 - <inline_response>
  <conformance>pass</conformance>
  </inline_response>
  </test_assertion>
```

Table 4. Test result of sample BSPs

Function	Company A	Company B	Company C	TestBSP for CTS *
BioSPI_BSPLoad	Pass	Pass	Pass	Pass
BioSPI_BSPUnload	Pass	Pass	Pass	Pass
BioSPI_BSPAttach	Pass	Pass	Pass	Pass
BioSPI_BSPDetach	Pass	Pass	Pass	Pass
BioSPI_QueryUnits	Pass	Pass	Pass	Pass
BioSPI_QueryBFPs	-	-	-	Pass
BioSPI_ControlUnit	-	-	-	Pass
BioSPI_FreeBIRHandle	Pass	Pass	Pass	Pass
BioSPI_GetBIRFromHandle	Pass	Pass	Pass	Pass
BioSPI_GetHeaderFromHandle	Pass	Pass	Pass	Pass
BioSPI_EnableEvents	Pass	Pass	Pass	Pass
BioSPI_SetGUICallbacks	-	Pass	-	Pass
BioSPI_Capture	-	Pass	Pass	Pass
BioSPI_CreateTemplate	-	Pass	Pass	Pass
BioSPI_Process	-	Pass	Pass	Pass
BioSPI_ProcessWithAuxBIR	-	Pass	Pass	Pass
BioSPI_VerifyMatch	-	Pass	Pass	Pass
BioSPI_IdentifyMatch	-	Pass	Pass	Pass
BioSPI_Enroll	Pass	Pass	Pass	Pass
BioSPI_Verify	Pass	Pass	Pass	Pass
BioSPI_Identify	-	-	Pass	Pass
BioSPI_Import	-	Pass	Pass	Pass
BioSPI_PresetIdentifyPopulation	-	-	Pass	Pass
BioSPI_DbOpen	-	-	-	Pass
BioSPI_DbClose	-	-	-	Pass
BioSPI_DbCreate	-	-	-	Pass
BioSPI_DbDelete	-	-	-	Pass
BioSPI_DbSetMarker	-	-	-	Pass
BioSPI_DbFreeMarker	-	-	-	Pass
BioSPI_DbStoreBIR	-	-	-	Pass
BioSPI_DbGetBIR	-	-	-	Pass
BioSPI_DbGetNextBIR	-	-	-	Pass
BioSPI_DbDeleteBIR	-	-	-	Pass
BioSPI_SetPowerMode	-	-	-	Pass
BioSPI_SetIndicatorStatus	-	-	-	Pass
BioSPI_GetIndicatorStatus	-	-	-	Pass
BioSPI_Cancel	Pass	Pass	Pass	Pass
BioSPI_Free	Pass	Pass	Pass	Pass

(*Note*) - : BioAPIERR_FUNCTION_NOT_SUPPORTED

5   Conclusions and Future Works

This paper designs and implements a conformance testing suite for BioAPI v2.0. The improved CTS can operate without the BioAPI frameworks. The weakness of the previous versions of BioAPI CTS was that they could not tell whether any test failure originates either from the BSP under test or from the BioAPI framework. The new BioAPI CTS is designed to be able to test BSPs and frameworks independently. The performance of the new BioAPI CTS was demonstrated by testing commercial fingerprint verification and identification BSPs.

The developed BioAPI CTS will make the process of manufacturing standard biometrics products with less expense in shorter period of time. In addition, the biometrics products compliant to international standards will promote the interoperability among different vendor's products and consequently enlarge the biometrics market worldwide.

The current BioAPI CTS uses XML only for outputting the test results. For further progress, XML will be used for writing scripts of test scenario and a parser of XML test-scripts needs to be developed in order to make the conformance-testing process more flexible.

Acknowledgments. This work was supported in part by the Korea Small and Medium Business Administration.

References

1. Korea Information Security Agency, Development of test technology for Korea BioAPI Standard (2002)
2. Korea Information Security Agency, A Study on Improvement of Conformance Test Suite Tool for Application Interface of Biometric System (2003)
3. Lee, Y.-Y., Kwon, Y.-B.: A Study on Conformance Testing Methods to Verify the BioAPI Based System Module. Korea Information Processing Society B 11(7), 759–768 (2004)
4. http://www.itl.nist.gov/div893/biometrics/BioAPI_CTS/index.htm
5. Biometric Consortium, BioAPI Specification Version 1.1 (2001)
6. ISO/IEC IS 19784-1, Information Technology - Biometric application programming interface - Part 1: BioAPI specification
7. ISO/IEC FDIS 24709-1, Information Technology - Conformance Testing for BioAPI - Part 1: Methods and Procedures
8. ISO/IEC FDIS 24709-2, Information Technology - Conformance Testing for BioAPI - Part 2: Test Assertions for Biometric Service Providers
9. SecuTronix, http://www.secutronix.com/
10. Suprema, http://www.supremainc.com/
11. Digent, http://www.digent.co.kr/

Information Hiding in Software with Mixed Boolean-Arithmetic Transforms

Yongxin Zhou, Alec Main, Yuan X. Gu, and Harold Johnson

Cloakware Inc., USA
{yongxin.zhou,alec.main,yuan.gu,harold.johnson}@cloakware.com

Abstract. As increasingly powerful software analysis and attack tools arise, we need increasingly potent software protections. We generate an *unlimited* supply of obscuring transforms via mixed-mode computation over Boolean-arithmetic (MBA) algebras corresponding to real-world functions and data. Such transforms resist reverse engineering with existing advanced tools and create NP-hard problems for the attacker. We discuss broad uses and concrete applications to AACS key hiding and software watermarking.

1 Introduction

With the increasing power of software analysis and attack tools and the ubiquity of open operating systems, ever stronger software data- and algorithm-hiding mechanisms are essential. (For existing protections, see, e.g., [3,4,5,6,7,10,18,21].)

We introduce Boolean-arithmetic (BA) algebras which model real-world software computation. Modern ALUs use (1) 2's complement arithmetic on n-bit words, which maps to the modular ring $Z/(2^n)$, and (2) bitwise operations over B^n where $B = \{0, 1\}$. Combining (1) and (2) gives the BA-algebra BA[n], over which we define highly simplification-resistant mixed Boolean-arithmetic (MBA) obfuscating transforms with NP-hard fragment recognition, for which we provide unlimited-volume generators, ensuring an ever-growing MBA protections database.

MBA transforms based on MBA expressions, MBA identities and invertible functions can be used to transform software code: functionality is preserved, but secret constants, intermediate values, and algorithms are hidden from static and dynamic reverse engineering and analysis. Perimeter software protection methods, that ultimately allowed the data or algorithm to appear in memory cannot provide a similar level of protection.

Moreover, transformed software simultaneously occupies multiple mathematical domains, creating worst-case NP-hard problems for the attacker, and making them highly resistant even to advanced analytical tools such as **Maple**[TM] or **Mathematica**[TM]. The unlimited supply of MBA transforms can be generated ensuring an ever-growing search space to protect against new tools for analyzing and attacking transformed software.

S. Kim, M. Yung, and H.-W. Lee (Eds.): WISA 2007, LNCS 4867, pp. 61–75, 2007.

We provide practical threat scenarios. We then introduce MBA transforms and their use for protection against such threats. Lastly, we provide practical examples of transformed algorithms.

2   Motivating Scenarios

2.1   Naïve Code

In Fig. 1(A)'s scenario, both algorithm and constant data C are unprotected, permitting algorithmic reverse engineering by static analysis and extraction of C by searching the executable file.

This is the normal state of software as written, compiled, and delivered.

2.2   Hiding Constants from Static Analysis

Hiding C in code gives us Fig. 1(B). The algorithm is still exposed to static analysis, but C (created at runtime) no longer appears in the executable file.

This (without MBA methods) was the situation in the Advanced Access Control System (AACS: see Fig. 2), a copy protection system adopted for HD-DVD^{TM} and **BluRay**^{TM} optical discs, which was hacked[22] by various parties by initially obtaining the title key, K_t, from memory, then working back through the chain to obtain earlier keys from memory, such as the media key, K_m. Since the algorithms are public, obtaining the keys allows for off-line decryption of the licensed content by an application that does not comply with licensing terms (e.g. writes decrypted content to a file). Obtaining the higher level keys allows the others to be calculated, making the memory-key-extraction step simpler. As in Fig. 1(B), while the software manufacturers made an effort to hide the device keys, they did not prevent intermediate values from appearing in memory.

2.3   Hiding Constants and Algorithms from Dynamic Analysis

Finally, in Fig. 1(C)'s scenario, we protect the value of C and its associated code by applying code and data transforms[3,10,21]. The constant code generates C^T (C under transformation T) with corresponding changes to the algorithm. Even if a dynamic attack recovers C^T, an attacker must reverse-engineer of the transformed algorithm to find T. E.g. if C is a cryptographic key, offline decryption is infeasible until T is found or the algorithm code is lifted, but transform diversity[21] makes lifting less useful. Moreover, lifting could be made difficult if the code surrounding decryptions were mathematically intermixed with the decryptions using MBA transforms.

Example: AACS. The above is the approach we would recommend for systems such as AACS: using MBA transforms would ensure that only *transformed* key values appear in memory or registers during computation, with a transform not useful for offline decryption without significant additional analysis.

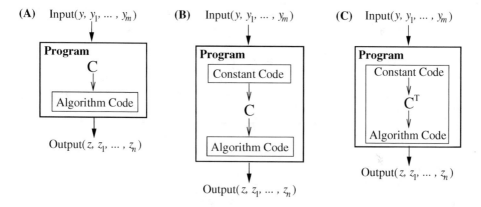

Fig. 1. Basic Scenarios

A possible attack point would be to compare known title keys (obtained from previously hacked titles) with the corresponding transformed keys. To render such an attack ineffective, the transformation must be sufficiently complex that determining its functionality from such isolated plain-key-to-transformed-key instances is infeasibly hard for the system's anticipated attackers.

AACS

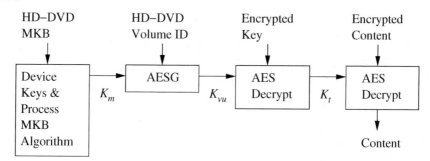

Fig. 2. AACS

Example: Software Watermarking. Another possible use for key and algorithm hiding is software watermarking in order to prove ownership of the software or intellectual property contained therein if the software is used without a license. Software watermarking is not to be confused with steganographic watermarking, where a message is hidden images or an audio or video stream, although some systems (e.g., DRM systems) permit both forms of protection to be used (software watermarking for DRM components, steganographic watermarking for the content they manage).

```
Q:  if  I = K  then
        K = E (K)
        W = emit_watermark ( P, K )
        output W
    else
        P (I)
```

Fig. 3. Watermarking

In §4.2, we will provide a simple example where software function is dependent on a secret key K which can be used to prove software ownership. MBA transforms effectively protect the software watermark algorithm by making it very hard to discover K and by interlocking (see §3.4) the constant code producing K and the watermark algorithm (see Fig. 3).

3   Mixed Boolean-Arithmetic (MBA) Transforms

3.1   Basic Definitions

Microprocessor arithmetic logic units (ALUs) use arithmetic operations including addition $+$, subtraction $-$ (whence comparisons $<, \leq, =, \geq, >$), multiply $\cdot$, left shift $\ll$, arithmetic right shift $\gg^s$, and logical right shift $\gg$. Bitwise operations include *exclusive-or* $\oplus$, *inclusive-or* $\vee$, *and* $\wedge$, and *not* $\neg$. With n-bit 2's complement integers, arithmetic operations are in integer modular ring $Z/(2^n)$. Bitwise operations operate over Boolean algebra $(B^n, \wedge, \vee, \neg)$. All above computations are captured in the BA-algebra, BA[n].

Definition 1. *With n a positive integer and $B = \{0, 1\}$, the algebraic system* $(B^n, \wedge, \vee, \oplus, \neg, \leq, \geq, >, <, \leq^s, \geq^s, >^s, <^s, \neq, =, \gg^s, \gg, \ll, +, -, \cdot)$, *where $\ll, \gg$ denote left and right shifts, $\cdot$ (or juxtaposition) denotes multiply, and signed compares and arithmetic right shift are indicated by ^{s}, is a Boolean-arithmetic algebra (BA-algebra), BA[n]. n is the dimension of the algebra.*

BA[n] includes the Boolean algebra $(B^n, \wedge, \vee, \neg)$, the integer modular ring $Z/(2^n)$, Galois field GF(2^n), and *p-adic* numbers[19]. The first two structures are most used in real applications and form the basis of our techniques for hiding keys (constants) and operations over BA[n].

Definition 2. *With BA[n] a BA-algebra and t a positive integer, a function* $f: (B^n)^t \mapsto B^n$ *of the form*

$$\sum_{i \in I} a_i \left(\prod_{j \in J_i} e_{i,j}(x_1, \ldots, x_t) \right),$$

where a_i are constants, $e_{i,j}$ are bitwise expressions of variables $x_1, \ldots, x_t$ over B^n, and $I, J_i \subset \mathsf{Z}$, are finite index sets, $\forall i \in I$, is a polynomial mixed Boolean-arithmetic expression, abbreviated to a polynomial MBA *expression. (If each of $x_1, \ldots, x_t$ is itself a polynomial* MBA *expression of other variables, the composed function is likewise a polynomial* MBA *expression over B^n.) Each non-zero summand in the expression is a* term. *A* linear MBA *expression is a polynomial* MBA *expression of the form*

$$\sum_{i \in I} a_i \, e_i(x_1, \ldots, x_t),$$

where e_i are bitwise expressions of $x_1, \ldots, x_t$ and a_i are constants.

Two examples of polynomial MBA expressions over BA$[n]$ are:

$$
\begin{aligned}
f(x, y, z, t) &= 8458(x \vee y \wedge z)^3 \left((xy) \wedge x \vee t\right) + x + 9(x \vee y)yz^3, \\
f(x, y) \quad &= x + y - (x \oplus (\neg y))) - 2(x \vee y) + 12564.
\end{aligned}
$$

The latter is a linear MBA expression. As indicated in [20], all integer comparison operations can be represented by polynomial MBA expressions with results in their most significant bit (MSB). For example, the MSB of

$$(x - y) \oplus ((x \oplus y) \wedge ((x - y) \oplus x))$$

is 1 if and only if $x <^s y$.

3.2   Linear MBA Identities and Expressions

We now show the existence of an unlimited number of linear MBA identities. We use truth tables, where the relationship of variables of the expression in the table and conjuncts is shown by example in Table 1.

Theorem 1. *Let n, s, t be positive integers, let x_i be variables over B^n for $i = 1, \ldots, t$, let e_j be bitwise expressions on x_i's for $j = 0, \ldots, s-1$. Let $e = \sum_{j=0}^{s-1} a_j \, e_j$ be a linear* MBA *expression, where a_j are integers, $j = 0, \ldots, s - 1$. Let f_j be the deduced Boolean expression from e_j, and let $(v_{0,j}, \ldots, v_{i,j}, \ldots, v_{2^t-1,j})^\mathsf{T}$ be the column vector of the truth table of f_j, $j = 0, \ldots s - 1$, and $i = 0, \ldots, 2^t - 1$. Let $A = (v_{i,j})_{2^t \times s}$, be the $\{0,1\}$-matrix of truth tables over $\mathsf{Z}/(2^n)$. Then $e = 0$ if and only if the linear system $AY = 0$ has a solution over ring $\mathsf{Z}/(2^n)$, where $Y_{s \times 1} = (y_0, \cdots, y_{s-1})^\mathsf{T}$ is a vector of s variables over $\mathsf{Z}/(2^n)$.*

Proof. If $e = 0$, $(a_0, a_1, \cdots, a_{s-1})^\mathsf{T}$ is plainly a solution of the linear system.

Assume a solution exists. Let z_{ji} represent the i−th bit value of e_j, $j = 0, 1, \cdots, s-1$, $i = 0, 1, \cdots, n-1$. Truth tables run over all inputs, so row vectors of matrix A run over all values of i-th bit vector $(z_{0,i}, \ldots, z_{s-1,i})$ in the Boolean expressions, and via the above solution, $\sum_{j=0}^{s-1} a_j z_{j,i} = 0$, for $i = 0, \ldots, n-1$.

From the arithmetic point of view, $e_j = \sum_{i=0}^{n-1} z_{j,i} 2^i$. Thus we have

$$\sum_{j=0}^{s-1} a_j e_j = \sum_{j=0}^{s-1} \sum_{i=0}^{n-1} a_j z_{j,i} 2^i = \sum_{i=0}^{n-1} \sum_{j=0}^{s-1} a_j z_{j,i} 2^i = \sum_{i=0}^{n-1} 2^i \left(\sum_{j=0}^{s-1} a_j z_{j,i}\right) = 0,$$

as required.   □

By this theorem, any $\{0,1\}$-matrix $(v_{ij})_{2^t \times s}$ with linearly dependent column vectors generates a linear MBA identity of t variables over B^n. For example, the $\{0,1\}$-matrix

$$A = \begin{pmatrix} 0 & 0 & 0 & 1 & 1 \\ 0 & 1 & 1 & 1 & 1 \\ 1 & 0 & 1 & 1 & 1 \\ 1 & 1 & 1 & 0 & 1 \end{pmatrix}$$

with column-vector truth-tables for $f_0(x,y) = x$, $f_1(x,y) = y$, $f_2(x_y) = x \vee y$, $f_3(x,y) = \neg(x \wedge y)$, $f_4(x,y) = 1$, respectively, with solution $(1,1,-1,1,-1)^\mathsf{T}$ over $\mathsf{Z}/(2^{32})$, generates linear MBA identity $x + y - (x \vee y) + (\neg(x \wedge y)) - (-1) = 0$, using $x_1 = x$, $x_2 = y$, and $-1 =$ all 1's. The interested reader can write $\mathbf{C}$ code to verify the identity for any $x, y \in \mathsf{B}^{32}$ by defining x and y as unsigned or signed 32-bit integers. Other linear MBA identities can be found in [20].

The following theorem states that any Boolean function has non-trivial linear MBA expressions. It allows us to embed hard Boolean functions into MBA transforms.

Table 1. Truth Table for $x_1 \vee (x_2 \oplus (\neg x_3))$

Conjunction	Binary	Result
$(\neg x_1) \wedge (\neg x_2) \wedge (\neg x_3)$	000	1
$(\neg x_1) \wedge (\neg x_2) \wedge (\ x_3)$	001	0
$(\neg x_1) \wedge (\ x_2) \wedge (\neg x_3)$	010	0
$(\neg x_1) \wedge (\ x_2) \wedge (\ x_3)$	011	1
$(\ x_1) \wedge (\neg x_2) \wedge (\neg x_3)$	100	1
$(\ x_1) \wedge (\neg x_2) \wedge (\ x_3)$	101	1
$(\ x_1) \wedge (\ x_2) \wedge (\neg x_3)$	110	1
$(\ x_1) \wedge (\ x_2) \wedge (\ x_3)$	111	1

Theorem 2. *Let e be a bitwise expression of m variables over B^n. Then e has a non-trivial linear MBA expression. That is $e = \sum_{i=0}^{2^m-1} a_i e_i$, where each $a_i \in \mathsf{B}^n$, each e_i is a bitwise expression of the m variables, and $e \neq e_i$ in B^n, for $i = 0, 1, \ldots, 2^m - 1$.*

Proof. Let $P_{2^m \times 1}$ be the column vector of the truth table of the deduced Boolean expression from e. Pick an invertible $\{0,1\}$-matrix $A_{2^m \times 2^m}$ over $\mathsf{Z}/(2^n)$. If a column vector of A is P, add another column vector to it. Then we have an invertible matrix A with all column vectors distinct from P. Suppose the solution of linear equation $AY = P_{2^m \times 1}$ is $Y = (y_0, y_1, \ldots, y_{2^m-1})^\mathsf{T}$. Let matrix $Q_{2^m \times (2^m+1)} = (P, A)$, and $X_{(2^m+1) \times 1} = (-1, y_0, y_1, \ldots, y_{2^m-1})^\mathsf{T}$. Because $AY = P$, it is easy to show that $QX = 0$.

Following the disjunctive normal form (or any standard form) of Boolean functions, for each column vector A_i of matrix A we have a unique Boolean expression e_i of m variables with A_i being its truth table, $i = 0, 1, \ldots, 2^m - 1$.

Since $QX = 0$, Theorem 1 gives a linear MBA identity $e - \sum_{i=0}^{2^m-1} y_i\, e_i = 0$. By our choice of A, $e_i \neq e$ for all i. □

3.3 Permutation Polynomials and Other Invertible Functions

We use polynomial functions over $Z/(2^n)$ to generate polynomial MBA expressions. We need invertible polynomials[15,13,12], and both the polynomial and its inverse must be of limited degree so that polynomial code transformations are efficient. We now show that there are many such invertible polynomials.

Theorem 3. *Let m be a positive integer and let $P_m(Z/(2^n))$ be a set of polynomials over $Z/(2^n)$:*

$$P_m(Z/(2^n)) = \left\{ \sum_{i=0}^m a_i x^i \;\middle|\; \forall a_i \in Z/(2^n), a_1 \wedge 1 = 1, a_i^2 = 0, i = 2, \ldots, m \right\}.$$

Then $(P_m(Z/(2^n)), \circ)$ is a permutation group under the functional composition operator $\circ$. For every element $f(x) = \sum_{i=0}^m a_i x^i$, its inverse $g(x) = \sum_{j=0}^m b_j x^j$ can be computed by

$$
\begin{aligned}
b_m &= -a_1^{-m-1} a_m, \\
b_k &= -a_1^{-k-1} a_k - a_1^{-1} \sum_{j=k+1}^m \binom{j}{k} a_0^{j-k} A_j, \, m-1 \geq k \geq 2, \\
b_1 &= a_1^{-1} - a_1^{-1} \sum_{j=2}^m j a_0^{j-1} A_j, \\
b_0 &= -\sum_{j=1}^m a_0^j b_j,
\end{aligned}
$$

where $A_m = -a_1^{-m} a_m$, and A_k are recursively defined by

$$A_k = -a_1^{-k} a_k - \sum_{j=k+1}^m \binom{j}{k} a_0^{j-k} A_j, \quad \text{for } 2 \leq k < m.$$

Proof. By definition of $P_m(Z/(2^n))$, the coefficient of x is odd, and coefficients of higher degrees are even. By [15], they are permutation polynomials. To show $(P_m(Z/(2^n)), \circ)$ is a group, we compute all coefficients of the composition $g(x) \circ f(x) = g(f(x)) = \sum_{j=0}^m b_j f(x)^j$ of any two elements $f(x) = \sum_{i=0}^m a_i x^i$ and $g(x) = \sum_{j=0}^m b_j x^j \in P_m(Z/(2^n))$. For any $j \in \{2, \ldots, m\}$, we have

$$
\begin{aligned}
b_j f(x)^j &= \sum_{(i_1 \cdots i_j), i_k \in \{0, \ldots, m\}, k=0, \ldots, j} b_j a_{i_1} \cdots a_{i_j} x^{i_1 + \cdots + i_j} \\
&= \sum_{(i_1 \cdots i_j), i_k \in \{0,1\}, k=0, \ldots, j} b_j a_{i_1} \cdots a_{i_j} x^{i_1 + \cdots + i_j} \quad (\text{since } b_j a_i = 0, \forall i \geq 2) \\
&= b_j \sum_{k=0}^j \binom{j}{k} a_1^k a_0^{j-k} x^k;
\end{aligned}
$$

$$
\begin{aligned}
g(f(x)) &= b_0 + \sum_{i=0}^m b_1 a_i x^i + \sum_{j=2}^m b_j \sum_{k=0}^j \binom{j}{k} a_1^k a_0^{j-k} x^k \\
&= b_0 + \sum_{k=0}^m \left(b_1 a_k + \sum_{j=2, j \geq k}^m b_j \binom{j}{k} a_1^k a_0^{j-k} \right) x^k \\
&= \left(\sum_{j=0}^m a_0^j b_j \right) + \left(\sum_{j=1}^m j a_0^{j-1} a_1 b_j \right) x \\
&\quad + \sum_{k=2}^m \left(a_k b_1 + \sum_{j=k}^m \binom{j}{k} a_0^{j-k} a_1^k b_j \right) x^k.
\end{aligned}
$$

Let $\sum_{i=0}^{m} c_i x^i$ denote $g(f(x))$. Then c_1 is odd since both a_1 and h_1 are odd, and all b_j, $j \geq 2$, are even. For all a_k and b_j, $k, j \geq 2$, $a_k^2 = b_j^2 = 0$, so we have $c_i^2 = 0, i \geq 2$. Therefore $g(f(x)) \in \mathsf{P}_m(\mathsf{Z}/(2^n))$ and $\mathsf{P}_m(\mathsf{Z}/(2^n))$ is a group.

Let us compute the inverse of $f(x)$. Assume $g(f(x)) = x$, which implies $c_1 = 1$ and $c_i = 0, i = 0, 2, \cdots, m$. From $c_m = 0$ we have $b_m = -a_1^{-m} a_m b_1$. Similarly, for all k, $m > k \geq 2$, $c_k = 0$ implies $b_k = -a_1^{-k} a_k - \sum_{j=k+1}^{m} b_j \binom{j}{k} a_0^{j-k}$. Observing that the second term of b_k is defined by $b_j, j > k$, and b_1 is a common factor of all these b_k starting at b_m, we can define $b_k = b_1 A_k$ such that all A_k can be computed from $A_m, A_{m-1}, \ldots, A_{k+1}$; i.e., $A_m = -a_1^{-m} a_m$, and $A_k = -a_1^{-k} a_k - \sum_{j=k+1}^{m} \binom{j}{k} a_0^{j-k} A_j$, from known coefficients of $f(x)$. From $c_1 = 1$ we obtain $b_1 = a_1^{-1}(1 + \sum_{j=2}^{m} j a_0^{j-1} A_j)^{-1} = a_1^{-1}(1 - \sum_{j=2}^{m} j a_0^{j-1} A_j)$. The latter identity holds because $A_k^2 = 0$ for all k, $m > k \geq 2$. Based on this formula for b_1 and the identities $b_k = b_1 A_k$, and $c_0 = 0$, we can compute all other coefficients recursively: $b_m = -a_1^{-m-1} a_m$, and for all k with $m > k \geq 2$,

$$b_k = a_1^{-1}(1 - \sum_{j=2}^{m} j a_0^{j-1} A_j)(-a_1^{-k} a_k - \sum_{j=k+1}^{m} \binom{j}{k} a_0^{j-k} A_j)$$
$$= -a_1^{-k-1} a_k - a_1^{-1} \sum_{j=k+1}^{m} \binom{j}{k} a_0^{j-k} A_j.$$

We then easily derive $b_0 = -\sum_{j=1}^{m} a_0^j b_j$.   □

$\mathsf{P}_1(\mathsf{Z}/(2^n))$ is used for data transforms in [10]. Formula of polynomial inverses of polynomials in $\mathsf{P}_2(\mathsf{Z}/(2^n))$ is given in [21]. Following Theorem 3, for cubic polynomial

$$f(x) = a_3 x^3 + a_2 x^2 + a_1 x + a_0$$

in $\mathsf{P}_3(\mathsf{Z}/(2^n))$, its inverse is

$$f^{-1}(x) = (-a_1^{-4} a_3)x^3 + (-a_2 a_1^{-3} + 3a_0 a_1^{-4} a_3)x^2$$
$$+(a_1^{-1} + 2a_0 a_1^{-3} a_2 - 3a_0^2 a_1^{-4} a_3)x - a_0 a_1^{-1} - a_0^2 a_1^{-3} a_2 + a_0^3 a_1^{-4} a_3.$$

The above theorem implies that all encoding, decoding and composition functions are in conveniently similar formats for generating code transforms.

Over BA[n], there are other types of invertible functions that can be used together with MBA identities and permutation polynomials. For example, $\mathsf{Z}/(2^n)$ invertible matrices can be composed with invertible polynomials to form polynomial matrices and matrix polynomials. The T-functions of [11,12] provide another example.

3.4   Code Transforms Via Zero and Invertible MBA Functions

Operating on transformed data requires that the data and code (see Fig. 1(A)) use corresponding transforms (see Fig. 1(C)). MBA transforms constructed using zero functions (functions returning zero irrespective of their inputs) and invertible functions achieve this while interlocking and hiding the original operations. Linear MBA identities and permutation polynomials over BA[n] are our main resources.

There are two basic methods to hide operation in polynomial MBA expressions. The first one is to treat code (possibly a single operation or variable) as a subexpression in a polynomial MBA zero function and replace it with the negated sum of the remaining terms (i.e., it performs an identity substitution $t_k = -\sum_{i=1}^{k-1} t_i + \sum_{i=k+1}^{n} t_i$ derived from a zero function of the form $\sum_{i=1}^{n} t_i = 0$).

The other method uses functional compositions of MBA functions and the first method. For example, given two invertible functions S and T, function f is $S^{-1} \circ S \circ f \circ T \circ T^{-1}$. The associative law of functional composition allows us to write f as $S^{-1} \circ (S \circ f \circ T) \circ T^{-1}$. Applying the first method to $(S \circ f \circ T)$ before compositions we obtain a new expression of f; i.e., we compute on 'encrypted' data with 'encrypted' functions[16,17].

A key technique is *interlocking*: (1) *reverse partially evaluate: at Y, replace a function $f: A \mapsto C$ with a function $g: A \times B \mapsto C$ such that $g(\cdot, b) = f(\cdot)$ but $g(\cdot, x)$ where $x \neq b$ gives a nonsense result and b (absent tampering) comprises value(s) computed at X, and then (2) make code at site Y highly dependent on code at site X by using values produced or obtained at X as coefficients in Y's transforms and finally (3) apply the remaining protections in this paper to make the interlock extremely hard to eliminate.* Removing such interlocks requires that the attacker fully understand what has been done (highly nontrivial, as we argue in §5), and tampering at X produces *chaotic* behavioral changes at Y. Thus dense interlocking renders code aggressively fragile under tampering. Interlocks also foil code-lifting.

Compositions of zero and/or invertible functions with original operations in specific orders give us desired polynomial MBA expressions, as shown in the proof below.

Proposition 1. *Let m be a positive integer. Then every operation in BA-algebra* $\text{BA}[n] = (\text{B}^n, \wedge, \vee, \oplus, \neg, \leq, \geq, >, <, \leq^s, \geq^s, >^s, <^s, \neq, =, \gg^s, \gg, \ll, +, -, \cdot)$ *can be represented by a high degree polynomial MBA expressions of multiple terms of m variables over B^n.*

Proof. It suffices to show that each operation can be represented by a linear MBA identity of at least two terms, since then we can apply operation and composition transforms with invertible polynomials according to Theorem 3 to obtain high degree polynomial MBA expressions of any desired number of variables.

Any single variable x over B^n can be represented by a linear MBA expression using any number of variables: this follows immediately from Theorem 2 by using x's truth table. If we have $x = \sum_{i \in I} e_i$, where e_i are bitwise expressions and $y = \sum_{s \in S} t_s$ where t_s are bitwise expressions, then $x \pm y$ is a linear MBA expression and by $\text{Z}/(2^n)$ distributivity, xy is in a polynomial MBA expression. So is $\ll$: it is a multiplication. For right shifts we have $x \gg^s y = -((-x - 1) \gg^s y) - 1$ and $x \gg y = -1 - ((-x - 1) \gg y) - (((-1) \gg y) \oplus (-1))$. Theorem 2 indicates that all bitwise operations can be a linear MBA expression with at least two terms. Formulas in [20] express arbitrary signed and unsigned comparisons as bitwise operations with subtraction. We then apply Theorem 2 to obtain expressions of more that two terms. (This construction is one of many due to $\text{BA}[n]$'s rich mathematical structure.) □

4   Protection Methods

4.1   Simple Constant Hiding Using MBA Transforms

In many applications, important information is represented by constants (keys).
Here, we provide methods to turn them into executable code which computes the
keys irrespective of its inputs, letting us seamlessly embed keys in applications.
WLOG, we consider n-bit key hiding in BA$[n]$ only: if the key size bigger than n, we
simply generate multiple n-bit keys which are concatenated to obtain the big key.

We start with the following result to show that for any constant over B^n, there
is a polynomial MBA expression computing that constant.

Proposition 2. *For any constant K in* BA$[n]$ *and any positive integer m there
is a multiterm polynomial* MBA *function f with $f(x_1, \ldots, x_m) = K$ for arbitrary
$x_1, \ldots, x_m$ in* BA$[n]$.

Proof. We use quadratic polynomial and linear MBA identities to construct f.
By Theorem 3, with $a \neq 0$, we have an invertible polynomial $p(x) = ax^2 + bx + c$
and its inverse $q(x) = \alpha x^2 + \beta x + \gamma$. Theorem 1 tells us that any singular matrix
of size $2^m \times t$, with s, t positive integers, produces an m-variable linear MBA
identity. Let $\sum_{i=1}^{r} a_i e_i = 0$ be an identity with multiple non-zero terms. Then
$K = q(p(K)) = q(\sum_{i=1}^{r} a_i e_i + p(K))$. Expanding the expression after rearranging
terms in $\sum_{i=1}^{r} a_i e_i + p(K)$ yields an m-variable polynomial MBA expression. (This
construction is one of many due to BA$[n]$'s rich mathematical structure.)   □

The variable inputs obfuscate the code, and its MBA expression frustrates simplification. The variables are typically shared with the remainder of the application.
Appendix A gives a practical example.

4.2   Algorithm and Data Hiding Example: Software Watermarking

As noted in §2.3, systems such as AACS can greatly benefit from MBA-based
algorithm and data hiding. As another example, we now show that they can
provide a secret watermark to prove identity of software[6], where a watermark
is an n-bit constant W, its extraction key is a k-bit constant K, where k is
large, and we must embed W in program **P** so that we can reliably extract it
under K, but an attacker (ignorant of K) cannot obliterate it. (To make n and k
large, we can compose W from $W_1, \ldots, W_w$ and K from $K_1, \ldots, K_w$; i.e., we can
use multiple sub-watermarks and multiple corresponding sub-keys. The methods
should be obvious: we need not discuss this further.)

Watermark Injection. We can represent W and $2^n - W$ as multiterm polynomial MBA expressions by Proposition 2:

$$W = f(x_1, \ldots, x_p) = \sum_{s \in S} a_s \prod_{j \in J_s} e_{s,j}(x_1, \ldots, x_p),$$

$$2^n - W = g(y_1, \ldots, y_q) = \sum_{i \in I} a_i \prod_{j \in J_i} e_{i,j}(y_1, y_2, \ldots, y_q),$$

for any integer variables $x_1, \ldots, x_p,\ y_1, \ldots, y_q \in$ B^n.

Suppose **P** has an MBA expression

$$h(z_1, \ldots z_r) = \sum_{t \in T} a_t \prod_{j \in J_t} e_{t,j}(z_1, \ldots z_r),$$

as an intermediate computation. For example, h could be any single BA operation, which can be represented by multiterm polynomial MBA expressions due to Theorem 3.

We can embed watermark W into h based on $h = W + h + (2^n - W)$. WLOG, assume index sets I, S and J are disjoint. Since $x_1, \ldots, x_p$, $y_1, \ldots, y_q$ are random variables, we can choose some of them from the set $\{z_1, \ldots, z_r\}$. Therefore, the intersection of variable sets $\{y_1, \ldots, y_q\} \cap \{x_1, \ldots, x_p\} \cap \{z_1, \ldots, z_r\}$ maybe nonempty. Represent all with the new set

$$\{u_1, \ldots, u_w\} = \{y_1, \ldots, y_q\} \cup \{x_1, \ldots, x_p\} \cup \{z_1, \ldots, z_r\}.$$

Let σ be any permutation of index set $I \cup S \cup J$. We have

$$h = \sum_{\sigma(t) \in I \cup S \cup J} a_{\sigma(t)} \prod_{j \in J_{\sigma(t)}} e_{\sigma(t),j}(u_1, u_2, \cdots, u_w).$$

Watermark W is computed by adding all terms with indices in $\sigma(S)$ and permutation σ is the watermark key K. To further obfuscate the watermark, apply permutation polynomial p to the watermark expression to mix its terms with terms in h. Then the table-concatenation of permutation σ and the the inverse permutation polynomial p^{-1}'s coefficients is watermark key K.

Following this general watermarking method, we can embed constant watermarks into any BA operations and MBA expressions. The embedding is stealthy because recovering a watermark without the key is an instance of the NP-complete Subset Sum problem, and can be made hard in practice by applying the protections of §3.4.

Watermark Extraction. For any program **P** there are likely to be inputs which are extremely improbable in normal use. Let **P** be a program containing an injected watermark W under key K as described above. At this point, extracting W from the executable code is awkward, and the techniques of this very paper could be used to obscure it and make it effectively impossible to extract.

Instead, the program extracts its own watermark by reüsing the above polynomial computations. (Generating code to do this which we are *building* the code is easy.) Let an extremely improbable lineup of inputs for **P** be **K**. Find an encoding or encodings E according to §3.4 such that $E(\mathbf{K}) = K$ (an easy problem). Then, replace **P** with **P**′ which, if its input-lineup $\mathbf{I} = \mathbf{K}$, computes $K = E(\mathbf{K})$ and uses K to extract and output W, but in all other circumstances, computes **P**(**I**) as in the original program (see Fig. 3).

Now, encode **P**′ according to §3.4, using interlocking to render the watermarking aspects of the code highly fragile under tampering, and making the normal behavior of **P**′ highly dependent on the watermarking code, producing final program **Q**, the final watermark protected version of **P**, with a watermark W protected under the new encoded key **K**.

Extensions to interactive or transaction programs and the like are straightforward and left as an exercise.

Watermark Robustness. The watermark in final watermarked program **Q** above is protected as follows. The attacker does not know **K** and so cannot directly attack the response to **K**. Attempting to otherwise change the I/O behavior of the program produces chaotic results: useless to the attacker since it simply destroys the program instead of obliterating the watermark. Further complicating the program by the methods in this paper does not obliterate the watermark, since so protecting programs by transforms and identities preserves functionality and the watermark extraction facility is a (very well hidden) part of that functionality. Of course, the attacker could add another such watermark, but that would not obliterate the original one.

5   Security of MBA Transforms

By experiment, analytical math tools (**Mathematica**^{TM}, **Maple**^{TM}) can't simplify most MBA expressions. Moreover, the following problems are NP-hard:

1. BA[n]-SAT: for a given polynomial MBA function $f(x_1, \ldots, x_m)$ over BA[n], find values $a_1, \ldots, a_m$ such that $f(a_1, \cdots, a_m) \neq 0$;
2. BA[n]-RECOG: for polynomial MBA functions $f(x_1, \ldots, x_m)$, $g(x_1, \ldots, x_m)$ over BA[n], find values $a_1, \ldots, a_m$ such that $f(a_1, \ldots a_m) \neq g(a_1, \ldots, a_m)$.

Proposition 3. BA[n]-SAT *and* BA[n]-RECOG *are* NP-*complete.*

Proof. The result follows trivially from NP-completeness of Boolean SAT.   □

(Efficient Boolean SAT-solvers can't directly solve these. Boolean SAT is a small subset of BA[n]-SAT: the above problems require solvers for vectors of mutually constrained Boolean SAT-problems.)

Average-case complexity theory is too preliminary for direct security proofs: in the *Average Case Complexity Forum*[2], the papers list was last updated in March of 2000; of roughly 1200 papers added to the *Electronic Colloquium on Computational Complexity*[8] since 1994, about one percent seem to be on average case complexity. We must argue our case by other means.

The best available theory on MBAs is provided in this very paper. We provide easy ways to complicate, but *not* to simplify, programs.

Consider a program whose computations are *interlocked* and *encoded* according to §3.4. Then consider any subexpression repeatedly transformed via the constructions of Theorems 1 and 2. Plainly the program interlocking and encoding and have vastly many choices, and by the nature of the constructions the identity-substitutions can each have vastly many choices as well.

The simplification problem for such programs is the problem of reversing the above process; the vast numbers of choices at every step make its search space vast. Indeed, as expressions grow during this process, the increase in choices with increasing numbers of steps is *hyperexponential*. We don't expect efficient simplifiers for such massively complex constructions any time soon. **Maple**^{TM}, **Mathematica**^{TM}, or similar foreseeable tools, need large databases of known identities and laws. As we have argued above, for MBAs, we should change 'large' to 'extremely large', and probably to 'infeasibly large'; methods depending on simple laws such as Karnaugh-map Boolean simplification are inadequate. New characterizations of NP problems, such as PCP, might eventually offer attack methods — but probably not soon.

Without an efficient simplifier, the limitless variety of polynomial MBA representations for any given BA operation, and the code composed of such operations, becomes an insurmountable BA[n]-RECOG function recognition burden for the attacker: the attacker must recognize the code functionality, but the search space for the attacker is vast and grows over time as increasing numbers of transforms are generated.

We can apply other protections before and/or after those in this paper: see [14] for an excellent survey. Such techniques are important to provide defense in depth and to address other attacks, for example, tampering or spoofing of system calls. This paper's methods proposed ensure viability of such additional protections by obviating any need for specialized hardware.

6   Conclusion

We have introduced powerful new methods for protecting constants, data, and code in software by converting computations into mixed Boolean-arithmetic computations, whether linear or polynomial, over BA-algebras, which provide a rich algebraic system based on the functionality of real-world computer instructions. Such protections are not penetrable using existing analytical tools such as **Maple**^{TM} or **Mathematica**^{TM}, since they combine multiple algebraic systems into one exceedingly complex system.

By basing our protections on ordinary computer instructions, we avoid the vulnerabilities of methods of protection which require code to appear in unexecutable forms or in forms which require an interpreter or a substantial supporting library.

These MBA transform methods provide open-ended generators for identities and transformations which provide an effectively *unlimited* supply of encodings for data and code, making the search-space for attackers very large, and increasingly large over time, as we accumulate more and more vast sets of identities and transforms.

We have described methods for hiding constants in code and for protecting code by keys, so that tampering with the code, with high probability, causes the code to malfunction, and given practical examples to demonstrate our methods.

Acknowledgements. The authors thank their colleagues Phil Eisen, Clifford Liem, and the anonymous referees, for valuable comments.

References

1. Arora, S., Safra, S.: Probabilistic checking of proofs: A new characterization of NP. Journal of the ACM 45(1), 70–122 (1998)
2. Average Case Complexity Forum, http://www.uncg.edu/mat/avg.html
3. Chow, S., Johnson, H., Gu, Y.X.: Tamper resistant software encoding, US Patent No. 6594761 (2003)
4. Chow, S., Gu, Y.X., Johnson, H., Zakharov, V.A.: An Approach to the Obfuscation of Control-Flow of Sequential Computer Programs. In: Davida, G.I., Frankel, Y. (eds.) ISC 2001. LNCS, vol. 2200, pp. 144–155. Springer, Heidelberg (2001)
5. Chow, S., Eisen, P., Johnson, H., van Oorschot, P.C.: White-Box Cryptography and an AES Implementation. In: Nyberg, K., Heys, H.M. (eds.) SAC 2002. LNCS, vol. 2595, Springer, Heidelberg (2003)
6. Collberg, C.S., Thomborson, C.: Watermarking, Tamper-Proofing, and Obfuscation - Tools for Software Protection. IEEE Trans. Software Eng. 28(6) (June 2002)
7. Chen, Y., Venkatesan, R., Cary, M., Pang, R., Sinha, S., Jakubowski, M.H.: Oblivious Hashing: A Stealthy Software Integrity Verification Primitive. In: Petitcolas, F.A.P. (ed.) IH 2002. LNCS, vol. 2578, pp. 400–414. Springer, Heidelberg (2003)
8. Electronic Colloquium on Computational Complexity, http://eccc.hpi-web.de/eccc/ ISSN 1433-8092
9. Garey, M.R., Johnson, D.S.: Computers and Intractability. W.H. Freeman and Company, New York (1979)
10. Kandanchatha, A.N., Zhou, Y.: System and method for obscuring bit-wise and two's complement integer computations in software, Canadian patent application 2456644, 2004; US Patent Application 20050166191 (2005)
11. Klimov, A., Shamir, A.: Cryptographic Applications of T-functions. In: Matsui, M., Zuccherato, R.J. (eds.) SAC 2003. LNCS, vol. 3006, pp. 248–261. Springer, Heidelberg (2004)
12. Klimov, A.: Applications of T-functions in Cryptography, PhD Thesis, Weizmann Institute of Science (2004)
13. Mullen, G., Stevens, H.: Polynomial functions (mod m). Acta Mathematica Hungarica 44(3-4), 287–292 (1984)
14. van Oorschot, P.C.: Revisiting Software Protection. In: Boyd, C., Mao, W. (eds.) ISC 2003. LNCS, vol. 2851, pp. 1–13. Springer, Heidelberg (2003)
15. Rivest, R.L.: Permutation Polynomials Modulo 2^w. Finite Fields and their Applications 7, 287–292 (2001)
16. Sander, T., Tschudin, C.F.: Towards Mobile Cryptography. In: Proceedings of the 1998 IEEE Symposium on Security and Privacy, pp. 215–224 (1998)
17. Sander, T., Tschudin, C.F.: Protecting Mobile Agents Against Malicious Hosts. In: Vigna, G. (ed.) Mobile Agents and Security. LNCS, vol. 1419, pp. 44–60. Springer, Heidelberg (1998)
18. Ogiso, T., Sakabe, Y., Soshi, M., Miyaji, A.: Software Tamper Resistance Based on the Difficulty of Interprocedural Analysis. In: Proceedings of WISA 2002 (2002)
19. Vuillemin, J.: Digital algebra and Circuits. In: Dershowitz, N. (ed.) Verification: Theory and Practice. LNCS, vol. 2772, Springer, Heidelberg (2004)
20. Warren Jr., H.S.: Hacker's Delight. Addison-Wesley, Boston (2002), www.hackersdelight.org
21. Zhou, Y., Main, A.: Diversity via Code Transformations: A Solution for NGNA Renewable Security, The NCTA Technical Papers[TM] 2006, The National Cable and Telecommunications Association Show, Atlanta, pp. 173–182 (2006)
22. http://www.aacsla.com

A   Example of Key Hiding in an MBA Polynomial

Let the key be $K = 0x87654321$ (hex). We use three input variables $x, x_1, x_2 \in B^{32}$, two linear MBA identities

$$2y = -2(x \vee (-y - 1)) - ((-2x - 1) \vee (-2y - 1)) - 3;$$
$$x + y = (x \oplus y) - ((-2x - 1) \vee (-2y - 1)) - 1;$$

and one polynomial transform

$$f(x) = 727318528x^2 + 3506639707x + 6132886 \in P_2(Z/(2^{32}))$$

to generate the following key code:

$$
\begin{aligned}
a =\ & x(x_1 \vee 3749240069); b = x((-2x_1 - 1) \vee 3203512843);\\
d =\ & ((235810187x + 281909696 - x_2) \oplus (2424056794 + x_2));\\
e =\ & ((3823346922x + 3731147903 + 2x_2) \vee (3741821003\\
     & + 4294967294x_2));\\
key =\ & 4159134852e + 272908530a + 409362795x + 136454265b\\
     & + 2284837645 + 415760384a^2 + 415760384ab + 1247281152ax\\
     & + 2816475136ad + 1478492160ae + 3325165568b^2 + 2771124224bx\\
     & + 1408237568bd + 2886729728be + 4156686336x^2 + 4224712704xd\\
     & + 70254592xe + 1428160512d^2 + 1438646272de + 1428160512e^2\\
     & + 135832444d,
\end{aligned}
$$

where $a, b, d, e \in B^{32}$ are intermediate variables. The output value of key is always the constant K regardless of values in x, x_1, and x_2.

Geometrically Invariant Image Watermarking in the DWT Domain

Shijun Xiang and Hyoung-Joong Kim

Graduate School of Information Security,
Center for Information Security Technologies (CIST),
Korea University, Seoul 136-701, Korea
xiangshijun@gmail.com, khj-@korea.ac.kr

Abstract. Watermark resistance to both geometric attacks and lossy compressions is a fundamental issue in the image watermarking community. In this paper, we propose a DWT (Discrete Wavelet Transform) based watermarking scheme for such a challenging problem. Watermark resistance to geometric deformations is achieved by using the invariance of the histogram shape. In both theoretical analysis and experimental way, we show that the invariance can be extended to the DWT domain thanks to the time-frequency localization property of DWT. Consequently, we achieve the goal to embed a geometrically invariant watermark into the low-frequency sub-band of DWT in such a way that the watermark is not only invariant to various geometric transforms, but also robust to common image processing operations. Extensive simulation results demonstrate the superiority of the proposed watermark strategy due to the use of the histogram shape invariance combined with the DWT technique.

1 Introduction

With the development of the Internet and image processing techniques, more and more digital media (e.g., image and video) become available from online sites and easy to distribute illegal copy. Image watermarking as a potential technical solution has been developed for copyright protection of owner [1]. For identifying the illegal use of digital products, the watermark should be resistant to two different kinds of content-preserving manipulations. One is noise-like image processing operations, which may fail the watermark extraction by reducing the watermark energy. The other includes various geometric attacks. From the image watermarking point of view, geometric attacks mainly introduce synchronization errors between encoder and decoder. The watermark is still present, but the detector is no longer able to detect it. Thus, watermark robustness to geometric attacks is taken as a challenging issue.

In the literature, only a few algorithms have presented the topic of how to achieve robustness against geometric attacks, which can be broadly classified into the following categories:

S. Kim, M. Yung, and H.-W. Lee (Eds.): WISA 2007, LNCS 4867, pp. 76–90, 2007.

i) Non-blind watermarking. The cost for resynchronization can be reduced by comparing the original image with the watermarked image which has undergone some geometric attacks, such as [2,3]. The non-blind watermarking schemes are limited for most of the practical applications.

ii) Exhaustive search: Another obvious solution to desynchronization is to randomly search for the space including a set of acceptable attack parameters. One concern in the exhaustive search is the computational cost and the false alarm probability in the larger search space.

iii) Invariant watermarking. Some researchers embedded the watermark into the affine invariant domain [4,5,6]. The watermark in the affine-invariant domains such as Fourier-Mellin transform can achieve the robustness to affine transforms. Though these techniques are robust to affine transform, they are vulnerable to cropping and difficult to implement.

iv) Using reference mark. The authors in [7,8] embedded a template invariant to affine transform in the DFT domain. By searching for the template to estimate the attacked parameters for recovery of the watermark. The template-based watermarking methods possibly suffer from the security issue [9].

v) Content-based invariance watermarking. By binding the watermark synchronization with the image characteristics, watermark detection avoids the synchronization errors. This class of watermarking methods usually exploit some special techniques to find those invariant features in an image. For instance, the watermark was embedded by using globally affine invariance of the moments [10,11,12] or locally invariant feature regions, such as image meshes [13] and Harris points [14]. A possible problem with content-based invariance watermarking is the computational burden in the detection due to the use of robust descriptor.

In this paper, we propose a histogram-based invariant watermarking solution, which has a satisfactory robustness to various geometric attacks. The basic idea is to apply geometrically invariant property of the histogram shape in a way that the watermark is embedded by controlling the number of samples in each two neighboring bins. Considering those noise-like image processing operations, we extend the invariance of the histogram shape to the DWT domain, so that the watermark can be embedded in the low-frequency component to improve robustness performance. Stirmark [15] and Checkmark [16] based simulation tests demonstrate that the proposed watermarking algorithm is very robust to various geometric attacks and has a satisfactory performance for common image processing operations.

The idea of modifying image statistics for watermarking is not new. For instance, patchwork-based watermarking methods (such as [17]) suppose that two sets of randomly selected pixels is Gaussian distributed with zero mean. The watermark sequence was embedded by shifting the mean among groups of two sets of pixels. The patchwork method is sensitive to geometric attacks since the detector can not find the patches correctly. In [18], a histogram specification was introduced for image watermarking. Later, the authors further presented some works to improve the watermarking method [19]. In [18,19], the watermark is in fact designed as a histogram. The basic idea is that the pixels in the original image are regrouped to achieve a desired histogram (the watermarked histogram). Also, the histogram has been applied in other watermarking applications such as lossless data hiding [20]. Our proposed watermarking method is based on the histogram shape invariance, which is distinctively different from the previous histogram-based ones.

In the next section, we will describe the characteristics of the histogram shape to geometric transforms via both the theoretical proof and the extensive testing. This is followed by a description of our proposed watermark embedding and detecting strategy. We then test and analyze the watermark robustness to geometric distortions and some common attacks. Finally, we draw the conclusions.

2   Invariant Features to Geometric Transformations

In this section, we first review geometric transformations briefly. We then investigate the insensitivity of the image histogram shape in the low-frequency of the DWT domain to geometric attacks.

2.1   Geometric Transformations

In [21], the authors introduced various geometric attacks on image watermarking system in detail. Common geometric distortions include affine transforms (such as rotation, scaling, translation and shearing) and cropping. RBAs (Random Bending Attacks) are recently reported geometric attacks, which are claimed as a challenging issue in image watermarking [21].

From the image watermarking point of view, all of the geometric attacks respect the rule that some or all of the pixels are displaced at a random amount under the constraint of visual coherence. Thus, geometric attacks mainly introduce desynchronization between encoder and decoder. Due to interpolation during geometric deformations, the pixel values will be modified slightly. Towards this direction, in the next section we investigate an invariant statistical feature (*the histogram shape*), which is mathematically invariant to affine transforms, as well as statistically resistant to those challenging geometric attacks, such as cropping and RBAs.

2.2   Invariance of the Histogram shape in the Spatial Domain

In [22], we analyzed the time-scale invariance of the histogram shape in 1-D audio signal. However, the image is quite different from the audio signal and the attacks the images may encounter are also different. In [23], we have addressed image histogram shape invariance in the spatial domain. There paper extends the invariance to the DWT domain for improving the robustness.

The image histogram with equal-sized bins may be described by

$$H_M = \{h_M(i)|i = 1, \cdots, L\}, \tag{1}$$

where H_M is a vector denoting the gray-level histogram of the image $F(i,j) = \{f(i,j)|i = 1, ..., R, i = 1, ..., C\}$, and $h_M(i), h_M(i) \geq 0$ denotes the number of pixels in the ith bin satisfying $\sum_{i=1}^{L} h_M(i) = R \times C$. Suppose that the resolution of the image is P bits, the relation between the number of bins L and the bin width M is calculated as

$$L = \begin{cases} 2^P/M & \text{if} \quad Mod(2^P/M) = 0 \\ \lfloor 2^P/M \rfloor + 1 & \text{otherwise,} \end{cases} \tag{2}$$

where $\lfloor \rfloor$ is the floor function.

Consider the case of pure non-proportional scaling over the image $F(i,j)$. Suppose that $F'(x',y') = \{f'(x',y')\}$ is the scaled image with the scaling factors α and β in both vertical and horizontal directions. $f'(x',y')$ is the value in the point (x',y'), theoretically satisfying the expression $f'(x',y') = f(x/\alpha, y/\beta)$. In the new version, the number of rows and columns are calculated as $R' = \alpha R$ and $C' = \beta C$. The histogram of $F'(x',y')$ can be formulated as

$$H'_M = \{h'_M(i)|i = 1, \cdots, L\}, \tag{3}$$

which satisfies the expression $h'_M(i) = h_M(i) \cdot \alpha \cdot \beta$ in theory, referred to Equation (1). Equation (3) indicates the invariance of the histogram shape to the scaling operation because under the scaling the number of elements in the bins are modified *linearly*. In practice, the number of the pixels in each bin may be slightly modified due to interpolation.

Rotation and *translation* are two common operations, which will be able to modify the pixel positions in the image plane. In the two cases, the histogram shape will be invariant due to the fact that the histogram is independent of the pixel position. This kind of special property also provides the histogram shape a capability against other challenging geometric attacks, such as cropping and RBAs. In practice, the interpolation errors during rotation and RBAs will distort the pixel slightly. As a result, the histogram shape will be changed a little.

2.3   The Histogram Shape Invariance in the DWT Domain

As we have known, the watermark can be embedded in the low-frequency component to improve watermark robustness performance, referred to the previous watermarking schemes in the DCT [1] and DWT [8] domain. Towards this direction, we extend the invariance of the histogram shape to the low-frequency sub-band of the DWT domain by exploiting the time-frequency localization property of DWT. The detailed procedure is described below.

Assume that $F(x/\alpha, y/\beta)$ is the scaled version of a digital image $F(x,y)$. The pixels in $F(x,y)$ and $F(x/\alpha, y/\beta)$ can be interpreted as the following 1-D vectors by using *zigzag* scanning, respectively:

$$V_1 = \{v_1(i)|i = 1, \cdots, R \times C\} \quad and \quad V_2 = \{v_2(j)|j = 1, \cdots, \alpha \cdot R \times \beta \cdot C\}, \tag{4}$$

where R and C respectively denote the size of rows and columns in $F(x,y)$. Let $\{c_{\alpha,\beta}^k(j)\}$ and $\{c^k(i)\}$ denote the low-frequency sub-band coefficients of V_1 and

V_2 after a k-level 1-D DWT, respectively. When k is 0, it is equivalent in the spatial domain. If k is 1, we have:

$$\begin{cases} c^k(i) = c^1(i) = \sum_{l=1}^{L_1} g(l) \cdot v_1(2(i-1)+l) \\ c^k_{\alpha,\beta}(j) = c^1_{\alpha,\beta}(j) = \sum_{l=1}^{L_1} g(l) \cdot v_2(2(j-1)+l), \end{cases} \tag{5}$$

where $\{g(l)|l = 1, \cdots, L_1\}$ is the low-pass filter. The DWT operation above will make the histogram difference between V_1 and V_2 in the DWT domain though the theoretical invariance to the scaling is right in the spatial domain. It is due to the fact that some of the neighboring samples belong to different bins.

This problem can be solved by regrouping the samples in V_1 and V_2 according to their spatial-domain histogram shape, and then applying the DWT to the pixels of each bin. Referred to Equation (5), the time-frequency localization characteristic of DWT shows that each transformed coefficient in the low-frequency sub-band is generated by filtering the neighboring L_1 samples with the low-pass filter $\{g(i)\}$. As a result, the DWT coefficients obey the same the histogram shape as the spatial-domain one. Let us take a simple example. Suppose that there are 6 neighboring samples, their intensity values denoted by a vector $X = [1, 6, 2, 5, 3, 4]$. We extract the histogram with 3 equal-sized bins. By regrouping X to generate a new vector $X_s = [1, 2, 3, 4, 5, 6]$. Then, to perform 1-level DWT on X and X_s with the $'db1'$ wavelet base with the low-pass filter of $[\frac{\sqrt{2}}{2}, \frac{\sqrt{2}}{2}]$. The low-frequency coefficients of X and X_s are respectively computed and denoted as

$$C = [(1+6) \times \tfrac{\sqrt{2}}{2}, (2+5) \times \tfrac{\sqrt{2}}{2}, (3+4) \times \tfrac{\sqrt{2}}{2}] = [\tfrac{7\sqrt{2}}{2}, \tfrac{7\sqrt{2}}{2}, \tfrac{7\sqrt{2}}{2}],$$
$$C_s = [(1+2) \times \tfrac{\sqrt{2}}{2}, (3+4) \times \tfrac{\sqrt{2}}{2}, (5+6) \times \tfrac{\sqrt{2}}{2}] = [\tfrac{3\sqrt{2}}{2}, \tfrac{7\sqrt{2}}{2}, \tfrac{11\sqrt{2}}{2}].$$

Obviously, there are 3 low-frequency coefficients after 1-level DWT in C and C_s. Without loss of generality, we compute the histograms of X, X_s, C and C_s with 3 equal-sized bins, respectively. It is noted that X or X_s (three bins, each bin including two samples) and C_s (three bins, each bin including one coefficient) have the same histogram shape, but the histogram of C (only one bin including 3 coefficients) is completely different from that of X (three bins, each bin including two samples). The simple example demonstrates that mapping image into 1-D signal and then regrouping are two crucial steps to exploit the time-frequency localization characteristics of 1-D DWT, so that the invariance of the histogram shape can be transferred to the DWT domain. Note that the invariance can not be equally extended to the DFT and DCT global transform domain.

Let $H_\mu^{r,k}$ denote the histogram of the image after the k-level DWT being performed. Here, μ is the bin width. Referred to Equation (1), the image histogram after regrouping may be rewritten as $H_M^{r,0} = \{h_M^{r,0}(i)|i = 1, \cdots, L\}$, and $H_M^{r,0} = H_M$. Referred to Equation (5)), the low-frequency band histogram shape of 1-level DWT domain may be mathematically formulated as,

$$H_\mu^{r,k} = H_{(\chi)^1 \cdot M}^{r,1} = \{\lfloor \frac{h_M^{r,0}(i) + L_1 - 1}{2} \rfloor\} = \{\lfloor \frac{h_M(i) + L_1 - 1}{2} \rfloor\}, \tag{6}$$

where $i = 1, \cdots, L$, and the bin width is changed from M in $H_M^{r,0}$ to $\chi \cdot M$ in $H_{\chi \cdot M}^{r,1}$, theoretically. If $k > 1$, according to the definition of k-level DWT and mathematical induction, $H_\mu^{r,k}$ may be formulated as,

$$H_\mu^{r,k} = H_{\chi^k \cdot M}^{r,k} = \{\lfloor \frac{h_{\chi^{k-1} \cdot M}^{r,k-1}(i) + L_1 - 1}{2} \rfloor\} \approx \{\frac{h_{\chi^{k-1} \cdot M}^{r,k-1}(i)}{2}\} \approx \{\frac{h_M(i)}{2^k}\}. \quad (7)$$

Referred to Equations (5), (6) and (7), after k-level DWT the bin width in the low-frequency sub-band is $\chi^k \cdot M$ instead of M in the spatial domain. Here, χ is

$$\chi = \sum_{l=1}^{L_1} g(l) \quad (8)$$

according to 1-D DWT theory. Corresponding to Equation (7), it is obvious that $H_{\chi^k \cdot M}^{r,k}$ keeps the same the histogram shape as the spatial-domain histogram H_M since the number of samples is almost *linearly* reduced.

The above proof process shows the spatial-domain histogram shape invariance and its extension in the DWT domain by: i) mapping image into 1-D signal, ii) regrouping the 1-D signal and iii) afterwards performing the DWT. Due to the fact that the *zigzag* mapped and regrouped 1-D signal can keep part of the original spectrum of image, the watermark based on the DWT-domain histogram shape can achieve a better performance for those common image processing operations while keeping its capability against geometric attacks.

2.4   Experimental Testing

In practice, the histogram shape is not invariant exactly due to interpolation errors during geometric deformations, such as scaling, rotation and many others. In order to tolerate the interpolation errors, the spatial-domain histogram bin width should be not less than 2 according to our observations.

In order to investigate the effect of interpolation during geometric attacks, we examine the histogram shape invariance by computing the relative relations of each two neighboring bins with *peppers* of size 512×512 as the example image. We also have tested the other well-known benchmark image (such as *lena* and *baboon*, etc.). The simulation results are similar. In order to satisfy the condition that the bins hold sufficient samples, we extract the histogram by referring to the mean value. For an image, we compute the histogram by the following steps:

i) Remove those non-zero value pixels. By doing this step, we can avoid the effect of those resulted zero-value samples during some geometric deformations (e.g., rotation and shearing).

ii) Extract the histogram by referring to the mean value and a parameter λ, which can be formulated as $B = [(1 - \lambda)\bar{A}, (1 + \lambda)\bar{A}]$. When $\lambda = 0.6$, we have achieve a satisfactory result.

iii) Finally, the histogram is extracted from the low-frequency sub-band of the 2-level DWT with the wavelet base of $'db5'$.

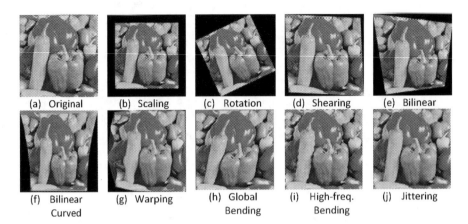

(a) Original   (b) Scaling   (c) Rotation   (d) Shearing   (e) Bilinear

(f) Bilinear   (g) Warping   (h) Global   (i) High-freq.   (j) Jittering
Curved   Bending   Bending

Fig. 1. *Peppers* and its deformed versions with 9 typical geometric transforms

In order to evaluate the histogram shape invariance in the DWT domain, we implement 9 typical geometric attacks including scaling, rotation, shearing, bilinear, bilinear curved, warping, global bending and high-frequency bending as shown in Fig. 1(b)~(j), as well as three different percentages of cropping. The relative relations of each two neighboring bins in the number of samples are designed to represent the histogram shape. By computing the alteration of the relative relations, we can examine the resistance of the histogram shape to various geometric attacks. The relative relation of two successive bins can be formulated as

$$\alpha(k) = \frac{h_M(k+1)}{h_M(k)}, 1 \leq k \leq L - 1, \tag{9}$$

where L is the number of the bins, and M is the bin width, referred to Equation (8).

Fig. 2 (a), (b) and (c) illustrate the relative relations of each two neighboring bins under the 9 typical geometric deformations. Fig. 2 (d) shows the effect of cropping of 5%, 15% and 25% by deleting the outer content, respectively. We can see that the relative relations in the number of pixels (or DWT coefficients) among groups of two *neighboring* bins are rather stable under these geometric attacks.

The above experimental works show the previous theoretical analysis on the spatial-domain histogram shape insensitivity to geometric attacks and its extension in the DWT domain in Section 2 is logical. This also implies a fact that if we embed the watermark based on the relative relations, it is expected that the watermark will be able to withstand those challenging geometric attacks. In addition, since the histogram is extracted from the low-frequency DWT coefficients of the preprocessed images, the watermark also can have a good capability against those common compressing and filtering operations.

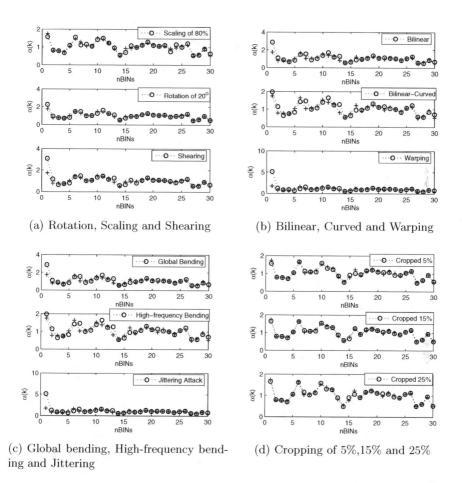

(a) Rotation, Scaling and Shearing

(b) Bilinear, Curved and Warping

(c) Global bending, High-frequency bending and Jittering

(d) Cropping of 5%,15% and 25%

Fig. 2. The effect of the geometric deformations and cropping on the histogram shape. This is evaluated by computing the relative relations of each two neighboring bins in the number of DWT coefficients, denoted by $\alpha(k)$. The bin relative relations of the original image *Peppers* are plotted with the points '+' for the purpose of comparing with the attacked ones plotted with 'o'. These results demonstrate the histogram shape invariance and the effect of the interpolation on the invariance.

3   Proposed Watermarking Algorithm

In this section, a geometrically invariant multi-bit image watermarking is presented. Watermark insertion and recovery are designed by the use of the histogram shape invariance. The histogram is extracted from the low-frequency sub-band of DWT for the purpose of improving robustness to those common image signal processing manipulations by *preprocessing* image (including mapping into 1-D signal and regrouping).

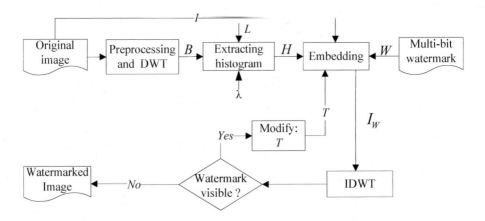

Fig. 3. Block Diagram of Watermark Embedding

3.1   Watermark Insertion

In the embedding phase, the image is first mapped into 1-D style, and then regrouped (keeping the index as ϖ). Furthermore, we extract the histogram as in the previous section (see Section 2.4). The k-level DWT is performed to extract the low-frequency coefficients. Divide the bins as groups, each two neighboring bins as a group is used to carry a bit of watermark information by reassigning the number of coefficients in each two bins. Finally, the inverse-DWT is performed to generate the watermarked image with the index ϖ. Fig. 3 illustrates block diagram of the embedding process.

Suppose that there is a binary sequence $W = \{w_i \mid i = 1, \cdots, L_w\}$ to be hidden into a digital image. The histogram in the low-frequency sub-band of DWT is denoted by $H = \{h_M(i) \mid i = 1, \cdots, L\}$. L should be not less than $2L_w$ in order to embed all bits.

Let Bin_1 and Bin_2 be two consecutive bins, which include a and b coefficients, respectively. We control the relative relation of the two bins to embed one bit of information, formulated as

$$\begin{cases} a/b \geq T & \text{if} \quad w(i) = 1 \\ b/a \geq T & \text{if} \quad w(i) = 0 \end{cases} \tag{10}$$

where T is a threshold selected with the consideration of the watermark robustness performance and the embedding distortion. How to embed one bit into two neighboring bins is depicted in Fig. 4.

Let us consider the case that $w(i)$ is $'1'$. If $a/b \geq T$, no operation is needed. Otherwise, the number of samples in two bins, a and b, will be adjusted until satisfying $a_1/b_1 \geq T$ for the insertion of the bit $'1'$. In the case of embedding the bit $'0'$, the procedure is similar. The watermark rules are referred to Equations (11) and (12).

If $w(i)$ is $'1'$ and $a/b < T$, some randomly selected samples from Bin_2, in the number denoted by I_2, will be modified to fall into Bin_1, achieving $a_1/b_1 \geq T$.

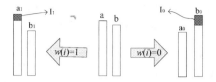

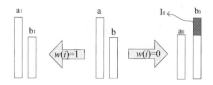

(a) 1<a/b<T; a₁/b₁=(a+I₁)/(b-I₁)≥T; b₀/a₀=(b+I₀)/(a-I₀)≥T

(b) a/b>T>1; a₁/b₁=a/b≥T; b₀/a₀=(b+I₀)/(a-I₀)≥T

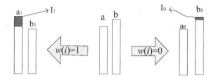

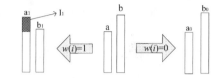

(c) 1<b/a<T; a₁/b₁=(a+I₁)/(b-I₁)≥T; b₀/a₀=(b+I₀)/(a-I₀)≥T

(d) b/a>T>1; a₁/b₁=(a+I₁)/(b-I₁)≥T; b₀/a₀=b/a≥T

Fig. 4. Illustration of embedding one bit of watermark information. There are four cases in total: (a) $a > b$ and $a/b < T$, (b) $a > b$ and $a/b \geq T$, (c) $b > a$ and $b/a < T$, and (d) $b < a$ and $b/a \geq T$. I_1 and I_0 are the numbers of the least modified coefficients according to the watermarking embedding rule.

If $w(i)$ is $'0'$ and $b/a < T$, some selected coefficients from Bin_1, in the number denoted by I_1, are adjusted into Bin_2 , satisfying $b_0/a_0 \geq T$. The rule for reassigning the coefficients is described as Equation (11).

$$\begin{cases} f'_1(i) = f_1(i) + M, & 1 \leq i \leq I_1 \\ f'_2(j) = f_2(j) - M, & 1 \leq j \leq I_2 \end{cases} \tag{11}$$

where M is the bin width. $f_1(i)$ and $f_2(j)$ denote the ith and j^{th} modified coefficient in Bin_1 and Bin_2, respectively. The modified coefficients $f'_1(i)$ fall into Bin_2 while $f'_2(i)$ move to Bin_1. I_1 and I_2 can be computed by using the following mathematical expressions,

$$\begin{cases} I_1 = (T * b - a)/(1 + T) & making \quad a_1/b_1 \geq T \quad from \quad a/b \leq T \\ I_2 = (T * a - b)/(1 + T) & making \quad b_0/a_0 \geq T \quad from \quad b/a \leq T, \end{cases} \tag{12}$$

where $a_1 = a + I_1$, $b_1 = b - I_1$, $a_0 = a - I_2$, and $b_0 = b + I_2$.

This procedure is repeated until all watermark bits are embedded. Finally, the inverse-DWT is implemented to generate the watermarked image, denoted by $F_w(x, y) = \{f_w(x, y) | x = 1 \sim R, y = 1 \sim C\}$.

3.2 Watermark Recovery

Our goal is to get an estimate of hidden bits, $W' = \{w'(i) \mid i = 1, \cdots, L_w\}$, at a low error rate. The histogram extracted from the low-frequency coefficients in $F'_w(x, y)$ is extracted as in the process of watermark insertion. Suppose that the number of coefficients in two consecutive bins are a' and b'. By comparing their values, we will be able to extract the hidden bit, formulated as

$$w'(i) = \begin{cases} 1 & \text{if} \quad a'/b' \geq 1 \\ 0 & \text{otherwise.} \end{cases} \qquad (13)$$

The same process is repeated to obtain all the hidden bits by computing all groups of two neighboring bins. In the watermarking decoder, the parameters, L_w, λ, are beforehand known. Thus, this is a blind watermarking algorithm.

4   Experimental Results

Below, we conduct experiments to demonstrate the performance of the proposed multi-bit watermarking scheme. The watermark is embedded in the low-frequency subband of 2-level DWT. The wavelet base $'db5'$ is adopted. In the experiments, a 10-bit watermark was embedded into a set of 512×512 example images (five of them in total, including *Boat*, *Peppers*, *Baboon* and *Lena* and *Clock*) using the proposed algorithm. The parameter $\lambda = 0.6$ is selected to compute the histogram with 20 bins. The embedding threshold, T, is 1.5. We assign $\triangle_1 = \triangle_2 = 6\%$ for the reliable watermark recovery.

4.1   Imperceptibility

In the embedding, only a small percent of pixels are modified with a smaller distortion magnitude (less than 6 gray levels). Since the probability of those selected samples being added or reduced is approximately equal, the watermark hardly has an effect on the image mean. The PSNR and mean values are tabulated in Table 1. $\hat{A}_o$ and $\hat{A}_w$ denote the mean before and after watermarking, respectively. For the five example images, the PSNR is over 40 dB. Usually, we consider that the watermark being embedded in the low-frequency sub-band will be able to cause the visual distortion. In order to better evaluate the watermark distortion, we plot the example images *Lena* and *Peppers* and their watermarked versions, as shown in Fig. 5. We can see that though the watermark is embedded into the low-frequency component, the distortion is imperceptible. The basic reason is that the distortion on the low-frequency coefficients has been evenly spread over times of pixels.

4.2   Robustness

Table 2 shows a list of attacks used to distort the images and their effects on the watermark in the experiments. In case of Stirmark attacks, the watermark can resist the cropping of 50%, JPEG compression of the quality factor 60, and all attacks regarding *Affine Transform*, *Rotation*, *Rotation+Scale*, *Rotation+Cropping*, and *Median filtering*.

Table 1. The distortions caused by the watermark in the spatial (denoted by $'S'$) and DWT Domain (denoted by $'D'$) (In PSNR and Mean)

Features	Boat (S/D)	Peppers (S/D)	Baboon (S/D)	Clock (S/D)	Lena (S/D)
Mean ($\hat{A}_o$)	117.53/235.06	119.83/239.65	98.84/197.68	70.48/140.88	115.14/230.29
Mean ($\hat{A}_w$)	117.51/235.03	119.63/239.26	98.65/197.37	70.58/140.95	115.07/230.15
PSNR (dB)	44.64/44.12	45.02/44.95	46.40/46.40	50.23/50.17	44.99/44.98

Table 2. Watermarking robustness to geometric attacks and common signal processing operations in the low-frequency subbabd of the DWT domäin

Strimarm4.0	BER	Checkmark	BER
AFFINE (all)	0	Linear Transform	0
CROP (50,75)	0	Aspect Ratio	0
ROT (all)	0	Projective	0
ROTSCALE (all)	0	Warping	0
ROTCROP (all)	0	Shearing	0
MEDIAN (all)	0	Row/Column Removal	0
RML (all)	0	Down/Up Sampling	0
JPEG (15-50)	0.1	JPEG2000 ($0.5 \sim 8.0$ bpp)	0
JPEG (60-100)	0	JPEG2000 ($0.2 \sim 0.4$ bpp)	0.1

The Checkmark benchmark is one of the second generation watermarking evaluation tools, which has incorporated some common but challenging geometric deformation operations, such as RBAs based on projective transform and image warping. Therefore, here we adopt the Checkmark for measuring the watermark performance to those challenging geometric attacks. In Table 2, the attack parameters are respectively given as: *Linear Transform* ($T_{11} = -0.85$; $T_{12} = -0.2$; $T_{21} = -0.05$; $T_{22} = 1.3$), *Aspect Ratio* (xscale=0.8 yscale=1.1), *projective* (30 degree rotation along x-axis + perspective projection), *Warping* (warpfactor =12), *Shearing* (xshear=5% yshear=5%), and *Row/Column removal* (12 rows and 9 columns removed) are implemented, respectively. In addition, the watermark is also robust to *Down/Up Sampling* and *JPEG2000* (with 0.5 bpp, compression rate of 16:1). We can see that the watermark also has a satisfactory robustness to those challenging geometric attacks.

Overall, in both the Stirmark and the Checkmark tests we show that in the low-frequency sub-band of 2-level DWT, the watermark has a satisfactory robustness to geometric attacks (even those challenging geometric attacks, such as cropping and RBAs) and common image processing operations (e.g., median filter, JPEG and JPEG2000 compressions). We believe that it is due to two main aspects: (i) The histogram-based watermark is insensitive to the shifting of the pixels on the image plane since the histogram is independent of the pixel position. As a result, the watermark is insensitive to those challenging geometric attacks and (ii) in the low-frequency sub-band of DWT, the watermark has a potential capability against those noise-like image processing operations.

(a) Lena.bmp   (b) Peppers.bmp

(c) Marked Lena   (d) Marked Peppers

Fig. 5. The original example images and the marked ones (resolution of 44%): (a) Lena (F), (b) Peppers, (c) Lena after watermarking, (d) Peppers after watermarking

5   Concluding Remarks

In both the theoretical analysis and the extensive experiments, in this paper we show that i) the histogram shape is insensitive to various geometric deformations, and ii) the histogram shape invariance property can be extended to the low-frequency sub-band of the DWT domain. Accordingly, a geometrically invariant image watermarking scheme is successfully designed by using the histogram shape invariance in the DWT domain. Extensive experimental works have shown that the watermark has a satisfactory robustness performance for those challenging geometric attacks (e.g., projective transform, image warping and random cropping). The watermark also achieves good robustness against those common image processing operations, such as JPEG compression, JPEG2000 compression, median filters, etc.

In theory, the watermark's embedding capacity is at most 128 bits. In practice, the watermark can achieve a satisfactory robustness only when the embedding capacity is less than 20 bits according to our observations. The more the embedding capacity, the lower the watermark robustness. Thus, how to improve data embedding capacity is a consideration of future works. In addition, our proposed watermarking scheme is suffering from its performance limitation for the image of smaller size since a smaller image can not provide efficient samples to satisfy the condition that the bins hold enough samples. Another note is that the proposed watermarking algorithm is not working well for those high-contrast images, which usually have a distinctive histogram.

Since the algorithm is very robust to geometric deformations under the constraint of visual coherence, we consider that our proposed watermarking scheme can combine with other robust watermarking algorithms together for better resisting those challenging geometric attacks and common image signal processing operations.

Acknowledgement

This work was supported by the Second Brain Korea 21 Project, and the MIC (Ministry of Information and Communication), Korea, under the ITRC (Information Technology Research Center) support program supervised by the IITA (Institute of Information Technology Advancement)" (IITA-2006-(C1090-0603-0025)).

References

1. Cox, I.J., Kilian, J., Leighton, T., Shamoon, T.: Secure Spread Spectrum Watermarking for Multimedia. IEEE Transaction on Image Proccess 6(6), 1673–1687 (1997)
2. Johnson, N., Duric, Z., Jajodia, S.: Recovery of Watermarks from Distorted Images. In: Pfitzmann, A. (ed.) IH 1999. LNCS, vol. 1768, pp. 318–332. Springer, Heidelberg (2000)
3. Davoine, F.: Triangular Meshes: A Solution to Resist to Geometric Distortions Based Watermark-Removal Softwares. In: Proc. Eurasip. Signal Processing Conference, vol. 3, pp. 493–496 (2000)
4. Ruanaidh, J., Pun, T.: Rotation, Scale and Translation Invariant Spread Spectrum Digital Image Watermarking. Signal Processing 66(3), 303–317 (1998)
5. Lin, C.Y., Wu, M., Bloom, J., Miller, M., Cox, I., Lui, Y.M.: Rotation, Scale, and Translation Resilient Public Watermarking for Images. IEEE Transaction on Image Processing 10(5), 767–782 (2001)
6. Zheng, D., Zhao, J., Saddik, A.: RST-Invariant Digital Image Watermarking Based on Log-Polar Mapping And Phase Correlation. IEEE Transactions on Circuits and Systems for Video Technology 13(8), 753–765 (2003)

7. Pereira, S., Pun, T.: Robust Template Matching for Affine Resistant Image Watermarks. IEEE Transaction on Image Processing 9(6), 1123–1129 (2000)
8. Kang, X., Huang, J., Shi, Y., Lin, Y.: A DWT-DFT Composite Watermarking scheme Robust to Both Affine Transform and JPEG Compression. IEEE Transactions on Circuits and Systems for Video Technology 13(8), 776–786 (2003)
9. Herrigel, A., Voloshynovskiy, S., Rytsar, Y.: The Watermark Template Attack. In: Proc. SPIE Electronic Imaging (2001)
10. Kim, H.S., Lee, H.K.: Invariant Image Watermark Using Zernike Moments. IEEE Transaction on Circuits and Systems for Video Technology 13(8), 766–775 (2003)
11. Alghoniemy, M., Tewfik, A.H.: Geometric Invariance in Image Watermarking. IEEE Transactions on Image Processing 13(2), 145–153 (2004)
12. Dong, P., Brankov, J.G., Galatsanos, N.P., Yang, Y.Y., Davoine, F.: Affine Transformation Resistant Watermarking Based on Image Normalizaton. IEEE Transactions on Image Processing 14(12), 2140–2150 (2005)
13. Lu, C.S., Sun, S.W., Hsu, C.Y., Chang, P.C.: Media Hash-Dependent Image Watermarking Resilient Against Both Geometric Attacks and Estimation Attacks Based on False Positive-Oriented Detection. IEEE Transactions on Multimedia 8(4), 668–685 (2006)
14. Seo, J.S., Yoo, C.D.: Image Watermarking Based on Invariant Regions of Scale-Space Representation. IEEE Transactions on Sginal Processing 54(4), 1537–1549 (2006)
15. http://www.cl.cam.ac.uk/~fapp2/watermarking/stirmark/
16. http://watermarking.unige.ch/Checkmark/
17. Yeo, I.K., Kim, H.J.: Generalized Patchwork Algorithm for Image Watermarking. Multimedia System 9(3), 261–265 (2003)
18. Coltuc, D., Bolon, P.: Watermarking by Histogram Specification. In: Proc. SPIE International Conference on Security and Watermarking of Multimedia Contents II, pp. 252–263 (1999)
19. Coltuc, D., Bolon, P., Chassery, J.M.: Fragile and Robust Watermarking by Histogram Specification. In: Proc. SPIE International Conference Security and Watermarking of Multimedia Contents IV, vol. 4675, pp. 701–710 (2002)
20. Lee, S., Suh, Y., Ho, Y.: Lossless Data Hiding Based on Histogram Modification of Difference Images. In: Aizawa, K., Nakamura, Y., Satoh, S. (eds.) PCM 2004. LNCS, vol. 3333, pp. 340–347. Springer, Heidelberg (2004)
21. Licks, V., Jordan, R.: Geometric Attacks on Image Watermarking Systems. IEEE Multimedia 12(3), 68–78 (2005)
22. Xiang, S., Huang, J., Yang, R.: Time-scale Invariant Audio Watermarking Based on the Statistical Features in Time Domain. In: Proc. of Information Hiding workshop (June 2006)
23. Xiang, S., Kim, H.J.: An Invariant Image Watermarking Against Geometric Attacks. In: Proc. International Joint Workshop on Information Security and Its Applications (February 2007)

Implementation of LSM-Based RBAC Module for Embedded System

Jae-Deok Lim[1], Sung-Kyong Un[1], Jeong-Nyeo Kim[1], and ChoelHoon Lee[2]

[1] Electronics and Telecommunications Research Institute (ETRI)
161 Gajung-dong, Yuseong-gu, Daejeon 305-700, Korea
{jdscol92,skun,jnkim}@etri.re.kr
[2] Computer Science & Engineering, Chungnam National University
220 Gung-dong, Yuseong-gu, Daejeon 305-764, Korea
clee@cnu.ac.kr

Abstract. Security requirements of the embedded system which were not considered when the embedded system is independently deployed are being increased because the embedded system is connected to an internet. Accordingly, the coverage of the system security is being expanded from the general server to the embedded system. And it is not enough that the embedded system supports only its inherent functions and it becomes the essential element to provide the security function to the embedded system. This paper implements the Role Based Access Control(RBAC) module which is designed using the Linux Security Module(LSM) for the embedded system. RBAC allows security management to be administrated easily and LSM is a lightweight, general purpose, access control framework for mainstream Linux kernel that enables many different access control models. The combination of RABC and LSM properties is very suitable for one of security solutions of embedded system because of the simplicity and flexibility of RBAC and a lightweight loadable mechanism of LSM. And we show the performance of our implementation that has very small overhead for the intended processing and is acceptable.

1 Introduction

The embedded system market is gradually enlarged to the request increment of the terminal performing the specific purpose. Particularly, the network-based service is generalized around the mobile personal digital assistants and the demand about the network service is more increased as the personal digital assistants have the high spec and high performance including the Smart phone, Ultra mobile PC(UMPC), Portable Multimedia Player(PMP), and etc. The usage of the internet service heightens the possibility of the external invasion and the sensitive personal data including the bank account, user certificates, personal address book, record of utilization, and etc. can be taken out stored in small and medium embedded system such as the personal digital assistant or the settop box, and etc. The embedded system using the internet service needs the security requirement which was not considered when being employed excluding network function.

S. Kim, M. Yung, and H.-W. Lee (Eds.): WISA 2007, LNCS 4867, pp. 91–101, 2007.
© Springer-Verlag Berlin Heidelberg 2007

In fact the Fsecure Mobile Anti virus site reports that the total number of mobile malware rose up to 344 by the end of December 2006[1]. Particularly F-Secure's research lab received samples of new mobile spying tools, running on Windows Mobile and Symbian S60 3rd Edition devices in May, 2007. According to the classification of a malware, the Trojan horse type occupied 76.6% to a most and the worm type occupied about 15.8%. Some of actually discovered viruses from [1] are as follows. *Doomboot.A* disguises as the crack file of the doom2 which is the game for the cellular phone and is distributed widely. The phone operation is interrupted in an infection and it has the information stored in the terminal and the concern losing data in a recovery. *Pbstealer.A* disguises as the useful utility and infects cellular phone. And it leaks the phone book data information of the corresponding terminal. *Sendtool.A* installs some of Trojan horse codes pretending to the useful program. And it is propagated through the bluetooth. To correspond to the threats as in the above, it is needed that the security function for protecting data and operating environment as well as the original function of embedded system, especially access control function.

This paper tries to strengthen the security of the embedded system by applying the Role Based Access Control(RBAC) function to the embedded linux to be used as OS of the embedded system and the role-based access control is implemented based on the Linux Security Module(LSM) framework and then able to be easily applied to the embedded system. In this paper, it is called L-RBAC that the implementation of role-based access control model using LSM framework.

RBAC is suitable to the access control model for an embedded system because of being the model which is more advantageous than the other access control model such as Discretionary Access Control (DAC) and Mandatory Access Control(MAC) as to the management and use[2][3]. DAC is an access policy that restricts access to files(and other system objects such as directories, devices, and IPC) based on the identity of users and/or the groups to which they belong. DAC is commonly implemented by Access Control List(ACL) and also is suitable for small system which has little users and resources. But DAC has the security hole that its policy can be modified and ignored without any restriction by user who has the super user right, that is 'root' user in linux system. Most malwares can acquire the super user right with various ways for example buffer-over-flow. RBAC provides the role based and strengthened access control function and is one of the access control models which is applied in order to intensify the security of the system. In RBAC, access to object by a subject is determined by role not the identity of subject. And it is the access control model providing the convenience of the management and many flexibilities unlike DAC, MAC, and etc. to the policy manager. A role is defined as the job function about the various tasks. Users are assigned to roles, permissions are assigned to roles and users acquire permissions by being members of roles.

The LSM framework meets the goal of enabling many different security models with the same base Linux kernel while minimally impacting the Linux kernel[4]. The generality of LSM permits enhanced access controls to be effectively implemented without requiring kernel patches. LSM also permits the existing security functionality of POSIX.1e capabilities to be cleanly separated from the base kernel. This allows users with specialized needs, such as embedded system developers, to reduce security features to a minimum for performance. So the combination of RABC and LSM properties is very suitable for one of security solutions of embedded system. Of cause LSM-based RBAC can be also applied to the general linux system such as servers and desktops. This paper shows that the LSM-based RBAC model is suitable for the embedded system and can be one solution for securing the embedded system.

The LSM is a lightweight, general purpose, access control framework for the mainstream Linux kernel that enables many different access control models to be implemented as loadable kernel modules. And a number of existing enhanced access control implementations have already been adapted to use the LSM framework, for example, POSIX.1e capabilities[5], SELinux[6], and Domain and Type Enforcement (DTE)[7]. Although SELinux supports RBAC, it was mainly designed for a desktop or a server. And it is not suitable for the embedded system because it has the difficulty of an operation and setting up and is the use of the concept complicated with the Type Enforcement, the MultiLevel Security, and etc.

The rest of this paper is organized as follows. A brief description of standard of RBAC is contained in section 2. Section 3 describes the design and implementation of L-RBAC module. Section 4 describes the performance overhead of L-RBAC. Section 5 shows the example of L-RBAC application. Finally conclusions and future work are discussed in section 6.

2   Standard of Role-Based Access Control

The standard for RBAC is proposed by NIST to have unified ideas from prior RBAC models, commercial products, and research prototypes[8]. It is intended to serve as a foundation for product development, evaluation, and procurement specification.

The RBAC reference model from [8] is defined in terms of four model components – Core RBAC, Hierarchical RBAC, Static Separation of Duty Relations, and Dynamic Separation of Duty Relations. Core RBAC defines a minimum collection of RBAC elements, element sets, and relations in order to completely achieve a Role-Based Access Control system. This includes user-role assignment and permission-role assignment relations, considered fundamental in any RBAC system. In addition, Core RBAC introduces the concept of role activation as part of a user's session within a computer system. Core RBAC is required in any RBAC system, but the other components are independent of each other and may be implemented separately. The Hierarchical RBAC component adds relations for supporting role hierarchies. A hierarchy is mathematically a partial order defining a seniority relation between roles, whereby senior roles acquire the permissions of their juniors and junior roles acquire users of their seniors.

Separations of duty relations are used to enforce conflict of interest policies. Conflict of interest in a role-based access control system may arise as a result of a user gaining authorization for permissions associated with conflicting roles. Static Separation of Duty(SSD) Relations adds exclusivity relations among roles with respect to user assignments. A common example is that of Static Separation of Duty (SSD) that defines mutually disjoint user assignments with respect to sets of roles. Dynamic Separation of Duty(DSD) Relations defines exclusivity relations with respect to roles that are activated as part of a user's session. DSD properties provide extended support for the principle of least privilege in that each user has different levels of permission at different times, depending on the role being performed.

In addition to [8], there is RBAC implementation standard of draft version 0.1[9]. The draft describes the requirement of RBAC implementation and requires that Administrative Commands and Supporting System Functions for Core RBAC must be provided at least.

In this paper, we comply with NIST RBAC standard and requirements[8][9]; that is, core RBAC component and separation of duty component are provided.

3   Design and Implementation of L-RBAC

L-RBAC was designed simply for the embedded system and designed in order to be satisfied the RBAC standard features[8]. Table 1 shows the function of a standard requesting and the function provided by L-RBAC.

STD-6.2 property, a hierarchy, is more suitable to the large server system which is used by multi-user and multi-tasking. But it may not be suitable to the embedded system which is mostly used by the single user. Therefore, the STD-6.2 property is excluded in our design. The core component, STD-6.1 property, must be provided in any RBAC and applied to our design though the commands shown at table 1 and the libraries corresponding to each command. Figure 1 shows the access policy between subject and object with role. The assumption

Table 1. The L-RBAC functions according to the Standard of RBAC

Command of L-RBAC	Standard number
System role : addrole, delrole, getallrole	STD-6.1 (Core RBAC)
User role : seturole, geturole	STD-6.1 (Core RBAC)
Process role : setprole, getprole	STD-6.1 (Core RBAC)
Object role : setfrole, getfrole	STD-6.1 (Core RBAC)
setssd, getssd	STD-6.3.1 (SSD relations)
setdsd, getdsd	STD-6.3.2 (DSD relations)
setcrole, getcrole	Cardinality (additional supported)

$$S_i \xrightarrow{\quad rwx \quad} O_{j\_any}$$

(a) Case that RBAC is not applied

$$S_i \xrightarrow{\quad rwx \quad} O_{Rj\_any} \qquad S_{Ri} \genfrac{}{}{0pt}{}{\xrightarrow{\quad r \quad}}{\xrightarrow{\quad wx \quad}} O_{Rj\_r}$$

$$S_{Ri} \genfrac{}{}{0pt}{}{\xrightarrow{\quad rw \quad}}{\xrightarrow{\quad x \quad}} O_{Rj\_rw} \qquad S_{Ri} \xrightarrow{\quad rwx \quad} O_{Rj\_rwx}$$

(b) Case that RBAC is applied

Fig. 1. Access model between subject and object. (a) Traditional situation. Subject S can do any type of access to object O if S has the ownership of O. (b) Secure situation. Subject S can do an only accepted type of access to object O if S has the permission of role assigned to O. In this case, S cannot access to O if S does not have the permission of role assigned to O even though S has the ownership to O

of Fig.1 is that S has the ownership to O, that is, a subject S can do any type of access to object O if O does not be set any role.

The meaning of symbols and assumption is as follows.

- S_i : a subject i
- S_{Ri} : a subject i which has a permission of role R
- O_{j_mode} : an object j with $mode$ permission. $mode$ indicate r for read, w for write, x for execute and any for any permission type.
- O_{Rj_mode} : an object j assigned role R with $mode$ permission but not assigned any role. $mode$ is the same above.

STD-6.3.1 and STD-6.3.2 show Static Separation of Duty (SSD) relations and Dynamic Separation of Duties(DSD) relations respectively. For example, if $role1$ and $role2$ were set up in SSD, they cannot be assigned to a user or an object simultaneously. And if $role1$ and $role2$ are set up in DSD, they cannot be activated at the same time but can be assigned to a user or an object. In our design, L-RBAC also provides the Cardinality that is the limitation of assignment of role. If $role1$ is set up in Cardinality with 3, the $role1$ cannot be assigned 4 times at the same time. This property can be used to prevent from abusing of role.

Now, we describe the implementation of L-RBAC with LSM properties. Figure 2 shows the architecture of L-RBAC. The process of enforcement is started from the request of LSM hooks. LSM allows module to mediate access to kernel objects by placing hooks in the kernel code just ahead of the access, as shown in left side of Fig.2[4]. Just before the kernel would have accessed an internal object, a hook makes a call to a function that the L-RBAC module

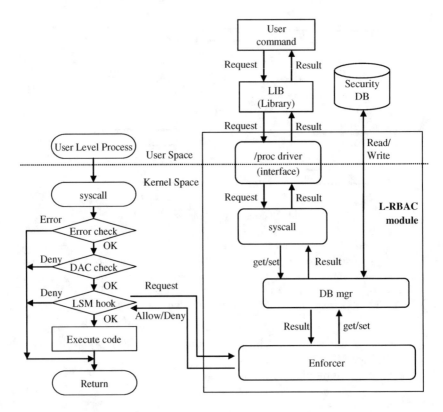

Fig. 2. The architecture of L-RBAC. There are two pathes for enforcement and management. Enforcement is requested from LSM hooks and Management is requested from /proc device driver.

must provide. The L-RBAC module can either let the access granted or denied forcing an error code return. LSM is the security framework of the kernel level provided from the linux kernel 2.6 and more. And LSM has total 88 hooks and calls the function provided by the LSM module in the place where it is necessary to have the security check including the program loading, the file access, the IPC use, and etc. L-RBAC module consists of enforcer for determining access, DB manager for searching and setting security DB, system call and /proc device driver interface for managing RBAC.

As shown Fig.2, RBAC management is achieved through /proc device driver. Each management command such as *addrole*, *delrole* and so on calls a correspondent system call and system call request a correspondent action to DB manager. DB manager modify or update the security DB and response to requester. Security DB stores the information that is used to determine if an access is granted or denied, in-cluding inode of object, role assigned to object, the device in which object is. To speed up to search DB, it is constructed by 4 hash list and is loaded into kernel mem-ory when L-RBAC is initialized.

4   Performance Overhead

The performance overhead of L-RBAC module is explained in this section. The overhead imposed by such a model is a composite of the LSM framework overhead and the actual RBAC enforcement overhead. We had two tests, macrobenchmark on PC and microbenchmark on target system.

At First we use the widely used kernel compilation benchmark for macrobenchmark, measuring the time to build the Linux Kernel. We ran this test on a Pentium IV 3.00Ghz processor with 1 GB RAM. The conditions of this test are that there is no network activity, caches are flushed(that is rebooted), compiled with pre-configured '.config' file and measurement values are acquired with *time* command. Table 2 shows the macrobenchmark test result. As shown at Table 2, the L-RBAC has 1.45% overhead at system space, 0.1% overhead at user space and just 0.24% overhead totally. We think that it is acceptable compared to the overhead of LSM only, 0–0.3%[4].

Table 2. The result of kernel compilation macrobenchmark

Space	Without L-RBAC(time)	With L-RBAC(time)	Overhead
Real(user+sys)	31m 41.067s	31m 45.691s	0.24%
User	28m 15.110s	28m 16.774s	0.1%
Sys	1m 58.371s	2m 0.092s	1.45%

Table 3. The result of kernel compilation macrobenchmark

Syscall	Without L-RBAC(time)	With L-RBAC(time)	Overhead
Open/close	11.8310ms	12.6815ms	7.2%
Stat	7.4214ms	8.0136ms	8.0%
Fork/exit	3,263.5000ms	3,263.5000ms	0%
Fork/exec	3,442.0000ms	3,438.5000ms	-0.1%

Secondly we used LMBench for microbenchmarking[10]. LMBench was developed specifically to measure the performance of core kernel system calls and facilities, such as file access, context switching, and memory access. We ran this test on a X-Hyper270A embedded system which is based on Intel PXA270 processor. It has the performance of the low power and high-end (520MHz) and then can be used for the mobile related products group. In addition, it also supports the Linux 2.6.11 and can use the LSM security framework. In target system, the macrobenmark (Kernel Soruce Compilation) is unable to be used due to the resources restriction of the Target System like the PC Version. Table 3 shows the result of a microbenchmark test and the values are the mean value at each test after 100 time repetition.

In [4], the *open/close* overhead of LSM only is 2.7% and that of L-RBAC is 7.2%. But the test of [4] was on high-end level system and just for LSM module without RBAC function and the test of L-RBAC was on low-end embedded system and for LSM module with RBAC function. So the overhead of L-RBAC is very acceptable.

5   Example of Application

In this section, the example in which the RBAC model is applied to the personal digital assistant such as smart phone which is the representative kind of the embedded system is illustrated. The current mobile smart phone provides various internet-based services and then stores personal data such as the personal identification number and authentication information etc. for the internet-based services.

Figure 3(a) shows the process of the personal information being taken out from the smart phone by the Trojan horse when using the internet service. Hacker inserts the malicious code into the popular programs like games and uploads the modified programs. The inserted malicious code can have the activities like the Trojan horse having the personal information outflow function. And then, user downloads the modified program into the smart phone and executes it. At this time, regardless of the original program operation, the malicious code accesses the personal information and delivers it to the hacker not knowing to the owner of smart phone. This example that is shown at Fig.3(a) can be enough issued with the malware and/or malicious software which is illustrated in section 1.

Figure 3(b) shows the process of protecting the personal information from the attack of the method as in the above by applying RBAC. A role is assigned to personal data like Fig.3(b) in advance for access control with RBAC by using one of L-RBAC commands introduced at Table 1, *setfrole* which can assign a permission to an object with a role. Now the only subject that has an assigned role to object can access the object. A malicious code tries to access the personal data through the process like Fig.3(a). The access request is captured by LSM hook in kernel and then the request is passed to the Enforcer of L-RBAC with the subject ID and object ID. Enforcer requests the access decision to the DB manager. DB manager determines if the access is granted or denied through the security DB. At this time, the object assigned the permission of a role and subject hoes not has a role, so DB manager returns that this access should be denied. Like this process, L-RBAC module determines the access based on a role and permission assigned to the data and a role assigned to the malicious code that tries to access the data. In this case, the malicious code does not have a role that is able to access to data because it is the abnormal program. So the malicious code cannot access the personalization data protected with a role. The example in this section is very simple model in which RBAC is applied, but the effectiveness is very good.

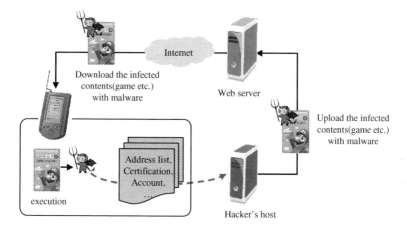

(a) Service without L-RBAC

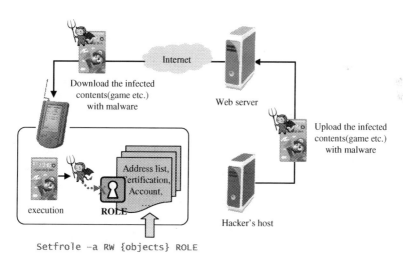

Setfrole −a RW {objects} ROLE

(b) Service with L-RBAC

Fig. 3. The example of L-RBAC application. In (a), personal data can be taken out by the Trajan horse. In (b), personal data can be protected by role of L-RBAC policy. The data had been set to be only accessed by the subject with role of *ROLE*. But malware code cannot access the data because it has been executed abnormally and then cannot have any role.

6   Conclusion

The embedded system is the particular system for the specific purpose. At the past, most embedded system was the stand-alone type and focused on performing function of the system itself. Now the network-based service is generalized

around the mobile personal digital assistants and the demand about the network
service has been more increased. The usage of the internet service heightens the
possibility of the external invasion and the sensitive personal data including the
financial information, user certificates, personal address book, record of utilization, and etc. can be taken out stored in small and medium embedded system.
In fact there are reported the presence of malicious code for embedded system
especially mobile phones. Therefore, the system resources and the user data are
needed to be safely protected from these crackings even though it is embedded
system.

This paper tries to strengthen the security of the embedded system by applying the Role Based Access Control(RBAC) function to the embedded linux to
be used as OS of the embedded system and the role-based access control is implemented based on the Linux Security Module(LSM) framework and then able
to be easily applied to the embedded system. The combination of RABC and
LSM properties is very suitable for one of security solutions of embedded system
because of the simplicity and flexibility of RBAC and a lightweight loadable
mechanism of LSM.

Although we introduced the simple example of application of RBAC for mobile
smart phone, there is few practical application of RBAC for embedded system
including home network devices, car computing system and so on as well as
mobile assistants. So it should be studied that the specified application model
of RBAC which is suitable for the various embedded computing environments
such as home networking, car computing, sensor networking and so on.

References

1. F-Secure Mobile Anti-virus, http://mobile.f-secure.com/
2. Sandhu, R.S., Coyne, E.J., Feinstein, H.L., Youman, C.E.: Role-based Access Control models. IEEE Computer 29(2), 38–47 (1996)
3. Ferraiolo, D., Cugini, J., Kuhn, D.R.: Role-based Access Control: Features and motivations. In: Annual Computer Security Applications Conference, IEEE Computer
   Society Press, Los Alamitos (1995)
4. Wright, C., Cowan, C., Smalley, S., Morris, J., Kroah-Hartman, G.: Linux Security
   Modules: General Security Support for the Linux Kernel. In: Proceedings of the
   11th USENIX Security Symposium, pp. 17–31 (2002)
5. Trumper, W.: Summary about POSIX.1e (1999),
   http://wt.xpilot.org/publications/posix.1e
6. Spencer, R., Smalley, S., Loscocco, P., Hibler, M., Andersen, D., Lepreau, J.: The
   Flask Security Architecture: System Support for Diverse Security Policies. In: Proceedings of the Eighth USENIX Security Symposium, pp. 123–139 (1999)
7. Hallyn, S., Kearns, P.: Domain and Type Enforcement for Linux. In: Proceedings
   of the 4th Annual Linux Showcase and Conference (2000)
8. American National Standard for Information Technology – Role Based Access Control. ANSI/INCITS 359-2004 (2004)

 9. Role Based Access Control Implementation Standard Version 0.1. draft-rbac-implementation-std-v01 (2006), http://csrc.nist.gov/rbac
10. McVoy, L.W., Staelin, C.: lmbench: Portable Tools for Performance Analysis. In: USENIX Annual Technical Conference (1996),
    http://www.bitmover.com/lmbench/

Iteration Bound Analysis and Throughput Optimum Architecture of SHA-256 (384,512) for Hardware Implementations

Yong Ki Lee[1], Herwin Chan[1], and Ingrid Verbauwhede[1,2]

[1] University of California, Los Angeles, USA
[2] Katholieke Universiteit Leuven, Belgium
{jfirst,herwin,ingrid}@ee.ucla.edu

Abstract. The hash algorithm forms the basis of many popular cryptographic protocols and it is therefore important to find throughput optimal implementations. Though there have been numerous published papers proposing high throughput architectures, none of them have claimed to be optimal. In this paper, we perform iteration bound analysis on the SHA2 family of hash algorithms. Using this technique, we are able to both calculate the theoretical maximum throughput and determine the architecture that achieves this throughput. In addition to providing the throughput optimal architecture for SHA2, the techniques presented can also be used to analyze and design optimal architectures for some other iterative hash algorithms.

Keywords: SHA-256 (384,512), Iteration Bound Analysis, Throughput Optimum Architecture.

1 Introduction

Hash algorithms produce a fixed size code independent of input size of messages. Generated codes from hash algorithms are commonly used for digital signature [1] and message authentication. Since the hash outputs are relatively small compared to the original messages, the hash algorithms take an important roll for computation efficiency. Considering the increasing data amount to store or communicate, the throughput of hash algorithms is an important factor. Common hash algorithms include SHA1, MD5, SHA2 family (SHA256, SHA384 and SHA512) and RMD family (RMD160, RMD256 and RMD320). The SHA2 family of hash algorithms [2] has become of particular interest lately due to the official support of the National Institute of Standards and Technology (NIST) in 2002.

Even though many publications were produced to show high throughput architectures of SHA2, there has been no mathematical analysis of the delay bound. In this paper, we analyze the iteration bound analysis of SHA2, which gives us the maximum theoretical throughput achievable by the algorithm. Knowing the iteration bound not only allows the designer a goal to design towards, but also signals the designer when an optimal architecture has been achieved.

S. Kim, M. Yung, and H.-W. Lee (Eds.): WISA 2007, LNCS 4867, pp. 102–114, 2007.

The remainder of this paper is organized as follows. We start with reviewing related work in Section 2 and introduce the iteration bound analysis and transformations in Section 3. In Section 4, we analyze the iteration bound of the SHA2 family of hash algorithms and show the procedure to design throughput optimum architectures. Some comments for implementation and synthesis results are given in Section 5 followed by the conclusion in Section 6.

2   Related Works

The most common techniques for high throughput hardware implementations of hash algorithms are pipelining, unrolling and using Carry Save Adder (CSA). Pipelining techniques are used in [4,5,6,7], unrolling techniques are used in [7,8,9,10], and CSA techniques are used in [4,5,6,7,10,11]. Some other interesting implementations can be found in [12,13].

Even though there are many published papers, the mathematical analysis of the iteration bound has rarely been performed. For example, even though the iteration bound for SHA2 was achieved in [4], no analysis or proof of optimality was given. Since there is no proof of theoretical optimality and systematic approach to achieve the optimality, many architectures seem to count on the designers' intuition. Actually the work of [4] achieved the theoretical optimum after another work [5]. Therefore, this work will not only prevent a futile attempt to design architecture achieving better throughput than the theoretical optimum but also will guide designers to achieve the theoretical optimum throughput in MD4-based hash algorithms.

3   The Iteration Bound Analysis and Transformations

The SHA2 family of hash algorithms are iterative algorithms, which means the output of one iteration is the input of the next. We use a Data Flow Graph (DFG) to represent dependencies. We continuously apply the techniques of retiming and unfolding to achieve the iteration bound. Even though the optimized SHA2 family of hash algorithms requires only the retiming transformations, both transformations are briefly discussed for a better understanding of the analysis technique. Some of the MD4-based hash algorithms may require the unfolding transformation. A more detailed discussion of the iteration bound and the transformations can be found in [3].

3.1   DFG Representation

The mathematical expression of our example is given in Eq. 1. A and B are variables which are stored in registers and the indices of the variables represent the number of iterations of the algorithm. C_1 and C_2 are some constants. According to the equation, the next values of variables are updated using the current values of variables and constants. This type of equations is very common in MD4-based hash algorithms.

$$A(n+1) = A(n) \mid B(n) * C_1 * C_2 \tag{1}$$
$$B(n+1) = A(n)$$

The DFG of Eq. 1 is shown in Fig. 1. Box A and B represent registers which give the output at cycle n, and circles represent some functional nodes which perform the given functional operations. A D on edges represents an *algorithmic delay*, i.e. a delay that cannot be removed from the system. Next to algorithmic delays, nodes also have functional delays. We express the functional delays, i.e. the delays to perform the given operations, of $+$ and $*$ as $Prop(+)$ and $Prop(*)$ respectively. The binary operators, $+$ and $*$, can be arbitrary operators but we assume $Prop(+) < Prop(*)$ in this example. The iteration bound analysis starts with an assumption that any functional operation is atomic. This means that a functional operation can not be split or merged into some other functional operations.

3.2   The Iteration Bound Analysis

A loop is defined as a path that begins and ends at the same node. In the DFG in Fig. 1, $A\longrightarrow +\underset{D}{\longrightarrow} A$ and $A\underset{D}{\longrightarrow}B\longrightarrow *\longrightarrow *\longrightarrow +\underset{D}{\longrightarrow} A$ are the loops. The loop calculation time is defined as the sum of the functional delays in a loop. If t_l is the loop calculation time and w_l is the number of algorithmic delays in the l-th loop, the l-th loop bound is defined as t_l/w_l. The iteration bound is defined as follows:

$$T_\infty = \max_{l \in L} \left\{ \frac{t_l}{w_l} \right\} \tag{2}$$

where L is the set of all possible loops. The iteration bound creates a link between the arithmetic delay and the functional delay. It is the theoretical limit of a DFG's delay bound. Therefore, it defines the maximally attainable throughput. Please note that every loop needs to have at least one algorithmic delay in the loop otherwise the system is not causal and cannot be executed.

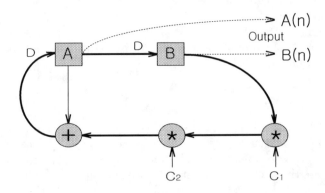

Fig. 1. An example of DFG

Since the loop marked with bold line has the maximum loop delay assuming that $Prop(+) < Prop(*)$, the iteration bound is as follows:

$$T_\infty = \max\left\{Prop(+), \frac{Prop(+) + 2 \times Prop(*)}{2}\right\} \tag{3}$$
$$= \frac{Prop(+) + 2 \times Prop(*)}{2}$$

This means that a critical path delay in this DFG can not be less than this iteration bound. The critical path delay is defined as the maximum calculation delay between any two consecutive algorithmic delays, i.e. D's. In our example (Fig. 1), the critical path delay is $Prop(+) + 2 \times Prop(*)$ which is larger than the iteration bound. The maximum clock frequency (and thus throughput) is determined by the critical path (the slowest path). The iteration bound is a theoretical lower bound on the critical path delay of an algorithm. We use the retiming and unfolding transformations to reach this lower bound.

3.3   The Retiming Transformation

The minimum critical path delay that can be possibly achieved using the retiming transformation is shown in Eq. 4.

$$\lceil T_\infty \rceil = \left\lceil \frac{Prop(+) + 2 \times Prop(*)}{2} \right\rceil = Prop(+) + Prop(*) \tag{4}$$

Assuming that a functional node can not be split into multiple parts, $\lceil \cdot \rceil$ is the maximum part when $Prop(+) + 2 \times Prop(*)$ is evenly distributed into N parts, where N is the number of algorithmic delays in a loop. This is denoted by the 2 in our example and sits in the denominator. Since the total delay $Prop(+) + 2 \times Prop(*)$ can be partitioned into one delay $Prop(+) + Prop(*)$ and the other delay $Prop(*)$, the attainable delay bound by the retiming transformation is $Prop(+) + Prop(*)$.

The retiming transformation modifies a DFG by moving algorithmic delays, i.e. D's, through the functional nodes in the graph. Delays of out-going edges can be replaced with delays from in-coming edges and vice versa. Fig. 2 shows the retiming transformation steps performed on Fig. 1.

Based on the + node in Fig. 1, the delay of the out-going edge is replaced with delays of the in-coming edges resulting in Fig. 2(a). Note that the out-going edges and the in-coming edges must be dealt as a set. By performing one more retiming transformation based on the left * node in Fig. 2(a), we obtain the DFG of Fig. 2(b). Therefore, the critical path becomes the path in bold between the two bolded D's in Fig. 2(b) and its delay is reduced to $Prop(+) + Prop(*)$ which is the same as Eq. 4. However, the iteration bound still has not been met.

3.4   The Unfolding Transformation

The unfolding transformation improves performance by calculating several iterations in a single cycle. For the unfolding transformation we expand the Eq. 1 by representing two iterations at a time, which results in Eq. 5.

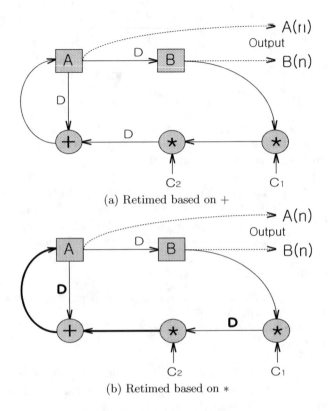

(a) Retimed based on +

(b) Retimed based on *

Fig. 2. Retiming Transformation

$$A(n + 2) = A(n + 1) + B(n + 1) * C_1 * C_2$$
$$= A(n) + B(n) * C_1 * C_2 + A(n) * C_1 * C_2 \qquad (5)$$
$$B(n + 2) = A(n + 1) = A(n) + B(n) * C_1 * C_2$$

Note that now $A(n+2)$ and $B(n+2)$ are expressed as a function of $A(n)$ and $B(n)$. By introducing a temporary variable Tmp, Eq. 5 can be simplified into Eq. 6.

$$Tmp(n) = A(n) + B(n) * C_1 * C_2$$
$$A(n + 2) = Tmp(n) + A(n) * C_1 * C_2 \qquad (6)$$
$$B(n + 2) = Tmp(n)$$

By doubling the number of functional nodes, we are able to unfold the DFG by a factor of two (Fig. 3(a)). Box A and B now give the outputs of every second iteration. By applying the retiming transformation to the unfolded DFG, the resulting critical path becomes the path in bold between the two bolded D's which is $D \rightarrow + \rightarrow A \rightarrow * \rightarrow * \rightarrow D$ (Fig. 3(b)). Therefore, the critical path delay is $Prop(+) + 2 \times Prop(*)$. Due to the unfolding factor of two, the

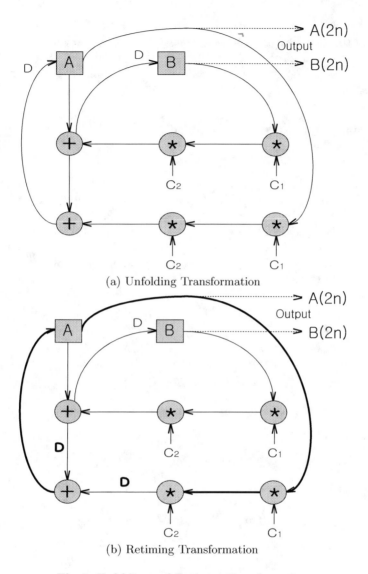

(a) Unfolding Transformation

(b) Retiming Transformation

Fig. 3. Unfolding and Retiming Transformation

normalized critical path delay, $\hat{T}$, can be calculated by dividing the critical path delay by two as shown in Eq. 7.

$$\hat{T} = \frac{Prop(+) + 2 \times Prop(*)}{2} = T_{\infty} \qquad (7)$$

This final transformation results in an architecture that achieves the iteration bound of the example DFG (Fig. 1).

Now the only remaining step is the implementation of the resulting DFG. Note that some of the square nodes are not any more paired with an algorithmic delay, which can be seen in Fig. 3(b). The explanation about how this issue is dealt with during implementation will be given in Section 5 where we synthesize the SHA2 family hash algorithms.

4   Iteration Bound Analysis and Throughput Optimum Architecture of SHA2

The SHA2 family of hash algorithms is composed of three parts: the padding, expander and compressor [2]. The padding extends an input message to be a whole number of 512-bit (for SHA-256) or 1024-bit (for SHA-384 and SHA-512) message blocks. The expander enlarges input messages of 16 words into 64 (for SHA-256) or 80 (for SHA-384 or SHA-512) words. The compressor encodes the expanded message into 256, 384 or 512 bits depending on the algorithm. For one message block, the required iterations are 64 (for SHA-256) or 80 (for SHA-384 or SHA-512).

$$Ch(x, y, z) = (x \wedge y) \oplus (\neg x \wedge z)$$
$$Maj(x, y, z) = (x \wedge y) \oplus (x \wedge z) \oplus (y \wedge z)$$
$$\Sigma_0^{\{256\}}(x) = ROTR^2(x) \oplus ROTR^{13}(x) \oplus ROTR^{22}(x)$$
$$\Sigma_1^{\{256\}}(x) = ROTR^6(x) \oplus ROTR^{11}(x) \oplus ROTR^{25}(x)$$
$$\sigma_0^{\{256\}}(x) = ROTR^7(x) \oplus ROTR^{18}(x) \oplus SHR^3(x)$$
$$\sigma_1^{\{256\}}(x) = ROTR^{17}(x) \oplus ROTR^{19}(x) \oplus SHR^{10}(x)$$

(a) SHA-256 Functions

$$W_t = \begin{cases} M_t^{(i)} & 0 \le t \le 15 \\ \sigma_1^{\{256\}}(W_{t-2}) + W_{t-7} + \sigma_0^{\{256\}}(W_{t-15}) + W_{t-16} & 16 \le t \le 63 \end{cases}$$

(b) SHA-256 Expend Computation

$$T_1 = h + \Sigma_1^{\{256\}}(e) + Ch(e, f, g) + K_t^{\{256\}} + W_t$$
$$T_2 = \Sigma_0^{\{256\}}(a) + Maj(a, b, c)$$
$$h = g$$
$$g = f$$
$$f = e$$
$$e = d + T_1$$
$$d = c$$
$$c = b$$
$$b = a$$
$$a = T_1 + T_2$$

(c) SHA-256 Compress Computation

Fig. 4. SHA-256 Hash Computation

In this paper, we consider only the implementation of the expander and compressor. Though the expander can be performed before the compressor, we chose to implement it to perform dynamically during compression in order to increase the overall throughput and minimize the gate area.

Fig. 4 describes the SHA-256 algorithm on which a DFG will be derived based. Since all the SHA2 family hash algorithms have the same architecture except for input, output and word sizes, constants, non-linear scrambling functions, i.e. Σ_0, Σ_1, Maj, Ch, σ_0 and σ_1, and the number of the iterations, they can be expressed in the same DFG.

4.1   DFG of SHA2 Compressor

Since within one iteration the order of additions in SHA2 does not affect the results, there are several possible DFG's. For example, $(a + b) + c$ and $(b + c) + a$ are equivalent in mathematics but will have different DFG's. As a starting point, the DFG having the minimum iteration bound must be chosen, transformations are then performed to find the architecture that achieves this bound. In SHA2 compressor, since there are only 7 adders, finding a DFG having the minimum iteration bound is not difficult as long as we understand how to calculate the iteration bound.

The DFG in Fig. 5 is a straightforward DFG. The shaded loop indicates the loop having the largest loop bound and gives the following iteration bound.

$$T_\infty^{(5)} = \max_{l \in L} \left\{ \frac{t_l}{w_l} \right\} = 3 \times Prop(+) + Prop(Ch) \tag{8}$$

However, by reordering the sequence of additions, the DFG of Fig. 6 can be obtained which has the smallest iteration bound. As we assume that $Prop(\Sigma 0) \approx Prop(Maj) \approx Prop(\Sigma 1) \approx Prop(Ch)$, the two bolded loops have the same maximum loop bound. Since the loop bound of the left hand side loop cannot be reduced further, no further reduction in the iteration bound is possible. Therefore, the iteration bound of Fig. 6 is as follows.

$$T_\infty^{(6)} = \max_{l \in L} \left\{ \frac{t_l}{w_l} \right\} = 2 \times Prop(+) + Prop(Ch) \tag{9}$$

If we assume that any operation in the DFG cannot be merged or split into other operations, the iteration bound of SHA2 is Eq. 9. However, if we are allowed to use a Carrier Save Adder (CSA), we can substitute two consecutive adders with one CSA and one adder. Since CSA requires less propagation delay than an adder, we replace adders with CSA's if it is possible. The resulting DFG is shown in Fig. 7. Note that some of the adders are not replaced with CSA since doing so would increase the iteration bound. Therefore, the final iteration bound is achieved as Eq. 10.

$$T_\infty^{(7)} = \max_{l \in L} \left\{ \frac{t_l}{w_l} \right\} = Prop(+) + Prop(CSA) + Prop(Ch) \tag{10}$$

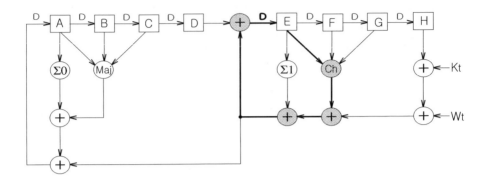

Fig. 5. Basic SHA2 Compressor DFG

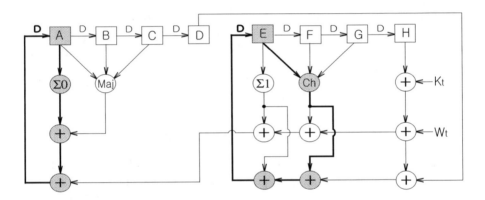

Fig. 6. Optimized SHA2 Compressor DFG

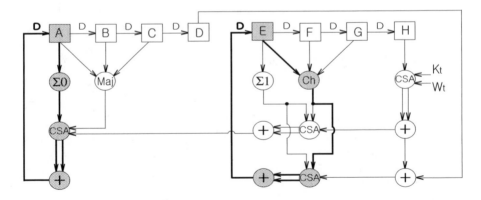

Fig. 7. Optimized SHA2 Compressor DFG with CSA

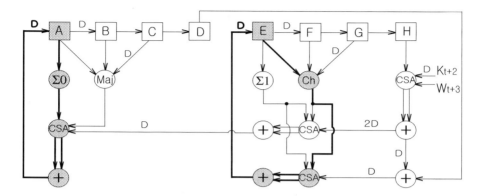

Fig. 8. Final SHA2 Compressor DFG with Retiming Transformation

In the next step, we perform transformations. Since there is no fraction in the iteration bound, we do not need the unfolding transformation. Only the retiming transformation is necessary to achieve the iteration bound. The retimed DFG achieving the iteration bound is depicted in Fig. 8. Note that the indexes of K_{t+2} and W_{t+3} are changed due to the retiming transformation. In order to remove the ROM access time for K_{t+2}, which is a constant value from ROM, we place an algorithmic delay, i.e. D, in front of K_{t+2}. This does not change the function.

4.2 DFG of SHA2 Expander

A straightforward DFG of the SHA2 expander is given in Fig. 9(a). Even though the iteration bound of the expander is much less than the compressor, we do not need to minimize the expander's critical path delay less than the compressor's iteration bound (the throughput is bounded by the compressor's iteration bound). Fig. 9(b) shows a DFG with CSA, and Fig. 9(c) shows a DFG with the retiming transformation where the critical path delay is $Prop(+)$.

5   Implementation and Synthesis Results

In the DFG of Fig. 8, some of the register values, i.e. A, B, ..., H, are no longer paired with an algorithmic delay D. For example, there is no algorithmic delay between registers F and H. Therefore, the values of H will be the same as F except for the first two cycles: in the first cycle, the value of H should be the initialized value of H according to the SHA2 algorithm; in the second cycle the value of H should be the initialized value of G. Therefore, the value of F will be directly used as an input of the following CSA.

Another register management problem is found in the path from the register H to the register A which includes four algorithmic delays. Therefore, register A has to hold its initial value until an effective value of H reaches to the register A, which means the register A must hold the first three cycles and then it can update

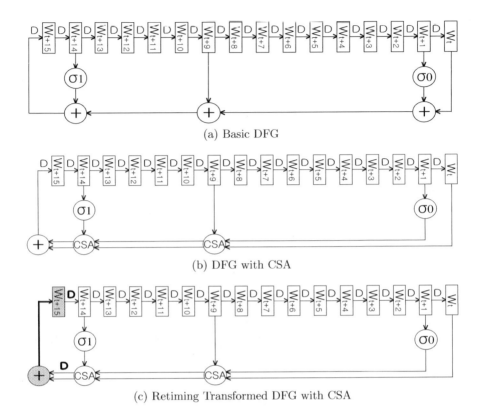

Fig. 9. SHA2 Expander DFG

with a new value. This causes overhead of three extra cycles. Therefore the total number of cycles required for one message block is the number of iterations plus one cycle for initialization and finalization plus three overhead cycles due to the retiming transformation, which results in 68 cycles for SHA256 and 84 cycles for SHA384 and SHA512.

We synthesized SHA2 for an ASIC by Synopsys Design Vision using a $0.13\mu m$ standard cell library whose results and a comparison with other works are shown in Table 1. The throughputs are calculated using the following equation.

$$Throughput^{256} = \frac{Frequency}{\#\ of\ Cycles} \times (512\ bits) \qquad (11)$$

$$Throughput^{384,512} = \frac{Frequency}{\#\ of\ Cycles} \times (1024\ bits)$$

Note that our purpose of the synthesis is not to beat the throughput record but to verify our architecture by checking the correct hash outputs and the actual critical path. Since our HDL programming is done at register transfer level and we have mostly concentrated on optimizing micro-architecture rather than focusing lower-level optimization, some other reported results, e.g. [4], achieve

Table 1. Synthesis Results and Comparison of SHA2 Family Hashes

	Algorithm	Technology (ASIC)	Area (Gates)	Frequency (MHz)	Cycles	Throughput (Mbps)
[14]	SHA256	$0.18\mu m$	22,000	200	65	1,575
[13]	SHA256	$0.13\mu m$	15,329	333.3	72	2,370
	SHA384/512		27,297	250.0	88	2,909
[4]	SHA256	$0.13\mu m$	N/A	>1,000	69	>7,420
Our	SHA256	$0.13\mu m$	22,025	793.6	68	5,975
Results	SHA384/512		43,330	746.2	84	9,096

*All our proposals include all the registers and ROM.

better performance with the same iteration bound delay. However the iteration bound analysis still determines the optimum high level architecture of an algorithm.

6 Conclusion

We analyzed the iteration bound of the SHA-256 (384,512) hash algorithms and showed architectures achieving the iteration bound. Since the iteration bound is a theoretical limit, there will be no further throughput optimization in micro-architecture level. We also synthesized our design to verify the correctness of our architecture design. Moreover, we illustrated detailed steps from a straight-forward DFG to a throughput optimized architecture. This approach will guide how to optimize some other iterative hash algorithms in throughput.

Acknowledgments. This work is supported by NSF CCF-0541472, FWO and funds from Katholieke Universiteit Leuven.

References

1. Digital Signature Standard. National Institute of Standards and Technology. Federal Information Processing Standards Publication 186-2,
   http://csrc.nist.gov/publications/fips/fips186-2/fips186-2-change1.pdf
2. Secure Hash Standard. National Institute of Standards and Technology. Federal Information Processing Standards Publication 180-2,
   http://csrc.nist.gov/publications/fips/fips180-2/fips180-2.pdf
3. Parhi, K.K.: VLSI Digital Signal Processing Systems: Design and Implementation, pp. 43–61, 119–140. Wiley, Chichester (1999)
4. Dadda, L., Macchetti, M., Owen, J.: An ASIC design for a high speed implementation of the hash function SHA-256 (384, 512). In: ACM Great Lakes Symposium on VLSI, pp. 421–425 (2004)
5. Dadda, L., Macchetti, M., Owen, J.: The design of a high speed ASIC unit for the hash function SHA-256 (384, 512). In: DATE 2004. Proceedings of the conference on Design, Automation and Test in Europe, pp. 70–75. IEEE Computer Society Press, Los Alamitos (2004)

6. Macchetti, M., Dadda, L.: Quasi-pipelined hash circuits. In: ARITH 2005. Proceedings of the 17th IEEE Symposium on Computer Arithmetic, pp. 222–229 (2005)
7. McEvoy, R.P., Crowe, F.M., Murphy, C.C., Marnane, W.P.: Optimisation of the SHA-2 Family of Hah Functions on FPGAs. In: ISVLSI 2006. Proceedings of the 2006 Emerging VLAI Technologies and Architectures, pp. 317–322 (2006)
8. Michail, H., Kakarountas, A.P., Koufopavlou, O., Goutis, C.E.: A Low-Power and High-Throughput Implementation of the SHA-1 Hash Function. In: ISCAS 2005. IEEE International Symposium on Circuits and Systems, pp. 4086–4089 (2005)
9. Crowe, F., Daly, A., Marnane, W.: Single-chip FPGA implementation of a cryptographic co-processor. In: FPT 2004. Proceedings of the International Conference on Field Programmable Technology, pp. 279–285 (2004)
10. Lien, R., Grembowski, T., Gaj, K.: A 1 Gbit/s partially unrolled architecture of hash functions SHA-1 and SHA-512. In: Okamoto, T. (ed.) CT-RSA 2004. LNCS, vol. 2964, pp. 324–338. Springer, Heidelberg (2004)
11. Ming-yan, Y., Tong, Z., Jin-xiang, W., Yi-zheng, Y.: An Efficient ASIC Implementation of SHA-1 Engine for TPM. In: The 2004 IEEE Asia-Pacific Conference on Circuits and Systems, pp. 873–876 (2004)
12. Ganesh, T.S., Sudarshan, T.S.B.: ASIC Implementation of a Unified Hardware Architecture for Non-Key Based Cryptographic Hash Primitives. In: ITCC 2005. Proceedings of the International Conference on Information Technology: Coding and Computing, pp. 580–585 (2005)
13. Satoh, A., Inoue, T.: ASIC-Hardware-Focused Comparison for Hash Functions MD5, RIPEMD-160, and SHS. In: ITCC 2005. Proceedings of the International Conference on Information Technology: Coding and Computing, pp. 532–537 (2005)
14. Helion IP Core Products. Helion Technology http://heliontech.com/core.htm

A Compact Architecture for Montgomery Elliptic Curve Scalar Multiplication Processor

Yong Ki Lee[1] and Ingrid Verbauwhede[1,2]

[1] University of California, Los Angeles, USA
[2] Katholieke Universiteit Leuven, Belgium
{jfirst,ingrid}@ee.ucla.edu

Abstract. We propose a compact architecture of a Montgomery elliptic curve scalar multiplier in a projective coordinate system over $GF(2^m)$. To minimize the gate area of the architecture, we use the common Z projective coordinate system where a common Z value is kept for two elliptic curve points during the calculations, which results in one register reduction. In addition, by reusing the registers we are able to reduce two more registers. Therefore, we reduce the number of registers required for elliptic curve processor from 9 to 6 (a 33%). Moreover, a unidirectional circular shift register file reduces the complexity of the register file, resulting in a further 17% reduction of total gate area in our design. As a result, the total gate area is 13.2k gates with 314k cycles which is the smallest compared to the previous works.

Keywords: Compact Elliptic Curve Processor, Montgomery Scalar Multiplication.

1 Introduction

Even though the technology of ASIC advances and its implementation cost decreases steadily, compact implementations of security engines are still a challenging issue. RFID (Radio Frequency IDentification) systems, smart card systems and sensor networks are good examples which need very compact security implementations. Public key cryptography algorithms seem especially taxing for such applications. However, for some security properties such as randomized authentications and digital signatures, the use of public key cryptography algorithms is often inevitable. Among public key cryptography algorithms, elliptic curve cryptography is a good candidate due to its efficient computation and relatively small key size.

In this paper, we propose an architecture for compact elliptic curve multiplication processors using the Montgomery algorithm [1]. The Montgomery algorithm is one of the most popular algorithms in elliptic curve scalar multiplication due to its resistance to side-channel attack. We use the projective coordinate system to avoid inverse operations.

In order to minimize the system size, we propose new formulae for the common projective coordinate system where all the Z-coordinate values are equal.

S. Kim, M. Yung, and H.-W. Lee (Eds.): WISA 2007, LNCS 4867, pp. 115–127, 2007.
© Springer-Verlag Berlin Heidelberg 2007

When we use López-Dahab's Montgomery scalar multiplication algorithm [2], two elliptic curve points must be kept where X and Z-coordinate values for each point. Therefore, by the use of the common Z projective coordinate property, one register for a Z-coordinate can be reduced. Considering that the register size is quite large, e.g. 163, reducing even one register is a very effective way to minimize the gate area. Moreover, efficient register management by reuse of the registers makes it possible to reduce two additional registers. Therefore, we reduce three registers out of nine in total compared to a conventional architecture. In addition, we design a unidirectional circular shift register file to reduce the complexity of the register file. While the multiplexer complexity of a register file increases as the square of the number of the registers, that of our register file is a small constant. Therefore, the proposed register file architecture effectively reduces the overall area. Though the register file is small (6 registers) an additional 17% of gate area is reduced using this technique. We also show the synthesis results for various digit sizes where the smallest area is 13.2k gates with the cycles of 314k.

The remainder of this paper is organized as follows. In Section 2, we review the background on which our work is based. In Section 3, the common Z projective coordinate system is introduced and its corresponding formulae are given. The proposed system architecture and the synthesis results are shown in Section 4 and Section 5 followed by the conclusion in Section 6.

2   Background

2.1   López-Dahab's Montgomery Scalar Multiplication

In this section we introduce López-Dahab's Montgomery scalar multiplication algorithm, which uses a projective coordinate system [2]. The algorithm is shown in Fig. 1. A non-supersingular elliptic curve E over $GF(2^m)$ is the set of coordinative points (x, y) satisfying $y^2 + xy = x^3 + ax^2 + b$ with the point at infinity O, where $a, b, x, y \in GF(2^m)$ and $b \neq 0$.

Input: A point $P = (x, y) \in E$ and a positive integer $k = 2^{l-1} + \Sigma_{i=0}^{l-2} k_i 2^i$
Output: $Q = kP$

    1.   if ($k = 0$ or $x = 0$) then output $(0,0)$ and stop
    2. $X_1 \leftarrow x$, $Z_1 \leftarrow 1$, $X_2 \leftarrow x^4 + b$, $Z_2 \leftarrow x^2$
    3.   for $i = l - 2$ to 0 do
           if $k_i = 1$ then
                $(X_1, Z_1) \leftarrow \mathrm{Madd}(X_1, Z_1, X_2, Z_2)$, $(X_2, Z_2) \leftarrow \mathrm{Mdouble}(X_2, Z_2)$
           else $(X_2, Z_2) \leftarrow \mathrm{Madd}(X_2, Z_2, X_1, Z_1)$, $(X_1, Z_1) \leftarrow \mathrm{Mdouble}(X_1, Z_1)$
    4.   return $Q \leftarrow \mathrm{Mxy}(X_1, Z_1, X_2, Z_2)$

Fig. 1. Montgomery scalar multiplication with López-Dahab algorithm

The adding formula of $(X_{Add}, Z_{Add}) \leftarrow \mathrm{Madd}(X_1, Z_1, X_2, Z_2)$ is defined in Eq. 1.

$$Z_{Add} = (X_1 \times Z_2 + X_2 \times Z_1)^2 \tag{1}$$
$$X_{Add} = x \times Z_{Add} + (X_1 \times Z_2) \times (X_2 \times Z_1)$$

The doubling formula of $(X_{Double}, Z_{Double}) \leftarrow \mathrm{Mdouble}(X_2, Z_2)$ is defined in Eq. 2.

$$Z_{Double} = (X_2 \times Z_2)^2 \tag{2}$$
$$X_{Double} = X_2^4 + b \times Z_2^4$$

$Q \leftarrow \mathrm{Mxy}(X_1, Z_1, X_2, Z_2)$ is the conversion of projective coordinate to affine coordinate. López-Dahab's adding and doubling algorithms are described in Fig. 2 where $c^2 = b$.

The total number of registers in Fig. 2 is six, i.e. the registers for X_1, Z_1, X_2, Z_2, T_1 and T_2. The total field operations of Adding Algorithm are 4 multiplications, 1 square and 2 additions, and those of Doubling Algorithm are 2 multiplications, 4 squares and 1 addition. Note that it is not necessary to maintain Y-coordinate during the iterations since it can be derived at the end of the iterations.

Adding Algorithm $(X_1, Z_1) \leftarrow \mathrm{Madd}(X_1, Z_1, X_2, Z_2)$		Doubling Algorithm $(X, Z) \leftarrow \mathrm{Mdouble}(X, Z)$	
1.	$T_1 \leftarrow x$	1.	$T_1 \leftarrow c$
2.	$X_1 \leftarrow X_1 \times Z_2$	2.	$X \leftarrow X^2$
3.	$Z_1 \leftarrow Z_1 \times X_2$	3.	$Z \leftarrow Z^2$
4.	$T_2 \leftarrow X_1 \times Z_1$	4.	$T_1 \leftarrow Z \times T_1$
5.	$Z_1 \leftarrow Z_1 + X_1$	5.	$Z \leftarrow Z \times X$
6.	$Z_1 \leftarrow Z_1^2$	6.	$T_1 \leftarrow T_1^2$
7.	$X_1 \leftarrow Z_1 \times T_1$	7.	$X \leftarrow X^2$
8.	$X_1 \leftarrow X_1 + T_2$	8.	$X \leftarrow X + T_1$

Fig. 2. López-Dahab's Adding and Doubling Algorithms

2.2 Modular Arithmetic Logic Unit (MALU) and Elliptic Curve Processor Architecture

In order to perform the field operations, i.e. the multiplications, squares and additions in Fig. 2, we need an Arithmetic Logic Unit (ALU). Fig. 3 shows the MALU architecture of K. Sakiyama et al [5]. This is a compact architecture which performs the arithmetic field operations as shown in Eq. 3.

$$C(x) = A(x) * B(x) \bmod P(x) \qquad \text{if } cmd = 1 \tag{3}$$
$$C(x) = B(x) + C(x) \bmod P(x) \qquad \text{if } cmd = 0$$

where $A(x) = \Sigma a_i x^i$, $B(x) = \Sigma b_i x^i$, $C(x) = \Sigma c_i x^i$ and $P(x) = x^{163} + x^7 + x^6 + x^3 + 1$.

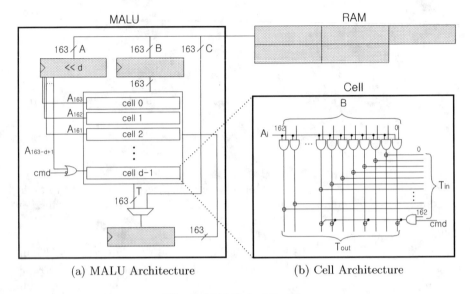

(a) MALU Architecture   (b) Cell Architecture

Fig. 3. MALU Architecture

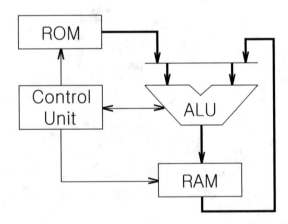

Fig. 4. MALU based Elliptic Curve Processor Architecture

d is the digit size and the number of cells. The square operation uses the same logic as the multiplication by duplicating the operand. The arithmetic multiplication and addition take $\lceil \frac{163}{d} \rceil$ and one cycle respectively. The benefit of this architecture is that the multiplication, the square and the addition operations share the XOR array and by increasing the digit size, the MALU can be easily scaled. The architecture of our ALU starts from this MALU.

ECP (Elliptic Curve Processor) architecture based on MALU is shown in Fig. 4 [6]. Note that in Fig. 4, ALU is implemented with MALU and hence includes three registers, and RAM contains five words of 163 bit size.

2.3   Implementation Consideration

If López-Dahab's Montgomery scalar multiplication algorithm is implemented using Sakiyama's MALU in a conventional way, the total number of registers is 9, i.e. 3 registers for MALU plus 6 registers for the Montgomery scalar multiplication. In [6], 3 registers and 5 RAMs are used (8 memory elements in total). One register is reduced by modifying López-Dahab's algorithm and assuming that constants are loadable directly to the MALU without using a register. In our architecture, we are able to reduce the number of registers to 6 even without constraining ourselves to these assumptions. This was accomplished by observing the fact that the area of a scalar multiplier is dominated by register area. Note that the registers occupy more than 80% of the gate area in a conventional architecture. Therefore, reducing the number of the registers and the complexity of the register file is a very effective way to minimize the total gate area.

Accordingly, our compact architecture is achieved in two folds: reducing the number of registers (one register reduction by using the common Z projective coordinate system and two register reduction by register reuse) and reducing the register file complexity by designing a unidirectional circular shift register file.

3   Common Z Projective Coordinate System

We propose new formulae for the common Z projective coordinate system where the Z values of two elliptic curve points in Montgomery scalar multiplication are kept to be the same during the process. New formulae for the common Z projective coordinate system have been proposed over prime fields in [3]. However, this work is still different from ours in that first, they made new formulae over prime field while ours is over binary polynomial field and second, they made new formulae to reduce the computation amount in special addition chain while our formulae slightly increase the computation amount in order to reduce the number of the registers. Please note that reducing even one register decreases the total gate area considerably.

Since in López-Dahab's algorithm, two elliptic curve points must be maintained, the required number of registers for this is four (X_1, Z_1, X_2 and Z_2). Including two temporary registers (T_1 and T_2), the total number of registers is six. The idea of the common Z projective coordinate system is to make sure that $Z_1 = Z_2$ at each iteration of López-Dahab's algorithm. The condition at the beginning of the iterations is satisfied since the algorithm starts the iterations with the initialization of $Z_1 = Z_2 = 1$. Even if $Z_1 \neq Z_2$, we can make it satisfy this condition using three field multiplications as shown in Eq. 4 where the resulting coordinate set is (X_1, X_2, Z).

$$
\begin{aligned}
X_1 &\leftarrow X_1 \times Z_2 \\
X_2 &\leftarrow X_2 \times Z_1 \\
Z &\leftarrow Z_1 \times Z_2
\end{aligned}
\tag{4}
$$

Table 1. The comparison between the original and the modified formulas

The original equation	The new equation assuming $Z = Z_1 = Z_2$
$Z_{Add} = (X_1 \times Z_2 + X_2 \times Z_1)^2$	$Z_{Add} = (X_1 + X_2)^2$
$X_{Add} = x \times Z_{Add} + (X_1 \times Z_2) \times (X_2 \times Z_1)$	$X_{Add} = x \times Z_{Add} + X_1 \times X_2$

Since we now assume $Z_1 = Z_2$, we can start the Adding Algorithm with the common Z projective coordinate system. With $Z = Z_1 = Z_2$, Eq. 1 is re-represented as shown in Eq. 5. Now Z_{Add} and X_{Add} have a common factor of Z^2.

$$Z_{Add} = (X_1 \times Z_2 + X_2 \times Z_1)^2 = (X_1 + X_2)^2 \times Z^2$$
$$X_{Add} = x \times Z_{Add} + (X_1 \times Z_2) \times (X_2 \times Z_1) \qquad (5)$$
$$= x \times Z_{Add} + (X_1 \times X_2 \times Z^2)$$

Due to the property of the projective coordinate system, we can divide Z_{Add} and X_{Add} by the common factor of Z^2. The comparison of the original equation and the modified equation is shown in Table 1. Note that the new formula of the Adding Algorithm is independent of the previous Z-coordinate value.

In Doubling Algorithm, there is no such reduction since it deals with only one elliptic curve point. Nevertheless, we can simplify the Doubling Algorithm by noticing that $T_1^2 + X^2 \equiv (T_1 + X)^2$ at the steps of 6, 7 and 8 in Fig. 2. One field multiplication can be reduced using this mathematical equality. The Eq. 2 is re-represented in Eq. 6 where $c^2 = b$.

$$Z_{Double} = (X_2 \times Z)^2 \qquad (6)$$
$$X_{Double} = (X_2^2 + c \times Z^2)^2$$

Note that the resulting Z-coordinate values are different between Adding and Doubling formulae. In order to maintain a common Z-coordinate value, some extra steps similar to Eq. 4 are required. These extra steps must follow every pair of Adding and Doubling Algorithm. The final mathematical expression and its algorithm are shown in Eq. 7 and Fig. 5 respectively.

$$X_1 \leftarrow X_{Add}Z_{Double} = \left\{ x(X_1 + X_2)^2 + X_1 X_2 \right\}(X_2 Z)^2 \quad ; P1 \leftarrow P1 + P2$$
$$X_2 \leftarrow X_{Double}Z_{Add} = (X_2^2 + cZ^2)^2(X_1 + X_2)^2 \quad ; P2 \leftarrow 2 \times P2 \qquad (7)$$
$$Z \leftarrow Z_{Add}Z_{Double} = (X_1 + X_2)^2(X_2 Z)^2 \quad ; \text{The new common Z-coordinate}$$

In Fig. 5 we mark with (T_1) at each square operation to indicate that the T_1 register is free to store some other value. The reason for this will be obvious in the next section. The comparison of the amount of field operations between López-Dahab's algorithm and our algorithm is shown in Table 2.

Noting that the multiplication and the square are equivalent in the MALU operation, the workload of our algorithm is the same as that of López-Dahab's algorithm and we still reduce one register.

Adding Algorithm	Doubling Algorithm	Extra Steps
1. $T_2 \leftarrow X_1 + X_2$	1. $X_2 \leftarrow X_2^2 \quad (T_1)$	1. $X_1 \leftarrow X_1 \times Z$
2. $T_2 \leftarrow T_2^2 \quad (T_1)$	2. $Z \leftarrow Z^2 \quad (T_1)$	2. $X_2 \leftarrow X_2 \times T_2$
3. $T_1 \leftarrow X_1 \times X_2$	3. $T_1 \leftarrow c$	3. $Z \leftarrow Z \times T_2$
4. $X_1 \leftarrow x$	4. $T_1 \leftarrow Z \times T_1$	
5. $X_1 \leftarrow T_2 \times X_1$	5. $Z \leftarrow Z \times X_2$	
6. $X_1 \leftarrow X_1 + T_1$	6. $X_2 \leftarrow X_2 + T_1$	
	7. $X_2 \leftarrow X_2^2 \quad (T_1)$	

Fig. 5. Proposing Adding and Doubling Algorithms

Table 2. Comparison of the computational workload

Field Operation	López-Dahab's algorithm	Our algorithm
Multiplication	6	7
Square	5	4
Addition	3	3

4   Proposing System Architecture

4.1   Arithmetic Logic Unit (ALU) Architecture

The ALU architecture in Fig. 6 is similar to MALU in Fig. 3. The only difference is in the placement of the registers and the control outside the ALU block. Therefore, the ALU block is equivalent to an array of cells in Fig. 3. The reason we separate the registers from the ALU block is for the reuse of the registers. Note that at the completion of the multiplication or addition operation, only the register Reg1 is updated while the registers Reg2 and Reg3 are remained as the beginning of the operations. Therefore, Reg2 and Reg3 can be used not only to store field operands but also to store some values of the proposed Adding and Doubling algorithm where we need five registers for X_1, X_2, Z, T_1, and T_2 in Fig. 5.

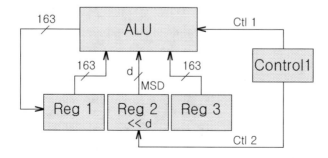

Fig. 6. ALU Architecture

A care should be taken at this point since the same value must be placed in the both of Reg2 and Reg3 for squaring. Therefore, during squaring, only one register can be reused. This fact would conflict with our purpose to reuse each of Reg2 and Reg3 as a storage of the adding and doubling algorithm. Fortunately, it is possible to free one of the registers to hold another value during squaring. As shown in Fig. 5, T_1 can be reused whenever a square operation is required.

In Fig. 6, the control line $Ctl1$ signals the command (multiplication or addition) and the last iteration of the multiplication. When ALU performs a multiplication, each digit of d bits of Reg2 must be entered into ALU in order. Instead of addressing each digit of the 163 bit word, the most significant digit (MSD) is entered and a circular shift of d bits is performed. The shift operation must be circular and the last shift must be the remainder of $163/d$ since the value must be kept as the initial value at the end of the operation. During performing the ALU operation, an intermediate result is stored in Reg1. Reg1, Reg2 and Reg3 are comparable with C, A and B in Fig. 3 respectively.

4.2   Circular Shift Register File Architecture

By reusing the registers, we reduce two of the registers in the previous subSection. This causes that all the registers should be organized in single register file. Therefore, the register file of our system consists of six registers. In our register file architecture, we use a circular shift register file with a minimum number of operations. The multiplexer complexity of a randomly accessible register file increases as the square of the number of registers. On the other hand, since the multiplexer complexity of a circular shift register file is a constant, this model effectively reduces the total gate area.

The operations defined in Fig. 7 are the minimum operations such that any replacement or reordering of the register values can be achieved. Since only Reg1 gets multiple inputs, only one multiplexer of fixed size is necessary.

Note that Reg1, Reg2 and Reg3 in Fig. 7 are the three registers which are connected to the ALU in Fig. 6. The assignment operation loads the constants of elliptic curve parameters into Reg1 which is the only register to be assigned a constant value. The shift operation shifts the register values in circular and the switch operation switches the values of Reg1 and Reg2. The copy operation replaces the value of Reg1 with Reg2. Note that the copy operation is required for the field square operation which is implemented as the field multiplication with two operands of the same value.

4.3   Overall System Architecture

The overall system architecture is shown in Fig. 8. Elliptic curve point add and doubler (EC Add&Doubler) consists of Control 1, ALU and the register file. Control 1 includes the hard-wired elliptic curve parameters and manages the register file. Control 2 detects the first bit of 1 in Key (or a scalar) and controls EC Add&Doubler depending on the Key values of the later bits according to the Montgomery algorithm in Fig. 1. Key and Tester are placed outside Montgomery

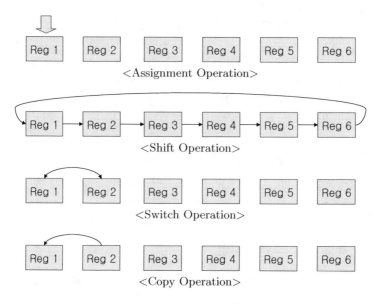

Fig. 7. Operations and Architecture of Register File

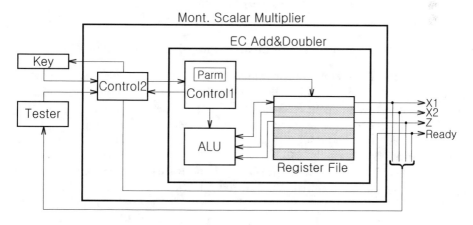

Fig. 8. Overall System Architecture

scalar multiplier. We assume that Key can be addressable in single bit and the addressed bit is forwarded into Control 2. Control 2 also generates the Ready signal to indicate when the final outputs of $X1$, $X2$ and Z are ready. The outputs are compared with the pre-computed results in Tester.

In our system, we suppose that the coordinate conversion into affine coordinate system and calculation of Y-coordinate value are performed in the counterpart of this system if it is needed. If we assume that this system is implemented in RFID tags, the counter part can be a tag reader or back-end system.

Step	Field Operation	Command	Reg1	Reg2	Reg3	Reg4	Reg5	Reg6
(1)	Initial		X1	X2	Z	–	–	–
(2)		Shift	–	X1	X2	Z	–	–
(3)		Copy	X1	X1	X2	Z	–	–
(4)	1. $T_2 \leftarrow X_1 + X_2$	Add	T2	X1	X2	Z	–	–
(5)		Shift	–	T2	X1	X2	Z	–
(6)		Copy	T2	T2	X1	X2	Z	–
(7)		Shift	–	T2	T2	X1	X2	Z
(8)	2. $T_2 \leftarrow T_2^2$	Multiply	T2	–	–	X1	X2	Z
(9)		Shift*4	–	X1	X2	Z	T2	–
(10)	3. $T_1 \leftarrow X_1 \times X_2$	Multiply	T1	–	X2	Z	T2	–
(11)		Switch	–	T1	X2	Z	T2	–
(12)	4. $X_1 \leftarrow x$	Load x	X1	T1	X2	Z	T2	–
(13)		Shift*2	T2	–	X1	T1	X2	Z
(14)		Switch	–	T2	X1	T1	X2	Z
(15)	5. $X_1 \leftarrow T_2 \times X_1$	Multiply	X1	T2	–	T1	X2	Z
(16)		Switch	T2	X1	–	T1	X2	Z
(17)		Shift*5	X1	–	T1	X2	Z	T2
(18)	6. $X_1 \leftarrow X_1 + T_1$	Add	X1	–	T1	X2	Z	T2

Fig. 9. Register File Management for Adding Algorithm

4.4   Register File Management for Algorithm Implementation

For better understanding how the system works, the register file management of
Adding Algorithm of Fig. 5 is shown in Fig. 9. Note that when the algorithm is
actually implemented, some more detailed controls are required. In this example,
only the register file rearrangement is shown. Remember that the field addition
and multiplication are performed as Reg1 ← Reg2 × Reg3 and Reg1 ← Reg1 +
Reg3 respectively. Initially, we assume that the arrangement of register values
are as step (1) in Fig. 9, and that Reg4, Reg5 and Reg6 are not available (marked
as –) since meaningful values are not stored yet. The commands of Assign, Shift,
Switch and Copy work as described in Fig. 7 and the rearrangements of register
values are shown in each step. Note that Shift*4 is the abbreviation of four
times Shift operation and some register values are changed to be – when the old
values are not used any more. The rest of the Montgomery scalar multiplication
algorithm can be also described similarly.

In fact, the use of this register file increases the number of cycles due to the
control overhead. However, considering that a field multiplication takes a large
number of cycles, the number of overhead cycles is relatively small. Note that
a field multiplication requires 163 cycles for 163 bit words and the digit size of
1 (reference Fig. 3 for the digit size). We compare synthesis results for various
cases in the following section.

5   Synthesis Results

In order to verify our algorithm and architecture, we synthesized the proposed architecture using TSMC $0.18\mu m$ standard cell library. Summarized results are shown in Table 3. While version 1 uses a randomly accessible register file, the other versions use the circular shift register file which is shown in the previous section. Comparing version 1 with version 2, we can see how changing the register file management strategy can effectively reduce the area (17% reduction of total gate area). The use of the circular shift register file requires more cycles. However, if we increase the digit size into 4 (version 5), a much smaller number of cycles can be achieved with even less gate area.

A comparison with other works is shown in Table 4. Since the architecture of [4] uses an affine coordinate system, it requires only 6 registers but require a larger number of cycles due to field inverse operations. The ALU of [4] has separate logic modules for multiplication, square and addition where multiplication requires 163 cycles and square and addition require 1 cycle.

Except for [6], all the reported results include memory area. In [6], the reported gate area of 8,214 does not include the required RAM area. For a fairer comparison, we estimate the total gate area assuming that 1 bit memory is equivalent to 10 gate area. Note that 1 bit register require 6 gates and there should be some extra area for addressing. According to our experiment of synthesis for a 163 bit register in standard CMOS compilers, the number of gates per bit is above 10 gates. Even in this under-estimation, our results show much smaller

Table 3. Synthesis Results

Version	Digit size (d)	Register Type	Gate Area	Cycle
Ver1	1	Random Access	15,894	295,032
Ver2	1		13,182	313,901
Ver3	2	Circular Shift	14,188	168,911
Ver4	3		14,896	120,581
Ver5	4		15,538	95,521

Table 4. Comparison with other works

	Technology	Key Size	Digit Size	Area (Gate)	Cycle	Memory Units
[7]	0.13	165	–	30,333	545,440	–
[8]	0.13	160	–	28,311	2,500,000	320∗8 bits
[4]	–	163	–	15,097	432,000	6∗163 bits
[6]	0.13	163	1	8,214 + 5 RAM ($\approx 16,364$)**	353,710	8∗163 bits
Our Work (Ver2)	0.18	163	1	13,182	313,901	6∗163 bits

**The gate area of 8,214 does not include RAM area. The gate area of 16,364 is an estimation including the RAM area.

gate number with a smaller cycle number. This result is obvious considering that our ALU is similar to [6] and the number of total memory units of our architecture is two less than [6]. In [8], among several implementations, we show the one having the smallest area, which is still much larger than our results and also has a much larger number of cycles. As a result, our implementation has not only the smallest area but also the smallest cycle.

6   Conclusion

We proposed a compact architecture for an elliptic curve scalar multiplier. This contribution has been achieved by reducing the number of the registers and the complexity of the register file.

The reduction of the number of the registers is done in two different approaches. By proposing new formulae for the common Z projective coordinate system, one register was reduced and by the reuse of the registers, two more registers were reduced. Accordingly, three registers were reduced in total. The reduction of the complexity of the register file is done by designing a circular shift register file.

As a result, for elliptic curve scalar multiplication, only 13.2k gates and 314k cycles are required. This result not only achieves the smallest area but also the smallest cycle number compared with fairly comparable architectures. Moreover, our processor architecture is secure against TA (Timing Analysis) and SPA (Simple Power Analysis) due to the property of Montgomery elliptic curve scalar multiplication.

Acknowledgments. This work is supported by NSF CCF-0541472, FWO and funds from Katholieke Universiteit Leuven.

References

1. Montgomery, P.: Speeding the Pollard and elliptic curve methods of factorization. Mathematics of Computation 48, 243–264 (1987)
2. López, J., Dahab, R.: Fast multiplication on elliptic curves over $GF(2^m)$ without precomputation. In: Koç, Ç.K., Paar, C. (eds.) CHES 1999. LNCS, vol. 1717, pp. 316–327. Springer, Heidelberg (1999)
3. Meloni, N.: Fast and Secure elliptic Curve Scalar Multiplication Over Prime Fields Using Special Addition Chains. Cryptology ePrint Archive: listing for 2006 (2006/216) (2006)
4. Paar, C.: Light-Weight Cryptography for Ubiquitous Computing. Invited talk at the University of California, Los Angeles (UCLA). Institute for Pure and Applied Mathematics (December 4, 2006)
5. Sakiyama, K., Batina, L., Mentens, N., Preneel, B., Verbauwhede, I.: Small-footprint ALU for public-key processors for pervasive security. In: Workshop on RFID Security, 12 pages (2006)

6. Batina, L., Mentens, N., Sakiyama, K., Preneel, B., Verbauwhede, I.: Low-cost Elliptic Curve Cryptography for wireless sensor networks. In: Buttyán, L., Gligor, V., Westhoff, D. (eds.) ESAS 2006. LNCS, vol. 4357, pp. 6–17. Springer, Heidelberg (2006)
7. OztÄurk, E.Ä., Sunar, B., Savas, E.: Low-power elliptic curve cryptography using scaled modular arithmetic. In: Joye, M., Quisquater, J.-J. (eds.) CHES 2004. LNCS, vol. 3156, pp. 92–106. Springer, Heidelberg (2004)
8. Satoh, A., Takano, K.: A Scalable Dual-Field Elliptic Curve Cryptographic Processor. IEEE Transactions on Computers 52(4), 449–460 (2003)

Windows Vault: Prevention of Virus Infection and Secret Leakage with Secure OS and Virtual Machine

Yoshiki Sameshima[1], Hideaki Saisho[1], Tsutomu Matsumoto[2], and Norihisa Komoda[3]

[1] Hitachi Software Engineering, Co., Ltd.
[2] Graduate School of Environment and Information Science,
Yokohama National University
[3] Graduate School of Information Science and Technology, Osaka University
{same,saisho}@hitachisoft.jp, tsutomu@ynu.ac.jp,
komoda@ist.osaka-u.ac.jp

Abstract. We present an integrated system of two Windows workstations; while the first workstation is prepared to process secret information, the second is for non-secret which may contain computer virus, and the two workstations are integrated into a PC with secure OS, virtual machine and gateways. Since the two workstations are virtually separated at the physical level, the first workstation is not infected by virus, nor is secret leaked out to the Internet, even if the second is infected by unknown virus. Comparing previous work which realizes complete data isolation for intelligence community, user of the proposed system can import data securely from the second workstation to the first through security guaranteed channel between the two workstations. The user can also read e-mail from the Internet on the first without fear of virus infection, and as a result the user does not need to be aware that she/he uses the two workstations.

Keywords: virus, secret leakage, information flow, virtual machine, secure OS.

1 Introduction

The top two IT security threats are virus infection and secret leakage including PC theft [1-3]. The best practice to prevent virus infection is to use virus protection software and install security patch. However, the practice is becoming less effective, because of the following two reasons: The first reason is zero-day attack [2]; the attack code appears soon after vulnerability is announced, for example the attack code of MS07-002 appeared three hours later after the patch was released. As a result, virus definition file cannot be in time. The second reason is targeted attack [4]; while existing attack codes aim to be spread over many victims, the target of the new attack is very limited, for example a single organization or few people. As a result, there is less chance to detect the target attack and the virus definition file may not be issued.

A solution against the virus threat is to utilize secure OS [5, 6]. The OS supports the Mandatory Access Control (MAC) [7], and the damage of attack to vulnerability

S. Kim, M. Yung, and H.-W. Lee (Eds.): WISA 2007, LNCS 4867, pp. 128–141, 2007.

of application is limited only to the application; the attack code cannot access file nor execute process which are not permitted in security policy, even if the code gets the administrator privilege. The secure OS is used mainly for server, but not client PC, because of management of the security policy; it is difficult for end user or system administrator to configure the security policy specifying which process is permitted to access to which resources with what kind of operations.

Another solution is behavior based virus detection [8]. Virus has some specific behavior; some of virus code is encrypted to bypass the virus protection system, and decryption of code is one of features of the virus. Another virus sends many e-mail messages of its own copy. The new technology watches such behavior of virus and detects the virus, but the new virus detection may miss targeted attack, because the virus targets specific organization or information, and the virus may be tuned so as not to be detected by such virus protection software.

On the other hand, more serious IT security threat is leakage of secret information or secret leakage [3]. The main reason of secret leakage is lost of PC or storage media, but other reason is intentional leakage by authorized user and exposition to the Internet by virus.

Solutions against secret leakage are file encryption and prohibition of portable storage media/printer. The Windows OS supports file encryption, and its security policy can enforce to stop use of USB memory. However, these solutions are not effective for intentional leakage through e-mail or HTTP by authorized user; it is possible to stop sending e-mail outside or posting via HTTP, however, this is not practical for commercial organizations.

NetTop [9, 10] is a countermeasure of the two threats; it is designed for intelligence community, and the goal is data isolation. User of NetTop accesses classified information of multiple categories and operates multiple workstations which are integrated into a single PC with Trusted Linux and Virtual Machine (VM). The workstations are separated virtually at physical level, so the threats do not happen. However, the user should always be aware that which workstation she/he is operating and needs to switch the two workstations. This is acceptable for users of intelligence community, but it is very troublesome for office workers of commercial companies.

The authors propose Windows Vault as system isolation which usage is as same as a normal Windows as possible. The user operates a safe workstation isolated from the Internet, but she/he can access the external information that comes from the Internet on the safe workstation without threats of virus infection or secret leakage. The word 'Vault' means a room with thick walls and strong doors where valuables can be kept safely; Windows Vault is a vault running Windows, that is, a Windows workstation guarded by secure OS and gateways which establish secure data exchange between the isolated workstation and the external environment including the Internet.

In the paper, the authors describe the architecture of Windows Vault in Section 2, evaluation of performance, security and usages in Section 3 through 5, compares with the previous works in Section 6, and conclude in Section 7.

2 Windows Vault

2.1 Concepts

The principal of Windows Vault is very simple; data is divided into two categories, safe secret and unsafe non-secret, and the later includes information on the Internet and may contain virus. Windows Vault processes the two data categories with two virtual workstations; Internal Workstation for safe secret, and External Workstation for unsafe non-secret, and the two workstations are integrated into a single physical PC with use of VM and secure OS. Network is also divided; Internal Workstation is connected to Internal Network and External Workstation to External Network including the Internet.

The above architecture realizes very high level security, as far as user processes the two categories in completely separated manner. But such use is not realistic. While main task of user of commercial company is processed on Internal Workstation, the user also needs to access the Internet and utilize information of the Internet as part of secret; text on Web and spread sheet data attached to e-mail from business partner are examples of such information. It is also desirable to use a single e-mail client; the user does not want to use two clients on Internal and External Workstations, because it is different from the current e-mail client usage. As for web browser, the other most used network application, it is normal that user operates multiple browser windows, and it is desirable that the user can operate browser window accessing a site on the Internet in the same operation of the window on Internal Network. As a result, the following functions are required with security guaranteed form:

(1) Data import: data is imported from External Workstation to Internal Workstation.
(2) Mail retrieval and sending on Internal Workstation: user operates e-mail client on Internal Workstation, retrieves and sends messages with the client from/to Internal and External Networks.
(3) Browsing Internet sites from Internal Workstation: user operates web browser on External Workstation from Internal Workstation.

With the above functions, the user needs to use Internal Workstation only and she/he can process information on External Workstation on Internal Workstation. Four gateways connect the two workstations and realize secure channel between the two workstations for e-mail and copy & paste operation. In the following, the overall architecture, platform OS, and four gateways are described.

2.2 Overall Architecture

The overall architecture of Windows Vault is shown in Figure 1. Platform OS is the base of security, and we adopt the Security-Enhanced Linux (SELinux) [6], which supports the MAC based on the Type Enforcement model. Each of Internal and External Workstations consists of VM, Windows OS, and applications.

Two LANs, Internal and External Networks, are connected to Platform OS. It is assumed that the network devices connected to Internal Network are managed, that is, only identified and authorized devices are connected to the network, and virus infected PCs are not connected.

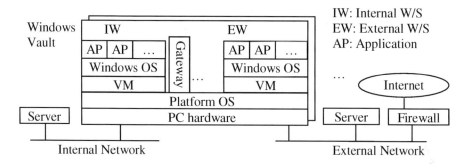

Fig. 1. Architecture of Windows Vault

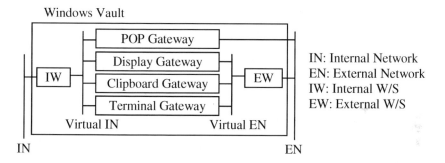

Fig. 2. Gateways on Virtual Internal Networks

The virtual networks on Platform OS are configured as shown in Figure 2; Internal Workstation is connected to Internal Network and the virtual Internal Network, so on External Workstation, and each gateway is connected to the virtual networks and External Network. Data exchanged between Internal and External Workstations is limited only through the gateways by the configuration of Platform OS.

2.3 Platform OS

In order to prevent user from changing configuration of Platform OS, direct access to Platform OS must be prohibited. The following configuration realizes this:

(1) The default run level is changed to level 4.
(2) The init process starts services required to manage Platform OS, for example syslogd, and does not start getty, nor trap ctl-alt-del.
(3) The starting script kicks the following programs: the X window system display server, four gateways, two VMs, and screen lock program.
(4) The shutdown process runs after both the VMs end.

The security policy of Platform OS is configured as shown in Figure 3. The init process launches the xinit command, and the command starts the X window system display server, VMs and gateways. Each VM accesses three files, log, configuration,

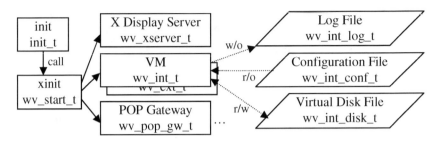

Fig. 3. Security Policy of Platform OS

and virtual disk image, and each of the files is assigned a different type of SELinux. The access kind of each type is minimal, for example, wv_int_log_t, the type of log file of Internal Workstation, is written only by wv_int_t, the domain of Internal Workstation.

2.4 Gateways

The first request, data import from External Workstation to Internal Workstation without virus infection, is realized by Clipboard Gateway, which works as follows:

(1) The clipboard watch agent on External Workstation transmits object on the clipboard to the gateway when the user copies object.
(2) The gateway checks the object type, and transmits the object if the type is not file. Otherwise the gateway does not transmit.
(3) The agent copies the object to the clipboard of Internal Workstation.

In order to realize part of the second requirement, e-mail retrieval from External Network, the e-mail client on Internal Workstation accesses two POP servers on Internal and External Networks, and the client accesses the later through POP Gateway, which encapsulates attached files. The encapsulation and decapsulation processes are shown in Figure 4.

POP gateway encrypts each attached file with a randomly generated AES key, encrypts the random key with an encryption key of RSA, and signs the encrypted random key and file with a signature key of RSA. When the user opens the attached file received from External Network, it is sent to Display Gateway, the gateway checks the signature with the verification key corresponding to the signature key, forwards the encrypted key and file to the display agent on External Workstation, and then the agent decrypts the file and displays it. The e-mail from Internal Network is opened normally on Internal Workstation.

Attached Files from the Internet are opened in External Workstation and they are accessed safely from Internal Workstation through Terminal Gateway. Actually the gateway is a remote access client or terminal client running on a remote access server or terminal server; as shown in Figure 5, combination of two remote accesses, one from Internal Workstation to Terminal Gateway and the other from the gateway to External Workstation, realized a remote access from Internal Workstation to External Workstation.

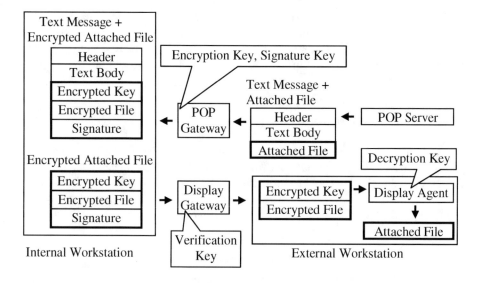

Fig. 4. Encapsulation and Decapsulation of Attached File

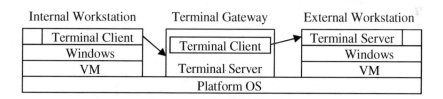

Fig. 5. Terminal Gateway as a Combination of Two Remote Accesses

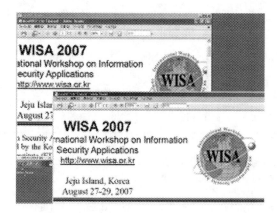

Fig. 6. The same files opened in Internal Workstation (right) and External Workstation (left)

With use of Terminal and Display Gateways, the user can open an attached file of e-mail from the Internet with the same operation of opening attached file from Internal Network; the file is automatically displayed in the terminal client on Internal Workstation, and it looks almost the same as file opened in Internal Workstation locally as shown in Figure 6.

3 Performance Evaluation

The authors have implemented a prototype of Windows Vault and measured performance in the environment shown in Table 1 with the benchmark program, CrystalMark 2004R2 [11], and result is shown in Table 2. The column M is the result of the mean score of Internal and External Workstations measured simultaneously, S is one of Internal Workstation, and W is a normal Windows PC with Intel Core Solo (1.66GHz).

Table 1. Environment

Item	Description
Platform OS	Cent OS release 5
VM	VMware Workstation 5.5.2
Windows	Windows XP Pro. + SP2
CPU	Intel Core 2 Duo (2.16GHz)
Memory	2GB

Table 2. CrystalMark Results

Item	M	S	W
Integer	8,361	8,383	3,901
Float	9,511	9,465	4,584
Memory	10,447	10,722	4,764
HD	11,457	11,985	4,485
GDI	1,979	2,205	1,426

Table 3. Performance of POP Gateway and Display Process

File Size (B)	Msg. Size (B)	N (sec)	P (sec)	P/N	D (sec)
10K	15K	0.198	0.198	1.00	0.018
345K	467K	0.206	0.280	1.36	0.438
3,262K	4,406K	0.522	0.977	1.87	1.954

Comparing with the normal Windows, the performance of Internal Workstation and External Workstation is better, and each of the workstations has shown enough performance as a Windows PC.

The performance of retrieving e-mail and opening attached file is shown in Table 3. The column N is the time without POP Gateway, and the column P is the case through the gateway. The overhead is about 0-90%. The column D is the transmission and decryption time of encrypted file through Display Gateway. There is overhead of encryption and decryption, however, it is not so heavy to give impact on usability.

4 Security Considerations

4.1 Attacks from External Workstation/Network to Internal Workstation

Internal Workstation is not directly connected to External Network, but there are four routes of attack from External Network to Internal Workstation. The first route is via e-mail; the e-mail client receives messages from External Network through POP Gateway which encrypts attached files, and the files cannot be opened on Internal Workstation. As a result, there is no possibility to infect virus via e-mail attached file. Virus might be included in header or text body, so the gateway should check character code and line length, and sanitize if they do not meet the protocol specification.

The second is via VM; External Workstation may be infected with virus which attacks the base VM, and such virus may attack Internal Workstation. But the MAC of Platform OS does not allow access between Internal and External Workstations, and such attack cannot happen.

The third is via Clipboard Gateway. Normally user sees and selects an object, and copies it to the clipboard, so the possibility of virus in clipboard object, which is not a file, is considered to be low, but the object might contain virus code. In order to avoid such possibility, the following object check functions of the gateway are useful:

(1) Plain text only: A clipboard object consists of type and data, and the gateway checks the type and only text object is transmitted to Internal Workstation. The size of text data and character code are also be checked.
(2) Strictly defined data: If the object data type is strictly defined, it is possible for the gateway to check the clipboard object meets the definition and does not contain virus.

The fourth route is via Terminal Gateway; basically the gateway transmits the keyboard and mouse events from Internal Workstation to External Workstation and graphical screen data from External Workstation to Internal Workstation, so virus code cannot come into Internal Workstation. Normally a remote access protocol supports clipboard sharing, however, Terminal Gateway kills the function, and virus infection through Terminal Gateway does not happen.

4.2 Attacks by User

User may try to leak a secret file on Internal Workstation to External Workstation through Display Gateway, but the file is not forwarded to External Workstation, because the signature verification at the gateway fails. Consequently, there is no secret leakage of file created on Internal Workstation to External Workstation or Network through Display Gateway. The information flow of POP Gateway and Clipboard Gateway is only from External Workstation to Internal Workstation, therefore secret leakage does not happen. Terminal Gateway transmits display image, mouse and keyboard events, and secret leakage from Internal Workstation to External Workstation cannot happen except that a malicious user leaks secret text by typing keyboard.

The user can change consoles of character terminals or X Window by typing ctl-alt-function key, however, Platform OS is configured as no getty and screen lock program is running on the X Window console, so the user can only access Internal and External Workstations. As a result, normal office worker cannot access Platform OS, nor change its configuration.

But the user who has knowledge of Linux management can access Platform OS by trapping the boot process or direct access to hard disk. Possible solutions are change of the init process program, physical lock of the PC hardware or use of the Trusted Platform Module (TPM) [12]. The TPM is a chip on a PC motherboard and calculates hash values of software components. On request from a remote challenger, the TPM returns the hash value with signature generated within the chip. With this attestation process, the remote challenger can authenticate PC hardware and verify software integrity of Platform OS, and as a result, it is possible to detect physical attacks such as replace of PC hardware, workstations and gateways. The TPM is also used as a key storage; it is possible to encrypt the virtual disk images of the two workstations and decrypt only on the specific PC hardware that has the TPM storing the decryption key, and this countermeasure makes the attack of direct access to hard disk useless.

A few services, such as system logging, are running on Platform OS, and it might be possible to attack such services. However, each service is given a domain and separated from the other processes by the MAC, so Internal Workstation cannot be attacked through a service even if there is vulnerability of the service.

4.3   Vulnerability of Gateways and Enhancements

If POP Gateway has vulnerability, attacker may get the control of the gateway and can inject virus to Internal Workstation or steal secret from Internal Workstation. It is the same as Clipboard and Display Gateways. The MAC of Platform OS cannot cover the weakness of the three gateways, and the security quality of the gateways is very important. However, it is possible to enhance the security by dividing function of each gateway as follows:

Display Gateway has three functions; firstly it receives encrypted and signed file from Internal Workstation, secondly verifies the signature and strips it, and finally sends the file to External Workstation. The three functions can be realized by three processes of different domains, receive process of r_display_t domain, verify process of v_display_t domain, and send process of s_display_t domain. Data between processes is passed via files of different types; the receive process receives file from Internal Workstation and saves it of rv_display_t type, the verify process verifies and strips the signature and saves data as file of vs_display_t type, and the send process sends it to External Workstation. The permitted operations between the domains and types are shown in Figure 7.

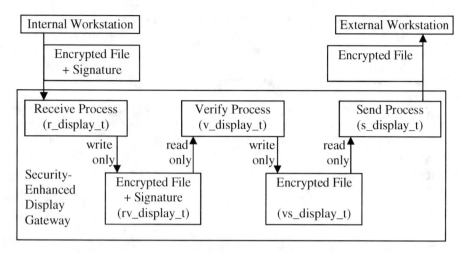

Fig. 7. Domains and Types of Security-Enhanced Display Gateway

Comparing the original implementation of the gateway, the new gateway is more secure, because of the following reasons:

(1) An attacker, which might be the user, must exploit the vulnerability through file, which is enforced by the MAC, and the attack through file is more difficult than one through TCP/IP communication channel, because the former is not interactive and less measures of attack.

(2) The order of attack is fixed; first the reception process, next the verification process, then the send process, and there is no other pass of attack, because the other pass is prohibited by the MAC, and the attacker has less means to attack.

(3) Each process realizes one function and the code is simpler, so that it is more secure than process supporting multiple functions.

(4) Even if an attacker succeeds to exploit all the processes, the information flow is limited from Internal Workstation to External Workstation by the MAC, and there is no chance virus infection of Internal Workstation.

The situation of Clipboard Gateway is very similar to Display Gateway. The gateway has three functions; firstly it receives clipboard object from External Workstation, secondly verifies the type object, and finally sends the object to Internal Workstation. The security of the gateway can be enhanced in the same way of Display Gateway.

Since the POP is an interactive protocol, the situation of POP Gateway is different from the other two gateways, but the basic idea is the same; the first process receives messages as a POP client, the next encrypts and signs the attached files, and the third behaves as a POP server and sends the messages to Internal Workstation.

While the fail of security of the three gateways before the enhancements leads to catalysis, the channel through Terminal Gateway is safe even if there is vulnerability in the gateway. The gateway consists of two applications, terminal server and terminal client which domains are different. As a result, if an attacker gets control of one application, the attacker cannot get one of the other. Even if one application has vulnerability and an attack code succeeds to transmit any type of data, the other application transmits only graphical display data, keyboard and mouse events, so that the security of the gateway is guaranteed.

4.4 Another Data Category: Unsafe Secret

Current Windows Vault processes two data categories, safe secret and unsafe non-secret, but there is another category data, unsafe secret. Online banking is a typical example; account number, password, balance sheet are secret, but the web page data sent from the server may contain virus. Another typical example is e-mail message sent from a business partner; an attached file contains business secret but the file might be infected with virus.

The current Windows Vault processes such data as unsafe non-secret, because it comes from External Network, and there is a risk that such secret data is stolen from External Workstation. A solution is the third type workstation, which can access only trusted web sites through encrypted and authenticated channel over the Internet. An attached file of e-mail is transmitted through Display Gateway and opened on this workstation; even if the workstation is infected with virus, secret cannot be leaked out to the Internet, because the workstation is connected only the trusted web sites.

5   Usability of Network Applications

In the following, usability of sending e-mail and web browsing is described.

5.1 Sending Message to External Network

In the current implementation, user can receive e-mail message from External Network with e-mail client on Internal Workstation, but cannot reply to the message, because Internal Workstation cannot access External Network, and this leads to inconvenience. It is also true that the user cannot send a new message from Internal Workstation to External Network. As far as user sends from Internal Workstation to External Network, the only solution is encryption; all messages from internal to trusted external recipient are encrypted by the fifth gateway, SMTP gateway, which is connected to the Virtual Internal Network and External Network, and encrypts all received e-mail from Internal Workstation.

A solution to reply to message from External Network is to add the original whole message as an attached file to the message; POP gateway encrypts and signs the whole message, and then adds it as the last attached file. When user wants to reply to the message, the user selects the last attached file to open, and then the file is sent to External Workstation through Display Gateway, an e-mail client opens the file and displays the original message, and then the user replies with normal operation through Terminal Gateway.

As for a new message to External Network, the user needs to send it with the e-mail client on External Network. However, by sending carbon copy to the user own account on Internal Workstation, the user can access the new message on Internal Workstation.

5.2 Web Browsing

With click of links, user can brows web pages without conscious of the page location. Windows Vault divides OS and network into internal and external, so the user needs to conscious of which network the accessing site belongs to, and changes browsers on Internal and External Workstations. This is big change of usage of web browser.

In order to realize 'smooth browsing from internal to external,' it is better that with click of link to external page on internal page, the external page is displayed on Internal Workstation. This function can be realized with HTTP Gateway which calls web browser on External Workstation. The gateway is connected to the virtual External Network and Internal Network, and behaves as follows:

(1) The web browser on Internal Workstation accesses the gateway according to the proxy configuration of the browser.
(2) The gateway returns an error page to the browser, and sends the requested URL to the HTTP agent on External Workstation.
(3) The agent directs browser on External Workstation to access the URL.
(4) The browser accesses the page of the URL, displays the external page, and user can access the page from Internal Workstation through Terminal Gateway.

With the gateway, the user can smoothly brows from a page on Internal Network to a page on External Network in the same as the current operation. The reverse direction browsing is also possible, but it needs to sanitize the URL in external page, since virus may be contained it the URL.

6 Related Works

NetTop also consists of Trusted Linux and VMs, and Windows' on VMs exchange data via 'Regrade Server' with explicit user authorization [10]. The user of NetTop is enforced to use two Windows OSes, two mail clients, two documentation tools, etc., and this is a burden for office workers of commercial companies. On the other hand, the user of Windows Vault accesses only Internal Workstation basically; the user can receive and read text body of e-mail from the Internet, open and read attached files with the same operation as the normal Windows. It is also true that the user can access web pages on the Internet from Internal Workstation through HTTP and Terminal Gateways. This is convenient for users who do not aware of multi-category security.

The Trusted Virtual Domains framework [13] is a kind of system isolation based on Trusted Platform Module [12]. The goal of the framework is to establish secure communication channels between software components with the integrity assurance of the other components. The framework also utilizes multiple VMs and software components of different domains running on a hardware platform. There is a secure communication channel between the software components of the same domain, but no communication between those of different domains. However, Windows Vault is focusing the air gap between the different domains or workstations, and has established secure user data exchange between the two workstations.

VIRTUS [14] is a new processor virtualization architecture for security-oriented next-generation mobile terminals. It creates OS instances, called domains, for pre-installed applications and downloaded native applications. VIRTUS supports inter-domain communications, but it does not clearly specify its security. On the other hand, in Windows Vault the communication between Internal Workstation and External Workstation/External Network is designed carefully not to cause virus infection nor secret leakage.

7 Conclusions

The authors have described Windows Vault, which consists of two Windows workstations, one for safe secret and the other for unsafe non-secret. The two workstations are integrated into a single PC with use of VM and secure OS, and connected securely by gateways. These gateways transmit data between the two workstations without virus infection of Internal Workstation or secret leakage from Internal Workstation to External Workstation. Comparing with the existing data isolation system, the proposed system realizes the same security without change of current user operations of e-mail or awareness of multi-category security of intelligence community.

References

1. Gordon, L.A., Loeb, M.P., Lucyshyn, W., Richardson, R.: 2006 CSI/FBI Computer Crime and Security Survey: Computer Security Institute (2006)
2. Symantec Reports Rise in Data Theft, Data Leakage, and Targeted Attacks Leading to Hackers' Financial Gain: News Release (19th March 2007), http://www.symantec.com/about/news/release/article.jsp?prid=20070319_01
3. McAfee, Inc. Releases New Research Suggesting Data Loss Will Lead To Next Major Corporate Collapse: Press Release (24th April 2007), http://www.symantec.com/about/news/release/article.jsp?prid=20070319_01
4. Frantzen, S.: Targeted attack: Experience from the trenches: The SANS Institute (May 21, 2006) http://isc.sans.org/diary.html?storyid=1345
5. Argus Systems Group, Inc.: PitBull.comPack, OS-level Security for Solaris and AIX: White Paper (March 2001), http://www.argus-systems.com/public/docs/pitbull. white paper.oss.pdf
6. Loscocco, P.A., Smalley, S.D.: Meeting Critical Security Objectives with Security-Enhanced Linux. In: Proceedings of the 2001 Ottawa Linux Symposium (2001), http://www.nsa.gov/selinux/papers/ottawa01.pdf
7. Trusted Computer System Evaluation Criteria; Department of Defense Standard 5200.28-STD (August 1983)
8. Christodorescu, M., Jha, S., Seshia, S., Song, D., Bryant, R.E.: Semantics-Aware Malware Detection. In: IEEE Symposium on Security and Privacy (2005)
9. HP NetTop: A Technical Overview (December 2004)
10. Meushaw, R., Simard, D.: Nettop, Commercial Technology in High Assurance Applications: NSA Tech Trend Notes (Fall 2000), http://www.vmware. com/pdf/TechTrendNotes.pdf
11. Crystal Dew World, http://crystalmark.info/?lang=en

12. Trusted Computing Group, TCG Specification Architecture Overview, Specification Revision 1.4 (August 2, 2007)
13. Griffin, J.L., Jaeger, T., Perez, R., Sailer, R., van Doorn, L., Caceres, R.: Trusted Virtual Domains: Toward Secure Distributed Services. In: The First Workshop on Hot Topics in System Dependability (June 30, 2005)
14. Inoue, H., Ikeno, A., Kondo, M., Sakai, J., Edahiro, M.: VIRTUS: A new processor virtualization architecture for security-oriented next-generation mobile terminals. In: Proceedings of the 43rd annual conference on Design automation, pp. 484–489 (2006)

An Architecture Providing Virtualization-Based Protection Mechanisms Against Insider Attacks

Frederic Stumpf*, Patrick Röder**, and Claudia Eckert

Department of Computer Science,
Technische Universität Darmstadt,
Darmstadt, Germany
{stumpf,roeder,eckert}@sec.informatik.tu-darmstadt.de

Abstract. Insider attacks are very powerful and are relevant in many scenarios, such as grid computing, corporate computing on home computers and electronic commerce of digital content. We present an example scenario to illustrate these attacks and perform a threat analysis to extract requirements for preventing insider attacks. We believe that these requirements are also representative of other scenarios. We develop a four layered protection architecture by using virtualization techniques based on these requirements. Therefore, the proposed architecture prevents insider attacks in scenarios with similar requirements as well.

1 Introduction

Insider attacks are relevant in scenarios where confidential data or intellectual property is processed, e.g., grid computing, corporate computing on home computers and electronic commerce of digital content. These attacks are more dangerous than outsider attacks, since the inside attacker can use his legitimate permissions to perform an attack, e.g., to steal data. An FBI/CSI survey [1] states that a substantial portion of losses is attributed to inside attackers, which shows that these attacks are important and must be considered.

Depending on the scenario, the corresponding attacks differ in the attacker's options to perform an attack. For example, a private user who is trying to bypass a digital rights management (DRM) protection mechanism has unlimited access to his computer. In contrast to this, office employees often do not have administrative access to their computers. The common problem of these attacks is that the attacker can modify his local system configuration to deactivate or bypass protection mechanisms.

As a result, each scenario requires different protection mechanisms. These mechanisms should be effective, but should not limit usability, e.g., mechanisms for multi-purpose computers should maintain the flexibility of these computers. Therefore, we develop a flexible protection architecture for general purpose

---

* The author is supported by the Germand Research Foundation (DFG) under grant EC 163/4-1, project *TrustCaps*.
** The author is supported by the PhD program *Enabling Technologies for Electronic Commerce* of the German Research Foundation (DFG).

S. Kim, M. Yung, and H.-W. Lee (Eds.): WISA 2007, LNCS 4867, pp. 142–156, 2007.

computers, which maintains the universal character of these computers. We introduce protection mechanisms which prevent software components on different trust levels from being able to influence each other. This gives us the ability to run additional software on the machine besides the software that requires protection.

We use the scenario of handling confidential documents in a business environment to perform a threat analysis. Next, we extract requirements for our protection architecture from this analysis. A central challenge is to detect when the attacker has modified his local system configuration. For this purpose, we use the concepts of the Trusted Computing Group (TCG) and virtualization techniques.

The remainder of this paper is organized as follows: We provide background information on the TCG concepts and virtualization techniques in Section 2. Section 3 explains our scenario. We perform a threat analysis for this scenario in Section 4. We extract requirements for the protection architecture which we present in Section 5. After that, we evaluate these mechanisms by discussing whether they prevent the attacks described before in Section 6. Section 7 discusses related work. Finally, we conclude and discuss future work in Section 8.

2   Background

In this section, we present background information on trusted computing and virtualization techniques, which are important for understanding our approach.

2.1   Trusted Computing

The core of the TCG mechanisms [2] is the Trusted Platform Module (TPM), which is basically a smart card soldered to the mainboard of a PC. The TPM serves as the *root of trust*. Tampering with the TPM is generally difficult, since it is implemented in hardware and uses non-migratable keys for certain cryptographic functions. Therefore, we assume that the TPM is trustworthy. One must also assume that the hardware vendor is trustworthy, and has designed the TPM chip according to the specifications. Although the TPM chip is not specified to be tamper-resistant, it is tamper-evident, meaning that unauthorized manipulations will at least be detected.

In this paper, the Platform Configuration Registers (PCRs) are of particular interest. These registers are initialized on startup and then used to store the software integrity values. The TPM calculates the hash value of software components before they are executed and writes this software integrity value to a specific PCR by combining the current result with the previous value of the PCR. The following cryptographic function is used to calculate the values for the specific registers:

$$Extend(PCR_N, value) = SHA1(PCR_N || value)$$

SHA1 refers to the cryptographic hash function used by the TPM, while the $||$ operation represents a concatenation of byte arrays. The trust-anchor for a so called trust-chain is the *Core Root of Trust Measurement* (CRTM) , which resides in the BIOS and is first executed when a platform is powered up. The CRTM then measures itself and the BIOS, and hands over control to the next software component in the trust-chain.

For each measured component, an event is created and stored in the stored measurement log (SML). The PCR values and SML are used to attest the platform's state to a remote party. In order to guarantee the authenticity of these values, they are signed with a non-migratable TPM signing key, namely the Attestation Identity Key (AIK). A remote platform can compare those signed values with reference values to check whether the platform is in a trustworthy state or not.

2.2 Virtualization

Virtualization allows the execution of several different virtual machines, with different operating systems, on a single host entity by the introduction of a hypervisor, also known as a virtual machine monitor (VMM) [3]. This hypervisor provides an abstract interface to the hardware and partitions the underlying hardware resources. The underlying resources are then available to the virtual machines through the VMM which maintains full control of the resource given to the VM. The main contribution of this technology is the provision of strong isolation between different virtual machines, established by the virtual machine monitor.

3   Example Scenario

In this section, we present the example scenario of handling confidential documents in a business environment. We use a client server based document processing architecture (DPA) as an example. This architecture enables the user to view and edit documents, while enforcing access control policies, which are defined by corresponding rules. We perform a threat analysis for this architecture in the next section. The DPA is depicted in Figure 1 and uses three databases. The document database (Doc DB) contains all documents of the system. The rule database (Rule DB) contains the access control rules, which specify allowed or denied accesses to the documents and their parts. Finally, the user database (User DB) stores the credentials of the users of the system, as well as the corresponding roles, including their hierarchy.

The document editor (DE) presents documents to the user and offers operations that can be performed on the documents. If the user invokes such an operation, the corresponding request is sent to the document processor (DP), which runs on the server and performs the requested operation if it is permitted. Inside the DP, the policy enforcement point (PEP) intercepts each operation and asks the policy decision point (PDP) whether the requested operation is allowed. The PDP uses the three databases to decide whether to allow or deny the requested operation. We believe that this scenario is a representative

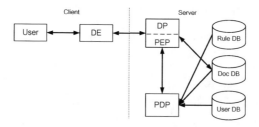

Fig. 1. Document processing architecture (DPA)

example for evaluating insider attacks in scenarios where all documents reside on the server. Moreover, the scenario has similarities with scenarios for DRM or corporate computing on home computers. The common requirement of these scenarios is that the corresponding architectures depend on the trustworthiness of the client configuration. In addition to this, these architectures must ensure that data is not extracted from the protected system on the client side.

4   Threat Analysis

In this section, we evaluate possible attacks on the components of the DPA mentioned above. We describe two different types of attackers, namely the inside attacker and the outside attacker.

Inside Attacker: An inside attacker is a legitimate user of the system who misuses his permissions to perform an attack. We assume that an inside attacker also has physical access to the client machine, which enables additional attacks. In addition to this, an inside attacker can perform remote attacks on the document processor. In a case, where the system is used within a company, an inside attacker is typically an employee of the company.

Outside Attacker: An outside attacker is a user who does not have legitimate access to the system, which means that he has no credentials to login to the server and also has no physical access to any machine of the system. The outside attacker can only perform remote attacks on the client and the document processor. For example, if our system is used within a company an outside attacker might be either a professional hacker hired by a competitor, a government spy performing industry espionage or a hacker who tries to perform attacks just for his own entertainment.

All together, an inside attacker can perform much more powerful attacks than an outside attacker. Since the attacks of an outside attacker are a subset of the attacks of an inside attacker, we focus on attacks by inside attackers. With this approach, we also prevent the attacks of an outside attacker. We assume the server to be trustworthy. Accordingly, we only examine attacks on the client.

4.1   Attacks on the Client

In this section, we describe possible attacks in the scenario mentioned above. We focus on attacks that compromise the confidentiality of the protected data.

Software Manipulations. In the following, we discuss software manipulations on the client, which can be performed on different components of the system.

Extract data from the document editor. An inside attacker can try to extract confidential information from the document editor. As a result, the document editor must be designed in a way, that it is not possible to extract confidential data from it and transfer it to another application, e.g., an e-mail client.

Manipulate the document editor. If the document editor prevents the extraction of confidential data, the attacker can try to manipulate the corresponding protection mechanisms. Alternatively, the attacker could use another document editor that is compatible with the protocols used in the DPA, but allows data to be extracted. Therefore, we must have a mechanism to ensure that the document editor is not modified and that it is the version that has been deployed originally.

Use the operating system mechanisms to extract data. The attacker could also use the underlying operating system on which the document editor runs to extract data. One such method is to extract the confidential data from the memory by writing the memory used by the document editor to a file, which is also referred to as a memory dump. An attack like this requires that the application of the attacker runs in kernel mode, which enables access to the entire physical memory of the machine. There are many other similar methods, which all have in common that they use the services offered by the underlying operating system. Consequently, we must configure the underlying operating system in a way that prevents the use of services like memory dumps to extract the confidential data from the document editor.

Manipulate operating system. If the underlying operating system is configured in a way that prevents the extraction of confidential data using its services, the attacker could modify the operating system or its configuration. The attacker could try to re-enable the mechanisms that we have disabled before. For example, he could exchange a system module, e.g., the module that performs memory management or the module that displays data on the screen. Another similar approach is to replace the entire operating system with a system that allows the extraction of data. As a result, we need a mechanism to ensure that the operating system is neither manipulated nor entirely replaced. This mechanism must ensure that the operating system is authentic, which means that it is the one that has been deployed and it is configured as we have defined.

Extract confidential data from the swap file. The DPA does not store documents permanently on the client. Instead, the DPA keeps them in the memory to display and edit them, which avoids attacks based on accessing the hard drive of a client machine. Nevertheless, we must also ensure that the operating system does not swap the memory used by the document editor to the hard disk, if available memory is getting low. This again must be done by configuring the operating system. As a consequence, there is no risk of losing confidential data by stealing a hard drive of an authorized client.

Masquerading Attacks. In the following, we discuss different types of masquerading attacks on the DPA. We describe the cloning of a client machine and the spoofing of the server of the DPA.

Clone a client machine. Another type of attack is to clone an authorized client machine by creating an exact copy of the configuration of an authentic machine, e.g., by creating an exact copy of the hard disk of the authentic client or by copying the authentication credentials to another client. For example, a legitimate user could set up such a cloned client machine in an area which is not under surveillance to extract data by taking pictures of the displayed data. To reduce the risk of this type of attack, we need a mechanisms that prevents the cloning of a client machine. This mechanism must ensure that the identity of the client machine is bound to the hardware of the machine.

Masquerade the server. The attacker can also masquerade the server, e.g., by redirecting the network traffic using a DNS poisoning attack. Therefore, we need mutual authentication between client and server. In our scenario, the masquerading of a server is less dangerous, since no confidential documents are uploaded to the server. However, this can be the case in the scenario of corporate computing on home computers.

Hardware Attacks and Analogue Attacks In the following, we discuss attacks on the hardware and analogue attacks. We consider DMA attacks as hardware attacks and discuss them in this section, too.

Use DMA to extract data. Another type of attack is to use a device with DMA to extract confidential data. DMA bypasses any protection managed by the CPU and allows to access the entire memory.

Extract data using probing attacks. Moreover, the attacker can perform probing attacks, such as mechanical or electrical probing attacks, on the hardware components of the DPA. Using this attack, he can extract confidential data directly from the hardware, e.g., from the TPM or from a memory module.

Use analogue channels to extract data. Besides the attacks mentioned above, the attacker can take an analogous screen shot of the display using a camera.

4.2   Requirements for the Protection Architecture

In this section, we present the requirements for the protection architecture. The first two requirements apply to any scenario, whereas the requirements that follow are specific for the DPA.

Requirement 1: *The operating system is configured to support only the minimum set of services and resources.* As we have discussed so far, some of the mechanisms for securing the client must be performed by configuring the operating system, e.g., configuring it to not swap the memory occupied by the document editor or disabling the possibility to take digital screen shots. Moreover, we must configure the operating system to allow only network connections to the document processor, which reduces the risk that data is sent to an unauthorized third party.

Requirement 2: *The number of software components of the operating system is minimal.* To reduce the risk of vulnerabilities, it is highly desirable to employ a small operating system that has the minimal set of functions that are required to execute the document editor, because the chance of vulnerabilities increases with the complexity of a system. Consequently, we must use a operating system with the minimal number of user space software and kernel components, e.g., device drivers.

Requirement 3: *Attestation of the client machine.* Moreover, we need to ensure that the operating system that we have supplied is neither exchanged with another operating system nor is its configuration manipulated to disable the security mechanisms of the protection architecture.

Requirement 4: *Authenticity of client and server.* The user of the client platform could manipulate his machine to forward an attestation request to another machine with authentic software. Therefore we must ensure that the provided configuration values refer to the attested system and that the authenticity of both client and server is guaranteed.

Requirement 5: *Completeness of attestation.* The definition of this state depends on what is measured on the client side. The usual approach [4] is to calculate the hash value of every executed binary and include it in the state definition. As a result, the verifier receives a list of all binaries that have been executed since the last reboot of the machine. However, this approach has two problems. First, the received list of executed binaries gives no hint about what was executed after the remote attestation. For example, a key logger or trojan horse can be started after the remote attestation. Although the malware was located on the client machine at the time of the remote attestation, it was not detected, because it was executed after the remote attestation. The second problem is, that using this approach, only the executable binaries of applications are inspected. Shell scripts and configuration files are not included in the measurement. This leads to the problem, that certain manipulations, e.g., manipulations of the configuration files, can not be detected by this approach. Consequently, we need an approach that measures the complete system configuration including scripts and configuration files.

5   Protection Architecture

As discussed before, we must ensure that the client machine can execute additional software, e.g., a web browser or an e-mail client, after the security mechanisms are applied. This can be a problem when requirements 1 and 2 are fulfilled, since they reduce the compatibility of the client machine with additional software. For this reason, it is desirable to have a different operating system for different applications. As a consequence, we need a method to run different operating systems on one client machine, which we achieve by using virtualization techniques and running different virtual machines on a client machine. Each operating system can be executed in a separate virtual machine. Concerning the security of the system, we must ensure that these virtual machines can not influence each other. For example, we must ensure that malware running in one virtual machine can not extract confidential data from another virtual machine. We apply our approach for providing different virtual machines [5] and analyze whether the attacks described in Section 4.1 can be solved with this approach. The strong isolation achieved through virtualization guarantees that different virtual machines can not influence each other. Our previous approach uses virtualization in combination with the mechanisms defined by the Trusted Computing Group. It establishes several different execution environments by using various types of virtual machines, which are strongly isolated from each other. It also provides an abstraction of the underlying hardware TPM through a virtualized TPM (vTPM) interface. This allows the different virtual machines to use the measurement and reporting facilities of the TPM, thus they benefit from a hardware-based trust anchor. This approach has the advantage over the others [6] that the binding between TPM and vTPM is already specified, which is useful for remote attestation of virtual machines.

We use this approach to execute the document editor in one such isolated virtual machine. Other applications are executed in a different virtual machine. Thus, they can not interfere with the document editor. Figure 2 depicts the approach applied to the DPA.

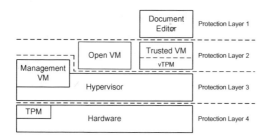

Fig. 2. Protection architecture organized in layers

The resulting protection architecture consists of components divided into four protection layers, in which components located on one layer provide security mechanisms to protect the components located on the layer directly above. In the case of a successful attack on one layer, the layers below can prevent the attacker from successfully transferring data to another physical machine.

These components include three virtual machines, namely the *open virtual machine*, a *management virtual machine* and the *trusted virtual machine* (TVM). Additionally, a hypervisor partitions the underlying hardware and a TPM serves as a hardware-based trust anchor. The TPM provides hardware-based tamper-evident cryptographic functions to protect the software components running on the layer directly above from unauthorized manipulations. Together with remaining hardware components, the TPM forms the lowest protection layer, more specifically, protection layer 4.

5.1   Protection Layer 4: TPM and Hardware

The TPM is the anchor of trust and the basis for the attestation. We store several non-migratable client-specific keys in the TPM, which are used for the challenge-response authentication with the server. This prevents the cloning of a client machine and additional attacks on the authenticity of the client machine. The attacker must perform a local physical attack, e.g., a mechanical or electrical probing attack, to the TPM to extract these keys. Since the TPM is specified to be tamper-evident, these attacks are not prevented, but can be detected afterwards. We assume that the hardware and the TPM behave as specified.

5.2   Protection Layer 3: Hypervisor and Management VM

The hypervisor is the first part of protection layer 3 and provides an abstraction layer to the underlying hardware. It has privileged access to the hardware and can grant and revoke resources, e.g., CPU cycles, to and from the running VMs. This hypervisor provides strong isolation of the virtual machines, which is the protection mechanism of this layer. It ensures that different virtual machines can not influence each other, e.g., by reading each others memory. In this approach, every virtual machine uses individual virtualized device drivers, which are executed within that VM. The hypervisor ensures, that these device drivers can only access the memory of the corresponding virtual machine. When running applications of different trust levels on a machine without virtualization, an attacker could use a malicious device driver to gain system wide access, e.g., to read the memory of the document editor and extract the confidential documents. We assume that the hypervisor and the management VM are set up by a trustworthy system administrator and that the user of the machine is not able to change this configuration.

Because of its privileged position, the hypervisor needs to be trustworthy, since it can manipulate the CPU instructions of every virtual machine. We assume that the hypervisor is trustworthy and therefore guarantees strong isolation. Currently available virtualization solutions provide strong isolation. However, this still can be circumvented with direct memory access (DMA) operations [7]. These operations access the memory without intervention by the CPU and therefore bypass the hypervisor's protection mechanisms. Hypervisors with *secure sharing* [8] prevent these attacks, but suffer from a high performance overhead, as well as a large trusted computing base, since the required I/O emulation is moved into the hypervisor layer.

The management virtual machine is the second part of protection layer 3. It is responsible for starting, stopping and configuring the virtual machines. It is part of this protection layer, since it is closely connected to the hypervisor and is a privileged VM, which has direct access to the hardware TPM.

5.3   Protection Layer 2: Open VM and Trusted VM

This protection layer consists of the open VM and the trusted VM. The open VM is allowed to run arbitrary software components. It runs applications with a lower trust level, such as web browsers or office applications. The open VM provides the semantics of today's open machines and therefore has no additional protection mechanisms for upper layers. Since this virtual machine is not of interest for our approach, we will not focus on it in the rest of our work.

The TVM runs the document editor and a tiny OS with a minimal number of software components, to reduce the possible number of security vulnerabilities. This fulfills requirements 1 and 2 without losing the ability to run other software on the client machine. The tiny OS and the document editor are part of a virtual appliance (VA), which is a fully pre-installed and pre-configured set of software for virtual machines. To ensure that the VA is not manipulated, the management VM measures its integrity before startup.

The TVM runs in protection layer 2 and provides a virtual TPM (vTPM) as an additional protection mechanism. The operating system of the TVM uses this vTPM to protect the document editor running in protection layer 1. We use this vTPM to perform a complete attestation of the entire hard disk of the TVM, to ensure that neither the operating system, its configuration, nor the document editor running on top of the operating system is manipulated. As a result, the verification of the state of the entire virtual machine requires only one reference value. This eliminates the need to maintain a large amount of reference values, which is the main disadvantage of the binary attestation. Moreover, the server checks in the attestation whether the protection layers below the operating system, e.g., the hypervisor, are trustworthy. As a result, this mechanism fulfills Requirement 5. In addition to that, we use the vTPM to establish an authenticated channel between client and server. We discuss the corresponding protocol in Section 5.5.

The TVM only accepts network requests from the server to reduce the chance of network attacks. After the booting process, which can not be interrupted, the operating system of the TVM directly executes the document editor. As a consequence, the only option for a user to interact with the TVM is to use the document editor provided by us. This improves the security of the TVM, since it limits the number of possible attacks.

All I/O interfaces which can be used to extract data from the system are either blocked or controlled. For example, the management VM ensures that the hard disk is read only, which prevents an attacker from temporarily storing confidential data on this disk to extract it afterwards by booting a different operating system. Additionally, the management VM has a configuration file for the TVM, which defines that network connections are only allowed to the

server of the DPA, which inhibits an attacker from sending confidential data
to a different host. As a consequence, even if an attacker exploits a vulnerability of the document editor, he can not transfer the confidential data out of the
TVM.

5.4   Protection Layer 1: Document Editor

This protection layer consists of the document editor. The document editor is
written in Java, which is expected to minimize the risk of buffer overflows. In
addition to this, the document editor can edit confidential documents in memory
and does not need to write them to disk. The server's authenticity is checked by
verifying the server's certificate before answering an attestation request.

5.5   Attestation Protocol

To prevent masquerading attacks on the authenticity of the platform configuration, we use an enhanced remote attestation protocol [9]. These attacks forward
the integrity measurements of a conform host to masquerade a conform client
state. The enhanced protocol adds a key establishment phase, to ensure that
the channel of attestation is authentic. It also guarantees an end-to-end communication and prevents the attestation channel from becoming compromised
by another application which could take over the attestation channel after the
attestation has succeeded.

The simplified process of our remote attestation protocol is illustrated in
Figure 3. It consists of an initialization phase and an attestation phase. The
initialization phase yields a vAIK credential which is then used in attestation
phase to sign the PCRs. This vAIK credential is signed by an AIK from the hardware TPM. In the first step of the initialization phase, the vTPM is initialized,

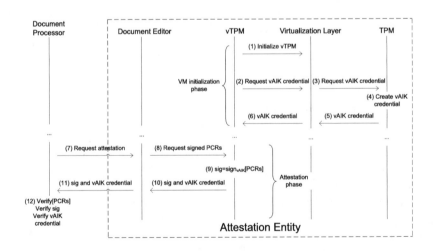

Fig. 3. Simplified attestation process

which in turn requests a new vAIK credential from the hardware TPM (steps 2 and 3). The hardware TPM issues a vAIK credential and sends it to the vTPM (steps 5 and 6). The attestation phase is triggered by the document processor, which sends an attestation request consisting of a *nonce* and its public Diffie-Hellman key pair g^a mod m for the key-establishment to the document editor (step 7). The document editor generates the corresponding Diffie-Hellman key pair g^b mod m and sends this, together with the *nonce*, to the vTPM (step 8). The vTPM generates a digital signature using the vAIK (step 9) and transfers it together with the vAIK credential, to the document editor (step 10). The document editor forwards this data to the DP (step 11). Next, the DP verifies the authenticity of the document editor and its platform by inspecting the platform configuration registers (step 12). Finally, both the DP and the document editor calculate the shared session key for the following communication (step 13, not illustrated).

The protocol for performing remote attestations guarantees that the endpoint of the communication is within the attested virtual machine. Therefore, relay or masquerading attacks are not possible. The combination of attestation and key establishment fulfills Requirement 4, since it prevents the masquerading of a trustworthy system configuration.

6   Evaluation of the Protection Architecture

In the following section, we evaluate whether the security mechanisms described in Section 5 prevent the attacks mentioned in Section 4.1.

Software Manipulations. Each of the protection layers can be either manipulated during runtime or before it is executed. Runtime attacks are especially critical, since they are not detected by the current method of integrity measurement, which only measures components when they are executed. The underlying protection layer must be manipulated to modify the current layer, because the integrity of each layer is measured before execution by the layer below. This results in a chain of trust, with the TPM as a hardware anchor. As a consequence, the manipulation of any layer either requires a runtime attack or a hardware attack on the TPM. In the following, we discuss possible runtime attacks on each layer. The document editor is robust against buffer overflow attacks, since it is written in Java, which is commonly believed to decrease the possibility of buffer overflows. On the downside, other attacks, such as exploiting other programming errors, are still possible. The risk of runtime attacks on the operating system is reduced, because software with lower complexity is expected to have less errors than software with higher complexity. Moreover, we choose a strict system configuration to minimize possible attack methods, e.g., network connections are restricted to the server, the hard disk of the TVM is read-only and swapping is disabled. As a consequence, in the case of a successful attack on the operating system, the attacker has no options to transfer confidential data to another machine. This is an example of a lower layer preventing a successful attack, when the protection mechanisms of the layer above failed. Runtime attacks on the hypervisor are difficult, since it has a lower complexity compared to operating systems and it does not expose interfaces to the user which could be used for an attack. Moving protection mechanisms of upper layers into this layer, simplifies the verification of the correctness of these mechanisms.

Masquerading attacks. Both client and server can be masqueraded, where the cloning of a machine is a special type of this attack. Since we assume that the server is trustworthy, we only focus on cloning attacks on the client. An attacker can create an exact copy of a client's hard drive, but he can not copy the content of the corresponding TPM. The attacker can not use this cloned client to access the server, since our attestation protocol uses secrets stored in the TPM and therefore detects that the client is not authentic. One such secret is the AIK of the hardware TPM, which is used to sign the vAIK of the vTPM. This vAIK in turn, is used in the attestation protocol. The server can check the authenticity of the vAIK with the corresponding AIK credential that was installed on the server when the system was set up. Using an honest system to masquerade a trustworthy system state is prevented by our attestation protocol. This protocol also detects and prevents masquerading of a server, since the server's certificate is checked by the document editor.

Hardware attacks and analogue attacks. DMA attacks can either be handled entirely in software by emulating all I/O devices, which causes a high performance degradation. Alternatively, DMA attacks can be prevented by using hardware support, e.g., Intel's Trusted Execution Technology. As a consequence, it depends on the implementation of our protection architecture whether or not DMA attacks are possible. Probing attacks are difficult to inhibit. At least the TPM is specified to be tamper-evident, which allows an attack to be detected afterwards. Analogue attacks are difficult to prevent with software mechanisms. Fortunately, the bandwidth of this channel is much lower compared to digitally copying confidential data. In addition to that, this attack method has a higher risk of being detected, if the machine is located at a monitored location, e.g., an office with many co-workers or an office that is under surveillance by security cameras. We do not provide a mechanism to prevent this type of attack.

7   Related Work

Terra [10] is an approach to create a virtual machine-based platform, which allows the attestation of virtual machines. It uses VMWare's ESX Server to establish two types of virtual machines (*Closed Box* and *Open Box*) and to report the state of a closed box machine to a remote entity. We could also use Terra's Closed Box for our scenario and perform the analysis of the protection mechanisms based on Terra. However, Terra suffers from using a large trusted computing base, which is a potential security threat, since the trusted computing base could be exploited to undermine the protection mechanisms.

A similar approach that enables attestation is used in the Integrity Measurement Architecture (IMA) [4]. The authors present a comprehensive prototype based on trusted computing technologies, where integrity measurement is implemented by examining the hashes of all executed binaries. However, the prototype is not based on virtualization technologies, and therefore no strong isolation between processes is achieved. This requires to transfer a complete SML to the remote entity, which in turn, needs to validate all started processes to determine the platform's trustworthiness.

Similar to our proposed protection architecture a number of additional projects, such as *EMSCB* [6] and Open-TC exist that also use virtualization to establish a trustworthy computing platform. These projects are either based on the L4 microkernel [11] or on the Xen hypervisor. In this context, Sadeghi et al. have presented a prototype for DRM [12] that uses the L4 and provides secure storage and attestation of compartments. Our concepts and how the different protection layers interact with each other to prevent insider attacks could also be analyzed based on these alternative approaches. However, these approaches do not use a virtual TPM, therefore their protection mechanisms differ from the ones presented in this paper.

Our concept of the DPA is very similar to server-based computing, where all documents remain on the server and are accessed by executing the corresponding applications on the server. Only the display content of these applications is transferred to the client. An example of such an architecture is the Display-Only File Server (DOFS) architecture [13]. However, in these approaches, a modified client is neither detected nor handled.

Kuhlmann et al. [14] discuss similar scenarios as in our paper. The key difference to our work is that they do not focus on insider attacks and do not analyze how different protection mechanisms prevent insider attacks.

This work is also based on [15], in which we have analyzed existing architectures that aim at preventing insider attacks and explained the need for protection mechanisms on the level of the operating system.

8   Conclusions and Future Work

In this paper, we presented an architecture for document processing, as an example, and analyzed insiders attacks on this architecture. Then, we performed a threat analysis and extracted requirements for a protection architecture that prevents these attacks. We introduced a four layer protection architecture based on virtualization techniques that fulfills these requirements. Among our mechanisms, we developed an authentication and communication protocol that is robust against masquerading attacks and ensures a confidential communication channel between client and server. We are finished with the implementation of this protection architecture. Currently, we are migrating the client of a document processing architecture developed by us into a trusted virtual machine. After that, we will perform penetration tests on the client and evaluate the effectiveness of the proposed protection mechanisms.

References

1. Gordon, L.A., Loeb, M.P., Lucyshyn, W., Richardson, R.: 2006 CSI/FBI Computer Crime and Security Survey. Technical report, CSI (2006)
2. Group, T.C.: Trusted Platform Module (TPM) specifications. Technical report (2006), https://www.trustedcomputinggroup.org/specs/TPM
3. Goldberg, R.P.: Survey of Virtual Machine Research. Computer 7, 34–45 (1974)
4. Sailer, R., Zhang, X., Jaeger, T., van Doorn, L.: Design and Implementation of a TCG-based Integrity Measurement Architecture. In: 13th USENIX Security Symposium, IBM T. J. Watson Research Center (2004)
5. Stumpf, F., Benz, M., Hermanowski, M., Eckert, C.: An Approach to a Trustworthy System Architecture using Virtualization. In: ATC-2007. Proceedings of the 4th International Conference on Autonomic and Trusted Computing, Hong Kong, China. LNCS, Springer, Heidelberg (2007)
6. Base, E.M.S.C.: Towards trustworthy systems with open standards and trusted computing (2006), http://www.emscb.de/
7. Fraser, K., Hand, S., Neugebauer, R., Pratt, I., Warfield, A., Williamson, M.: Safe Hardware Access with the Xen Virtual Machine Monitor. In: 1st Workshop on Operating System and Architectural Support for the on demand IT InfraStructure (OASIS) (2004)
8. Karger, P.A., Zurko, M.E., Bonin, D.W., Mason, A.H., Kahn, C.E.: A Retrospective on the VAX VMM Security Kernel. IEEE Trans. Softw. Eng. 17, 1147–1165 (1991)
9. Stumpf, F., Tafreschi, O., Röder, P., Eckert, C.: A Robust Integrity Reporting Protocol for Remote Attestation. In: Second Workshop on Advances in Trusted Computing (WATC 2006 Fall) (2006)
10. Garfinkel, T., Pfaff, B., Chow, J., Rosenblum, M., Boneh, D.: Terra: a virtual machine-based platform for trusted computing. In: SOSP 2003. Proceedings of the nineteenth ACM symposium on Operating systems principles, pp. 193–206. ACM Press, New York (2003)
11. Liedtke, J.: On Micro-Kernel Construction. In: SOSP 1995. Proceedings of the fifteenth ACM symposium on Operating systems principles, pp. 237–250. ACM Press, New York (1995)
12. Sadeghi, A.R., Scheibel, M., Stüble, C., Wolf, M.: Play it once again, sam - enforcing stateful licenses on open platforms. In: 2nd Workshop on Advances in Trusted Computing (WATC 2006 Fall) (2006)
13. Yu, Y., Chiueh, T.: Display-Only File Server: A Solution against Information Theft Due to Insider Attack. In: DRM 2004. Proceedings of the 4th ACM workshop on Digital rights management, pp. 31–39. ACM Press, New York (2004)
14. Kuhlmann, D., Landfermann, R., Ramasamy, H., Schunter, M., Ramunno, G., Vernizzi, D.: An open trusted computing architecture - secure virtual machines enabling user-defined policy enforcement. Technical report, Open Trusted Computing consortium (OpenTC) (2007)
15. Röder, P., Stumpf, F., Grewe, R., Eckert, C.: Hades - Hardware Assisted Document Security. In: Second Workshop on Advances in Trusted Computing (WATC 2006 Fall), Tokyo, Japan (2006)

Detecting Motifs in System Call Sequences

William O. Wilson, Jan Feyereisl, and Uwe Aickelin

School of Computer Science, The University of Nottingham, UK
{wow,jqf,uxa}@cs.nott.ac.uk

Abstract. The search for patterns or motifs in data represents an area of key interest to many researchers. In this paper we present the Motif Tracking Algorithm, a novel immune inspired pattern identification tool that is able to identify unknown motifs which repeat within time series data. The power of the algorithm is derived from its use of a small number of parameters with minimal assumptions. The algorithm searches from a completely neutral perspective that is independent of the data being analysed and the underlying motifs. In this paper the motif tracking algorithm is applied to the search for patterns within sequences of low level system calls between the Linux kernel and the operating system's user space. The MTA is able to compress data found in large system call data sets to a limited number of motifs which summarise that data. The motifs provide a resource from which a profile of executed processes can be built. The potential for these profiles and new implications for security research are highlighted. A higher level system call language for measuring similarity between patterns of such calls is also suggested.

1   Introduction

The investigation and analysis of time series data is a popular and well studied area of research. Common goals of time series analysis include the desire to identify known patterns in a time series, to predict future trends given historical information and the ability to classify data into similar clusters. Historically, statistical techniques have been applied to this problem domain whilst Immune System (IS) inspired techniques have remained fairly limited [1]. In this paper we describe the Motif Tracking Algorithm (MTA), a deterministic but non-exhaustive approach to identifying repeating patterns in time series data. The MTA abstracts principles from the human immune system, in particular the immune memory theory of Eric Bell [2]. Implementing principles from immune memory to be used as part of a solution mechanism is of great interest to the immune system community and here we are able to take advantage of such a system. The MTA implements the Bell immune memory theory by proliferating and mutating a population of solution candidates using a derivative of the clonal selection algorithm [3].

A subsequence of a time series that is seen to repeat within that time series is defined as a motif. The objective of the MTA is to find those motifs. The power of the MTA comes from the fact that it has no prior knowledge of the time series

S. Kim, M. Yung, and H.-W. Lee (Eds.): WISA 2007, LNCS 4867, pp. 157–172, 2007.

to be examined or what motifs exist. It searches in a fast and efficient manner and the flexibility incorporated in its generic approach allows the MTA to be applied across a diverse range of problems. The MTA has already been applied to motif detection in industrial data sets [2]. Here we test its generic properties by applying it to motif identification in system call data sets.

Considerable research has already been performed on identifying *known* patterns in time series [4]. In contrast little research has been performed on looking for *unknown* motifs in time series. A distinguishing feature of the MTA is its ability to identify *variable length unknown* patterns that repeat in a time series. This focus on the detection of unknown patterns makes it an ideal tool for investigating underlying patterns in low level system data generated from the execution of processes on a computer system. The nature of program execution, with the re-use of functions and methods, along with standardised programming structures, implies a set of motifs do exist within each running process. Each process on a system is executed by issuing sequences of system calls which are translated by the kernel into data understandable by the underlying hardware. All processes rely on such system calls making them of high interest to the security community. By looking at the sequences of such system calls, we can observe repeating motifs, which will be identifiable and explainable in terms of higher level functions. The MTA provides an ideal mechanism to compress the data found in these large system call data sets to a limited number of motifs which effectively summarise that data. The motifs could then provide a resource from which we can build a profile of executed processes. These profiles could be used to identify sequences that indicate potentially anomalous process behaviour.

Related work on motif detection is discussed in Section 2 with details of system calls found in Section 3. Terms and definitions used are covered in Section 4 followed by the MTA pseudo code and the problem to be addressed in Sections 5 and 6. Results and future work are found in Sections 7 and 8 before concluding in Section 9.

2   Related Work

The search for patterns in data is relevant to a diverse range of fields, including biology, business, finance and computer security. For example, Guan [5] addresses DNA pattern matching using lookup table techniques that exhaustively search the data set to find recurring patterns. Investigations using a piecewise linear segmentation scheme [6] and discrete Fourier transforms [7] provide examples of mechanisms to search a time series for a particular motif of interest. An underlying assumption in all these common approaches is that the pattern to be found is known in advance. The matching task is much simpler as the algorithm just has to find re-occurrences of the required pattern.

The search for unknown motifs is at the heart of the work conducted by Keogh et al. Keoghs probabilistic [8] and Viztree algorithms [9] are very successful in identifying unknown motifs but they require additional parameters compared to the MTA and they also assume prior knowledge of the length of the motif to be found. Motifs longer and potentially shorter than this predefined length may remain undetected in full. Work by Tanaka [10] attempts to address this issue by using minimum description length to discover the optimal length for the motif. Fu et al. [11] use self-organising maps to identify unknown patterns in stock market data, by representing patterns as perceptually important points. This provides an effective solution but again the patterns found are limited to a predetermined length.

This prior awareness of the patterns to find, or their lengths, is not appropriate for intrusion detection systems as by their very nature intrusion techniques are constantly changing to avoid detection. This represents an ideal application for the MTA as it makes no such pre-assumptions and aims to find all unknown motifs of variable length from the data set. Security researchers have been investigating system calls for a number of years. System calls represent a low level communication mechanism between processes and the systems' underlying hardware, providing a high enough level of abstraction for intelligent process behaviour analysis and modelling. The use of system calls for anomaly detection was first introduced by Forrest et al. [12]. Their IS inspired work looks at sequences of system calls using a sliding window mechanism. System calls are used to generate a database of normal behaviour, i.e. self, which is consequently used to capture anomalous behaviour, non-self.

Forrest's work instigated a new stream of intrusion detection research, with some researchers taking the idea of generating a database of normal behaviour and extending it further [13]. Novel approaches to solving related issues by varying the methods and types of signals used to generate a set of normal behaviour were also proposed [14]. Tandon et al. have looked at system call motifs as a source for their normal behaviour profile generation, however this differs from our approach because it uses an exhaustive search mechanism [15].

3   Intrusion Detection and System Calls

System calls are lower level functions/methods, which act as a communication channel between higher level processes (e.g. executable commands) and the lower level kernel of an operating system (OS). The system calls perform system actions on behalf of a user. Each system call performs a slightly different atomic task, yet in combination they achieve much more complex functionality. Examples of some of the simplest system calls are the file I/O calls, such as *open()*, *read()*, *write()* and *close()*. An application or a process can produce on average between a dozen and thousands of system calls per execution, depending on the complexity of the task. As such system calls are ideal data signals from a security point of view, they provide a detailed view of a system or process operation while avoiding complex issues such as encryption or other possible higher level evasion mechanisms.

The focus of the MTA is to look for variable length unknown motifs in the data. This fits nicely with system calls as we are interested in seeing if motifs exist in system call execution sequences. Our inspiration originates from the way that programs are written, compiled and executed. An application usually consists of various classes, objects, methods or functions, along with variables and constants. All these structures are high level constructs, that are processed by lower level libraries which execute appropriate system calls accordingly. These atomic functions, which are deterministic as they do not depend on any variable input, are likely to form the building blocks of our motifs of interest, no matter what application calls them. The combination of such motifs could then provide a resource to generate a profile for a process that distinguishes a permitted execution from a malicious one.

The MTA provides a mechanism for compressing and summarising all this system call data into a number of repeating motifs that are prevalent in the data. The MTA would highlight consistent patterns in the data that are understandable and of value to the user, to aid in the generation of these process profiles. The ability of the MTA to find variable length motifs, with no assumptions about the data or the motifs to find, ensures it is flexible enough to carry out such a task.

4   Motif Detection: Terms and Definitions

Whilst immunology provides the inspiration for the theory behind the MTA (see [2] for more information), the work of Keogh et al. [8] is the inspiration for the time series representation used by the MTA. Keogh's Symbolic Aggregate approXimation (SAX) technique for representing a time series was utilised. Many of the following definitions used by the MTA are adapted from the work of Keogh [8], as summarised below.

Definition 1. *Time series.* A time series $T = t_1,...,t_m$ is a time ordered set of m real or integer valued variables. In order to identify patterns in T in a fast and efficient manner we break T up into subsequences.

Definition 2. *Subsequence.* "Given a time series T of length m, a subsequence C of T consists of a sampling of length $n \leq m$ of contiguous positions from T." [8]. Subsequences are extracted using a sliding window technique.

Definition 3. *Sliding window.* Given a time series T of length m, and a subsequence C of length n, a symbol matrix S of all possible subsequences can be built by sliding a window of size n across T, one point at a time, placing each subsequence into S. After all sliding windows are assessed S will contain ($m - n + 1$) subsequences. Each subsequence generated could represent a potential match to any of the other subsequences within S. If two subsequences match, we have found a pattern in the time series that is repeated. This pattern is defined as a motif.

Definition 4. *Motif.* A subsequence from T that is seen to repeat at least once throughout T is defined as a motif. The re-occurrence of the subsequence need not be exact for it to be considered as a motif. The relationship between two subsequences C_1 and C_2 is assessed using a match threshold r. We use the most common distance measure (Euclidean distance) to examine the match between two subsequences C_1 and C_2, $ED(C_1, C_2)$. If $ED(C_1, C_2) \leq r$ the subsequences C_1 and C_2 are deemed to match and thus are saved as a motif. The motifs prevalent in a time series are detected by the MTA through the evolution of a population of trackers.

Definition 5. *Tracker.* A tracker represents a signature for a motif sequence that is seen to repeat. It has within it a sequence of 1 to w symbols that are used to represent a dimensionally reduced equivalent of a subsequence. The subsequences generated from the time series are converted into a discrete symbol string using an intuitive technique described in Section 5. The trackers are then used as a tool to identify which of these symbol strings represent a recurring motif. The trackers also include a match count variable to indicate the level of stimulation received during the matching process.

5   The Motif Tracking Algorithm

The MTA pseudo code is detailed in Program 1. and a brief summary of this algorithm as applied to system call analysis is described in the subsequent sections. The MTA parameters include the length of a symbol s, the match threshold r, and the alphabet size a.

Convert Time Series T to Symbolic Representation. The MTA takes as input a univariate time series data set consisting of system call data which has been converted to a list of integers as described in Section 6. To minimise amplitude scaling issues with subsequence comparisons across T we normalise the time series. We then use the SAX representation [8] to discretise the time series under consideration. SAX is a powerful compression tool that uses a discrete, finite symbol set to generate a dimensionally reduced version of a time

---

Program 1. MTA Pseudo Code

```
Initiate MTA (s, r, a)
Convert Time series T to symbolic representation
Generate Symbol Matrix S
Initialise Tracker population to size a
While ( Tracker population > 0 )
{
    Generate motif candidate matrix M from S
    Match trackers to motif candidates
    Eliminate unmatched trackers
    Examine T to confirm genuine motif status
    Eliminate unsuccessful trackers
    Store motifs found
    Proliferate matched trackers
    Mutate matched trackers
}
Memory motif streamlining
```

---

series consisting of symbol strings. This intuitive representation has been shown to rival more sophisticated reduction methods such as Fourier transforms and wavelets [8].

Using SAX we slide a window of size s across the time series T one point at a time. Each sliding window represents a subsequence of system calls from T. The MTA calculates the average of the values from the sliding window and uses that average to represent the subsequence.

The MTA now converts this average value into a symbol string. The user pre-defines the size a of the alphabet used to represent the time series T. Given T has been normalised we can identify the breakpoints for the alphabet characters that generate a equal sized areas under the Gaussian curve [8]. The average value calculated for the sliding window is then examined against the breakpoints and converted into the appropriate symbol. This process is repeated for all sliding windows across T to generate m-s+1 subsequences, each consisting of symbol strings comprising one character.

Generate Symbol Matrix S. The string of symbols representing a subsequence is defined as a *word*. Each word generated from the sliding window is entered into the symbol matrix S. The MTA examines the time series T using these words and not the original data points to speed up the search process. Symbol string comparisons can be performed efficiently to filter out bad motif candidates, ensuring the computationally expensive Euclidean distance calculation is only performed on those motif candidates that are potentially genuine.

Having generated the symbol matrix S, the novelty of the MTA comes from the way in which each generation a selection of words from S, corresponding to the length of the motif under consideration, are extracted in an intuitive manner as a reduced set and presented to the tracker population for matching.

Initialise Tracker Population to Size a. The trackers are the primary tool used to identify motif candidates in the time series. A tracker comprises a sequence of 1 to w symbols. The symbol string contained within the tracker represents a sequence of symbols that are seen to repeat throughout T. Tracker initialisation and evolution is tightly regulated to avoid proliferation of ineffective motif candidates. The initial tracker population is constructed of size a to contain one of each of the viable alphabet symbols predefined by the user. Each tracker is unique, to avoid unnecessary duplication of solution candidates and wasted search time.

Trackers are created of a length of one symbol. The trackers are matched to motif candidates via the words presented from the stage matrix S. Trackers that match a word are stimulated; trackers that attain a stimulation level ≥ 2 indicate repeated words from T and become candidates for proliferation. Given a motif and a tracker that matches part of that motif, proliferation enables the tracker to extend its length by one symbol each generation until its length matches that of the motif.

Generate Motif Candidate Matrix M from S. The symbol matrix S contains a time ordered list of all the words, each containing just one symbol, that are present in the time series. Neighbouring words in S contain significant overlap as they were extracted via the sliding windows. Presenting all words in S to the tracker population would result in potentially inappropriate motifs being identified between neighbouring words. To prevent this issue such 'trivial' match candidates are removed from the symbol matrix S. Trivial match elimination (TME) is achieved as a word is only transferred from S for presentation to the tracker population if it differs from the previous word extracted. This allows the MTA to focus on significant variations in the time series and prevents excessive time being wasted on the search across uninteresting variations.

Excessively aggressive trivial match elimination is prevented by limiting the maximum number of consecutive trivial match eliminations to s, the number of data points encompassed by a symbol. In this way a subsequence can eliminate as trivial all subsequences generated from sliding windows that start in locations contained within that subsequence (if they generate the same symbol string) but no others. The reduced set of words selected from S is transferred to the motif candidate matrix M and presented to the tracker population for matching.

Match Trackers to Motif Candidates. During an iteration each tracker is taken in turn and compared to the set of words in M. Matching is performed using a simple string comparison between the tracker and the word. We define a match to occur if the comparison function returns a value of 0, indicating a perfect match between the symbol strings. Each matching tracker is stimulated by incrementing its match counter by 1.

Eliminate Unmatched Trackers. Trackers that have a match count >1 indicate symbols that are seen to repeat throughout T and are viable motif candidates. Eliminating all trackers with a match count < 2 ensures the MTA only searches for motifs from amongst these viable candidates. Knowledge of possible motif candidates from T is therefore carried forward by the tracker population. After elimination the match count of the surviving trackers is reset to 0.

Examine T to Confirm Genuine Motif Status. The surviving tracker population indicates which words in M represent viable motif candidates. However motif candidates with identical words may not represent a true match when looking at the time series data underlying the subsequences comprising those words. In order to confirm whether two matching words X and Y, containing the same symbol strings, correspond to a genuine motif we need to apply a distance measure to the original time series data associated with those candidates. The MTA uses the Euclidean distance to measure the relationship between two motif candidates $ED(X, Y)$.

If $ED(X, Y) \leq$ r a motif has been found. The match count of that tracker is stimulated to indicate a match. A memory motif is created to store the symbol string associated with X and Y. The start locations of X and Y are also saved.

For further information on the derivation of this matching threshold please refer to [2]. The MTA then continues its search for motifs, focusing only on those words in M that match the surviving tracker population in an attempt to find all occurrences of the potential motifs. The trackers therefore act as a pruning mechanism, reducing the potential search space to ensure the MTA only focuses on viable candidates.

Eliminate Unsuccessful Trackers. The MTA now removes any unstimulated trackers from the tracker population. These trackers represent symbol strings that were seen to repeat but upon further investigation with the underlying data were not proven to be valid motifs in T.

Store Motifs Found. The motifs identified during the confirmation stage are stored in the memory pool for review. Comparisons are made to remove any duplication. The final memory pool represents the compressed representation of the time series, containing all the re-occurring patterns present.

Proliferate Matched Trackers. Proliferation and mutation are needed to extend the length of the tracker so it can capture more of the complete motif. At the end of the first generation the surviving trackers, each consisting of a word containing a single symbol, represent all the symbols that are applicable to the motifs in T. The complete motifs in T can only consist of combination of these symbols. This subset of trackers is therefore stored as the mutation template for use by the MTA.

Proliferation and mutation to lengthen the trackers will only involve symbols from the mutation template and not the full symbol alphabet, as any other mutations would lead to unsuccessful motif candidates. During proliferation the MTA takes each surviving tracker in turn and generates a number of clones equal to the size of the mutation template. The clones adopt the same symbol string as their parent.

Mutate Matched Trackers. The clones generated from each parent are taken in turn and extended by adding a symbol taken consecutively from the mutation template. This creates a tracker population with maximal coverage of all potential motif solutions and no duplication. The tracker pool is fed back into the MTA ready for the next generation. A new motif candidate matrix M consisting of words with two symbols is now formulated to present to the evolved tracker population. In this way the MTA builds up the representation of a motif one symbol at a time each generation to eventually map to the full motif.

Given the symbol length s we generate a word consisting of two consecutive symbols by taking the symbol from matrix S at position i and that from position $i+s$. Repeating this across S, and applying trivial match elimination as per Section 5, the MTA obtains a new motif candidate matrix M in generation two, each entry of which contains a word of two symbols, covering a length of 2 x s.

The MTA continues to prepare and present new motif candidate matrix data to the evolving tracker population each generation. The motif candidates are built up one symbol at a time and matched to the lengthening trackers. This flexible approach enables the MTA to identify unknown motifs of a variable length. This process continues until all trackers are eliminated as non matching and the tracker population is empty. Any further extension to the tracker population will not improve their fit to any of the underlying motifs in T.

Memory Motif Streamlining. The MTA streamlines the memory pool, removing duplicates and those encapsulated within other motifs to produce a list of motifs that it associates with T.

6   Detection of System Call Patterns

This paper demonstrates that an execution of a process shall produce a sequence of system calls containing a number of motifs of variable lengths and these shall be identifiable by the MTA. Such motifs should re-occur when the same or similar processes are run. The motifs in system call sequences can be used in various security applications, for example as a data reduction tool for behaviour profiling within an Intrusion Detection System (IDS).

In our experiments we have two machines connected by a local network. The client machine (Windows XP machine running an SSH client PuTTY version 0.57) connects to the server machine (Debian Linux) which then performs actions based on commands sent by the client. Our experiments use a VMware virtual machine, running a Debian Linux distribution, v.3.3.5-13, with a Linux kernel, v.2.4.27-2, as our SSH server. The SSH daemon process (OpenSSH 3.8.1p1 Debian-8.sarge.6) is monitored along with all its children, using the standard *strace* utility. All system calls generated by the SSH daemon and its child processes are logged and stored in separate files based on their process ID (PID).

The following sequence of actions is executed to generate our data set. The client connects to the server and an SSH session is established. The following commands, chosen at random, are then issued by the client: *ls, ls, ls -lsa, pwd, ls, ps, ps aux, ls -lsa, chmod a+x file, chmod a+x directory, ls -lsa, chmod a-x file*. The client then disconnects from the SSH server.

The PID files generated are concatenated to produce one file. During concatenation the PID file from the child with the smallest PID is added to the parent data, this is then repeated for each remaining child process. Concatenation results in a single data set containing system call names with their respective arguments. The data is further pre-processed by converting the individual system call names to their appropriate Linux OS id numbers and removing their arguments. This generates a one dimensional data set comprising a sequence of 8,040 system call numbers.

From the data set generated it can be observed that a small sequence of system calls relating to one particular monitored child process is repeated across a large proportion of the data. This process looks after the SSH terminal operation for the duration of the whole SSH session. Repeated *read()* and *write()* calls and various real time system call actions are performed over and over again. Due to the basic nature of this repeating sequence, it is not deemed of interest to our analysis. Instead we focus on the last 1,000 system calls from the data set, to investigate motifs that occur during the last seven commands issued by the client. The data set generated is available at *http://cs.nott.ac.uk/~jqf/MTA_scdata.dat*.

7   Results

Having introduced the MTA we now provide some experimental results which examine the ability of the MTA to identify motifs present in system call data. As defined in Section 6 the data set examined consists of 1,000 system calls represented by an ordered list of 1,000 integers. A bind threshold $r = 0$ was set since system call sequences need to match identically. Symbol length s and alphabet size a values were varied to investigate the sensitivity of the MTA to these parameters. The MTA was written in C++ and run on a Windows XP machine with a Pentium M 1.7 Ghz processor with 1.0 Gb of RAM.

7.1   System Call Motifs Identified by the MTA

In this scenario $a = 10$ to give a large alphabet diversity and s took the values 10, 20 and 40. To evaluate the impact on speed and accuracy the MTA was run with trivial match elimination (TME) and with no trivial match elimination (NTME). We focus on significant motifs whose length exceeds 40 system calls to enable fair comparison across different values of s. With $s = 10$ and NTME eight motifs are identified. Table 1 lists these motifs with the number of system calls they encompass and the start locations where they occur in the data set.

Motif 1 dominates the data set, it consists of 280 system calls and occurs twice in the data set from locations 386 and 717. Figure 1 presents the list of system calls from location 350 to 1,000 and motif 1 is clearly evident in this sequence. From the commands issued during the SSH session (Section 6), we observe the existence of motifs within the command list itself as there are repetitions of the *ls* and *chmod* commands. From the MTA's analysis of the system

Table 1. List of motifs found by the MTA

Motif No.	Length	Start Locations
1	280	386, 717
2	80	0, 227
3	70	8, 160, 235
4	50	198, 262
5	50	668, 950
6	40	39, 191, 266, 324
7	40	619, 668, 950
8	40	77, 120

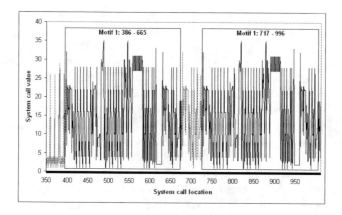

Fig. 1. Illustration of system calls 350 to 1,000, highlighting the occurrence of Motif 1 from system call 386 to 665 and 717 to 996

call data set, motif 1 relates to the repetition of these two observed commands. The *ls* commands contain the same arguments (*-lsa*) across both repetitions, whilst the *chmod* command includes execute permissions for all users to a file in the first occurrence and removes those same privileges from the file during the second occurrence. Motif 1 represents two processes occurring in succession at two different time points within the overall SSH session. Motif 1 also contains other sub-motifs such as motif 7. Motif 7 occurs at three different positions as seen from Table 1. This motif represents the *chmod* command that was executed three times during the session, each time with different arguments. The motifs found by the MTA are a super-set of those evident in the original command list, validating the accuracy of the MTA. The existence of motif 7 shows that applications with varying arguments (i.e. performing different actions), have atomic motifs that could be used for data reduction in a security application.

Motif 2 is the second largest motif, which has two repetitions in the data set. It relates to the execution of the *ps* command. This command occurred twice in succession, with different arguments, spawning a new process each time. Motif 2 represents 80 system calls that are identical across these two spawned processes. Motifs 3, 4 and 8 partly overlap with motif 2 indicating a subset of system calls from motif 2 that is consistent across all these motifs. However this subset occurs with a higher frequency than motif 2, representing similarities between atomic parts of the *ps* processes not fully captured by the motif 2. This highlights parts of the process execution that are more dynamic and input dependent and which need to be dealt with when considering an IDS.

Motif 6 again relates to a component of the *ps* command. At a lower level, the *ps* command reads a number of small files from the /proc/ directory of the Linux OS and prints the read information onto the screen. This information shows the running processes on the system to the user. From this a recurring sub-pattern of *open()*, *read()* and *close()* system calls with various arguments is observed. This sub-pattern is largely dependant on the input of the *ps* command.

In this case it is the number of running processes on the monitored system, which in turn is the number of files in the aforementioned /proc/ directory. The motifs generated by the MTA are formed by such atomic system call sequences. The randomness in the input, which results in motifs of variable lengths is of major importance when considering IDS systems. For this purpose a system call expression language is proposed which, besides giving the MTA an alternative representation to assess system call similarity, gives security researchers a regular expression type language for describing system call motifs at a higher level. This language is described in more detail in Section 8.

In the above analysis we have focused on significant motifs with sequences exceeding 40 system calls. The advantage of using the MTA on system call data and not the command list becomes apparent when we look at the shorter motifs that are generated, as these indicate atomic motifs that are found across varying command instructions. One such motif, referred to as Z, has a length of 30 system calls and occurred five times at positions 387, 620, 669, 718 and 951. Motif Z relates to the re-occurrence of a sequence that occurs during the initialisation of newly spawned processes executed across the commands *ls -lsa, chmod a+x file, chmod a+x directory, ls -lsa* and *chmod a-x file* respectively. Each C application under Linux, when it starts, calls and loads the standard C library, *libc*. The occurrences of motif Z corresponds to the loading of this library. Thus the MTA has found a motif that is present but embedded across differing commands. This approach of using system calls as input to the MTA, and not the commands, would aid in the detection of exploits that are far smaller than the commands themselves. An example of such an exploit is the *SQL slammer* worm which is only 376 bytes long, compared to the text segment of the *chmod* command of 29,212 bytes.

7.2   Sensitivity to Changes in the Symbol Length s

In total 961 of the 1,000 system calls are identified as being part of one or more of these eight motifs. From these results it is clear the MTA is able to successfully identify a reduced set of motifs from the large system call data set. By varying the value of s and the use of trivial match elimination we can examine the sensitivity of the MTA and assess its ability to retain knowledge of these eight motifs. The results of this sensitivity analysis can be seen in Table 2.

Table 2 shows the total number of motifs found and the execution time of the MTA for the various values of s. In addition a measure of the quality of

Table 2. Sensitivity of the MTA to variations in the symbol length s

s	Motifs found		Execution time (sec)		Motif quality measure	
	NTME	TME	NTME	TME	NTME	TME
10	8	6	315.8	262.0	1,490	1,230
20	5	4	56.9	26.5	1,140	940
40	4	3	12.1	1.9	960	720

the motifs found is included by multiplying the identified length of the motif by the identified frequency and summing for all motifs found. Any omissions in the length or frequency of the complete motif will cause a decline in this quality measure.

As the symbol length s increases, the number of motifs detected declines. This appears logical as a higher s implies the search is less fine grained. Introducing TME also reduces the number of motifs found. TME significantly reduces the size of the motif candidate matrix M resulting in fewer candidates being examined. TME is key to the dimensionality reduction of the original data set leading to a fast search process, however it would appear that its inclusion does lead to a loss in detection accuracy.

Given NTME, the MTA is only able to identify four of the eight motifs (1, 2, 6 and 7) if s rises from 10 to 40. The quality measure also indicates that, of the motifs found, there appears to be a loss in the detection of the full length or frequency of occurrence. The quality measure falls from 1,490 to 960. Of the four motifs still detected we lose 40 system calls from motif 1 and we only detect two of the three repetitions of motif 7. However raising the symbol length from 10 to 40 results in a 96.2% reduction in the MTA execution time, taking only 12.1 seconds compared to 315.8.

7.3 Sensitivity to Changes in the Alphabet Size a

Adjusting the alphabet size alters the symbol set used to represent the time series. Reducing a means a greater diversity of sequences are now grouped together as similar. TME with a reduced alphabet set should lead to a larger number of trivial match eliminations, leading to a faster but potentially less accurate search. This hypothesis is confirmed when we look at Table 3 which lists the motifs found for various alphabet sizes. In this scenario $s = 20$, $r = 0$ and a took the values 10, 8, 6, and 4.

Table 3 shows the alphabet size has no impact on the detection ability of the MTA if there is NTME. The five motifs detected when $s = 20$, $a = 10$ (Table 2) are always found and have the same quality measurement. However the search time of the MTA with NTME improves by 30.1% as a is reduced from 10 to 4.

With TME activated, changes to a have a more significant impact on the motifs detected. Reducing a from 10 to 8 causes the MTA to lose track of motif 8 but it now finds motif 2. As motif 2 is longer than motif 8 we get an improvement

Table 3. Sensitivity of the MTA to variations in the alphabet size a

a	Motifs found		Execution time (sec)		Motif quality measure	
	NTME	TME	NTME	TME	NTME	TME
10	5	4	56.9	26.5	1,140	940
8	5	5	48.0	19.8	1,140	1,140
6	5	3	43.3	16.1	1,140	860
4	5	5	39.8	6.3	1,140	1,140

in the overall motif quality measure from 940 to 1,140. Reducing a further from 8 to 4 causes the MTA to lose motif 6 but gain knowledge of motif 4. Thus we see that TME causes a change in the location in search space where the MTA conducts its search, resulting in less consistent results.

One could imply that this inconsistency due to trivial match elimination is detrimental to this particular search problem but this need not be the case. As is evident from Table 3 trivial match elimination significantly improves the search time of the MTA and the results from including trivial match elimination are still satisfactory. When $a=4$ activating trivial match elimination results in the MTA still finding five motifs but it reduces the search time by 84.2% from 39.8 seconds to 6.3 seconds and with no loss to the quality of those five motifs found.

7.4   Summary Discussion of Results

From these results it is apparent that the MTA is able to identify motifs that are present in this system call data set. The MTA can compress the original data set of 1,000 system calls down to eight repeating motifs. A trade off between speed and accuracy becomes apparent as the user is able to adjust the parameters of the algorithm to speed up the search process at the cost of a reduction in detection capability, allowing a flexible search mechanism.

The sensitivity to changes in s and a noted here is due to the nature of system call data. In this paper we group system calls together as similar by averaging their system call values over a fixed sized window. These are then grouped by boundary conditions and represented by a symbol which is then subject to trivial match elimination. With system calls there is no real relationship between two separate system call values, i.e. system call 2 is not twice as large as system call 1. Therefore one could argue that a more appropriate representation may be more suitable as is discussed in Section 8.

The results show that the MTA, developed to identify motifs in financial and industrial data sets, is successful in identifying motifs in system call data due to its generic and flexible approach. It provides a useful tool to compress a large data set into small subset of repeating patterns that are of immediate value to the user.

8   Future Work

The difficulty with analysing system call sequences for the purposes of intrusion detection is that the variety of sequences generated is largely dependant on the diversity of the application's input. This potential variety sidesteps most forms of pattern detection as long as the detection mechanism is not able to encode the variations in a manner that is granular enough to be able to distinguish between normal and anomalous patterns. To address this issue, as part of our future work we propose a system call expression language (SCEL), which acts as a higher level regular expression type language consisting of constructs representing atomic system call motifs of meaningful actions.

An example of this language can be presented using motif Z of length 30 as described in Section 7. In the SCEL motif Z could be represented by a higher level construct, such as *lib_loading(libc)*. Where *lib_loading* represents a particular set of motifs for that action and *(libc)* denotes the class to which those motifs belong. Similar constructs could be devised for other operations which contain atomic motifs, representative of a higher level functionality. The motifs 2, 3, 4, and 8 in Table 1 indicate the re-occurrence of the *open()*, *read()* and *close()* system calls. These three calls could now be represented as one *file_read(small)* construct to be used for files below a certain size threshold. In addition a *file_read(large)* construct containing a wild card for the number of *read()* system calls between the *open()* and *close()* calls can be generated for instances when reading larger files, where numerous *read()* calls are executed depending on the file's size. When reading such a file an attribute of the language construct could denote the number of motifs present in an observed process.

For example ***lib_loading(libc)[1], file_read(small)[*], other(*)[*]*** could denote a complete *ps* command being executed. This language tool would prove of value to a user as it focuses on a high level of abstraction while maintaining the ability to conduct fine grained analysis of system calls. This new representation for system call similarity could now also be used as input for the MTA to enhance its motif detection ability.

9   Conclusion

The search for patterns or motifs in data represents a generic problem area that is of great interest to a huge variety of researchers. By extracting motifs that exist in data we gain some understanding as to the nature and characteristics of that data, so that we can benefit from that knowledge. The motifs provide an obvious mechanism to cluster, classify and summarise the data, placing great value on these patterns.

Little research has been performed looking for *unknown* motifs in time series. The MTA takes up this challenge using a novel immune inspired approach to evolve a population of trackers that seek out and match motifs present in a time series. The MTA uses a minimal number of parameters with minimal assumptions and requires no knowledge of the data examined or the underlying motifs, unlike other alternative approaches.

In this paper the MTA was applied to motif detection in system call data. The MTA was shown to compress the data set into a limited number of motifs that provide good coverage of the original data set resulting in a minimal loss of information. The authors propose that these motifs highlight repeating or atomic functions that can be used to build profiles of "system behaviour". These profiles could then assist in tasks such as anomaly detection or behaviour classification.

The authors provide information on a system call expression language that addresses system call granularity issues for computer security applications in the future. In its current form we believe the MTA offers a valuable contribution to an area of research that at present has received surprisingly little attention.

References

1. Nunn, I., White, T.: The application of antigenic search techniques to time series forecasting. In: GECCO, pp. 353–360 (June 2005)
2. Wilson, W.O., Birkin, P., Aickelin, U.: Motif detection inspired by immune memory. In: ICARIS 2007. Proceedings of the 6th International Conference on Artificial Immune Systems, Santos, Brazil. LNCS, Springer, Heidelberg (2007)
3. de Castro, L.N., Von Zuben, F.J.: Learning and optimization using the clonal selection principle. IEEE Transactions on Evolutionary Computation 6(3), 239–251 (2002)
4. Lin, J., Keogh, E., Lonardi, S., Patel, P.: Finding motifs in time series. In: The 2nd workshop on temporal data mining, at the 8th ACM SIGKDD international conference on knowledge discovery and data mining (July 2002)
5. Guan, X., Uberbacher, E.C.: A fast look up algorithm for detecting repetitive DNA sequences. In: Pacific symposium on biocomputing, Hawaii IEEE Tran. Control Systems Tech. (December 1996)
6. Keogh, E., Smyth, P.: A probabilistic approach to fast pattern matching in time series databases. In: Proceedings of the third international conference of knowledge discovery and data mining, pp. 20–24 (1997)
7. Faloutsos, C., Ranganathan, M., Manolopoulos, Y.: Fast subsequence matching in time series databases. In: Proceedings of the SIGMOD conference, pp. 419–429 (1994)
8. Chiu, B., Keogh, E., Lonardi, S.: Probabilistic discovery of time series motifs. In: SIGKDD (August 2003)
9. Lin, J., Keogh, E., Lonardi, S.: Visualizing and discovering non trivial patterns in large time series databases. Information visualization 4(2), 61–82 (2005)
10. Tanaka, Y., Uehara, K.: Discover motifs in multi-dimensional time series using the principal component analysis and the MDL principle. In: 3rd international conference on machine learning and data mining in pattern recognition, Leipzig, Germany, pp. 252–265 (2003)
11. Fu, T.C., Chung, F.L., Ng, V., Luk, R.: Pattern discovery from stock market time series using self organizing maps. In: Workshop notes of KDD 2001 workshop on temporal data mining, San francisco, CA, pp. 27–37 (2001)
12. Forrest, S., Hofmeyr, S.A., Somayaji, A., Longstaff, T.A.: A sense of self for UNIX processes. In: IEEE Symposium on Security and Privacy, pp. 120–128. IEEE Computer Society Press, Oakland, CA (1996)
13. Sekar, R., Bowen, T., Segal, M.: On preventing intrusions by process behavior monitoring. In: Proceedings of the Workshop on Intrusion Detection and Network Monitoring, pp. 29–40. USENIX Association, Berkeley, CA (1999)
14. Warrender, C., Forrest, S., Pearlmutter, B.: Detecting intrusions using system calls: Alternative data models. In: Proceedings of the 1999 Conference on Security and Privacy (S&P-99), pp. 133–145. IEEE Press, Los Alamitos (1999)
15. Tandon, G., Chan, P., Mitra, D.: Morpheus: Motif oriented representations to purge hostile events from unlabeled sequences. In: Proceedings of the 2004 ACM workshop on Visualization and data mining for computer security, pp. 16–25. ACM Press, New York (2004)

Comparative Studies in Key Disagreement Correction Process on Wireless Key Agreement System

Toru Hashimoto[1,*], Takashi Itoh[1], Masazumi Ueba[1], Hisato Iwai[2], Hideichi Sasaoka[2], Kazukuni Kobara[4,3], and Hideki Imai[3,4]

[1] ATR Wave Engineering Laboratories, Japan
[2] Doshisha University, Japan
[3] Chuo University, Japan
[4] National Institute of Advanced Industrial Science and Technology (AIST), Japan
hashi@atr.jp

Abstract. This paper describes the comparison of the error-correcting codes that is adopted by the key disagreement correction process about wireless key agreement system called ESPARSKEY that is expected to achieve information-theoretic security. This system consists of AP with a variable directional antenna, that is, an ESPAR antenna, and UT with an omni-directional antenna. We employ conditional mutual information as the evaluation index. From experimental evaluation results, we clarified that the best way is adopting BCH(31,16,7) with table-aided soft-decision decoding as the key disagreement process where one eavesdropper exists more than 40cm from UT. After adopting this error-correcting code, we should transact 200 wireless packets between the nodes to share a 128-bit unguessable key against an eavesdropper.

1   Introduction

The rapid progress of such wireless communication technologies as RF devices, signal processing, modulation methods, antennas, and so on have greatly contributed to the cost reduction of terminals and the speed-up of wireless communication. As a result, such wireless communication as Wireless LAN or Personal Digital Cellular has become more popular and convenient.

On the other hand, this popularization causes threats, such as tapping by eavesdroppers (passive attacks) and impersonations from third parties (active attacks). For active attacks, mutual authentication is the best solution, many kinds of which are incorporated in much application software.

* This work is part of "Research and development of ultra-high speed giga-bit rate wireless LAN systems" granted by National Institute of Information and Communications Technology (NICT).

S. Kim, M. Yung, and H.-W. Lee (Eds.): WISA 2007, LNCS 4867, pp. 173–187, 2007.

The easiest way to protect wireless communication data from passive attackers is to encrypt the data with either public key encryption or common key encryption. The public key encryption system does not need an identical key for encryption and decryption, which is an advantage from view of the key management that includes key distribution, generation, sharing, and so on.

But it has the disadvantage of low speed. Therefore, it has mainly been used for key exchange, authentication schemes, and digital signatures. Though a common key encryption system can encrypt and decrypt at high speed, it must manage common secret keys between nodes. For secure encryption using common key encryption schemes, key management between nodes is crucial.

In the past, many kinds of key management schemes, especially key sharing or generating methods, have been proposed and adopted at many established wireless networks. Representative examples include the Diffie-Hellman key exchange algorithm [1] and key distribution methods using public key encryption such as RSA cryptosystem [2]. Both methods can be decoded in practical time if eavesdroppers have high computational power, which continues to increase rapidly, because the security of both is based on the difficulty of calculation, such as the Discrete Logarithm Problem or prime factorization called "computational security."

On the other hand, some methods are "unconditional (information-theoretic) secure," based on quantum cryptography [3], noisy communication channels [4] [5], fluctuation of radio wave channels [6], and so on. Even assuming that eavesdroppers have infinite computational power, these methods are secure since they are based on information-theoretic security.

In these methods, the most practical solution for wireless communication systems is the fluctuation of the radio wave channel response. Aono et al. [7] proposed a system based on the fluctuation of radio wave channels called ESPARSKEY that generates and shares keys without distributing them. In addition, for the intentional fluctuation of radio waves, this system exploits a variable directional antenna that is called Electronically Steerable Parasitic Array Radiator (ESPAR) antenna [8]. In this system, security evaluation studies have been performed. Imai et al. [9] reported that this system can achieve unconditionally secure key agreement as long as the passive eavesdropper is not located too close (on the order of tens of centimeters) to the players.

In this paper, we describe the comparison of the error-correcting codes that is adopted by the key disagreement correction process for secure key generating concerning ESPARSKEY. The key disagreement correction process has possibilities not only of increasing the mutual information between AP and UT but also decreasing of the mutual information between EV and UT for miscorrection by error-correcting codes. As the result, the possibility to achieve unconditionally secure key agreement increases. We give the details of the wireless key generation system including its components, principle, and procedure in Section 2, an evaluation index in Section 3, and experiments and evaluations in Section 4. Finally we conclude this paper in Section 5.

Fig. 1. Outline of AP

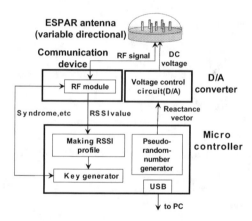

Fig. 2. Function block diagram of AP

2 Wireless Key Agreement System

2.1 System Configuration

This system consists of Access Point(AP) and User Terminal(UT). AP's outline drawing is shown in Fig. 1, and its function block diagram is shown in Fig. 2 and consists of four parts: "Communication device," "Microcontroller," "D/A converter," and "7-element ESPAR antenna."

- The "Communication device" is a CC2420 [10], which is a single-chip 2.4 GHz IEEE 802.15.4 compliant RF transceiver with baseband modem and MAC support. The simple specifications of the IEEE802.15.4 standard are shown in Table. 1. IEEE 802.15.4 is used at "ZigBee" as a physical layer and a MAC layer specification [11]. Such data as syndrome, initial value, etc.

Table 1. Specifications of IEEE802.15.4

Frequency	2.4 GHz (ISM band)
	· same as wireless LAN
	(IEEE802.11b/g)
Channel number	16 CH (CH 11~CH 26)
	· use all CH for key generation
	· use arbitrary 1 CH for control
Transmission power	1 mW
Data rate	250 kbps

are set with a microcontroller and communicate with packets through an ESPAR antenna. The received power of packets is measured and converted into an RSSI value in this chip.

- "Microcontroller" carries out the "making RSSI profile" and "generating the key" steps in the "key generator" function. These steps are based on the RSSI value from the "Communication device." "Microcontroller" has a USB port to send the generated keys to a PC by USB cable. The "7-element ESPAR antenna" needs DC voltage to control the beam pattern of the antenna. The seeds of DC voltage, called reactance vectors, are made in the "Pseudo random number generator" function in the "Microcontroller," which is set to the "D/A converter."

- The "D/A converter" changes the digital value of the reactance vectors into analog DC voltage and sets this voltage to the varactor in the "ESPAR antenna." The DC voltage, which ranges from 0 to 5 [V], is set randomly in 4 bits resolution at the "D/A converter." For example, the radiation patterns of the 7-element ESPAR antenna result in $2^{4^6} = 16^6 = 16777216$ patterns, because it has six parasitic elements.

- The "ESPAR antenna," which is a variable-directional array antenna with a single central active radiator surrounded by parasitic elements, is a component of AP. The six parasitic elements are located at equal intervals around a single central active radiator, and each is loaded with a varactor diode, which is a variable-capacitance diode. By adjusting the DC voltage given to the varactors with reverse bias, the antenna's beam can be formed. Because it only has a single RF radiator, it is expected to have lower power consumption than Digital Beam-Forming (DBF) array antennas. Many studies using this antenna have been performed for personal wireless communication or the direction of arrival estimation.

UT's outline drawing is shown in Fig. 3, and its function block diagram is shown in Fig. 4. They consist of three parts: "an omni-directional patch antenna," "a communication device," and "a microcontroller." The role of each block is identical to AP except for the antenna. The node is connected to the PC by a USB interface.

Fig. 3. Outline of UT

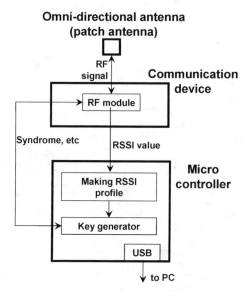

Fig. 4. Function block diagram of UT

2.2   Key Generation

Principle of Key Generation. This key generation system is based on the reciprocity theorem of radio wave propagation between AP and UT. In addition, a variable directional antenna called ESPAR antenna is used for intentional fluctuation. The key is made by this fluctuation of radio waves.

We describe the principle of key generation in detail. We use the beam-forming technique of the ESPAR antenna; that is, by adjusting the DC voltage given to the varactors with reverse bias, we can intentionally undulate the response of the propagation channels between the two nodes. In this condition, we measure the Received Signal Strength Indicator (RSSI) by alternately transmitting short packets between nodes. From this measurement, AP and UT can independently obtain RSSI profiles whose characteristics are identical due to the reciprocity theorem of radio wave propagation. The same value is provided by making these

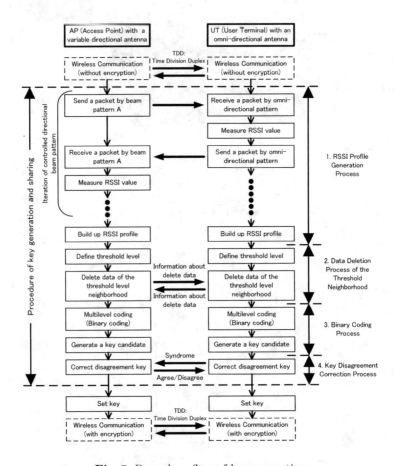

Fig. 5. Procedure flow of key generation

profiles multilevel coding, for example, binary coding. As a result, these values
are generated keys in this system.

An eavesdropper (EV), who is a passive attacker listening at another place,
has difficulty obtaining the same key between nodes because EV cannot obtain
the same RSSI profile from AP and UT since their propagation characteristics
are different.

Procedure. Here we describe in detail the procedure of our key generation system. The preconditions are set as follows. AP has a 7-element ESPAR antenna,
and UT has a conventional omni-directional antenna. EV is identical as UT
except for the location. AP and UT can communicate at the same frequency by
a method such as Time Division Duplex (TDD). The DC voltage sets at each
varactor diode are connected to the parasitic element of the 7-element ESPAR
antenna using a pseudorandom number.

The procedure of this system is shown in Fig. 5 and described as follows.

1. **RSSI Profile Generation Process**

   AP decides a certain directional beam pattern by obtaining pseudorandom numbers and sending a short packet to UT, which receives a packet from AP and computes the RSSI value by measuring the received power. A computed RSSI value is recorded in UT's memory. UT returns a short packet to AP as soon as possible to maintain a propagation environment. AP receives a packet from UT and computes and records the RSSI value as well as UT. If a packet isn't received by UT or AP, a packet-send-error is recognized by timeout, and AP will change the beam pattern and retry transmission.

   Next, AP changes the directional beam pattern and repeats the above procedure N times. Here, N consists of key length K and the length of redundant bit α, $N = K + \alpha$. AP and UT can independently compile a RSSI data profile. Thanks to the reciprocity theorem of radio wave propagation between AP and UT, this profile in the nodes is identical, except for the random noise, the differences in transmission power, the receiver's noise figures, and such antenna performance factors as sensitivity or directivity. From each profile, AP and UT independently define a threshold level that is considered the median value of each RSSI profile in this system. Now the value of the RSSI profile includes noise components. To reduce their influence, this system has a data deletion process of the threshold neighborhood, which is shown in Fig. 6.

2. **Data Deletion Process of the Threshold Neighborhood**

   AP and UT have an RSSI profile the size of N. As shown above, N consists of key length K and the length of redundant bit α. In Fig. 6, K is defined as 6 and α as 4. From this profile, the threshold level is decided by the median value of each RSSI profile sorted afterwards in each node by ascending order. At AP, a subset of the RSSI value is chosen as the most susceptible place for noise by picking the largest $K/2 + \beta$ and the smallest $K/2 + \beta$ RSSI values, with $\beta < \alpha/2$ (in Fig. 6, β is defined as 1). The positions of the unchosen RSSI values are transmitted to UT and deleted at AP and UT. At UT, the RSSI values undeleted by transmitted information from AP are sorted again and the process is repeated, this time choosing the largest $K/2$ and smallest $K/2$ RSSI values from the remaining RSSI values. Again, the positions of the unchosen RSSI values are transmitted to AP, and unchosen RSSI values are deleted at both nodes. The remaining RSSI profiles whose size is K are sorted again by original number.

3. **Binary Coding Process**

   These RSSI profiles that have been coded to binary using the threshold level defined above are candidates for the shared key.

4. **Key Disagreement Correction Process**

   The key disagreement correction process is carried out on these candidates by an error-correcting code to produce the shared secure keys. In this process, we basically consider the bit patterns of key candidates a series of such block code as BCH code. In this condition, we calculate each syndrome,

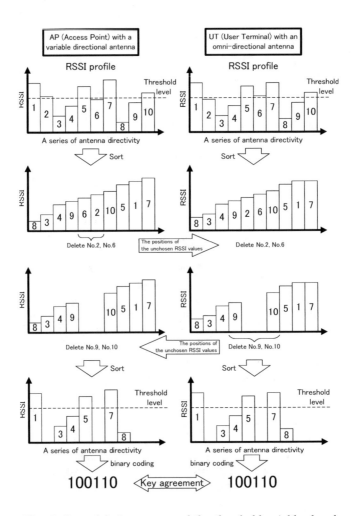

Fig. 6. Data deletion process of the threshold neighborhood

$S_{AP} = x_{AP}\mathbf{H^T}$, and $S_{UT} = x_{UT}\mathbf{H^T}$, where x_{AP} and x_{UT} are bit patterns in the key candidates of AP and UT, respectively, $\mathbf{H^T}$ denotes a check matrix, and superscript ^{T} is the transpose of the matrix. Calculated syndrome S_{UT} is transmitted from UT to AP. At AP, we define the differences in the syndrome as $S = S_{AP} - S_{UT}$ and in the bit patterns as $e = x_{AP} - x_{UT}$. The relationship between these parameters is expressed as $S = e\mathbf{H^T}$. If $S = 0$ is true, then $e = 0$ is true, and both bit patterns of the key candidates are considered to be in agreement. If $S = 0$ is false, then we will correctly estimate e to minimize the number of disagreement bits by an error correction technique. If no agreement is obtained after the key disagreement correction process, the generated key is rejected, and the entire process is repeated.

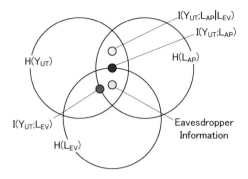

Fig. 7. Entropy relation of L_{AP}, Y_{UT}, and L_{EV}

3   Security Evaluation Index

Fig. 7 denotes the entropies and their relation of L_{AP}, Y_{UT}, and L_{EV}. In this figure, L is the set of levels, and Y is the binary encoded data, $Y \in \{0,1\}^N$. Each node obtains these values from RSSI profiles. We calculate entropies (H) and information (I) by estimating the error rate. To estimate the error rate, we tried the time of the N_p key generation procedure to show in Fig. 5. This error rate estimation procedure is described as the following protocol [9]:

Protocol

1. For $i = 1$ *to* N_p do:
   (a) For $i = 1$ *to* N do:
      i. *AP* sends a packet to *UT*, who receives it, measures its RSSI value, and records it as $R_{UT}(i)$.
      ii. As soon as possible *UT* returns a packet to *AP*, who receives it, measures its RSSI value, and records it as $R_{AP}(i)$.
      iii. *AP* changes the radiation pattern.
      Endfor.
      AP and *UT* conclude with their RSSI value sets R_{AP} and R_{UT}, respectively.
   (b) Both AP and UT perform the following:
      i. R is sorted by ascending order $L \in \{1, 2, \dots, N\}$ and is coded to binary using threshold level T_{N_p}, which is the median value of each RSSI profiles, that is, $Y_i = 0$, if $R(i) < T_{N_p}$ and otherwise $Y_i = 1$. *AP* and *UT* conclude with Y_{AP} and Y_{UT}, respectively.
      ii. *AP* and *UT* announce Y_{AP} and Y_{UT} to each other. For $i = 1, 2, \dots, N$, *AP* and *UT* calculate: $err(i) = err(i) + 1$, if $Y_{AP}(i) \neq Y_{UT}(i)$.
      Endfor.
2. *AP* and *UT* compute the estimated error rate(p_i) for each level as follows:
   For $i = 1, 2, \dots, N,\ :\ p_i = err(i)/N_p$

EV can get its own RSSI value and estimate the error rate by tapping the communication between AP and UT. After this procedure, we can calculate entropies $H(L_{AP})$, $H(Y_{UT})$, and so on.

In Fig. 5, the intersection of $H(L_{AP})$ and $H(Y_{UT})$ is the amount of information about Y_{UT} obtained from L_{AP}. In other words, it is mutual information $I(Y_{UT}; L_{AP})$ between $H(Y_{UT})$ and $H(L_{AP})$.

Evaluation of only this quantity presents a problem because this quantity does not consider the eavesdropper. Because this mutual information $I(Y_{UT}; L_{AP})$ includes information obtained by eavesdroppers, their influence must be removed. The information obtained by the eavesdropper is shown at the intersection of $H(L_{AP})$, $H(Y_{UT})$, and $H(L_{EV})$ and is marked "Eavesdropper Information" in Fig. 7. For simplicity, we consider this value mutual information $I(Y_{UT}; L_{EV})$ between $H(Y_{UT})$ and $H(L_{EV})$, and we can get the upper bound of the information obtained by the eavesdropper. This quantity is shown at the intersection of $H(Y_{UT})$ and $H(L_{EV})$ in Fig. 7. We need to evaluate mutual information $I(Y_{UT}; L_{EV})$ in addition to the former evaluation.

From these evaluations, the lower bound of mutual information $I(Y_{UT}; L_{AP}|L_{EV})$ (based on L_{AP}) that an eavesdropper can't know is shown as:

$$I(Y_{UT}; L_{AP}|L_{EV}) \geq I(Y_{UT}; L_{AP}) - I(Y_{UT}; L_{EV}) \tag{1}$$

In the same way, the lower bound of $I(Y_{AP}; L_{UT}|L_{EV})$ (based on L_{UT}) is shown as:

$$I(Y_{AP}; L_{UT}|L_{EV}) \geq I(Y_{AP}; L_{UT}) - I(Y_{AP}; L_{EV}) \tag{2}$$

In this paper, we show the calculation result of Eq. (1) defined as the "conditional mutual information per round" because there is little difference between the calculation result of Eqs. (1) and (2).

4   Evaluation Experiments and Simulations

4.1   Experimental Condition

The conditions of the key generation method are described as follows. Key length K is 128 bits, and the length of redundant bit α, described in Subsection 2.2, is 256 bits. In other words, the number of RSSI value N is 384 at each node. N_p is at least 100 key generations.

This experimental system has an eavesdropper (EV), whose figure and function block diagram is the same as UT. The difference between UT and EV is the positions in which the packet was received.

The experimental room in which we carried out key generation experiments is shown in Fig. 8. Each node was arranged in 141 points all over the experiment room that has three metal walls and one concrete wall. The experiment was performed in turn by each node.

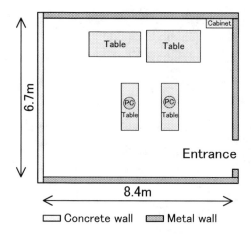

Fig. 8. Sketch of experimental room

4.2 Security Evaluation without Key Disagreement Correction Process

First, we evaluated the security on this wireless key agreement system. Fig. 9 shows the security evaluation results by conditional mutual information. The vertical scale of this graph is the mutual information per round in each result. The word "round" means the process by which AP sends a packet to UT and UT returns it to AP. In this result, we find the following three things:

- The mutual information between AP and UT shown in (a) is high level at any distance.
- The mutual information between EV and UT shown in (b) is high level when the distance between EV and UT is close.
- The system exhibits conditional mutual information 0.6 or higher when there is one EV more than 40 cm from UT.

This means that to share a 128-bit unguessable key against an eavesdropper in this procedure without the key disagreement correction process, we should transact 214 wireless packets between the nodes.

4.3 Comparison of Error-Correcting Codes Concerning Key Disagreement Correction Process by Computer Simulation

Preparation. When we compare the differences between the error-correctiong codes concerning key disagreement correction processes by computer simulation, the following four types of coding methods have been prepared that mainly focus on implementation for this system:

Method 1. BCH(31,21,5) with table-aided hard-decision decoding.
Method 2. BCH(31,16,7) with table-aided hard-decision decoding.

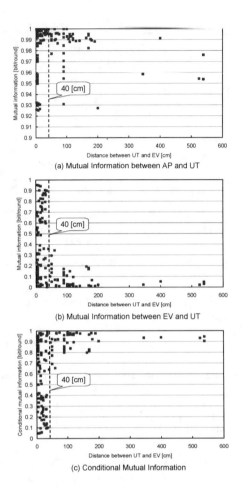

Fig. 9. Mutual information without key disagreement correction process whose function is distance between UT and EV

Method 3. BCH(31,21,5) with table-aided soft-decision decoding.
Method 4. BCH(31,16,7) with table-aided soft-decision decoding.

The aided table for decoding is pre-shared by all terminals.

Comparison of Mutual Information between AP and UT. Table 2 shows the mutual information between AP and UT. This value is the first term in Eq. (1). Five methods, one of which is the case of whthout a key disagreement correction process and another is described as the method of the key disagreement correction process in the previous subsection, are shown in this table. In addition, they divided by arranging EV. Case 1 is all the points in this experiment, case 2 is the points whose EV is located within 40 cm from UT, and case 3 is the other points.

Table 2. Comparison of Mutual Information between AP and UT

	no error correction	Coding Method 1	Coding Method 2	Coding Method 3	Coding Method 4
Case 1 141 points	0.9854 (—)	0.9915 (0.0061)	0.9921 (0.0069)	0.9920 (0.0066)	0.9923 (0.0069)
Case 2 89 points	0.9857 (—)	0.9927 (0.0070)	0.9938 (0.0081)	0.9935 (0.0078)	0.9939 (0.0082)
Case 3 52 points	0.9848 (—)	0.9894 (0.0045)	0.9893 (0.0045)	0.9895 (0.0047)	0.9896 (0.0047)

(bit/round)

Table 3. Comparison of Mutual Information between EV and UT

	no error correction	Coding Method 1	Coding Method 2	Coding Method 3	Coding Method 4
Case 1 141 points	0.2729 (—)	0.2518 (-0.0211)	0.2719 (-0.0010)	0.2486 (-0.0243)	0.2645 (-0.0084)
Case 2 89 points	0.3788 (—)	0.3535 (-0.0253)	0.3836 (0.0048)	0.3556 (-0.0232)	0.3866 (0.0078)
Case 3 52 points	0.0917 (—)	0.0776 (-0.0141)	0.0808 (-0.0109)	0.0655 (-0.0262)	0.0555 (-0.0362)

(bit/round)

This table means that the key disagreement correction process is effective for mutual information between AP and UT for all methods regardless of the distance between EV and UT.

Comparison of Mutual Information between EV and UT. Table 3 shows the mutual information between EV and UT. This value is the second term in Eq. (1). When EV is located near UT, methods 1 and 3 are more effective for the mutual information between EV and UT than methods 2 or 4 because the possibility that the RSSI profile of EV is similar to UT's profile increases when the distance of each node is short. Moreover, a different feature is found in which method 4 is the most effective in case 3. Miscorrection occurs in the key disagreement correction process based on the syndrome received by EV because the RSSI profile of EV is different from that of UT in case 3.

Comparison of Conditional Mutual Information. Table 4 shows the conditional mutual information defined in Eq.(1). In this result, we clarified the effectiveness of the key disagreement correction process based on the error-correcting codes. Conditional mutual information has only increased 0.04 bit or less using this process. In fact, the best way is to adopt BCH(31,16,7) with table-aided soft-decision decoding as the key disagreement correction process when there is one EV more than 40 cm from UT. To share a 128-bit unguessable key against

Table 4. Comparison of Conditional Mutual Information

	no error correction	Coding Method 1	Coding Method 2	Coding Method 3	Coding Method 4
Case 1 141 points	0.7125 (—)	0.7397 (0.0273)	0.7202 (0.0077)	0.7434 (0.0309)	0.7278 (0.0154)
Case 2 89 points	0.6069 (—)	0.6392 (0.0323)	0.6101 (0.0033)	0.6378 (0.0310)	0.6073 (0.0004)
Case 3 52 points	0.8932 (—)	0.9118 (0.0186)	0.9085 (0.0154)	0.9241 (0.0309)	0.9341 (0.0409)

(bit/round)

an eavesdropper in this procedure with the key disagreement correction process, we should transact 200 wireless packets between the nodes.

5   Conclusion

As a result of experiments and computer simulation, we clarified the following:

- The system that has no key disagreement correction process exhibits conditional mutual information 0.6 or higher when there is one EV more than 40 cm from UT.
- In this case, to share a 128-bit unguessable key against an eavesdropper, we should transact 214 wireless packets between the nodes.
- The key disagreement correction process based on error-correcting code contributes to the improvement not only of the mutual information between AP and UT but also the mutual information between EV and UT.
- The best way is to adopt BCH(31,16,7) with table-aided soft-decision decoding as the key disagreement correction process under the same conditions.
- After this improvement, to share a 128-bit unguessable key against an eavesdropper, we should transact 200 wireless packets between nodes.

References

1. Diffie, W., Hellman, M.E.: New Directions in Cryptography. IEEE Trans. Information Theory 22(6), 644–654 (1976)
2. Rivest, R.L., Shamir, A., Adleman, L.M.: A Method for Obtaining Digital Signatures and Public-key Cryptosystems. Communications of the ACM 21, 120–126 (1978)
3. Bennett, C.H., Brassard, G.: Quantum Cryptography: Public Key Distribution and Coin Tossing. In: Proc. IEEE Int. Conf. Com. Sys. and Signal Processing, Bangalore, India (December 1984)
4. Maurer, U.: Secret Key Agreement by Public Discussion from Common Information. IEEE Trans. Inf. Theory 39(3), 733–742 (1993)
5. Maurer, U.: Information-Theoretically Secure Secret-Key Agreement by NOT Authenticated Public Discussion. In: Fumy, W. (ed.) EUROCRYPT 1997. LNCS, vol. 1233, pp. 209–225. Springer, Heidelberg (1997)

6. Hershey, J.E., Hassan, A.A., Yarlagadda, R.: Unconventional Cryptographic Keying Variable Management. IEEE Trans. Commun. 43, 3–6 (1995)
7. Aono, T., Higuchi, K., Ohira, T., Komiyama, B., Sasaoka, H.: Wireless Secret Key Generation Exploiting Reactance-domain Scalar Response of Multipath Fading Channels. IEEE Trans. Antennas Propag. 53(11), 3776–3784 (2005)
8. Ohira, T., Cheng, J.: Analog smart antennas, Adaptive Antenna Arrays, pp. 184–204. Springer, Heidelberg (2004)
9. Imai, H., Kobara, K., Morozov, K.: On the Possibility of Key Agreement Using Variable Directional Antenna. In: JWIS 2006. The 1st Joint Workshop on Information Security 2006, Seoul, Korea, pp. 153–167 (September 2006)
10. http://focus.ti.com/docs/prod/folders/print/cc2420.html
11. http://www.zigbee.org/

Breaking 104 Bit WEP in Less Than 60 Seconds

Erik Tews, Ralf-Philipp Weinmann, and Andrei Pyshkin[*]

TU Darmstadt, FB Informatik
Hochschulstrasse 10, 64289 Darmstadt, Germany
{e_tews,weinmann,pyshkin}@cdc.informatik.tu-darmstadt.de

Abstract. We demonstrate an active attack on the WEP protocol that is able to recover a 104-bit WEP key using less than 40,000 frames with a success probability of 50%. In order to succeed in 95% of all cases, 85,000 packets are needed. The IV of these packets can be randomly chosen. This is an improvement in the number of required frames by more than an order of magnitude over the best known key-recovery attacks for WEP. On a IEEE 802.11g network, the number of frames required can be obtained by re-injection in less than a minute. The required computational effort is approximately 2^{20} RC4 key setups, which on current desktop and laptop CPUs is negligible.

1 Introduction

Wired Equivalent Privacy (WEP) is a protocol for encrypting wirelessly transmitted packets on IEEE 802.11 networks. In a WEP protected network, all packets are encrypted using the stream cipher RC4 under a common key, the *root key*[1] Rk. The root key is shared by all radio stations. A successful recovery of this key gives an attacker full access to the network. Although known to be insecure and superseded by Wi-Fi Protected Access (WPA) [18], this protocol is still is in widespread use almost 6 years after practical key recovery attacks were found against it [5,15]. In this paper we present a new key-recovery attack against WEP that outperforms previous methods by at least an order of magnitude.

First of all we describe how packets are encrypted: For each packet, a 24-bit initialization vector (IV) IV is chosen. The IV concatenated with the root key yields the per packet key K = IV||Rk. Over the data to be encrypted, an Integrity Check Value (ICV) is calculated as a CRC32 checksum. The key K is then used to encrypt the data followed by the ICV using the RC4 stream cipher. The IV is transmitted in the header of the packet. Figure 1 shows a simplified version of an 802.11 frame.

A first analysis of the design failures of the WEP protocol was published by Borisov, Goldberg and Wagner [2] in 2001. Notably, they showed that the ICV merely protects against random errors but not against malicious attackers. Furthermore, they observed that old IV values could be reused, thus allowing

---

[*] Supported by a stipend of the Marga und Kurt-Möllgaard-Stiftung.

[1] The standard actually allows for up to four different root keys; in practice however, only a single root key is used.

S. Kim, M. Yung, and H.-W. Lee (Eds.): WISA 2007, LNCS 4867, pp. 188–202, 2007.

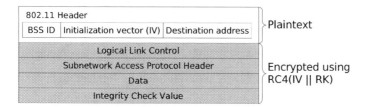

Fig. 1. A 802.11 frame encrypted using WEP

to inject messages. In the same year, Fluhrer, Mantin and Shamir presented a related-key ciphertext-only attack against RC4 [5]. In order for this attack to work, the IVs need to fulfill a so-called "resolved condition". This attack was suspected to be applicable to WEP, which was later demonstrated by Stubblefield et al [15]. Approximately 4 million different frames need to be captured to mount this attack. Vendors reacted to this attack by filtering IVs fulfilling the resolved condition, so-called "weak IVs". This countermeasure however proved to be insufficient: In 2004, a person using the pseudonym KoreK posted a family of statistical attacks against WEP that does not need weak IVs [9,3]; moreover the number of frames needed for key-recovery was reduced to about 500,000 packets.

More recently, Klein [7] showed an improved way of attacking RC4 using related keys that does not need the "resolved condition" on the IVs and gets by with a significantly reduced number of frames.

Table 1 shows a statistic of employed encryption methods in a sample of 490 networks, found somewhere in the middle of Germany in March 2007. Another survey of more than 15.000 networks was performed in a larger German city in September 2006 [4]. Both data sets demonstrate that WEP still is a popular method for securing wireless networks. Similar observations have been made by Bittau, Handley and Lackey [1]. Their article also give an excellent history of WEP attacks and describes a real-time decryption attack based on packet fragmentation that does not recover the key.

The structure of the paper is as follows: In Section 2 we introduce the notation that is used throughout the rest of this paper, in Section 3.1 we present a summary of Klein's attack on RC4, in Section 4 we specialize Klein's Attack to WEP, Section 5 describes how sufficient amounts of key stream can be obtained for the attack, Section 6 describes extensions of the attack such as key ranking techniques in detail and Section 7 gives experimental results.

2 Notation

For arrays or vectors we use the $[\cdot]$ notation, as used in many programing languages like in C or $Java$. All indices start at 0. For a permutation P denote the inverse permutation by P^{-1}; meaning $P[i] = j \Leftrightarrow P^{-1}[j] = i$. We will use $x \approx_n y$ as a short form for $x \approx y \bmod n$.

Table 1. Methods used for securing wireless networks

Time	No Encryption	WEP	WPA1/2
March 2007	21.8%	46.3%	31.9%
Middle of 2006	23.3%	59.4%	17.3%

Rk is the WEP or root key and IV is the initialization vector for a packet. K = Rk‖IV is the session or per packet key. X is a key stream generated using K. We will refer to a key stream X with the corresponding initialization vector IV as a session.

3   The Stream Cipher RC4

RC4 is a widely used stream cipher that was invented by Ron Rivest in 1987. It was a trade secret of RSA Security until 1994 when the algorithm was published anonymously on the Internet. RC4's internal state consists of a 256-byte array S defining a permutation as well as two integers $0 \leq i, j \leq 255$ acting as pointers into the array.

The RC4 key setup initializes the internal state using a key K of up to 256 bytes. By exchanging two elements of the state in each step, it incrementally transforms the identity permutation into a "random" permutation. The quality of randomness of the permutation after the key setup will be analyzed in Section 3.1.

The RC4 key stream generation algorithm updates the RC4 internal state and generates one byte of key stream. The key stream is XORed to the plaintext to generate the ciphertext.

Listing 1.1. RC4 key setup

```
1   for i ← 0 to 255 do
2     S[i] ← i
3   end
4   j ← 0
5   for i ← 0 to 255 do
6     j ← j+S[i]+K[i mod len(K)] mod 256
7     swap(S, i, j)
8   end
9   i ← 0
10  j ← 0
```

Listing 1.2. RC4 key stream generation

```
1   i ← i + 1 mod 256
2   j ← j + S[i] mod 256
3   swap(S, i, j)
4   return S[ S[i] + S[j]  mod 256 ]
```

We have a closer look at the RC4 key setup algorithm described in listing 1.1, especially at the values for S, i and j. After line 4, S is the identity permutation and j has the value 0. We will use S_k and j_k for the values of S and j after k iterations of the loop starting in line 5 have been completed. For example, if the key CA FE BA BE is used, S_0 is the identity permutation and $j_0 = 0$. After the first key byte has been processed, $j_1 = 202$ and $S_1[0] = 202$, $S_1[202] = 0$, and $S_1[x] = S_0[x] = x$ for $0 \neq x \neq 202$. For the rest of this paper, let $n = 256$. It is possible to generalize our results for modified versions of the RC4 algorithm, but we will only focus on the original algorithm as printed in listing 1.1 and 1.2.

3.1   Klein's Attack on RC4

Suppose w key streams were generated by RC4 using packet keys with a fixed root key and different initialization vectors. Denote by $K_u = (K_u[0], \ldots, K_u[m]) = (\mathsf{IV}_u \| \mathsf{Rk})$ the u-th packet key and by $X_u = (X_u[0], \ldots, X_u[m-1])$ the first m bytes of the uth key stream, where $1 \leq u \leq w$. Assume that an attacker knows the pairs (IV_u, X_u) – we shall refer to them as *samples* – and tries to find Rk.

In [7], Klein showed that there is a map $\mathcal{F}_i \colon (\mathbb{Z}/n\mathbb{Z})^i \to \mathbb{Z}/n\mathbb{Z}$ with $1 \leq i \leq m$ such that

$$\mathcal{F}_i(K[0], \ldots, K[i-1], X[i-1]) = \begin{cases} K[i], & \text{with Prob} \approx \frac{1.36}{n} \\ a \neq K[i], & \text{with Prob} < \frac{1}{n} \text{ for all } a \end{cases}$$

So $\mathcal{F}_i$ can be seen as a kind of approximation for $K[i]$, and we can write $\mathcal{F}_i \approx_n K[i]$. If the first i bytes of a packet key are known, then the internal permutation S_i and the index j at the ith step of the RC4 key setup algorithm can be found. We have

$$\mathcal{F}_i(K[0], \ldots, K[i-1], X[i-1]) = S_i^{-1}[i - X[i-1]] - (j_i + S_i[i]) \bmod n$$

The attack is based on the following properties of permutations.

Theorem 1. *For a random number $j \in \{0, \ldots, n-1\}$ and a random permutation P, we have*

$$\mathrm{Prob}(P[j] + P[P[i] + P[j] \bmod n] \equiv i \bmod n) = \frac{2}{n}$$

$$\mathrm{Prob}(P[j] + P[P[i] + P[j] \bmod n] \equiv c \bmod n) = \frac{n-2}{n(n-1)}$$

where $i, c \in \{0, \ldots, n-1\}$ are fixed, and $c \neq i$.

Proof. see [7].

In the case of $n = 256$, the first probability is equal to $2^{-7} \approx 0.00781$, and the second one is approximately equal to 0.00389.

From Theorem 1 it follows that for RC4 there is a correlation between i, $S_{i+n}[S_{i+n}[i] + S_{i+n}[j] \bmod n]$, and $S_{i+n}[j] = S_{i+n-1}[i]$.

Next, the equality $S_{i+1}[i] = S_{i+n-1}[i]$ holds with high probability. The theoretical explanation of this is the following. If we replace the line 6 of the RC4 key setup, and the line 2 of the RC4 key stream generator by $j \leftarrow \mathrm{RND}(n)$, [2] then

---

[2] Some publications approximate $\left(1 - \frac{1}{n}\right)^{n-2}$ by $\frac{1}{e}$. We will use $\left(1 - \frac{1}{n}\right)^{n-2}$ for the rest of this paper.

$$\text{Prob}(\mathsf{S}_{i+1}[i] = \mathsf{S}_{i+n-1}[i]) = \left(1 - \frac{1}{n}\right)^{n-2} \approx e^{-1}$$

Moreover, we have $\mathsf{S}_{i+1}[i] = \mathsf{S}_i[j_{i+1}] = \mathsf{S}_i[j_i + \mathsf{S}_i[i] + \mathsf{K}[i] \bmod n]$. Combining this with Theorem 1, we get the probability that

$$\mathsf{K}[i] = \mathsf{S}_i^{-1}[i - \mathsf{S}_{i+n}[\mathsf{S}_{i+n}[i] + \mathsf{S}_{i+n}[j] \bmod n] \bmod n] - (j_i + \mathsf{S}_i[i])$$

is approximately

$$\left(1 - \frac{1}{n}\right)^{n-2} \frac{2}{n} + \left(1 - \left(1 - \frac{1}{n}\right)^{n-2}\right) \frac{n-2}{n(n-1)} \approx \frac{1.36}{n}$$

4   Extension to Multiple Key Bytes

With Klein's attack, it is possible to iteratively compute all secret key bytes, if enough samples are available. This iterative approach has a significant disadvantage: In this case the key streams and IVs need to be saved and processed for every key byte. Additionally correcting falsely guessed key byte is expensive, because the computations for all key bytes following $\mathsf{K}[i]$ needs to be repeated if $\mathsf{K}[i]$ was incorrect.

We extend the attack such that is it possible to compute key bytes independently of each other and thus make efficient use of the attack possible by using key ranking techniques. Klein's attack is based on the the fact that

$$\mathsf{K}[i] \approx_n \mathsf{S}_i^{-1}[i - \mathsf{X}[i - 1]] - (\mathsf{S}_i[i] + j_i) \tag{1}$$

$$\mathsf{K}[i + 1] \approx_n \mathsf{S}_{i+1}^{-1}[(i + 1) - \mathsf{X}[(i + 1) - 1]] - (\mathsf{S}_{i+1}[i + 1] + j_{i+1}) \tag{2}$$

We may write j_{i+1} as $j_i + \mathsf{S}_i[i] + \mathsf{K}[i]$. By replacing j_{i+1} in equation 2, we get an approximation for $\mathsf{K}[i] + \mathsf{K}[i + 1]$:

$$\mathsf{K}[i] + \mathsf{K}[i + 1] \approx_n \mathsf{S}_{i+1}^{-1}[(i + 1) - \mathsf{X}[(i + 1) - 1]] - (\mathsf{S}_{i+1}[i + 1] + j_i + \mathsf{S}_i[i]) \tag{3}$$

By repeatedly replacing j_{i+k}, we get an approximation for $\sum_{l=i}^{i+k} \mathsf{K}[l]$. Because we are mostly interested in $\sum_{l=3}^{3+i} \mathsf{K}[l] = \sum_{l=0}^{i} \mathsf{Rk}[l]$ in a WEP scenario, we will use the symbol σ_i for this sum.

$$\sigma_i \approx_n \mathsf{S}_{3+i}^{-1}[(3 + i) - \mathsf{X}[2 + i]] - \left(j_3 + \sum_{l=3}^{i+3} \mathsf{S}_l[l]\right) = \tilde{\mathcal{A}}_i \tag{4}$$

The right side of equation 4 still depends on the key bytes $\mathsf{K}[3]$ to $\mathsf{K}[i - 1]$, because they are needed to compute S_l and S_{3+i}^{-1}. By replacing them with S_3, we get another approximation $\mathcal{A}_i$ for σ_i, which only depends on $\mathsf{K}[0]$ to $\mathsf{K}[2]$.

$$\sigma_i \approx_n \mathsf{S}_3^{-1}[(3 + i) - \mathsf{X}[2 + i]] - \left(j_3 + \sum_{l=3}^{i+3} \mathsf{S}_3[l]\right) = \mathcal{A}_i \tag{5}$$

Under idealized conditions, Klein derives the following probability for the event $\tilde{A}_i = \sigma_i$:

$$\text{Prob}\left(\sigma_i = \tilde{A}_i\right) \approx \left(1 - \frac{1}{n}\right)^{n-2} \cdot \frac{2}{n} + \left(1 - \left(1 - \frac{1}{n}\right)^{n-2}\right) \cdot \frac{n-2}{n(n-1)} \quad (6)$$

The first part of sum represents the probability that $S[i+3]$ remains unchanged until $X[2+i]$ is generated, the second part represents the probability that $S[i+3]$ is changed during key scheduling or key stream generation with A_i still taking the correct value. By replacing S_l and S_{i+3} with their previous values, we have reduced that probability slightly.

$S_{k+3}[k+3]$ differs from $S_3[k+3]$ only if one of the values of j_3 to j_{k+2} has been $k+3$. All values of $S_l[l]$ will be correct, if for all j_z with $3 \leq z \leq 3+i$ the condition $j_z \notin \{z, \ldots, 3+i\}$ holds. Assuming j changes randomly, this happens with probability $\prod_{k=1}^{i}\left(1 - \frac{k}{n}\right)$. Additionally $S_{3+i}[j_{i+3}]$ should not be changed between iteration 3 and $3+i$. This is true if j does not take the value of j_{i+3} in a previous round, which happens with probability $\approx \left(1 - \frac{1}{n}\right)^i$ and i does not take the value of j_{i+3}, which happens with probability $\approx \left(1 - \frac{i}{n}\right)$. To summarize, the probability that replacing all occurrences of S in $\tilde{A}_i$ with S_3 did not change anything is:

$$q_i = \left(1 - \frac{1}{n}\right)^i \cdot \left(1 - \frac{i}{n}\right) \cdot \prod_{k=1}^{i}\left(1 - \frac{k}{n}\right) \quad (7)$$

This results in the following probability p_{correct_i} being a lower bound for $\mathcal{A}_i$ taking the correct value for σ_i.

$$\text{Prob}\left(\sigma_i = \mathcal{A}_i\right) \approx q_i \cdot \left(1 - \frac{1}{n}\right)^{n-2} \cdot \frac{2}{n} + \left(1 - q_i \cdot \left(1 - \frac{1}{n}\right)^{n-2}\right) \cdot \frac{n-2}{n(n-1)} (8)$$

Experimental results using more than *50,000,000,000* simulations with 104 bit WEP keys show that this approximations differs less than 0.2% from values determined from these simulations.

5   Obtaining Sufficient Amounts of Key Stream

The Internet Protocol (IP) is the most widely deployed network protocol. For our attack to work, we assume that version 4 (IPv4) of this protocol is used on the wireless networks we attack.

If host A wants to send an IP datagram to host B, A needs the physical address of host B or the gateway through which B can be reached. To resolve IP addresses of hosts to their physical address, the Address Resolution Protocol (ARP) [13] is used. This works as follows: Host A sends an ARP request to the link layer broadcast address. This request announces that A is looking for the physical address of host B. Host B responds with an ARP reply containing his

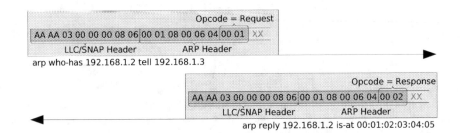

Fig. 2. Cleartext of ARP request and response packets

own physical address to host A. Since the Address Resolution Protocol is a link layer protocol it is typically not restricted by any kind of packet filters or rate limiting rules.

ARP requests and ARP replies are of fixed size. Because the size of a packet is not masked by WEP, they can usually be easily distinguished from other traffic. The first 16 bytes of cleartext of an ARP packet are made up of a 8 byte long 802.11 Logical Link Control (LLC) header followed by the first 8 bytes of the ARP packet itself. The LLC header is fixed for every ARP packet (AA AA 03 00 00 00 08 06). The first 8 bytes of an ARP request are also fixed. Their value is 00 01 08 00 06 04 00 01. For an ARP response, the last byte changes to 02, the rest of the bytes are identical to an ARP request. An ARP request is always sent to the broadcast address, while an ARP response is sent to a unicast address. Because the physical addresses are not encrypted by WEP, it is easy to distinguish between an encrypted ARP request and response.

By XORing a captured ARP packet with these fixed patterns, we can recover the first 16 bytes of the key stream. The corresponding IV is transmitted in clear with the packet.

To speed up key stream recovery, it is possible to re-inject a captured ARP request into the network, which will trigger another reply. The destination answers the request with a new response packet that we can add to our list of key streams. If the initiator and the destination of the original request have been both wireless stations, every re-injected packet will generate three new packets, because the transmission will be relayed by the access point. Because ARP replies expire quickly, it usually takes only a few seconds or minutes until an attacker can capture an ARP request and start re-injecting it. The first public implementation of a practical re-injection attack was in the BSD-Airtools package [6].

It is even possible to speed up the time it takes to capture the first ARP request. A *de-authenticate* message can be sent to a client in the network, telling him that he has lost contact with the base station. In some configurations we saw clients rejoining the network automatically and at the same time flushing their ARP cache. The next IP packet sent by this client will cause an ARP request to look up the Ethernet address of the destination.

6   Our Attack on WEP

The basic attack is straightforward. We use the methods described in Section 5 to generate a sufficient amount of key stream under different IVs. Initially we assume that a 104 bit WEP key was used. For every σ_i from σ_0 to σ_{12}, and every recovered key stream, we calculate A_i as described in equation 5 and call the result a *vote* for σ_i having the value A_i. We keep track of those votes in separate tables for each σ_i.

Having processed all available key streams, we assume that the correct value for every σ_i is the one with the most votes received. The correct key is simply $\mathsf{Rk}[0] = \sigma_0$ for the first key byte and $\mathsf{Rk}[i] = \sigma_i - \sigma_{i-1}$ for all other key bytes. If the correct key was a 40 bit key instead of a 104 bit key, the correct key is just calculated from σ_0 to σ_4.

6.1   Key Ranking

If only a low number of samples is available, the correct value for σ_i is not always the most voted one in the table, but tends to be one of the most voted. Figure 3 contains an example in which the correct value has the second most votes after 35.000 sessions. Instead of collecting more samples, we use another method for finding the correct key. Checking if a key is the correct key is simple, because we have collected a lot of key streams with their corresponding IV. We can just generate a key stream using an IV and a guessed key, and compare it with the collected one. If the method used for key stream recovery did not always guess the key stream right, the correct value just needs to match a certain fraction of some key streams.

For every key byte $\mathsf{K}[i]$, we define a set M_i of possible values σ_i might have. At the beginning, M_i is only initialized with the top voted value for σ_i from the table. Until the correct key is found, we look for an entry $\tilde{\sigma}_i \notin M_i$ in all tables having a minimum distance to the top voted entry in table i. We then add $\tilde{\sigma}_i$ to M_i and test all keys which can now be constructed from the sets M that have not been tested previously.

6.2   Handling Strong Keys

For equation 5 we assumed S_3 to be an approximation of S_{3+i}. This assumption is wrong for a fraction of the key space. We call these keys *strong keys*. For these keys, the value for j_{i+3} with high probability is taken by j in a iteration before $i + 3$ and after 3. This results in $\mathsf{S}[j_{i+3}]$ being swapped with an unknown value, depending on the previous key bytes and the IV. In iteration $i + 3$, this value instead of $\mathsf{S}_3[j_{i+3}]$ is now swapped with $\mathsf{S}[i]$.

More formally, let Rk be a key and $\mathsf{Rk}[i]$ a key byte of Rk. $\mathsf{Rk}[i]$ is a *strong key byte*, if there is an integer $l \in \{1, \ldots, i\}$ where

$$\sum_{k=l}^{i} (\mathsf{Rk}[k] + 3 + k) \equiv_n 0 \tag{9}$$

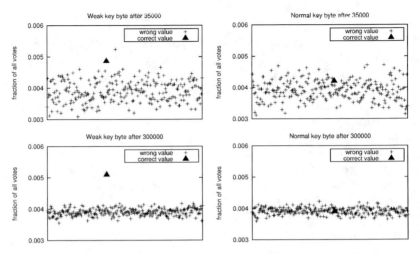

Fig. 3. Distribution of votes for a strong and a normal key byte

A key Rk is a *strong key*, if at least one of its key bytes is a *strong key byte*. On the contrary, key bytes that are not *strong key bytes* are called *normal key bytes* and keys in which not a single *strong key byte* occurs are called *normal keys*.

Assuming that S is still the identity permutation, the value 0 will be added to j_{l+3} from iteration $l + 3$ to $i + 3$, making j_{i+3} taking his previous value j_{l+3}. This results in the value q_i of equation 7 being close to 0 and $\text{Prob}(\sigma_i = A_i)$ is very close to $\frac{1}{n}$.

Figure 3 shows the distribution of votes for a strong and a non strong key byte after 35.000 and 300.000 samples. It is easy to see that the correct value for strong key byte has not received the most votes of all key bytes any longer. An alternative way must be used to determine the correct value for this key byte. Our approach can be divided into two steps:

1. *Find out which key bytes are strong key bytes:*
   If a key byte Rk[i] is a normal key byte, the correct value for σ_i should appear with probability $\approx p_{\text{correct}_i}$ (see equation 8). We assume that all other values are equidistributed with probability $p_{\text{wrong}_i} = \frac{(1 - p_{\text{correct}_i})}{n-1}$. If Rk[$i$] is a strong key byte we assume that all values are equidistributed with probability $p_{\text{equal}} = \frac{1}{n}$.
   Let N_{i_b} the fraction of votes for which $\sigma_i = b$ holds. We calculate

$$\text{err}_{\text{strong}_i} = \sum_{j=0}^{n} \left(N_{i_j} - p_{\text{equal}}\right)^2 \tag{10}$$

$$\text{err}_{\text{normal}_i} = \left(\max_b(N_{i_b}) - p_{\text{correct}_i}\right)^2 +$$

$$\sum_{j=0, j \neq \text{argmax}_b(N_{i_b})}^{n} \left(N_{i_j} - p_{\text{wrong}_i}\right)^2 \tag{11}$$

If enough samples are available, this can be used as a test if $\text{err}_{\text{strong}_i}$ is smaller than $\text{err}_{\text{normal}_i}$. If that is the case, it is highly likely that key byte $\text{Rk}[i]$ is a strong key byte. If only a small number of samples are available, $\text{err}_{\text{strong}_i} - \text{err}_{\text{normal}_i}$ can be used as an indicator for the likelihood of key byte $\text{Rk}[i]$ being a strong key byte.

2. *Find the correct values for these key bytes:*
   Assuming that $\text{Rk}[i]$ is a strong key byte and all values for $\text{Rk}[0] \ldots \text{Rk}[i-1]$ are known, we can use equation 9 and get the following equation for $\text{Rk}[i]$:

$$\text{Rk}[i] \equiv_n -3 - i - \sum_{j=l}^{i-1} (\text{Rk}[j] + 3 + j) \tag{12}$$

Because there at most i possible values for l, we can try every possible value for l and restrict $\text{Rk}[i]$ to at most i possible values (12 if $\text{Rk}[i]$ is the last key byte for a 104 bit key). This method can be combined with the key ranking method as described in Section 6.1. Instead of taking possible values for σ_i from the top voted value in the table for key byte i, we ignore the table and use the values calculated with equation 12 for $\text{Rk}[i]$ and assume that $\sigma_{i-1} + \text{Rk}[i]$ was top voted in the table. Possible values for σ_i for all assumed to be normal key bytes are still taken from the top voted values in their tables.

This approach is only feasible if the number of strong bytes in the key is small. For a 104 bit key all 12 key bytes can be strong key bytes. For such a key, we need to test up to $12! \approx 2^{28.8}$ different keys, which is possible, but slows down our attack. Because *Klein's attack* as described in Section 3.1 is not hindered by strong keys, we suggest to additionally implement this attack without key ranking, to be able to attack even keys with the maximum number of strong key bytes in a reasonable time.

6.3   A Passive Version

For the attack in the previous section we assumed that an attacker obtains a sufficient amount of encrypted ARP packets by actively injecting ARP requests into the network. This attack strategy however might be detected by an intrusion detecting system (IDS). In this section we present a passive version of the attack.

As we have seen, an ARP packet can be detected by its destination address and size. For our attack we will assume every packet which is not an ARP packet to be an IPv4 packet. This is expected to be true with a high probability for most networks in use today. Figure 4 shows the first 15 bytes of an IPv4 packet [14].

There are three fields in the first 7 bytes of the the IPv4 header which do not contain fixed values. These are:

Total Length. This is the total length of the packet, starting from the IPv4 header. We can calculate this value from the length of the 802.11 frame, which can be observed.

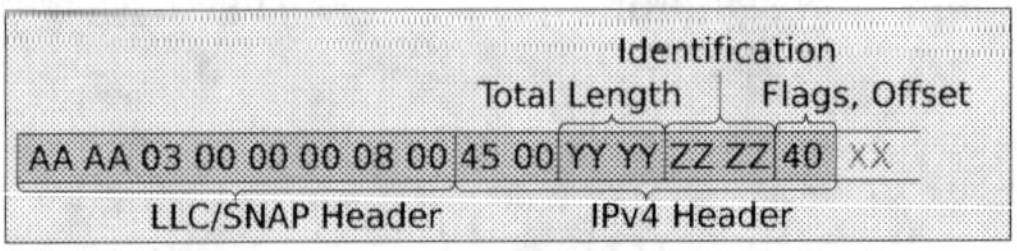

Fig. 4. First 15 bytes of a 802.11 frame containing an IPv4 packet

Identification. This field is used to keep track of packets for the reassembly of fragments and must be assumed to be random.

Flags and Fragment Offset. This byte contains the most significant bits of the fragment offset and two control flags. Because IPv4 packets are usually short, the most significant bits of the fragment offset can be assumed to be zero, even if the packet was fragmented. After having analyzed traffic from various sources, we found that about 85% of all packets were sent with the *don't fragment* flag set and about 15% had all flags cleared.

In total, this means that we cannot guess two bytes at all, and one byte can be restricted to two possible values with high probability.

We can now modify our attack as follows. The values for σ_{10} and σ_{11} are not determined by statistical tests, because we cannot recover $X[12]$ and $X[13]$. Instead, we just iterate over all 2^{16} possible values when it comes to determine these values. To prevent a slowdown of our attack by a factor of 2^{16}, we do less key ranking.

To determine the value of σ_{12}, we now introduce the concept of a "weighted vote". Until now, we counted the output of the function $\mathcal{A}_i$ as a vote for σ_i having a specific value. We now calculate $\mathcal{A}_{12}$ two times, once under the assumption that $X[12] = 64$ (which is equivalent to *don't fragment* flag set), and count it as a $\frac{220}{256}$ vote for σ_{12}, and once with the assumption that $X[12] = 0$ (which is equivalent to no flags set), and count it as a $\frac{36}{256}$ vote for σ_{12}.

Of course, the exact success rate of this passive attack heavily depends on the nature of the traffic captured, but some simulations have shown that it works with reasonable reliability and just needs some more captured packets than the active version just using ARP packets. Most of the work on the passive attack has been done by Martin Beck who also integrated our attack in the aircrack-ng toolsuite [16].

6.4   Breaking Implementations Using Larger WEP Keys

Some vendors implemented WEP using *root keys* longer than 104 bit. We have seen implementations using up to 232 bit key length for the *root key*. Attacking such networks is not as easy as attacking a 104 bit key, because only the first 16 bytes of cleartext of an ARP packet are known, but 31 bytes of the cleartext would be needed. The missing 15 bytes are constant for every request or response, if only a single ARP packet was used for injection.

Using the *chopchop attack* invented by KoreK [8] or the *fragmentation attack* published by Bittau, Handley and Lackey [1] allows us do decrypt the request packet we used and one of the response packets. The decrypted packets can then be used for the ARP injection attack. Because ARP responses contain packet-unique values, we can assume that all other responses contain exactly the same plaintext. This allows us to recover enough plaintext for breaking even implementations with *root keys* longer than 232 bit.

7   Experimental Results

We wrote an implementation using the parallelized computation as described in Section 4 and the key ranking methods described in Section 6.1 and 6.2. At the beginning an upper bound on the number of keys to be tested is fixed (key limit). A limit of 1,000,000 keys seems a reasonable choice for a modern PC or laptop. Three different scenarios of attacks cover the most likely keys:

scenario 1 tests 70% of the limit and uses key ranking as described in Section 6.1. As long as the set of possible keys does not exceed 70% of the key limit, a new value $v \notin M_i$ is added to a set M_i. The value v is chosen to have minimal distance to the top voted entry.

scenario 2 tests 20% of the limit and uses the key ranking method in combination with strong byte detection. We use the difference $\text{err}_{\text{strong}_i} - \text{err}_{\text{normal}_i}$ to determine which key byte is the most likely to be strong. We then use equation 12 to get possible values for this key byte. As long as the number of possible keys does not exceed 20% of the key limit all other key bytes are determined as in scenario 1.

scenario 3 tests 10% of the limit and works like scenario 2, with the exception that 2 key bytes are assumed to be strong.

To verify a possible key Rk for correctness, 10 sessions $(\text{IV}_i, \text{X}_i)$ are chosen at random. If the key stream generated using $\text{IV}_i \| \text{Rk}$ is identical to X_i in the first 6 bytes for all sessions, we assume the key to be correct. If all three scenarios where unsuccessful, the attack is retried using just 10% of the key limit, this time under the assumption that the root key is a 40 bit key instead of a 104 bit one.

Figure 5 shows the result from a simulation, showing that a 50% success rate is possible using just 40,000 packets.

To test whether this attack works in a real world scenario we used the *aircrack-ng* tool suite [16]. *aircrack-ng* contains *aireplay-ng*, a tool which is able to capture and replay 802.11 frames; for example, frames containing ARP requests or other kinds of packets that cause traffic on the target network. Additionally, *airodump-ng* can be used to capture and save the generated traffic including all needed IEEE 802.11 headers.

On a mixed IEEE 802.11 b/g network, consisting of cards with chipsets from Atheros, Broadcom, Intersil and Intel, we achieved a rate of 764 different captured packets per second, using *aireplay-ng* and a network card with a *PrismGT* chipset for injecting and an *Atheros* based card for capturing. This number might vary, depending on the chipsets and the quality of the signal. This allowed us to

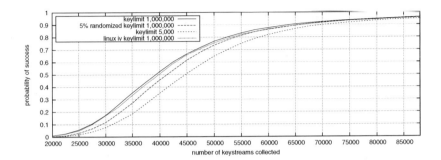

Fig. 5. Success rate

recover 40,492 key streams in 53 seconds. Additional 2 seconds can be added for deauthenticating one or all clients forcing them to send out new ARP requests. The final cryptographic computation requires 1 to 3 seconds of CPU-time, depending on the CPU being used. For a 104 bit key we were able to consistently and successfully recover keys from a packet capture in less than 3 seconds on a Thinkpad T41p (1.7 GHz Pentium-M CPU) – this includes reading and parsing the dump file, recovering key streams and performing the actual attack. On more recent multi-core CPUs we expect this figure can be brought down to less than a second with a parallelized key space search. This results in 54 to 58 seconds to crack a 104 bit WEP key, with probability 50%.

Main memory requirements for an efficient implementation are quite low. Our implementation needs less than 3 MB of main memory for data structures. Most of the memory is consumed by a bit field for finding duplicate IVs, this is 2 MB in size. CPU-time scales almost linearly with the number of keys tested. By reducing the number of keys tested to 5,000, this attack is suitable for PDA or embedded system usage too, by only reducing its success probability a little bit. The success rate with this reduced key limit is included in Figure 5 with label *keylimit 5,000*.

7.1   Robustness of the Attack

The key stream recovery method we used might not always be correct. For example, any kind of short packet (TCP, UDP, ICMP) might be identified as an ARP reply resulting in an incorrect key stream. To find out how our attack performs with some incorrect values in key streams, we ran a simulation with 5% of all key streams replaced with random values. The result is included in Figure 5, labeled "5% randomized key limit 1,000,000". Depending on the number of packets collected, the success rate is slightly reduced by less than 10%. If enough packets are available, there is no visible difference.

In all previous simulations, we assumed that IVs are generated independently, using any kind of pseudo random function. Some drivers in fact do use an PRNG to generate the IV value for each packet, however others use a counter with some modifications. For example the 802.11 stack in the Linux 2.6.20 kernel uses an counter, which additionally skips IVs which where used for an earlier attack on RC4 by Fuller, Mantin and Shamir which became known as FMS-weak-IVs. Using this modified IV generation scheme, the success rate of our attack (label *linux iv keylimit 1,000,000*) was slightly reduced by less than 5%, depending on the number of packets available. As before, there are no noticeable differences, if a high number of packets are available.

8   Related and Further Work

After we made a draft of this paper available on the IACR's Cryptology ePrint Archive in early April 2007, other researchers published similar analyses. Sub-hamoy Maitra and Goutam Paul gave an independent analysis [10] of Klein's attack with results similar to our multiple key bytes extension. Additionally, they found new correlations in RC4 independent of Klein's analysis.

Vaudenay and Vuagnoux presented a similar attack at SAC2007 [17], which additionally makes use of the fact that the RC4 key is stretched to 256 bytes by repeating it. The same trick was discovered by Ohigashi, Ozasa, Fujikawa, Kuwadako and Morii [12], who developed an improved version of our attack. Vaudenay and Vuagnoux additionally make use of a modified *FMS attack*, to improve their results. Still ongoing research of Ohigashi, Ozasa, Fujikawa, Kuwadako and Morii is expected to halve the number of packets needed for similar success rates as ours [11].

9   Conclusion

We have extended Klein's attack on RC4 and have applied it to the WEP protocol. Our extension consists in showing how to determine key bytes independently of each other and allows us to dramatically decrease the time complexity of a brute force attack on the remaining key bytes. We have carefully analyzed cases in which a straightforward extension of Klein's attack will fail and have shown how to deal with these situations.

The number of packets needed for our attack is so low that opportunistic attacks on this security protocol will be most probable. Although it has been known to be insecure and has been broken by a key-recovery attack for almost 6 years, WEP is still seeing widespread use at the time of writing this paper. While arguably still providing a weak deterrent against casual attackers in the past, the attack presented in this paper greatly improves the ease with which the security measure can be broken and will likely define a watershed moment in the arena of practical attacks on wireless networks.

References

1. Bittau, A., Handley, M., Lackey, J.: The final nail in WEP's coffin. In: IEEE Symposium on Security and Privacy, pp. 386–400. IEEE Computer Society Press, Los Alamitos (2006)
2. Borisov, N., Goldberg, I., Wagner, D.: Intercepting mobile communications: the insecurity of 802.11. In: ACM MobiCom 2001, pp. 180–189. ACM Press, New York (2001)

3. Chaabouni, R.: Break WEP faster with statistical analysis. Technical report, EPFL, LASEC (June 2006), http://lasecwww.epfl.ch/pub/lasec/doc/cha06.pdf
4. Dörhöfer, S.: Empirische Untersuchungen zur WLAN-Sicherheit mittels Wardriving. Diplomarbeit, RWTH Aachen (September 2006) (in German)
5. Fluhrer, S.R., Mantin, I., Shamir, A.: Weaknesses in the key scheduling algorithm of RC4. In: Vaudenay, S., Youssef, A.M. (eds.) SAC 2001. LNCS, vol. 2259, pp. 1–24. Springer, Heidelberg (2001)
6. Hulton, D. (h1kari).: bsd-airtools, http://www.dachb0den.com/projects/bsd-airtools.html
7. Klein, A.: Attacks on the RC4 stream cipher. Designs, Codes and Cryptography (submitted, 2007)
8. KoreK. chopchop (experimental WEP attacks) (2004), http://www.netstumbler.org/showthread.php?t=12489
9. KoreK. Next generation of WEP attacks (2004), http://www.netstumbler.org/showpost.php?p=93942&postcount=35
10. Maitra, S., Paul, G.: Many keystream bytes of RC4 leak secret key information. Cryptology ePrint Archive, Report2007/261(2007), http://eprint.iacr.org/
11. Ohigashi, T., Kuwakado, H., Morii, M.: A key recovery attack on WEP with less packets (2007)
12. Ozasa, Y., Fujikawa, Y., Ohigashi, T., Kuwakado, H., Morii, M.: A study on the Tews, Weinmann, Pyshkin attack against WEP. In: IEICE Tech. Rep., Hokkaido, July 2007. ISEC2007-47, vol. 107, pp. 17–21 (2007) Thu, Jul 19, 2007 - Fri, Jul 20 : Future University-Hakodate (ISEC, SITE, IPSJ-CSEC)
13. Plummer, D.C.: RFC 826: Ethernet Address Resolution Protocol: Or converting network protocol addresses to 48.bit Ethernet address for transmission on Ethernet hardware (November 1982)
14. Postel, J.: Internet Protocol. Request for Comments (Standard) 791, Internet Engineering Task Force (September 1981)
15. Stubblefield, A., Ioannidis, J., Rubin, A.D.: A key recovery attack on the 802.11b wired equivalent privacy protocol (WEP). ACM Transactions on Information and System Security 7(2), 319–332 (2004)
16. The Aircrack-NG team. Aircrack-ng suite (2007), http://www.aircrack-ng.org
17. Vaudenay, S., Vuagnoux, M.: Passive-only key recovery attacks on RC4. In: Selected Areas in Cryptography 2007. LNCS, Springer, Heidelberg (to appear, 2007)
18. Wi-Fi Alliance. Wi-Fi Protected Acccess (WPA) (2003), http://www.wi-fi.org

Efficient Implementation of the Pairing on Mobilephones Using BREW

Motoi Yoshitomi[1], Tsuyoshi Takagi[1], Shinsaku Kiyomoto[2], and Toshiaki Tanaka[2]

[1] Future University - Hakodate, School of System Information Science
116-2, Kamedanakano-cho, Hakodate, 041-0806, Japan
[2] KDDI R&D Laboratories Inc.
2-1-15, Ohara, Fujimino, Saitama, 356-8502, Japan

Abstract. Pairing based cryptography can accomplish novel security applications such as ID-based cryptosystems, which have not been constructed efficiently without the pairing. The processing speed of the pairing based cryptography is relatively slow compared with the other conventional public key cryptography. However, several efficient algorithms for computing the pairing have been proposed, namely Duursma-Lee algorithm and its variant η_T pairing. In this paper, we present an efficient implementation of the pairing over some mobilephones, and examine the feasibility of the pairing based cryptosystems on ubiquitous devices. Indeed the processing speed of our implementation in ARM9 processors on BREW achieves under 100 milliseconds using the supersingular curve over $\mathbb{F}_{3^{97}}$. It has become fast enough for implementing security applications using the pairing on mobilephones.

Keywords: Pairing Based Cryptosystem, Mobilephone, BREW, Efficient Implementation.

1 Introduction

Tate pairing can realize novel cryptographic applications e.g. short signature [5], ID-based cryptography [4], which have not been achieved by conventional public key cryptosystems. Short signature is a digital signature suitable for applications on memory-constrained devices because the signature length in Tate pairing becomes about a half of that in elliptic curve cryptography. ID-based cryptosystems can replace the public key with an E-mail address or an IP address which can be easily memorized. However, the processing speed is slower than that of other public key cryptography. The timing in paper [2] shows that the processing speed of pairing-based cryptography is about 5 times or more slower than that of RSA cryptography or elliptic curve cryptography. Recently, Duursma and Lee proposed a very efficient algorithm for computing the pairing over supersingular curves [6]. Barreto et al. then presented η_T pairing which is about twice faster than Duursma-Lee algorithm [1]. The two algorithms can compute the pairing relatively efficient.

S. Kim, M. Yung, and H.-W. Lee (Eds.): WISA 2007, LNCS 4867, pp. 203–214, 2007.
© Springer-Verlag Berlin Heidelberg 2007

By the recent progress of devices technology, we are able to implement pairing based cryptosystems on ubiquitous devices that the processing speed is comparatively slow. Especially, it is important to implement and evaluate of a pairing based cryptography on mobilephones which are the most familiar as ubiquitous devices. There are two kinds of platforms for mobilephones, JAVA and BREW. An implementation of the pairing with mobilephones for JAVA was already reported [11].

In this paper, we report about an efficient implementation of the pairing by mobilephones in ARM9 processors on BREW. Indeed we implement both Duursma-Lee algorithm and η_T pairing over finite fields $\mathbb{F}_{3^m}$ for extension degrees $m = 97, 167, 193, 239, 313$. We try to improve the efficiency of pairing by the following procedures (mainly with engineering efforts). At first, functions of the finite field and the pairing are implemented from scratch in C language. Then, we investigate the functions which requires a lot of the processing time by using a profiling tool. It turns out that the multiplications in the finite field are about 80% of the whole computation of the pairing programs, and thus we focus on enhancing the speed of multiplication in $\mathbb{F}_{3^m}$.

Note that a substitution operation in $\mathbb{F}_{3^m}$ on ARM9 processors is relatively slow to our experiments. Comb method can perform the polynomial multiplication fast because there are few substitution operations than normal multiplication algorithm [10]. In this paper, we propose the improved Comb method which reduces the number of substitution operations by eliminating the first loop of the Comb method. The improved Comb method enhances the whole speed of pairing by about 20%. In addition, the unrollment of the loop in the programs further improves the speed due to the reduction of pipeline hazard.

Finally, we examine the speeds of Duursma-Lee algorithm and η_T pairing using the above improvements. The processing speed of our implementation in ARM9 processors on BREW achieves under 100 milliseconds using the supersingular curve over $\mathbb{F}_{3^{97}}$. Therefore the pairing on BREW mobilephones has become practical enough.

2   Algorithms for Implementing the Pairing

We explain some efficient algorithms for computing in finite fields and Tate pairing.

2.1   The Elements Representation in $\mathbb{F}_{3^m}$

Let $\mathbb{F}_3[x]$ be the polynomials with coefficients over field $\mathbb{F}_3 = \{0, 1, 2\}$. Finite field $\mathbb{F}_{3^m}$ is the set of all polynomials represented by $\mathbb{F}_{3^m} = \mathbb{F}_3[x]/f(x)$, where $f(x)$ is an irreducible polynomial. An element $A(x)$ in $\mathbb{F}_{3^m}$ can be represented as follows:

$$A(x) = (a_{m-1}, a_{m-2}, \cdots, a_1, a_0), \ a_i \in \mathbb{F}_3,$$

where a_i is an element in $\mathbb{F}_3$ for $i = 0, 1, \cdots, m-1$. Note that $\mathbb{F}_3$ has the three values 0,1 and 2. Therefore, we represent an element in $\mathbb{F}_3$ as (hi, lo)-bit, where hi and *lo* are binary bits. Let W be the word size of a targeted computer, and let $A[i]$ be a sequence of (hi, lo)-bits with size of W, where i is a positive integer including zero. Let $t = \lceil m/W \rceil$. Then $A(x)$ can be represented by the right-to-left array $A[t - 1], \cdots, A[1], A[0]$. In this case of $W = 32$ and $m = 97$, $A(x)$ in $\mathbb{F}_{3^{97}}$ is represented by the array such that $A[3] = (0, 0, \cdots, 0, a_{96}), A[2] = (a_{95}, a_{94}, \cdots, a_{65}, a_{64})$, $A[1] = (a_{63}, a_{62}, \cdots, a_{33}, a_{32}), A[0] = (a_{31}, a_{30} \cdots, a_1, a_0)$. Finally, let $A[i]_k$ be the k-th element of $A[i]$ (for example, $A[1]_0$ is a_{32}).

2.2 Arithmetic in Finite Field $\mathbb{F}_{3^m}$

Addition/Subtraction $A(x) \pm B(x)$ in $\mathbb{F}_{3^m}$ can be efficiently implemented by logical operations such as AND, OR and XOR [7].

Shift-and-Add method [10] is well known as a standard algorithm for computing the polynomial multiplication over finite fields. This method is an algorithm which shifts $A(x)$ from right to left, and performs addition $C(x) \leftarrow A(x) \pm B(x)$ based on each (hi, lo)-bit of $B(x)$, where $A(x), B(x)$ and $C(x)$ are elements in $\mathbb{F}_{3^m}$. Therefore Shift-and-Add method requires $\frac{2}{3}m^2$ additions $a + b$ for $a, b \in \mathbb{F}_3$ and $\frac{2}{3}m^2$ substitution operations $c \leftarrow a + b$ for the resulting addition. In this paper the leftarrow ($\leftarrow$) is called the substitution operation. Comb method [10] is another efficient algorithm for computing the polynomial multiplication, which shifts $A(x)$ from right to left only after performing t additions in $\mathbb{F}_{3^m}$ based on each (hi, lo)-bit of the array $B[t - 1], \cdots, B[1], B[0]$. $A(x) \cdot x^{iW+k}$ is computed by shifting $A(x)$ for $k \in [0, W - 1], j \in [0, t - 1]$ and the word size W. Therefore the number of the substitution operations in Comb method becomes $\lceil m/W \rceil$ times smaller than that of Shift-and-Add method, namely it is $1/t$. In our implementation in Section 3, we use the Comb method because the substitution operations on ARM9 processors are inefficient to our experiment.

In characteristic 3, cube can be computed as $A(x)^3 = \sum_{i=0}^{m-1} a_i x^{3i}$. Cube can be computed analogously to square in characteristic 2 by using table look-up [7]. Therefore, this process is fast because it does not require the multiplication step actually. Inversion can be computed by using the extended Euclidean algorithm for the polynomials over $\mathbb{F}_3[x]$ [11]. This algorithm was improved extended Euclidean algorithm in characteristic 2.

Note that each operation in $\mathbb{F}_{3^m}$ has the following relationship of the cost:

$$A < C < M < I,$$

where A, C, M and I are the cost for addition/subtraction, cube, multiplication and inversion, respectively. In our implementation in $\mathbb{F}_{3^{97}}$, the difference of the costs in each inequality sign ($<$) is about 10 times (see for Section 3.4).

2.3 Arithmetic in Extended Field $\mathbb{F}_{3^{3m}}$ and $\mathbb{F}_{3^{6m}}$

We can represent $\mathbb{F}_{3^{3m}}$ and $\mathbb{F}_{3^{6m}}$ by a tower of extensions to use the operations of $\mathbb{F}_{3^m}$. Let $\mathbb{F}_{3^{3m}} = \mathbb{F}_{3^m}[\rho]/(\rho^3 - \rho - 1)$ and $\mathbb{F}_{3^{6m}} = \mathbb{F}_{3^{3m}}[\sigma]/(\sigma^2 + 1)$. An element A in $\mathbb{F}_{3^{6m}}$ is represented as follows:

$$\Lambda = \alpha_1 \sigma + \alpha_0 \tag{1}$$
$$= a_5 \sigma \rho^2 + a_4 \sigma \rho + a_3 \sigma + a_2 \rho^2 + a_1 \rho + a_0 \tag{2}$$
$$= (a_5, a_4, a_3, a_2, a_1, a_0) \tag{3}$$

where α_i is an element in $\mathbb{F}_{3^{3m}}$, a_j be an element in $\mathbb{F}_{3^m}$ and $i = 0, 1, j = 0, 1, \cdots, 5$. Operations in $\mathbb{F}_{3^{3m}}$ and $\mathbb{F}_{3^{6m}}$ are addition, subtraction, cube, multiplication and inversion, and the operations require operations in $\mathbb{F}_{3^m}$. The operations in $\mathbb{F}_{3^{3m}}$ and $\mathbb{F}_{3^{6m}}$ are computed the same way in [8].

We show the costs of operations in $\mathbb{F}_{3^{3m}}$ and $\mathbb{F}_{3^{6m}}$ in Table 1. The operations cost of addition/subtraction and cube in $\mathbb{F}_{3^{6m}}$ is just 2 times of that in $\mathbb{F}_{3^{3m}}$. Meanwhile the operation cost of multiplication and inversion in $\mathbb{F}_{3^{6m}}$ is more than 2 times of that in $\mathbb{F}_{3^{3m}}$.

Table 1. The costs of operations in $\mathbb{F}_{3^{3m}}$ and $\mathbb{F}_{3^{6m}}$

Operations	$\mathbb{F}_{3^{3m}}$	$\mathbb{F}_{3^{6m}}$
Addition / Subtraction	3A	6A
Multiplication	12A + 6M	51A + 18M
Cube	3A + 3C	6A + 6C
Inversion	6A + 15M + 1I	57A + 38M + 1I

2.4   Tate Pairing

Tate pairing requires operations of elliptic curve over finite fields. In this paper, we use the following supersingular elliptic curve over $\mathbb{F}_{3^m}$,

$$E(\mathbb{F}_{3^m}) = \{(x, y) \in (\mathbb{F}_{3^m})^2 \mid y^2 = x^3 - x + 1\} \cup \{\mathcal{O}\}$$

where $\mathcal{O}$ is the point at infinity. The group order $\sharp E$ of $E(\mathbb{F}_{3^m})$ is $\sharp E = 3^m + 3^{(m+1)/2} + 1$. Let r be a prime number which satisfies with $r | \sharp E$ and $r | (3^{6m} - 1)$. Tate pairing is defined as follows:

$$e\langle \cdot, \cdot \rangle : E(\mathbb{F}_{3^m})[r] \times E(\mathbb{F}_{3^{6m}})[r] \rightarrow \mathbb{F}_{3^{6m}}^* / (\mathbb{F}_{3^{6m}}^*)^r$$

where $E(\mathbb{F}_{3^m})[r]$ is the subgroup of order r in $E(\mathbb{F}_{3^m})$. Point in $E(\mathbb{F}_{3^{6m}})$ is generated from point in $E(\mathbb{F}_{3^m})$ by using distortion map $\phi(x, y) = (-x + \rho, y\sigma)$. The pairing $e\langle P, Q \rangle$ satisfies bilinearity $e\langle aP, Q \rangle = e\langle P, aQ \rangle = e\langle P, Q \rangle^a$, where P, Q are points in $E(\mathbb{F}_{3^m})[r]$ and a is an integer.

Miller proposed the first polynomial time algorithm for computing Tate pairing [14]. Duursma and Lee proposed an efficient algorithm using supersingular elliptic curve over finite fields in characteristic 3 [6]. Kwon proposed an improved algorithm of Duursma-Lee algorithm which requires no cube root. We present Duursma-Lee algorithm without cube root in Algorithm 1.

Duursma-Lee algorithm has the step which is called the final exponentiation. The step is necessary to compute $T^{(3^{3m}-1)}$, where $T = \tau_1 \sigma + \tau_0$ is the representation in equation (2). One final exponentiation usually requires $3m$ multiplications and 1 inversion in $\mathbb{F}_{3^{6m}}$. However it can be computed by 1 multiplication and 1 inversion due to $T^{(3^{3m}-1)} = (-\tau_1 \sigma + t_0)(\tau_1 \sigma + \tau_0)^{-1}$ [12].

Algorithm 1. Duursma-Lee algorithm [13]

INPUT: $P = (x_p, y_p), Q = (x_q, y_q) \in E(\mathbb{F}_{3^m})[r]$
OUTPUT: $e\langle P, Q \rangle \in \mathbb{F}_{3^{6m}}$
1: initialization:
   $T \leftarrow 1$ (in $\mathbb{F}_{3^{6m}}$)
   $a \leftarrow x_p, b \leftarrow y_p, x \leftarrow x_q{}^3, y \leftarrow y_q{}^3$ (in $\mathbb{F}_{3^m}$)
   $d \leftarrow 1$ (in $\mathbb{F}_3$)
2: **for** $i \leftarrow 0$ to $m - 1$ **do**
3:     $a \leftarrow a^9, b \leftarrow b^9$ (in $\mathbb{F}_{3^m}$)
4:     $c \leftarrow a + x + d$ (in $\mathbb{F}_{3^m}$)
5:     $R \leftarrow -by\sigma - \rho^2 - c\rho - c^2$ (in $\mathbb{F}_{3^{6m}}$)
6:     $T \leftarrow T^3$ (in $\mathbb{F}_{3^{6m}}$)
7:     $T \leftarrow TR$ (in $\mathbb{F}_{3^{6m}}$)
8:     $y \leftarrow -y$ (in $\mathbb{F}_{3^m}$)
9:     $d \leftarrow d - 1$ (in $\mathbb{F}_3$)
10: **end for**
11: final exponentiation:
    $T \leftarrow \text{Algorithm\_2} (T)$
12: **return** T

Algorithm 2. Final exponentiation (Duursma-Lee algorithm) [12]

INPUT: $T = \tau_1\sigma + \tau_0 \in \mathbb{F}_{3^{6m}}$
OUTPUT: $T^{(3^{3m}-1)} \in \mathbb{F}_{3^{6m}}$
   $U \leftarrow T^{-1}$ (in $\mathbb{F}_{3^{6m}}$)
   $\tau_1 \leftarrow -\tau_1$ (in $\mathbb{F}_{3^{3m}}$)
   $T \leftarrow UT$ (in $\mathbb{F}_{3^{6m}}$)
   return T

2.5 η_T Pairing

η_T pairing can reduce the cost of Duursma-Lee algorithm to the half by using Frobenius map [1]. An improved algorithm without cube root was also proposed in η_T pairing [3]. We show η_T pairing without cube root in Algorithm 3. η_T pairing need a final exponentiation step to compute T^S, where $S = (3^{3m} - 1)(3^m + 1)(3^m - 3^{(m+1)/2} + 1)$. Because S is a large value, it takes much time to compute the final exponentiation compared with Duursma-Lee algorithm. However, an efficient algorithm which uses the torus T_2 for $\mathbb{F}_{3^{6m}}^*$ was proposed, where T_2 is defined $T_2(\mathbb{F}_{3^{3m}}) = \{A_0 + A_1\sigma \in \mathbb{F}_{3^{6m}}^* : A_0{}^2 + A_1{}^2 = 1\}$ [15]. This algorithm for computing T^S is shown in Algorithm 5.

The output of Duursma-Lee algorithm and η_T pairing relates as follows:

$$(\eta_T\langle P, Q \rangle^S)^{3(3^{(m+1)/2}+1)^2} = e\langle P, Q \rangle^{-3^{(m+3)/2}},$$

and $e\langle P, Q \rangle$ can compute from $U = \eta_T\langle P, Q \rangle^S$ as follows [3]:

$$e\langle P, Q \rangle = \left(U^2 \cdot U^{3^{(m+1)/2}} \cdot \sqrt[3^m]{U^{(m-1)/2}} \right)^{-1}.$$

Algorithm 3. η_T pairing [3]

INPUT: $P = (x_p, y_p), Q = (x_q, y_q) \in E(\mathbb{F}_{3^m})[r]$,
$\qquad S = (3^{3m} - 1)(3^m + 1)(3^m - 3^{(m+1)/2} + 1)$

OUTPUT: $(\eta_T \langle P, Q \rangle^S)^{3^{(m+1)/2}} \in \mathbb{F}_{3^{6m}}$

1: initialization:
$\qquad a \leftarrow x_p, b \leftarrow -y_p, x \leftarrow x_q, y \leftarrow y_q \quad$ (in $\mathbb{F}_{3^m}$)
$\qquad d \leftarrow 1 \quad$ (in $\mathbb{F}_3$)
$\qquad c \leftarrow a + x + d \quad$ (in $\mathbb{F}_{3^m}$)
$\qquad T \leftarrow y\sigma + b\rho - bc \quad$ (in $\mathbb{F}_{3^{6m}}$)
2: **for** $i \leftarrow 0$ to $(m-1)/2$ **do**
3: $\quad c \leftarrow a + x + d \quad$ (in $\mathbb{F}_{3^m}$)
4: $\quad R \leftarrow by\sigma - \rho^2 - c\rho - c^2 \quad$ (in $\mathbb{F}_{3^{6m}}$)
5: $\quad T \leftarrow TR \quad$ (in $\mathbb{F}_{3^{6m}}$)
6: $\quad T \leftarrow T^3 \quad$ (in $\mathbb{F}_{3^{6m}}$)
7: $\quad b \leftarrow -b \quad$ (in $\mathbb{F}_{3^m}$)
8: $\quad x \leftarrow x^9, \ y \leftarrow y^9 \quad$ (in $\mathbb{F}_{3^m}$)
9: $\quad d \leftarrow d - 1 \quad$ (in $\mathbb{F}_3$)
10: **end for**
11: final exponentiation:
$\qquad T \leftarrow$ Algorithm_5 (T)
12: **return** T

Table 2. Computation costs of Duursma-Lee algorithm and η_T pairing in $\mathbb{F}_{3^{97}}$

Duursma-Lee algorithm (Alg. 1)	4635A + 972C + 1511M + 1I	≈ 1664M
(final exponentiation (Alg. 2))	(108A + 56M + 1I)	(≈ 67M)
η_T pairing (Alg. 3)	2785A + 784C + 871M + 1I	≈ 987M
(final exponentiation (Alg. 5))	(496A + 294C + 86M + 1I)	(≈ 130M)

Here we estimate the computational costs of Duursma-Lee algorithm and η_T pairing. The extension degree of the underlying finite fields is usually chosen as $m = 97, 167, 193, 239, 313$ [1,2,3,8,11,12]. The computational cost with $m = 97$ is shown in Table 2. The third column is the estimated number of multiplications with A= 0.01M, C= 0.1M, I= 10M appeared in Section 3.4. Actually, the cost of η_T pairing is smaller than that of Duursma-Lee algorithm.

3   Implementation of the Pairing on BREW

In this section, we explain our efficient implementation of the pairing in mobile-phones on BREW[1].

---

[1] BREW is a registered trademark of Qualcomm company and it is an application platform developed for mobilephones of cdmaOne and cdma2000.

3.1 Experimental Environment and Analysis of the Program

In this paper, we try to implement the pairing on ARM9 processors which is currently often used for mobilephones. BREW supports an emulator of ARM processors on a PC whose programs are written in C language. A source file in C is complied using an ARM compiler on BREW, and then an executable file (*.mod) of BREW applications for ARM processors is generated.

Table 3. Timings by profiling the functions in $\mathbb{F}_{3^{97}}$

Duursma-Lee algorithm

Time of Function	%	Hit Count	Function
927.176	84.1	199900	FF_Multi
83.649	7.6	97776	FF_Cube
22.580	2.0	408606	FF_Add

η_T pairing

Time of Function	%	Hit Count	Function
338.506	78.6	113200	FF_Multi
53.508	12.4	165976	FF_Cube
10.281	2.4	351406	FF_Add

Here we are interested in the timing of the executable files on ARM processors. The same source code can be also compiled using a standard C compiler, and we can examine the timing of the compiled codes on a PC. We deploy a PC (AMD Opteron Processor 246 (2.0 GHz), RAM : 1 GByte) with GCC version 3.4.2 using the flags "-O2 -fomit-frame-pointer", and mobilephones (150MHz ARM9 processor and 225MHz ARM9 processor) with an ARM complier using "-Otime" for optimizing the speed.

In order to implement the pairing, we implement the functions of the finite field in Section 2.2 and the pairing in Sections 2.4-2.5 from scratch in C language. The extension degrees and their irreducible trinomial are chosen as $m = 97, 167, 193,$ $239, 313$ and $x^{97} + x^{12} + 2$, $x^{167} + x^{96} + 2$, $x^{193} + x^{12} + 2$, $x^{239} + x^{24} + 2$, $x^{313} + x^{126} + 2$, respectively. The functions in our implementation are named as follows: FF_Add (addition in $\mathbb{F}_{3^m}$), FF_Multi (Comb method in $\mathbb{F}_{3^m}$), FF_Cube (cube in $\mathbb{F}_{3^m}$) and so on. Then we examine the timing of the basic functions (FF_Add, FF_Multi, FF_Cube, etc) by GCC using a profiling tool. The timings by profiling for Duursma-Lee algorithm and η_T pairing on $\mathbb{F}_{3^{97}}$ is shown in Table 3.

In Table 3, the multiplication speeds of both Duursma-Lee algorithm and η_T pairing are about 80% in the whole program of the pairing. Accordingly, we try to optimize the speed of multiplication in $\mathbb{F}_{3^m}$.

3.2 Optimized Multiplication for BREW

In the following we propose *the improved Comb method*, which reduces the number of the substitution operations by unrolling the first loop of Comb method.

Here we explain the improved Comb method with extension degree $m = 97$, but it can be applicable to other extension degrees $m = 167, 193, 237, 313$.

We now focus on $B[3]$ which is one of the array representing $B(x) \in \mathbb{F}_{3^{97}}$. Note that $B[3]$ only contains the 96-th coefficient of $B(x)$ as $B[3]_0$, namely,

$$B[3] = (B[3]_{31}, B[3]_{30}, \cdots, B[3]_1, B[3]_0) = (0, 0, \cdots, 0, b_{96}).$$

When we compute $A(x) \cdot B(x)$ using Comb method in Section 2.2, we have to perform the addition of $A(x) \cdot B[3]$ and substitution operations for a temporary save of the addition even $B[3]_j = 0$ for $j = 31, 30, \cdots, 1$. There are many substitution operations and additions which do not affect the result of $A(x) \cdot B(x)$. Those operations can be eliminated by unrolling the loop of computing $B[3]$. In other words, the loop corresponding to $B[i]_j$ with $j > 0$ is not computed for $i = 3$, and we only fulfill the complete loop for $B[i]_0$ with $i = 0, 1, 2, 3$. As a result, the proposed scheme can save 31 substitution operations compared with Comb method, and we achieve about 20% faster multiplication. We show the improved Comb method in Algorithm 4.

Algorithm 4. Improved Comb method $m = 97$

INPUT: $A(x), B(x) \in \mathbb{F}_{3^m}$, $W = 32$: word length
OUTPUT: $C(x) = A(x) \cdot B(x) \bmod f(x) \in \mathbb{F}_{3^m}$
1: $C(x) \leftarrow 0$
2: **for** $i \leftarrow 0$ to 3 **do**
3:     $C(x) \leftarrow C(x) + B[i]_0 A(x) x^{iW}$
4: **end for**
5: **for** $j \leftarrow 1$ to W **do**
6:     **for** $i \leftarrow 0$ to 2 **do**
7:         $C(x) \leftarrow C(x) + B[i]_j A(x) x^{iW+j}$
8:     **end for**
9: **end for**
10: **for** $i \leftarrow 2m - 2$ downto m **do**
11:     $c_{i-85} \leftarrow c_{i-85} - c_i$
12:     $c_{i-97} \leftarrow c_{i-97} + c_i$
13:     $c_i \leftarrow 0$
14: **end for**
15: **return** $C(x)$

This algorithm has two steps, the polynomial multiplication step (line 1-9) and the reduction step (line 10-14), where the reduction step is the computation of $c(x) \bmod f(x)$. The main loop is line 5-9, and process of loop unrolling is line 2-4. The difference of the proposed scheme from Comb method is line 6. The number of iteration in the loop of line 6 becomes one time shorter, and the omitted process is moved to line 2.

3.3   Further Discussion on Speed-Up

We carry out the following two methods for speed-up of the pairing.

In the one method, we perform effectively multiplication in $\mathbb{F}_{3^{6m}}$ in the pairing algorithms. The multiplication $T \cdot R$ in $\mathbb{F}_{3^{6m}}$ is computed in line 7 of Algorithm 1 and line 5 of Algorithm 3. Kerins et al. pointed out the element $R = r_5 \sigma \rho^2 + r_4 \sigma \rho + r_3 \sigma + r_2 \rho^2 + r_1 \rho + r_0$ in $\mathbb{F}_{3^{6m}}$ satisfies $r_4 = r_5 = 0$ and $r_2 = 2$ [12]. The number of multiplication in $\mathbb{F}_{3^m}$ required for $T \cdot R$ is reduced because the multiplication with the constants $(r_2, r_4$ and $r_5)$ is virtually for free. We can reduce the speed of the whole pairing about 10% by developing the optimized multiplication for $T \cdot R$.

In the other method, we unroll the loop used in the functions of $\mathbb{F}_{3^m}$. The functions in $\mathbb{F}_{3^m}$ processes 32 coefficients depending on word length at a time. For example, the addition of m (hi, lo)-bits is constructed $\lceil m/W \rceil$ times of loop. By unrolling this loop, the count of a pipeline hazard in the target processor can be reduced and can be speeded up. Actually, the processing speed can be improved about 30% by unrolling the loop.

Finally, we also implemented a window method in Algorithm 4. However the speed of the window method of width 2 was slower on the ARM9 processors (Note that it was faster on the Opteron processor). Therefore we do not use a window method in this paper. One of the reasons is that the precomputation table in a window method cannot store in the CPU cache.

3.4   Implementation Result

We show the average time of the operations in $\mathbb{F}_{3^m}$ and the pairing algorithms, Duursma-Lee algorithm and η_T pairing, on the ARM9 processors and on the Opteron processor in Table 4-6. We compute the average time for the pairing algorithm with random input at least 200 times on the ARM9 processors and at least 20,000 times on the Opteron processor. The optimized program at $m = 97$ is denoted by "$opt\mathbb{F}_{3^{97}}$". This program uses the improved Comb method with unrolling the loop, and other programs use Comb method without it in $\mathbb{F}_{3^m}$.

Table 4. The average time of the operations in $\mathbb{F}_{3^m}$ and the pairing algorithms on the 150MHz ARM9 processor (msec)

150MHz ARM9	$opt\mathbb{F}_{3^{97}}$	$\mathbb{F}_{3^{97}}$	$\mathbb{F}_{3^{167}}$	$\mathbb{F}_{3^{193}}$	$\mathbb{F}_{3^{239}}$	$\mathbb{F}_{3^{313}}$
Addition (A)	0.0006	0.0009	0.0012	0.0014	0.0016	0.0020
Subtraction (A)	0.0006	0.0009	0.0012	0.0014	0.0016	0.0019
Cube (C)	0.0070	0.0067	0.0156	0.0189	0.0229	0.0261
Multiplication (M)	0.0642	0.0852	0.2055	0.2200	0.3410	0.5308
Inversion (I)	0.6915	0.8360	1.8540	2.3765	3.4115	5.8725
Duursma-Lee algorithm	98.96	129.19	549.39	701.18	1303.07	2616.63
η_T pairing	56.50	76.68	337.25	401.27	738.23	1459.65

Table 5. The average time of the operations in $\mathbb{F}_{3^m}$ and the pairing algorithms on the 225MHz ARM9 processor (msec)

225MHz ARM9	$opt\mathbb{F}_{3^{97}}$	$\mathbb{F}_{3^{97}}$	$\mathbb{F}_{3^{167}}$	$\mathbb{F}_{3^{193}}$	$\mathbb{F}_{3^{239}}$	$\mathbb{F}_{3^{313}}$
Addition (A)	0.0004	0.0005	0.0007	0.0008	0.0009	0.0012
Subtraction (A)	0.0004	0.0005	0.0007	0.0008	0.0010	0.0012
Cube (C)	0.0050	0.0051	0.0107	0.0133	0.0155	0.0162
Multiplication (M)	0.0393	0.0530	0.1448	0.2313	0.2200	0.3420
Inversion (I)	0.4590	0.5825	1.6890	1.4480	2.3040	3.7280
Duursma-Lee algorithm	66.00	84.70	356.11	457.93	847.56	1702.64
η_T pairing	37.52	50.34	218.27	261.88	478.54	947.30

Table 6. The average time of the operations in $\mathbb{F}_{3^m}$ and the pairing algorithms on the 2.0 GHz Opteron processor (μ sec)

2.0 GHz Opteron	$opt\mathbb{F}_{3^{97}}$	$\mathbb{F}_{3^{97}}$	$\mathbb{F}_{3^{167}}$	$\mathbb{F}_{3^{193}}$	$\mathbb{F}_{3^{239}}$	$\mathbb{F}_{3^{313}}$
Addition (A)	0.0118	0.0158	0.0219	0.0250	0.0280	0.0421
Subtraction (A)	0.0118	0.0160	0.0221	0.0250	0.0281	0.0421
Cube (C)	0.1631	0.1631	0.3062	0.3406	0.4151	0.4440
Multiplication (M)	1.5955	2.3438	5.1805	5.9468	8.6590	14.7052
Inversion (I)	16.6686	19.7985	44.3534	62.2334	86.1984	137.4680
Duursma-Lee algorithm	2,610	3,810	13,980	18,531	32,800	71,780
η_T pairing	1,480	2,240	8,540	10,473	18,400	39,720

In $opt\mathbb{F}_{3^{97}}$ and $\mathbb{F}_{3^{97}}$, it turns out that the addition/subtraction (A) was about 0.01 times of the multiplication (M), the cube (C) was about 0.1 times and the inversion (I) was about 10 times. This estimation have little differences with the ARM9 processors and the Opteron processor. Based on the values, we can estimate the ratios of final exponentiation of Duursma-Lee algorithm and η_T pairing as 4.03% and 13.2%, respectively. The ratios required in $\mathbb{F}_{3^m}$ in the pairing computation become 2.78% addition/subtraction (A), 5.84% cube (C), 90.78% multiplication (M) and 0.60% inversion (I) in Duursma-Lee algorithm, and 2.82% addition/subtraction (A), 7.94% cube (C), 88.22% multiplication (M) and 1.01% inversion (I) in η_T pairing, respectively. In our programs except $opt\mathbb{F}_{3^{97}}$, when extension degree becomes about 2 times, the processing speed becomes about 5 times slower on both the ARM9 processors and the Opteron processor.

The total size of executable files (*.mod) in $opt\mathbb{F}_{3^{97}}$ was 36,528 Bytes. The size of other programs for each degree ($m = 97, 167, 193, 239, 313$) is smaller than that of $opt\mathbb{F}_{3^{97}}$. As an average size of executable files currently, 300 Kbytes or less is standard. Then, the size of our executable files becomes the size of around 10% in BREW applications.

η_T pairing is more efficient than Duursma-Lee algorithm in ARM9 processors and an Opteron processor. The processing speed achieves 56.5 msec in the

150MHz ARM9 processor and 37.52 msec in the 225MHz ARM9 processor for computing η_T pairing on the supersingular curve over $\mathbb{F}_{3^{97}}$.

4   Conclusion

In this paper, we presented efficient implementation of Duursma-Lee algorithm and η_T pairing over $\mathbb{F}_{3^m}$ using BREW mobilephones. From our initial implementation in $\mathbb{F}_{3^{97}}$, the whole timing required for the multiplication is about 80% in the computation of the pairings. We thus proposed *improved Comb method*, which is an optimized multiplication for BREW mobilephones, namely with fewer substitution operations. Moreover, we improved the multiplication $T \cdot R$ in $\mathbb{F}_{3^{6m}}$ of the pairing algorithms and we performed loop unrolling in the finite field.

As a result, the processing speed of our optimized pairing implementation using BREW on the 150MHz ARM9 and the 225MHz ARM9 achieved under 100 milliseconds. It has become efficient enough to implement security applications, such as short signature or ID-based cryptosystems, using the pairing on BREW mobilephones.

References

1. Barreto, P., Galbraith, S., O'hEigeartaigh, C., Scott, M.: Efficient Pairing Computation on Supersingular Abelian Varieties. Designs, Codes and Cryptography 42(3), 239–271 (2007)
2. Barreto, P., Kim, H., Lynn, B., Scott, M.: Efficient Algorithms for Pairing-Based Cryptosystems. In: Yung, M. (ed.) CRYPTO 2002. LNCS, vol. 2442, pp. 354–368. Springer, Heidelberg (2002)
3. Beuchat, J., Shirase, M., Takagi, T., Okamoto, E.: An Algorithm for the η_T Pairing Calculation in Characteristic Three and its Hardware Implementation. In: IEEE International Symposium on Computer Arithmetic, ARITH-18, pp. 97–104 (2007)
4. Boneh, D., Franklin, M.: Identity Based Encryption from the Weil Pairing. SIAM J. Comput. 32(3), 514–532 (2001)
5. Boneh, D., Lynn, B., Shacham, H.: Short Signatures from the Weil Pairing. In: Boyd, C. (ed.) ASIACRYPT 2001. LNCS, vol. 2248, pp. 514–532. Springer, Heidelberg (2001)
6. Duursma, I., Lee, H.: Tate Pairing Implementation for Hyperelliptic Curves $y^2 = x^p - x + d$. In: Laih, C.-S. (ed.) ASIACRYPT 2003. LNCS, vol. 2894, pp. 111–123. Springer, Heidelberg (2003)
7. Galbraith, S., Harrison, K., Soldera, D.: Implementing the Tate Pairing. In: Fieker, C., Kohel, D.R. (eds.) Algorithmic Number Theory. LNCS, vol. 2369, pp. 324–337. Springer, Heidelberg (2002)
8. Granger, R., Page, D., Stam, M.: On Small Characteristic Algebraic Tori in Pairing-Based Cryptography. LMS Journal of Computation and Mathematics 9, 64–85 (2006)
9. Granger, R., Page, D., Stam, M.: Hardware and Software Normal Basis Arithmetic for Pairing-Based Cryptography in Characteristic Three. IEEE Transactions on Computers 54(7), 852–860 (2005)

10. Hankerson, D., Menezes, A., Vanstone, S.: Guide to Elliptic Curve Cryptography. Springer, Heidelberg (2004)
11. Kawahara, Y., Takagi, T., Okamoto, E.: Efficient Implementation of Tate Pairing on a Mobile Phone using Java. In: CIS 2006. LNCS (LNAI), vol. 4456, pp. 396–405 (2007)
12. Kerins, T., Marnane, W., Popovici, E., Barreto, P.: Efficient Hardware for the Tate Pairing Calculation in Characteristic Three. In: Rao, J.R., Sunar, B. (eds.) CHES 2005. LNCS, vol. 3659, pp. 412–426. Springer, Heidelberg (2005)
13. Kwon, S.: Efficient Tate Pairing Computation for Supersingular Elliptic Curves over Binary Fields. Cryptology ePrint Archive, Report 2004/303 (2004)
14. Miller, V.: Short Programs for Functions on Curves (unpublished Manuscript)
15. Shirase, M., Takagi, T., Okamoto, E.: Some efficient algorithms for the final exponentiation of η_T pairing. In: ISPEC 2007. LNCS, vol. 4464, pp. 254–268 (2007)

A   Final Exponentiation for Pairing

In this appendix, we describe the algorithms used for the pairing in this paper.

Algorithm 5. Final exponentiation (η_T pairing) [15]

INPUT: $K \in \mathbb{F}_{3^{6m}}$, $S = (3^{3m} - 1)(3^m + 1)(3^m - 3^{(m+1)/2} + 1)$
OUTPUT: $K^S \in \mathbb{F}_{3^{6m}}$

1: $K \leftarrow K^{3^{3m}-1}$, $G \leftarrow \Lambda(K) = K^{3^m+1}$
2: $K \leftarrow G$, $K \leftarrow \Lambda(K) = K^{3^m+1}$
3: **for** $i \leftarrow 0$ to $(m-1)/2$ **do**
4:    $G \leftarrow G^3$
5: **end for**
6: $g_2 \leftarrow -g_2$, $g_1 \leftarrow -g_1$, $g_0 \leftarrow -g_0$
7: **return** $K \cdot G$

Algorithm 6. Computation of $\Lambda(K)$ [15]

INPUT: $K = (k_5, k_4, k_3, k_2, k_1, k_0) \in \mathbb{F}_{3^{6m}}$
OUTPUT: $\Lambda(K) = K^{3^m+1} \in T_2(\mathbb{F}_{3^{3m}})$

1: $v_0 \leftarrow k_0 k_2$, $v_1 \leftarrow k_3 k_5$, $v_2 \leftarrow k_1 k_2$, $v_3 \leftarrow k_4 k_5$, $v_4 \leftarrow (k_0 + k_3)(k_2 - k_5)$
2: $v_5 \leftarrow k_3 k_1$, $v_6 \leftarrow k_0 k_4$, $v_7 \leftarrow (k_0 + k_3)(k_1 + k_4)$, $v_8 \leftarrow (k_1 + k_4)(k_2 - k_5)$
3: $c_0 \leftarrow 1 + v_0 + v_1 \mp v_2 \mp v_3$
4: $c_1 \leftarrow v_7 - v_2 - v_3 - v_5 - v_6$ $(m \equiv 1 \bmod 12)$
    $c_1 \leftarrow v_5 + v_6 - v_7$ $(m \equiv -1 \bmod 12)$
5: $c_2 \leftarrow v_2 + v_3 + v_7 - v_5 - v_6$
6: $c_3 \leftarrow v_1 + v_4 \pm v_5 - v_0 \mp v_6$
7: $c_4 \leftarrow v_3 + v_8 \pm v_0 - v_2 \mp v_1 \mp v_4$
8: $c_5 \leftarrow \pm v_3 \pm v_8 \mp v_2$
9: **return** $C = (c_5, c_4, c_3, c_2, c_1, c_0)$

Security Analysis of MISTY1

Hidema Tanaka[1], Yasuo Hatano[2], Nobuyuki Sugio[3], and Toshinobu Kaneko[4]

[1] National Institute of Information and Communications Technology,
4-2-1 Nukui-Kitamachi, Koganei, Tokyo, 184-8795, Japan
[2] Systems Development Laboratory, Hitachi, Ltd.
Yokohama Laboratory, 292, Yoshida-cho, Totsuka-ku, Yokohama, Kanagawa,
244-0817, Japan
[3] Service & Solution Development Department, NTT DoCoMo, Inc.
NTT DoCoMo R&D Center 3-5, Hikarinooka, Yokosuka, Kanagawa 239-8536, Japan
[4] Tokyo University of Science
2641 Yamazaki Noda, 278-8510, Japan

Abstract. We analyze 64-bit block cipher MISTY1 from several standpoints. Our analysis consists of two algorithms based on the higher order differential property of the S-box. The first succeeds in attacking a six round MISTY1 provided $2^{18.9}$ chosen plaintexts and $2^{80.9}$ computational cost. The second succeeds in attacking a seven round MISTY1 with no FL functions by controlling the value of the fixed part of the plaintext and using a 2-round elimination method provided $2^{11.9}$ chosen plaintexts and $2^{125.1}$ computational cost. Both algorithms exceeds the existing attack algorithms against MISTY1 and give new perspectives for the security of MISTY1.

Keywords: MISTY1, Higher order differential, Chosen plaintext attack.

1 Introduction

MISTY1 is a 64-bit block cipher with a 128-bit secret key [6]. It has an eight round Feistel structure with FO functions and FL functions. Since its security is basically guaranteed by FO functions only, a three round MISTY1 with no FL functions is still provably secure against differential cryptanalysis and linear cryptanalysis. It has relatively high performance on both software environments and hardware platforms compared with other 64-bit block ciphers. Because of these desirable security properties and the high performance, MISTY1 is considered as one of the strongest 64-bit block ciphers and it has been widely evaluated by some international cryptographic technology evaluation projects such as NESSIE [8]. And it is considered as a strong candidate for several international standardization [9]. We also note that KASUMI, a variant of MISTY1, is the standard cipher within 3GPP systems [10]. Hence, it is significant for information security community to understand the precise security level of MISTY1.

In this paper, we show a new development of security evaluation for MISTY1 by describing two attack algorithms using the higher order differential property

S. Kim, M. Yung, and H.-W. Lee (Eds.): WISA 2007, LNCS 4867, pp. 215–226, 2007.
© Springer-Verlag Berlin Heidelberg 2007

216   H. Tanaka et al.

of S-box. By analyzing the key schedule and relation among sub-keys, we derive the condition for the secret key to be insecure. Under the condition, we can construct an attack algorithm against a six round MISTY1 that has FL functions in the last round. This algorithm needs $2^{18.9}$ chosen plaintexts and $2^{80.6}$ computational cost. Knudsen and Wagner have shown that a five round MISTY1 is attackable by integral cryptanalysis [2]. Their method needs 2^{34} chosen plaintexts and 2^{48} computational cost. MISTY1 has FL functions in the last round, however, Knudsen and Wagner study a five round MISTY1 that has no FL function in the last round. We study a six round MISTY1 that has FL functions in the last round. Therefore, our target is more realistic and harder to attack than the model in [2].

Next, we invent a technique that controls the value of the fixed part of the plaintext. Using this technique and the 2-round elimination method, we can construct an attack algorithm against a seven round MISTY1 with no FL functions. This needs $2^{11.9}$ chosen plaintexts and $2^{125.1}$ computational cost. Kühn shows that a six round structure of MISTY1 with no FL functions is attackable by impossible differential cryptanalysis [5]. His method needs 2^{54} chosen plaintexts and 2^{61} computational cost. So, we improve the number of attackable rounds from [5].

These results indicate that MISTY1's simple key schedule and low order of S-boxes may be its weaknesses.

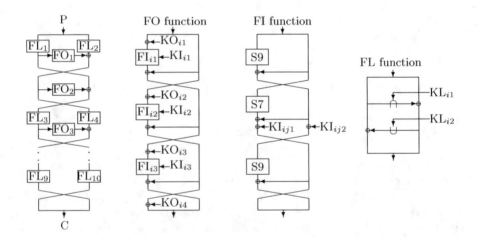

Fig. 1. MISTY1

Table 1. Key schedule

Sub-key	KO_{i1}	KO_{i2}	KO_{i3}	KO_{i4}	KI_{i1}	KI_{i2}	KI_{i3}	KL_{i1}	KL_{i2}
Secret key sub-block	K_i	K_{i+2}	K_{i+7}	K_{i+4}	K'_{i+5}	K'_{i+1}	K'_{i+3}	K_i (odd i) K'_{i+1} (even i)	K'_{i+6} (odd i) K_{i+3} (even i)

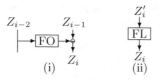

Fig. 2. Variables

2 Preliminaries

2.1 Notation

We explain briefly the notations in this paper. See Figure 1 for the structure of MISTY1. A plaintext P is expressed as follows :

$$P = (P_L || P_R)$$
$$= (X_{15}, \ldots, X_8 || X_7, \ldots, X_0), \quad X_i \in \begin{cases} \text{GF}(2)^7 : i = \text{even} \\ \text{GF}(2)^9 : i = \text{odd} \end{cases} \quad (2.1)$$

MISTY1 has two types of S-box; S7 and S9 in the FI function. S7 is a 7-bit S-box whose order is 3. And S9 is a 9-bit S-Box whose order is 2.

We summarize the key schedule in Table 1. The sub-keys are defined as follows.

$$K = (K_7, \ldots, K_0), \quad K_i \in \text{GF}(2)^{16}$$
$$K_i' = \text{FI}(K_i; K_{i+1}) \quad (2.2)$$

We define the variables Z_i and Z_i' as follows (see Figure 2). When FL functions are operated after the FO function, Z_i is rewritten as Z_i', and the output from the FL function is redefined as Z_i (see Figure 2 (ii)). Therefore, $Z_{-1}' = P_L$ and $Z_0' = P_R$.

We denote the left-most m-bit of the sub-block Q_i by Q_i^{Lm}, and the value of n-th order differential of the sub-block Q_i by $\Delta^{(n)} Q_i$, respectively.

2.2 Higher Order Differential Property

Babbage and Frisch analyzed the details of the relation between the linear and differential properties and the seventh order differential property [1]. Then they found an important property of the MISTY-structure and S-boxes. The property plays a crucial role in this paper.

Property 1: When MISTY1 has no FL functions, if the most-right seven bits of the input of FO_i consists of seventh order differential, the following holds for any value of the fixed part of the input or sub-keys.

$$\Delta^{(7)} Z_{i+1}^{L7} = \text{0x6d} \quad (2.3)$$

For example, $\Delta^{(7)} Z_3^{L7} = \text{0x6d}$ holds for the variable sub-block $X_0 \in \text{GF}(2)^7$. Our algorithms against MISTY1 exploit the property 1. In Section 3, we show that the condition of the secret key satisfies the equation (2.3) in the case of MISTY1 with FL functions as well. Our algorithm exploits the simple relation among sub-keys to make successful attack. In Section 4, we show an attack algorithm which exploits the property 1 as effective as possible. It focuses on the low cost of solving the attack equation because of the low order of S-box.

3   Weakness of Key Schedule

3.1   Basic Idea

In this section, we analyze MISTY1 with FL functions. The MISTY1's compact key schedule contributes to high implementing performance. However, there are very simple relations among sub-keys produced by the key schedule. Therefore, the number of unknowns in an attack equation is small, and so the necessary complexity to solve it turns out to be small actually appeared.

If the sub-key used by the AND operation contains only zeros and the sub-key used by the OR operation contains only ones, the output of the FL function is the EX-OR of its input and a constant. Thus, if we fix the sub-keys as follows,

$$\mathrm{KL}_{21} = \mathrm{KL}_{31} = 0\mathrm{x}0000, \qquad \mathrm{KL}_{22} = \mathrm{KL}_{32} = 0\mathrm{xffff} \qquad (3.1)$$

the higher order differential property of Z_3' is same as the property of output from third round of MISTY1 with no FL functions. Thus $\Delta^{(7)} Z_3'^{\mathrm{L7}} = 0\mathrm{x}6\mathrm{d}$ holds from equation (2.3) (see Figure 3).

The following condition for the secret key K is derived using the key schedule.

$$K_3' = K_2 = 0\mathrm{x}0000, \qquad K_5 = K_8' = 0\mathrm{xffff} \qquad (3.2)$$

where

$$K_3' = \mathrm{FI}(K_3; K_4), \qquad K_8' = \mathrm{FI}(K_8; K_1). \qquad (3.3)$$

Consequently, we need to fix the secret key sub-blocks K_1, K_2, K_3, K_4, K_5 and K_8.

However, we can show that the number of fixed secret key sub-blocks becomes small if we use an eighth order differential for the attack. In the case of fixed KL_3, from the formal analysis, the degree of the left-most 7 bits in the output of $\mathrm{FO}_3(Z_3'^{\mathrm{L7}})$ is 9 (see left part of figure 4). However, equation (2.3) implies that $\Delta^{(7)} Z_3'^{\mathrm{L7}} = 0\mathrm{x}6\mathrm{d}$. In the case of NOT fixed KL_3, the formal degree of $Z_3'^{\mathrm{L7}}$ is estimated to be 8 (see right part of figure 4). Comparing these estimations, we conjecture that the degree of $Z_3'^{\mathrm{L7}}$ for NOT fixed KL_3 is 7 and the value of its seventh order differential depends on the value of the fixed part of the plaintext and sub-keys.

From the properties of higher order differentials, it is easy to see that if $\Delta^{(n)} Z$ is constant, then $\Delta^{(n+1)} Z$ is equal to 0. Since the attacker cannot specify the value of the seventh order differential of $Z_3'^{\mathrm{L7}}$, we consider an attack using the

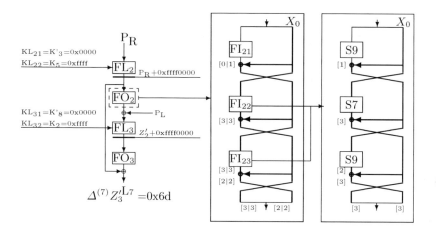

Fig. 3. Formal analysis

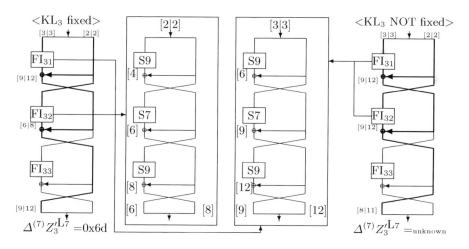

Fig. 4. Formal analysis of FO_3

eighth order differential. Moreover, we consider the case of NOT fixed KL_{21}. The plaintext sub-blocks X_2 and X_3 affect the maximum degree of output because they are inputted to FI_{21}. Therefore we cannot use them as variable sub-blocks. Thus we consider an eighth order differential using X_0 and one bit selected from among X_1. We confirmed that $\Delta^{(8)} Z_3'^{L7} = 0$ for such an eighth order differential by computer simulation although we have to omit the details of the simulation due to the limitted space. The attack equation derived from the equation $\Delta^{(8)} Z_3'^{L7} = 0$ has unknowns with respect to sub-keys for FL_6 and FO_5. However, if we fix the value of the secret key sub-block as $K_7 = KL_{62} = 0\text{xffff}$, we have $\Delta^{(8)} Z_3'^{L7} = 0$. We can neglect the unknowns with respect to the sub-keys for FL_6.

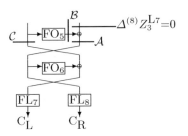

Fig. 5. Relation of the variables $\mathcal{A}$, $\mathcal{B}$ and $\mathcal{C}$ in equation (3.4)

Our attack succeeds under the condition that the secret key sub-blocks satisfy $K_5 = K_7 =$ 0xffff.

inter.tex

3.2   Attack Equation

In general, an attack equation is derived by calculating a higher order differential from the ciphertext side step by step. So, the attacker starts to derive an equation to solve the sub-keys in the last round. Then he derives a new equation to determine the next level unknown sub-keys using the information already obtained. So it is necessary for attacker to solve many attack equations. Contrary to such a general approach, we employ a different method, that is, we derive an attack equation for a secret key directly. So it suffices for us to construct an attack equation only once, and solve it.

We apply a method in [7] to solve the attack equation. In this paper, we call it an *algebraic method*. The algebraic method was proposed by Moriai, Shimoyama and Kaneko, to solve $\mathcal{KN}$ cipher and CAST. This method solves higher order equations by regarding them as linear equations: basically, every product of (more than two) variables is identified to a new variables, and the resulting equation has order 1, that is, every term of the resulting equation contains only one variables. Let us demonstrate an example of higher order equation with three variables (x_2, x_1, x_0) and the equation transformed. The equation $a_0x_0 \oplus a_1x_1 \oplus a_2x_0x_2 = 1$ is transformed to $a_0x_0 \oplus a_1x_1 \oplus a_2x_3 = 1$, where x_3 is a new variable which is identified to x_0x_2. We should note that the resulting equation is linear, that is, every term contains at most one variable. So we can regard the equation as a linear equation which contains at most $_3C_1 + {}_3C_2 + {}_3C_3 = 7$ new variables if the original equation contains three variables. Since the higher order equation with three variables is defined as the linear equation with seven variables by this procedure, to determine variables, we need more linear independent equations than equations required by a brute force search. However, the computational cost to solve linear equations is much smaller than the cost required by a brute force search. The reader is referred to [7] for the precise definition and detailed discussion of the algebraic method.

The number of the independent unknown terms turns out to be large if the number of secret key sub-blocks inputted to S-boxes is large. On the other hand, it is hard to solve a system of equations with a large number of independent unknown terms. Therefore, we need to keep the number of secret key sub-blocks inputted to S-boxes to a minimum in order to make the attack equation easily solvable. Following such a strategy, we construct an attack equation with a small number of independent unknown terms, and then present an attack algorithm against a six round MISTY1 using 2-round elimination method that estimates a part of the secret key sub-blocks with a brute force search.

Let us see the construction of our attack equation as follows. First of all, the following attack equation can be derived using 2-round elimination method.

$$\Delta^{(8)} Z_3^{\mathrm{L7}} = \Delta^{(8)} \{\mathcal{A} + \mathcal{B}\} = 0,$$

$$
\begin{cases}
\mathcal{A} = \mathrm{FL}_8(C_\mathrm{R}; \mathrm{KL}_8)^{\mathrm{L7}} \\
\quad = \mathrm{FL}_8(C_\mathrm{R}; K_6', K_8)^{\mathrm{L7}} \\[2mm]
\mathcal{B} = \mathrm{FO}_5(\mathcal{C}; \mathrm{KO}_5, \mathrm{KI}_5)^{\mathrm{L7}} \\
\quad = \mathrm{FO}_5(\mathcal{C}; K_1, K_2', K_4, K_5, K_6', K_7, K_8')^{\mathrm{L7}} \\[2mm]
\mathcal{C} = \mathrm{FL}_7(C_\mathrm{L}; \mathrm{KL}_7) + \mathrm{FO}_6(\mathrm{FL}_8(C_\mathrm{R}; K_6', K_8); \mathrm{KO}_6, \mathrm{KI}_6) \\
\quad = \mathrm{FL}_7(C_\mathrm{L}; K_2', K_4) + \mathrm{FO}_6(\mathrm{FL}_8(C_\mathrm{R}; K_6', K_8); K_1, K_2, K_3', K_5, K_7', K_8)
\end{cases}
$$

$$(3.4)$$

The relation of the variables $\mathcal{A}$, $\mathcal{B}$ and $\mathcal{C}$ is shown in Figure 5.

Next, we consider the optimal combination which divides unknowns into the group determined by an algebraic method and the group determined by a brute force search. Since K_5 and K_7 are fixed, we have 6 secret key sub-blocks (total: 96 bits) as unknowns. Since the number of terms inputted to the S-boxes becomes the maximum, it is difficult to solve KO_{61}, KO_{62} and KI_{61} by using the algebraic method. Thus we use a brute force search to estimate the secret key sub-blocks, $K_6(= \mathrm{KO}_{61})$, $K_8(= \mathrm{KO}_{62})$ and $K_3'(= \mathrm{KI}_{61})$. Since $K_7'(= \mathrm{FI}(K_7; K_8))$, we can treat the terms with respect to $\mathrm{KI}_{62} = K_7'$ as known values. Consequently,

$$
\begin{aligned}
&K_5, K_7 = \text{fixed}, \\
&K_3', K_6, K_8 = \text{estimated by brute force search}, \\
&K_7' = \text{calculated},
\end{aligned}
$$

$$(3.5)$$

and we have K_1, K_1', K_2, K_2' and K_4 as unknowns. Note that $K_1 = \mathrm{KO}_{54}$ is a constant term in the attack equation. Thus the terms with respect to K_1 do not exist in the eighth order differential. Thus we can omit terms with respect to K_1 and determine K_1', K_2, K_2' and K_4 (total 64 bit) by using the algebraic method.

Consequently, our attack equation consists of equation (3.4) and (3.5). By solving the attack equation, we can determine secret key sub-blocks K_1', K_2, K_2', K_3', K_4, K_5, K_6, K_7 and K_8. Since $K_1' = \mathrm{FI}(K_1; K_2)$ and $K_3' = \mathrm{FI}(K_3; K_4)$, secret key sub-block K_1 and K_3 can be determined by using (K_1', K_2), or (K_3', K_4).

3.3 Complexity

Let us assume that an attack equation derived from the value of the n-th order differential of the b-bit sub-block among the output. Let L be the number of independent unknowns in the attack equation. To determine all the unknowns, we need at least L linear equations. Since we can derive b linear equations from one n-th order differentials, we need $\lfloor L/b \rfloor$ different n-th order differential to derive the $L \times L$ coefficient matrix. If we use the same techniques shown in [7] to derive the matrix, we need to calculate the F function operation using L different temporary sub-keys. Thus we need $2^n \times \lfloor L/b \rfloor$ chosen plaintexts and $2^n \times \lfloor L/b \rfloor \times L$ F function operations (computational cost). After deriving the coefficient matrix, we can solve the equation by Gauss - Jordan elimination. In general, the cost required by Gauss - Jordan elimination can be negligible comparing with the cost required to calculate the $L \times L$ coefficient matrix.

We consider the complexity to solve the attack equation by estimating the other unknown S (s bits). If we solve the attack equation using $L + \alpha$ linear equations, the equation holds a false value of S, with probability $2^{-\alpha}$. Therefore, if we have additional α linear equations for such that $2^{s-\alpha} << 1$, we are able to eliminate all false value of S. Thus we need $2^n \times \lfloor (L + \alpha)/a \rfloor$ chosen plaintexts and $2^{n+s} \times \lfloor (L + \alpha)/a \rfloor \times L$ computational cost.

We counted the number of independent unknown terms appeared in the attack equation (3.4) and (3.5) by computer simulation. Although the details are omitted, we found 13,269 independent unknown terms. Since we estimated an $s = 48$ bit unknown with the brute force search, we set $\alpha = 64$ ($2^{48-64} = 2^{-16} << 1$). And since we derive the attack equation (3.4) focusing on 7-bit output sub-block Z_3^{L7}, b is equal to 7. Consequently, we estimate that $2^8 \times \lfloor (13269 + 64)/7 \rfloor \simeq 2^{18.9}$ chosen plaintexts and $2^{8+48} \times \lfloor (13269 + 64)/7 \rfloor \times 13269 \simeq 2^{80.6}$ computational cost are needed to determine a 128-bit secret key.

In this section, we attacked 6 round MISTY1 with FL functions, and succeeded in attacking because we could make the complexity for solving the attack equation relatively small ($2^{80.6}$). There are two reasons that we could make it. First, the key schedule for MISTY1 makes only 16 combinations of sub-keys. Second, the relation between 16 combinations of secret key sub-blocks is relatively simple because the key schedule is simple. MISTY1 has high performance because of its simple key schedule whereas our result suggests its key schedule might be a weakness in its security.

4   Low Order of S-Box

4.1   Basic Idea

In this section, we analyze MISTY1 with no FL functions (no FL version). We omit the key schedule in the following, because it is not defined for no FL version. The structure of no FL version is shown in Figure 6. We uses equivalent functions and sub-keys to simplify the attack algorithm. Our goal is to know the maximum attackable number of rounds for the no FL version using property 1.

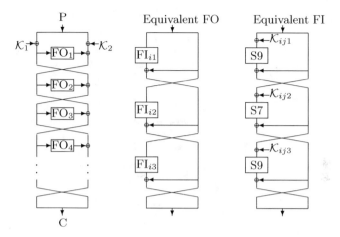

Fig. 6. MISTY1 with no FL functions

We consider an attack using the chosen plaintext $\mathcal{P}$ which has the following form :

$$\mathcal{P} = (V||\mathcal{P}_R), \quad V = (0, 0, 0, 0, 0, 0, 0, X_8) \tag{4.1}$$

where "0" denotes a fixed plaintext sub-block. In this case, since the variable sub-block is inputted to the first round, $\Delta^{(7)} Z_2^{L7} = 0\text{x}6\text{d}$ holds from the equation (2.3).

However, if the attacker can select the value of $\mathcal{P}_R$ which satisfies

$$Z_1 \oplus \mathcal{P}_R = \text{constant}, \tag{4.2}$$

he can get $\Delta^{(7)} Z_4^{L7} = 0\text{x}6\text{d}$.

Let us discuss the details of FO_1. The structure of FO_1 is shown in Figure 7. Since the output of FI_{11} and the outputs of the first S9 in FI_{12} and FI_{13} are constants, the value of the output of FO_1 is determined by the value of equivalent sub-keys $\mathcal{K}_{122}$, $\mathcal{K}_{123}$, $\mathcal{K}_{132}$ and $\mathcal{K}_{133}$ (total: 32 bits).

Let us consider the technique to adjust the value of $\mathcal{P}_R$ using the equation

$$\mathcal{P}_R = FO(V; \mathbf{K}) \tag{4.3}$$

where $\mathbf{K}$ denotes a 32 bit variable corresponding to equivalent sub-keys $\mathcal{K}_{122}$, $\mathcal{K}_{123}$, $\mathcal{K}_{132}$ and $\mathcal{K}_{133}$. The other equivalent sub-keys in FO are fixed to some constant value (for example, all zeros). As a result, equation (4.2) holds with probability 2^{-32}. If the attacker has all the value of $\mathbf{K}$, he can get $\Delta^{(7)} Z_4^{L7} = 0\text{x}6\text{d}$.

4.2   Attack Equation

From the discussion above, $\Delta^{(7)} Z_4^{L7} = 0\text{x}6\text{d}$ holds with probability 2^{-32}. Thus we can derive the following attack equation by calculating the seventh order differential from the ciphertext side.

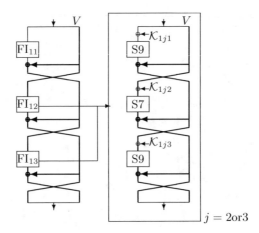

Fig. 7. Structure of FO_1

$$\Delta^{(7)}\{FO_6(C_L; \mathcal{K}_{611}, \mathcal{K}_{612}, \mathcal{K}_{621}, \mathcal{K}_{622},) + C_R\}^{L7} = 0x6d \qquad (4.4)$$

We solve the equation using the algebraic method. Although the details are omitted, we found that the number of independent unknown terms appeared in the attack equation (4.4) is 74 by computer simulation.

We use a brute force search for **K**. If **K** satisfies equation (4.2), the attack equation (4.4) holds and we can determine the unknown terms. But if it does not satisfy equation (4.2), the attack equation does not hold. In the same way as in Section 3.3, we set $\alpha = 48$ ($2^{32-48} = 2^{-16} << 1$) to solve the equation. And since we derive the attack equation (4.4) focusing on 7-bit output sub-block Z_4^{L7}, b is equal to 7. As a result, we need $2^7 \times \lfloor(74 + 48)/7\rfloor \simeq 2^{11.2}$ chosen plaintexts and $2^{7+32} \times \lfloor(74 + 48)/7\rfloor \times 74 \simeq 2^{49.4}$ computational cost. This computational cost is much smaller than 2^{128} needed for brute force search for secret key. Therefore a 2-round elimination method using a brute force search for the sub-key in the seventh round (total: 75 bits) works.

4.3   Complexity

Since we determine a 107-bit unknown (a 32-bit **K** and 75-bit sub-key in the seventh round), we set $\alpha = 123$ ($2^{107-123} = 2^{-16} << 1$). Thus we need $2^7 \times \lfloor(74 + 123)/7\rfloor \simeq 2^{11.9}$ chosen plaintexts and $2^{7+32+75} \times \lfloor74 + 123/7\rfloor \times 74 \simeq 2^{125.1}$ computational cost to attack a seven round MISTY1 with no FL functions.

In this section, we attacked 7 round MISTY1 with no FL functions, and succeeded in attacking because our technique enable us to raise the number of rounds.

The computational cost can be divided into three tasks: 2-round elimination, adjusting the value of $\mathcal{P}_R$, and matrix computation. Since S-boxes has low order, the order of the attack equation turns out to be low. Then the number of the independent unknown terms is small. This makes the cost for the matrix computation small. Then we can use our computation resource to the other tasks, that is, computation for the 2-round elimination and adjusting the value of $\mathcal{P}_R$.

Our technique enables us to determine the output of FO_1 for the input V using only 32-bit sub-key satisfying (4.2). Note that this is a big improvement because 75-bit $\mathbf{K}$ satisfying (4.2) is necessary to determine the output of FO_1 unless a certain trick is employed. Because the cost for matrix computation is kept small, we have more computation cost available and then the reduction from 75-bit to 32-bit helps to raise the number of rounds, that is, we could attack seven round MISTY1 with no FL.

Table 2. Comparison of results

	#rounds	#chosen plaintexts	comput. cost	method
MISTY1	5	2^{34}	2^{48}	integral [2]
with FL	6	$2^{18.9}$	$2^{80.9}$	Section 3
MISTY1	6	2^{54}	2^{61}	impossible differential [4,5]
with no FL	7	2^{39}	$2^{125.1}$	Section 4

5 Conclusions

First, we showed the attack of a six round MISTY1 with FL functions. This attack algorithm takes advantage of the simplicity of the key schedule. We gave the condition for the secret key to satisfy $\Delta^{(8)} Z_3^{L7} = 0$. And we also showed the technique to reduce the complexity to solve the attack equation using the simple relation among sub-keys. Consequently, we showed the attack equation for a six round MISTY1 with FL functions and the effective algorithm to determine a 128-bit secret key. Our algorithm needs $2^{18.9}$ chosen plaintexts and $2^{80.6}$ computational cost. Since our target, reduced round MISTY1, has FL functions in the last round, our algorithm is more realistic and powerful than the existing methods. Although it may be unfair to compare only the number of rounds and the number of chosen plaintexts, our algorithm can attack more rounds using less number of chosen plaintexts than Knudsen and Wagner's integral cryptanalysis.

We also succeeded in attacking MISTY1 with no FL functions that has more rounds than the model attacked previously. We presented a novel technique to control the value of fixed part of plaintext. Since the order of S-boxes is very small and unknown terms are very few, the algebraic method works very efficiently. The 2-round elimination method works because the complexity needed by the algebraic method in the procedure of solving the attack equation is very small. Our algorithm needs $2^{11.9}$ chosen plaintexts and $2^{125.1}$ computational cost, and is superior to the previous ones, in the sense that it can attack more rounds with fewer chosen plaintexts.

We summarize our results and the related works in table 2.

Acknowledgements

We would like to thank Ms. Makiko Shirota for her contribution to the computer simulations.

References

1. Babbage, S., Frisch, L.: On MISTY1 Higher Order Differential Cryptanalysis. In: Won, D. (ed.) ICISC 2000. LNCS, vol. 2015, pp. 22–36. Springer, Heidelberg (2001)
2. Knudsenand, L.R., Wagner, D.: Integral Cryptanalysis. In: Daemen, J., Rijmen, V. (eds.) FSE 2002. LNCS, vol. 2365, pp. 114–129. Springer, Heidelberg (2002)
3. Jakobsen, T., Knudsen, L.R.: The Interpolation Attack on Block Cipher. In: Preneel, B. (ed.) Fast Software Encryption. LNCS, vol. 1008, pp. 28–40. Springer, Heidelberg (1995)
4. Kühn, U.: Cryptanalysis of Reduced-Round MISTY. In: Pfitzmann, B. (ed.) EUROCRYPT 2001. LNCS, vol. 2045, pp. 325–339. Springer, Heidelberg (2001)
5. Kühn, U.: Improved Cryptanalysis of MISTY1. In: Daemen, J., Rijmen, V. (eds.) FSE 2002. LNCS, vol. 2365, pp. 61–75. Springer, Heidelberg (2002)
6. Matsui, M.: New block encryption algorithm MISTY. In: Biham, E. (ed.) FSE 1997. LNCS, vol. 1267, pp. 54–68. Springer, Heidelberg (1997)
7. Moriai, S., Shimoyama, T., Kaneko, T.: Higher Order Differential Attack of a CAST Cipher. In: Vaudenay, S. (ed.) FSE 1998. LNCS, vol. 1372, pp. 17–31. Springer, Heidelberg (1998)
8. NESSIE, https://www.cosic.esat.kuleuven.ac.be/nessie/
9. RFC2994, http://www.faqs.org/rfcs/rfc2994.html
10. 3GPP, http://www.3gpp.org/

A Generic Method for Secure SBox Implementation

Emmanuel Prouff[2] and Matthieu Rivain[1,2]

[1] University of Luxembourg
Faculty of Sciences, Technology and Communication
6, rue Richard Coudenhove-Kalergi
L-1359 Luxembourg
[2] Oberthur Card Systems,
71-73 rue des Hautes Pâtures,
92726 Nanterre Cedex, France
{m.rivain,e.prouff}@oberthurcs.com

Abstract. Cryptographic algorithms embedded in low resource devices are vulnerable to side channel attacks. Since their introduction in 1996, the effectiveness of these attacks has been highly improved and many countermeasures have been invalidated. It was especially true for countermeasures whose security was based on heuristics and experiments. Consequently, there is not only a need for designing new and various countermeasures, but it is also necessary to prove the security of the new proposals in formal models. In this paper we provide a simple method for securing the software implementation of functions called SBoxes that are widely used in symmetric cryptosystems. The main advantage of the proposed solution is that it does not require any RAM allocation. We analyze its efficiency and we compare it with other well-known countermeasures. Moreover, we use a recently introduced proof-of-security framework to demonstrate the resistance of our countermeasure from the viewpoint of Differential Power Analysis. Finally, we apply our method to protect the AES implementation and we show that the performances are suitable for practical implementations.

1 Introduction and Motivations

Side Channel Analysis are powerful attacks that utilize side channel leakage of embedded devices such as timing execution or power consumption to obtain information about secret data. It essentially allows two kinds of *Power Attacks*: the *Simple Power Analysis* (SPA) and the *Differential Power Analysis* (DPA). SPA consists in directly interpreting power consumption measurements and in identifying the execution sequence. In a DPA, the attacker focuses on the power consumption of a single instruction and performs statistical tests to reveal some correlations between the distribution of the measurement values and the *sensitive data* (*i.e.* depending on a secret value) manipulated by the instruction. Since the publication of the first DPA, many papers describing either countermeasures or attack improvements have been published (see [1,3,4,12] for example). Among

S. Kim, M. Yung, and H.-W. Lee (Eds.): WISA 2007, LNCS 4867, pp. 227–244, 2007.

these improvements, *Higher order DPA attacks* (HODPA) are of particular interest. They extend the DPA by considering a set of several instructions instead of a single one. The number d of instructions targeted by the attack is called *order* of the DPA.

The most common way of thwarting DPA involves random values (called *masks*) to de-correlate the leakage signal from the sensitive data which are manipulated [4, 6, 1]. If every sensitive variable is protected with a single mask, the implementation may thwart first order DPA but it can be theoretically attacked by a second order DPA targeting both the mask and the masked value. To thwart second order DPA (and more generally d-th order DPA), every sensitive variable must be masked with 2 (resp. d) random values. This implies that the timing-memory cost of the existing masking countermeasures increases greatly with the order of the DPA they aim to counteract. For applications where time constraints are very strong (such as contact-less applications), it may be considered as sufficient to mask all the sensitive data with a small number of random values generated at the beginning of the algorithm execution. The performances of many DPA countermeasures have been studied in this model. However recent results (see [13]) showed that second order DPA represents a real practical threat, especially when the same value is used to mask several intermediate results throughout the algorithm. Therefore, as noticed in [5, 15], the masks must be re-generated as often as possible and the analysis of the efficiency of a countermeasure has to take this fact into account. In this model, it appears that only a few among the existing countermeasures are still efficient in a low resource context and there is therefore still a need for investigating new and various countermeasures that thwart first order DPA efficiently when the masks change frequently.

Due to the very large variety of Side Channel Attacks reported against cryptosystems and devices, sensitive applications (*e.g.* Banking, GSM or Identity Card) cannot make use of countermeasures with *ad hoc* security but need countermeasures which are provably secure against a precisely modeled adversary. Recently, new notions and tools have been introduced to evaluate the security of an implementation against Side Channel Attacks [20, 18, 17]. They allow for the formal validation or the formal invalidation of the resistance of a countermeasure under some realistic assumptions on the behavior of the device and on the power of the adversary.

In this paper, we focus on DPA against block cipher algorithms. The most critical part when securing implementations of such algorithms against DPA is to protect their non-linear operations (*i.e.* the calls to the SBoxes). In the next section, we recall the methods which have been proposed in the Literature. Then, we introduce in Sect. 3 a new and simple countermeasure which counteracts first order DPA against SBox implementations whatever the algebraic structure of the SBox. When the masks change frequently, we argue that the new method has a good efficiency compared to the other generic methods. In Sect. 4, we analyze the security of our proposal by following the methodology described in [20]. In Appendix A, we apply our method to protect the implementation of the AES SBox and we compare its efficiency and its security with the ones of other existing countermeasures.

2   Secure Implementation of Non-linear Functions in the Literature

2.1   State of the Art of the Generic Methods

To counteract DPA attacks, one usually tries to make the power consumption signal as independent as possible of the sensitive data manipulated by the algorithm. Goubin and Patarin proposed in [6] a general solution, called *duplication method*, to protect the implementation of an algorithm. In this approach, every sensitive variable x is split into d blocks r_1, ..., r_d and every cryptographic primitive F that manipulates x is associated to d functions F_1, ..., F_d and to a simple transformation σ (*e.g.* a simple bitwise addition) such that $F(x) = \sigma(F_1[r_1, ..., r_d], \cdots, F_d[r_1, ..., r_d])$. Goubin and Patarin showed that an implementation protected by duplication method thwarts first order DPA if for every x (resp. every $F[x]$) the d blocks r_1, ..., r_d (resp. $F_1[r_1, ..., r_d]$, ... , $F_d[r_1, ..., r_d]$) are never manipulated at the same time.

Another approach consists in masking all the sensitive internal data with random values. Depending on the kind of operations performed by the linear parts of the algorithm, the mask values are introduced by modular addition, bitwise addition or multiplication. After selecting the masking operation $\star$, the implementation of a cryptographic function F is rendered resistant to first order DPA by solving the following problem:

Problem 1. Knowing $x \star r$, r and s, compute $F(x) \star s$ such that every value of the power consumption signal is independent of x.

If the function F is linear for the law $\star$, then solving the above problem is a simple task. Indeed, since $F(x \star r)$ equals $F(x) \star F(r)$, we have $F(x) \star s = F(x \star r) \star F(r) \star s$. If F is non-linear for the law $\star$ (which is the case when F is a SBox), then designing an implementation solving Problem 1 is much more difficult. Several kinds of methods have been proposed in the Literature and we recall two of them hereafter.

The first one, called *re-computation method* [1,11], involves the computation of a table corresponding to the masked SBox and the generation of one or several random value(s). In its most elementary version, two random values r and s are generated and the table $T^\star$ representing the function $F^\star : x \mapsto F(x \star r) \star s$ is computed from F and stored in the RAM of the device. Then, each time the masked value $F[x] \star s$ has to be computed from the masked input $x \star r$, the table $T^\star$ is accessed. For such a method, the number of tables to be recomputed during the execution of the algorithm equals the number of different input/output masks which is allowed.

Remark 1. The re-computation method is a particular case of the duplication method where d equals 2, where the sensitive value x is split into $r_1 = x \star r$

and $r_2 = r$ and where the functions F_1 and F_2 equal $r_1 \mapsto S[r_1] \star s$ and $r_2 \mapsto s$ respectively.

The second kind of methods, that we call here *SBox secure calculation*, has been essentially applied to protect AES implementations [4, 7, 18, 19, 21] due to the strong algebraic structure of the AES SBox. The SBox outputs are not directly obtained by accessing a table but are computed *on-the-fly* by using a mathematical representation F of the SBox. Then, each time the masked value $F[x] \star s$ must be computed from the pair $(x \star r, r)$, an algorithm performing F and parameterized by the 3-tuple $(x \star r, r, s)$ is executed. The computation of F is split into elementary operations (bitwise addition, bitwise multiplication, addition, multiplication, ...) and/or is performed in spaces of small dimensions (*e.g.* 4) by accessing one or several look-up table(s) (see [15]). The security of such a method is achieved by protecting each elementary operation and each memory transfer.

When the same pair of input/output masks is used throughout the algorithm, the latter is said to be protected in the *single-mask protection mode*. In such a mode, a new pair of input/output masks (r, s) is generated at each execution of the algorithm and every computation $F(x)$ performed during the execution is protected with this single pair. When the algorithm is protected in this mode, SBox secure calculation methods are often much more costly than the re-computation methods since they essentially replace a single access to a table by numerous logical operations and memory transfers. This difference between the performances of the two methods decreases when the number of different masks generated to protect the SBox calculations increases. In the *multi-mask protection mode*, the pair of masks (r, s) is re-generated each time a calculation $F(x)$ must be protected (and thus many times per algorithm execution). In such a context, the SBox secure calculation methods become more appropriate and induce a smaller timing/memory overhead than the re-computation methods. Indeed, when re-computation methods are used in the multi-mask protection mode, a new table must be computed from F after each re-generation of masks (*i.e.* before every computation $F(x)$).

As discussed in the previous paragraph, the choice between the first and the second category of methods highly depends on the protection mode, single-mask or multi-mask, in which the algorithm is implemented. We compare the two modes in the next section.

2.2   Single-Mask Protection Mode *versus* Multi-mask Protection Mode

When it is only required to thwart first order DPA, then implementing the algorithm in the single mask protection mode is sufficient. However recent results (*e.g.* [13]) show that second order DPA can represent a real practical threat when the amount of information leaking in the two consumption points targeted by the attacker is sufficiently high to make the effects of the de-synchronization and of the noise negligible. More generally, the analyses of second order DPA published in [8,13,23] illustrate that the complexities of the various second order DPA are very different and show that some of them must be considered when implementing an algorithm for secure applications. In fact, as already put forward in [5,15], second order DPA are especially effective when the same pair of masks is used to protect all the inputs/outputs of the cryptographic primitives (*e.g.* all the inputs/outputs $(x, F(x))$ of the SBoxes) involved in the algorithm. Indeed, the beginning and the end dates of the execution of these primitives are quite easy to localize in the power consumption curves. Consequently, when all the inputs (resp. all the outputs) of the primitives are masked with the same value, then an attacker can precisely isolate two consumption points manipulating the same masks and is therefore able to unmask a sensitive data. A straightforward solution to make this particular class of second order DPA difficult to perform in practice consists in re-generating the masks as often as possible. Even if such a solution does not ensure that the algorithm thwarts all kinds of second order DPA, it allows to counteract those among the most efficient ones.

For the reasons detailed above, we think that there is a practical interest to introduce an intermediate resistance level between the *first order DPA-resistance*, in which every first order DPA is counteracted, and the *second order DPA-resistance*, in which every second order DPA is also counteracted. We call this intermediate level, *first order DPA-resistance in the multi-mask protection mode*. In this new level, the pair of masks (r, s) is re-generated each time a calculation $F(x)$ must be protected (and thus many times per algorithm execution). Since the implementation of an algorithm perfectly thwarting second-order DPA requires a great timing and memory overhead and since an implementation thwarting only first order DPA does no longer provide enough security, we think that the *first order DPA-resistance in the multi-mask protection mode* nowadays offers the better security/efficiency trade-off.

Analyzing the security of an implementation of an SBox for the new resistance level is equivalent to study the first order DPA resistance of the SBox implementation. The difference appears when it comes to investigate the efficiency of the countermeasure. For instance, a technic efficient in the single-mask mode (*e.g.* the re-computation method) can become much more costly in the multi-mask mode.

In the next section, we present a simple SBox secure calculation method which resolves Problem 1 and we compare its performances with other generic methods in the multi-mask protection mode.

3   The New *S*-Box Secure Calculation Method

3.1   Our Proposal

Let x denote a sensitive variable, let r and s be an input mask and an output mask and let F denote an SBox function mapping $\mathbb{F}_2^n$ into $\mathbb{F}_2^m$. The core idea of our proposal is to compute $F((x \oplus r) \oplus a) \oplus s$ for every value a, storing the result in a register R_0 if a equals r and in a second register R_1 otherwise.

Let *compare* : $x, y \mapsto compare(x, y)$ be the function returning 0 if $x = y$ and 1 otherwise, we depict our proposal in the following algorithm.

Algorithm 1. Computation of a masked S-Box output from a masked input

INPUT: a masked value $\tilde{x} = x \oplus r$, an input mask r, an output mask s, a look-up table for F

OUTPUT: the masked S-Box output $F(x) \oplus s$

---

1. **for** $a = 0$ **to** $2^n - 1$ **do**
2. $cmp \leftarrow compare(a, r)$
3. $R_{cmp} \leftarrow F(\tilde{x} \oplus a) \oplus s$
4. **return** R_0

Remark 2. Many microprocessors implement the function *compare* by a single instruction. Thus, we will assume in the rest of the paper that this function is an elementary operation.

To verify the correctness of Algorithm 1., it can be checked that Step 3 performs the following operation:

$$\begin{cases} R_0 \leftarrow F(\tilde{x} \oplus a) \oplus s & \text{if } a = r \ , \\ R_1 \leftarrow F(\tilde{x} \oplus a) \oplus s & \text{otherwise} \ . \end{cases} \tag{1}$$

Hence, R_0 contains the value $F(\tilde{x} \oplus r) \oplus s = F(x) \oplus s$ when the loop is completed.

The security of the new method highly depends on the assumption that the leakage generated by a register transfer is the same whatever is the register. This assumption is commonly accepted and it is the security core of SPA countermeasures used to protect asymmetric cryptosystems (see for instance [9]).

As every variable manipulated during the execution of the algorithm is masked by a random value, it can be proven (in a similar way as done in Sect. 4) that it thwarts DPA in both Hamming Weight and Hamming Distance models. Nevertheless, Algorithm 1. has a potential security weakness because it involves dummy operations (*i.e.* operations which do not impact the value returned by the algorithm)[3]. This flaw could be exploited by an attacker who would disrupt the Step 3 operation (for instance by fault injection [2]) during a chosen loop iteration $a = a_0$. By checking if Algorithm 1. output is erroneous or not, the attacker would be able to detect when the mask r equals the known loop index a_0. Finally, for the power consumption measurements corresponding to the cases $r = a_0$, the attacker would be able to unmask $\tilde{x}$ and to perform a classical first order DPA.

To circumvent the flaw, dummy operations must be avoided. When F is *balanced*[4], *i.e.* when $\#F^{-1}(y)$ equals 2^{n-m} for every $y \in \mathbb{F}_2^m$, then we propose in

---

[3] Attacks exploiting dummy operations have been mainly applied to attack SPA-resistant implementations of RSA (see [24] for an example of such attacks).

[4] For security reasons, functions F involved in cryptographic applications are always balanced.

Algorithm 2. Computation of a masked S-Box output from a masked input

INPUT: a masked value $\tilde{x} = x \oplus r$, an input mask r, an output mask s, a look-up table for F

OUTPUT: the masked S-Box output $F(x) \oplus s$

---

1. $R_0 \leftarrow s$
2. $R_1 \leftarrow s$
3. **for** $a = 0$ **to** $2^n - 1$ **do**
4. $cmp \leftarrow compare(a, r)$
5. $R_{cmp} \leftarrow R_{cmp} \oplus F(\tilde{x} \oplus a)$
6. $cmp \leftarrow compare(R_0, R_1)$
7. **return** $R_0 \oplus (cmp \times R_1)$

---

the following a slightly modified version of Algorithm 1. where both registers R_0 and R_1 are involved in the computation of the output value.

According to (1), register R_0 contains the value $F(x) \oplus s$ at the end of the loop. Moreover it can be checked that the content of R_1 equals $s \oplus \bigoplus_{\substack{a \in \mathbb{F}_2^n \\ a \neq r}} F(\tilde{x} \oplus a)$. As F is balanced, the summation $\bigoplus_{\substack{a \in \mathbb{F}_2^n \\ a \neq r}} F(\tilde{x} \oplus a)$ equals $F(\tilde{x} \oplus r)$ that is $F(x)$ since we have $\tilde{x} = x \oplus r$. Indeed, the summation $\bigoplus_{a \in \mathbb{F}_2^n} F(x)$ can be rewritten $\bigoplus_{y \in \mathbb{F}_2^m} (\bigoplus_{a \in \mathbb{F}_2^n; \ F(a)=y} y)$. As F is assumed to be balanced, each term $\bigoplus_{a \in \mathbb{F}_2^n; \ F(a)=y} y$ corresponds to 2^{n-m} times the sum of the vector y with itself. Thus, each term $\bigoplus_{a \in \mathbb{F}_2^n; \ F(a)=y} y$ equals the null vector if $n > m$ and equals y if $n = m$. This implies that $\bigoplus_{a \in \mathbb{F}_2^n} F(a)$ equals 0 if $n > m$ and equals $\bigoplus_{y \in \mathbb{F}_2^m} y$ if $n = m$. Since the sum of all the elements of a space equals the zero vector, one deduces that $\bigoplus_{a \in \mathbb{F}_2^n} F(a)$ is also equal to 0 if n and m are equal. Consequently, when F is balanced, the equality $R_1 = s \oplus F(\tilde{x} \oplus r) = F(x) \oplus s$ holds at the end of the loop.

Finally, Step 6 aims at verifying that the contents of the two registers R_0 and R_1 are equal. Then, Step 7 returns either the expected result if no perturbation occurred or an erroneous result otherwise. This simple improvement of Algorithm 1. ensures that the attacker is no longer able to determine when the index a_0 of the targeted loop iteration equals the input mask r.

Algorithm 1. requires $2^n \times 3$ logical operations (2 x-or operations and 1 comparison per loop iteration) and 2^n memory transfers (1 table look-up per loop operation). For Algorithm 2., two assignments (Steps 1 and 2), one comparison (Step 6), one multiplication and one x-or operation (Step 7) are added.

Since changing the input and output masks at each execution of Algorithm 2. has no impact on its performances, our proposal is efficient in the multi-mask protection mode. Moreover, it is generic in the sense that it can be applied to any balanced SBox F without any assumption on the algebraic structure of F. In what follows, we compare the performances of our proposal with the ones of other generic methods.

3.2   Comparison with Other Generic Methods

We focus here on two well-known elementary masked SBox computation methods. The first one is the table re-computation method recalled in Sect. 2. The second one, that we call here the *global look-up table method*, uses a large look-up table addressed with the mask and the masked value.

Re-computation method. Let T denote a 2^n bytes table allocated in RAM[5]. When the block cipher algorithm is protected in the multi-mask protection mode, a new pair of input/output masks is generated each time an SBox output is computed and the following sequence of operations is performed:

> 1. **for** $x = 0$ **to** $2^n - 1$ **do**
> 2. $T[x] \leftarrow F(x \oplus r) \oplus s$
> 3. **return** $T[\tilde{x}]$

This algorithm requires $2^n \times 2$ logical operations (2 x-or operations per loop iteration) and $2^n \times 2 + 1$ memory transfers (1 read operation and 1 write operation per loop iteration and one access to the re-computed table). The computational cost of the table re-computation method is approximatively the same as for Algorithm 2.. However, it also requires the allocation of 2^n bytes of RAM which can be problematic in a low resource context, especially when several SBoxes need to be protected.

Global look-up table method. Let $T^\star$ denote the look-up table associated to the function $(x, y) \mapsto F(x \oplus y) \oplus y$. To compute $F(x) \oplus r$ from $x \oplus r$ and r, the global look-up table method performs a single operation: the table look-up $T^\star[\tilde{x}, r]$. Its timing performances are ideal since it requires only one memory transfer. However, the size 2^{2n} of the look-up table $T^\star$ makes an application of the method difficult in a low resource context. For instance, if n is greater than or equal to 7, the amount of ROM required is definitely too great (at least 16 KB!). When n is lower than or equal to 6, the feasibility of the method depends on the amount of ROM of the device and on the number of different SBoxes which must be protected. The method can become interesting when it comes to protect SBoxes mapping $\mathbb{F}_2^4$ into itself (as it is the case for FOX [10] where three such SBoxes are involved) or when the SBox calculus can be performed in spaces of dimensions lower than or equal to 4 (as it is the case for the AES SBox - see Appendix A -).

From a security point of view, the global look-up table method has a flaw since it manipulates the mask r and the masked data $\tilde{x}$ at the same time. Indeed $\tilde{x}$ and r are concatenated to address the look-up table $T^\star$ and thus, the value $\tilde{x}||r$ is transferred through the bus. Since the variables $\tilde{x}||r$ and x are statistically dependent, the leakage on $\tilde{x}||r$ is potentially exploitable by a first order DPA.

---

[5] To make the description easier, we assume that every element of $\mathbb{F}_2^m$ is stored on one byte.

Table 1. Comparison of methods solving Problem 1 for the bitwise addition

Method	Masking Mode	Pre-computation	SBox calculation	RAM	ROM
Table recomp.	Single-masking	$2^{n+1}MT + 2^{n+1}RLO$	$1MT$	2^n	2^n
Table recomp.	Multi-masking	0	$(2^{n+1}+1)MT + 2^{n+1}RLO$	2^n	2^n
Global LUT	Multi-masking	0	$1MT$	0	2^{2n}
Algo. 2.	Multi-masking	0	$2^n MT + (3 \times 2^n + 5)RLO$	0	2^n

Table 1 summarizes the costs of the three previously considered methods according to the number of register logical operations (RLO), the number of memory transfers (MT), the memory size (bytes in RAM) and the code size (bytes in ROM).

4 Security Analysis

To study the security of our proposal we will use some basic notions of information Theory. We recall them in the next section.

4.1 Preliminaries

We use the calligraphic letters, like $\mathcal{X}$, to denote finite sets. The corresponding large letter X is then used to denote a random variable over $\mathcal{X}$, while the lowercase letter x - a particular element from $\mathcal{X}$. The probability of the event $(X = x)$ is denoted $P[X = x]$. The *entropy $H(X)$* of a random variable X aims at measuring the amount of information provided by an observation of X and satisfies $H(X) = -\sum_{x \in \mathcal{X}} P[X = x] \log(P[X = x])$. The *conditional entropy* of X given Y, denoted by $H(X|Y)$, equals $-\sum_{y \in \mathcal{Y}} P[Y = y] \sum_{x \in \mathcal{X}} P[X = x|Y = y] \log(P[X = x|Y = y])$. To quantify the amount of information that Y reveals about X, the notion of *mutual information* is usually involved. The mutual information of X and Y is the value $\mathcal{I}(X, Y)$ defined by $\mathcal{I}(X, Y) = H(X) - H(X|Y)$. The random variables X and Y are *independent* if and only if $\mathcal{I}(X, Y)$ equals 0. Moreover, the mutual information is always positive or null and it satisfies the following property.

Property 1. Let X and Y be two random variables respectively defined over $\mathcal{X}$ and $\mathcal{Y}$. For every function f defined over $\mathcal{Y}$, we have $\mathcal{I}(X, f(Y)) \leq \mathcal{I}(X, Y)$.

For our security analysis, we shall also use the following proposition.

Proposition 1. *Let X and Y be two random variables defined over $\mathcal{X}$ and let Z be a random variable defined over $\mathcal{Z}$. If Z is mutually independent of X and Y and has a uniform distribution over $\mathcal{Z}$, then for every measurable function f defined from $\mathcal{X}^2$ into $\mathcal{Z}$, we have $\mathcal{I}(X, Z \oplus f(X, Y)) = 0$.*

As a consequence of Proposition 1, we have $\mathcal{I}(X, Z \oplus X) = 0$ when X and Z satisfy the conditions of Proposition 1.

4.2   Evaluation Methodology

To evaluate the security of our proposal, we follow the outlines of the methodology depicted in [20]. This methodology holds in five steps: specify the target implementation, specify the target secret, define the adversary model, evaluate the information leakage and define a metric to evaluate the security.

The target implementation is Algorithm 2. running on a smart card.

The target secret is the un-masked value x corresponding to the masked input $\tilde{x}$ of Algorithm 2..

The adversary model. We assume that the attacker can query the targeted cryptographic primitive with an arbitrary number of plaintexts and obtain the corresponding physical observations, but cannot choose its queries in function of the previously obtained observations (such a model is called *non-adaptive known plaintext model* in [20]). We also assume that the attacker has access to the power consumption and electromagnetic emanations of the device and applies a first order DPA attack but is not able to perform HODPA.

The effectiveness of the *prediction* made by the adversary is strongly related to the amount of information provided by the physical observations. In our analysis, we assume that the attacker knows how information leaks from the device and straightforwardly makes its prediction based on the leakage model (such a prediction is called *device profiled prediction* in [20]). Moreover, the physical observations are assumed to be perfect *i.e.* matching exactly the leakage model (which is a very favorable situation from the attacker's viewpoint).

For our analysis, we choose to consider a general leakage model that can be used for both power consumption or electromagnetic emanations.

The leakage model. Different models coexist to quantify the leakage of CMOS circuits with respect to the data handled but two of them are predominantly used: the *Hamming Weight* model (where the leakage is related to the Hamming Weight of the data handled) and the *Hamming Distance* model (where the leakage is related to the Hamming Distance between the previous and the current data handled in a register or transmitted through a bus - see [3]). In the Hamming Distance model, the leakage of the bit-transitions $0 \rightarrow 1$ and $1 \rightarrow 0$ are assumed to be equal, which makes the leakage analysis much simpler. However this assumption, which is adequate when trying to attack an unprotected implementation, is not relevant to model a strong opponent against a secure implementation. Indeed, in practice CMOS gates leak differently when charging or discharging the load capacitance (especially in the case of electromagnetic emanations [17]). Hence, as mentioned in [17,20], a more accurate leakage model must be defined to model an attacker who is able to observe these differences.

Definition 1. *[17] In the Hamming Distance Extended (HDE) model, the leakage $\mathcal{L}_{HDE}(s, y)$ related to a variable y that replaces an initial state s, satisfies*

$$\mathcal{L}_{HDE}(s, y) = N_{0 \to 1}(s, y) \times P_{0 \to 1} + N_{1 \to 0}(s, y) \times P_{1 \to 0} + \beta , \qquad (2)$$

where $N_{0 \to 1}(s, y)$ (resp. $N_{1 \to 0}(s, y)$) denotes the number of transitions $0 \to 1$ (resp. $1 \to 0$) from s to y, $P_{0 \to 1}$ (resp. $P_{1 \to 0}$) denotes the average energy consumed by a transition $0 \to 1$ (resp. $1 \to 0$) and where β denotes some noise.

Denoting by δ the normalized difference $\frac{P_{0 \to 1} - P_{1 \to 0}}{P_{0 \to 1}}$ and by ε the leakage $P_{0 \to 1}$, we have $P_{1 \to 0} = \varepsilon(1 - \delta)$ and Relation (2) can be rewritten:

$$\mathcal{L}_{HDE}(s, y) = \varepsilon \left(1 - \frac{\delta}{2} \right) \mathrm{HW}(s \oplus y) + \varepsilon \frac{\delta}{2} \left(\mathrm{HW}(y) - \mathrm{HW}(s) \right) + \beta . \qquad (3)$$

From Relation (3), it can be verified that the HDE model includes the Hamming Weight (HW) and the Hamming Distance (HD) models. Indeed, when there is no difference between the transitions $0 \to 1$ and $1 \to 0$ (*i.e.* when $\delta = 0$), we have $\mathcal{L}_{HDE}(s, y) = \varepsilon HW(s \oplus y) + \beta$ and the HDE model is equivalent to the HD model. On the other hand, when the initial state s is constant, equal to 0, then we have $\mathcal{L}_{HDE}(s, y) = \varepsilon HW(y) + \beta$ and the HDE model is equivalent to the HW model. The HDE model is also appropriate to quantify electro-magnetic emanations leaking in the *signed distance model* which assumes that $P_{1 \to 0}$ equals $-P_{0 \to 1}$ [17]. In this case, we have $\delta = 2$ and the leakage satisfies $\mathcal{L}_{HDE}(s, y) = \varepsilon(HW(y) - HW(s)) + \beta$.

Once the behavior of the device and the attacker capacities are modeled, a method can be deduced from Standaert *et al.* [20] to prove the security of a countermeasure.

Evaluation of the security. Let us denote by X, Y and IS the random variables respectively corresponding to the sensitive data targeted by the attacker, the data manipulated at the date of a leakage and the initial state replaced by Y. In the theoretical model depicted by the four steps above, it has been proved in [18] and [20] that a first order DPA does not succeed in extracting information about X if and only if X and $\mathcal{L}_{HDE}(IS, Y)$ are independent for every pair (IS, Y) appearing during the execution of the algorithm.

In the following section, we evaluate $\mathcal{I}(X, \mathcal{L}_{HDE}(IS, Y))$ for every pair (IS, Y) appearing during the execution of Algorithm 2..

4.3   Proof of Security

If IS is an operation code, a constant memory address or a system variable which is independent of the intermediate results of the algorithm, then Property 1 and the positivity of the mutual information imply the following inequality:

$$0 \leq \mathcal{I}(X, \mathcal{L}_{HDE}(IS, Y)) \leq \mathcal{I}(X, Y) . \qquad (4)$$

In such a case, proving $\mathcal{I}(X, Y) = 0$ is sufficient to prove $\mathcal{I}(X, \mathcal{L}_{HDE}(IS, Y)) = 0$.

If IS corresponds to an intermediate result of the algorithm, then Property 1 and the positivity of the mutual information imply the following inequality:

$$0 \leq \mathcal{I}(X, \mathcal{L}_{HDE}(IS, Y)) \leq \mathcal{I}(X, (IS, Y)) , \tag{5}$$

where (IS, Y) denotes the random variable that has the joint distribution of IS and Y. In this case, proving that $\mathcal{I}(X, (IS, Y))$ equals 0 is sufficient to prove that $\mathcal{I}(X, \mathcal{L}_{HDE}(IS, Y))$ equals 0.

To show that $\mathcal{I}(X, \mathcal{L}_{HDE}(IS, Y))$ equals 0 for every pair (IS, Y) appearing during the execution of Algorithm 2., we decompose our security proof into two steps, depending on the nature of IS. In a first step, we show that for every intermediate variable Y manipulated by Algorithm 2., the mutual information $\mathcal{I}(X, Y)$ equals 0. According to Inequality (4), this will prove that X and $\mathcal{L}_{HDE}(IS, Y)$ are independent when IS is assumed to be an operation code, a constant memory address or a system variable: we shall say in this case that there is no *variables leakage*. In a second time, we show that for every transition occurring between two intermediate results Y_1 and Y_2, the mutual information $\mathcal{I}(X, (Y_1, Y_2))$ equals 0. According to Inequality (5), this will prove that X and $\mathcal{L}_{HDE}(IS, Y)$ are independent when IS corresponds to an intermediate result of the algorithm: we shall say in this case that there is no *transitions leakage*.

Variables leakage. We decompose Algorithm 2. into several elementary operations each manipulating an intermediate result computed from the sensitive variable X, the input mask R and the output mask S. Since the random variables R and S correspond to randomly generated values, we can assume that they have a uniform distribution and that X, R and S are mutually independent.

Let $sum_a(X, R)$ denotes the sum $\bigoplus_{\substack{j=0 \\ j \neq R}}^{a} F(X \oplus R \oplus j)$ and let tmp denote the register used to store the intermediate results at Step 5. Table 2 lists the intermediate values that occur during an execution of Algorithm 2.

As R and S have a uniform distribution and as X, R and S are mutually independent, one straightforwardly deduces from Proposition 1 that all the intermediate results listed in Table 2 are independent of X.

Table 2. Intermediate results manipulated during Algorithm 2

Step	Instruction	Intermediate results
5.	$tmp \leftarrow \tilde{x}$	$X \oplus R$
	$tmp \leftarrow tmp \oplus a$	$X \oplus R \oplus a$
	$tmp \leftarrow F(tmp)$	$F(X \oplus R \oplus a)$
	$R_{cmp} \leftarrow R_{cmp} \oplus tmp$	$S \oplus \begin{cases} 0 & \text{if } R = a \\ sum_{a-1}(X, R) & \text{otherwise} \end{cases}$
		$S \oplus \begin{cases} F(X) & \text{if } R = a \\ sum_a(X, R) & \text{otherwise} \end{cases}$
6.	$cmp \leftarrow compare(R_0, R_1)$	$F(X) \oplus S$
7.	**return** $R_0 \oplus (cmp \times R_1)$	$F(X) \oplus S$

Table 3. Transitions between intermediate results occurring during Algorithm 2

Step	Operation	Target	Initial State IS	New State Y
5	$tmp \leftarrow \bar{x}$	tmp	$F(X \oplus R \oplus (a-1))$	$X \oplus R$
5	$tmp \leftarrow tmp \oplus a$	tmp	$X \oplus R$	$X \oplus R \oplus a$
5	$tmp \leftarrow F(tmp)$	A-BUS	$ad_F + (X \oplus R \oplus (a-1))$	$ad_F + (X \oplus R \oplus a)$
5	$tmp \leftarrow F(tmp)$	D-BUS	$F(X \oplus R \oplus (a-1))$	$F(X \oplus R \oplus a)$
5	$tmp \leftarrow F(tmp)$	S-BUS	$F(X \oplus R \oplus (a-1))$	$ad_F + (X \oplus R \oplus a)$
5	$tmp \leftarrow F(tmp)$	S-BUS	$ad_F + (X \oplus R \oplus a)$	$F(X \oplus R \oplus a)$
5	$tmp \leftarrow F(tmp)$	tmp	$X \oplus R \oplus a$	$F(X \oplus R \oplus a)$
5	$R_{cmp} \leftarrow R_{cmp} \oplus tmp$	R_{cmp}	$S \oplus \begin{cases} 0 & \text{if } R = a \\ sum_{a-1}(X,R) & \text{otherwise} \end{cases}$	$S \oplus \begin{cases} F(X) & \text{if } R = a \\ sum_a(X,R) & \text{otherwise} \end{cases}$
7	$R_1 \leftarrow R_1 \oplus cmp$	cmp	$F(X \oplus S)$	$F(X \oplus S)$

Transitions leakage. We consider hereafter the transitions between intermediate results that occur either on the bus or in the registers R_0, R_1, cmp and tmp. For the bus, we consider transitions that appear when memory addresses and data transit either on the same bus (here denoted S-BUS for single bus) or on different bus (an address bus denoted A-BUS and a data bus denoted D-BUS).

Let ad_F denote the memory address of the look-up table F. In Table 3, we list the successive bus or register transitions occurring during an execution of Algorithm 2.. We only list the transitions involving the sensitive data X.

For all except the fifth row of Table 3, Proposition 1 and Property 1 straightforwardly imply that $\mathcal{I}(X,(IS,Y))$ equals 0. For the fifth row, which corresponds to the update of R_{cmp}, let us study (IS,Y) for $R = a$ and $R \neq a$. If R equals a, then (IS,Y) can be written $(S, S \oplus F(X \oplus R \oplus a))$ where S is uniformly distributed over $\mathbb{F}_2^m$ and is independent of the pair (X,R). If R differs from a, then (IS,Y) can be written $(S \oplus sum_{a-1}(X,R), S \oplus sum_a(X,R))$ that is $(S', S' \oplus F(X \oplus R \oplus a))$ after denoting $S \oplus sum_{a-1}(X,R)$ by S'. It can be verified that S' has a uniform distribution over $\mathbb{F}_2^m$. Thus, due to Proposition 1, S' is independent of (X,R). One deduces that (IS,Y) is equivalent to a random variable $(U, U \oplus F(X \oplus R \oplus a))$ where U is uniformly distributed over $\mathbb{F}_2^m$ and independent of the pair (X,R). Then, from Property 1, we get $\mathcal{I}(X,(IS,Y)) \leq \mathcal{I}(X,(U,X \oplus R))$ and Proposition 1 implies that $\mathcal{I}(X,(IS,Y))$ equals 0.

We showed in this section that the sensitive variable X is independent of every intermediate result Y and every transition $IS \rightarrow Y$ that occurs during the execution of Algorithm 2.. As argued in Sect. 4.2, this implies that there is no mutual information between the sensitive variable and the instantaneous power consumption leakages. We can therefore conclude that Algorithm 2. is secure against first order DPA in the HDE model.

5 Conclusion

In this paper we have presented a new masking scheme for software SBox implementations that requires no RAM allocation. Since our method does not rely on specific SBox properties, it is generic and can thus be applied to protect any symmetric cryptosystem. We have argued that a first order DPA countermeasure must be efficient not only in the single-mask protection mode but also in the multi-mask mode. In this mode, we have shown that our countermeasure is as efficient as the other classical generic methods and does not require RAM allocation. We have evaluated our solution within the framework recently introduced by Standaert *et al.* in [17, 20], proving its security against first order DPA under realistic assumptions about the attacker and the device behaviors. Finally, we have applied our method to AES and we have compared its efficiency with other secure implementations. Based on this analysis, we think that the timing and memory overhead of our countermeasure are suitable for practical implementations of the AES algorithm when a protection in multi-mask protection mode is required.

Acknowledgements

We would like to thank Christophe Giraud and Emmanuelle Dottax for their fruitful comments and suggestions on this paper.

References

1. Akkar, M.-L., Giraud, C.: An Implementation of DES and AES, Secure against Some Attacks. In: Koç, Ç.K., Naccache, D., Paar, C. (eds.) CHES 2001. LNCS, vol. 2162, pp. 309–318. Springer, Heidelberg (2001)
2. Boneh, D., DeMillo, R., Lipton, R.: On the Importance of Eliminating Errors in Cryptographic Computations. Journal of Cryptology 14(2), 101–119 (2001)
3. Brier, E., Clavier, C., Olivier, F.: Correlation Power Analysis with a Leakage Model. In: Joye, M., Quisquater, J.-J. (eds.) CHES 2004. LNCS, vol. 3156, pp. 16–29. Springer, Heidelberg (2004)
4. Chari, S., Jutla, C., Rao, J., Rohatgi, P.: Towards Sound Approaches to Counteract Power-Analysis Attacks. In: Wiener, M.J. (ed.) CRYPTO 1999. LNCS, vol. 1666, pp. 398–412. Springer, Heidelberg (1999)
5. Golić, J., Tymen, C.: Multiplicative Masking and Power Analysis of AES. In: Kaliski Jr., B.S., Koç, Ç.K., Paar, C. (eds.) CHES 2002. LNCS, vol. 2523, pp. 198–212. Springer, Heidelberg (2003)
6. Goubin, L., Patarin, J.: DES and Differential Power Analysis – The Duplication Method. In: Koç, Ç.K., Paar, C. (eds.) CHES 1999. LNCS, vol. 1717, pp. 158–172. Springer, Heidelberg (1999)
7. Gueron, S., Parzanchevsky, O., Zuk, O.: Masked Inversion in $GF(2^n)$ Using Mixed Field Representations and its Efficient Implementation for AES. In: Embedded Cryptographic Hardware: Methodologies and Architectures, pp. 213–228. Nova Science Publishers (2004)
8. Joye, M., Paillier, P., Schoenmakers, B.: On Second-Order Differential Power Analysis. In: Rao, J.R., Sunar, B. (eds.) CHES 2005. LNCS, vol. 3659, pp. 293–308. Springer, Heidelberg (2005)
9. Joye, M., Yen, S.-M.: The Montgomery Powering Ladder. In: Kaliski Jr., B.S., Koç, Ç.K., Paar, C. (eds.) CHES 2002. LNCS, vol. 2523, pp. 291–302. Springer, Heidelberg (2003)

10. Junod, P., Vaudenay, S.: FOX: a new family of block ciphers. In: Handschuh, H., Hasan, M.A. (eds.) SAC 2004. LNCS, vol. 3357, pp. 114–129. Springer, Heidelberg (2004)
11. Messerges, T.: Securing the AES Finalists Against Power Analysis Attacks. In: Schneier, B. (ed.) FSE 2000. LNCS, vol. 1978, pp. 150–164. Springer, Heidelberg (2001)
12. Messerges, T.: Using Second-Order Power Analysis to Attack DPA Resistant software. In: Paar, C., Koç, Ç.K. (eds.) CHES 2000. LNCS, vol. 1965, pp. 238–251. Springer, Heidelberg (2000)
13. Oswald, E., Mangard, S., Herbst, C., Tillich, S.: Practical Second-Order DPA Attacks for Masked Smart Card Implementations of Block Ciphers. In: Pointcheval, D. (ed.) CT-RSA 2006. LNCS, vol. 3860, Springer, Heidelberg (2006)
14. Oswald, E., Mangard, S., Pramstaller, N., Rijmen, V.: A Side-Channel Analysis Resistant Description of the AES S-box. In: Gilbert, H., Handschuh, H. (eds.) FSE 2005. LNCS, vol. 3557, pp. 413–423. Springer, Heidelberg (2005)
15. Oswald, E., Schramm, K.: An Efficient Masking Scheme for AES Software Implementations. In: Song, J., Kwon, T., Yung, M. (eds.) WISA 2005. LNCS, vol. 3786, pp. 292–305. Springer, Heidelberg (2006)
16. Oswald, E.: Stefan, and N. Pramstaller. Secure and Efficient Masking of AES – A Mission Impossible? Cryptology ePrint Archive, Report 2004/134 (2004)
17. Peeters, E., Standaert, F.-X., Quisquater, J.-J.: Power and Electromagnetic Analysis: Improved Model, Consequences and Comparisons. In Integration, the VLSI Journal. Elsevier, Spring (to appear)
18. Prouff, E., Giraud, C., Aumonier, S.: Provably Secure S-Box Implementation Based on Fourier Transform. In: Goubin, L., Matsui, M. (eds.) CHES 2006. LNCS, vol. 4249, pp. 216–230. Springer, Heidelberg (2006)
19. Rudra, A., Bubey, P.K., Jutla, C.S., Kumar, V., Rao, J., Rohatgi, P.: Efficient Rijndael Encryption Implementation with Composite Field Arithmetic. In: Koç, Ç.K., Naccache, D., Paar, C. (eds.) CHES 2001. LNCS, vol. 2162, pp. 171–184. Springer, Heidelberg (2001)
20. Standaert, F.-X., Malkin, T.G., Yung, M.: Side-Channel Resistant Ciphers: Model, Analysis and Design. Cryptology ePrint Archive, Report 2006/139 (2006)
21. Trichina, E.: Combinatorial Logic Design for AES SubByte Transformation on Masked Data. Cryptology ePrint Archive, Report 2003/236 (2003)
22. Trichina, E., Korkishko, L.: Secure and Efficient AES Software Implementation for Smart Cards. In: Lim, C.H., Yung, M. (eds.) WISA 2004. LNCS, vol. 3325, pp. 425–439. Springer, Heidelberg (2005)
23. Waddle, J., Wagner, D.: Toward Efficient Second-order Power Analysis. In: Joye, M., Quisquater, J.-J. (eds.) CHES 2004. LNCS, vol. 3156, pp. 1–15. Springer, Heidelberg (2004)
24. Yen, S.-M., Joye, M.: Checking before output may not be enough against fault-based cryptanalysis. IEEE Transactions on Computers 49(9), 967–970 (2000)

A   Application to AES

We recall that the AES SBox is composed of two parts: a non-linear function and an affine mapping. In the following we focus on the non-linear part, which will be denoted here by F. Let $p(x)$ denotes the irreducible polynomial $x^8 \oplus x^4 \oplus$

$x^3 \oplus x \oplus 1 \in \mathbb{F}_2[x]$. The function F is defined in $\mathbb{F}_2[x]/p(x)$ by $F(a) = 0$ if $a = 0$ and by $F(a) = a^{-1}$ otherwise.

At first, we applied the method depicted in Algorithm 2. for $n = 8$ to protect the SBox access of the AES algorithm. We implemented the solution on a classical 8051 chip running at 8 Mhz and we studied the performances of the implementation. Clearly, the timing of the resulting AES algorithm was not interesting (around 115 ms and $1,8$ KB of ROM) compared to 5ms for an implementation without countermeasures.

Secondly, we represented $\mathbb{F}_{2^8}$ has an extension of $\mathbb{F}_{2^4}$, allowing us to perform the computations in $\mathbb{F}_{2^4}$ instead of $\mathbb{F}_{2^8}$ (such a method is usually called *composite field approach*). We chose the two irreducible polynomials $p'(x) = x^2 + x + \{e\}$ and $p''(x) = x^4 + x + 1$ in $\mathbb{F}_4[x]$ and $\mathbb{F}_2[x]$ respectively and we denoted by *map* the field isomorphism which takes an element a of $\mathbb{F}_2[x]/p(x)$ as input and outputs the pair $(a_h, a_l) \in (\mathbb{F}_2[x]/p''(x))^2$ corresponding to the coefficients of the linear polynomial $(a_h x + a_l) \in \mathbb{F}_{2^4}[x]/p'(x)$. Moreover, we denoted by $Inv_{\mathbb{F}_{2^4}}$ the function which corresponds to the inverse function over $\mathbb{F}_2[x]/(x^4 + x + 1)\backslash\{0\}$ and which maps 0 into itself. In the following, we depict the different steps of our computation:

Algorithm 3. Inversion of a masked element $\widetilde{a} = a \oplus m_a$ in $\mathbb{F}_{2^8}$

INPUT: $(\widetilde{a} = a \oplus m_a, m_a) \in \mathbb{F}_{2^8}{}^2$
OUTPUT: $(\widetilde{a^{-1}} = a^{-1} \oplus m'_a, m'_a)$

1. Pick up three 4-bit random m_d, m'_h and m'_l
2. $(m_h, m_l) \in \mathbb{F}_{2^4}^2 \leftarrow map(m_a)$
3. $(\widetilde{a_h}, \widetilde{a_l}) \in \mathbb{F}_{2^4}^2 \leftarrow map(\widetilde{a})$ $\qquad\qquad\qquad [(\widetilde{a_h}, \widetilde{a_l}) = (a_h \oplus m_h, a_l \oplus m_l)]$
4. $\widetilde{d} \leftarrow \widetilde{a_h}^2 \otimes \{e\} \oplus \widetilde{a_h} \otimes \widetilde{a_l} \oplus \widetilde{a_l}^2 \oplus m_d \oplus \widetilde{a_h} \otimes m_l$ $\qquad\qquad [\widetilde{d} = d \oplus m_d]$
   $\oplus \widetilde{a_l} \otimes m_h \oplus m_h^2 \otimes \{e\} \oplus m_l^2 \oplus m_h \otimes m_l$
5. $\widetilde{d^{-1}} \leftarrow$ Algorithm 2.$(\widetilde{d}, m_d, m_{d-1}, Inv_{\mathbb{F}_{2^4}})$ $\qquad\qquad [\widetilde{d^{-1}} = d^{-1} \oplus m_{d-1}]$
6. $\widetilde{a'_h} \leftarrow \widetilde{a_h} \otimes \widetilde{d^{-1}} \oplus m'_h \oplus m_h \otimes \widetilde{d^{-1}} \oplus m_{d-1} \otimes \widetilde{a_h} \oplus m_{d-1} \otimes m_h$ $\qquad [\widetilde{a'_h} = a'_h \oplus m'_h]$
7. $\widetilde{a'_l} \leftarrow \widetilde{a_l} \otimes \widetilde{d^{-1}} \oplus m'_l \oplus \widetilde{a'_h} \oplus \widetilde{d^{-1}} \otimes m_l \oplus \widetilde{a_l} \otimes m_{d-1} \oplus m'_h \oplus m_l \otimes m_{d-1} [\widetilde{a'_l} = a'_l \oplus m'_l]$
8. $m'_a \leftarrow map^{-1}(m'_h, m'_l)$
9. $\widetilde{a^{-1}} \leftarrow map^{-1}(\widetilde{a'_h}, \widetilde{a'_l})$ $\qquad\qquad\qquad\qquad\qquad [\widetilde{a^{-1}} = a^{-1} \oplus m'_a]$
10. **return** $(\widetilde{a^{-1}}, m'_a)$

For this version, the timing of the resulting AES algorithm are very interesting and the input and output masks can be changed at each execution of the algorithm.

In the following table, we have listed the timing/memory performances of our proposal and the ones of other methods proposed in the Literature. As the performances have been measured for a particular implementation on a particular architecture, the table above does not aim at arguing that a method is better than another but aims at enlightening the main particularities (timing performances and ROM/RAM requirements) of each method.

Table 4. Comparison of several methods to protect AES against DPA

Method	Timings (ms)	RAM (bytes)	ROM (bytes)	Multi-masking
Straightforward implementation	5	0	1150	-
Re-computation Methods in the single-mask mode				
Re-computation Method in $\mathbb{F}_{2^8}$ [11]	×1.42	+256	+49%	not allowed
Re-computation Method in $\mathbb{F}_{2^4}$ [11]	×2.60	+16	+150%	not allowed
Re-computation Methods in the multi-mask mode				
Re-computation Method in $\mathbb{F}_{2^8}$ [11]	×50,60	+256	+49%	allowed
Re-computation Method in $\mathbb{F}_{2^4}$ [11]	×5.86	+16	+150%	allowed
Secure SBox computation methods based on the composite field approach				
Oswald et al. [14,16]	×5.20	0	+173%	allowed
This paper (Algo. 3.)	×5.30	0	+150%	allowed
Prouff et al. [18]	×6.40	0	+147%	allowed
Methods with security under discussion				
Oswald and Schramm [15]	×2.40	0	+200%	allowed
Trichina et al. [22]	×4.20	+256	+165%	not allowed

The AES implementations listed above only differ in their approaches to protect the SBox access. The linear steps of the AES have been implemented in the same way and the internal sensitive data have been masked by bitwise addition of a random value. We chose to protect only rounds 1 to 3 and 8 to 10, assuming that the diffusion properties of the AES algorithm make DPA attacks impossible to mount on inner rounds 4 to 7 (this implies that the SBox calculations made in rounds 4 to 7 are performed by simply accessing the table representation of F which is stored in ROM).

In the single mask mode, the re-computation method in $\mathbb{F}_{2^8}$ has the best timing performances but at least 256 bytes of RAM must be allocated to store the re-computed SBox table. As RAM is a sensitive resource in the area of embedded devices, we implemented a second version which follows the outlines of the composite field approach and then applies the re-computation method in $\mathbb{F}_{2^4}$. Because only 16 bytes of RAM are required to store the table re-computed from the $Inv_{\mathbb{F}_{2^4}}$ function, the new implementation requires much less RAM than the version in $\mathbb{F}_{2^8}$ and the timing performances are suitable for practical applications.

As the multi-mask protection mode offers better security with respect to power analysis attacks [5,15], we tested the re-computation method in this mode. As expected, the re-computation method in $\mathbb{F}_{2^8}$ no longer gives full satisfaction in this mode (requiring 253 ms for one AES execution). The timing performances of the re-computation method in $\mathbb{F}_{2^4}$ are acceptable in the multi-mask protection mode, however they are close to (and even slightly greater than) the performances of the SBox secure calculation methods. Moreover, 16 bytes of RAM are required.

The SBox secure calculation methods of Oswald et al., Prouff et al. and our proposed approach only differ in the ways of securely computing the value $d^{-1} \oplus m_{d-1}$ from $\tilde{d}$, m_d and m_{d-1} (i.e. to securely perform the fifth Step of Algorithm 3.):

- In [14,16], the inversion is performed by going down to $\mathbb{F}_4$ and its complexity approximatively equals the one of Algorithm 3. excluding the 5th Step which is replaced by a square operation (since the inversion operation in $\mathbb{F}_4$ is equivalent to squaring). For our implementation of [14, 16], the number of cycles required for the fifth step is 267.

- In [18], the inversion is essentially performed by computing a Fourier transform on $\mathbb{F}_2^4$. For our implementation of [18], the number of cycles required for the fifth step is 468.
- For the new solution presented here, the fifth step essentially corresponds to the computation of $y^{-1} \oplus m_{d-1}$ for every $y \in \mathbb{F}_2^4$. For our implementation, the number of cycles required by the fifth step is 270.

The three methods can be used in the multi-mask protection mode without decreasing the performances of the implementation and they offer approximatively the same (good) level of security related to first order DPA attacks. The execution timings of AES implementations based on our proposal or on Oswald et al.'s method are very close and their RAM requirements are almost equal. The additional time required by the Prouff et al. method is slightly greater, however the code seems to be shorter (2844 bytes of ROM versus 2881 and 3144 bytes of ROM for our method and the Oswald et al.'s method).

The methods proposed by Trichina [22] and Oswald-Shramm [15] have good timing performances but are not perfectly resistant to first order DPA attacks.

- In the method of Trichina et al., a primitive element of $\mathbb{F}_{2^8}$ is computed and every non-zero element of $\mathbb{F}_{2^8}$ is expressed as a power of that element. To resolve Problem 1 for the bitwise operation, Trichina et al. use pre-computed discrete logarithm and exponentiation tables to realize the SBox operation. As argued in [15], the method has a faulty behavior when some intermediate values are null and to correct the method without introducing a flaw with respect to first order attacks seems to be an issue.
- The method proposed by Oswald and Shramm offers the best timing performances. As for Algorithm 3., it is based on the composite field approach but steps 4 to 7 are replaced by a sequence of table look-ups and bitwise additions. The table look-ups have been render resistant to first order DPA attacks by applying the global look-up table method (which is recalled in Sect. 3). For example, the computation of $d^{-1} \oplus m_{d-1}$ (Step 5) is performed by accessing the table T_{inv} associated to the function $((d \oplus m_d), m_d) \in (\mathbb{F}_{2^4})^2 \mapsto (d^{-1} \oplus m_d) \in \mathbb{F}_{2^4}$. As argued in Sect. 3, the global look-up table method has a flaw with respect to first order DPA attacks. Indeed, to address the T_{inv} table the value $(d \oplus m_d) \| m_d$ is manipulated, which results in a power consumption that leaks information on the sensitive value d. For instance, it can be checked that $\mathcal{I}(d, H((d \oplus m_d) \| m_d))$ is not null, which results in an information leakage in the Hamming Weight model. Moreover, the input and output masks being equal, this method has also a potential flaw in the Hamming Distance model. Indeed, if a transition occurs between the index $(d \oplus m_d) \| m_d$ and the value $d^{-1} \oplus m_d$ accessed in the look-up table (which is very likely in a single bus architecture), the mask m_d is canceled and information leaks about d and/or d^{-1}.

On the Security of a Popular
Web Submission and Review Software (WSaR)
for Cryptology Conferences

Swee-Won Lo[1,*], Raphael C.-W. Phan[2], and Bok-Min Goi[3]

[1] School of Electrical & Electronics Engineering & Computer Science,
Kyungpook National University, Sankyuk-dong, Buk-gu, Daegu 702-701, Korea
swlo@ee.knu.ac.kr
[2] Laboratoire de sécurité et de cryptographie (LASEC),
Ecole Polytechnique Fédérale de Lausanne (EPFL),
CH-1015 Lausanne, Switzerland
raphael.phan@epfl.ch
[3] Centre for Cryptography and Information Security (CCIS)
Faculty of Engineering, Multimedia University, 63100 Cyberjaya, Malaysia
bmgoi@mmu.edu.my

Abstract. Most, if not all, conferences use an online system to handle paper submissions and reviews. Introduction of these systems has significantly facilitated the administration, submission and review process compared to traditional paper-based ones. However, it is crucial that these systems have strong resistance against Web attacks as they involve confidential data and privacy. Some submissions could be leading edge breakthroughs that authors do not wish to leak out and be subtly plagiarized. Also, security of the employed system will attract more submissions to conferences that use it and gives confidence of the quality that the conferences uphold. In this paper, we analyze the security of the Web-Submission-and-Review (WSaR) software - latest version 0.53 beta at the time of writing; developed by Shai Halevi from IBM Research. WSaR is currently in use by top cryptology and security-related conferences including Eurocrypt 2007 & 2008, Crypto 2007, and Asiacrypt 2007, annually sponsored by the International Association for Cryptologic Research (IACR). We present detailed analysis on WSaR's security features. In particular, we first discuss the desirable security features that are designed into WSaR and what attacks these features defend against. Then, we discuss how some untreated security issues may lead to problems, and we show how to enhance WSaR security features to take these issues into consideration. Our results are the first known careful analysis of WSaR, or any type of online submission system for that matter.

Keywords: Web submission and review software, security analysis, privacy, passwords, email, protocol.

---

* Part of work done while the author was at CCIS@Multimedia University (Cyberjaya campus) and iSECURES Lab@Swinburne University of Tech (Sarawak campus).

S. Kim, M. Yung, and H.-W. Lee (Eds.): WISA 2007, LNCS 4867, pp. 245–265, 2007.
© Springer-Verlag Berlin Heidelberg 2007

1   Introduction

About two decades ago, authors interested to submit papers to a conference would submit via postal service or airmail. After being reviewed, papers (together with the reviews) would be sent back by similar means. Before the camera-ready deadline, authors of accepted papers would need to race against time to send their camera-ready versions over, and hope that they do not get lost in transit. This method of correspondence is not only costly, it is also time-consuming. More notably, it will be hard to trace lost or delayed papers and reviews since it all depends on the reliability of the postal system. Fast forward a few years, technology advances introduce the use of email (attachments) and facsimile. Although most email services are free of charge, this method is often limited in terms of the size of the attachment(s). Facsimile, on the other hand, can be costly although fast.

Thus, the introduction of online web-based systems significantly facilitates the paper submission and review process [26], and overcomes shortfalls in the traditional paper-based system. Authors and reviewers can track their papers' progress anytime, anywhere, as long as they have an Internet connection. In addition, the conference Chair is now capable of managing papers and reviews more effectively, as well as reacting quickly to feedback and complaints.

According to a survey [26] by ALPSP[1] on web submission and review systems for journals, among the 442 respondents selected at random from the ISI Web of Knowledge database, 81 per cent preferred to use web submission and review systems and 36 per cent said that they would think twice when choosing a journal without online submission for their work. Following the introduction of online submission, there was a 25 per cent increase in submission volumes and publishers reported a 30 per cent decrease in administration time. From this survey, we see that online submission and review systems are playing a significant role. Nevertheless, popular though they be, there is still an issue involved that should be a major concern among the community - how secure are the data handled by these systems?

In this setting, security and privacy can be seen from two opposite perspectives. One, arguably less eminent, is the risk of malicious individuals attempting to obtain unauhorized access to leading edge research results and thus idea theft, or cause unfair dismissal of submitted papers. On the other is the case of honest paper authors desiring that the submission system maintains their privacy and secrecy of research ideas, and be able to verify to themselves and prove later to others that their submissions are properly handled by the system; at least that any errors should be detectable without unnecessary delay. Also desirable to the honest reviewer is that reviewer anonymity is upheld.

In this paper, we analyze the web-submission-and-review system (known as WSaR from here onwards) [10] developed by Shai Halevi from IBM Research. WSaR is currently in use by top cryptology conferences including Eurocrypt 2007 & 2008, Crypto 2007 and Asiacrypt 2007, annually sponsored by the International Association for Cryptologic Research (IACR) [11]. See Appendix B for a longer list.

---

[1] Association of Learned and Professional Society Publishers.

2   WSaR and Its Security Features

WSaR is open source and is hosted at SourceForge [23]. While analyzing its HyperText Preprocessor (PHP) scripts, we found some security features that have been designed into WSaR to protect against several common Web attacks. This section will analyze how the features are added and the type of attacks the features defend against.

2.1   Password Strength

Passwords are often the first defense against intrusion. Relative to online submission and review systems, passwords are the first fortification to ensure the quality of conference proceedings because they are used to safeguard the submissions and their reviews.

In order to gain initial access to the administration or review sites, WSaR computes and generates unique passwords for the conference Chair and reviewers respectively. Firstly, after the customization phase, the Chair will be given a 10-alphanumeric-character password to log in to the administration site. Once logged in, he has the option to change the default password.

The same goes to the reviewers (in most security conferences, a reviewer with access to the online system is called a program committee member) - soon after the Chair grants the reviewers access to the review site, they will receive a notification email that gives them the password to log on to their own review sites. Here, they will be able to view the list of submissions (for which they have no conflict of interest), change their reviewing preferences, post their reviews, participate in paper discussions or take part in a ballot. On the other hand, throughout the submission phase, a distinct submission-ID and password will be generated for every paper. Authors will need these parameters to revise or withdraw the papers. However, they do not have the option to change the submission password.

These "WSaR-generated" passwords are 10-alphanumeric-character strings. Each character is either uppercase (A-Z), lowercase (a-z), numerals (0-9), or sometimes a tilde (~) or an underscore (_). Figure 1 illustrates how passwords are generated in WSaR:

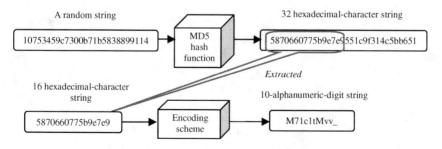

Fig. 1. Password generation process for the reviewer

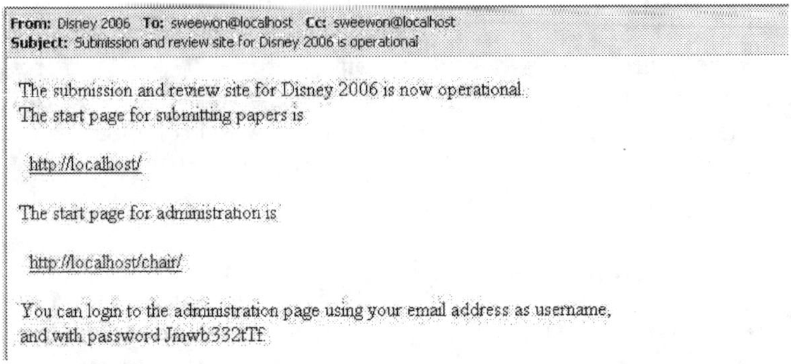

From: Disney 2006 To: sweewon@localhost Cc: sweewon@localhost
Subject: Submission and review site for Disney 2006 is operational

The submission and review site for Disney 2006 is now operational.
The start page for submitting papers is

  http://localhost/

The start page for administration is

  http://localhost/chair/

You can login to the administration page using your email address as username,
and with password Jmwb332tTf.

Fig. 2. An example email where generated password is emailed to the conference Chair

1. For the Chair and PC members: A long random string is generated using PHP functions such as `uniqid()`, `mt_rand()`, and `rand()`. This random string has length between 15 to 28 digits.
   For the submissions: A long random string is generated using the similar functions as above. This string is then appended by the submission's title and the author's name.
2. The hash of the resulting string is then computed via PHP's MD5 function.
3. The first 16 hexadecimal digits of the resulted message digest are extracted.
4. A custom WSaR encoding function is used to compress these extracted digits into a 10-digit alphanumeric string.
5. The resulting string (which is the password) will be emailed to the user (see Figure 2).

Note that an alphanumeric character corresponds to 6-bit entropy, so the entire 10-alphanumeric-character string requires an exhaustive effort of 2^{60} to brute force. Therefore, the passwords generated by WSaR are deemed to be secure.

2.2   Password Storage for Conference Chair and PC Members

No matter where passwords are stored on the online system server, they should be stored in encrypted or hashed form, similar to multi-user operating systems like Unix, Linux etc. The most popular way to seal passwords in a database is via password hashing. There are currently two most commonly used hash functions, namely the Secure Hash Algorithm-1 (SHA-1) and the Message Digest 5 (MD5).

MD5 produces a hash that is 128 bits long (equivalent to 32 hexadecimal characters) while SHA-1 computes a hash that is 160 bits long (equivalent to 40 hexadecimal characters). Among these two, MD5 is the more commonly used hash function to safeguard passwords as well as to ensure message or software integrity. Likewise, this function is also employed in WSaR when it comes to storing passwords.

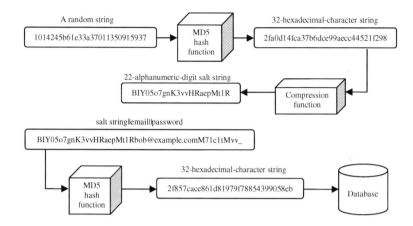

Fig. 3. Generation of salt string and password storing process

Here, we look at how WSaR protects the Chair and PC members' passwords stored in the system database (see Figure 3):

1. Upon customization, a random string is generated using PHP functions such as `uniqid()`, `mt_rand()`, and `rand()`. The string's message digest is computed and the digest is then compressed using a custom WSaR function into a 22-alphanumeric-character salt string. This salt string is saved and is constant throughout the entire conference.
2. The user's email address and password are retrieved.
3. The salt string is then appended by the user's email address and password, and it is fed to the MD5 hash function.
4. The resulting digest is stored into the database table (see Figure 4).

```
mysql> select revId,revPwd,name from committee;
+-------+----------------------------------+----------------------+
| revId | revPwd                           | name                 |
+-------+----------------------------------+----------------------+
|     1 | e81bf9d3b0cf5bc462f41b0221fbc0b9 | Disney2006 Chair     |
|     2 | 8285ced9fc7aa1339dcf0cafc93e76fa | John Smith           |
|     3 | ec739037e723790de8b4f30212e82c2d | Jane Doe             |
+-------+----------------------------------+----------------------+
```

Fig. 4. The digests are stored in the database instead of the passwords

In this case, users' passwords are not stored in the clear in the database, and it is infeasible for an attacker to reverse on the hash values to retrieve the pre-images (passwords). In Section 3.5, we will discuss an issue with the storage of submissions' passwords.

Furthermore, this technique of appending a salt string to the email address and password before hashing it increases the difficulty in cracking the passwords using brute-force attack even if an attacker has access to the hash table. In Section 3.4, we discuss how using different salt strings (instead of a constant one) can increase the difficulty in cracking users' passwords.

2.3   Input Sanitization

As discussed in [8], SQL injection is considered one of the most dangerous threats to Web applications because it allows an attacker to connect to the back-end database and extract any data as he wants. An example of an SQL injection attack is the log in form where a user enters his username and password to be authorized, and the server will retrieve the user's ID and credit card number, for example. Generally, the SQL query is shown in Table 1.

Table 1. SQL statement to retrieve user's ID and credit card number

SELECT	ID, CREDIT_NUM
FROM	users
WHERE	username = '$username'
AND	password = '$password'

Assuming an attacker enters "Jane" in the username field and provides the string "anything' OR 'a'='a" in the password field. The SQL query would become:

Table 2. SQL statement as "modified" by the attacker

SELECT	ID, CREDIT_NUM
FROM	users
WHERE	username = 'Jane'
AND	password = 'anything' OR 'a'='a'

The 'a'='a' part is always true regardless of what the first part of the query contains, thus the attacker would be able to trick the application to obtain database data that is not supposed to be returned by the application. Successful SQL injection attack will also result in authentication bypass and database modification [15].

The "one rule" to defend against SQL injection (as well as cross-site scripting, buffer overflows etc.) is input sanitization. If this is done, the Web application will be 80 per cent more secure.

There are two commonly used ways to validate input: (1) strip off any undesirable characters (such as meta-characters) and (2) check input data for expected data type [12]. Both ways are implemented in WSaR. We note that the potential SQL injection characters include: (''*;&<>/'^) [7]. In WSaR, a possible exploitation of special characters for an SQL Injection attack is in the "Submission/Revision Receipt" page where, as an example, the receipt page's URL for submission A with password 'ABC' will be"http://localhost/receipt.php? subId=A&subPwd=ABC". In this case, query to the database will be as in Table 3 (as an example).

Table 3. SQL statement to retrieve submission with subId=A and subPwd=ABC

SELECT	title, authors, abstract
FROM	submissions
WHERE	subId='A'
AND	subPwd='ABC'

Firstly, WSaR uses the `my_addslashes()` function in PHP to remove undesirable characters. If an attacker happens to be one of the submitters to the conference, she would know the pattern of the receipt page's URL. Now, she is interested in finding out the paper submitted by her rival, so she launches an SQL Injection attack on the receipt page by changing the URL to "`http://localhost/receipt.php?subId=1&subPwd=1'% 20OR% 20'1'='1`, where %20 represents a space in its HTML entity. This time, the query will be as follows:

Table 4. SQL query for an SQL Injection attack

SELECT	title, authors, abstract
FROM	submissions
WHERE	subId='1'
AND	subPwd='1' OR '1'='1'

However, since all special characters are removed by the `my_addslashes()` function - single quotes are ignored using backslashes (commented out), the '1'='1' part no longer makes sense. Thus, the attacker will receive a generic error message as shown in the screen shot in Figure 5.

If the software does not sanitize user's input in all PHP scripts (i.e. all `my_addslashes()` functions are removed from every WSaR scripts), the URL

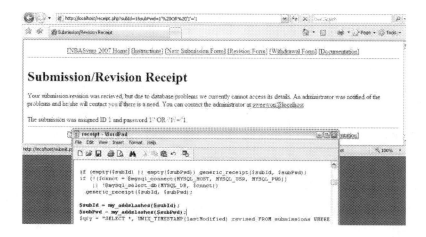

Fig. 5. Attacker receives an error message

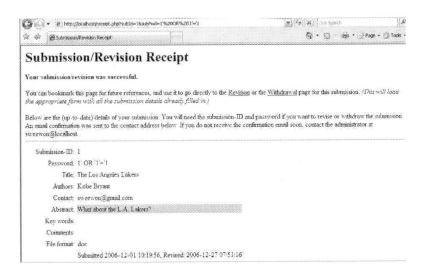

Fig. 6. An attacker can click on the Revision or Withdrawal link to revise or withdraw the submission

constructed by the attacker will return submission 1's receipt page and from there, she can redirect to the revision page and revise her rival's paper or even withdraw it from the conference without her rival knowing it (see Figure 6).

Secondly, developers should specify the type of input that is expected for certain form fields, and that the unexpected input will be removed. As an example, a form field that requests for user's phone number should accept only numbers as input. WSaR always has a specific input type that is expected for the submission ID - it processes only integers for the submission ID field. In spite of that, developers can make use of regular expressions to tell the program the type of pattern in the text that it should look for [19]. If the data submitted does not match the regular expression, it will be ignored [7] or error messages will be generated.

Both the above mentioned methods are employed in WSaR. Therefore, this system is not categorized as one of the 60 per cent of Web applications that is vulnerable to SQL injection (or other attacks due to invalidated input) [24].

2.4   Resistance to Bypass of Access Control Checks Through Forced Browsing

Forced browsing refers to a technique used by attackers to access to resources that are not referenced, but are nevertheless accessible [25]. Access control checks are normally performed after a user gets authenticated and it monitors what authorized users are allowed to do. As an example, if a reviewer is blocked from reviewing certain submissions due to conflict of interest, he should not be able to bypass the access control checks by requesting the review form of that submission directly in the URL.

Fig. 7. Review form for submission 1

Taking a look at the URL of a review form; to review submission A, reviewer will access the review form at the URL "`http://localhost/review/`
`review.php?subId=A`" (see Figure 7).

Assume that the insider attacker is one of the reviewers in a conference and she
is blocked from reviewing submission 1 since she is one of the authors of that submission. In order to make sure that her submission is accepted to the conference,
the attacker needs good reviews for her paper. Thus, she tries to change submission
A's review form URL to which she has access, from "`http://localhost/review/`
`review.php?subId=A`" to "`http://localhost/ review/review.php?subId=1`"
since she is prohibited to access the link directly from her review page. If the system then displays the review form for submission 1, the attacker has bypassed the
access control checks through forced browsing.

Fortunately, the attempt to bypass WSaR's access control check is forbidden
in the review form page, as well as the voting page and the reviewers' discussion forum. Whenever a reviewer attempts to access a blocked submission by
directly specifying the submission-ID in the URL, WSaR will firstly perform an
authorization check in the reviewer table; if the reviewer is blocked from that
submission, it will display an error message indicating that the submission is not
found, or the reviewer has a conflict as shown in Figure 8.

Fig. 8. WSaR prevents broken access control

3   Security Issues and Enhancements

In addition to the security features already designed into WSaR discussed in
Section 2, we have also discovered some security issues not treated in WSaR
and in this section, we discuss them in detail and then describe ways to enhance
WSaR security by taking them into consideration.

For any security issue, we will discuss its implications from the two opposing perspectives motivated in Section 1. We also highlight whether exploitation of issues can be traceable or uniquely pointing the finger to the culprit. This has devastating consequences if the attacker cannot be traced since it means even a curious (if not malicious) researcher from the scientific community could have mounted the attack without any counter-incentives i.e. no adverse effects on his reputation. Furthermore, issues that lead to attacks for which the culprit cannot be unambiguously accused will cause disputes for which a malicious attacker could deny his involvement or an honest user be unfairly thought by peers to have mounted an attack.

3.1   Browser Caching

Browser caching is categorized as one of the critical areas in OWASP's Top Ten projects under "Broken Authentication and Session Management" [25].

In WSaR, the submission-ID and password are sent by the HTTP GET method. Information sent in such way will be displayed in the browser's URL [18] and it is extremely undesirable (see Figure 9).

Fig. 9. Submission-ID and password are displayed in the page's URL

This means the submission-ID and password are part of the URL. As has been highlighted in [25], authentication and session data should not be submitted as part of a GET to prevent someone malicious from using the "Back" button in an authorized user's browser to backup the page and hence obtain the password from the URL.

Alternatively, even if a browser window is closed, the URL info can also be obtained from the browser's cache and history. Recall that browsers *cache* most of the contents of frequently visited pages so that the pages will load faster the next time they are visited, including images, sounds, cookies, web pages and their URLs. Information stored in browsers' cache is not encrypted [1] and it can be obtained by anyone who accesses the computer. Both Netscape Navigator and Mozilla Firefox, by default require users to clear the browser's cache (and disk cache - also known as "Temporary Internet Files") manually. On the other hand, Internet Explorer will clear the browser's cache but not the "Temporary Internet Files", once the browser is restarted. In addition, previously visited URLs are typically stored in the browser's *history*; for instance the latest versions (at the time of writing) of Netscape Navigator and Mozilla Firefox by default will only clear browser's history every nine days, while the default for Internet Explorer is 20 days.

Fig. 10. Internet Explorer's temporary internet files that stores the receipt page's URL

Figure 10 shows the receipt URLs stored in the "Temporary Internet Files" folder. In spite of that, if the user does not clear the browser's cache or history after he uses the computer, the URLs will also be displayed in the browser's history pane as shown in Figure 11.

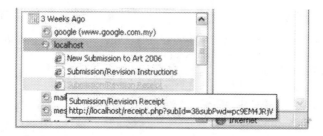

Fig. 11. Submission ID and password are exposed to the attacker

This threat can be launched by any individual having access to a common machine previously utilized by a WSaR user, and upon retrieving the login information (ID and password), he can login as the WSaR victimized user. This attack is non-traceable in the sense that the attacker cannot be later pinpointed, so he can mount the attack without any risk of jeopardizing his reputation. Thus, the counter-incentive is non-existent that it will indeed be tempting for any individual to abuse this issue to the victim's disadvantage.

Browser caching can be prevented by submitting the submission-ID and password as part of a `HTTP POST` method [25] instead. If the `POST` method is used, we can employ the PHP's predefined variable "$_POST" to retrieve the values entered in the submission-ID and password fields respectively. In this case, both submission-ID and password will not be displayed in the page's URL.

Other than this, WSaR users are advised to clear the browser's cache before they leave the computer. In Netscape Navigator, users would have to clear both the memory and disk cache; in Mozilla Firefox, users should check all fields when clearing their private data [4]; in Internet Explorer, users should clear the history and all temporary internet files [21]. This way, users can ensure the security of their private information.

3.2   Constant Salt String for Reviewer and Chair Passwords

In Section 2.2, we discussed how WSaR uses a salt string appended to the reviewer's email address and password to build a stronger defense in securing his passwords. However, this salt string is constant throughout the entire conference for any party, thus all users of the same conference will have the same salt appended to their password. So what differentiates each user is just the email address (which is typically public information) and his password. This indicates that the salt string does not really provide better strength against insider attackers (users of the same conference) than conventional password-based authentication systems. Therefore, we recommend the use of different salt strings for different users.

These salt strings will be stored in a single PHP script upon customization of WSaR, and they will be labeled in the sense that "SALT_2" will be used for PC member with the ID of 2 and so on. In this case, since the salt strings will be random and of different lengths, the attacker would have a much harder time trying to guess the exact salt that is appended to a specific user's email address and password.

Again, this threat is non-traceable as it allows a malicious insider individual to brute-force the password, upon which he can login as the victim without any evidence pointing back to him.

3.3   Storage of Submission Passwords

Throughout our analysis, we discovered that although WSaR stores the hashes of reviewers' passwords, it does not do the same when it comes to storing submissions' passwords (see Figure 12). For someone who manages to gain access to the database, he has the ID and password for every submission as well. We recommend that the submission passwords to be salted and hashed as well to secure them so that even if a hacker manages to penetrate the database's security, he would face the prospect of a potentially expensive search for the exact password.

```
mysql> select subId,title,subPwd from submissions;
+-------+--------------------------------------------------------------------------------------+------------+
| subId | title                                                                                | subPwd     |
+-------+--------------------------------------------------------------------------------------+------------+
|     1 | Hardening Network Security                                                           | 1yZrHxZa4o |
|     2 | Multiband PIFAs (planar inverted-F antenna) for Internal Mobile Phone Antennas       | KUuGRUFAcb |
|     3 | Implementation of Cryptographic Pseudorandom Generator in 8-bit Microcontroller      | fCbk_MkFi_ |
|     4 | Intelligent Health System                                                           | ZEQjc44ktk |
|     5 | Trellis coding                                                                      | 2H0xeSxMcC |
|     6 | Chess-Playing Robot                                                                 | Ady4i4D0_8 |
|     7 | Intelligent Car Alarm System                                                        | xO8qBFvk3q |
+-------+--------------------------------------------------------------------------------------+------------+
7 rows in set (0.00 sec)
```

Fig. 12. Submissions' passwords are stored in the clear in the database

3.4   Password Policy and Strength Checking

Using a good password by every user is vital to defending a system. The components of a good password should be at least eight characters long, should not consist of dictionary words (would be vulnerable to dictionary attack otherwise), should never be the same as the user's log in name, should not consist of any item that is easily identified with the user, and have at least three of the following elements [5]:

 – One or more uppercase letters (A-Z)
 – One or more lowercase letters (a-z)

- One or more numerals (0-9)
- One or more special characters or punctuation marks

However, it is worth noting that some systems do not permit the use of certain special characters in user's password string.

Although the passwords supplied by WSaR fulfill all the mentioned requirements, users might find the password hard to remember and opt to change it. Therefore, we analysed WSaR's password change mechanism. WSaR does not have any password policies imposed to ensure the strength of new passwords, thus a careless user may happen to employ a password which is easily cracked by any password-cracking tools, without being reminded not to do so. Hence, we suggest that WSaR should force its users to adopt passwords that cannot be easily cracked. Google mail [9] uses a scale to show its users the strength of their passwords with parameters such as "Too short", "Weak", "Fair", "Good" or "Strong". This is a feature that could be added to WSaR.

Fig. 13. Google mail's password strength evaluation

However, careless users tend to ignore the password strength evaluation and proceed to employing the new password. Consequently, the system's security could still be breached.

Having said that, WSaR's password changing mechanism should perform an assessment on the new password - whether it is too short or it contains dictionary words or even a row of letters from a standard keyboard layout (e.g., ertyui) [14]. If a user's new password happens to be a weak password, a pop up window should be issued to require him to re-enter a new password.

Besides that, a password policy should also be implemented to require frequent change of passwords. If an attacker uses brute-force attack to crack a password, it is possible that he would be taking a long time (depending on the length of the password, speed of both the machine and network connection) to complete the attack [14]. In this case, if the user changes his password frequently, he could avoid his password from being cracked via brute-force attack.

3.5   Absence of File Integrity and Binding

Whenever we download any files or software, the first thing we would want to do is to check the file's integrity. Presently, the most popular method used to verify a file's integrity is via the use of the MD5 function. If the file content is modified, it can be easily detected by re-computing its hash value. In an online submission and review system, calculating a submission's message digest is important both to ensure message integrity and to bind the author to the submitted paper due to absence of face-to-face communication.

We note that WSaR does not have this feature, i.e. upon submission the file's message digest is not computed and thus not supplied to both the author and the

Chair. Therefore, considering the case of malicious users, if an author happens to submit a not-so-perfect paper in order to meet the submission deadline, he can later deny that he submitted that version of the paper, then claim that the file is corrupted and request for a second-time submission, thus gaining advantage over other authors. More devastatingly, an honest author could have submitted a proper paper but the file became corrupted by the server machine; in which case it is desirable to be able to unambiguously prove that the corrupted version is not the submitted file, or at least be able to check during submission that it was properly received. This avoids ambiguity when a Chair notes during review phase that a file is corrupted and is unsure if it was intentionally submitted in that form in order to buy authors some time, or if it was indeed submitted properly but was corrupted in transit.

Indeed, this issue is often not so much to guard against malicious authors but rather so as to allow a scientifically honest author in this situation to be able to prove his innocence beyond any doubt.

To counter this issue, we recommend that authors be presented with a 128-bit hash of his submission file and that this hash value is kept as a record for the Chair. Since WSaR is developed in PHP, we can apply the "md5_file()" function where it calculates the message digest of the given file [18].

Firstly, a new column has to be created in the "submissions" table to record the message digest by adding a "msgDigest varchar(255) BINARY NOT NULL" statement in the "create_table( )" function, which can be found in WSaR's database.php script. Subsequently, we added a statement to calculate the file's message digest in the act-submit.php and act-revise.php scripts, which are used in WSaR to process all parameters entered in the submission and revision form respectively. The resulted digest is inserted into the database under the "msgDigest" column and authors will be redirected to the receipt page. An email will also be generated to the author, and carbon-copied to the Chair with all submission details listed (including the message digest). Now, we can be assured of the file's integrity as well as binding the author to his submission. The screenshots are shown as Figure 14 and Figure 15 in Appendix A for further illustration.

4   Protocol Sketch for Password Distribution Via Email

In general (not specific to WSaR), passwords for reviewers are commonly sent via emails to the reviewers' email addresses. This is indeed the most practical way to distribute passwords, although it is known that email formats by default (and this is the setting that users commonly use) do not provide any form of confidentiality nor authenticity, unless explicit email clients or plug-ins like PGP are applied.

We take what we view as a concrete step towards securing online systems by motivating here and sketching the basic idea of our ongoing work: a proposal for an email-based password distribution protocol for security conferences. Having this kind of protocol in place will prevent reviewer passwords from being easily compromised through attacks mounted not on the system itself but on how this password is distributed. Indeed, it is well known that the study of password-based key exchange protocols is a long-standing research topic in cryptology, thus we should avoid having security conferences using in practice the email-based password distribution protocols that are not securely designed.

The setting for an email ID-based password distribution protocol is different from those in typical key exchange protocols [3]. The protocol involves two parties, the program chair C and the reviewer R. Rather than requiring any public-key infrastructure (PKI), only a trusted web site bulletin board is used, for instance the IACR website (http://www.iacr.org), where URLs for different IACR conferences or workshops are hosted or mirrored. On this website is listed the email address ID_C of the program chair. Meanwhile, it is common that the chair invites program committee members (the reviewers) who are experts in the field and for whom the chair knows the authentic email addresses ID_R either himself, or for which he can ask from other experts through some out of band mechanism. Alternatively, the email addresses can be obtained from the IACR membership database.

Thus, when a reviewer R receives an email from the chair C, it can check to be certain that the email came from the chair; vice versa a chair knows if an email came from a particular reviewer. This provides source authentication without resorting to any PKI.

Then a general sketch of this kind of protocol proceeds as follows:

1. C generates an ID-based public and private key pair based on his ID_C. Denote these as pk_C and sk_C. Then C computes the message sig_{SK_C} $(ID_C, ID_R, \text{INVITE})$ where sig_{SK} denotes signing under a person's private key SK, and INVITE contains a one-way (e.g. hashed) representation of a typical invitation email stating the conference name etc.
2. C sends $m_1 = sig_{SK_C}(ID_C, ID_R, \text{INVITE})$ to R.
3. R generates an ID-based public and private key pair based on his ID_R. Denote these as pk_R and sk_R. Then R computes the message $sig_{SK_R}(ID_R, ID_C, \text{ACCEPT})$.
4. R sends $m_2 = sig_{SK_R}(ID_R, ID_C, \text{ACCEPT})$ to C.
5. C generates a password pwd_R for R.
6. C sends $m_3 = \langle sig_{SK_C}(ID_C, ID_R, m_1, m_2, Enc_{PK_R}(pwd_R)), Enc_{PK_R}(pwd_R)\rangle$ to R, where $Enc_{PK}(\cdot)$ denotes encryption under a person's public key PK.
7. R obtains pwd_R by decrypting $Enc_{PK_R}(pwd_R)$.

In fact, this can be a concrete step to a long-term setting where one submission and review system is used for all conferences that use WSaR, so only a one-time setup cost e.g. the ID-based password distribution protocol as above, is incurred for new users, while existing users can update their passwords online through the system at any time; and new membership in conference program committees of existing users only require the program chair to email to a PC member R asking him to update his password himself rather than having to email newly generated passwords every time R is involved in a new conference program commitee. Indeed, this centralization is possible since conferences using WSaR are typically hosted on a central machine e.g. at `http://ε1.iacr.org`, unlike some other submission software that need to be locally set up. Furthermore, conferences using WSaR commonly involve program committee members who are involved in multiple conferences so the setup cost will be amortized over time and this centralization makes sense compared to treating each conference system separately.

We emphasize here that the above is a sketch of a protocol design that we are currently working on, whose formal security we are in the process of proving. This should therefore preclude the sprouting of future papers that propose informal "breaks" on the above enumerated steps. The above sketch should only be taken as a basic template and taken for the general idea that it is sketching and nothing more. We do welcome comments for which will be acknowledged in future work, or collaborations in this direction.

5   Concluding Remarks

In this paper, we have seen that WSaR is built with a strong defense against a number of known attacks in the Web. We have also discovered and discussed the absence of several features that could jeopardise the security of WSaR users and we proposed suggestions to further enhance WSaR's security that address these issues. As a side remark, we recommend that besides strengthening the defense of the software itself e.g. WSaR, Web administrators should secure the Web server as well as the back-end database and constantly monitor the activities going on in the Web server to detect any malicious behaviour.

In addition, as a further step to securing these types of systems, we have also motivated the design of an email-based password distribution protocol for WSaR users and argued that together with such a design, there are advantages in centralizing conferences that use WSaR.

Acknowledgement

The first author thanks Shai Halevi for encouragement during the initial stages of this research, for patiently answering queries about WSaR and for detailed comments on an early version of this paper. The second author thanks Thomas Baignères for stimulating discussions on another popular submission and review system iChair. Nous avons eu un temps merveilleux pendant la pause de café, ou bien? We thank an anonymous referee for motivational comments especially on the need to make clear the distinction between pro- and counter-incentives for an attacker; and for acknowledging the fun of this research work :-)

References

1. AICT Security - Empty your Cache. Available online at
   `https://www.ualberta.ca/AICT/Security/BrowserCache.html#private`
2. Archer, T.: Are Hash Codes Unique? Available online at
   `http://blogs.msdn.com/tomarcher/archive/2006/05/10/594204.aspx`

3. Bellare, M., Rogaway, P.: Entity Authentication and Key Distribution. In: Stinson, D.R. (ed.) CRYPTO 1993. LNCS, vol. 773, pp. 232–249. Springer, Heidelberg (1994)
4. CIBC - Clear Your Browser's Cache. Available online at http://www.cibc.com/ca/legal/clear-browsers-cache.html
5. Conklin, W.A., White, G.B., Cothren, C., Williams, D., Davis, R.L.: Principles of Computer Security: Security+ TM and Beyond. McGraw-Hill, New York (2005)
6. EasyChair Conference System. Available online at http://www.easychair.org/
7. Foster, J.C.: Defense Tactics for SQL Injection Attacks. Available online at http://searchappsecurity.techtarget.com/tip/0,289483,sid92_gci1219912, 00.html
8. Fyre, C.: One Simple Rule to Make your Web Apps more Secure (2006), Available online at http://searchappsecurity.techtarget.com/qna/0,289202, sid92_gci1225425,gci1225425,00.html00.html
9. Google Mail. Available online at http://gmail.google.com
10. Halevi, S.: Web Submission and Review Software. Available online at http://theory.csail.mit.edu/~shaih/websubrev
11. IACR Conferences. Available online at http://www.iacr.org/conferences/
12. McClure, S., Shah, S., Shah, S.: Web Hacking: Attacks and Defense. Addison-Wesley, Reading (2003)
13. Microsoft Corporation. Microsoft's Conference Management Toolkit. Available online at http://msrcmt.research.microsoft.com/cmt/
14. Password Cracking: Information from Answers.com (2006), Available online at http://www.answers.com/topic/password-cracking
15. Peikari, C., Chuvakin, A.: Security Warrior. O'Reilly (2004)
16. Phan, R.C.-W., Goi, B.-M.: Flaw in IEEE Trans on Consumer Electronics Online Submission System. In: Dawson, E., Vaudenay, S. (eds.) Mycrypt 2005. LNCS, vol. 3715, Springer, Heidelberg (2005)
17. Phan, R.C.-W., Ling, H.-C.: On the Insecurity of the Microsoft Research Conference Management Tool (MSRCMT) System. In: CITA 2005. Proceedings of International Conference on IT in Asia, pp. 75–79 (2005) Also presented at the rump session of Asiacrypt 2004, Jeju Island, Korea
18. PHP Manual. Full version available online at http://www.php.net/manual/en/
19. Regular Expressions (2006), Available online at http://searchappsecurity. techtarget.com/sDefinition/0,290660,sid92_gci517740,00.html
20. ScholarOne, Inc. Manuscript Central: About Manuscript Central. Available online at http://www.scholarone.com/products_manuscriptcentral_aboutMC.shtml
21. Security Information Clearing Browser Cache and History. Available online at http://www.hlasset.com/files/Clearing_Cache_History.pdf
22. SoftConf.com - Software for Conferences. Available online at http://www.softconf.com/index.html
23. SourceForge.net: Web Submission and Review Software. Available online at http://sourceforge.net/projects/websubrev
24. What is SQL Injection? (2006), Available online at http://searchappsecurity. techtarget.com/sDefinition/0,290660,sid92_gci1003024,00.html
25. The Ten Most Critical Web Application Security Vulnerabilities (2004) Available online at http://osdn.dl.sourceforge.net/sourceforge/owasp/OWASPTop Ten2004.pdf
26. Ware, M.: Online Submission and Peer-Review System (2005) Available online at www.zen34802.zen.co.uk/Learned_Publishing_offprint.pdf

A   Storage and Display of Submissions' Digests

We present below the screen shots of the "submissions" table, and the submission/revision receipt after the calculation of submission's digest is incorporated.

```
mysql> select subId,title,authors,msgDigest from submissions where subId=2;
+-------+--------------------+----------------+----------------------------------+
| subId | title              | authors        | msgDigest                        |
+-------+--------------------+----------------+----------------------------------+
|     2 | The Indiana Pacers | Jermaine O'Neal| e12ad858eef40ad7229d7a400483806f |
+-------+--------------------+----------------+----------------------------------+
```

Fig. 14. Digest of submission is stored in the database for Chair's reference

Fig. 15. Digest of submission is presented in the receipt for the author

B   Conferences That Have Used or Are Using WSaR

In reverse chronological order:

1. EUROCRYPT 2008: 27th Annual International Conference on the Theory and Applications of Cryptographic Techniques
2. CT-RSA 2008: RSA Conference 2007, Cryptographers' Track
3. LATIN 2008: 8th Latin American Theoretical Informatics
4. TCC 2008: 5th Theory of Cryptography Conference
5. PKC 2008: 11th International Conference on Theory and Practice in Public-Key Cryptography
6. ASIACRYPT 2007: 13th Annual International Conference on the Theory and Application of Cryptology and Information Security
7. ISC 2007: 10th Information Security Conference
8. CRYPTO 2007: 27th Annual International Cryptology Conference
9. ICALP 2007: Track C of the 34th International Colloquium on Automata, Languages and Programming

10. GOCP 2007: 1st International Workshop on Group-Oriented Cryptographic Protocols
11. ACNS 2007: 5th International Conference on Applied Cryptography and Network Security
12. EUROCRYPT 2007: 26th Annual International Conference on the Theory and Applications of Cryptographic Techniques
13. USEC 2007: Usable Security Workshop
14. TCC 2007: 4th Theory of Cryptography Conference
15. CT-RSA 2007: RSA Conference 2007, Cryptographers' Track
16. HVC 2006: 2nd Annual Haifa Verification Conference
17. PKC 2006: 9th International Conference on Theory and Practice of Public-Key Cryptography

C   Related Work

Many online paper submission and review systems are emerging. For the context of cryptology and information security, the predecessor to WSaR is the collection of PHP/Perl scripts written progressively by Chanathip Namprempre, Andre Adelsbach, Andrew Clark and the Computer Security and Industrial Cryptography (COSIC) group at Katholieke Universiteit Leuven.

These scripts were used for almost all mainstream cryptology and information security conferences till 2006 when building on ideas in these scripts, two successor systems were developed independently: WSaR by Shai Halevi of IBM Research and iChair by Thomas Baignères and Matthieu Finiasz of LASEC at EPFL. These two systems are now used by almost all mainstream cryptology and information security conferences.

A few other major submission and review systems used in other fields deserve some mention here:

1. Manuscript Central
   Manuscript Central [20], developed by ScholarOne, Inc., is the online submission and peer review system used to handle manuscript submissions to journals. It manages over 44,000 submissions per month and its comprehensive and user-friendly features result in reports that most journals using Manuscript Central achieve gains in submissions of 20 to 40 per cent per annum. This system is currently used by most IEEE and Association of Computing Machinery (ACM) journals. Manuscript Central is a fully-developed software with 24-hour support on weekdays. By contacting the sales representative, one would be able to obtain and understand the system's functionalities, features, pricing and get the system running in two weeks' time.
2. Microsoft Research Conference Management Tool (MSRCMT)
   Firstly developed for ACM SIGKDD 1999, the MSRCMT [13] is an academic conference management service sponsored by Microsoft Research. Surajit Chaudhuri, a Research Area Manager at Microsoft Research is the architect of MSRCMT. Since the year 1999, this system has been used in over 500

conferences, among them are the International Conference on Security of Information and Networks (SIN 2007) and the ACM SIGCOMM 2007 Data Communication Festival. Similar to Manuscript Central, the MSRCMT is also a fully-developed system. It is free and hosted by Microsoft Research, but with limited support since it is developed and managed by a small team.

3. EasyChair

   Developed in the year 2002 by Andrei Voronkov, a Professor from the University of Manchester, EasyChair [6] is used by over 600 conferences in year 2007 alone. EasyChair is free and it is currently hosted by University of Manchester's Computer Science Department. EasyChair is capable of supporting two models: (1) the standard model for conferences having one program committee and (2) the multi-track version for conferences having multiple tracks that have their own program committee. There are a number of ACM and IEEE conferences/workshops that have used or are using EasyChair. Among them are the 8th IEEE/ACM International Conference on Grid Computing (Grid 2007), the 2nd ACM Workshop on Scalable Trusted Computing (STC'07) and the 20th IEEE Computer Security Foundation Symposium (CSF 20).

4. START V2 ConferenceManager

   START V2 [22], written by Rich Gerber, is a product from SoftConf.com. Apart from EasyChair, several IEEE and ACM conferences have, or are employing START V2 as the submission and peer review system since the year 2002. The IEEE Symposium on Intelligence and Security Informatics (ISI 2007), the 2007 IEEE Symposium on Security and Privacy, the 5th ACM Workshop on Recurring Malcode (WORM 2007) and the 40th Annual IEEE/ACM International Symposium on Microarchitecture (MICRO 2007) are among the many IEEE and ACM conferences using START V2. Users would need to contact the developer to order the system; the pricing depends on whether one needs the system to be hosted at softconf.com, and on the different types of licensing arrangements. This system is constantly improving based on the users' feedback.

It is worth to note two earlier work related to the security of online submission and review systems, although our work here is the first detailed analysis of this type of system. Phan and Goi [16] pointed out the lack of privacy in a system used by an IEEE Transactions where the URL of pages that disclose paper information and that allow paper revision for a particular submitted paper, differ from pages of other papers by an ID counter. Thus if the URL to revise author A's submitted paper is uniquely identified by ID 100, then A can also view the revision page for the paper submitted right after (resp. before) his, which he knows will be uniquely identified by ID 101 (resp. 99). Correspondence with the administrator of the system obtained the response that this was not a significant issue.

Phan and Ling [17] discovered by accident when submitting their paper to a conference using the Microsoft Research Conference Management Tool (MSR-CMT) that the system automatically creates an account for co-authors of a corresponding author who submitted a paper, where email addresses of these co-authors are used as login usernames and the numeric 0 is used as the default password. This applied for any co-author(s) of any paper. Correspondence with developers of MSRCMT obtained the response that this was an exercise of regression testing, though the flaw was present for some months in the actual online system used by several conferences. As of 2005 it was verified that both the above systems no longer exhibit those issues.

Authorization Constraints Specification of RBAC

Lilong Han, Qingtan Liu, and Zongkai Yang

Department of Information and Technology&Engineering Research Center on Education
Information Technology, Central China Normal Uninversity, 430079,Wuhan, China
{Lilong Han,Qingtan Liu,Zongkai Yang,hanlilong2001}@yahoo.com.cn

Abstract. Constraints are an important aspect of role-based access control (RBAC) and are often regarded as one of the principle motivations behind RBAC. Although the importance of the constraints in RBAC has been recognized for a long time, they have not received much attention. In this article, we introduce an intuitive formal language for specifying role-based authorization constraints named *RCL2000* including its basic elements, syntax and semantics. We show how previously identified role-based authorization constraints such as separation of duty (SOD) can be expressed in this language, and that there are other significant SOD properties that have not been previously identified in the literature. Our work indicates that there are many alternate formulations of even the simplest SOD properties, with varying degree of flexibility and assurance. So this language provides us a rigorous foundation for systematic study of role-based authorization constraints.

Keywords: RBAC, Constraints, RCL2000, SOD, DSOD.

1 Introduction

Role-based access control (RBAC) has emerged as a widely accepted alternative to classical discretionary and mandatory access controls. RBAC regulates the access of users to information and system resources on the basis of activities that users need to execute in the system, and requires the identification of roles in the system. Since roles in an organization are relatively persistent with respect to user turnover and task reassignment, RBAC provides a powerful mechanism for reducing the complexity, cost, and potential for error in assigning permissions to users within the organization. Because roles within an organization typically have overlapping permissions, RBAC models include features to establish role hierarchies, where a given role can include all of the permissions of another role. Another fundamental aspect of RBAC is authorization constraints (also simply called constraints). Although the importance of constraints in RBAC has been recognized for a long time [1], they have not received much attention in the research literature, while role hierarchies have been practiced and discussed at considerable length.

In this article, our focus is on constraint specifications, that is, on how constraints can be expressed, whether in natural languages, such as English, or in more formal languages. Natural language specification has the advantage of ease of comprehension by human beings, but may be prone to ambiguities, and the specifications do not lend themselves to the analysis of properties of the set of constraints.

S. Kim, M. Yung, and H.-W. Lee (Eds.): WISA 2007, LNCS 4867, pp. 266–276, 2007.

To specify these constraints we introduce the specification language *RCL2000* (for Role-Based Constraints Language 2000, pronounced Ríckle2000) which is the specification language for role-based authorization constraints [2]. In this article, we describe its basic elements, syntax, and the formal foundation of *RCL2000*. *RCL2000* is a substantial generalization of RSL99 [Ahn and Sandhu 1999], which is the earlier version of *RCL2000*. It encompasses obligation constraints in addition to the usual separation of duty and prohibition constraints.

2 Role-Based Constraints Language (*RCL 2000*)

RCL2000 is defined in context of the well-known family of models for RBAC of Sandhu et al. This model has become a widely cited authoritative reference and is the basis of a standard currently under development by the National Institute of Standards and Technology. Here we use a slightly augmented form of the model illustrated in Figure 1. We decompose permissions into operations and objects to enable formulation of certain forms of constraints. Also in Figure 1 we drop the administrative roles since they are not germane to *RCL2000*.

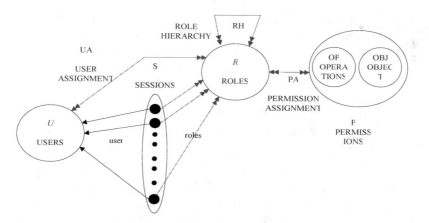

Fig. 1. Basic elements and system functions

Constraints are an important aspect of role-based access control and are a powerful mechanism for laying out higher-level organizational policy. The importance of flexible constraints to support emerging applications has been recently discussed by many scholars. Consequently, the specification of constraints needs to be considered. To date, this topic has not received much formal attention in the context of role-based access control. A notable exception is the work of Giuri and Iglio who defined a formal model for constraints on role-activation. *RCL2000* considers all aspects of role-based constraints, not just those applying to role activation. *RCL2000* goes beyond separation of duty to include obligation constraints such as those used in the constructions of Sandhu and Osborn et al. for simulating mandatory and discretionary access controls in RBAC.

One of our central claims is that it is futile to try to enumerate all interesting and practically useful constraints because there are too many possibilities and variations. Instead, we should pursue an intuitively simple yet rigorous language for specifying constraints such as *RCL2000*. The expressive power of *RCL2000* is demonstrated in Section 4, where it is shown that many constraints previously identified in the RBAC literature and many new ones can be conveniently formulated in *RCL2000*.

2.1 Basic Components

The basic elements and system functions on which *RCL2000* is based are defined in Figure 2. Figure 1 shows the RBAC model which is the context for these definitions. *RCL2000* has six entity sets called users (U), roles (R), objects (OBJ), operations (OP), permissions (P), and sessions (S). These are interpreted as in RBAC model as discussed above. OBJ and OP are not in RBAC model. OBJ is the passive entities that

—U=a set of users, $\{u_1, \cdots, u_n\}$

—R=a set of roles, $\{r_1, \cdots, r_m\}$

—OP=a set of operations, $\{op_1, \cdots, op_o\}$

—OBJ=a set of objects, $\{obj_1, \cdots, obj_r\}$

—P=OP×OBJ, a set of permissions, $\{p_1, \cdots, p_q\}$

—S=a set of sessions, $\{s_1, \cdots, s_r\}$

—RH⊆R×R is a partial order on R called the role hierarchy or role dominance relation, written as $\leq$

—UA⊆U×R, a many-to-many user-to-role assignment relation

—PA⊆P×R=OP×OBJ×R, a many-to-many permission-to-role assignment relation

—user :S→U, a function mapping each session s_i to the single user.

   user: R→2^U, a function mapping each role r_i to a set of users.

—roles :U∪P∪S→2^r, a function mapping the set U,P and S to a set of roles R.

   roles*: U∪P∪S→2^r, extends roles in presence of role hierarchy.

      roles(u_i)=$\{r \in R | (u_i, r) \in UA\}$

      roles*(u_i)=$\{r \in R | (\exists r' \geq r)[(u_i, r') \in UA]\}$

      roles(p_i)=$\{r \in R | (p_i, r) \in PA\}$

      roles*(p_i)=$\{r \in R | (\exists R' \leq r)[(p_i, r') \in PA]\}$

      roles(s_i)=$\{r \in R | (sessions(s_i),r) \in UA\}$

      roles*(s_i)=$\{r \in R | (\exists R' \geq r)[r' \in roles(s_i)]\}$

—sessions: U→2^{s_i} a function mapping each user u_i to a set of sessions

—permissions :R→2^P, a function mapping each role r_i to a set of permissions.

   permissions*: R→2^P, extends permissions in presence of role hierarchy.

      permissions(r_i)=$\{p \in P | (p,r_i) \in PA\}$

      permissions*(r_i)=$\{p \in P | (\exists r \leq r_i)[(p,r_i) \in PA]\}$

—Operations: R×OBJ→2^{OP}, a function mapping each role r_i and

         object obj_i to a set of operations

   Operations(r_i,obj_i) =$\{op \in OP | (op,obj_i,r_i) \in PA\}$

—object: P→2^{OBI}, a function mapping each permissions p_i to a set of objects

Fig. 2. Basic elements and system functions

contain or receive information. OP is an executable image of a program, which upon execution causes information flow between objects. P is an approval of a particular mode of operation to one or more objects in the system.

2.2 Additional Elements

Additional elements and system functions used in *RCL2000* are defined in Figure 3. The precise meaning of conflicting roles, permissions, and users will be specified as per organizational policy in *RCL2000*. For mutually disjoint organizational roles such as those of purchasing manager and accounts payable manager, the same individual is generally not permitted to belong to both roles. We defined these mutually disjoint roles as conflicting roles. We assume that there is a collection CR of sets of roles that have been defined as conflicting.

—CR=a collection of conflicting role sets,$\{cr_1, \cdots, cr_s\}$.where $cr_i=\{r_i, \cdots, r_t\} \subseteq R$
—CP=a collection of conflicting permission sets,$\{cp_1, \cdots, cp_u\}$.where $cp_i=\{p_i, \cdots, p_v\} \subseteq P$
—CU=a collection of conflicting user sets,$\{cu_1, \cdots, cu_w\}$.where $cu_i=\{u_i, \cdots, u_t\} \subseteq U$
—oneelement(X)=x_i.where $x_i \in X$
—allother(X)=X-$\{OE(X)\}$

Fig. 3. Additional elements and nondeterministic functions

The concept of conflicting permissions defines conflict in terms of permissions rather than roles. Thus the permission to issue purchase orders and the permission to issue payments are conflicting, irrespective of the roles to which they are assigned. We denote sets of conflicting permissions as CP. As we show, defining conflict in terms of permissions offers greater assurance than defining it in terms of roles. Conflict defined in terms of roles allows conflicting permissions to be assigned to the same role by error (or malice). Conflict defined in terms of permissions eliminates this possibility. In the real world, conflicting users also should be considered. For example, for the process of preparing and approving purchase orders, it might be company policy that members of the same family should not prepare the purchase order, and also be a user who approves that order.

RCL2000 has two nondeterministic functions, *oneelement* and *allother*. The *oneelement*(X) function allows us to get one element X_i from set X. We usually write *oneelement* as OE. Multiple occurrences of OE(X) in a single *RCL2000* statement all select the same element X_i from X. With *allother*(X) we can get a set by taking out one element. We usually write *allother* as AO. These two nondeterministic functions are related by context, because for any set S, $\{OE(S)\} \cup AO=S$, and at the same time, neither is a deterministic function.

In order to illustrate how to use these two functions to specify role-based constraints, we take the requirement of the static separation of duty (SOD) property which is the simplest variation of SOD [3]. For simplicity assume there is no role hierarchy (otherwise replace roles by roles*). Requirement: No user can be assigned to two conflicting roles. In other words, conflicting roles cannot have common users. We can express this requirement as below.

Expression: $|\text{roles}(OE\ (U)) \cap OE(CR)| \leq 1$

OE(CR) means a conflicting role set and the function roles(OE(U)) returns all roles that are assigned to a single user OE(U). Therefore this statement ensures that a single user cannot have more than one conflicting role from the specific role set OE(CR). We can interpret the above expression as saying that if a user has been assigned to one conflicting role, that user cannot be assigned to any other conflicting role. We can also specify this property in many different ways using *RCL2000*, such as OE(OE (CR)) $\in$ Roles(OE(U)) $\Rightarrow$ AO(OE(CR)) $\cap$ roles(OE(U))= ϕ or user(OE(OE(CR))) $\cap$ User(AO(OE(CR)))= ϕ.

The expression $|\text{roles}(OE\ (U)) \cap OE(CR)| \leq 1$ specifies dynamic separation of duties (DSOD) applied to active roles in a single session as opposed to static separation applied to user-role assignment. Dynamic separation applied to all sessions of a user is expressed by $|\text{roles}(\text{sessions}(OE\ (U))) \cap OE(CR)| \leq 1$.

A permission-centric formulation of separation of duty is specified as roles(OE(OE(CP))) $\cap$ roles(AO(OE(CP)))= ϕ .The expression roles(OE(OE(CP))) means all roles that have a conflicting permission from, say cp_i, and roles(AO(OE(CP))) stands for all roles that have other conflicting permissions from the same conflicting permission set cp_i. This formulation leaves open the particular roles to which conflicting permissions are assigned but requires that they be distinct. This is just a sampling of the expressive power of *RCL2000* discussed in Section 4.

2.3 Syntax of RCL 2000

The syntax of RCL 2000 is defined by the syntax diagram and grammar given in Figure 4. The rules take the form of flow diagrams. The possible paths represent the possible sequence of symbols. Starting at the beginning of a diagram, a path is followed either by transferring to another diagram if a rectangle is reached or by reading a basic symbol contained in a circle. Backus Normal Form (BNF) is also used to describe the grammar of *RCL2000* as shown in the bottom of Figure 4. The symbols of this form are "::=" meaning "is defined as" and "|" meaning "or." Figure 4 shows that *RCL2000* statements consist of an expression possibly followed by implication ($\Rightarrow$) and another expression. Also *RCL2000* statements can be recursively combined with a logical AND operator ($\wedge$). Each expression consists of a token followed by a comparison operator and token, size, set, or set with cardinality. Also a token itself can be an expression. Each token can be just a term or a term with cardinality. Each term consists of functions and sets including set operators. The sets and system functions described earlier in Section 2.1 are allowed in this syntax. Also, we denote *oneelement* and *allother* as OE and AO, respectively.

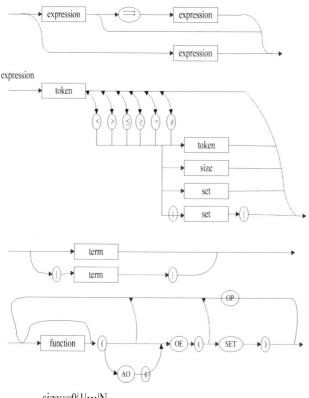

size::=0|1|...|N
Set::=U|R|OP|OBJ|P|S|CR|CP|CU
Function::=user|roles|roles*|sessions|permissions|permissions*|operations|object|OE|AO

Fig. 4. Syntax of language

3   Formal Semantics of RCL2000

In this section, the formal semantics for *RCL2000* is discussed. We do so by identifying a restricted form of first-order predicate logic called RFOPL which is exactly equivalent to *RCL2000*. Any property written in *RCL2000*, called a *RCL2000* expression, can be translated to an equivalent expression in RFOPL and vice versa. The translation algorithm, namely, Reduction, converts a *RCL2000* expression to an equivalent RFOPL expression. The Reduction algorithm eliminates AO function(s) from a *RCL2000* expression in the first step. Then we translate OE terms iteratively introducing universal quantifiers from left to right. If we have nested OE functions in the *RCL2000* expression, translation will start from the innermost OE terms. This algorithm translates the *RCL2000* expression to an RFOPL expression in time $O(n)$, supposing that the number of OE terms is n.

For example, the following expression can be converted to an RFOPL expression according to the sequences below.

Example 1. $OE(OE(CR)) \in roles(OE(U)) \Rightarrow AO(OE(CR)) \cap roles(OE(U)) = \phi$

(1) $OE(OE(CR)) \in roles(OE(U) \Rightarrow (OE(CR) - \{OE(OE(CR))\} \cap roles(OE(U)) = \phi$

(2) $\forall cr \in CR : OE(cr) \in roles(OE(U)) \Rightarrow (cr - \{OE(cr)\}) \cap roles(OE(U)) = \phi$

(3) $\forall cr \in CR, \forall r \in cr : r \in roles(OE(U)) \Rightarrow (cr - \{r\}) \cap roles(OE(U)) = \phi$

(4) $\forall cr \in CR, \forall r \in cr, \forall u \in U : r \in roles(u) \Rightarrow (cr - \{r\}) \cap roles(u) = \phi$

The resulting RFOPL expression will have the following general structure.

(1) The RFOPL expression has a (possibly empty) sequence of universal quantifiers as a left prefix, and these are the only quantifiers it can have. We call this sequence the quantifier part.

(2) The quantifier part will be followed by a predicate separated by a colon(:) (i.e., universal quantifier part : predicate).

(3) The predicate has no free variables or constant symbols. All variables are declared in the quantifier part (e.g., $\forall r \in R, \forall u \in U: r \in roles(u)$).

(4) The order of quantifiers is determined by the sequence of OE elimination. In some cases this order is important so as to reflect the nesting of OE terms in the *RCL2000* expression. For example, in $\forall cr \in CR, \forall r \in cr, \forall u \in U$: predicate; the set cr, which is used in the second quantifier, must be declared in a previous quantifier as an element, such as cr in the first quantifier.

(5) Predicate follows most rules in the syntax of *RCL2000* except the term syntax in Figure 4.

Because the reduction algorithm has a nondeterministic choice for reduction of the OE term, we may have several RFOPL expressions that are translated from a *RCL2000* expression.

4   Expressive Power of RCL2000

In this section, we demonstrate the expressive power of *RCL2000* by showing how it can be used to express a variety of separation of duty properties. As a security principle, SOD is a fundamental technique for prevention of fraud and errors, known and practiced long before the existence of computers [4]. It is used to formulate multi-user control policies, requiring that two or more different users be responsible for the completion of a transaction or set of related transactions. The purpose of this principle is to minimize fraud by spreading the responsibility and authority for an action or task over multiple users, thereby raising the risk involved in committing a fraudulent act by requiring the involvement of more than one individual. A frequently used example is the process of preparing and approving purchase orders. If a single individual prepares and approves purchase orders, it is easy and tempting to prepare and approve a false order and pocket the money. If different users must prepare and approve orders, then committing fraud requires a conspiracy of at least two, which significantly raises the risk of disclosure and capture.

Although separation of duty is easy to motivate and understand intuitively, so far there is no formal basis for expressing this principle in computer security systems. Several definitions of SOD have been given in the literature. For the purpose of this article, we use the following definition. Role-based separation of duty ensures SOD requirements in role-based systems by controlling membership in, activation of, and use of roles as well as permission assignment.

There are several papers in the literature over the past decades that deal with separation of duty. During this period various forms of SOD have been identified. Attempts have been made to systematically categorize these definitions. However, this work has significant limitations. It omits important forms of SOD including session-based dynamic SOD needed for simulating lattice-based access control and Chinese Walls in RBAC. It also does not deal with SOD in the presence of role hierarchies. Moreover, as shown, there are additional SOD properties that have not been identified in the previous literature. Here, we take a different approach to understanding SOD. Rather than simply enumerating different kinds of SOD we show how *RCL2000* can be used to specify the various separation of duty properties.

4.1 Static SOD

Static SOD (SSOD) is the simplest variation of SOD. In Table 1, we show our expression of several forms of SSOD. These include new forms of SSOD that have not previously been identified in the literature. This demonstrates how *RCL2000* helps us in understanding SOD and discovering new basic forms of it.

Property 1 is the most straightforward property. The SSOD requirement is that no user should be assigned to two roles which are in conflict with each other. In other words, it means that conflicting roles cannot have common users. *RCL2000* can clearly express this property, which is the classic formulation of SSOD. It is a role-centric property.

Property 2 follows the same intuition as Property 1, but is permission-centric. Property 2 says that a user can have at most one conflicting permission acquired through roles assigned to the user. Property 2 is a stronger formulation than Property 1, which prevents mistakes in role permission assignment. This kind of property has not been previously mentioned before [5]. *RCL2000* helps us discover such omissions in previous work. In retrospect, Property 2 is an "obvious property" but there is no mention of it in over a decade of SOD literature. Even though Property 2 allows more flexibility in role-permission assignment since the conflicting roles are not predefined, it can also generate roles that cannot be used at all. For example, two conflicting permissions can be assigned to a role. Property 2 simply requires that no user can be assigned to such a role or any role senior to it, which makes that role quite useless. Thus, Property 2 prevents certain kinds of mistakes in role-permissions but tolerates others.

Property 3 eliminates the possibility of useless roles with an extra condition, $|\text{permissions}^*(OE(R)) \cap OE(CP)| \leq 1$. This condition ensures that each role can have at most one conflicting permission without consideration of user-role assignment.

Property 4 can be viewed as a reformulation of Property 3 in a role-centric manner. Property 3 does not stipulate a concept of conflicting roles. However, we can interpret conflicting roles to be those that happen to have conflicting permissions assigned to them. Thus, for every cp_i, we can define $cr_i = \{r \in R \mid cp_i \cap \text{permissions}(R) \neq \phi\}$. With this interpretation, Properties 3 and 4 are essentially identical. The viewpoint of Property 3 is that conflicting permissions get assigned to distinct roles which thereby become conflicting, and therefore cannot be assigned to the same user. Which roles are deemed conflicting is not determined a priori but is a side-effect of permission-role assignment. The viewpoint of Property 4 is that conflicting roles are designated in advance and conflicting permissions must be restricted to conflicting roles. These properties have different consequences on how roles get designed and managed but essentially achieve the same objective with respect to separation of conflicting permissions. Both properties achieve this goal with much higher assurance than Property 1. Property 2 achieves this goal with similar high assurance but allows for the possibility of useless roles. Thus, even in the simple situation of static SOD, we have a number of alternative formulations offering different degrees of assurance and flexibility.

Table 1. Static separation of duty

Properties	Expressions
1.SOOD-CR	$\mid\text{roles}*(\text{OE(U)}) \cap \text{OE(CR)}\mid \leq 1$
2.SOOD-CP	$\mid\text{permissions}(\text{roles}*(\text{OE(U)})) \cap \text{OE(CP)}\mid \leq 1$
3.Variation of 2	$(2) \wedge \mid\text{permissions}*(\text{OE(R)}) \cap \text{OE(CP)}\mid \leq 1$
4.Variation of 1	$(1) \wedge \mid\text{permissions}*(\text{OE(R)}) \cap \text{OE(CP)}\mid \leq 1$
	$\wedge\ \text{permissions}(\text{OE(R)}) \cap \text{OE(CP)} \neq \phi \Rightarrow \text{OE(R)} \cap \text{OE(CR)} \neq \phi$
5.SOOD-CU	$(1) \wedge \mid\text{user}(\text{OE(CR)}) \cap \text{OE(CU)}\mid \leq 1$
6.Yet another variation	$(4) \wedge (5)$

Property 5 is a very different property and is also new to the literature. With a notion of conflicting users, we identify new forms of SSOD. Property 5 says that two conflicting users cannot be assigned to roles in the same conflicting role set. This property is useful because it is much easier to commit fraud if two conflicting users can have different conflicting roles in the same conflicting role set. This property prevents this kind of situation in role-based systems. A collection of conflicting users is less trustworthy than a collection of non-conflicting users, and therefore should not be mixed up in the same conflicting role set. This property has not been previously identified in the literature.

We also identify a composite property that includes conflicting users, roles, and permissions. Property 6 combines Properties 4 and 5 so that conflicting users cannot have conflicting roles from the same conflict set while ensuring that conflicting roles have at most one conflicting permission from each conflicting permission set. This property supports SSOD in user-role and role-permission assignment with respect to conflicting users, roles, and permissions.

4.2 Dynamic SOD

In RBAC systems, a dynamic SOD property with respect to the roles activated by the users requires that no user can activate two conflicting roles. In other words, conflicting roles may have common users but users can not simultaneously activate roles that are in conflict with each other. From this requirement, we can express user-based Dynamic SOD as Property 1. We can also identify a session-based DSOD property that can apply to the single session as Property 2. We can also consider these properties with conflicting users such as Properties 1-1 and 2-1. Additional analysis of DSOD properties based on conflicting permissions can also be pursued as was done for SSOD.

Table 2. Dynamic separation of duty

Properties	Expressions
1.Used-based DSOD	$|Roles^*(sessions(OE(U))) \cap OE(CR)| \leq 1$
1-1.Used-based DSOD with CU	$|Roles^*(sessions(OE(OE(CU)))) \cap OE(CR)| \leq 1$
2.Session-based DSOD	$|Roles^*(OE(sessions(OE(U)))) \cap OE(CR)| \leq 1$
2-2.Session-based DSOD with CU	$|Roles^*(OE(sessions(OE(OE(CU))))) \cap OE(CR)| \leq 1$

5 Conclusion

In this article, we have described the specification language *RCL2000*. This language is built on RBAC components and has two nondeterministic functions OE and AO. We have given a formal syntax and semantics for *RCL2000*. Any property written in *RCL2000* may be translated to an expression written in a restricted form of first order predicate logic, which we call RFOPL.

There is room for much additional work with *RCL2000* and similar specification languages [6]. The language can be extended by introducing time and state. Analysis of *RCL2000* specifications and their composition can be studied. The efficient enforcement of these constraints can also be investigated. A user-friendly front-end to the language can be developed so that it can be realistically used by security policy designers.

Acknowledgments. This work was supported by National Science Foundation under Grant No:60673010 and supported by the Natural Science Foundation of Hubei Province under Grant No:2006ABC011 and supported by National Great Project of Scientific and Technical Supporting Programs Funded by Ministry of Science & Technology of China During the 11th Five-year Plan under Grant No: 2006BAH02A24.

References

1. Chen, F., Sandhu, R.S.: Constraints for Role-based Access Control. In: Proceedings of the First ACM Workshop on Role-Based Access Control, pp. 39–46. ACM Press, New York (1995)
2. Ahn, G.J., Sandh, R.: The RSL99 Language for Role-based Separation of Duty Constraints. In: Proceedings of 4th ACM Workshop on Role-Based Access Control, pp. 43–54. ACM Press, New York (1999)

3. Giuri, L., Iglio, P.: A Formal Model for Role-based Access Control with Constraints. In: Proceedings of 9th IEEE Workshop on Computer Security Foundations, pp. 136–145. IEEE Press, Piscataway, NJ (1996)
4. Gligor, V.D., Gavrila, S., Ferraiolo, D.: On the Formal Definition of Separation-of-duty Policies and Their Composition. In: Proceedings of the 1998 IEEE Computer Society Symposium on Research in Security and Privacy, pp. 172–183. IEEE Computer Society Press, Los Alamitos, CA (1998)
5. Jaeger, T.: On the Increasing Importance of Constraints. In: Proceedings of 4th ACM Workshop on Role-Based Access Control, pp. 33–42. ACM Press, New York (1999)
6. Osborn, S., Sandhu, R., Munawer, Q.: Configuring Role-based Access Control to Enforce Mandatory and Discretionary Access Control Policies. ACM Trans. Inf. Syst. Secur. 3(2) (2000)

Dynamic Access Control Research for Inter-operation in Multi-domain Environment Based on Risk*

Zhuo Tang, Ruixuan Li, Zhengding Lu, and Zhumu Wen

School of Computer Science and Technology,
Huazhong University of Science and Technology, Wuhan 430074, Hubei, China
hust_tz@126.com, {rxli,zdlu}@hust.edu.cn, zoomer@thinkbank.com.cn

Abstract. For the complexity of the multi-domain environment and the ceaseless evolvement of the information secure sharing, the traditional access control method can not ensure the absolute security for the exchange of data resources. Through introducing the concept of risk, this paper proposes a dynamic access control model for multi-domain environment based on risk of inter-operations. The risk rank of an access policy can be calculated by the history of the inter-operations among domains, the security degree of the objects and the safety factor of the access events. Through adjusting the access policies which be considered the high risk, the risk in the system can be controlled in real time. The security analysis shows that this method can reinforce the facility of the access control and the security of the multi-domain environment.

1 Introduction

With the increase in information and data accessibility, there is a growing concern for security and privacy of data. The realization of the connections and the inter-operations among the different data sources under the distributed heterogeneous environment is becoming the practical problem. There is a growing concern for the security problem for the inter-operations between multi-domains. More and more researches try to resolve the defense for the vicious behaviors through the economic methods. In fact, recent research in these directions has suggested some economical models for a wide range of secure distributed systems, including a payment based security system for mobile agents [1] and game based model for secured grid computing [2]. However, risk remains un-quantified in these proposals. In fact, there exists an emerging consensus that every security question is indeed an economical question concerning the utility of the underlying system [3]. For example, it is easy to show that in a mobile agent based e-commerce system, both the protection of agents and hosts have a direct impact

---

* This work is partially supported by National Natural Science Foundation of China under Grant 60403027, Natural Science Foundation of Hubei Province under Grant 2005ABA258, Open Foundation of State Key Laboratory of Software Engineering under Grant SKLSE05-07.

S. Kim, M. Yung, and H.-W. Lee (Eds.): WISA 2007, LNCS 4867, pp. 277–290, 2007.

on the utility: attacks on a host by malicious agents will cause loss of commercial secrets such as customers private information, downtime to the system, loss of customers, which will eventually be counted as utility loss. Attacks on agents will result in similar consequences that will also lead to the lost of utility. Thus utility maximization and risk minimization are important issues in the design of a secure distributed system if we seek to gain maximum economical benefits from the underlying system. This is also an important target of the distributed system security. But at present, there are little literatures to demonstrate the actual signification of the risk of distributed system [4].

In the economic area, there exist the consanguineous relations between the risk and trust. Mayer and Rousseau [5] discussed the difference and the relationship between the risk and trust. Jarvenpaa [6] proposed definitely: trust can influence the risk in a certain extent. Further more, it can influence the subjects' behaviors. For example, there is the lower risk when you loan money to the familiar than stranger. Moreover, this literature considers that the extent of trust can influence the cognitive extent of the risk.

The objective of the inter-operations is to offer the rational distributing and effective share of the resource, and the cooperation of the distributed systems. It means the ability of the two software components to communicate and co-operate to complete a common task. It contains two meanings: the basic and the application. The basic inter-operations mean the communications and coop-eration among the different platforms. And the applied inter-operations mean the cooperation among the distributed application components which above the computational platforms. This paper mainly discusses the later.

The multi-domain environment has the characteristic of dynamic and inde-termination. As the frequent changes of the security policies in individual au-tonomy, the changes of the relationship among the domains, even the birth and the death of the individual domains, the any security polices can not insure the absolute security of the data resource in the process of inter-operations. For the access control method of the traditional model, the subject sometimes can use its permissions constantly once been authorized. It hardly satisfies the dynamic changes of the multi-domain environment. And it will bring many security risks and hidden trouble to the inter-operations among multi-domain environment.

In order to decrease the risk of inter-operations, for the problems of trust and risk of the security inter-operations under the application tier, which base the mappings between the users and roles in the different domains, this paper pro-poses a risk based dynamic access control model for multi-domain environment. In this model, through calculating the trust degree between the subjects firstly, we can ascertain the risk extent when a subject in one domain has an operation to the objects in the other domains. Therefore, we can receive the risk degree of the inter-operations. Using this risk degree, we can adjust the subjects' access privilege dynamically. The risky permissions will be revoked, and the utility of the system will be maximized.

The rest of the paper is organized as follows. Section 2 describes the re-lated works. Section 3 presents algorithms for the calculating the risk of the inter-operations. Section 4 describes the dynamic access control model for multi-domain environment, followed by the conclusion in Section 5.

2   Related Works

In the recently 20 years, people have acquired the plentiful achievement for the research of the access control. Many access control models have been proposed. The most popular models include discretionary access control (DAC), mandatory access controls (MAC) and role based access control (RBAC). In the RBAC family which be proposed by Sandhu in 1996[7], the users' privilege is related with their roles, and the users acquire their privilege through roles. A role is a permission set for a special work station. When the users' privilege needs to be changed, we can do it by revoking the roles or re-distributing the user's roles.

Michael J. Covington et al [8] have proposed the Generalized Role Based Access Control (GRBAC) model. In this model, they extend the traditional RBAC by applying the roles to all the entities in a system. (In RBAC, the role concept is only used for subjects). By defining three types of roles, i.e., Subject roles, Environment roles, and Object roles, GRBAC uses context information as a factor to make access decisions. Guangsen Zhang et al. [9] also uses context parameters in their dynamic role-based access control model under the two key ideas: (1) A user's access privileges should be changed when the user's context changes. (2) A resource must adjust its access policy when the environment context information (e.g., network bandwidth, CPU usage, memory usage) changes. These above two papers make the access control dynamic and flexible but the decision-making process is not as powerful and precise as that in our model. They did not consider the aspect of security in making-decision process and the impact of security problems on the system.

The Nathan Dimmock's paper [10] uses the concept of outcome to calculate cost for each outcome and risk value. Comparing to this paper, they do not consider the context for risk assessment. So it loses the flexibility characteristic in evaluating risk. They did not consider risk as an important factor in their access control mechanism and they did not use risk directly in making decision.

There is little attention to the trust and risk in the access control research [11]. The term trust management system was introduced by Blaze et al. in [12], but the solution it proposes involves an unduly static notion of trust application programmers choose where to insert code to evaluate their notion of trust, for example at the starting point of a given execution session. Most of the past research combining access control with trust concepts focuses on a trust-management approach in which trust values flow in a manually defined way through access control policy. For example, in literature [13] and [14], the mutual trust relationship is founded by the continuously negotiation. Literature [15] illuminates the relationship between the trust management and distributed access control, and it extends the access control system of OASIS and the access control language. So, the access policy can be decided base on the trust and risk. But the trust mentioned in this paper is defined by the special operation, and the relationship between risk and trust is faint in this paper.

The above access control methods mostly base the traditional model. They are all short of the dynamic description for the subjects. With the complexity of the system and the dynamics of the applications, the changes of the access control objects are very large. Hence, these methods may increase the difficulty of the authorization. These access control models all try to protect the resource from the perspective of system. The weakness of these passive security models is that they cannot manage the privilege according to the environment dynamically. Once the subject acquire the privilege, it can use this privilege until it be revoked. It can bring the risk easily.

Compared with the traditional RBAC model, the paper's main contributions are as follows:

1. Introducing of a concept of risk into access control area. This method can ascertain the risk of inter-operations between the different domains in real time through the histories of the interactive events. It is better able to adapt to the distributed, complex, and diverse multi-domain environment.
2. Through adjusting the privilege of the subjects dynamically according to the risk levels of the access events, the functions of the access control system can be changed from the static protect for the resources to the dynamic authorization. The system can detect the environment and the security venture in real time, and the permissions of the subjects are not unchangeable anymore since be authorized. The system can identify the risky permissions automatically and revoke them duly.
3. This method can bring the convenience to the security management. The difference between this dynamic model and the traditional access control models is as follows: The management for the user's permission settings is according to the actual events and historical records. In this way, the permission management is more convenient, and the control to the authorization is more convincing.

3   The Risk of the Inter-operation in Multi-domains

In the traditional model of the trust relationship, trust was usually defined as a Boolean variable, that is to say, in the session of both trust entities, one trust another entirely, or absolutely not, there would never be middle status. For instance, the entity A trusts entity B, but it is hard to tell how much they trust each other. For this reason, we have to quantify their trust. In this section, firstly, we formalize the definitions of the permissions and the operations between the permissions in the multi-domain environment. On this basis, we introduce the description of the trust in multi-domains.

3.1   The Formalization of the Permissions

Definition 1. *Authorization Term. Authorization terms are 2-tuple of the form:* $< object, accessmode >$, *which is denoted as* $< O, A >$ *for short. It is the basic form of the permission. The set of authorization terms is denoted as* P. *We have* $P = \{< O, A >\}$.

Definition 2. *Permission Set. Permission set represents all permissions of some subject, which is the set of the authorization terms. We can formulize it as PS.*

For example, we can describe a role r_1's all permission as: $PS(r_1) = \{< file1, +read >, < file2, -write >\}$. That is to say the users, which are assigned to r_1, can read file1 and write file2. The denotation PS_u can also express the permission set of the user u. obviously, if a role r is assigned to a user u, then $PS(u) \supseteq PS(r)$.

In this paper, the denotation $role(u)$ represents the role set, which is assigned to user u. We can define the basic operators of the *PS*. The BNF definition for permission set as follows:

$$PS = PS|PS \cup PS|PS \cap PS|PS - PS|SoD(PS, PS)$$

Where the $\cup, \cap$ and $-$ are the basic operation in set theory, $SoD(PS_1(r), PS_2(r))$ denotes the separation of duties, it returns $PS_1(r)$ or $PS_2(r)$, but it can return the $PS_1(r)$ and $PS_2(r)$ concurrently.

$OS = \{O/D\}$ returns the controlled objects set for a subject. D denotes the object's domain. For instance $OS(r_1) = \{file1/A, file2/A\}$.

3.2   The Role-Mappings Based Trust Degree Between Domains

In a typical multi-domain environment, we partition the domains into external and local domains. The role mapping can be formalized as a 4-tuple: $< r_1, d_1, r_2, d_2 >$, r_1 is a role in domain d_1, r_2 is a role in domain d_2 respectively, in general, d_1 is the local domain, and d_2 is the external domain. A subject in the local domain can access the objects in the external through the inter-domain mappings. As the mapping exhibits, the permissions of the role r_1 in the domain d_1 is $PS(r_1) = PS(r_1) \cup PS(r_2)$ and $OS(r_1) = OS(r_1) \cup OS(r_2)$.

Trust is one entity assessing to behavior credibility, reliability, integrity and performance of other entity. Trust relationship is such a case: if the subject meets the object's expectation, then the subject is trustable to the object.

Definition 3. *The trust degree denotes the trust extent between the different domains which be formed by the role-mappings. Which is formalized: C (d_1, d_2), depict the trust relationship between the domain d_1 and d_2. As its value range*

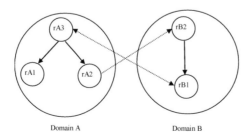

Fig. 1. The role-mappings between two domains

is $[0, 1]$, supposing a role-mapping $< r_1, d_1, r_2, d_1, false >$, $C(d_1, d_2) = 1$ means the complete trust, that is to say the all permissions of the role r_2 in the domain d_2 can be inherited by the role r_1 in the domain d_1; by contraries, $C(d_1, d_2) = 0$ means the complete distrust, that is to say the all permissions of the role r_2 in the domain d_2 are forbidden to be inherited by the role r_1 in the domain d_1.

The trust degree between domains is changed according to the inter-operation events. This is denoted by the function as follows:

$$\delta : C \times E \to C \tag{1}$$

Where, E denotes the set of the inter-operation events. In general, if there are role-mappings exist between two domains, for each inter-operation, if the result is successful, the trust degree will be strengthened; by contraries, if the result is failed, it will be weakened.

The following subsection discusses how to found the trust relationship between two domains. In this paper, we consider the trust in the multi-domain environment through their past transaction experiences. Considering the inter-operations between the domain i and j, if the subject in domain i request to access the resources in domain j, according the estimate of each event, if the request is be satisfied, then the estimate from i to j is positive, that is denoted as $tr_k(i, j) = 1$, by contraries, if the estimate is passive, then $tr_k(i, j) = -1$. This paper defines the denotation s_{ij} as the appraisement for the all transactions between the domain i and j: $s_{ij} = \sum(tr_{(}ij)$. Let's use $sat(i, j)$ to denote the total of the positive appraisement, while the denotation $unsat(i, j)$ is used to denote the total of the passive appraisement. Then,

$$s_{ij} = sat(i, j) - unsat(i, j) \tag{2}$$

For the convenience of the denotation, we mapping the value of the trust value to $[0, 1]$:

$$C(i, j) = \begin{cases} \frac{s_{ij}}{sat(i,j)+unsat(i,j)} & s_{ij} \geq 0 \\ 0 & \text{otherwise} \end{cases} \tag{3}$$

In this way, every domain maintains local trust degrees of the other domains which the local ever affiliates with. We can use a vector to describe the trust of a local domain to the externals: $T = \{C(i, 1), c(i, 2), \ldots, C(i, n)\}$, n is the number of the external domains.

3.3   The Risk of the Inter-operations in Multi-domain Environment

In general, a domain can maintain the trust vector for the externals domains which it interact with. As mentioned above, in the multi-domain environment, the risk of the inter-operations is up to the trust value of the domains $C(i, j)$, the security level of the operation object O_s, and the safety factor of the access action A_s. The following function defines the risk of the interoperation between the different domains:

Definition 4. $R_i = F(C(i,j), O_s, A_s)$. *The parameter O_s denotes the security level of the operation object, the more high level the role, the more security level the objects can be accessed. The A_s denotes the security extent of the access operation. In general, the risk of the inter-operations will be increased with the heightener of the security level of the objects. Reversely, it will be decreased with the heightener of the trust between the interrelated domains and the safety factor of the access action.*

The function of the risk for the inter-operations is defined as follows:

$$F(C(i,j), O_s, A_s) = O_s \times (1 - C(i,j)) \times (1 - A_s) \qquad (4)$$

By (1), we can see the value of R_i is in the range of $[0, 1]$. Where, the value 0 denotes no risk, and the value 1 denotes the maximal risk. The following is the algorithm for the security level of all operation objects in the special domain. The basic idea is that the leaf nodes in a role hierarchy only access the objects with the lowest security level in a special domain. That is to say, if the objects can be only accessed by the senior role, their security level is higher in the domain. The detailed algorithm is as follows. The parameter k is the basic security parameter in a special domain. k is an integers. $k \geq 1$.

Algorithm 1. The calculation for the security level of the access control objects.
  program Obj_Security_level()
  begin
  1. Searching the role hierarchy, find the deepest leaf nodes.
  2. Setting the value of the security level of the objects which can be controlled by the leaf node as k. While, the "visited" flags of the nodes are modified as "already visited".
  3. Finding the directly senior up from the leaf node, the security level of the objects which directly under the next senior node is on the basis of an increase for the objects controlled by the directly junior nodes.
  4. Searching the all unvisited nodes down from the root node, the security level of the objects which directly under the next junior node is on the basis of a decrease for the objects controlled by the directly senior nodes.
  5. Adjusting the security level of all nodes in the role hierarchy. The value of security level of all nodes is divided by the value of the root to be mapped to the range [0, 1]
  end.

There is a role-mapping $< A_4, A, B_2, B, false >$ exist between the domains in the figure 2. In a moment, a user in the domain A requests the operation "write" to the object O_5 which is in the domain B: $< O_5, write >$. We set the basic security parameter k in this example as 1. Firstly, according to algorithm 1, We set security level of the directly controlled objects of the deepest leaf nodes B_4, O_7 and O_8, as 1. Followed up, we can get that the security level of the directly controlled objects of B_2 is 2, and the security level of the directly controlled objects of B_1 is 3. By the step 5, we can get the security level of O_5: $\frac{(k+1)}{(k+2)} = \frac{2}{3} = 0.67$.

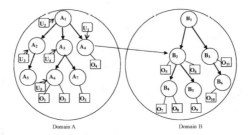

Fig. 2. The inter-operations between domain A and domain B

Table 1. The historical inter-operations between domain A and domain B

Sequence	Subject	Object	Operation	Status
1	U_1	O_5	read	successful
2	U_2	O_6	write	successful
3	U_3	O_7	read	failed
4	U_4	O_5	execute	successful
5	U_5	O_8	copy	failed
6	U_1	O_9	write	successful
7	U_1	O_{10}	read	successful

The safety factor for all access events in this example, which are denoted as *read, copy, write, execute*, is set as $(0.8, 0.6, 0.4, 0.2)$ respectively. We suppose that the inter-operation history between domain A and B is as the table 1 shows. There are seven access events which the subject is in domain A and the object is in domain B. And five of them are successful and two failed. By the above method to compute the trust degree between domain A and B, we have: $\frac{(5-2)}{7} = 0.43$. So, According to (4), we can get the risk of the above 2-tuple $< O_5, write >$ as:

$$R_i(O_s, C(i,j), A) = O_s \times (1 - C(i,j)) \times (1 - A_s) = 0.67 \times (1 - 0.43) \times (1 - 0.4) = 0.23$$

Thus, we can educe the risk rank in the multi-domain environment. In this instance, the risk is divided as 5 levels, which are as $\{potty, little, general, grave, verygrave\}$. The mapping from risk values to the risk ranks is as table 2 shows. This table can be configured by the administrators according to the special context.

Table 2. The mapping from risk values to the risk ranks

Sequence	ranks	values	description
1	I	$0 \le R_i < 0.2$	potty
2	II	$0.2 \le R_i < 0.4$	little
3	III	$0.4 \le R_i < 0.6$	general
4	IV	$0.6 \le R_i < 0.8$	grave
5	V	$0.8 \le R_i < 1.0$	very grave

We can conclude from the table 2 that the above operation $< O_5, write >$, a user in the domain A requests the operation "write" to the object O_5 which is in the domain B, it's risk rank is II. This means that the operation $< O_5, write >$ has little risk. It may bring the failure for the operation. In the following sections, we will discuss how to avoid the risk through adjusting the privileges of the subjects.

4   The Risk-Based Dynamic Access-Control Model for Multi-domain

4.1   The Model of MD-R²BAC

The traditional security mechanism is generally designed for static network and closed system. In these systems, the authorizations of the users are determinate, and the relationship between user's privileges and resources are found early. Based this, the protected resource are only be accessed by the authorized users. As these security models are simpler, we can call them traditional security model. But in the multi-domain environment, as the requestor and the provider of the resource can be in the different domains, because there is no absolute trust between these domains, it can not satisfy the all requests of the requestors through the traditional access control mechanism. Further more, the multi-domain environment changes frequently, and the real-time update is also unpredictable, so, the requestor and the provider of the resource may do not know each other. Therefore, the traditional models do not match the multi-domain environment well. This paper proposes a risk-based dynamic access-control model through importing the risk of the event context to the policies of RBAC.

The authorization of the traditional is general denoted as 3-tuple: $< S, O, A >$, where S represents the subject, O represents the object, and A is the set of the actions. If a 3-tuple $< s, o, a >$ exist, that is to say, the subject S can do the operation A on the object O. These 3-tuples are all predefined in the security system, and they are effective of all times. For the privilege constrain to the users, this access control method is passive and negative.

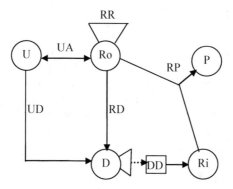

Fig. 3. The model of MD-R²BAC

The following definitions contain some elements in the literature. The relationship between these definitions is as the figure 3.

Definition 5. *The variables and the relationships in this model.*

1. $MD - R^2BAC = (U, Ro, P, D, Ri)$, *where* U *is the set of the users,* Ro *is the set of the roles,* P *is the set of the permissions,* D *is the set of the domains, and* Ri *denotes the set of the risk banks.*
2. *User Assignment. This is a many-to-many relationship between users and roles. It is denoted as* UA, $UA \subseteq U \times Ro$. *This function can be expressed as* $assigned - user(ro) = \{u \in U | (u, ro) \in UA\}$.
3. *Permission Assignment. This is a one-to-many relationship from roles to permissions. And it is a function which from the roles and risk ranks to the permissions. It is denoted as* RP, $Ro \times Ri \rightarrow P$. *The function can be expressed as: assigned* $-$ *permission*$(ro : Ro, ri : Ri) \rightarrow 2^P$.
4. *Role Relation. This relationship contains the hierarchy and inheriting between the roles. We denote the set of the relationship of roles as* RR, $RR \subseteq R \times R$.
5. *Risk between Domains. This is a mapping from the inter-operation between the domains to the risk rank. It is a function from a special inter-operation event to a certain risk rank. We can denote as* $DR : D \times D \times P' \rightarrow Ri$, $P' \subseteq P$.
6. *User Hypotaxis. This is a one-to-many relationship from roles to domains. It is denoted as* $RD : R \rightarrow D$.

Each user and role in the model must belong to a special domain, and a user or role can not be subject to two or more domains synchronously. This constrain is defined as follows:

- Constrain 1. Each user in the model must only subordinate to only domain.

$$< u, d_1 >\in UD \cap < u, d_2 >\in UD \rightarrow d_1 = d_2$$

- Constrain 2. Each role in the model must only subordinate to only domain.

$$< r, d_1 >\in RD \cap < r, d_2 >\in RD \rightarrow d_1 = d_2$$

The dynamic distribution of permission in the MD-R^{2}BAC is mainly embodied in relation of DR, RP. The ration DR can acquire the trust degree of two domains through the inter-operation history. All the more, it can acquire the risk rank of an access event according to the security extent of the access operation and the security level of the operation object. Where, the access event between different domains can also be denoted as 6-tuple: ¡S, O, A, D_1, D_2, ri¿. The meaning of the elements is the same as the authorization item. Hence, in the relation DR, we have $P' \subseteq P$.

RP is a real-time implementation of the dynamic function. It can adjust the authorization to a subject in a domain duly according to the risk rank of the inter-operation. This paper will detail the authorization and the adjustment in the following sections.

4.2   The Policy and Mechanism of the Access Control in MD-R^{2}BAC Model

MD-R^{2}BAC is an access control model which can be changed with the inter-operation history between different domains. It is a dynamic process that the users acquire the permissions through the roles. In this process, system can adjust the subject's permissions according to the risk rank of its operation. In this way, the access control implementation process can be divided into three steps: privilege distribution, ascertaining the risk rank, and dynamic adjustment of the privilege.

Privilege distribution. The privilege distribution includes that the administrator assigns the roles to user and predefine the permissions of the roles. Referred to above, the users' permissions can be denoted as a 2-tuple :¡ u, ro¿, the set is formalized as $ua(u,ro)$. We use $UA(ro)$ to denote that assigning the role ro to a set of users

$$UA(ro) = \{ua(ui, ro)|ua(ui, ro) \in UA(i = 1, 2, \ldots, n)\}$$

In the multi-domain environment, the privilege usually performs as the power of the subject to access the objects which in the different domain. The basic authorization item can be formalized as the 6-tuple $< s, o, a, d_1, d_2, ri >$,which is denoted as $atomp(s, o, a, d_1, d_2, ri)$. It means that a subject s in the domain d_1 can do the operation a to the object o which is in the domain d_2, and the risk rank of this operation is ri in the current context.

$$RP(ro) = \{atomp(s, o, a, d_1, d_2, ri)|atomp(s, o, a, d_1, d_2, ri) \in P\}$$

Ascertaining the risk rank. The risk rank ri in authorization item is a function of the access history events in the multi-domain environment. We have detail the process of calculation for the risk rank in the third part of this paper. The function which acquires the risk rank of an inter-operation is recorded as $risk\_count(s,o,a,d_1,d_2)$. It returns the risk rank of a subject s in the domain d_1 do the operation a to the object o which is in the domain d_2

$$Ri = \{ri|ri = risk\_count(s, o, a, d_1, d_2)\}$$

Dynamic adjustment of the privilege. The prominent character of MD-R^{2}BAC is that it can adjust the subject's privilege according to the risk rank of its operation to the objects. We can set a risk threshold RV between two different domains. For the subject which acquire the access permissions to the objects in the other domains through the role-mappings, we can check each authorization items, and revoke the items whose risk rank over the predefined threshold RV.

The dynamic adjustment of the privilege mainly reflected in the relation of privilege distribution RP. It is a function which from the roles and risk ranks to the permissions.

$$F(Ro, Ri) \to P, P = \{atomp_1, atomp_2, \ldots, atomp_n\},$$

this is the initial permission set.

$$G(Ro, Ri, P_1) \rightarrow P_2, P_1 \subseteq P, P_2 \subseteq P, P_2 = P - P_1,$$

G is the revoke function.

Return to the example in the third section, suppose that the initial permission set of the role A_4 in the domain A to the objects in the domain B is $PS(A_4) = \{< O_5, write >, < O_6, read >, < O_7, read >, < O_8, write >, < O_9, read >$, we can acquire the risk value of these five authorization items:

$risk\_count(A_4, O_5, write, A, B) = Ri(O_s(O_5), C(A,B), A_s(write)) = 0.23$, the risk rank is II;

$risk\_count(A_4, O_6, read, A, B) = Ri(O_s(O_6), C(A,B), A_s(read)) = 0.08$, the risk rank is I;

$risk\_count(A_4, O_7, read, A, B) = Ri(O_s(O_7), C(A,B), A_s(read)) = 0.04$, the risk rank is I;

$risk\_count(A_4, O_8, write, A, B) = Ri(O_s(O_8), C(A,B), A_s(write)) = 0.11$, the risk rank is I;

$risk\_count(A_4, O_9, read, A, B) = Ri(O_s(O_9), C(A,B), A_s(read)) = 0.04$, the risk rank is I;

If the predefined threshold RV is set as 0.2, base the policy of dynamic adjustment of the privilege, we will revoke the write permission of the subject A_4 to the object O_5 between domains A and B:

$$PS(A_4) = \{< O_6, read >, < O_7, read >, < O_8, write >, < O_9, read >\}$$

Through the privilege's dynamic adjustment, whether the subject can acquire some privilege lie on the risk rank of the relevant authorization items. The course which the subjects acquire the privilege is a dynamic and frequent process. We can decide on that whether the operation is can be executed base the operations history, the security level of the operation object, and the security extent of the access operation. Hence, the authorization is dynamic which will be adjusted with the time and the hierarchy of the subjects and objects.

4.3   The Security Analyses for the MD-R^{2}BAC

Comparing with the traditional security model, the contribution of the MD-R^{2}BAC is as follows:

1. It is adapted well to the dynamic change in the multi-domain environment. In the MD-R^{2}BAC, the change of operations and objects can bring the change of the authorization. Through the risk rank, this model can reflect the change of the operations and the hierarchy of the access objects. Further more, these changes in this model will not affect the special authorizations. Hence, it can be adapted well to the frequently change of the multi-domain environment.

2. The more security
   MD-R^{2}BAC first imports the concept of risk to access control model, and the ultimately minimal of a subject is up to the conclusion of the access history. The risky permissions will be revoked in the dynamic adjustment

for the authorizations. It will restrict the risky event from the source and advance the success probability of the inter-operations. Through the dynamic adjustment, this model supports these two famous security principles:

- The least of privilege. Through the risk control, the privilege with high risk rank will be revoked in time. When the subject accesses the other domain's objects, it only holds on the relative security privilege.
- The separation of duty. Sometimes, there are some sensitive objects can not be accessed by one subjects at the same time, and two different subjects also do not hope access one object simultaneity. These above can be regarded as the high risky events. These events can be identified by the estimate of the risk rank. And the system can revoke some part of the privileges to implement this security principle.

5 Conclusion and Future Work

In the multi-domain environment, the randomicity exist in the share of the information, the validity of the security mechanism, and the demand of the information exchange between users. For the complexity of the multi-domain environment and the ceaseless evolvement of the information secure share, the traditional access control method can not ensure the absolute security for the exchange of data resource. The traditional security mechanism is always designed for static network or closed system. As lacking the dynamic description of the subjects and objects, the traditional security mechanism hardly to adjust the subjects' privilege base the security status of the system.

Through introducing the concept of risk, this paper proposes a dynamic access control model MD-R^{2}BAC for multi-domain environment based the risk of inter-operations. This model can acquire the risk of the authorization items of the subject's privilege base the operations history, the security level of the operation object, and the security extent of the access operation. And the risky permissions will be revoked in the dynamic adjustment for the authorizations. The security analyses for the MD-R^{2}BAC indicate that this model can reduce the risk and hidden trouble for the information exchange in the multi-domain environment, and advance the security of the system obviously.

In this paper, we only discuss the risk for a single access operation in the multi-domain environment. When an attacker who combines multiple low risk operations into a new operation, how to assess the risk for the new multiple operation is a problem being worth paying close attention to. It will be our future works.

References

1. Sonntag, M., Hrmanseder, R.: Mobile agent security based on payment. Operating Systems Review 34(4), 48–55 (2000)
2. Kwok, Y.K., Song, S., Hwang, K.: Selfish grid computing: Game-theoretic modeling and nas performance results cardiff. In: CCGrid-2005. Proceedings of the International Symposium on Cluster Computing and the Grid, Cardiff, UK, May, pp. 9–12 (2005)

3. IEEE (ed.): IEEE Security and Privacy. Economics of Information Security, vol. 3. IEEE Computer Society, Los Alamitos (2005)
4. Grandison, T., Sloman, M.: A Survey of Trust in Internet Applications. IEEE Communications Surveys 3(4), 2–16 (2000)
5. Mayer, R.C., Davis, J.H., Schoorman, F.D.: An Integrative Model of Organizational Trust. Academy of Management Review (20), 75–91 (1995)
6. Jarvenpaa, S.L., Leidner, D.E.: Communication and trust in global virtual teams. Organization Science 10(6), 791–815 (1999)
7. Sandhu, R., Coyne, E.J., Feinstein, H.L., Youman, C.E.: Role Based Access Control Models. Computer 29(2) (1996)
8. Moyer, M.J., Covington, M.J., Ahamad, M.: Generalized role-based access control for securing future applications. In: NISSC 2000. 23rd National Information Systems Security Conference, Baltimore, Md, USA (October 2000)
9. Zhang, G., Parashar, M.: Context-Aware Dynamic Access Control for Pervasive Applications. In: Proceedings of the Communication Networks and Distributed Systems Modeling and Simulation Conference (CNDS 2004), Western MultiConference (WMC), San Diego, CA, USA (January 2004)
10. Dimmock, N., Belokosztolszki, A., Eyers, D., Bacon, J., Moody, K.: Using Trust and Risk in Role-Based Access Control Policies. In: Proceedings of Symposium on Access Control Models and Technologies (2004)
11. Grandison, T., Sloman, M.: A Survey of Trust in Internet Applications. IEEE Communications Surveys 3(4), 2–16 (2000)
12. Blaze, M., Feigenbaum, J., Lacy, J.: Decentralized trust management. In: Proc. IEEE Conference on Security and Privacy. AT&T (May 1996)
13. Li, N., Mitchell, J.C., Winsborough, W.H.: Design of a role-based trust management framework. In: 2002 IEEE Symposium on Security and Privacy, pp. 114–131. IEEE, Los Alamitos (2002)
14. Teh-Ming, W., Fidelis, Y.: A policy-driven trust management framework. In: Nixon, P., Terzis, S. (eds.) iTrust 2003. LNCS, vol. 2692, Springer, Heidelberg (2003)
15. Dimmock, N., Belokosztolszki, A., Eyers, D., et al.: Using Trust and Risk in Role based Access Control Policies. In: SACMAT 2004, New York, USA, June 2-4, 2004 (2004)

A Compositional Multiple Policies Operating System Security Model

Lei Xia, Wei Huang, and Hao Huang

State Key Laboratory for Novel Software Technology,
Department of Computer Science and Technology,
Nanjing University, 22 Hankou Road, Nanjing 210093, China
xiaxlei@gmail.com, whuang.nju@gmail.com, hhuang@nju.edu.cn

Abstract. Multilevel security policies aim at only confidentiality assurance, with less consideration on integrity assurance and weakness in expressing channel control policies. Besides, the trusted subjects it introduces to handle the information flow "downgrade" have many security flaws. Moreover, increasing diversity of the computing environments results in various security requirements. However, current mainstream security models are aiming at only one or few requirements of them each. The Multi-Policy Views Security Model is presented, which is based on the MLS model, combining the domain and role attributes to the model, to enforce the expression power in channel control policies, make permission management more fine-grained and enhance the ability of confining the permission of the trusted subjects. Moreover, MPVSM has integrated the properties and functions of MLS, Domain-Type and Role Based models into one unified model. It is able to enforce multi-policy views in operating system in a flexible way.

Keywords: security model, multiple policy views, integrity assurance, confidentiality assurance, least privilege, separation of duties.

1 Introduction

Multilevel Security Model (MLS) [1] is one of the most widely used security model in various system. MLS aims at confidentiality assurance of the information, preventing the unauthorized leakage of the data in high security level. However, it rarely considers the integrity assurance, which is also a very critical security requirement [2,7,11].

Biba model is a mathematical dual of BLP, intending to protect integrity of information. However, they are both based on lattice mechanism, and information policies based on the lattice are transitive. Therefore, MLS models are weak in expressing channel control policies [22]. A firewall's control policy is a typical channel control policy. As an example in Figure 1.1, Information is allowed to flow from the Outside component to the Inside component via the Access Control, but is forbidden to do so directly. Such policies are hardly expressed in the MLS models.

S. Kim, M. Yung, and H.-W. Lee (Eds.): WISA 2007, LNCS 4867, pp. 291–302, 2007.

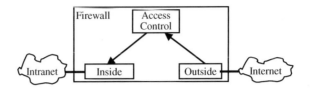

Fig. 1. Information channel control in a firewall

In addition, in MLS models, information is not allowed to flow "downward", such as from high confidentiality level to lower, or from lower integrity level to higher. However, in many situations, information flow "downward" is needed. Such an example of information flow from lower integrity level to the higher is the system call between user process and operating system. Data at a higher integrity level is more accurate and/or reliable than data at a lower integrity level. And the integrity level of user's data is usually lower than the operating system's data. Therefore, according to multilevel policies, user's data is not allowed to flow to the operating system data objects. However, in actual computer system, though user applications are not permitted to violate the integrity of operating system data, they should be given appropriate ways to pass the information or parameters to operating system.

To handle these problems, many MLS systems (such as HP-UX/CMW [8]) introduce some special trusted subjects outside the TCB. These special subjects are given privileges to bypass the MLS access control mechanisms. For they are not controlled by the access control mechanisms, they have almost all of privileges, which is far more than what they need to do they jobs. It is obviously a violation to the Principle of Least Privileges. These subjects turn to be the potential targets for malicious attacks. Once they are compromised, they can bring huge damages to the system.

Moreover, various security requirements are coming up with the sharply increased diversity and complexity of the computing environments. To satisfy these security requirements, a variety of security models were proposed in last twenty years. Widely-used security policies in current mainstream systems include multi-level military security model (Bell-LaPadula model, BLP) [1] and its variants (Biba [6], Dion model), Domain and Type Enforcement (DTE) [9], Role-based access control (RBAC) [14], and etc. Each of these models aims mainly at one or several security requirements, such as BLP aiming at the confidentiality of the information, Biba aiming at data integrity assurance, DTE aiming at confining the information flow channels, etc.

Previous trusted operating system usually enforced only one kind of mandatory access control model, for instance, Multics[3] implemented only BLP model in it. However, as mentioned above, the security goals in different applications are various. The different security requirements of applications result in different security models needed for them. How operating system to support this kind of multiple security model views--the access control model different applications can perceive in the system is different.

Recently, as a policy neutral security model, RBAC provides a valuable level of permission abstraction. However, using RBAC to simulate multi-level security level or discretionary access control models [12] is over complex and therefore unpractical in real-world operating system.

In this paper, a Compositional Multiple Policy Security Model (MPVSM) is presented. MPVSM is a hybrid security model, which is based on Multi-level Security models. It combines confidentiality and integrity lattices into a unified security lattice for confidentiality and integrity assurance. It then divides the subjects and objects in the same security level into different domains and types, using access control mechanisms in DTE to make the permission assignment and management more fine-grained and flexible, meantime enforce the separation of duties between subjects in the same security level. In addition, using the thought of RBAC, role is added in MPVSM. Roles are assigned the extra permissions, which are independent of MLS and Domain-Type parts of the model. MPVSM makes use of the flexible permission assignment and revocation mechanisms in RBAC to confine the permissions of those special "trusted subjects", provides a way to make them do they job out of control range of the MLS and Domain-type access control parts, but meanwhile prevent them from too powerful to be potential security holes of the system.

MPVSM has integrated the properties and functions of Multiple Level Security, Domain-Type and Role Based models into one unified model. By combining the elements and attributes of DTE and RBAC to the MLS model, MPVSM avoids the drawbacks of MLS. MPVSM is able to enforce channel control and assured pipelines policies, with providing fine-grained permissions management. In addition, MPVSM owns an enhanced ability of policy expression. It can ensure the enforcement of least privilege to these special "trusted subjects" in the MPVSM model. Moreover, MPVSM provides a framework to enforce multiple policy views in operating system. It can not only enforce the equivalent functions of these three kinds of models independently in the system, but also can enforce multi-policy views between different applications in system.

The remainder of the paper is organized as follows. Section 2 describes the MPVSM formally. Section 3 gives the example policy configurations in MPVSM. Section 4 is the related works. And section 5 is the conclusion.

2   Multiple Policy Security Model

2.1   Overview

The architecture of the MPVSM is shown in figure 2. MPVSM comprises of elements, relations and mappings. A *user* in the framework is a system user. A *role* is a job function or job title within some associated semantics regarding the authority. *Subjects* are active entities in the system, usually processes or transactions. *Objects* are data objects as well as resource objects. *Domain* is a control access attribute associated with each subject. And *type* is the other control attribute associated with objects. Two global matrixes are defined to represent allowed access or interaction modes between domains and types or domains and domains respectively. *Permission* is an approval of a particular mode of access to object or interaction to subject. *Security label* is a 2-tuple, containing a *confidentiality label* and an *integrity label*.

There are several relations and mappings between elements. The relation between users and roles are defined in *user-role* assignment relation. The *user-subject* relation gives relation between subjects and users, while *subject-role* mapping figures out a subject's current running role. Permissions in system can be authorized to roles. Roles' authorized permissions are given in the *role-permission authorization* relation. Each role in system can have many authorized domains. *Role-domain authorization* relation gives the authorized domains of each role. Each subject has only one running domain, which is given in *subject-domain* mapping. Besides, each subject has a security label. The security labels are assigned to roles, and subject's security label is determined by the label of its running role. Each object has a *security attribute* which includes the *type* and *security label* of that object.

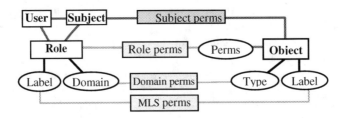

Fig. 2. The MPVSM

The *final permissions* that a subject gets are based on three kinds of permissions corresponding to that subject: *MLS permissions*, *Domain permissions* and *Role-based permissions*. *MLS Permissions* are coarse-grained base permissions, indicating the subject has the read-related permission or write-related permission. *Domain permissions* are the fine-grained permissions based on the *MLS Permissions*. *Role-based permissions* is independent from *MLS permissions* and *domain permissions*.

Correspond to the three kinds of permissions, MPVSM model contains three access control views: **1)** Multi-level Security Access Control. The *MLS permissions* given to the subject are based on the security level of the subject and the target object. **2)** Domain Access Control. Subjects run in different domains. A subject's *Domain permissions* are based on its running domain and the target objects' types. **3)** Role-Based Access Control. The subject has the permissions of its running role as its *Role-based permissions*.

In addition, MPVSM model is also an extensible security model, by adding other attributes to the role and object, besides the label and domain or type attributes of current role and object, more functions or properties can be added.

2.2 Formal Definitions

The following definitions formalize the discussion above:

Definition 2.1. Elements Sets
- Users: U
- Subjects: S

- Objects: O
- Roles: R
- Domains: D
- Types: T
- Confidentiality Labels: C
- Integrity Labels: I
- Security Labels: $SL \subseteq C \times I$
- Access modes: P, containing of two disjointed subsets: Read-related Modes $RP=\{read(r), execute(e), getattr(g)$ ... $\}$; Write-related Modes $WP=\{$ $write(w)$, append(a), create(c), delete(d), setattr(s)$ ... $\}$; $P=RP \cup WP$.
- Domain transfer operation: $transfer(t)\square transfer$ denotes the subject can transfer from one domain to another domain.
- Role Permissions $CAP \subseteq P \times O$, $(p, o) \in CAP$ denotes the permission to access o in mode p.

Definition 2.2. $US \subseteq U \times S$, *user-subject* relation. More than one subject can run on behalf of one user at the same time. But each subject can only run on behalf of one user, called its running user.

- *user*: $S \rightarrow U$, mapping from subject to its running user. $user(s) =u$ if and only if $u \in U$ $\wedge (u, s) \in US$.

Definition 2.3. $UA \subseteq U \times R$, *user-role assignment* relation. Each user can be assigned many roles and each role can be assigned to many users.

- UR: $U \rightarrow 2^R$, mapping from user to the set of roles assigned to that user. $UR(u) =\{r \in R | (u, r) \in UA\}$.
- SR: $S \rightarrow R$, *subject-role* mapping, from the subject to its running role. Each subject has a running user and running role at anytime, and the role must have been assigned to that user: $SR(s) \in UR(user(s))$.

Definition 2.4. role's *security label*
- RL: $R \rightarrow SL$, mapping from role to its security label.
- Ssl: $S \rightarrow SL$, mapping from subject to its security label. Subject's security label is the same as its running role's security label: $Ssl(s)=RL(SR(s))$.

Definition 2.5. $RD \subseteq R \times D$, *role-domain authorization* relation. Each role has many authorized domains and each domain can be authorized to many roles.

- $RDom$: $R \rightarrow 2^D$, mapping from role to its authorized domains set. $RDom(r) =\{d \in D | (r, d) \in RD\}$.
- $SDom$: $S \rightarrow D$, mapping from subject to its running domain. Each subject is running in only one domain at anytime, and the domain is authorized to that subject's running role: $SDom(s) \in RDom(SR(s))$.

Definition 2.6. object's *security attribute*
- OT: $O \rightarrow T$, mapping from object to its type.
- OL: $O \rightarrow SL$, mapping from object to its security label.

Definition 2.7. $RCAP \subseteq R \times CAP$, role-permission authorization relation. $(r_l, cap) \in RCAP$ denotes that role r_l has the role permission *cap*.

- *Rolecap*: $R \rightarrow 2^{CAP}$, mapping from role to its authorized *Role permissions* set. *Rolecap*(r)={cap|(r,cap)∈*RCAP*}.

Definition 2.8. Two control matrixes
- *DTM*: $D \times T \rightarrow 2^P$, *domain-type access control matrix*. $p \in DTM(d, t)$ denotes that the subjects in domain d can access objects with type t in mode p.
- *DDI*: $D \times D \rightarrow \{\Phi, \{transfer\}\}$, *domain-domain interaction control matrix*. *transfer*∈ $DDI(d_1, d_2)$ denotes that subjects in domain d_1 can transfer into domain d_2.

Definition 2.9. Multiply Levels Security rule: *MLS_rule*: $SL \times SL \rightarrow 2^P$, $a \in MLS\_rule$ (*ls*, *lo*) implies that subjects with security label *ls* can access objects with security label *lo* in mode *a*. This rule combines the BLP confidentiality and Biba integrity lattices. Let $ls=(cs, is), lo=(co, io)$:

- If cs⩾co, permit all read-related operations, that is: $RP \subseteq MLS\_rule$(ls, lo).
- If cs<co, deny all read-related operations, that is: ∀p∈*RP*, p∉ *MLS_rule* (ls, lo).
- If is⩾io, permit all write-related operations, that is: $WP \subseteq MLS\_rule$(ls, lo).
- If is<io, deny all write-related operations, that is: ∀p∈*WP*, p∉ *MLS_rule* (ls, lo).

2.3 Permission Decision

Definition 2.10
- *MLS permission (MLP)*: a subject's *MLP* on an object is determined as follow: $mlp(s, o)=\{(o, p)|p \in MLS\_rule (Ssl(s), OL(o))\}$
- *Domain permission (DP)*: a subject's *DP* on an object is determined as follow: $dp(s, o)=\{(o, p)|p \in DTM(SDom(s), OT(o))$
- *Role permission (RP)*: a subject's *RP* on an object is determined as follow: $rp(s, o)=\{(o, p)|(o, p) \in Rolecap(SR(s))\}$

    A subject's *Final permissions* on an object is determined as: $fp(s, o)=(mlp(s, o) \cap dp(s, o)) \cup rp(s, o)$.

3   Examples of Policy Configuration

3.1   Trusted Subjects' Permission Confinement

We take the information interaction between user process and operating system as an example on the information flow from lower integrity level to higher integrity level. As shown in Figure 3. User data is in lower integrity level, and operating system data in higher integrity level. In order to satisfy the needs of system calls, User process is permitted to write to the buffer data space of the operating system, but no permission to the other data object of the OS. Similarly, operating system writes the data to the buffer object of the user process.

    To enforce the policy described above, each process is assigned a security attribute {*role, domain*}, denoting the process's running role and running domain. And each data object is assigned a security attribute {(*c, i*), *t*}, denoting the object's confidentiality level c, integrity level i and type t, as shown in Figure 3. And *Rolecap*(usr_r)={(w, kerbuffer)}, role *usr_r* has *write* permission to the *kerbuffer* object, its security label is (0,1),

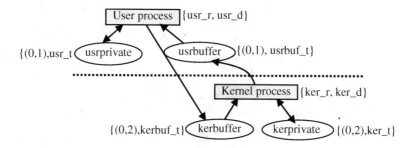

Fig. 3. Information interaction between user process and operating system

Table 1. *DTM*

	ker_t	Kerbuf_t	usr_t	usrbuf_t
ker_d	r,w	r	·	w
usr_d			r,w	r

and its authorized domains set is {usr_d}. *Rolecap*(ker_r)= Φ, ker_r has no role permission, its security label is (0,2), and its authorized domains set is {ker_d}. The *DTM*
and *DDI* between the domains and types are shown in Table 3.1.

We isolate the operating system data and user data from each other by dividing them
into different integrity level. The *usrbuffer* and *usrprivate* data objects which are in the
same integrity level are divided into different types, therefore User process can have
different fine-grained permissions to these two objects. According to the MLS policy,
User process has no write permission to the *kerbuffer* objects for its integrity level is
lower than the object. However, this write permission is necessary for getting job done.
So, we assign write permission on object *kerbuffer* to the role usr_r, this permission is
independent of MLS and Domain permissions. In this way, the function of system call
is achieved without giving too much permission to the User process to bring potential
security flaws to system.

3.2 Channel Control

We design a simplified firewall system to demonstrate the use of MPVSM in configuring channel control policies. The firewall is shown in Figure 4. The security policy of
the firewall is that all information flow from outside network to inside network or in
reverse direction must be checked by the access control component. It can be described
as follow: information is only allowed to flow from the Outside to the Inside or in reverse direction via the Access Control. It can not be flowed directly between them.
Besides, all components are permitted to read the Config without modifying it. And all
components can append information to the Log, but can not read it.

Our configurations to enforce this policy are shown in Figure 3.2. The *DTM* and
DDI between domains and types are shown in Table 3.2. And *Rolecap*(fw_r) =Φ, role

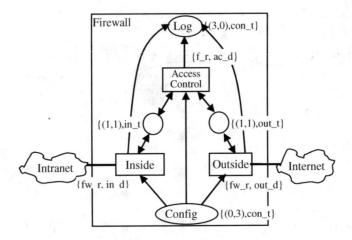

Fig. 4. Policy configuration of the Firewall

Table 2. The DTM and DDI

	in_t	out_t	con_t	in_d	out_d	ac_d
in_d	r,w		r,a			
out_d		r,w	r,a			
ac_d	r,w	r,w	r,a			

fw_r has no *Role permissions*. The security label of the *fw_r* is (1,1), and its authorized domains are {ac_d, in_d, out_d}, there is no *transfer* permission between any two of these three domains.

We upgraded the confidentiality level of the Log to make it unreadable to the components, upgraded the integrity level of the Config to make it unmodifiable by components. Then we divided the subjects of the same security level to different domains, and objects of the same security level to different types. By controlling the fine-grained permissions between the domains to types, information channel control policy between the inside and outside network is enforced.

3.3 Enforcing Multiple Security Policies

Through different configuring ways, Multi-Level security model, DTE and RBAC can be enforced separately in the MPVSM, and multi-policy views between different user groups can be enforced too.

3.3.1 Enforcing Multi-level Security model
The way configuring MPVSM to enforce Multi-Level Security model, which based on both confidentiality and integrity lattices, is described as following:

1. $|R|=|SL|$, number of roles in the system is the same as the number of the security labels. Each role corresponds to one security label.
2. $D=\{gen\_d\}$, $T=\{gen\_t\}$, there are only one domain and one type in the system. $RD=\{(r, gen\_d)|r{\in}R\}$, indicates that all roles' authorized domain is gen_d. The type of all objects is gen_t: $OT=\{(o, gen\_t)|\ o{\in}O\}$.
3. $DTM=\{(d, t, p)|d{\in}D, t{\in}T, p{\in}P\}$, which indicates domain gen_d have all domain permissions to type gen_t.
4. $Rolecap(r:R)=\Phi$, no role permission is authorized to every role.

3.3.2 Enforcing DTE

1. $R=\{gen\_r\}$, only one role in system. $UA=\{(u, gen\_r)|u{\in}U\}$, role gen_r is assigned to every users.
2. $RD=\{(gen\_r, d)|d{\in}D\}$, indicates that all domains in system are authorized to the role gen_r.
3. $SL=\{(Only\_C,Only\_I)\}$, only one security label in the system, therefore: $RL=\{(r, Only\_C, Only\_I))|r{\in}R\}$.
4. $Rolecap(r:R)=\Phi$.

3.3.3 Enforcing RBAC

1. $D=\{gen\_d\}$, $T=\{gen\_t\}$, only one domain and one type in system. $RD=\{(r, gen\_d)|\ r{\in}R\}$, gen_d is authorized to every role in system. The type of all objects is gen_t, $OT=\{(o, gen\_t)|\ o{\in}O\}$.
2. $DTM(gen\_d, gen\_t)=\Phi$, denotes subjects in gen_d domain have no domain permissions to objects in type gen_t.
3. $SL=\{(Only\_C, Only\_I)\}$, only one security label. $RL=\{(r,(Only\_C,Only\_I))\ |r{\in}R\}$.

3.3.4 Enforcing Multiple Model Views

Assume all users in the system can be divided into three groups: $Grpa$, $Grpb$ and $Grpc$. Now we may hope that users in each group can perceive different access control model views. For instance, users in $Grpa$ think that the security model enforced in system is MLS, users in $Grpb$ think that is RBAC and users in $Grpc$ think that is DTE. The configuring method that enforces this multi-model views in one system is given as below.

1. $U=Grpa{\cup}Grpb{\cup}Grpc$, the three sets are disjointed each other.
2. $R=mls\_rs{\cup}rbac\_rs{\cup}\{dte\_r\}$. mts_rs is the roles set corresponding to MLS model. $rbac\_rs$ is the roles set corresponding to RBAC model. And dte_r is the role corresponding to DTE model.
3. $D=\{mls\_d\}{\cup}\{rbac\_d\}{\cup}dte\_ds$.
4. $(u, r){\in}UA{\wedge}(u, r'){\notin}UA$, where $u{\in}Grpa$, $r{\in}mls\_rs$, $r'{\notin}mls\_rs$, the roles in mls_rs are only permitted to be assigned to users in $Grpa$. $(u, r){\in}UA{\wedge}(u, r'){\notin}UA$, where $u{\in}Grpb$, $r{\in}rbac\_rs$, $r'{\notin}rbac\_rs$, the roles in $rbac\_rs$ can only be assigned to users in $Grpb$. Similarly, $(u, dte\_r){\in}UA{\wedge}(u, r){\notin}UA$, where $u{\in}Grpc$, $r{\neq}dte\_r$, every user in $Grpc$ is assigned the only role dte_r.
5. $|mls\_rs|=|SL|$, number of roles in set mls_rs is the same as the number of security labels in system. Each role in mls_rs corresponds to one security label. $MLS\_rule(Ssl(r), tsl)=M$, $r{\in}rbac\_rs$, $tsl{\in}SL$, have all of possible MLS permis-

sions to other subjects or objects. *MLS_rule(Ssl(dte_r)*, *tsl)=M*, *tsl∈ SL*, role *dte_r*'s *MLS permissions* to other subjects or objects include all of possible permissions too.

6. The security label of the roles in *rbac_rs* is the lowest level label of the system, that is: $\forall$ r∈rbac_rs, *RL*(r)=(cs, is), $\forall$ c∈ *C*, cs≤c and $\forall$ i∈*I*, is≤i. the security label of *dte_r* is the highese level label of the system, that is: *RL*(dte_r)=(cs, is), $\forall$ c∈ *C*, cs≥c and $\forall$ i∈*I*, is≥i.

7. (r, *mls_d*)∈*RD*∧(r,d)∉ *RD*, where r∈*mls_rs*, d≠*mls_d*, every roles in *mls_rs* is authorized the only domain *mls_d*. (dte_r, d) ∈*RD*∧(r', d)∉ *RD*, where r'≠*dte_r*, d∈*dte_ds*, all domains in *dte_ds* are authorized to role *dte_r*. Simliarly, (r,*rbac_d*) ∈*RD*∧(r,d)∉ *RD*, where r∈*rbac_rs*, d≠*rbac_d*, every role in *rbac_rs* is authorized the only domain *rbac_d*.

8. (mls_d,t,p)∈*DTM*,t∈*T*, p∈*P*. *DDI*(*mls_d*, d)=Φ, d∈*D*, subjects in domain *mls_d* can not transfer to other domains.

9. (rbac_d, t, p)∈*DTM*, t∈*T*, p∈*P*, the subjects in domain *rbac_d* have all *domain permission* to all types' objects in system. *DDI*(*rbac_d*, d)=Φ, d∈*D*, subjects in domain *rbac_d* can not transfer to other domains.

10. For every r∈*mls_rs* ∪ {*dte_r*} and c∈*CAP*, (r, c)∉ *RCAP*, there is no role permission authorized to roles in set *mls_rs* and the role *dte_r*.

4 The Related Works

Bell-LaPadula [1] (BLP) model mainly emphasizes the protection of confidentiality. It is able to limit flow of information and unauthorized information leakage. However, it does not care about the integrity, which is also important [2,7,11]. Besides, BLP is weak in channel control of information flow [22]. Biba Integrity Model [6] is the mathematical dual of BLP, intending to protect the integrity in system.

Type enforcement is a table-oriented mandatory access control policy for confining applications and restricting information flows. DTE [9] is an enhanced version of type enforcement designed to provide needed simplicity and compatibility. Role-based access control [14] provides a valuable level of abstraction to promote security administration at a business level.

The Flask [10] security architecture emphasizes diverse security policies support. However, it applies only MAC to the Fluke Microkernel. It provides the mechanisms for diverse policies without giving how to enforce multiple policies in system.

One of the earliest MAC mechanisms in operating system is Lattices [1, 20]. For instance, LOMAC [13] enforces Biba integrity. CMW [8] can dynamically relabel the current object for increased flexibility.

Recently, Asbestos [17] provides labeling and isolation mechanisms that can support applications to express a wide range of policies and make MAC more practical. KernelSec [18] aims at improving the effectiveness of the authorization model and the security policies that can be implemented.

In capability-based confinement systems, KeyKOS [21] achieved military-grade security by isolating processed into compartments and interposing reference monitors to control the use of capabilities. EROS [19] later successful realized this principles on the modern hardware. And the Coyotes kernel [5] mainly explores use of software verification techniques to achieve higher confidence in the correctness and security of the kernel.

Mandatory access control can also be achieved with unmodified traditional operating system through virtual machines [16, 4].

5 Conclusions

The Compositional Multiple Policy Security Model is presented, which is based on the MLS model, combining the domain and type attributes to the model, to eliminate the limitations of MLS models. It has enforced expression power in channel control policies, and made permission management more fine-grained and enhanced the ability of confining the permission of the trusted subjects. MPVSM is also able to enforce multiple policy views in operating system in a flexible way.

References

1. Bell, D., La Padula, L.: Secure Computer Systems: Mathematical Foundations. Technical Report MTR-2547, vol. I, MITRE Corporation (1975)
2. Amoroso, E., Nguyen, T., Weiss, J., et al.: Towards an Approach to Measuring Software Trust. In: 1991 IEEE Symposium on Research in Security and Privacy, pp. 198–218 (1991)
3. Organick, E.: The MULTICS System: An Examination of Its Structure. MIT Press, Cambridge (1972)
4. Karger, P.A., Zurko, M.E., Bonin, D.W., et al.: A VMM security kernel for the VAX architecture. In: 1990 IEEE Symposium on Security and Privacy, pp. 2–19 (1990)
5. Shapiro, J., Doerrie, M.S., Northup, E., et al.: Towards a Verified, General-Purpose Operating System Kernel. In: 1st NICTA Workshop on Operating System Verification (2004)
6. Biba, K.: Integrity Considerations for Secure Computer Systems. Technical Report MTR-3153, MITRE Corporation (1977)
7. Eswaran, K., Chamberlin, D.: Functional Specifications of Subsystem for Database Integrity. In: The International Conference on Very Large Data Bases (1975)
8. Berger, J.L., Picciotto, J., Woodward, J.P.L., Cummings, P.T.: Compartmented mode workstation: Prototype highlights. IEEE Transactions on Software Engineering, Special Section on Security and Privacy 16, 608–618 (1990)
9. Badger, L., Sterne, D.F., Sherman, D.L., et al.: A Domain and Type Enforcement UNIX Prototype. In: 5th USENIX UNIX Security Symposium (1995)
10. Spencer, R., Smalley, S., Hibler, M., et al.: The Flask Security Architecture: System Support for Diverse Security Policies. In: 8th USENIX Security Symposium, pp. 123–139 (1999)
11. Lipner, S.: Non-Discretionary Controls for Commercial Applications. In: 1982 Symposium on Privacy and Security (1982)
12. Osborn, S., Sandhu, R., Munawer, Q.: Configuring Role-based Access Control to Enforce Mandatory and Discretionary Access Control Policies. ACM Transactions on Information and System Security 3, 85–106 (2000)
13. Fraser, T.: LOMAC–low water-mark mandatory access control for Linux. In: 9th USENIX Security Symposium (1999)

14. Sandhu, R., Coyne, E., Feinstein, H., Youman, C.: Role-Based Access Control. IEEE Computer 29 (1996)
15. Loscocco, P., Smalley, S.: Meeting critical security objectives with security-enhanced linux. In: Ottawa Linux Symposium 2001 (2001)
16. Goldberg, R.P.: Architecture of virtual machines. In: AFIPS National Computer Conference, vol. 42, pp. 309–318 (1973)
17. Efstathopoulos, P., Krohn, M., VanDeBogart, S., et al.: Labels and Event Processes in the Asbestos Operating System. In: 20th Symposium on Operating Systems Principles (2005)
18. Radhakrishnan, M., Solworth, J.A.: Application Support in the Operating System Kernel. In: ACM Symposium on Information, Computer and Communications Security (2006)
19. Shapiro, J.S., Smith, J.M., Farber, D.J.: EROS: A Fast Capability System. In: 17th ACM symposium on Operating systems principles (1999)
20. Saltzer, J.H., Schroeder, M.D.: The protection of information in computer system. Proceedings of the IEEE 63, 1278–1308 (1975)
21. Key Logic. The KeyKOS/KeySAFE System Design (1989), http://www.agorics.com/ Library/KeyKos/ keysafe/Keysafe.html
22. Rushby, J.: Noninterference, Transitivity, and Channel-Control Security Policies. Technical Report CSL-92-02, Computer Science Lab, SRI International (1992)

Longer Randomly Blinded RSA Keys May Be Weaker Than Shorter Ones

Colin D. Walter

Comodo Research Laboratory
7 Campus Road, Bradford, BD7 1HR, UK
Colin.Walter@comodo.com

Abstract. Side channel leakage from smart cards has been of concern since their inception and counter-measures are routinely employed. So a number of standard and reasonable assumptions are made here regarding an implementation of RSA in a cryptographic token which may be subjected to non-invasive side-channel cryptanalysis. These include blinding the re-usable secret key, input whitening, and using an exponentiation algorithm whose operation sequence partially obscures the key.

The working hypothesis is that there is limited side channel leakage which only distinguishes very imprecisely between squarings and multiplications. For this typical situation, a method is described for recovering the private exponent, and, realistically, it does not require an excessive number of traces. It just requires the modulus to be public and the public exponent not to be too large.

The attack is computationally feasible unless parameters are appropriately adjusted. It reveals that longer keys are much more vulnerable than shorter ones unless blinding is proportional to key length. A further key conclusion is that designers must assume that the information theoretic level of leakage from smart cards can be transformed into usable key information by adversaries whatever counter-measures are put in place.

Keywords: Side channel leakage, power analysis, SPA, DPA, RSA.

1 Introduction

Side channel leakage of secret key information from cryptographic devices has been known publicly for a number of years [1], and very widely since the work of Kocher [6,7]. In the case of RSA, the main software counter-measures to this have included message whitening, key blinding and more complex exponentiation algorithms. These, therefore, form the main assumptions here.

In the past, there were no obvious ways of extracting weak leaked information from this and using it to recover the secret key. Either the leaked information had to distinguish clearly between squarings and multiplications for individual uses of the key [3] or, with less precise leakage, the same key had to be re-used many times in an unblinded state so that the leakage could be averaged to reduce noise [6,2,13].

S. Kim, M. Yung, and H.-W. Lee (Eds.): WISA 2007, LNCS 4867, pp. 303–316, 2007.

However, from the information-theoretic standpoint, it is clear that there can be enough data for the key to be recovered when blinding is used but side channel leakage is imprecise. Here a means for obtaining the key is given for that situation, developed from the case of perfect, but partial, side channel information described by Fouque *et al.* [3]. One of the main contributions here is a metric for evaluating choices and enabling the best to be investigated first.

The first objective is to determine the blinding factor for several dozen cases. This is done by brute force: testing every possible value until one is found which would provide a trace that matches the measured trace sufficiently well under a suitable metric. The analysis is complicated by an unknown factor k equal to the size of the public exponent E. That factor must also be determined from the side channel leakage in the same way, and therefore affects the computational feasibility of the method if E is large. However, there is no obvious way to avoid the exhaustive search.

Once the blinding factors are determined for as many traces as are needed, the second objective is to determine the unblinded private exponent. Its bits are guessed from most to least significant by looking at both possible values and selecting the one which matches the observed leakage better. Incorrect choices are quickly noticed, and corrected by back-tracking and lookahead. This phase of the attack is less computationally intensive than the first, but it requires more traces when the leakage is weaker – a number inversely proportional to the strength of leakage.

The adversary makes use of certain properties of the exponentiation algorithm which lead to the leakage. The standard 4-ary sliding windows [4] considered here has a pattern of squarings and multiplications which contains information about the bit pattern of the exponent. The method applies equally well to any other algorithm with a variable pattern of operations where the variation is derived from a local property of the secret key, such as bit values.

Finally, the complexity of the attack is considered. There is low space complexity and the attack is highly, and easily, parallelisable to make full use of computing resources. The total time complexity is of order which is the product of the public key, the maximum blinding factor and a measure of the unreliability of the side-channel leakage. Thus, it appears to be computationally feasible to extract the key in many normal circumstances.

A significant conclusion is that, for a fixed amount of blinding, longer keys are less secure because blinding factors are determined more accurately. This means that blinding should be increased in proportion to key length in order to thwart the attack.

The organisation of the paper is as follows. The main assumptions, the leakage model, pre-requisite notation and background algorithms are covered in sections §2 to §5. Phase 1 of the attack, during which the blinding factors are recovered, is treated in §6. Phase 2 of the attack, namely the recovery of the secret key, is described in §7. The computational cost is reviewed in §8 and wide-ranging conclusions are drawn in §9.

2   Notation

The n-bit RSA modulus N and public exponent E are assumed to be known by the attacker. His aim is to recover the private key D which is re-used a number of times but only in the blinded form $D_i = D+r_i\phi(N)$ where $r_i < R$ is a small random number (typically up to 32 bits) and $\phi(N)$ is unknown.

The modulus is a product of two primes $N = PQ$ which must be of similar magnitude. For convenience, we assume P and Q have the same number of bits. Then, without loss of generality, $P < Q < 2P$ so that $2\sqrt{N} < P+Q < 3\sqrt{N/2}$ and $\phi(N) = N-(P+Q)+1$ is bounded by

$$N - 3\sqrt{N/2} + 1 < \phi(N) < N - 2\sqrt{N} + 1 \tag{1}$$

This interval has length less than $\frac{1}{8}\sqrt{N}$, so that more than half of the most significant bits of $\phi(N)$ are known by the attacker from those of N.

The exponents D and E are related by

$$D \times E = 1 + k\phi(N) \tag{2}$$

for some k. Without loss of generality, let D be the smallest non-negative solution to this congruence, so that $D < \phi(N)$ and $k < E$. When key D is re-used many times, blinding factors are normally added to produce the randomly different exponents which are actually used for decryption or signing [6]:

$$D_i = D + r_i\phi(N) \tag{3}$$

where r_i is a random number, usually of 16 to 32 bits. Thus,

$$D_i = \frac{1 + (k + r_iE)\phi(N)}{E} \tag{4}$$

Let R be an upper bound on such r_i. Then the coefficient $k+r_iE$ of $\phi(N)$ is, in effect, a random number in the range 1 to RE. (So it is irrelevant whether k and D were chosen minimally in equation (2)). In equation (4) the adversary is initially only interested in the most significant half of the bits. He ignores the 1 and approximates $\phi(N)/E$ by computing N/E. By the earlier remarks this gives him at least the top $n/2$ bits of $\phi(N)/E$. So,

$$D_i \approx (k + r_iE)N/E \tag{5}$$

The attacker now has to generate each of the RE possible values of the random coefficient of N/E in order to obtain a set containing an approximation to the value of D_i used in the exponentiation which he has observed.

3   The Exponentiation

For convenience we assume that the exponentiation algorithm is 4-ary sliding windows using the re-coding in Fig. 1 [4,5]. This uses a window of 1 bit width

Input: Binary $D - (b_{n-1}...b_2 b_1 b_0)_2$
Output: Recoding $D = (d_{m-1}...d_2 d_1 d_0)$

```
i ← 0 ;
m ← 0 ;
While i < n do
If b_i = 0 then
Begin
    d_m ← 0 ;
    i ← i+1 ;
    m ← m+1 ;
End
else
Begin
    d_m ← 2b_{i+1} + 1 ;
    i ← i+2 ;
    m ← m+1 ;
End
```

Fig. 1. Quaternary Sliding Windows Recoding

when there is a digit zero in the recoded exponent, and otherwise a window of 2 bits width, for which the digit is 1 or 3. Although this does not provide the same protection against side channel cryptanalysis as the square-and-always multiply algorithm, it is more time efficient even than the usual square-and-multiply algorithm and also creates some difficulty for an attacker who may have to distinguish whether the multiplications pertain to digit 1 or digit 3.

This algorithm, or its fixed-width equivalent, is typical of a smart card because of its speed and low storage overhead: only the first and third powers of the input message need storing for the exponentiation. Both algorithms generate a pattern of squarings and multiplications which is related to occurrences of the zero digit. This is the property that can be exploited here by an attacker.

4   The Leakage Model

With expected counter-measures in place it is unrealistic to assume that every long integer multiplicative operation in an RSA exponentiation can be identified and distinguished as a squaring or not. However, some imperfect deductions may be possible from a side channel trace, particularly in contactless cards where severe resource limitations and an explicit aerial limit the scope and effectiveness of any counter-measures. The following two leakage scenarios are likely in practice. Others are certainly possible.

First, because the conditional subtraction in a Montgomery modular multiplication ([8], *see* Fig. 2) consumes a number of extra clock cycles, there is a possibility that it may be observed in a side channel trace via the longer time for the operation. The slightly different frequencies of the subtraction for squares and multiplies mean that each occurrence or absence of the subtraction makes

Input: A and B such that $0 \le A, B < N < r^n$ and N prime to r.
Output: $C = ABr^{-n} \bmod N$

```
C ← 0 ;
For i ← 0 to n-1 do
Begin
    qᵢ ← -(c₀+aᵢb₀)n₀⁻¹ mod r ;
    C ← (C+aᵢB+qᵢN) div r ;
End ;
```
$\{$ Assertion: $Cr^n \equiv A \times B \bmod N$ and $ABr^{-n} \le C < N + ABr^{-n}\}$
```
If C ≥ N then C ← C-N ;
```

Fig. 2. Montgomery's Modular Multiplication Algorithm (MMM)

a square or multiplication marginally more likely [13]. As previous attacks have been unable to use this information in the presence of exponent blinding and message whitening, implementors may not perceive the leakage as a threat when such counter-measures are in place. One can therefore expect many of them to prefer more widely applicable code which includes the conditional subtraction, despite the existence of straightforward and efficient alternatives [12].

Secondly, the data loading cycles for multiplications and squarings are different and therefore vulnerable. For example, the Hamming weight of the words of the arguments may leak when they pass along the internal bus [7]. A squaring is almost certain where the Hamming weights are equal, and a multiplication must be the case if they are different. However, this information is usually well submerged in noise, and in a well designed implementation it should only yield a minimal bias towards a squaring or a multiplication.

The above are very much more realistic leakage models than that of [3] where it was assumed that each multiplicative operation was known to be a squaring or a multiplication. In practice, only weak probabilistic information is known.

In order to obtain specific measures of implementation strength, the attack here is modelled on the level of data leakage from observing every conditional subtraction in Montgomery modular multiplication. However, the attack is generic, and applies to both of the above scenarios as well as many others.

5   Selecting the Leakiest Traces

The word-based algorithm for Montgomery multiplication (MMM) is given in Fig. 2 where the digits a_i, b_i etc. are for the base r representation of the long integers A, B etc. From the assertion after the loop it is easy to establish the frequency of the conditional subtraction under the reasonable assumption of the output residues being uniformly distributed modulo N. The probability is proportional to the fraction of the interval which is greater than N, namely $ABr^{-n}N^{-1}$. For a typical multiplication with independent arguments, this can be summed with respect to A and B over the interval $[0, N)$ to obtain the average probability of

$$p_M \approx \frac{1}{4} N r^{-n} \qquad (6)$$

Similarly, setting $A = B$ and summing gives the probability of the subtraction for a squaring, namely

$$p_S \approx \frac{1}{3} N r^{-n} \qquad (7)$$

The difference between p_M and p_S shows that the occurrences of a conditional subtraction indicate a squaring is slightly more likely to be the case than a multiplication. The difference, however, is small. Early attacks on Montgomery's algorithm relied on being able to perform hundreds or thousands of exponentiations with the same key in order to observe enough subtractions to conclude with high probability whether the operation was a squaring or a multiplication.

The formulae (6) and (7) also indicate that decreasing N or increasing the number of iterations n will reduce the occurrences of the conditional subtraction and so make the algorithm more secure.

However, the multiplications in individual exponentiations are not as random as used for the formula (6). For 4-ary sliding windows, one of the two pre-computed powers of the input message is used as one of the arguments, the other being a random output from an earlier Montgomery multiplication. So only one argument is uniformly distributed in a given exponentiation. Let A be the fixed input to such a multiplication. Then, summing $ABr^{-n}N^{-1}$ with respect to B yields the true probability of a subtraction, $viz.$

$$p_A \approx \frac{1}{2} A r^{-n} \qquad (8)$$

Thus, when the pre-computed powers of the input are small (resp. large) there will be very few (resp. many) conditional subtractions resulting from multiplications. This increases the probability of distinguishing between squarings and multiplications. Overall, this will be noticed by an adversary because the total number of conditional subtractions will be less (resp. greater) than the average for such exponentiations. This provides the opportunity for the adversary to select the leakiest traces with very little computational effort.

Similarly, in the Hamming weight leakage scenario, instead of an enhanced or reduced frequency of conditional subtractions from large or small values of A, the adversary homes in on the argument pairs A, B which are the highest Hamming distance apart. They have the highest probability of being multiplications. This occurs most frequently when the re-used, pre-computed multiplier A has the highest number of extreme Hamming weights. So, by screening for extreme Hamming weights, traces which leak significantly more information than average can be identified easily by the adversary.

In both leakage models, the attacker can therefore begin by selecting side channel traces which yield the greatest amount of information, and these can be chosen without excessive computational effort for the initial phase of data capture, signal processing and selection.

6   The Attack: Phase 1

In the leakage scenarios of §4, the attacker is expected to obtain little or no useful information about a multiplicative operation in many cases, and only a very weak probability in favour of a squaring rather than a multiplication (or *vice versa*) in other cases. However, as described in §5, he begins his attack by collecting as many traces as possible and selecting those for which the leakage promises to be greatest. Phase one of his attack then progresses as follows.

Suppose he has selected a promising trace corresponding to the use of the blinded exponent D_i. He first determines the top half of the digits of $\phi(N)/E$ as in §2 and then guesses the values of k and r_i. Equation (5) gives him a possible approximation D_i' for D_i. He then compares the side channel leakage expected from D_i' with that obtained from D_i and discards the guessed pair (k, r_i) if the match is poor. Repeating this for all pairs leaves him with a set S_i of the most likely blinding values for D_i. This process is repeated with more traces – enough for him to complete the second phase successfully.

The decision about whether guesses are good enough is based on a metric $\mu(tr(D_i), ops(D_i', m))$. The first parameter $tr(D_i)$ is the processed side channel leakage from use of the unknown blinded key D_i. Specifically, it is a list of probabilities $pr(op)$ that the operations op of the exponentiation using D_i were squares rather than multiplications. Thus $tr(D_i) = [pr(op_s), pr(op_{s-1}), ..., pr(op_3), pr(op_2), pr(op_1)]$ where $s = len(tr(D_i))$ is the total number of operations in the exponentiation with key D_i. In the second parameter, D_i' is the bit sequence for the guessed value of D_i, and $ops(D_i', m)$ is the sequence of multiplicative operations carried out in an exponentiation with key $\lfloor D_i'/2^m \rfloor$. So the m least significant bits of D_i' are irrelevant, and need not have been guessed yet. This parameter will be a list containing, say, '0' to denote a squaring, and '1' a multiplication. In this phase we will set $m = n/2 + \log_2 R$.

If the side channel leakage $tr = tr(D_i)$ for D_i indicates with probability tr_j that the jth operation was a squaring and the jth operation in $ops(D_i', m)$ is also a squaring then $tr_j - \frac{1}{2}$ is added to the metric. However, if a multiplication occurs as the jth element in $ops(D_i', m)$, then $\frac{1}{2} - tr_j$ is added. So 0 is added if the leakage provides no information since then $tr_j = \frac{1}{2}$, but there is a positive contribution to the sum when the operation in $tr(D_i)$ is more likely to be the same as that in $ops(D_i', m)$, and there is a negative contribution when the two operations are more likely to be different. Thus, the sum for calculating the metric is

$$\mu(tr, ops(D', m)) \quad = \sum_{1 \leq j \leq nops(\lfloor D'/2^m \rfloor)} (-1)^{ops(D', m)_j}\left(tr_j - \frac{1}{2}\right) \qquad (9)$$

when $ops(D', m)_j \in \{0, 1\}$ as suggested above, and $nops(D'')$ is the number of operations in exponentiating to the power D''. Here the lists tr and $ops(D', m)$ are in temporal execution order assuming an exponentiation algorithm which processes bits from most to least significant. This correctly aligns corresponding elements of the lists when the lowest bits of D' are ignored.

If the guess (k, r_i) is correct, the value $D_i{}'$ provides the same pattern of squarings and multiplications as D_i over the first (approximately) half of the operations of the exponentiation. So, unless the noise is overwhelming, this should maximise the value for the sum when restricted to those operations. Therefore larger values for μ imply a better match between the guessed value $D_i{}'$ and the targetted exponent D_i, whereas smaller and negative values indicate a poor match. Because of the unknown difference between N and $\phi(N)$, the $n/2 + \log_2 R$ least significant bits of $D_i{}'$ are unreliable even when (k, r_i) is guessed correctly. By taking $m = n/2 + \log_2 R$ the operations corresponding to them are ignored.

The metric could be improved by taking account of the dependence between consecutive operations: for example, the probable occurrence of a multiplication implies that the next operation is more likely to be a squaring. Schindler [9,11,10] treats this in detail and provides theory about the best choice of metric.

6.1   Phase 1 Simulation

In our simulation, values were chosen which correspond to a leaky implementation of MMM where every conditional subtraction is observed and $N \approx r^n$. Conditional subtractions were generated randomly with frequencies in accordance with the model described in §5. There was no selection of "better" traces on the grounds of fewer or more subtractions than normal. Since conditional subtractions occur with slightly greater frequency for squarings than for multiplications, the metric was (arbitrarily) incremented by $p_j - \frac{1}{2} = 0.1$ for every conditional subtraction in the trace when there was a squaring in the guessed value and therefore incremented by $\frac{1}{2} - p_j = -0.1$ (i.e. decremented) for every conditional subtraction that coincided with a multiplication.

Table 1. Proportion of Guesses returning a Higher Value of μ than the Correct One

$\log_2 RE$	8	12	16	32	48
$n = 384$	7.9×10^{-3}	8.0×10^{-3}	8.2×10^{-3}	5.0×10^{-3}	3.6×10^{-3}
512	2.7×10^{-3}	2.4×10^{-3}	3.4×10^{-3}	2.0×10^{-3}	1.0×10^{-3}
768	5.3×10^{-4}	3.2×10^{-4}	1.0×10^{-3}	1.4×10^{-4}	1.2×10^{-4}
1024	2.0×10^{-5}	1.9×10^{-5}	8.7×10^{-4}	1.7×10^{-5}	8.0×10^{-6}
1536	$< 2.5\times10^{-7}$	$< 2.5\times10^{-7}$	$< 2.5\times10^{-7}$	...	...

With only this weak knowledge to distinguish between squarings and multiplications, the "best" guess is rarely the correct one. The correct values are ranked among the best, but do not usually come top. Therefore, to assess the feasibility of the attack, it is necessary to know the size of the set S of best guesses which is big enough to include the correct guess. This depends on the strength of the leakage. With the parameters just described, the results in Table 1 were obtained. It gives a good indication of how well the matching process works and shows the minimum proportion of all guesses which must be considered if the correct one is not to be excluded. For example, with a modulus of $n = 1024$ bits, and

$RE = 2^{32}$, the leakage of interest is from the top 512 or so bits. Then the metric μ places the correct values (k, r_i) above all but about $RE \times 1.7 \times 10^{-5} \approx 2^{16}$ incorrect values, on average.

In information theoretic terms, the metric has extracted about 16 bits from the side channel, i.e. about 1 bit in every $512/16 = 32$. This is the case for all the entries in the table: they all correspond to about 1 bit per 32 in the top half of the key, i.e. $n/64$ bits in total. An improved metric is possible (e.g. taking into account multiplications having to be next to squarings) and this would enable more information bits to be obtained. However, for 2048-bit keys (not tabulated), this means about 32 bits' worth of information is recovered, so that k and r_i should be determined almost uniquely when $RE \le 2^{32}$. This is indeed what was found in the simulation. Clearly, longer keys are more vulnerable:

- *For a given size of blinding and public exponent, the longer the key, the more likely (k, r_i) is to be guessed correctly and uniquely.*

The figures in the table show little effect from increasing RE. k and r_i blind information equivalent to about $\log_2 RE$ bits' worth of operations. However, longer blinding factors also seem to constrain the pattern of the blinded key more tightly. With these conflicting forces, the average success of the method is little changed: the number of bits leaked depends almost entirely on the length n of the key. Consequently, for a given key length, the same proportion of choices (k, r_i) are removed irrespective of the value of RE. Of course, the number of accepted pairs must still increase directly in proportion to RE. Thus,

- *Typical leakage from 2048-bit or longer keys will usually reveal (k, r_i) correctly with current standards for key blinding and a small public exponent;*

and

- *In these cases, an exhaustive search is computationally feasible to find the correct blinding factors (k, r_i).*

Incidentally, a powerful counter-measure in the case of Montgomery conditional subtractions is just to halve the modulus. This halves the number of conditional subtractions, and so halves the number of bits which are leaked.

6.2   Combining Traces to Determine k in Phase 1

The leakage from t traces can be processed for an outlay of t times the effort for one. If these traces are independent, t times as much bit information is extracted. Thus, a very small number of traces should result in k being determined with some confidence, since the same k is used in all cases. In fact, the correct value of k should have been guessed for all or almost all traces, and, if there is any bias, the correct value for k should be one of the most popular among the best guesses for an individual trace.

Guesses at k are ranked as follows. For each sufficiently good guess $k + r_i E$, the value of $k = (k + r_i E) \bmod E$ is extracted and the associated value of the metric μ is added to the weighting of k. The higher the total weight for a guess at k, the more likely that value is to be correct. The possible values of k are then considered in descending order of weight in Phase 2, the heaviest first.

Our simulation did not investigate how much this ranking reduces the search space in Phase 2 as a function of t; from the information theoretic point of view, it seems possible that k is almost completely determined by only a very small number of traces. This is an important detail that still needs to be researched as it affects the effectiveness of the blinding.

7   The Attack: Phase 2

Let S_i be the set of plausible guesses at (k, r_i) for the ith trace, and suppose S_i is partitioned into subsets S_{ik} which share the same k. Armed with these sets, the adversary progresses to phase 2, which is the recovery of the remaining, least significant bits of $\phi(N)$. He repeats this phase for each k separately, choosing the most likely k first. $\phi(N)$ is constructed bit by bit from the most significant end. The first half of $\phi(N)$ was obtained already from the public N and equation (1).

Let $\phi(N)_j = (\phi_{n-1}\phi_{n-2}...\phi_j)_2$ be the part of $\phi(N)$ already determined, so ϕ_{j-1} is the next bit to be guessed. Let $\Phi_j = (\phi_{j-1}\phi_{j-2}...\phi_{j-w})_2$ be a guess at the next w bits of $\phi(N)$. For each possible value of word Φ_j, the right side of equation (4) is evaluated with $\phi(N)_{j-w}$ in place of $\phi(N)$. This yields an approximation $D_{r_i,j-w}$ to D_i in which only the most significant $n-j+w$ bits are of interest. The same metric as in Phase 1 is used again to measure how well this matches the leakage from D_i, namely $\mu(tr(D_i), ops(D_{r_i,j-w}, j-w+\log_2 R))$. (As before, at the point before division by E, we ignore the lowest $\log_2 RE$ bits containing a contribution from ϕ_{j-w} because they are too contaminated by the carries up from less significant bits of $\phi(N)$.) For the given k, the sum

$$\mu_w(k, j, \Phi_j) = \sum_i \sum_{r_i \in S_{ik}} \mu(tr(D_i), \ ops(D_{r_i,j-w}, \ j-w+\log_2 R)) \qquad (10)$$

over all guesses is used to assess the worth of the choice for Φ_j. The leading bit of Φ_j from the maximum $\mu_w(k, j, \Phi_j)$ is selected as the value for ϕ_{j-1}.

Correct bit choices amplify any peak (i.e. maximum) values of the metric μ_w whilst incorrect choices decrease it. Moreover, previous mistakes reduce any peaks. When that happens, it is necessary to backtrack and select the most promising previous value. The difference between the two cases is determined using a threshold value for the metric which is obtained by experience. When it becomes too low for every value of Φ_j, it is necessary to backtrack and select the most promising previously untried value. The least significant bits of Φ_j are partly masked by carries up, and contribute less to the peak values than the more significant bits. So only the top one or two bits of the best Φ_j are chosen each time. In this way the bits ϕ_j are chosen from most to least significant. Once most bits have been guessed, the final $\log_2 E$ bits are fully determined by the division being exact in equation (4).

Table 2. Probability of predicting the correct bit of $\phi(N)$ from t correct guesses r_i with w lookahead bits when $n = 1024$ and $\log_2 RE = 16$

w	1	2	3	4	6	8
$t = 25$	0.613	0.767	0.833	0.868	0.914	0.930
$t = 50$	0.642	0.819	0.896	0.939	0.973	0.989
$t = 100$	0.673	0.846	0.922	0.954	0.981	0.994
$t = 250$	0.706	0.863	0.930	0.971	0.991	0.995

7.1 Phase 2 Simulation

For the simulation it was assumed that the correct (k, r_i) had been chosen for each i, i.e. that k had been deduced correctly and for the ith trace only the correct r_i had been selected. So $|S_{ik}| = 1$ and $|S_{ik'}| = 0$ if $k' \neq k$. From the conclusions about Phase 1, this should usually be the case for long keys.

As long as there is a reasonable probability of detecting the correct bit each time, all of $\phi(N)$ can be determined. Typical probabilities can be seen in Table 2. There seems little to be gained from having more than 100 traces; more is achieved by having more lookahead bits. In fact, the probability of picking the wrong bit seems to fall exponentially as the number w of lookahead bits increases[1]. From Table 3, $w \geq 8$ allows a significant proportion of keys to be recovered if the k and the randoms r_i have been guessed correctly. The figures are for an implementation of the algorithm without backtracking. When incorrect bits are predicted, the process does not recover and random bits are generated thereafter. With most bits being correct, backtracking is a cheaper alternative to solve this than increasing the number of lookahead bits. Assuming that Table 2 probabilities are constant over the length of the key and are independent of the key length, it is possible to compute the probability of successfully recovering the key: approximately $p^{n/2}$ where p is the table entry and n the key length.

Table 3 gives these probabilities as obtained from a simulation with 100 traces and $w = 8$. This corresponds to $p = 0.9973$. With 10 lookahead digits the simulation shows there is a 60% chance of recovering 2048-bit keys, and this corresponds to $p = 0.999512$. Lastly, with 50 traces but w varying dynamically between 8 and 16 as necessary, 2048-bit keys were recovered in 11% of cases. Since the values of k and r_i from Phase 1 will be mostly correct for 2048-bit keys with $\log_2 RE \leq 32$,

- *It is computationally feasible to recover a substantial number of 2048-bit keys using 50 traces, current standards for random blinding, typical small public exponents, and expected levels of weak side channel leakage.*

---

[1] The maximum values of $\mu_w(k, j, \Phi_j)$ were computed where Φ_j ranged over i) values with $\phi_j = 0$ and ii) values with $\phi_j = 1$. The difference between these was a good indicator of the reliability of the choice of ϕ_j. Increasing w just for the cases for which this difference was smallest led to a remarkable improvement in accuracy. Moreover, decreasing w for other cases led to a considerable computational saving. Many 2048-bit keys were recovered successfully using just 50 traces and varying w between 8 and 16.

Table 3. Probability of success in determining $\phi(N)$ from $t = 100$, correct r_is and key length n with $w = 8$ lookahead bits, no back-tracking and $\log_2 RE = 16$

n	512	768	1024	1536	2048
$prob$	0.50	0.40	0.29	0.13	0.04

7.2   The Case of Some Incorrect Phase 1 Deductions

Now consider the case where not all pairs (k, r_i) are correct. If (k, r_i) is incorrect then the above process applied only to this pair (i.e. $t = 1$ and $|S_{ik}| = 1$) would result in choosing the lower bits of $\phi(N)$ to satisfy (4) with the incorrect values (k, r_i) and the correct D_i. This makes the lower bits incorrect by a multiplication factor of $(k'+r_i'E)/(k+r_iE)$ where (k', r_i') is the correct pair. Moreover, for these bit choices the metric retains the peak values associated with a correct choice. So, without the context of other traces, the error will remain undetected and the pair (k, r_i) cannot be removed from consideration.

Thus, if the above process is performed with a set of pairs (k, r_i), some of which are correct and others incorrect, then the incorrect values predict random bits, while the correct ones predict the correct bits. This averages to a weaker prediction of the correct bits. However, the incorrect choices become more apparent as more correct bits are appended to $\phi(N)$. Eventually this is noticed and those choices can be dropped to speed up the process. It is easy to choose threshold values for the metric – several standard deviations below the average, say – to guide this decision.

So the Phase 2 process is applied to all the outputs of Phase 1 for a given k, i.e. every $(k, r_i) \in S_{ik}$ for every trace, and the sum of all the metric values is used to choose the lower bits of $\phi(N)$. Clearly, however, the limiting factor in this phase is the ratio of correct to incorrect predictions (k, r_i). If this is too small it will not be possible to identify correct bits through peaks in the value of the metric. Table 1 shows that key length is a very strong contributor to this: longer keys improve the ratio, making recovery of $\phi(N)$ much easier.

7.3   Comparison with Fouque

In this algorithm the bits of $\phi(N)$ are determined in the reverse order from that used by Fouque *et al.* [3]. This has several advantages. It makes the transition between the known upper half of $\phi(N)$ and unknown lower half seamless, it allows the metric easily to include the value of all previous decisions, and it allows the division by E to be done straightforwardly. The problems of carry influence in the multiplications of equation (4) is similar for both directions.

8   Complexity

The first phase has time complexity $O(REt \log(RE))$ where t is the number of traces needed to complete the second phase, and depends on the level of leakage.

This complexity results from an exhaustive search over all possible (k, r_i). It was remarked that there was an information leakage which is proportional to the length of the traces. Therefore, recovering the $\log_2(RE)$ bits of each (k, r_i) only requires processing a part of the traces with length $O(\log(RE))$, not the whole length. Space is not an issue in this phase as only one pair (k, r_i) need be considered at any one time. The pairs are treated independently and so the work can be completely parallelised. For standard choices of $E = 2^{16}+1$, $R = 2^{32}$ and a similar level of leakage to the example, this is clearly computationally feasible.

In the second phase the worst situation is that all RE guesses are considered for every trace at each bit selection, making a total time complexity $O(REnt)$, which is at worst similar to the first phase. However, if only $R'E'$ guesses survive then the complexity is reduced to $O(R'E'nt)$. This assumes that metrics do not have to be recomputed over the whole length of the trace every time another bit is guessed; instead the incremental effect of the new bit is used to update the preceding value. This approach requires $O(R't)$ space as different values of k are processed sequentially. The second phase requires strong leakage or a high ratio of correct pairs (k, r_i) to have a chance of working. Therefore practical limitations on the number of traces that can be obtained guarantees that space will not be the overriding problem. Furthermore, the work can be parallelised without difficulty at least as far as distributing the effort for each k to different processors. This would reduce the time complexity by a factor of $O(E)$.

9 Conclusion

The scope of the attack of Fouque *et al.* [3] has been extended to include imprecise leakage by introducing a practical metric which prioritises the selection of guesses at the random blinding factors and bits of $\phi(N)$ for an RSA modulus N. Both attacks target the typical set-up for RSA decryption/signing in a smartcard with standard counter-measures which include exponent blinding.

It was found that very weak, imprecise leaked data could be successfully manipulated to reduce the ambiguity in the blinding factors by a factor essentially proportional to the length of the keys, so that the blinding factors are fully determined when the key is long enough. For typical choices of public exponent and blinding parameters, and a leakage rate equivalent to only 1 bit per 32 bits of key per trace, the blinding factors can be recovered correctly for keys above about 2048 bits in length.

Reconstruction of the unknown lower bits of $\phi(N)$ requires most of the blinding factors to be recovered correctly and sufficiently many traces to be available. With a leakage rate of 1 bit per r key bits, $1.5r$ traces suffice to recover $\phi(N)$ and hence factor N without any need for an expensive search. In a simulation, a sizeable proportion of 2048-bit keys were successfully recovered using leakage from only 50 traces ($r=32$). Thus the attack is certainly computationally feasible with only weak, imprecise leakage.

So longer keys were found to be *more vulnerable*. The best counter-measure is to ensure that blinding increases with key length at least until it becomes computationally infeasible to test every blinding value individually. The attack illustrates that the information theoretic level of leakage can be into converted successfully into the secret key even in the presence of a typical collection of standard counter-measures.

References

1. Portable Data Carrier including a Microprocessor, Patent 4211919, US Patent and Trademark Office (July 8, 1980)
2. Dhem, J.-F., Koeune, F., Leroux, P.-A., Mestré, P., Quisquater, J.-J., Willems, J.-L.: A practical implementation of the Timing Attack. In: Schneier, B., Quisquater, J.-J. (eds.) CARDIS 1998. LNCS, vol. 1820, pp. 175–190. Springer, Heidelberg (2000)
3. Fouque, P.-A., Kunz-Jacques, S., Martinet, G., Muller, F., Valette, F.: Power Attack on Small RSA Public Exponent. In: Goubin, L., Matsui, M. (eds.) CHES 2006. LNCS, vol. 4249, pp. 339–353. Springer, Heidelberg (2006)
4. Knuth, D.E.: The Art of Computer Programming, 3rd edn. Seminumerical Algorithms, vol. 2. Addison-Wesley, Reading (1997)
5. Koç, Ç.K.: High Radix and Bit Recoding Techniques for Modular Exponentiation. International J. of Computer Mathematics 40(3-4), 139–156 (1991)
6. Kocher, P.: Timing attack on implementations of Diffie-Hellman, RSA, DSS, and other systems. In: Koblitz, N. (ed.) CRYPTO 1996. LNCS, vol. 1109, pp. 104–113. Springer, Heidelberg (1996)
7. Kocher, P., Jaffe, J., Jun, B.: Differential Power Analysis. In: Wiener, M.J. (ed.) CRYPTO 1999. LNCS, vol. 1666, pp. 388–397. Springer, Heidelberg (1999)
8. Montgomery, P.L.: Modular Multiplication without Trial Division. Mathematics of Computation 44(170), 519–521 (1985)
9. Schindler, W.: A Combined Timing and Power Attack. In: Naccache, D., Paillier, P. (eds.) PKC 2002. LNCS, vol. 2274, pp. 263–279. Springer, Heidelberg (2002)
10. Schindler, W.: On the Optimization of Side-Channel Attacks by Advanced Stochastic Methods. In: Vaudenay, S. (ed.) PKC 2005. LNCS, vol. 3386, pp. 85–103. Springer, Heidelberg (2005)
11. Schindler, W., Walter, C.D.: More detail for a Combined Timing and Power Attack against Implementations of RSA. In: Paterson, K.G. (ed.) Cryptography and Coding. LNCS, vol. 2898, pp. 245–263. Springer, Heidelberg (2003)
12. Walter, C.D.: Precise Bounds for Montgomery Modular Multiplication and Some Potentially Insecure RSA Moduli. In: Preneel, B. (ed.) CT-RSA 2002. LNCS, vol. 2271, pp. 30–39. Springer, Heidelberg (2002)
13. Walter, C.D., Thompson, S.: Distinguishing Exponent Digits by Observing Modular Subtractions. In: Naccache, D. (ed.) CT-RSA 2001. LNCS, vol. 2020, pp. 192–207. Springer, Heidelberg (2001)

Differential Power Analysis of HMAC Based on SHA-2, and Countermeasures

Robert McEvoy, Michael Tunstall, Colin C. Murphy, and William P. Marnane

Department of Electrical & Electronic Engineering, University College Cork, Ireland
{robertmce,miket,cmurphy,liam}@eleceng.ucc.ie

Abstract. The HMAC algorithm is widely used to provide authentication and message integrity to digital communications. However, if the HMAC algorithm is implemented in embedded hardware, it is vulnerable to side-channel attacks. In this paper, we describe a DPA attack strategy for the HMAC algorithm, based on the SHA-2 hash function family. Using an implementation on a commercial FPGA board, we show that such attacks are practical in reality. In addition, we present a masked implementation of the algorithm, which is designed to counteract first-order DPA attacks.

1   Introduction

In today's modern society of e-mail, internet banking, online shopping and other sensitive digital communications, cryptography has become a vital tool for ensuring the privacy of data transfers. To this end, Message Authentication Code (MAC) algorithms are used to verify the identity of the sender and receiver, and to ensure the integrity of the transmitted message. These algorithms process the message to be authenticated along with a secret key, which is shared between the sender and receiver. The result is a short string of bits, called a MAC. HMAC [1] is a popular type of MAC algorithm which is used in the IPsec [14] and TLS protocols [6], and is based on a cryptographic hash function such as SHA-2 [16].

The last decade has also seen the emergence of attacks which target cryptographic algorithms that are implemented in embedded hardware [9]. Of particular interest are differential side-channel attacks, such as Differential Power Analysis (DPA) [12]. These non-invasive attacks exploit information that leaks from a cryptographic device via some side channel, such as timing information, power consumption, or electromagnetic emanations. Comparing small variations in the side-channel information as a device processes different messages can potentially allow an attacker to recover secret information stored within the device. In this paper, we examine the susceptibility to differential side-channel attacks of the HMAC algorithm based on the SHA-2 family of hash functions.

Side-channel attacks on hash functions and the HMAC algorithm have been discussed in the past, but specific attack details for the SHA-2 family have not been given, nor have countermeasures been designed. In 2001, Steinwandt et al. [21] presented a theoretical attack on the SFLASH signature scheme, which

S. Kim, M. Yung, and H.-W. Lee (Eds.): WISA 2007, LNCS 4867, pp. 317–332, 2007.

targeted an exclusive-OR (XOR) operation in SHA-1. Coron and Tchoulkine [5] noted the vulnerability of the HMAC algorithm to a DPA attack. Lemke et al. [10] described a theoretical DPA attack on the HMAC algorithm based on the hash function RIPEMD-160, noting that a similar approach could be taken for a HMAC scheme based on SHA-1. Okeya et al. [18,19] highlight the susceptibility of MAC and HMAC algorithms to side-channel attacks, but the exposition is for the HMAC algorithm based on block-cipher based hash functions, in contrast with SHA-2, which is a dedicated cryptographic hash function.

In this paper, we characterise a differential side-channel attack on an implementation of the HMAC algorithm that uses the SHA-2 hash function family. Furthermore, we provide attack results on a FPGA implementation of the algorithm. We also describe countermeasures that could be used to prevent such side-channel attacks, by designing masked circuits for the vulnerable SHA-2 operations. The rest of this paper is organised as follows. In Section 2, the necessary background theory regarding the HMAC algorithm, the SHA-2 family, and DPA attacks is introduced. Section 3 gives a detailed account of how the SHA-256 based HMAC scheme can be broken by a side-channel attacker. Results from a practical FPGA-based implementation of this attack are presented in Section 4. In Section 5, a masking scheme is designed as a countermeasure against the attack, and the resulting FPGA-based scheme is tested in Section 6. Section 7 concludes the paper.

2   Background Theory

2.1   HMAC Algorithm Overview

The HMAC authentication scheme was first introduced by Bellare et al. at CRYPTO'96 [1]. The scheme was designed such that the security of the MAC is built upon the security of the underlying hash function h. The MAC is calculated as follows:

$$\text{HMAC}_k(m) = h((k \oplus opad)\|h((k \oplus ipad)\|m)) \tag{1}$$

where k is the secret key (padded with zeros to equal the block size of h), and m is the message to be authenticated. $ipad$ is a fixed string whose length equals the block size of h; generated by repeating the hexadecimal byte 0x36. Similarly, $opad$ is fixed and is formed by repeating the hexadecimal byte 0x5C. $\oplus$ and $\|$ denote XOR and concatenation respectively.

Clearly, in order to calculate $\text{HMAC}_k(m)$, the hash function h must be invoked twice. In this paper, we focus on the first call to the hash function, which calculates the partial MAC:

$$\text{HMAC}'_k(m) = h((k \oplus ipad)\|m) \tag{2}$$

In [1], the authors suggested using MD5 or SHA-1 to instantiate the hash function h. In 2002, the HMAC algorithm was released as a standard by NIST [17], in which h is defined as a NIST-approved hash function. In this paper, we adhere to this standard and choose SHA-256 to instantiate h. This follows a recent trend in the cryptographic community away from older hash functions, for which weaknesses have been identified [11], and towards newer constructions like the SHA-2 family [16]. We use the term "HMAC-SHA-256" to denote the HMAC algorithm that uses SHA-256 to instantiate h.

2.2 SHA-256 Description

There are four hash functions in the SHA-2 family: SHA-224, SHA-256, SHA-384 and SHA-512. Each algorithm generates a fixed-length hash value; SHA-224 produces a 224-bit output, SHA-256 has a 256-bit output, etc. The compression functions in SHA-224 and SHA-256 are based on 32-bit operations, whereas the compression functions for SHA-384 and SHA-512 are based on 64-bit operations. We focus on SHA-256 in our attacks, because it is easier in practice to perform a side-channel attack on a 32-bit word than on a 64-bit word. However, in theory, the side-channel attacks and countermeasures described in this paper should also be applicable to HMAC-SHA-384 and HMAC-SHA-512.

The SHA-256 algorithm essentially consists of three stages: (i) message padding and parsing; (ii) expansion; and (iii) compression.

Message Padding and Parsing. The binary message to be processed is appended with a '1' and padded with zeros until its bit length $\equiv 448 \bmod 512$. The original message length is then appended as a 64-bit binary number. The resultant padded message is parsed into N 512-bit blocks, denoted $M^{(i)}$, for $1 \leq i \leq N$. These $M^{(i)}$ message blocks are passed individually to the message expansion stage.

Message Expansion. The functions in the SHA-256 algorithm operate on 32-bit words, so each 512-bit $M^{(i)}$ block from the padding stage is viewed as sixteen 32-bit blocks denoted $M_t^{(i)}$, $1 \leq t \leq 16$. The message expansion stage (also called the message scheduling stage) takes each $M^{(i)}$ and expands it into sixty-four 32-bit W_t blocks for $1 \leq t \leq 64$, according to equations given in [16].

Message Compression. The W_t words from the message expansion stage are then passed to the SHA compression function, or the 'SHA core'. The core utilises eight 32-bit working variables labelled $A, B, \ldots, H$, which are initialised to predefined values $H_0^{(0)}$–$H_7^{(0)}$ (given in [16]) at the start of each call to the hash function. Sixty-four iterations of the compression function are then performed, given by:

$$A = T1 \boxplus T2 \tag{3}$$
$$B = A \tag{4}$$
$$C = B \tag{5}$$
$$D = C \tag{6}$$

$$E = D \boxplus T1 \tag{7}$$
$$F = E \tag{8}$$
$$G = F \tag{9}$$
$$H = G \tag{10}$$

where

$$T1 = H \boxplus \sum\nolimits_1 (E) \boxplus Ch(E, F, G) \boxplus K_t \boxplus W_t \tag{11}$$

$$T2 = \sum{}_0(A) \boxplus Maj(A, B, C) \tag{12}$$

$$Ch(x, y, z) = (x \wedge y) \oplus (\bar{x} \wedge z) \tag{13}$$

$$Maj(x, y, z) = (x \wedge y) \oplus (x \wedge z) \oplus (y \wedge z) \tag{14}$$

$$\sum{}_0(x) = ROT_2(x) \oplus ROT_{13}(x) \oplus ROT_{22}(x) \tag{15}$$

$$\sum{}_1(x) = ROT_6(x) \oplus ROT_{11}(x) \oplus ROT_{25}(x) \tag{16}$$

and the inputs denoted K_t are 64 32-bit constants, specified in [16]. All additions in the SHA-256 algorithm are computed modulo 2^{32}, denoted by $\boxplus$. The logical AND operator is denoted by $\wedge$, and $\bar{x}$ denotes the logical NOT operator. After 64 iterations of the compression function, a 256-bit intermediate hash value $H^{(i)}$, comprising $H_0^{(i)}$–$H_7^{(i)}$, is calculated:

$$H_0^{(i)} = A \boxplus H_0^{(i-1)}, H_1^{(i)} = B \boxplus H_1^{(i-1)}, \ldots, \ H_7^{(i)} = H \boxplus H_7^{(i-1)} \tag{17}$$

The SHA-256 compression algorithm then repeats and begins processing another 512-bit block from the message padder. After all N data blocks have been processed, the output, $H^{(N)}$, is formed by concatenating the final hash values:

$$H^{(N)} = H_0^{(N)} \ || \ H_1^{(N)} \ || \ H_2^{(N)} \ || \ \cdots \ || \ H_7^{(N)} \tag{18}$$

2.3   Differential Side-Channel Analysis

Some of the most common forms of side-channel analysis are Differential Power Analysis (DPA) [9] and related attacks such as Correlation Power Analysis (CPA) [2]. In this type of attack, a series of power consumption traces are acquired using an oscilloscope, where each trace has a known associated input (e.g. the message block being processed). A comprehensive guide to this class of attacks is provided in [12].

The fundamental principle behind all DPA attacks is that at some point in an algorithm's execution, a function f exists that combines a fixed secret value with a variable which an attacker knows. An attacker can form hypotheses about the fixed secret value, and compute the corresponding output values of f by using an appropriate leakage model, such as the Hamming Distance model [2]. The attacker can then use the acquired power consumption traces to verify her hypotheses, by partitioning the acquisitions or using Pearson's correlation coefficient. These side-channel analysis attacks are aided by knowledge of details of the implementation under attack. Moreover, these attacks can be used to validate hypotheses about implementation details. In subsequent sections, these side-channel analysis attacks are referred to as DPA attacks.

3   Attacking HMAC-SHA-256

In this section, we describe an attack on HMAC-SHA-256 using DPA. This attack does not allow recovery of the secret key itself, but rather a secret intermediate state of the SHA-256 hash function. Knowledge of this intermediate state would allow an attacker to forge MACs for arbitrary messages. We note that the attack is not limited to DPA, and other side-channels, such as the electromagnetic side-channel, could also be used.

3.1   Goal of the Attack

We assume that the attacker has access to a device that performs the HMAC algorithm, and that she has knowledge of the messages being processed by the device. This target device contains a basic implementation of the SHA-256 algorithm, and does not include any side-channel analysis countermeasures. Furthermore, we assume that the attacker has access to some side-channel information (e.g. the power consumption) while the device is calculating the MAC, which leaks the Hamming Distance between the internal signals as they change from one state to the next. As is common, we assume that the secret key is stored in a secure environment, which does not leak side-channel information.

The attack focuses on the first execution of SHA-256, given in equation (2). The block size of SHA-256 is 512 bits; therefore, using the notation from Section 2.2, $|k| = |ipad| = 512$. Without loss of generality, we can assume that the size of the message m is such that $N = 2$, i.e. the device will run through the 64 iterations of the compression function twice, in order to calculate equation (2).

When $i = 1$, the hash function is operating on $(k \oplus ipad)$, which clearly does not change from one execution of the HMAC algorithm to the next. Hence, the intermediate hash $H^{(1)}$ is also fixed and unknown. Recall that in order to perform a differential side-channel attack, we require fixed unknown data to be combined with variable known data. This criterion is fulfilled during the calculation of $H^{(2)}$, when the variable m is introduced and combined with the previous intermediate hash $H^{(1)}$. Therefore, in theory, a differential side-channel attack could be launched on a device calculating equation (2), in order to recover $H^{(1)}$. This knowledge would allow the attacker to create partial MACs of her choice. Reapplying the side-channel attack on the second invocation of SHA-256 in the HMAC algorithm would allow the attacker to forge full MACs for messages of her choosing. Consequently, the goal of the attacker is to recover the secret intermediate hash value $H^{(1)}$.

3.2   Attack Strategy

The secret intermediate hash $H^{(1)}$ manifests itself as the initial values of the eight 32-bit working variables A–H, when $i = 2$. We use the subscript $t, 1 \leq t \leq 64$ to denote the round number, e.g. A_1 refers to the value of A at the start of round 1 of the compression function, etc. The side-channel attacker's goal is to uncover the eight variables A_1–H_1. A strategy for such an attack is now described.

1. With reference to equations (3) and (7), it is clear that at some point in the first round, the variable $T1_1$ must be calculated. $T1_t$ is a large sum with 5 terms, and can be re-written as:

$$T1_t = \theta_t \boxplus W_t \tag{19}$$

where

$$\theta_t = H_t \boxplus \sum_1 (E_t) \boxplus Ch(E_t, F_t, G_t) \boxplus K_t \qquad (20)$$

In round 1, θ_1 is fixed and unknown, and W_1 is known by the attacker, since it is related to m. Therefore, a DPA attack can be launched by making hypotheses about θ_1, and computing the corresponding values of $T1_1$. Since SHA-256 uses 32-bit words, 2^{32} hypotheses for θ_1 are required. Furthermore, since we assume that the target device leaks the Hamming Distance (HD), the 2^{32} possibilities for the previous state, $T1_0$, must also be taken into account. Therefore, the attacker correlates the power traces with her 2^{64} hypotheses for $HD(T1_0, T1_1)$. This allows the attacker to recover $T1_0$ and θ_1, and then calculate $T1_1$ for any message m.

Clearly, correlating with 2^{64} hypotheses would be computationally infeasible, even for well-resourced attackers. In Section 3.3, we describe how the Partial CPA technique [22] can be used to significantly reduce the attack's complexity.

2. The above attack stage gives the attacker control over the value of $T1_1$, so it is now a known variable. Using equation (7), the attacker can now make hypotheses on the (fixed) bits of D_1, using the bits of E_2 as selection bits. Using the Hamming Distance model, hypotheses for the previous (secret) state E_1 are also generated. In this way, the attacker can recover her first secrets, D_1 and E_1, and accurately predict the value of E_2 for any message m.

3. Focusing on equation (3), we observe that $T1_1$ is variable and known, whereas $T2_1$ is fixed and unknown. The attacker can launch a DPA attack on A_2 by forming hypotheses about $T2_1$ and the previous state A_1. Hence, the secret value of A_1 is revealed. Furthermore, with knowledge of both $T1_1$ and $T2_1$, the attacker can now accurately predict A_2 for any message m.

Therefore, by analysing the side-channel signals from the first round, the attacker can recover the fixed secret values of θ_1, D_1, E_1, $T2_1$ and A_1, and also predict the values of variables $T1_1$, A_2 and E_2.

4. The attacker now turns her attention to the second SHA-256 round. Here, the Ch function is calculated as:

$$Ch(E_2, F_2, G_2) = (E_2 \wedge F_2) \oplus (\overline{E_2} \wedge G_2) \qquad (21)$$

where E_2 is variable, and known by the attacker. From equations (8) and (9), we observe that F_2 and G_2 are fixed at E_1 and F_1, respectively. Therefore, the attacker can generate hypotheses about the unknown values F_1, and attack the output of the Ch function. Of course, 2^{32} hypotheses for the previous state $Ch(E_1, F_1, G_1)$ are also required. Recovering F_1 means that the attacker can now accurately predict the variable $Ch(E_2, F_2, G_2)$.

5. The next point of attack is the calculation of $T1_2$ (equation (11)). At this stage, the only fixed unknown value in the equation is H_2, as every other variable can be predicted. The attacker already knows the previous state $T1_1$ from stage 1 above. Mounting a DPA attack uncovers H_2, and allows

$T1_2$ to be predicted. From equation (10), it can be seen that H_2 is equivalent to G_1.

6. The knowledge of $T1_2$ gained from the previous attack stage can be applied to equation (7). Using the bits of E_3 as the selection function, the attacker can mount a DPA attack that uncovers D_2. From equation (6), we observe that D_2 is equivalent to C_1.

7. The Maj function in the second round can be expressed as:

$$Maj(A_2, B_2, C_2) = (A_2 \wedge B_2) \oplus (A_2 \wedge C_2) \oplus (B_2 \wedge C_2) \qquad (22)$$

where A_2 is variable, and known by the attacker. From equations (4) and (5), we observe that B_2 and C_2 are fixed at A_1 and B_1, respectively. Using a similar approach to that taken in stage 4 above, the attacker can perform DPA on Maj and discover the secret value of B_1.

8. By following the above strategy, the attacker can recover the fixed secrets A_1–G_1. The last remaining secret variable, H_1, can be found by reverting the focus to round 1, and substituting into equation (11), where the only unknown value is that of H_1. The eight 32-bit secret values are thus recovered, using seven first-order DPA attacks.

3.3 Complexity of the Attack

As noted above, it is currently computationally infeasible for an attacker to compute 2^{64} hypotheses for a DPA attack. However, as indicated in [2] and illustrated in [22], a partial correlation may be computed, rather than the full correlation. If a correlation coefficient of ρ is obtained by correctly predicting all 32 bits of an intermediate variable, then we would expect to obtain a partial correlation of $\rho\sqrt{l/32}$ by predicting l bits correctly. Hypotheses can be made on smaller sets of bits at a time, e.g. $l = 8$, and this strategy can be employed to keep only those hypotheses that produce the highest partial correlations. In this way, the full 32-bit correlation can be built up in stages, thereby reducing the complexity of the attack. This is similar to the 'extend-and-prune' strategy employed by a template attack [3].

4   Attack on FPGA Implementation

4.1   Implementation Details

In order to demonstrate the feasibility of a DPA attack on HMAC-SHA-256, we implemented the algorithm on a Xilinx FPGA Board. FPGAs are attractive for implementing cryptographic algorithms because of their low cost (relative to ASICs), and their flexibility when adopting security protocol upgrades. FPGAs also allow rapid prototyping of various designs. For our experiments, we implemented SHA-256 on Xilinx's low-cost Spartan™-3E Development Kit, which contains the Spartan™XC3S500E FPGA [23]. FPGAs consist mostly of Configurable Logic Blocks (CLBs), arranged in a regular array across the chip. In our

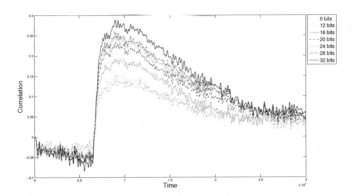

Fig. 1. Correlation and partial correlations between the power consumption and E_2, given the correct prediction of D_1 and the previous state E_1

case, each CLB contains 4 logic "slices", which is the basic unit used to quantify the area occupied by a design. Each slice contains two four-input Look-Up Tables (LUTs) and two registers. Logic also exists within a slice which allows fast implementation of carry look-ahead addition. Each slice has a dedicated multiplexer, which is hard-wired to provide a fast carry chain between consecutive slices and CLBs. Indeed, fast carry logic is a feature of many modern FPGAs. We will make use of this dedicated addition circuitry in Section 5.

Several optimisations for the SHA-2 family exist, such as pipelining and loop unrolling [4]. However, for simplicity, it was decided to implement a basic design without such optimisations. The design was captured using VHDL, and synthesis, placing and routing were performed using Xilinx ISE™v9.1i. The processor and interface circuitry utilise 951 slices, corresponding to 20% of the FPGA resources. The critical path in the design (i.e. the longest combinational path) is 16.4 ns, during the calculation of A (equation (3)). Block RAMs (BRAMs) on the FPGA are used to store the various messages to be processed; this reduces the communication requirements with the FPGA board.

4.2   Experimental Results

In order to obtain DPA power traces from the design, the FPGA board was configured with the basic SHA-256 design, and a 10 Ω resistor was inserted in the FPGA power supply line. Using a LeCroy WaveRunner 104Xi oscilloscope and a differential probe, we could measure the voltage fluctuations across the resistor as the SHA-256 algorithm was being executed. Therefore, the traces recorded on the oscilloscope were proportional to the power consumption of the FPGA during the execution of the algorithm. Traces for the first three rounds were captured while 4000 random messages were being processed by the FPGA. In order to reduce acquisition noise, each captured trace corresponded to the average of 700 executions with the same message. Figure 1 shows the correlation trace achieved when D_1 and the unknown previous state E_1 are correctly predicted.

The different levels correspond to the correlation coefficients achieved when a certain number of bits are correctly predicted.

5   Masking the SHA-256 Algorithm

The preceding sections have demonstrated the susceptibility of hardware implementations of the HMAC algorithm to first-order DPA attacks. We now examine how to use masking as a countermeasure to such attacks. The masking technique aims to use random values to conceal intermediate variables in the implementation of the algorithm, thereby making the side-channel leakage independent of the secret intermediate variables. Much of the literature has focused on masking techniques for software implementations of cryptographic algorithms (e.g. [5,8,15]). In [7], Golić detailed techniques for masking hardware implementations, which we build upon below in order to mask HMAC-SHA-256.

5.1   Requirements

Consider a function f and intermediate variables x, y and z, such that $z = f(x, y)$. If x or y are key-dependent or data-dependent, then masking is required. We introduce random masks r_x, r_y and r_z such that $x' = x \circ r_x$, $y' = y \circ r_y$ and $z' = z \diamond r_z$; where $\circ$ is the group operation masking the input data, and $\diamond$ is the group operation masking the output z. In order to prevent differential side-channel attacks, the function f must be modified to the function f', such that $z' = f'(x', y', r_x, r_y, r_z) = z \diamond r_z$. If the group operation is XOR, the masking scheme is termed Boolean masking. The SHA-256 algorithm also uses addition modulo 2^{32}, which requires arithmetic masking.

In [7], Golić described the goal of designing a secure masked hardware implementation for a function f, using the "secure computation condition". This condition states that the output value of each logic gate in the design should be statistically independent of the original data (i.e. the secret key and the input data). In the case of a Boolean logic circuit implementing f, this condition is satisfied if all of the inputs to the circuit are jointly statistically independent of the original data. In the case of a multiplexer-based design for f: (i) the data inputs to the multiplexer should be identically distributed; (ii) each data input should be statistically independent of the original data; and (iii) for each fixed value of the original data, each data input should be statistically independent of the control input. In order to mask our SHA-256 design correctly, care must be taken that these conditions are met.

5.2   Masking the Original Data

In Section 3, the eight variables A–H in the SHA-256 algorithm were identified as the secret values which are of interest to the side-channel attacker. Therefore, we begin the first iteration of the compression function by XOR-ing these values with eight 32-bit random masks denoted r_A–r_H, so that they become A'–H'. Furthermore, the variable input data W_t to the SHA-256 compression algorithm

Table 1. Linear and non-linear functions (with respect to XOR) used in SHA-256

Linear	Non-Linear
NOT $(\bar{x})$	Ch
σ_0	Maj
σ_1	AND
$\sum_0, \sum_1$	addition modulo 2^{32}

requires masking. Since this data is perfectly predictable by the attacker, it must be XOR-ed with a new 32-bit random value r_W in every SHA-256 round.

Recall that the fixed secret data mixes with the attacker's variable known data within the SHA-256 compression algorithm. Therefore, we must also mask the individual functions in the SHA-256 compression algorithm. If a function f is linear with respect to the mask, then it is easy to mask, as $z' = f(x', y')$, and $r_z = f(r_x, r_y)$. Conversely, non-linear functions require modification in order to achieve secure masking. Therefore, new circuits implementing these non-linear functions must be designed, with respect to the secure computation condition given above. Table 1 outlines the linear and non-linear functions used by SHA-256. In the following sub-sections, we present our designs for the secure circuits implementing the non-linear functions of Table 1 on an FPGA.

5.3   The Ch and Maj Functions

The logical functions Ch and Maj are described by equations (13) and (14) respectively. The non-linearity in both of these functions stems from the AND operations. Therefore, Ch and Maj cannot be implemented using ordinary AND gates, and masked AND gates must be used instead.

In [7], Golić proposed masking the AND function $z = x \wedge y$, using Boolean masking, as follows:

$$z' = \wedge'(x', y', r_x, r_y)$$
$$= \overline{y'} \wedge (\overline{r_y} \wedge r_x \vee r_y \wedge x') \vee y' \wedge (r_y \wedge r_x \vee \overline{r_y} \wedge x') \tag{23}$$

where $\vee$ denotes logical OR. This approach has the advantage that the output mask r_z is equal to the input mask r_x; therefore, a new mask for z is not required.

When implementing this masked AND circuit (denoted $\wedge'$) on an FPGA, we can take advantage of the underlying slice structure. Equation (23) is a four-input function, which is perfectly suited for implementation in one of the FPGA slice's four-input LUTs. A two-input or three-input XOR operation can also be implemented using a single four-input LUT. Note that care must also be taken when describing masked circuits, so that the HDL synthesis tool does not remove the redundancy in the design, or combine two variables that are not statistically independent.[1]

---

[1] In VHDL, this can be achieved by asserting the "keep_hierarchy" attribute within the masked AND gate's architecture.

Our design for masked $Maj(A, B, C)$, denoted $Maj'(A', B', C', r_A, r_B, r_C)$, is as follows:

$$Maj'(A', B', C', r_A, r_B, r_C) = (\wedge'(A', B', r_A, r_B)) \oplus (\wedge'(A', C', r_A, r_C)) \\ \oplus (\wedge'(B', C', r_B, r_C)) \quad (24)$$

Therefore, three LUTs (per bit) are required for the three masked AND operations, and one LUT (per bit) is required for the three-input XOR. Since the variables are 32-bit, Maj' requires 128 LUTs or 64 Spartan-3E slices. This is four times larger than a basic unmasked implementation of Maj. By choosing the order for the operands of the masked AND functions appropriately, the output mask becomes $r_{Maj} = r_A \oplus r_A \oplus r_B = r_B$.

Similarly, our design for masked $Ch(E, F, G)$ is

$$Ch'(E', F', G', r_E, r_F, r_G) = (\wedge'(E', F', r_E, r_F)) \oplus (\wedge'(G', \overline{E'}, r_G, r_E)) \quad (25)$$

which requires two LUTs (per bit) for the two masked AND operations, and one LUT (per bit) for the 2-input XOR. Care must be taken regarding the order of the operands of the masked AND functions. If E' was the first operand of both masked AND gates, then the output mask would be $r_{Ch} = r_E \oplus r_E = 0$, i.e. the output would be unmasked. Therefore, we choose the order such that $r_{Ch} = r_E \oplus r_G$, which requires one extra LUT (per bit) to compute the XOR. Hence, a total of 128 LUTs or 64 Spartan-3E slices are required, which is four times the size of a Ch implementation not protected by Boolean masking.

5.4   Addition Modulo 2^{32}

All of the masks that have been introduced up to this point have been Boolean masks. However, the SHA-256 compression algorithm makes extensive use of consecutive additions modulo 2^{32}, denoted $\boxplus$, which are arithmetic functions and are non-linear with respect to Boolean masking. This presents the designer with a choice: (i) a new masked function $\boxplus'$ can be created, which uses Boolean masking; or (ii) a Boolean-to-Arithmetic conversion can be applied prior to the $\boxplus$ operations. The latter choice converts a variable masked with a Boolean mask to a variable masked with an arithmetic mask, meaning that subsequent additions are linear with respect to the arithmetic mask. Arithmetic-to-Boolean conversion is required before the results of the additions are fed back to the Boolean part of the function. In [7], Golić investigated this design choice, and concluded that choice (i) above is effective only if a small number of consecutive masked additions (e.g. one to three) is required. This is verified by our experiments on the FPGA (not detailed here). The masked adder produced in design (i) has large area and large latency, which greatly adds to the critical path in the circuit. On the other hand, design (ii) uses the conversion functions along with ordinary addition operations, both of which can take advantage of the underlying structure of the FPGA, leading to a much shorter critical path than in design (i). Our designs for the conversion functions are detailed below.

5.5 Boolean-to-Arithmetic Conversion

The circuits implementing the Boolean-to-Arithmetic and Arithmetic-to-Boolean conversion functions must themselves be secure against side-channel attacks. Several software-based algorithms have been proposed for performing these conversions [5,8,15]; however, these solutions are not suitable for efficient hardware implementation. Golić [7] developed hardware solutions based on the basic method of ripple-carry addition. Here, we present solutions tailored for FPGA implementation, based on the carry look-ahead addition method. We take advantage of the dedicated carry logic that is hard-wired into the FPGA, which allows carry bits to quickly propagate through columns of FPGA slices.

Henceforth, we will use single prime notation (x') to denote Boolean masking, and double prime notation (x'') to denote arithmetic masking (with respect to $\boxplus$). The goal is to securely convert a variable $x' = x \oplus r_x$ into a variable x'' such that $x'' = x \boxplus r_x$, without compromising the secret value x. Following the analysis in [7], we use a subscript j, $0 \leq j \leq 31$ to index the individual bits of x', x'' and r_x. The addition, with carry word c, can be expressed as:

$$x''_j = x_j \oplus r_{x,j} \oplus c_{j-1} \tag{26}$$
$$= x'_j \oplus c_{j-1} \tag{27}$$

where $c_{-1} = 0$, and c_{31} is not used. The carry bits are described by the recursive equation $c_j = (x_j \wedge r_{x,j}) \vee c_{j-1} \wedge (x_j \oplus r_{x,j})$. In order to suit a carry look-ahead implementation, the equation for the carry bits can be restated as:

$$c_j = ((x'_j \oplus r_{x,j}) \wedge r_{x,j}) \vee (c_{j-1} \wedge (x'_j \oplus r_{x,j} \oplus r_{x,j}))$$
$$= \overline{x'_j} \wedge r_{x,j} \vee x'_j \wedge c_{j-1} \tag{28}$$

Clearly, equation (28) is suitable for implementation by a multiplexer in the FPGA's dedicated carry chain, with $r_{x,j}$ and c_{j-1} as data inputs, and x'_j as the control input. Therefore, the Boolean-to-Arithmetic conversion circuit should have similar area requirements and similar latency to an ordinary adder.

However, the above multiplexer-based design contravenes the secure computation condition, because the data input $r_{x,j}$ is not statistically independent of the control input x'_j. In theory, this dependence could be used by an attacker to launch a side-channel attack. In order to remove this dependence, we introduce a further Boolean masking bit q to mask the carry chain. The same bit q can be re-used for each multiplexer in the conversion circuit. The resulting scheme is described as follows:

$$c_j \oplus q = \overline{x'_j} \wedge (r_{x,j} \oplus q) \vee x'_j \wedge (c_{j-1} \oplus q) \tag{29}$$
$$x''_j = x'_j \oplus (c_{j-1} \oplus q) \oplus q \tag{30}$$

The carry look-ahead structure is maintained, which allows fast calculation of equation (29) on the FPGA. One extra LUT per bit is required by equation (30), to remove the mask from the masked carry bits.

5.6   Arithmetic-to-Boolean Conversion

The aim of an Arithmetic-to-Boolean conversion is to use x'' and r_x to derive the Boolean-masked variable x'. From equation (27), we have $x'_j = x''_j \oplus c_{j-1}$. In order to obtain a recursive expression for c_j in terms of x'', we substitute x'_j into equation (28), giving $c_j = \overline{(x''_j \oplus c_{j-1})} \wedge r_{x,j} \vee (x''_j \oplus c_{j-1}) \wedge c_{j-1}$. After some algebraic manipulation, the following can be derived:

$$c_j = (x''_j \oplus r_{x,j}) \wedge r_{x,j} \vee (\overline{x''_j \oplus r_{x,j}}) \wedge c_{j-1} \tag{31}$$

The conversion function is now in the carry look-ahead form that is required for fast calculation on the FPGA; with $r_{x,j}$ and c_{j-1} as the data inputs to the multiplexers, and $(\overline{x''_j \oplus r_{x,j}})$ as the control input. As above, we must now determine if the multiplexers comply with the secure computation condition. It appears that data input $r_{x,j}$ is statistically independent of the control input $(\overline{x''_j \oplus r_{x,j}})$, because x''_j incorporates randomness from bit c_{j-1} as well as from bit $r_{x,j}$ (equation (26)). However, when $j = 0$, c_{-1} is fixed at zero, and the control input becomes simply $\overline{x_0}$, i.e. one secret bit is unmasked.

Clearly, we must avoid computing $(\overline{x''_j \oplus r_{x,j}})$ when $j = 0$. Our solution is to remove one multiplexer from the carry chain, and to use an FPGA LUT to calculate c_0 directly. From equation (31), $c_0 = \overline{x''_0} \wedge r_{x,0}$, which could itself be the focus of a side-channel attack. Therefore, as in the case of the Boolean-to-Arithmetic conversion, we introduce a Boolean masking bit q, giving:

$$c_0 = (\overline{x''_0} \wedge r_{x,0}) \oplus q \tag{32}$$

Technically, this equation violates the secure computation condition, as the intermediate result $(\overline{x''_0} \wedge r_{x,0})$ is not independent of the secret bit x_0. However, if an FPGA LUT is used to calculate c_0, it can be shown that the LUT output is statistically independent of x_0, therefore the LUT does not leak information.

Finally, the other 31 masked values of c_j can be calculated using the fast carry chain, according to:

$$c_j \oplus q = (x''_j \oplus r_{x,j}) \wedge (r_{x,j} \oplus q) \vee (\overline{x''_j \oplus r_{x,j}}) \wedge (c_{j-1} \oplus q) \tag{33}$$

As in the case of Boolean-to-Arithmetic masking, additional LUTs are required to remove the masking bit q, via $x'_j = x''_j \oplus (c_{j-1} \oplus q) \oplus q$.

6   Masked FPGA Implementation

The above section detailed the proposed masking schemes for the SHA-256 compression function. Note that in order to remove the masks r_A–r_H at the end of the 64th iteration of the compression function, it is necessary to compute mask update terms in parallel with the masked compression function. The complete masked core design contains: sixteen 32-bit registers; thirteen adders; seven Boolean-to-Arithmetic conversion blocks; two Arithmetic-to-Boolean conversion blocks; as well as circuits implementing the $\sum_0$, $\sum_1$, Maj' and Ch' functions.

On our Spartan-3E chip, the masked processor and interface circuitry utilise 1734 slices (37% of FPGA resources), and the design's critical path is 18.6 ns. Hence, although the area has almost doubled compared with the unprotected implementation, the speed has not been overly affected. The required random bits could be generated, for example, by a cryptographically secure pseudo-random number generator implemented on the FPGA, as described in [20]. For simplicity, in our case we pre-generated the required random bits, and stored them in BRAM on the FPGA. By repeating the experiments described in section 3, we verified that the data-dependence of the power consumption has been removed; therefore, the design is resistant to standard first-order DPA attacks.

We note that more sophisticated first-order DPA attacks are still possible, for example by considering the side-channel leakage due to glitches [13]. However, such attacks rely on the strong assumption that the attacker has very detailed knowledge of the design, such as a back-annotated netlist, from which an exact power model can be extracted.

7   Conclusions

It has been shown that implementations of the HMAC algorithm are susceptible to side-channel attacks. An explicit DPA attack strategy for HMAC-SHA-2 has been presented, and the attacks have been verified with actual FPGA-based experiments. A hardware-based masked core for SHA-2 hash functions has been designed, which counteracts first-order DPA attacks. The Boolean-to-Arithmetic and Arithmetic-to-Boolean conversion circuits, which are traditionally considered to be slow, have been optimised for implementation on FPGAs. This useful adaptation can be used to mask other algorithms that mix Boolean and arithmetic functions, such as IDEA or RC6. Future work will focus on securing the HMAC algorithm against other forms of side-channel attack, such as higher-order DPA and template attacks. Another avenue for further research is to investigate how throughput optimisation techniques can be applied to SHA-2 implementations, while maintaining the DPA attack countermeasures.

Acknowledgements

The authors would like to acknowledge the comments of the anonymous reviewers, as well as the reviewers of an earlier draft of this paper. This work was supported in part by the Embark Initiative, operated by the Irish Research Council for Science, Engineering and Technology (IRCSET).

References

1. Bellare, M., Canetti, R., Krawczyk, H.: Keying hash functions for message authentication. In: Koblitz, N. (ed.) CRYPTO 1996. LNCS, vol. 1109, pp. 1–15. Springer, Heidelberg (1996)
2. Brier, E., Clavier, C., Olivier, F.: Correlation power analysis with a leakage model. In: Joye, M., Quisquater, J.-J. (eds.) CHES 2004. LNCS, vol. 3156, pp. 16–29. Springer, Heidelberg (2004)
3. Chari, S., Rao, J.R., Rohatgi, P.: Template attacks. In: Kaliski Jr., B.S., Koç, Ç.K., Paar, C. (eds.) CHES 2002. LNCS, vol. 2523, pp. 13–28. Springer, Heidelberg (2003)
4. Chaves, R., Kuzmanov, G., Sousa, L., Vassiliadis, S.: Improving SHA-2 hardware implementations. In: Goubin, L., Matsui, M. (eds.) CHES 2006. LNCS, vol. 4249, pp. 298–310. Springer, Heidelberg (2006)
5. Coron, J.-S., Tchoulkine, A.: A new algorithm for switching from arithmetic to boolean masking. In: D.Walter, C., Koç, Ç.K., Paar, C. (eds.) CHES 2003. LNCS, vol. 2779, pp. 89–97. Springer, Heidelberg (2003)
6. Dierks, T., Rescorla, E.: The Transport Layer Security (TLS) Protocol, Version 1.1. RFC 4346 (April 2006), http://tools.ietf.org/html/rfc4346
7. Golić, J.D.: Techniques for random masking in hardware. IEEE Transactions on Circuits and Systems — I 54(2), 291–300 (2007)
8. Goubin, L.: A sound method for switching between boolean and arithmetic masking. In: Koç, Ç.K., Naccache, D., Paar, C. (eds.) CHES 2001. LNCS, vol. 2162, pp. 3–15. Springer, Heidelberg (2001)
9. Kocher, P., Jaffe, J., Jun, B.: Differential power analysis. In: Wiener, M.J. (ed.) CRYPTO 1999. LNCS, vol. 1666, pp. 388–397. Springer, Heidelberg (1999)
10. Lemke, K., Schramm, K., Paar, C.: DPA on n-bit sized boolean and arithmetic operations and its application to IDEA, RC6, and the HMAC-Construction. In: Joye, M., Quisquater, J.-J. (eds.) CHES 2004. LNCS, vol. 3156, pp. 205–219. Springer, Heidelberg (2004)
11. Lenstra, A.K.: Further progress in hashing cryptanalysis (white paper) (February 2005), http://cm.bell-labs.com/who/akl/hash.pdf
12. Mangard, S., Oswald, E., Popp, T.: Power Analysis Attacks: Revealing the Secrets of Smart Cards. Springer, Heidelberg (2007)
13. Mangard, S., Pramstaller, N., Oswald, E.: Successfully attacking masked AES hardware implementations. In: Rao, J.R., Sunar, B. (eds.) CHES 2005. LNCS, vol. 3659, pp. 157–171. Springer, Heidelberg (2005)
14. Manral, V.: Cryptographic Algorithm Implementation Requirements for Encapsulating Security Payload (ESP) and Authentication Header (AH). RFC 4835 (April 2007), http://tools.ietf.org/html/rfc4835
15. Neiße, O., Pulkus, J.: Switching blindings with a view towards IDEA. In: Joye, M., Quisquater, J.-J. (eds.) CHES 2004. LNCS, vol. 3156, pp. 230–239. Springer, Heidelberg (2004)
16. National Institute of Standards and Technology. FIPS PUB 180-2. Secure Hash Standard (August 2002)
17. National Institute of Standards and Technology. FIPS PUB 198. The Keyed-Hash Message Authentication Code (HMAC) (March 2002)
18. Okeya, K.: Side channel attacks against HMACs based on block-cipher based hash functions. In: Batten, L.M., Safavi-Naini, R. (eds.) ACISP 2006. LNCS, vol. 4058, pp. 432–443. Springer, Heidelberg (2006)

19. Okeya, K., Iwata, T.: Side channel attacks on message authentication codes. In: Molva, R., Tsudik, G., Westhoff, D. (eds.) ESAS 2005. LNCS, vol. 3813, pp. 205–217. Springer, Heidelberg (2005)
20. Schellekens, D., Preneel, B., Verbauwhede, I.: FPGA vendor agnostic true random number generator. In: FPL 2006. 16th International Conference on Field Programmable Logic and Applications, pp. 139–144. IEEE (August 2006)
21. Steinwandt, R., Geiselmann, W., Beth, T.: A theoretical DPA-based cryptanalysis of the NESSIE candidates FLASH and SFLASH. In: Davida, G.I., Frankel, Y. (eds.) ISC 2001. LNCS, vol. 2200, pp. 280–293. Springer, Heidelberg (2001)
22. Tunstall, M., Hanley, N., McEvoy, R., Whelan, C., Murphy, C.C., Marnane, W.P.: Correlation power analysis of large word sizes. In: IET Irish Signals and Systems Conference (ISSC) 2007. IEEE (submitted, 2007)
23. Xilinx. Spartan-3 Generation FPGA User Guide (July 2007), http://direct.xilinx.com/bvdocs/userguides/ug331.pdf

Provably Secure Countermeasure Resistant to Several Types of Power Attack for ECC*

JaeCheol Ha[1], JeaHoon Park[2], SangJae Moon[2], and SungMing Yen[3]

[1] Dept. of Information Security, Hoseo Univ., 336-795, Korea
jcha@hoseo.edu
[2] School of Electrical Eng. and Computer Science, Kyungpook National Univ.,
702-701, Korea
{jenoon65,sjmoon}@ee.knu.ac.kr
[3] Dept. of Computer Science and Information Eng., National Central Univ.,
Chung-Li, Taiwan 320, R.O.C.
yensm@csie.ncu.edu.tw

Abstract. Recently, it has been shown that some cryptographic devices, such as smart card, RFID and USB token, are vulnerable to the power attacks if they have no defence against them. With the introduction of new types of power analysis attack on elliptic curve cryptosystem (ECC) which is implemented in these secure devices, most existing countermeasures against differential power analysis (DPA) are now vulnerable to new power attacks, such as a doubling attack (DA), refined power analysis attack (RPA), and zero-value point attack (ZPA). Mamiya et al. recently proposed a countermeasure (so-called BRIP) against the DPA, RPA, ZPA, and simple power analysis (SPA) by introducing a random initial value. Yet, the BRIP was also shown to be vulnerable to the address-bit DPA by Itoh et al. and the 2-torsion attack by Yen et al.. Accordingly, this paper proposes a secure countermeasure based on a message-blinding technique. A security analysis demonstrates that the proposed countermeasure is secure against most existing power attacks with just a few additional registers.

Keywords: ECC, Side channel attack, Power analysis attack, Smart card.

1 Introduction

In ubiquitous environments, some cryptographic devices become very useful tools to provide security services due to its portability, arithmetic power, storage capacity, and so on. In 1999, Kocher introduced power analysis attacks to cryptographic devices such as smart card, RFID, and USB token [15]. Since then, many power analysis attacks have been proposed and countermeasures presented

---

* This research was supported by the MIC of Korea, under the ITRC support program supervised by the IITA(IITA-2007-C1090-0701-0026).

S. Kim, M. Yung, and H.-W. Lee (Eds.): WISA 2007, LNCS 4867, pp. 333–344, 2007.

using various hardware and software techniques. Specifically, to implement elliptic curve cryptosystems (ECCs) with many cryptographic advantages, several types of countermeasure have been suggested, including a random scalar multiplication algorithm [5], random blinding on a point [5], random projective coordinate algorithm [5], and several approaches using special forms of elliptic curve (e.g., Montgomery form [9], Jacobian form [17], and Hessian form [13]). While Coron's countermeasures in [5] seemed to provide good security against a differential power analysis (DPA), recent research has highlighted new weaknesses related to new types of power analysis attacks. Coron's first countermeasure involves an additional computational overhead due to the large bit-length of the secret key, and his second countermeasure, the point blinding method, has been shown to be vulnerable to the Doubling Attack (DA) proposed by Fouque and Valette [16]. Furthermore, most randomization techniques (including Coron's third countermeasure, random elliptic curve isomorphism and random field isomorphism), which were originally considered to be secure against the DPA, have been shown to be vulnerable to the refined power analysis (RPA) proposed by Goubin [10] and a recent extension of the RPA, called the zero-value point attack (ZPA), proposed by Akishita et $al.$ [19]. Thus, at this time, none of the many countermeasures, including Coron's three methods, is secure against the above attacks.

To defeat these power attacks, Itoh et $al.$ proposed two countermeasures, the Randomized Linearly-transformed Coordinates(RLC) and the Randomized Initial Point(RIP) which scans the key from LSB to MSB [6]. In CHES-2004, Mamiya et $al.$ proposed a new countermeasure (called the BRIP [4]) which also uses a random initial point. However, this method is still vulnerable to the 2-torsion attack (($N - 1$) attack applied to an RSA system) based on exploiting specially chosen input messages and doesn't care about address-bit DPA. Even the exponent splitting(ES) method, thought to be secure against almost power attacks until now, can be threatened by the 2-torsion attack.

Accordingly, to solve the above mentioned problems of new vulnerability, this paper presents an enhanced countermeasure involving a message-blinding technique and Shamir's trick. The proposed countermeasure has several advantages compared with previous methods, providing a strong security against power analysis attacks using message-blinding multiplication with random point $P + R$ for each iterative operation. Additionally, we in detail give some fundamental reason and formulated analysis about power analysis attacks.

The rest of this paper is organized as follows. The next section describes the fundamental operations of an ECC and provides a brief review of power analysis attacks (including SPA, DPA, DA, RPA, ZPA, 2-torsion attack, and address-bit DPA). Section 3 then presents the proposed countermeasure based on an enhanced message-blinding technique. Previous power attack techniques are analyzed to prove the strength of the proposed countermeasure in Section 4, and some implementation considerations and final conclusions are given in Section 5, 6.

2   Elliptic Curve Cryptosystem and Power Attacks

2.1   Elliptic Curve Cryptosystems

The security of an ECC over finite group depends on the intractability of the elliptic curve analogue of the discrete logarithm problem. This problem has already been extensively studied and is well known to be computationally intensive.

An elliptic curve E over a finite group K is a set of points (x, y) that are solutions of a bivariate cubic equation. This curve has one point $\mathcal{O}$ at infinity that is the identity element of the group. For example, the elliptic curve defined on a field $K = GF(2^n)$ where n is prime, is the set of solution point (x, y) to an equation of the form

$$y^2 + xy = x^3 + ax^2 + b \tag{1}$$

with $a, b \in K$. Let $P = (x_1, y_1) \neq \mathcal{O}$ be a point, then the inverse of P is $-P = (x_1, x_1 + y_1)$. Let $Q = (x_2, y_2) \neq \mathcal{O}$ be a second point with $Q \neq -P$, the addition $P + Q$ can be computed as follows.

$$x_3 = \lambda^2 + \lambda + x_1 + x_2 + a$$

$$y_3 = \lambda(x_1 + x_3) + x_3 + y_1$$

where

$$\lambda = \frac{y_1 + y_2}{x_1 + x_2}.$$

And next is doubling operation $2P$.

$$x_3 = \lambda^2 + \lambda + a$$

$$y_3 = x_1^2 + \lambda x_3 + x_3$$

where

$$\lambda = x_1 + \frac{y_1}{x_1}.$$

To compute the subtraction of point $P = (x, y)$, add point $-P$. The addition of point P to itself d times is called a scalar multiplication by d and denoted as $Q = dP$. A binary algorithm is normally used to compute the scalar multiplication $Q = dP$. Here, we assume that d is a secret scalar integer and target information of attacker.

2.2   Power Analysis Attacks

To be resistant to the SPA attack, Coron proposed a simple countermeasure based on modifying the standard binary L-R method [5]. Nonetheless, even though the algorithm is resistant to the SPA attack, it remains vulnerable to the DPA and other power attacks. Coron suggested three countermeasures to protect against the DPA: randomizing the private exponent, blinding point P, and randomizing the projective coordinates. An improved version of Coron's third countermeasure has also been proposed by Joye and Tymen[14]. However, most countermeasures, including the above methods, have a computational overhead and are vulnerable to the DA, RPA, ZPA, and address-bit DPA.

In 2003, Goubin proposed a new power analysis, namely a refined power analysis (RPA), which assumes that an adversary can input adaptively chosen messages on elliptic curve points to the target scalar multiplication algorithm [10]. However, the RPA attack is still a threat to many countermeasures.

A ZPA is an extensive RPA attack, where the attacker uses a special point that has a zero-value on coordinate. Meanwhile, a ZPA attack utilizes an auxiliary register that may take a zero-value in the definition field [19]. Coron's third or random field isomorphism countermeasures do not protect against ZPA attack. Thus, to protect against RPA and ZPA attacks, the base point P or secret scalar d should be randomized.

The address-bit DPA is based on the fact that when data is loaded from various addresses, the power consumption changes in according to Hamming weight of addresses [7]. In [8], the authors used about 10,000 power traces to perform an address-bit DPA in their experiment. Also, they presented a practical countermeasure against address-bit DPA, which used the randomized addressing technique without additive computational cost.

2.3   The Mamiya *et al.*'s Method and the 2-Torsion Attack

To protect against the above new power attacks, Mamiya *et al.* recently proposed a countermeasure called the BRIP(Binary Random Initial Point) that uses a random point R. In their method, $dP + R$ is computed using the simple algorithm depicted in Fig. 1, then R is subtracted to get dP. Moreover, $(dP + (1\bar{1}\bar{1}\cdots\bar{1}\bar{1})R) - R$ is computed to protect against the SPA where $\bar{1}$ denotes -1. Kim *et al.* independently proposed an RSA version to protect against power attacks [2]. Yet, the RSA version should involve the computation of an inversion of a random number r because ECC version of BRIP uses a negative random point $-R$ shown as Fig. 1.

However, the BRIP was recently attacked using special input $(N - 1)$ data (so called $(N-1)$ attack) developed by Yen *et al.* in RSA or the 2-torsion attack in an ECC [18]. The attack uses the unique property of the BRIP, where the intermediate values during their execution are always the original ones plus a

Input: $d = (d_{n-1}, \cdots, d_0)_2$, P	
Output: $Q = dP$	
1.	$R =$ randompoint()
2.	$T[0] = R,\ T[1] = -R,\ T[2] = P - R$
3.	for i from $n - 1$ downto 0 do
3.1	$T[0] = 2T[0]$
3.2	$T[0] = T[0] + T[d_i + 1]$
4.	return($Q = T[0] + T[1]$)

Fig. 1. The binary expansion with RIP (BRIP)

random point R. Thus, if a malicious 2-torsion point G(a point which becomes $\mathcal{O}$ after a doubling operation, $2G = \mathcal{O}$) generated by an attacker is inputted into the algorithm, then the intermediate values will be R or $G + R$ in Step 3.2 of Fig. 1, which are dependent on a secret key d. Another approach to mount this attack is possible in the operation of Step 3.1. At the end of each iteration, there are only two possible computations, if $d_i = 0$, then $T[0] = 2R$, if $d_i = 1$, then $T[0] = 2(G+R)$. As only two possible keys can be derived, a trial-and-error approach attack can be used to select the correct d. In this 2-torsion attack, only one power consumption trace is needed. Even though this attack is applicable to special elliptic curves with a 2-torsion point, there is a point with an order of 2 for standard recommended curves over binary fields, although not over prime fields. So the BRIP has a similar security flaw, such as small subgroup attacks as presented in [11]. Also, BRIP has to be considered about address-bit DPA, because BRIP only uses constant three registers for every execution $(T[0], T[1], T[2])$.

2.4   The Exponent Splitting Method and the 2-Torsion Attack

As a countermeasure against the DPA, Clavier and Joye presented a method called ES-I(Exponent Splitting) that splits the scalar(exponent in exponentiation) and computes $dP = rP + (d - r)P$ for a random number r [1]. This ES-I requires at least twice the processing time. In another method(ES-II) by Ciet and Joye, the scalar multiplication is computed using $\lfloor d/r \rfloor (rP) + (d \bmod r)P$ [12]. In [4], Mamiya et al. also said that ES is a secure method against the DPA, RPA, and ZPA. However, the ES-I has recently been known to be vulnerable by Muller and Valette using various high-order attacks such as safe-error, fault, address-bit, and combined attacks[3]. Among these four attacks, only address-bit attack belongs to power attack.

Next, the 2-torsion attack is applied to ES-I. Suppose an attacker can find the 2-torsion point G and inputs it to compute rP. Even though rP can be computed with other power attack countermeasures, such as the BRIP or doubling-and-add-always algorithm, the attacker can derive a secret random number r and $d - r$ in two independent scalar multiplications using the 2-torsion attack. Thus, each term in ES-I should be computed using an algorithm resistant to all existing power attacks, including the 2-torsion attack. In the ES-II method, r is detected during the computation of $S = rP$ using 2-torsion attack. Also, $\lfloor d/r \rfloor$ and $(d \bmod r)$ are detected during the computation of $\lfloor d/r \rfloor S + (d \bmod r)P = \lfloor d/r \rfloor P + (d \bmod r)P$, because all intermediate values are 3 types P, $2P$ or $\mathcal{O}$ when r is odd. If r is even and input point is $G = 2P = \mathcal{O}$ then $S = rP = rG = \mathcal{O}$. The $(d \bmod r)$ are also detected during the computation of $(d \bmod r)P$.

3   New Countermeasure Against Power Analysis Attacks

This section describes the proposed countermeasure that can protect against all existing power attacks, including the SPA, DPA, DA, RPA, ZPA, 2-torsion attack, and address-bit DPA. The basic idea of the proposed countermeasure with message-blinding method is blind of a point using a random point $(P + R)$. Here, it is assumed that the number of points on the curves, $\#\varepsilon$ is n-bit. Thus, $t(P + R) + sR + (2^n - 1)(P + R)$ is finally computed instead of dP, where t and s are n-bit positive integers. The final result dP is obtained by computing

$$
\begin{aligned}
dP &= (k\#\varepsilon + d)P \\
&= (k\#\varepsilon + d - (2^n - 1))(P + R) + (\#\varepsilon - d)R + (2^n - 1)(P + R) \\
&= t(P + R) + sR + (2^n - 1)(P + R) \\
&= \sum_{i}^{n-1} 2^i(t_i(P + R) + s_iR + (P + R)),
\end{aligned}
\tag{2}
$$

where $\#\varepsilon R$ is equal to a point $\mathcal{O}$ at infinity. Now, let $t = k\#\varepsilon + d - (2^n - 1)$ and $s = \#\varepsilon - d$ be n-bit integers, then the smallest integer k is chosen such that $(k - 1)\#\varepsilon + d < (2^n - 1) < k\#\varepsilon + d$. Thus, k is 1 or 2. The core idea of the algorithm is the simultaneous scalar multiplication of the above three operations $t(P + R)$, sR, and $(2^n - 1)(P + R)$, as described in Fig. 2. By using a message-blinding technique, the intermediate values of the temporary registers used in each iteration are randomly changed.

Input: $d = (d_{n-1}, \cdots, d_0)_2$, P
Output: $Q = dP$
Pre-computation
1. $t = k\#\varepsilon + d - (2^n - 1)$, $s = \#\varepsilon - d$
2.   choose a random elliptic point R and random bits u, v
3. $T[00 \oplus uv] = P + R$, $T[01 \oplus uv] = P + 2R$, $T[10 \oplus uv] = 2P + 2R$, $T[11 \oplus uv] = 2P + 3R$
Evaluation
4. $Q = T[t_{n-1}s_{n-1} \oplus uv]$
5.   for i from $n - 2$ downto 0 do
5.1 $Q = 2Q$
5.2 $Q = Q + T[t_is_i \oplus uv]$
6.   return(Q)

Fig. 2. The proposed message-blinding scalar multiplication algorithm

Even if an attacker tries to input special points to attempt the RPA or ZPA, the proposed method remains effective, as point P is blinded by the random point R in Eq. (2). Point R should be changed for each scalar multiplication, otherwise the randomized projective coordinate technique can be used to generate a random point. Also, two random bit u and v can be used to defeat the address-bit DPA with just XORs. This method is a simple countermeasure by randomizing registers according to random bits during a scalar multiplication[8]. Therefore, the proposed countermeasure in Fig. 2 can protect against the power attacks (DPA, DA, RPA, ZPA, and address-bit DPA), as well as 2-torsion attack. Above mentioned roughly security analysis is summarized in Table 3.

Table 1. Comparison of security

Algorithm	SPA	DPA	DA	RPA/ ZPA	2-torsion attack	Address- bit DPA
Scalar Multiplication with Dummy Operation [5]	O	×	×	×	×	×
BRIP Algorithm [4]	O	O	O	O	×	×
Exponent Splitting Algorithm(ES-II) [12]	O	O	O	O	×	×
Proposed Algorithm	O	O	O	O	O	O

O : secure or support   × : insecure or not support.

4   Security Analysis

For a security analysis of the proposed countermeasure, it was assumed that the attacker could collect side-channel information, simulate a target algorithm in off-line using a guessed key, detect a resemblance when the same operation is done twice, and detect a register having a special point, for example, $(x, 0)$ or $(0, y)$. The following attack scenario describes the typical side-channel attack method.

- **Setup.** Attacker makes a chosen message set to input into the target device.
- **Challenge.** The device operates a cryptographic algorithm as soon as the attacker sends an input message. However, the device always leaks side-channel information during cryptographic operations. The attacker can measure this power signal.
- **Analysis.** The attacker analyzes the correlation between the input message and the side-channel information collected during the cryptographic operations. The attacker then deduces the real secret information used in certain operations by the device when adopting the countermeasure algorithm.

As seen in Fig. 3, P_i is the i-th input message and d is the secret key used in certain operations in the device. The device sends the cipher text $C_i = d \cdot P_i$ to the attacker along with side-channel information. Next, the security of the

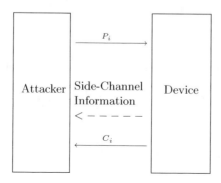

Fig. 3. Typical side-channel attack scenario

proposed countermeasure against existing power analysis attacks is evaluated using the analysis procedure in the side-channel attack scenario. The attacks are classified into two types using the power analysis model.

4.1 Attack Type-I

Assuming that the attacker already knows the key from MSB to the $(j-1)$-th bit of the secret key, the attacker guesses the j-th bit of the secret key, then analyzes the collected side-channel information using intermediate values resulting from the operation with P_i and from MSB to the j-th bit of the secret key. Among the existing power analysis attacks, the DPA, RPA, and ZPA can all be included in Attack Type-I.

Security against Attack Type-I. The attacker guesses the j-th secret key bit, and computes an intermediate value using an off-line simulation. The attacker then sends some messages to the device and monitors the symptoms of the power signal using side-channel information. By finding a special signal peak, the attacker confirms whether the guessed secret key is correct or not.

Theorem 1. The success probability of Attack Type-I, against the proposed countermeasure, is less than or equal to $\frac{1}{l}$. Here, l is the order of an EC over K.

Proof. We denote that this $f_d(\cdot)$ is a proposed algorithm with secret key d. The equation $f_{d_j}(P)$ represents an intermediate value after the operation of the proposed algorithm with point P and the secret key from MSB to the j-th bit, where d is the n-bit secret key and d_i is the i-th bit of the secret key. Then we have

$$f_{d_j}(P) = \sum_{i=0}^{j-1} t_{n-1-i} \cdot 2^{j-1-i}(P+R) + \sum_{i=0}^{j-1} s_{n-1-i} \cdot 2^{j-1-i}R + \sum_{i=0}^{j-1} 2^{j-1-i}(P+R)$$

$$= \sum_{i=0}^{j-1}(t_{n-1-i}+1) \cdot 2^{j-1-i}P + \sum_{i=0}^{j-1}(t_{n-1-i}+s_{n-1-i}+1) \cdot 2^{j-1-i}R. \quad (3)$$

Above Eq. (3) consists of $\sum_{i=0}^{j-1}(t_{n-1-i}+1) \cdot 2^{j-1-i} \cdot P$ and $\sum_{i=0}^{j-1}(t_{n-1-i}+s_{n-1-i}+1) \cdot 2^{j-1-i} \cdot R$, that is, the intermediate value which contains P and a random value. Even though the attacker guesses the j-th bit of the secret key, then computes an intermediate value using the guessed secret key and analyzes the side-channel information, they cannot obtain any useful information when the guessed intermediate value is not correct. So, the probability of an attacker correctly computing $f_{d_j}(P)$ is $\frac{1}{l}$, where l is the order of an EC over K, because of intermediate value's random factor.

Because $\frac{1}{l}$ is the probability of making correct intermediate value only at once, DPA attacker's success probability decreases. In other word, DPA attacker should collect power consumption signal of correct intermediate value at the some threshold ratio among the collected power consumption signals, in case of guessed key is correct, in order to have a special signal peak during analysis procedure.

And, if RPA, ZPA attacker guesses intermediate value with R according to secret key d, then attack success probability can be $\frac{1}{l}$.   □

If the attacker does not know the random point R or intermediate multiplicative results of R, which are stored at the end of every iteration, they can obtain some information about the secret key with negligible probability. Therefore, this analysis confirms that the proposed countermeasures can resist the Attack Type-I, including DPA, RPA, and ZPA.

4.2   Attack Type-II

The attacker creates a malicious message that causes a distinguishable pattern according to a secret key during a cryptographic operation, then observes the pattern in the measured side-channel information. Thus, the attacker can exploit the secret key that causes the distinguishable pattern. Among the existing power analysis attacks, a DA and 2-torsion attack can be included as Attack Type-II which is based on simple power analysis.

Security against Attack Type-II. The attacker creates a malicious message $2P$ or G(2-torsion point on an elliptic curve) that causes a significant pattern, then inputs the message and observes the side-channel information.

Plus, $f'_d(\cdot)$ is denoted as an add-and-double-always algorithm. The core idea of a doubling attack is summarized as follows. The intermediate value $f'_{d_j}(P)$ of an add-and-double-always algorithm with P and from MSB to the j-th bit of the secret key d is represented as follows.

$$
\begin{aligned}
f'_{d_j}(P) &= \sum_{i=0}^{j-1} d_{n-1-i} \cdot 2^{j-1-i} \cdot P \\
&= d_{n-1} \cdot 2^{j-1} \cdot P + \ldots + d_{n-j+1} \cdot 2^1 \cdot P + d_{n-j} \cdot 2^0 \cdot P \quad (4)
\end{aligned}
$$

In the case of d_{n-j} is zero, the above equation can be transformed as follows.

$$
\begin{aligned}
f'_{d_j}(P) &= d_{n-1} \cdot 2^{j-1} \cdot P + \ldots + d_{n-j+1} \cdot 2^1 \cdot P \\
&= d_{n-1} \cdot 2^{j-2} \cdot 2P + \ldots + d_{n-j+1} \cdot 2^0 \cdot 2P = f'_{d_{j-1}}(2P) \quad (5)
\end{aligned}
$$

When d_{n-j} is zero, doubling related to $j+1$-th bit with input P and doubling related to the j-th bit with input point $2P$ are the same operation with an identical intermediate value. Thus, the attacker can exploit the secret key by detecting the same power consumption signal during two scalar multiplications, inputted P and $2P$.

Theorem 2. The proposed countermeasure is secure against Attack Type-II.

Proof. Following equations are intermediate value of the proposed countermeasure with P and from MSB to the $(j+1)$-th bit of the secret key in Fig. 2.

Step 5.1 $Q = 2 \cdot f_{d_j}(P)$ $\hfill(6)$

Step 5.2 $Q = Q + (t_{n-j-1} + 1) \cdot P + (t_{n-j-1} + s_{n-j-1} + 1) + R$

$$= \sum_{i=0}^{j}(t_{n-1-i} + 1) \cdot 2^{j-i}P + \sum_{i=0}^{j}(t_{n-1-i} + s_{n-1-i} + 1) \cdot 2^{j-i}R$$

$$= f_{d_{j+1}}(P) \hfill(7)$$

As shown in the Eq. (7), the random value $((t_{n-1-i} + 1) \cdot P + (t_{n-1-i} + s_{n-1-i} + 1) \cdot R)$ is always added to each iteration. Moreover, even if the attacker inputs a malicious message P' instead of P, the intermediate value of every step contains the random value of $(t_{n-1-i} + s_{n-1-i} + 1) \cdot R$ regardless of the point P'. Therefore, the 2-torsion attack cannot be applied by any adversary.

Here, $f_{d_{j+1}}(P)$ consists of two terms which are the intermediate value, which contains P, and a random value $\sum_{i=0}^{j}(t_{n-1-i} + s_{n-1-i} + 1) \cdot 2^{j-i} \cdot R$ that can be written as follows.

$$\sum_{i=0}^{j}(t_{n-1-i} + s_{n-1-i} + 1) \cdot 2^{j-i} \cdot R$$

$$= (t_{n-1} + s_{n-1} + 1) \cdot 2^{j} \cdot R + ...$$
$$+ (t_{n-j} + s_{n-j} + 1) \cdot 2^{1} \cdot R + (t_{n-j-1} + s_{n-j-1} + 1) \cdot 2^{0} \cdot R \hfill(8)$$

Suppose a special case, where the random value R', for next operation, is updated by $2R$ for the next scalar multiplication, i.e. $R' = 2R$. By the fact that $(t_{n-j-1} + s_{n-j-1} + 1)$ can not be zero. That is, no attacker can make equation $f_{d_j}(P) = f_{d_{j-1}}(2P)$, even if random point was updated by $2R$. Due to the randomness of the intermediate value, it is difficult to make the same value as $f_{d_j}(P)$ for any bit iteration, even when inputting a message. $\hfill\square$

Consequently, an attacker who does not know the random point R cannot acquire any information about the secret key using Attack Type-II. As a result of security analysis about the proposed countermeasure, the attacker who don't know about the random point R cannot acquire any information about the secret key in actually, using Attack Type-I or Attack Type-II.

5   Implementation Consideration

To compare the efficiency, the number of required registers and computation load is considered. Following Table 2 shows the brief comparison where, n is bit length of secret key, D is doubling operation and A is addition operation.

In practical implementation, to provide randomness for the random point, it is assumed that the initial random point R is generated by finding the x-coordinate randomly and computing the corresponding y-coordinate. A simple way is to update the stored random point by $R' = kR$ (k is a small integer ($k \geq 2$)). However, we want to emphasize that if the RIP is updated by $R' = 2R$

Table 2. The Number of Required Register and Computational Cost

Algorithm	♯ of register	Computational Cost
Scalar Multiplication with Dummy Operation [5]	2	$n \cdot D + n \cdot A$
BRIP Algorithm [4]	3	$n \cdot D + (n + 3) \cdot A$
Exponent Splitting Algorithm(ES-II) [12]	4	$2n \cdot D + 2n \cdot A$
Proposed Algorithm	5	$(n + 1) \cdot D + (n + 4) \cdot A$

for each scalar multiplication, in BRIP this can be attacked by doubling attack by selecting P and $2P$ as inputs. The reason is that the intermediate values of BRIP are always $X + R$ type where X is the original (unmasked) intermediate values and R is the RIP (Random Initial Point) in each scalar multiplication. But, the intermediate values of ours are $X + Y$ type where Y is a random value but not the simple RIP. So, even though the random point is updated by $R' = 2R$, our countermeasure is not vulnerable to the doubling attack. Furthermore, the RSA version of proposed algorithm does not involve the computation of an inversion because ECC version have no negative random point $-R$.

6 Conclusion

Most existing countermeasures against power attacks are vulnerable to the new types of attack, such as the DA, RPA, ZPA, and address-bit DPA. In addition, the more recently proposed countermeasure, BRIP, is also vulnerable to 2-torsion attack and address-bit DPA. Accordingly, this paper presented a countermeasure against the new types of power attacks, as well as the 2-torsion attack and address-bit DPA that threatens the BRIP and ES method. Moreover, we offer the formulated security analysis about proposed countermeasure. The proposed algorithm has a similar computational cost when compared to previous SPA countermeasures and only requires three additional registers. Note, the proposed countermeasure can be applied to RSA as well as ECC systems without any inversion, and has a strong security based on a message-blinding technique.

References

1. Clavier, C., Joye, M.: Universal exponentiation algorithm. In: Koç, Ç.K., Naccache, D., Paar, C. (eds.) CHES 2001. LNCS, vol. 2162, pp. 300–308. Springer, Heidelberg (2001)
2. Kim, C., Ha, J., Kim, S., Kim, S., Yen, S., Moon, S.: A secure and practical CRT-based RSA to resist side channel attacks. In: Laganà, A., Gavrilova, M., Kumar, V., Mun, Y., Tan, C.J.K., Gervasi, O. (eds.) ICCSA 2004. LNCS, vol. 3043, pp. 150–158. Springer, Heidelberg (2004)
3. Muller, F., Valette, F.: High-order attacks against the exponent splitting protection. In: Yung, M., Dodis, Y., Kiayias, A., Malkin, T.G. (eds.) PKC 2006. LNCS, vol. 3958, pp. 315–329. Springer, Heidelberg (2006)

4. Mamiya, H., Miyaji, A., Morimoto, H..: Efficient countermeasure against RPA, DPA, and SPA. In: Joye, M., Quisquater, J.-J. (eds.) CHES 2004. LNCS, vol. 3156, pp. 343–356. Springer, Heidelberg (2004)
5. Coron, J.: Resistance against differential power analysis for elliptic curve cryptosystems. In: Koç, Ç.K., Paar, C. (eds.) CHES 1999. LNCS, vol. 1717, pp. 292–302. Springer, Heidelberg (1999)
6. Itoh, K., Izu, T., Takenaka, M.: Efficient countermeasure against power analysis for elliptic curve cryptosystems. In: Smart Card Research and Advanced Applications VI – CARDIS 2004, pp. 99–113. Kluwer Academic Pub, Dordrecht (2004)
7. Itoh, K., Izu, T., Takenaka, M.: Address-differential power analysis of cryptographic scheme OK-ECDH and OK-ECDSA. In: Kaliski Jr., B.S., Koç, Ç.K., Paar, C. (eds.) CHES 2002. LNCS, vol. 2523, pp. 129–143. Springer, Heidelberg (2003)
8. Itoh, K., Izu, T., Takenaka, M.: A practical countermeasure against address-bit differential power analysis. In: D.Walter, C., Koç, Ç.K., Paar, C. (eds.) CHES 2003. LNCS, vol. 2779, pp. 382–396. Springer, Heidelberg (2003)
9. Okeya, K., Sakurai, K.: Power analysis breaks elliptic curve cryptosystems even secure against the timing attack. In: Roy, B., Okamoto, E. (eds.) INDOCRYPT 2000. LNCS, vol. 1977, pp. 178–190. Springer, Heidelberg (2000)
10. Goubin, L.: A refined power-analysis attack on elliptic curve cryptosystems. In: Desmedt, Y.G. (ed.) PKC 2003. LNCS, vol. 2567, pp. 199–210. Springer, Heidelberg (2002)
11. Law, L., Menezes, A., Qu, M., Solinas, J., Vanstone, S.: An efficient protocol for authenticated key agreement at Technical Report CORR 98-05, Univ. of Waterloo (1998)
12. Ciet, M., Joye, M. (Vertually)Free randomization technique for elliptic curve cryptography. In: Qing, S., Gollmann, D., Zhou, J. (eds.) ICICS 2003. LNCS, vol. 2836, pp. 348–359. Springer, Heidelberg (2003)
13. Joye, M., Quisquater, J.: Hessian elliptic curves and side-channel attacks. In: Koç, Ç.K., Naccache, D., Paar, C. (eds.) CHES 2001. LNCS, vol. 2162, pp. 402–410. Springer, Heidelberg (2001)
14. Joye, M., Tymen, C.: Protections against Differential Analysis for Elliptic Curve Cryptography. In: Koç, Ç.K., Naccache, D., Paar, C. (eds.) CHES 2001. LNCS, vol. 2162, pp. 377–390. Springer, Heidelberg (2001)
15. Kocher, P., Jaffe, J., Jun, B.: Differential power analysis. In: Wiener, M.J. (ed.) CRYPTO 1999. LNCS, vol. 1666, pp. 388–397. Springer, Heidelberg (1999)
16. Fouque, P., Valette, F.: The doubling attack– why upwards is better than downwards. In: D.Walter, C., Koç, Ç.K., Paar, C. (eds.) CHES 2003. LNCS, vol. 2779, pp. 269–280. Springer, Heidelberg (2003)
17. Liardet, P., Smart, N.: Preventing SPA/DPA in ECC systems using the Jacobi form. In: Koç, Ç.K., Naccache, D., Paar, C. (eds.) CHES 2001. LNCS, vol. 2162, pp. 391–401. Springer, Heidelberg (2001)
18. Yen, S., Lien, W., Moon, S., Ha, J.: Power Analysis by Exploiting Chosen Message and Internal Collisions - Vulnerability of Checking Mechanism for RSA-Decryption. In: Dawson, E., Vaudenay, S. (eds.) Mycrypt 2005. LNCS, vol. 3715, pp. 183–195. Springer, Heidelberg (2005)
19. Akishita, T., Takagi, T.: Zero-value point attacks on elliptic curve cryptosystem. In: Boyd, C., Mao, W. (eds.) ISC 2003. LNCS, vol. 2851, pp. 218–233. Springer, Heidelberg (2003)

Risk & Distortion Based K-Anonymity

Shenkun Xu and Xiaojun Ye

Key Laboratory for Information System Security, School of Software
Tsinghua, Beijing 100084, China
xsk@mails.tsinghua.edu.cn, yexj@tsinghua.edu.cn

Abstract. Current optimizations for K-Anonymity pursue reduction of data distortion unilaterally, and rarely evaluate disclosure risk during process of anonymization. We propose an optimal K-Anonymity algorithm in which the balance of risk & distortion (RD) can be equilibrated at each anonymity stage: we first construct a generalization space (GS), then, we use the probability and entropy metric to measure RD for each node in GS, and finally we introduce releaser's RD preference to decide an optimal anonymity path. Our algorithm adequately considers the dual-impact on RD and obtains an optimal anonymity with satisfaction of releaser. The efficiency of our algorithm will be evaluated by extensive experiments.

1 Introduction

K-Anonymity model proposed by Samarati & Sweeney [17,18] can resolve various issues of linkage attack in microdata releasing. The core requirement is that each value of quasi-identifier (QI [3]) in released microdata should appears at least K times. Generalization is the main anonymization mechanism for QI attributes: it extends QI values according to their logical hierarchies to guarantee the probability of identification for each individual is no more than $1/K$.

Microdata usability is the key concern of K-Anonymity, and previous optimizations focus on elusion of data distortion. However the following issues deserve to be investigated:

1) Previous K-Anonymity algorithms don't implement generalization options adequately. E.g. for a single QI attribute, all its values should be generalized into same layer in its hierarchy [17,19]; for multiple QI attributes, their generalizations can't be implemented synchronously [18]. As a result, some efficient generalization options might get lost. We propose a generalization space (GS) construction, where all candidates of generalization are enumerated at each anonymity stage.

2) Although K-Anonymity model guarantees the disclosure risk for each released individual is no more than $1/K$, the risk might be larger than $1/K$ before end of anonymization. And risk can make interaction with distortion, which means less distortion generally induces smaller reduction of risk. Therefore, the risk factor can't be ignored along anonymity path. We propose a probability model to evaluate risk and an entropy model to evaluate distortion, which can measure the integrated dual-impact on risk & distortion (RD) for anonymity.

S. Kim, M. Yung, and H.-W. Lee (Eds.): WISA 2007, LNCS 4867, pp. 345–358, 2007.
© Springer-Verlag Berlin Heidelberg 2007

3) Current K-Anonymity algorithms don't have theoretical mechanism to choose candidate from possible generalizations. E.g. The *Datafly* [17] system makes generalization on QI attribute which has largest number of distinct values. We adopt utility theory to make decision of generalization option, which integrates releaser's preference about RD.

The remainder of this paper is organized as follows: In Sect. 2 we construct a GS to enumerate all eligible candidates. Then we proceed in Sect. 3 to present the RD metric and outline the search strategy of anonymity path. In Sect. 4 we design a greedy K-Anonymity algorithm involved with issues discussed above. In Sect. 5 we experimentally evaluate the effectiveness of our solution. In Sect. 6 we review some related works and conclude the paper with our future work in Sect. 7.

2   Construction of Generalization Space

First, we use set partition theory to enumerate generalizations for each QI attribute. Second, we make combination of multiple QI attributes' generalization to construct a GS which supplies entire candidates for search of anonymity path.

2.1   Enumeration of Generalizations for Single Attribute

Many studies [10,19] generalize values into the same layer in each QI attribute's hierarchy. This mode is so strict that lots of information might be lost. In fact, we can generalize them into different layers and make them reasonable according to their logical topology. We first introduce generalization for single QI attribute formally, and then enumerate all possible generalizations based on set partition algorithm.

Definition 1 (Generalization). *For a QI attribute's value domain $D = \{v_1, v_2, \ldots, v_n\}$, if there exists $D = D_1 \cup D_2 \cup \ldots \cup D_k$ and $\forall i, j \in \{1, 2, \ldots, k\}$ $D_i \cap D_j = \phi$, then $D_1, D_2, \ldots, D_k$ is a generalization g for D, each D_i is a subset of generalization g.*

We use set partition theory in combinational mathematics [12] to enumerate all generalizations. The generalization sequence defined below is used to map generalization in Algorithm 1.

Definition 2 (Generalization Sequence). *For a value domain $D = \{v_1 \prec v_2 \prec \ldots \prec v_n\}$ and a given generalization g, sort all subsets of g relied on their minimum value, label them start with 0 by order, mark all elements in one subset with same label. Then the labels of v_i construct a generalization sequence for g, this is called serializing of g.*

Example 1. For a value domain $D = \{x_1 \prec x_2 \prec \ldots \prec x_6\}$, the generalization is $g = \{\{x_2, x_4\}, \{x_1, x_6, x_3\}, \{x_5\}\}$, we can get $\left\langle \frac{\{x_1, x_6, x_3\}}{0}, \frac{\{x_2, x_4\}}{1}, \frac{\{x_5\}}{2} \right\rangle$, so the generalization sequence is $\kappa = \langle 0, 1, 0, 1, 2, 0 \rangle$.

Definition 3 (Max Generalization Sequence). *For a sequence κ of generalization g, $\lambda = \langle \lambda_0, \lambda_1, \ldots, \lambda_{n-1} \rangle$ is the max generalization sequence of g, where $\lambda_i = max\{\kappa_0, \kappa_1, \ldots, \kappa_i\}$.*

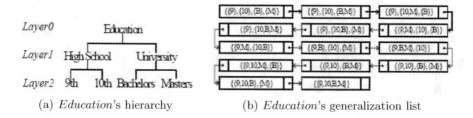

(a) *Education*'s hierarchy   (b) *Education*'s generalization list

Fig. 1. Enumeration of generalizations for attribute: *Education*. Each rectangle in (b) stands for a generalization and 9 is *9th*, 10 is *10th*, B is *Bachelors* and M is *Masters*.

The definitions above are used in Algorithm 1 which is a revision of set partition algorithm [15]. In algorithm *SGE*, the initial generalization needs each value to be a subset separately and the generalization sequence is $\kappa = \langle 0, 1, \ldots, n-1 \rangle$. This algorithm guarantees that each generalization can be generated only once, which is circumstantiated in [7].

   Algorithm 1. Single attribute generalization enumeration algorithm (*SGE*)

```
Input: value domain Dₐ, generalization g;
Output: list GL starts with g and contains all siblings of g.
  1 Serialize g based on Dₐ, get the generalization sequence κ according to definition 2;
  2 Get the max generalization sequence λ for κ according to definition 3;
  3 For i=|Dₐ|-1 to 1;
     If κᵢ>λ₉, then κᵢ=κᵢ-1, λᵢ=λᵢ₋₁, and from j=i+1 to |Dₐ|-1;
        Set κⱼ=λⱼ=λᵢ+j-1;
        Get the next sibling g′ for g according to updated κ;
        GL→head=g, g→next=SGE(Dₐ,g′);
        Return GL.
  4 GL→head=g, g→next=null, Return GL.
```

Fig. 2. Enumeration algorithm for single attribute' generalization

Although algorithm *SGE* can get all generalizations, some of them are not coincidental to attribute's hierarchy. So the ineligible node in generalization list should be removed. This is called generalization validation. The eligible generalization node should be: 1) For each generalization subset, all child of subset's least common ancestor should be gathered into it together. 2) All subsets shouldn't have same values. 3) The combination of subsets should contain all values. The eligible generalization list of Fig.1(b) is shown in Fig.3(a).

2.2 Combination of Generalizations for Multiple Attributes

Synchronous generalization for multiple attributes can make efficient results than asynchronous one. In this part, we make combination of generalizations for multiple attributes to gather multidimensional generalizations in GS.

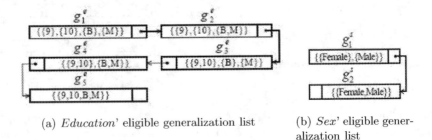

(a) *Education'* eligible generalization list

(b) *Sex'* eligible generalization list

Fig. 3. Eligible generalization list for *Education* and *Sex*

Definition 4 (Generalization Space). *The QI attributes are formed by $QI = \{a_1, a_2, \ldots, a_n\}$, and generalizations of $a_i \mid i \in \{1, 2, \ldots, n\}$ are $g^{a_i} = \{g_1^{a_i}, g_2^{a_i}, \ldots, g_{m_i}^{a_i}\}$, then the generalization space of QI is $GS = \{(g_{i_1}^{a_1}, g_{i_2}^{a_2}, \ldots, g_{i_n}^{a_n}) \mid 1 \leq i_j \leq m_j\}$. And the number of elements in GS is $\prod_{i=1}^{n} m_i$.*

The Algorithm 2 needs all QI attributes' own eligible generalization list, which can be combined into a GS for QI. The process of combination guarantees that all generalizations can be generated once and only once, which is shown as follows:

Algorithm 2. Multiple attributes generalization space construction algorithm (MGS)

Input: eligible generalization node $G=\{g^1, g^2, \ldots, g^n\}$ of multiple QI attributes $\{a^1, a^2, \ldots, a^n\}$, initial start index *isn*;

Output: generalization space tree GT with root G.

1 GT=*makeNode(G)*;

2 For *i=isn* to *n*

    If g^i→*next*≠*null*

    Then set $g=g^i$→*next*, $G'=\{g^1, \ldots, g^{i-1}, g, g^{i+1}, \ldots, g^n\}$ and

    GT→*AddChilds(MGS(G',i))*;

3 Return GT.

Fig. 4. Construction algorithm for multiple QI attributes' generalization space

In algorithm MGS, the GS is formed by a tree and the initial eligible generalization root node contains all heads of each QI attribute's generalization list. The initial start index is $isn = 1$ and the generalization tree for *Education* and *Sex* is shown in Fig.5.

3 Search Strategy of Anonymity Path

We need to measure utilities of possible generalizations at each K-Anonymity stage in GS. The measure factors include disclosure risk and data distortion of generalizations. This section presents models of RD measure and gives the search strategy of anonymity path by releaser's preference.

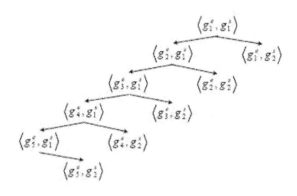

Fig. 5. *Education* & *Sex'* generalization tree for Fig.3

3.1 Risk Measure

Frequency of individual's QI value is the main factor of risk measure. In a microdata PT, for each tuple r, we set $freq(qi(r))$ as the frequency of r's QI value. If $freq(qi(r))$ is less than K, then r is an unsafe tuple. We define risk as a series of ordered pairs [9]:

$$risk \equiv \{(R_1, P_1), \ldots, (R_i, P_i), \ldots, (R_n, P_n)\} \ . \tag{1}$$

$R_i(i = 1, 2, \ldots, n)$ is a series of unexpected occurrences, and $P_i(i = 1, 2, \ldots, n)$ is the probability of R_i. E.g. R_i represents that the ith tuple is unsafe, and $P_i = \frac{1}{freq(qi(r))}$ is the probability of R_i. To normalize risk metric, we set the risk of PT as follows:

$$Risk = \frac{\sum\limits_{r \in PT, freq(qi(r)) < K} \frac{1}{freq(qi(r))}}{\#(r)} \ . \tag{2}$$

The risk value calculated by Formula 2 falls into interval $[0 \sim 1]$. When each tuple has a unique QI value, the risk of PT reaches maximum 1, which indicates that each tuple can be identified by linkage attract; when each tuple has a frequency larger than K for QI value, the risk of PT can be ignored as zero.

3.2   Distortion Measure

Shannon entropy [22] is a useful tool to measure information and appears to capture most successfully the general trend indicated by all measures. It is given by:

$$Entropy = - \sum_{qi \in QI(PT)} freq\,(qi) \times \log\,(freq\,(qi))\,. \qquad (3)$$

Where $QI(PT)$ is the value domain of QI attributes in PT. This formula leads to the natural interpretation of *Shannon entropy* as the expectation of a random variable that takes values $\log(freq(qi))$ with probability $freq(qi)$.

Shannon entropy has been used as a distortion measure by other authors [13]. They consider adjusted entropy, whereas we use pre-anonymity entropy minus post-anonymity entropy to quantify distortion. We denote the normalized distortion as:

$$Distortion = \frac{Entropy\,(QI_{\mathrm{pre}}) - Entropy\,(QI_{\mathrm{post}})}{\log\,(\#\,(r))}\,. \qquad (4)$$

In Formula 4, the distortion of generalization for PT falls into interval $[0 \sim 1]$. When each tuple in original PT has a unique QI value and all of them have been generalized into the same value, the distortion reaches maximum 1, which is the suppressive distortion; when all frequencies are not changed after generalization, the distortion can be ignored as zero.

3.3   Preference Model

To make trade offs between risk and distortion which are inversely proportional to each other, we adopt utility theory raised in insurance economics, which can make qualitative and quantitative analysis in search strategy of anonymity path.

In economics, utility estimates satisfaction of people with some substance or service. *Welfare* function is one of the common utility functions. Meanwhile, risk aversion measure based on utility is an important issue of insurance. James Cox & Vjollca Sadiraj [6] proposed a risk aversion model using two parameters: income and wealth, which comprehensively takes influence of them into account. In insurance, these issues are solved by multi-attribute utility theory ($MAUT$) [8].

Definition 5 (Utility Function). *Define $\mu(risk, distortion)$ as the utility function about RD, which describes the comprehensive utility of anonymity. Theoretically, data holder wants to release microdata with less risk and distortion. So the utility function needs to satisfy: $\frac{\partial \mu}{\partial risk} < 0$ and $\frac{\partial \mu}{\partial distortion} < 0$.*

This utility function has two dimensional parameters and can be predigested into three categories (Table 1). The additive one is adopted in the rest of paper.

Table 1. Styles of function with two parameters

	Function styles with parameters X and Y
Additive utility function	$\mu(X,Y) = a \cdot \mu_X(X) + b \cdot \mu_Y(Y)$
Multiplicative utility function	$\mu(X,Y) = (a \cdot \mu_X(X)) \cdot (b \cdot \mu_Y(Y))$
Synthesis utility function	$\mu(X,Y) = a \cdot \mu_X(X) + b \cdot \mu_Y(Y) + c \cdot \mu_X(X) \cdot \mu_Y(Y)$

Definition 6 (Satisfaction Degree). *The satisfaction degree (SD) indicates the degree of releaser's satisfaction with the process of anonymity. It is relative to current utility value and the changes of utility. We can define it formally:* $\rho = \partial'' \mu$. *When* $\rho < 0$, *it's a descending SD; when* $\rho > 0$, *it's an ascending SD; when* $\rho = 0$, *it's an invariable SD.*

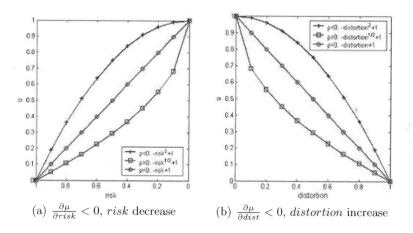

(a) $\frac{\partial \mu}{\partial risk} < 0$, *risk* decrease   (b) $\frac{\partial \mu}{\partial dist} < 0$, *distortion* increase

Fig. 6. Relationships between μ and *risk/distortion* separately

The change of risk is one of the factors for SD. E.g. some releasers' satisfaction increases as risk decreases, which is strong risk aversion (Sra, ascending SD in Fig.6(a)); contrarily, some releasers' satisfaction decreases as risk decreases, which is weak risk aversion (Wra, descending SD in Fig.6(a)); and if satisfaction is not changed as risk decreases, it is neutral risk aversion (Nra, invariable SD in Fig.6(a)).

The SD is also relative to change of distortion. E.g. some releasers' satisfaction decreases as distortion increases, which is strong distortion aversion (Sda, descending SD in Fig.6(b)); contrarily, some releasers' satisfaction increases as risk increases, which is weak distortion aversion (Wda, ascending SD in Fig.6(b)); and if satisfaction is not changed as distortion increases, it is neutral distortion aversion (Nda, invariable SD in Fig.6(b)).

The risk-distortion aversion categories are combined as nine kinds of utility function (Table 2). The form of them can be polynomial, exponential and logarithm. To unify RD measure metric, the polynomial utility function is adopted below.

Table 2. Nine kinds of polynomial utility functions

Preference	$\rho(risk)$	$\rho(distortion)$	Example of utility functions
Sra-Sda	ascending	descending	$\mu = -a \cdot \sqrt{risk} - b \cdot dist^2 + c$
Sra-Nda	ascending	invariable	$\mu = -a \cdot \sqrt{risk} - b \cdot dist + c$
Sra-Wda	ascending	ascending	$\mu = -a \cdot \sqrt{risk} - b \cdot \sqrt{dist} + c$
Nra-Sda	invariable	descending	$\mu = -a \cdot risk - b \cdot dist^2 + c$
Nra-Nda	invariable	invariable	$\mu = -a \cdot risk - b \cdot dist + c$
Nra-Wda	invariable	ascending	$\mu = -a \cdot risk - b \cdot \sqrt{dist} + c$
Wra-Sda	descending	descending	$\mu = -a \cdot risk^2 - b \cdot dist^2 + c$
Wra-Nda	descending	invariable	$\mu = -a \cdot risk^2 - b \cdot dist + c$
Wra-Wda	descending	ascending	$\mu = -a \cdot risk^2 - b \cdot \sqrt{dist} + c$

The utility functions above stand for nine categories of releaser's preference, which treat RD differently. At each anonymity stage, releasers use some utility function to balance RD according to their different preference for search of anonymity path.

4   Risk & Distortion Based K-Anonymity Algorithm

The RD based K-Anonymity algorithm ($RDKA$) is made up of two main factors: 1) Risk-distortion measures, which is the foundation of algorithm. We adopt RD measure model and utility function to satisfy requirement of releaser's preference among different generalization options. 2) Greedy approach. At each anonymity step, utility is estimated for each node in GS and the best anonymity path is selected to converge to optimal anonymity. Meanwhile, we use greedy idea to generalize only unsafe tuples, which leads less distortion. The $RDKA$ algorithm is described below.

Algorithm 3. Risk & Distortion based K-Anonymity algorithm ($RDKA$))

Input: microdata PT, quasi-identifier $QI=\{a_1,a_2...,a_n\}$, K, hierarchy trees for QI attributes HT_i, $i=1,2,...,n$ and utility function of releaser RDP;
Output: K-Anonymity table KAT.
  1 Initiate $KAT=PT$, $freq=frequency\_list(QI(KAT))$;
  2 If there is a tuple r in KAT, and $freq(qi(r))<K$, then repeat execute follows:
    2.1 Label all unsafe tuples with $flag(r)=\kappa$;
    2.2 If the number of unsafe tuples is less than K, then delete them and break;
    2.3 Construct all generalization lists for single QI attribute using SGE algorithm;
    2.4 Set up or update generalization space using MGS algorithm;
    2.5 Generalize unsafe tuples in generalization space and estimate its RD;
    2.6 Select the best generalization node using RDP, update KAT and $freq$;
  3 Return KAT.

Fig. 7. $RDKA$ algorithm

In step 2.5 of $RDKA$, the root node of GS should be removed because it means there isn't any change for generalization and infinite loop will be generated. In step 2.2, if the number of unsafe tuples is less than K, any generalization can't satisfy requirement of K-Anonymity. These tuples should be deleted to avoid disclosure.

5   Experiment

This section verifies the efficiency of our solution and compare it with classic anonymity algorithms ($Datafly$ [17], $Basic Incognito$ [10], $Naive Classfly^+$ [24]). The microdata is American census [25] about annual income in 1994. It contains sensitive attribute $\{Salary\}$ and QI attributes $\{Marital\text{-}status, Race,$ $Sex, Education\}$. The default premise condition of experiment without special illumination is: $Sra\text{-}Sda$ Preference, $QI = \{Marital\text{-}status, Race, Sex\}$ and the total number of tuples is 32561. All experiments were implemented on an Intel Pentium IV3.4 GHz PC with 1 GB RAM and MS Visual C++ IDE.

5.1   Information Loss Analysis

Fig.8 shows the relationships of $Distortion \sim K$ and $Distortion \sim \#(tuple)$. For all algorithms, the distortion increases as K increases, because the number of unsafe tuples is increased and stricter global generalization is used to satisfy requirement of anonymity; the distortion decreases as the number of tuples increases, because the number of tuples in same anonymity group increases, there are more tuples satisfying requirement of anonymity, and the distortion of generalization will be decreased.

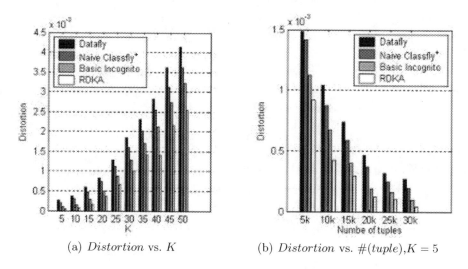

(a) $Distortion$ vs. K (b) $Distortion$ vs. $\#(tuple), K = 5$

Fig. 8. Comparison of distortion using different K or $\#(tuple)$

RDKA & *Incognito* both have less distortion than others because they adopt greedy idea, which generalizes unsafe tuples and select the best generalization at each anonymity stage. *Incognito* generalizes values into the same layer in hierarchy and makes more distortion than *RDKA*, which generalizes values into different layers.

Meanwhile, in Fig.8(a), *RDKA* makes more distortion as K increases, but there are some exceptions, where distortion won't be changed or even be decreased. The reasons are: 1) the requirement of anonymity might be satisfied because of large number of unsafe tuples as K increases. E.g. suppose the number of unsafe tuples is $num(k)$ and $num(35) = 50$, $num(40) = 100$, if all of their unsafe tuples are generalized into two groups, then the former is $\frac{25}{group}$ and the latter is $\frac{50}{group}$. Obviously, the latter satisfies requirement of anonymity, whereas the former still keeps its unsafe tuples risky and needs more generalization with larger distortion; 2) as K increases, the number of unsafe tuples changes a bit and same generalization might be used for different K. This is more frequent when K increases tardily; 3) when K reaches boundary, the distortion will keep smooth. This is because nearly all attributes are generalized completely, which makes distortion to be closed to each other.

5.2   Releaser's Preference Analysis

The distortions for different preference will differ with each other. Fig.9 shows the relationship between distortion and releaser's preference. In (a), all releasers detest risk and *Wda* gets more information loss because it has less weight in utility function than *Sda*. In (b), all releasers choose *Sda*, and *Wra* makes less information loss because it has less weight in utility function than *Sra*. In (c), if the risk aversion is stronger and distortion aversion is weaker, the distortion will be larger because all their weights in utility function are extremely conduce to distortion.

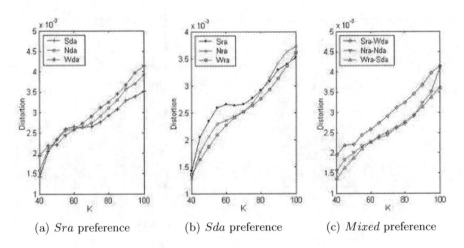

     (a) *Sra* preference   (b) *Sda* preference   (c) *Mixed* preference

Fig. 9. Comparison of distortion using different preferences

However, in some cases, this rule will be broken. E.g. when $K = 50$ in Fig.9(a), Sda makes more information loss than Wda. This is because Sda aims to keep data quality and adds weight of distortion in utility function, which can't make risk to be decreased quickly and need more generalizations. The anonymity path becomes longer with more distortion. So for different K, releaser can choose different utility functions to satisfy their preference and get more control modes.

5.3   Elapsed Time Analysis

Fig.10 shows the complexity of elapsed time for $RDKA$. In (a), the elapsed time increases acutely as the number of QI increases. The reason is: the value domain and number of QI attributes become larger; a huge GS is generated and needs more time to estimate utilities. However, other algorithms implement one generalization at each step, the elapsed time increases only with number of steps, so the time rises smoothly.

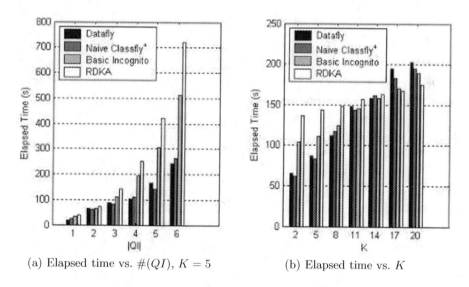

(a) Elapsed time vs. $\#(QI)$, $K = 5$ (b) Elapsed time vs. K

Fig. 10. Comparison of elapsed time using different QI or K

In (b), the elapsed time of $RDKA$ increases smoother than other algorithms as K increase. The reasons are: 1) for $RDKA$, no matter how K is changed, the GS is approximate and anonymity path is nearly same to each other. The little increase of elapsed time for $RDKA$ is used for more unsafe tuples' generalization; 2) other algorithms need more steps of generalization and the path is longer as K increases. E.g. when K is very large, $RDKA$ needs only one step of generalization and other algorithms need at least five steps to satisfy requirement of anonymity. So $RDKA$ use main of elapsed time to construct GS and the elapsed time has little relation with K.

Therefore, if the $\#(QI)$ is small, the value domain is narrow and K is very large, $RDKA$ gets efficient anonymity with less distortion and elapsed time. But if the value domain is large, $RDKA$ uses more time to construct GS and expends time for better data quality. In addition, the single attribute generalization link contains many invalid nodes, which will be deleted according to hierarchy tree. If we can get all eligible node directly, the elapsed time will be decreased faster.

6   Related Works

K-Anonymity has been studied for more than ten years, which gradually becomes an important preprocess of data mining and its risk and distortion measures are hot issues in this field. They are summarized as follows:

Optimization of K-Anonymity. Many algorithms[2,4,5,10,21] lucubrate in generalization for K-Anonymity. We can divide them into two categories: 1) represented by [5,10] studies on global generalization of QI attributes, which modifies all values into one topological layer. 2) represented by [4,21] studies how to generalize QI values into different layers, which reduce the information loss for masking operations.

Measure of Information Loss. Realizing optimal K-Anonymity is NP-Hard [1,14]. Therefore, lots of algorithms can only converge to the optimal K-Anonymity gradually: [4,5,17,21] adopt greedy idea, while [2,10,16,19] use expanded upgrade idea to optimize the information loss due to K-Anonymity. Whereas, measure of information loss usually adopts straightforward category measures [5], hierarchy measures [2] and other methods based on special application scenarios [16,17].

Extension of K-Anonymity. [11] proposes the multiple QI attributes anonymity mechanism and applies K-Anonymity to classification scenarios; [24] discusses multiple constraints of K-Anonymity; [13] studies the homogeneity attack and proposes diversity solution; [23] proposes personalization of K-Anonymity, which considers individuals' privacy purpose; and [20] studies the K-Anonymity using sequential releasing, etc. Future work might consider techniques for integrating these and other extensions into the scalable algorithm described in this paper.

7   Conclusion

In this paper, we adopt RD based decision-making mechanism in K-Anonymity, which use utility function to make tradeoffs between risk and distortion at each anonymity stage and choose the optimal anonymity path. Meanwhile, we develop GS construction, which enumerates all eligible generalization nodes. The experiment shows that our solution can achieve more efficient anonymity with less distortion and provide optional manners for releasers' preference control. This is a new approach for dealing with RD conflict and also leads to a full-scale study for privacy protection in microdata releasing.

Acknowledgments

This work was supported by NSFC 60673140 and HTRDP 2007AA01Z156.

References

1. Aggarwal, G., Feder, T., Kenthapadi, K., Motwani, R., Panigrahy, R., Thomas, D., Zhu, A.: Approximation algorithms for k-anonymity. Journal of Privacy Technology no. 20051120001 (2005)
2. Bayardo, R., Agrawal, R.: Data privacy through optimal k-anonymization. In: ICDE, pp. 217–228 (2005)
3. Bettini, C., Wang, X.S., Jajodia, S.: The Role of Quasi-identifiers in k-Anonymity Revisited. TR 11-06, DICo, University of Milan, Italy (July 2006)
4. Fung, B.C.M., Wang, K., Yu, P.S.: Top-down specialization for information and privacy preservation. In: ICDE, pp. 205–216 (2005)
5. Iyengar, V.: Transforming data to satisfy privacy constraints. In: SIGKDD, pp. 279–288 (2002)
6. Cox, J.C., Sadiraj, V.: Small-and Large-Stakes Risk Aversion: Implications of Concavity Calibration for Decision Theory. Games and Economic Behavior 56(1), 45–60 (2006)
7. Kawano, S.-I., Nakano, S.-I.: Constant Time Generation of Set Partitions. IEICE Trans. Fundamentals E88-A(4) (2005)
8. Keeney, R., Raiffa, H.: Decisions with Multiple Objectives: Preferences and Value Trade Offs. John Wiley & Sons, Chichester (1976)
9. Kevin, J., Soo, H.: How much is enough? A risk-management approach to computer security[D]. School of Engineering, Stanford University (2000)
10. Lefevre, K., Dewitt, D.J., Ramakrishnan, R.: Incognito: Efficient full-domain k-anonymity. In: SIGMOD, pp. 49–60 (2005)
11. LeFevre, K., DeWitt, D.J., Ramakrishnan, R.: Mondrian multidimensional k-anonymity. In: ICDE (2006)
12. Kai-cheng, L., Hua-ming, L.: Combinational Mathematics, 3rd edn. pp. 179–184. Tsinghua University Press, Beijing (in Chinese) (2002)
13. Machanavajjhala, A., Gehrke, J., Kifer, D.: l-diversity: Privacy beyond k-anonymity. In: ICDE (2006)
14. Meyerson, A., Williams, R.: On the complexity of optimal k-anonymity. In: PODS. Proc. Of the 23rd ACM Symposium on Principles of Database Systems, pp. 223–228 (2004)
15. Orlov, M.: Efficient Generation of Set Partitions (2002), http://www.informatik. uni-ulm.de/ni/Lehre/WS03/DMM/Software/partitions.pdf
16. Samarati, P.: Protecting respondents' identities in microdata releas. IEEE TKDE 13(6), 1010–1027 (2001)
17. Samarati, P., Sweeney, L.: Protecting privacy when disclosing information: k-anonymity and its enforcement through generalization and suppression. SRI Technical Report SRI-CSL-98-04 (1998)
18. Sweeney, L.: K-anonymity: A model for protecting privacy. International Journal on Uncertainty, Fuzziness, and Knowledge-based Systems 10(5), 557–570 (2002)
19. Sweeney, L.: Achieving k-anonymity privacy protection using generalization and suppression. International Journal on Uncertainty, Fuzziness and Knowledge-based Systems 10(5), 571–588 (2002)

20. Wang, K., Fung, B.C.M.: Anonymizing sequential releases. In: KDD. Proc. of the 12th ACM SIGKDD International Conference on Knowledge Discovery and Data Mining, Philadelphia, PA, pp. 414–423 (2006)
21. Wang, K., Yu, P.S., Chakraborty, S.: Bottom-up generalization: A data mining solution to privacy protection. In: ICDM, pp. 249–256 (2004)
22. Willenborg, L.C.R.J., de Waal, T.: Elements of Statistical isclosure Disclosure Control. Lecture Notes in Statistics. Springer, New York (2000)
23. Xiao, X., Tao, Y.: Personalized Privacy Preservation. In: Proc. of the SIGMOD, Chicago, Illinois, USA, June 27-29, 2006 (2006)
24. Xiao-chun, Y., Xiang-yu, L., Bin, W., Ge, Y.: K-Anonymization Approaches for Supporting Multiple Constraints. Journal of Software 17(5), 1222–1231 (2006), http://www.jos.org.cn/1000-9825/17/1222.htm
25. ftp://ftp.ics.uci.edu/pub/machine-learning-databases/adult

Optimizing Quality Levels and Development Costs for Developing an Integrated Information Security System[*]

Myeonggil Choi and Sangmun Shin

Department of Systems Management Engineering, INJE University, 607 Obang-dong, Gimhae, Gyeongnam, 621-749, Korea
{mgchoi,sshin}@inje.ac.kr

Abstract. Increased Internet threats make many kinds of information security systems performing various functions, which can often be combined into functions of an integrated information security system. To load various functions to an integration information system, much development resources should be invested to a development life cycles. The constraints of development resources force developers not to achieve a balanced quality of the system. To attain the specified quality of the system within the given development resources, the relative weights among quality factors of the system on a development life cycle should be measured and a balance between the levels of quality and development costs should be optimized, simultaneously. This paper suggests the relative weights of the quality factors influencing operations of the system, and shows an optimal solution for the quality levels and development costs using desirability function (DF). For optimization, this paper employs AHP as multiple criteria decision making (MCDM) technique and DF.

1 Introduction

Rapid growing Internet threats force organizations to deploy many kinds of information security systems, which perform various functions from detecting penetration to encrypting communication channels. A burden of purchasing costs and a discomfort management make the various functions of many kinds of information security systems transformed to functions of an integrated information security system in the industry world [7,8]. An integrated information security system can perform functions of firewall, intrusion detection, intrusion prevention, virus vaccine and virtual packet networks (VPN) systems. Currently, many integrated information security systems are adopted in Korea government and related institutions [9]. Deploying various security functions to an integrated information security system demands that many quality factors should be balanced on a development life cycle within the given resources. Constraints of development resources make developers focus mainly on developing functions of the system. Therefore, other quality factors on a development life cycle, which could be often less attracted than those of functionality, could cause the system to frequently halt and malfunction [7]. The failure of distributing development resources to overall quality factors makes organizations exposed to Internet threats.

---

[*] This work was supported by the 2006 Inje University research grant.

S. Kim, M. Yung, and H.-W. Lee (Eds.): WISA 2007, LNCS 4867, pp. 359–370, 2007.

To solve this problem, two kinds of approaches should be considered, simultane ously. First, the relative weights among the quality factors of the system should be measured by comparing the importance of the quality factors. The quality factors, which can influence the operation of an integrated information security system, could be regarded as reliability, usability, maintainability and functionality. Second, an optimal solution with consideration of tradeoff between the quality levels and development costs should be suggested by calculating the relative weights of quality factors using desirability function (DF). To solve the tradeoff, developers who charge in an integrated information security system usually distribute development costs with their experience.

This paper suggests the relative weights of the quality factors influencing operations of the system, and shows an optimal solution associated with the levels of quality and development costs using DF. This paper employs analytic hierarchy process (AHP) as multiple criteria decision making (MCDM) to decide the relative weights of the quality factors on a development life cycle, and DF to optimize the levels of the system quality and development costs. To illustrate the proposed approach, we use ISEM (High Secure Engineering Methodology), which has been created in a Korea security research institution and has been used to develop integrated information security systems.

2   Measuring the Relative Weights of Quality Factors

To obtain highly qualitative information security systems, the security engineering methodologies such as CC, ITSEC, SSE-CMM, SPICE have been introduce. The security engineering methodologies could be divided into two approaches in terms of assuring objects. The first approach is a product assurance approach and the second approach is a production process approach. The product assurance approach focuses the assurance of products through evaluating functions and assurances of information security systems. CC (Common Criteria), ITSEC (Information Technology Security Evaluation Criteria) and TCSEC (Trusted Computer Security Evaluation Criteria) could be included in the product assurance approach. Although the product assurance approach could assure high quality, it takes high costs and periods. The production process approach focuses the assurance of production process. The production process approach shifts its focus from assuring products to assuring production processes. SSE-CMM (System Security Engineering-Capability Mature Model), SPICE, ISO 9000-3 (Guidelines for the development supply and maintenance of software) could be included in the production process approach. Although the costs and periods of the production process approach are lower than those of the product assurance approach, the assurance level should have been lower than that of the first approach. The product assurance approach has been frequently introduced in developing high reliable information [12,13,16].

A security research institution in Korea has tried to solve a trade-off between costs and quality. The institute in Korea has created ISEM assuring both products and production process. ISEM could make up for shortcomings of the product assurance

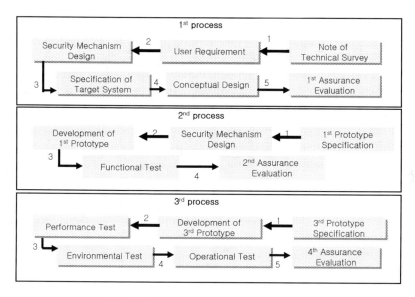

Fig. 1. The development life cycle of ISEM

approach and could reflect the advantages of the production process approach [12]. In this paper, we assume ISEM for the purpose of deciding the relative weights of quality factors on the development life cycle. ISEM has also been applied to develop integrated information security systems. As fig.1 shows, ISEM consists of 3 developmental processes, which are the 1st process (design process), the 2nd process (prototypes development process), and the 3rd process (test process).

To apply quality factors to ISEM, we select quality factors from ISO/IEC 9126 characteristics of software quality [2,10]. To select appropriate characteristics of software quality as quality factors, we formed a focus group, which consists of 4 researchers, 3 developers and 3 faculties. The members of the focus group have experience in developing information security systems. We asked the focus group to select the appropriate software quality characteristics as scales to measure the relative weights among quality factors in developing an integrated information system. As table 1 shows, they select 4 quality factors and 13 quality sub-factors as criteria to measure relative weights among qualities of an integrated information security system. The quality factors and quality sub-factors identified through the survey were used as input of AHP.

Table 1. Quality factors and sub-factors used in AHP technique

Factors	Sub-factors
Functionality	suitability, accuracy, interoperability, security
Reliability	maturity, fault tolerance, recoverability
Usability	understandability, operability
Maintainability	analyzability, changeability, stability, testability

To measure the relative weights of the quality factors influencing quality of an integrated information security system on the development life cycle, we conduct AHP as MCDM. AHP helps to set priorities and to make the best decision when both qualitative and quantitative aspects of a decision need to be considered. It serves as a framework for decision maker to structure complex decision problems and to provide judgments based on knowledge, experience [14]. We prepare a questionnaire based on the hierarchy of the quality factors and the quality sub-factors. In the questionnaire, pairwise comparisons are made between all the factors at each level in the hierarchy. The pairwise comparison process elicits qualitative judgmental statements that indicate the strength of the decision maker's preference in a particular comparison. Saaty suggests the use of a 1-9 scale to quantify the strength of decision maker's feeling between any two alternatives with respect to a given attribute [14]. An explanation of this scale is presented in table 2. We send 20 questionnaires to developers and evaluators, who have participated in developing and evaluating integrated information security systems. We asked them to assign weight values to the each quality factors and subfactors on the development life cycle of ISEM. The number of returned questionnaire is 11 and the return rate is 55 %.

Table 2. Scale used for pairwise comparison

Intensity of importance	Definition	Explanation
1	Equal importance	Both factors contribute equally to the objective or criteria
3	Weak importance of one over another	Experience and judgment slightly favor one factor over another
5	Essential or strong importance	Experience and judgment strongly favor one factor over another
7	Very strong or demonstrated importance	A factor is flavored very strongly over another, its dominance demonstrated in practice
9	Absolute importance	The evidence favoring one factor over another is unquestionable

Table 3 shows results of AHP evaluation analysis, which shows the weights of the quality factors. The weights of the quality factors could be applied to develop an integrated information system on the life cycle. In AHP technique, Geometric Consistency Index (GCI) is calculated for the verification of the result of AHP. When the value of GCI is less than 0.3526, 0.3147 (n=4, n=3, CR=0.1), respectively, the evaluation of experts can be considered meaningful [11]. As the values of GCI of the AHP are under 0.3526, 0.2147(n=3, n= 4, CR=0.1), the results of evaluation could be seen as meaningful.

Table 3. Results of AHP evaluation analysis

Quality factors	Quality Sub-factors	1st process		2nd process		3rd process	
		global weight	ra nk	global weight	ra nk	global weight	ra nk
Functionali ty	Suitability	0.1670	2	0.1386	2	0.0392	12
	Accuracy	0.0716	6	0.1689	1	0.0346	13
	interoperability	0.0799	4	0.1168	3	0.0505	9
	Security	0.0793	5	0.0843	5	0.0439	10
reliability	Maturity	0.0993	3	0.0746	7	0.1018	3
	fault tolerance	0.0672	9	0.0590	9	0.1359	2
	recoverability	0.0732	8	0.0644	8	0.0885	7
usability	understandabilit y	0.1968	1	0.1152	4	0.1580	1
	Operability	0.0793	7	0.0765	6	0.0888	5
Maintainab ility	analyzability	0.0265	10	0.0269	10	0.0418	11
	changeability	0.0212	11	0.0254	12	0.0563	8
	Stability	0.0195	12	0.0201	13	0.0979	4
	Testability	0.0193	13	0.0293	11	0.0866	6

In the 1st process, the ranks of understandability, suitability, maturity, interoperability and security are the 1st, the 2nd, the 3rd, the 4th, and 5th, respectively. In the 2nd process, accuracy, suitability, interoperability, understandability, and security rank the 1st, the 2nd, the 3rd, the 4th, and 5th.respectively. In the 3rd process, understandability,fault tolerance, maturity, stability, and operability rank the 1st, the 2nd, the 3rd, the 4th, and 5th.respectively. Although the ranks of each quality sub-factor in each process are different, understandability, suitability, maturity, interoperability and security are regarded as important quality sub-factors. The weights of the quality sub-factors could be used as a key scale to distribute the development resources for developing an integrated information security system on a development life cycle. Developers, who are in charge of developing integrated information security systems, can control quality of the systems, referring the weights.

3 Optimizing the Levels of Quality and Development Costs on ISEM

When an integrated information security system is developed, there exists a tradeoff between two primary objectives (i.e., the levels of a system quality and its associated development costs) in real industrial situations [4,6]. A high level of development resource in developing an integrated information security system usually incurs a high development cost. To achieve a specific quality factor of an integrated information security system, a high level of the development resource should be assigned to the quality factors. On the other hand, a low level of the development resource reduces a cost in developing an integrated information security system, resulting to the considerably lower quality level of the system. Thus, determining the level of the development resource involves a tradeoff between the levels of the system quality and the development costs.

In order to facilitate the economic tradeoff, researchers typically express quality in monetary terms using a quality function. One of the most applicable methods to the development of the system is a DF approach that is first introduced by Harrington [5]. This DF approach could be explained as following. If the preference of a decision-maker can be assessed, the optimal solution to a multi-objective problem can be found by maximizing the preference function. Once relevant information is received from the developer, the preference structure can be expressed as a functional form. However, it is usually very difficult to obtain an exact representation of the preference function. In this paper, the preference function for the quality factors, called DFs, are obtained by AHP discussed in the previous chapter.

For the cost-effective development, the DF approach can be used to optimize the two objectives (i.e., the levels of the system quality and costs of developing an integrated information security system) as an approximate representation of the preference, resulting to deciding the levels of the system quality considering development costs. Any quality levels of a development resource can be mapped onto DF, which ranges from zero to one. A zero-level of desirability implies that the quality level may not be acceptable, while one-level of desirability can be considered as the satisfactory quality level. Thus, the DF can be obtained by transforming a quality level into a desirability value. This is one of the most useful approaches for optimizing multiple objectives in order to use the simultaneous optimization technique [15].

The primary objective of using DF is to find the optimal level of a development resource in order to maximize overall desirability. DF is modified by Derringer and Suich [3], Borror [1], and Shin [15] proposed the optimization model using DF as follows:

$$\text{Maximize} \quad D = (d_1 \cdot d_2 \cdots d_m)^{1/m} = \left(\prod_{i=1}^{m} d_i \right)^{1/m} \tag{1}$$

$$\text{Subject to} \quad 0 \le d_i \le 1$$

where D and m represent the overall desirability which are the geometric mean of the number of the quality levels. Individual desirability d_i represents the desirability of achieving the goal set for particular the quality level, which is defined by fig. 2. If any of the individual quality factors is completely undesirable, then the overall desirability is also completely undesirable. Similarly, the overall desirability is 1 if and only if all of the individual quality factors are completely desirable. The optimal operating conditions are chosen to maximize the overall desirability $D = (d_1 \cdot d_2 \cdots d_m)^{1/m}$ with m quality levels. There are two different types of DF defined by characteristics: smaller-the-better (S-type) that is associated with the quality factors and larger-the-better (L-type) that is associated with the costs. Fig. 2 provides these two types of DFs and their graphical views.

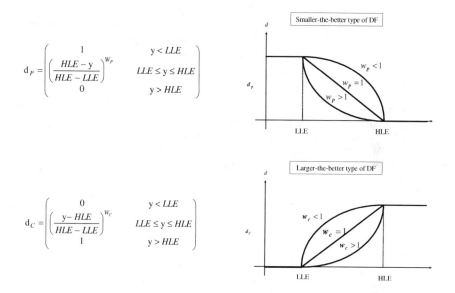

$$d_P = \left(\begin{array}{ll} 1 & y < LLE \\ \left(\dfrac{HLE - y}{HLE - LLE} \right)^{W_P} & LLE \leq y \leq HLE \\ 0 & y > HLE \end{array} \right)$$

$$d_C = \left(\begin{array}{ll} 0 & y < LLE \\ \left(\dfrac{y - HLE}{HLE - LLE} \right)^{W_C} & LLE \leq y \leq HLE \\ 1 & y > HLE \end{array} \right)$$

Fig. 2. Two types of DF(S and L type)

where LLE, HLE, d_p, and d_c are denoted by the lowest level of the resource in developing an integrated information security system, the highest level of the resource in developing an integrated information security system, the system quality levels and development costs of an integrated information security system, respectively. Superscripts, w_p and w_c, are denoted by the weights based on the AHP results to accommodate the nonlinear effect of a preference and cost structures, respectively. If the values are set to one, the desirability functions are linear.

Table 4 shows a process to transform the global weights of sub-factors in AHP to superscripts in a DF approach. We could calculate 0.0769, 0.0193, and 0.1968 as average, minimum, maximum of global weight, respectively. To get transformed superscripts, we establish 1, 100, and 0.01 as average, minimum, maximum in a DF approach, respectively.

In table 4, Min AHP $[W_{y_i}]$ (2) could be obtained through comparing the values of AHP $[W_{y_i}]$ (1) with the average of AHP $[W_{y_i}]$ (8). If the values of AHP $[W_{y_i}]$ are greater than the average of AHP $[W_{y_i}]$ (0.0769), 0.0769 could be assigned to (2). On the other hand, if the values of AHP $[W_{y_i}]$ are smaller than the average of AHP $[W_{y_i}]$, the minimum of AHP $[W_{y_i}]$ (0.0193) could be assigned to the values of MIN AHP $[W_{y_i}]$. Max AHP $[W_{y_i}]$ (3) could be obtained as MIN AHP $[W_{y_i}]$. If AHP $[W_{y_i}]$ is greater than 0.0769, 0.1968 could be assigned to the values of MAX AHP $[W_{y_i}]$. On the other hand, if AHP $[W_{y_i}]$ is smaller than 0.0769, 0.0769 could be assigned to the values of MAX AHP $[W_{y_i}]$.

Table 4. DF quality weights of the 1ˢᵗ process

Sub-factors (Y_i)	AHP $[W_{y_i}]$ (1)	Min AHP $[W_{y_i}]$ (2)	Max AHP $[W_{y_i}]$ (3)	Min $[W_{y_i}]$ DF (4)	Max $[W_{y_i}]$ DF (5)	Transf ormed $[W_{y_i}]$ (6)
suitability	0.1670	0.0769	0.1968	1	100	75.434
accuracy	0.0716	0.0193	0.0769	0.01	1	0.9078
interoperability	0.0799	0.0769	0.1968	1	100	3.4928
security	0.0793	0.0769	0.1968	1	100	2.9759
maturity	0.0993	0.0769	0.1968	1	100	19.457
fault tolerance	0.0672	0.0193	0.0769	0.01	1	0.8329
recoverability	0.0731	0.0193	0.0769	0.01	1	0.9352
understandability	0.1967	0.0769	0.1968	1	100	100
operability	0.0792	0.0769	0.1968	1	100	2.9280
analyzability	0.0264	0.0193	0.0769	0.01	1	0.1328
changeability	0.0211	0.0193	0.0769	0.01	1	0.0414
stability	0.0194	0.0193	0.0769	0.01	1	0.0125
testability	0.0193	0.0193	0.0769	0.01	1	0.0100
Min (7)	0.0193	Average(8)		0.0769	Max (9)	0.1968

Min $[W_{y_i}]$ DF (4) could be obtained through assigning the average of DF (8), and the minimum of DF (7). If the values of (2) are 0.0193, then 0.01(the minimum of DF) could be assigned. On the other hand, if the values of (2) are 0.0769, 1 (the average of DF) could be assigned. Max $[W_{y_i}]$ DF (5) could be obtained as Min $[W_{y_i}]$ DF. If the values of (3) are 0.1968, then 100 (the maximum of DF) could be assigned. On the other hand, if the values of (3) are 0.0769, 1 (the average of DF) could be assigned.

Finally, transformed weights for utilizing desirability function can be calculated by

$$W_{T_i} = Max[W_{y_i}]_{DF} - \frac{\left(Max\ AHP[W_{y_i}] - AHP[W_{y_i}]\right)\left(Max[W_{y_i}]_{DF} - Min[W_{y_i}]_{DF}\right)}{\left(Max\ AHP[W_{y_i}] - Min\ AHP[W_{y_i}]\right)} \quad (2)$$

As table 4 shows, the quality levels of understandability should be increased to 100, suitability 75.434, maturity 19.457, interoperability 3.4928, security 2.9759, and operability 2.9280. The levels of the quality sub-factors, which can be considered as important in the table 4, appropriately represent the nature of the 1ˢᵗ development process. In the 1ˢᵗ process of ISEM, user requirement analysis and conceptual design are stressed. For complete user requirement analysis and conceptual design of an integrated information system, the quality sub-factors, which are understandability, suitability, maturity, interoperability, security, and operability, should be naturally stressed as table 4 shows. The prototype in the 2ⁿᵈ process should reflect the user requirements and conceptual design and can operate in a secure way. As table 5 shows, the high levels of the quality sub-factors such as accuracy, operability, and security can reflect the nature of the 2nd process. In 3rd process which mainly focuses on the test of the 2nd prototype, the quality sub-factors such as fault-tolerance, stability, maturity, and recoverability could be considered important. The results of the DF approach, therefore, well reflect the different purposes of each development process.

Table 5. DF quality weights of the 2nd and 3rd process

Process	2nd Process			3rd Process		
Sub-factors (Y_i)	Min $[W_{y_i}]$ DF	Max $[W_{y_i}]$ DF	Trans formd $[W_{y_i}]$	Min $[W_{yi}]$ DF	Max $[W_{yi}]$ DF	Trans formed $[W_{yi}]$
suitability	1	100	67.434	0.01	1	0.1175
accuracy	1	100	100	0.01	1	0.0100
interoperability	1	100	43.978	0.01	1	0.3827
security	1	100	8.9235	0.01	1	0.2269
maturity	0.01	1	0.9597	1	100	31.341
fault tolerance	0.01	1	0.6885	1	100	73.036
recoverability	0.01	1	0.7811	1	100	15.104
understandability	1	100	42.164	1	100	100
operability	0.01	1	0.9931	1	100	15.498
analyzability	0.01	1	0.1278	0.01	1	0.1794
changeability	0.01	1	0.1030	0.01	1	0.5181
stability	0.01	1	0.0100	1	100	26.677
testability	0.01	1	0.1703	1	100	12.769
2nd Process	MIN	0.0193	AVG	0.0769	MAX	0.1968
3rd Process	MIN	0.0020	AVG	0.0769	MAX	0.1689

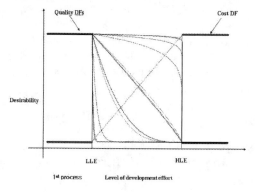

Fig. 3. Desirability functions for the quality levels and development cost on the 1st process

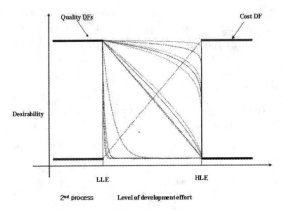

Fig. 4. Desirability functions for the quality levels and development cost on the 2nd process

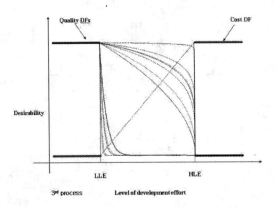

Fig. 5. Desirability functions for the quality levels and development cost on the 3rd process

We can optimize the levels of system quality and development costs using DFs. As shown in Figs. 3, 4, and 5, different DFs can be obtained because different weights are assigned to the quality sub-factors based on the results of AHP while assuming an equal weight for development costs. The optimal solution for the level of the each quality sub-factor and its associated development cost can be obtained at the cross points of Quality DFs and Cost DF. At the cross points, developers can assign an optimal development resource to the each quality sub-factor.

4 Conclusion

Many organizations deploy integrated information security systems to protect their information resources. The failure of an effective distribution of development resources to the quality factors on a development life cycle could make the systems frequently half and malfunction. To solve this problem, this paper suggested the weight values of quality factors as criteria, which direct developers to distribute development resources on a development life cycle and try to optimize the quality levels and development costs based on the DF approach.

To identify the quality factors influencing the quality of an integrated information security system on the development life cycle, we surveyed an opinion of a focus group. Based on the quality factors identified through the survey, we conducted AHP and found the relative weights of the quality factors on the development life cycle of ISEM. With the results of AHP, we obtained transformed weights of the quality factors. Finally, we elicited an optimal solution for the levels of the system quality and development costs.

An optimal solution provides a guidance to invest an amount of development resource to each quality factor in consideration of development costs. The relative quality weights and transformed weights used in the DF approach could be used to solve the tradeoff between the levels of the system quality and development costs when an organization tries to develop an integrated information security system. In this paper, we assume a fixed development costs to utilize the DF approach. The approach, suggested in this paper, could be applied to manage the quality levels and development costs in developing other information security systems. The development costs could be different in each organization. To overcome shortcomings of our research, we need to obtain transformed weights of development costs with the DF approach as the levels of the calculated system quality

References

1. Borror, C.M.: Mean and Variance Modeling with Qualitative Responses: A Case Study. Quality Engineering 11(1), 141–148 (1998)
2. Côté, et al.: The evolution Path for Industrial Software Quality Evaluation Methods Applying ISO/IEC 9126: 2001 Quality Model: 2001 Quality Model: Example of MITRE's SQAE Method. Software Quality Journal 13, 17–39 (2005)
3. Derringer, G.C., Suich, R.: Simultaneous Optimization of Several Response Variables. Journal of Quality Technology 12, 214–219 (1980)
4. Eloff, M., Solms, S.H.: Information Security Management, Hierarchical Framework for Various Approaches. Computers & Security 19, 243–256 (2000)
5. Harrington Jr., E.C.: The Desirability Function. Industrial Quality Control 21, 494–498 (1965)
6. Hefner, R., Monroe, W.: System Security Engineering Capability Maturity Model. In: Conference on Software Process Improvement (1997)
7. http://www.itstv.net/broad/news_list.asp?opt=contents&wrd=&page=2&status=list
8. http://www.3com.com/en_US/jump_page/embedded_firewall.html
9. The list of certified products http://www.ncsc.go.kr/
10. ISO/IEC: Software Engineering-Product Quality-Part1: Quality Model (2001)
11. Aguarón, J., et al.: The Geometric Consistency Index: Approximated threshold. European Journal of Operation Research Wood, C. and Snow, K.: ISO 9000 and information, Security, Computer & Security 147(1), 137–145 (2003)

12. Choi, M., et al.: An Empirical Study of Quality and Cost Based Security Engineering. In: Chen, K., Deng, R., Lai, X., Zhou, J. (eds.) ISPEC 2006. LNCS, vol. 3903, Springer, Heidelberg (2006)
13. Varnovsky, N.P., Zakharov, V.A.: On the Possibility of Provably Secure Obfuscating Programs. In: Broy, M., Zamulin, A.V. (eds.) PSI 2003. LNCS, vol. 2890, pp. 91–102. Springer, Heidelberg (2004)
14. Satty, T.L.: Decision Making for Leaders: The Analytical Hierarchy Process for Decision in a Complex World. RWS Publications (1995)
15. Shin, S.M., Cho, B.R.: Trade-off Studies on Process Parameters: A Robust Design Perspective. In: The 11th Industrial Engineering Research Conference, Orlando, FL (2002)
16. Wood, C., Snow, K.: ISO 9000 and information. Security, Computer & Security 14(4), 287–288 (1995)

ICRep: An Incentive Compatible Reputation Mechanism for P2P Systems*

Junsheng Chang, Huaimin Wang, Gang Yin, and Yangbin Tang

School of Computer, National University of Defense Technology,
HuNan Changsha 410073, China
cjs7908@163.com

Abstract. In peer-to-peer (P2P) systems, peers often must interact with unknown or unfamiliar peers without the benefit of trusted third parties or authorities to mediate the interactions. Trust management through reputation mechanism to facilitate such interactions is recognized as an important element of P2P systems. It is, however, faced by the problems of how to stimulate reputation information sharing and honest recommendation elicitation. This paper presents ICRep − an incentive compatible reputation mechanism for P2P systems. ICRep has two unique features: (i) a recommender's credibility and level of confidence about the recommendation is considered in order to achieve a more accurate calculation of reputations and fair evaluation of recommendations. (ii) Incentive for participation and honest recommendation is implemented through a fair differential service mechanism. It relies on peer's level of participation and on the recommendation credibility. Theoretic analysis and simulation show that ICRep can help peers effectively detect dishonest recommendations in a variety of scenarios where more complex malicious strategies are introduced. Moreover, it can also stimulate peers to send sufficiently honest recommendations.

1 Introduction

P2P (Peer-to-Peer) technology has been widely used in file-sharing applications, distributed computing, e-market and information management [1]. The open and dynamic nature of the peer-to-peer networks is both beneficial and harmful to the working of the system. Problems such as free-riders and malicious users could lead to serious problems in the correct and useful functioning of the system. As shown by existing work, such as [2, 3, 4, 5, 6, 7], reputation-based trust management systems can successfully minimize the potential damages to a system by computing the trustworthiness of a certain peer from that peer's behavior history.

However, the design of a reputation mechanism is faced by a number of challenges, including: (i) the under-participation problem, i.e., peers do not share reputation information with peers. There are multiple reasons for peers to be reluctant to report evaluations or to do so honestly [8], peers may be reluctant to give positive

* Supported by National Basic Research Program of china under Grand (No.2005CB321800), National Natural Science Foundation of China under Grant (No.90412011, 60625203) and National High-Tech Research and Development Plan of China under Grant (2005AA112030).

S. Kim, M. Yung, and H.-W. Lee (Eds.): WISA 2007, LNCS 4867, pp. 371–386, 2007.

recommendations because they lift the reputation of the trustees, which are potential competitors; peers may be afraid of retaliation for negative feedbacks; last but not least, the (truthful) recommendations only benefit others; and (ii) the honest elicitation problem, i.e., peers may report false reputation information. A malicious peer may submit dishonest recommendations in order to boost the ratings of other malicious peers or bad-mouth non-malicious peers. The situation is made much worse when a group of malicious peers make collusive attempts to manipulate the ratings [9, 10]. The two above issues pose obstacles for designing a reputation mechanism that is capable of recognizing the real trustworthiness of a peer. Thus, it is necessary to consider how to make a reputation mechanism incentive-compatible, i.e. how to ensure that it is in the best interest of a rational peer to report reputation information truthfully and actively [8].

With these issues in mind, we present ICRep: an incentive compatible reputation mechanism for P2P systems. Within this system a peer can reason about trustworthiness of other peers based on the available local information which includes past interactions and recommendations received from others. Peers collaborate to establish trust among each other without using a priori information or a trusted third party. Our contributions include: (1) When evaluating a recommendation, recommender's trustworthiness and confidence about the information provided are considered. (2) Incentive for participation and honest recommendation is implemented through a fair differential service mechanism. (3) To assess the effectiveness of our approach, we have conducted extensive analytical and experimental evaluations. As a result, ICRep can help peers effectively detect dishonest recommendations in a variety of scenarios where more complex malicious strategies are introduced. Moreover, it can also stimulate peers to send sufficiently honest recommendations.

The reminder of this paper is structured as follows. In the second section, the related works are introduced; ICRep will be illuminated in the third section; and in the fourth section, a simulation about this reputation mechanism is laid out. Conclusions and future works are in the end.

2 Related Work

In this section, we first survey existing reputation mechanisms for P2P system, especially focusing on their handing of recommendations, then give an overview on truthtelling mechanisms that are not specific to P2P systems concludes.

Measures Against Dishonest Feedback in P2P Systems. Effective protection against unfair ratings is a basic requirement in order for a reputation system to be robust. The methods of avoiding bias from unfair ratings can broadly be grouped into two categories, endogenous and exogenous [11], as described below.

1. Endogenous Discounting of Unfair Ratings. This category covers methods that exclude or give low weight to presumed unfair ratings based on analysing and comparing the rating values themselves. The assumption is that unfair ratings can be recognised by their statistical properties only. Proposals in this category include Dellarocas [12] and Chen & Singh [13]. The implicit assumption underlying endogenous approaches is that the majority of recommendations are honest such that

they dominate the lies. Therefore, a recommendation that deviates from the majority is considered a lie. This assumption is not solid in open environments where recommendations can be very few in number, most of which can be untruthful.

2. Exogenous Discounting of Unfair Ratings. This category covers methods where external factors, such as recommendation credibility, are used to determine the weight given to ratings. In order to calculate the recommendation credibility, PeerTrust [5] proposes to use a personalized similarity measure (PSM for short) to rate the recommendation credibility of another node x through node n's personalized experience, the evaluation of recommendation credibility is depending on the common set of peers that have interacted with requestor and the recommendatory peers. As the increase of peers' quantity, the common set is always very small [14]. Eigentrust [3] considers the recommendation credibility as being equal to the service trust. This metric is not suitable in circumstances where a peer may maintain a good reputation by providing high quality services but send malicious feedbacks to its competitors. Research [21] presents a new recommendation credibility calculation model, but there exists unfairness to blameless peers. Research [6] proposes the weighted majority algorithm (WMA), the main idea is to assign and tune the weights so that the relative weight assigned to the successful advisors is increased and the relative weight assigned to the unsuccessful advisors is decreased. But, the approaches mentioned above don't consider more complex malicious strategies, for example, peers could try to gain trust from others by telling the truth over a sustained period of time and only then start lying, colluding peers could inflate reputation using unfair ratings flooding. Moreover, a peer may be penalized for an incorrect opinion that was based on a small number of interactions and/or a large variation in experience. Then, honest peers will be falsely classified as lying.

Truthtelling Mechanisms. In order to stimulate reputation information sharing and honest recommendation elicitation, Jurca and Faltings [8] propose an incentive compatible reputation mechanism to deal with inactivity and lies. A client buys a recommendation about a service provider from a special broker named R-nodes. After interacting with the provider, the client can sell its feedback to the same R-node, but gets paid only if its report coincides with the next client's report about the same service provider. One issue is that if the recommendation from an R-node is negative such that a client decides to avoid the service provider, the client will not have any feedback to sell. Or in the existence of opportunistic service providers that, for example, behave and misbehave alternatively, an honest feedback does not ensure payback. This opens up the possibility of an honest entity to have negative revenue and thus is unable to buy any recommendation. Besides, the effectiveness of their work depends largely on the integrity of R-nodes, which is assumed to be trusted a priori. To encourage the exchange of reputation information, Pinocchio [16] rewards participants that advertise their experience to others and uses a probabilistic honesty metric to detect dishonest users and deprive them of the rewards. The reward can be used to query the reputation of others. Pinocchio does not intend to protect against conspiracies or bad-mouthing. Research [17] proposes a mechanism for providing the incentives for reporting truthful feedback in a P2P system for exchanging services. Under their approach, both transacting peers submit ratings on performance of their mutual transaction. If these are in disagreement, then both transacting peers are punished, since such an occasion is a sign that one of them is lying. The severity of each peer's punishment is determined by his corresponding non-credibility metric; this is maintained by the mechanism and evolves according to the peer's record. But their proposal still avoids the fundamental problem that peers have no incentive to provide reputation feedback. Even peer can provide feedback, but, obviously, malicious peers may collude to weaken the mechanism (two colluding peers can provide the consistent rating for each other to increase their reputation value.). In contrast to these works, we propose a fully distributed mechanism based on local knowledge that provides malicious and non-participating entities an incentive for participation and honest behavior.

3   Incentive-Compatible Reputation Mechanism

We adopt the terminology witness to denote a peer solicited for providing its recommendation. Finding the right set of witnesses is a challenging problem since the reputation value depends on their recommendations. Our approach for collecting recommendations follows the solution proposed by Yu et al [6], in which recommendations are collected by constructing chains of referrals through which peers help one another to find witnesses. In order to stimulate peers to send sufficiently honest recommendations, we make some changes (see Sect. 3.3 for details).

In this section, we first introduce our trust valuation algorithm used by a peer to reason about trustworthiness of other peers based on the available local information which includes past interactions and recommendations received from witnesses. Then, we present our recommendation credibility calculation model, which can effectively detect dishonest recommendations in a variety of scenarios where more complex malicious strategies are introduced. Last, a simple yet effective trust information exchange protocol is proposed to stimulate sufficiently honest recommendations.

3.1   Trust Evaluation Algorithm

In respect that peers may change their behaviors over time, and the earlier ratings may have little impact on the calculation result, it is desirable to consider more recent ratings, that is, to consider only the most recent ratings, and discard those previous ones. Such a restriction is motivated by game theoretic results and empirical studies on ebay that show that only recent ratings are meaningful [15]. Thus, in the following, only interactions that occur within a sliding window of width D are considered. Moreover, by doing so, the storage costs of our reputation system are reasonable and justified given its significant benefits.

There are two kinds of trust relationships among peers, namely, direct trust and indirect trust [19]. The direct trust of peer i to peer j can be evaluated from the direct transaction feedback information between i and j. The indirect trust of i to j can be computed according to the recommendations of peers who have interacted with j. The overall trust of peer i to peer j is produced by combining these two trust value.

Direct Trust. Any peer in our system will maintain a direct trust table for all the other peers it has interactions with directly. Suppose peer i has some interactions with peer j during the last D time units, the entry for peer j is denoted as

$Exp(i, j) = \langle n, EXP\_LIST \rangle$, where n is the number of ratings, and EXP_LIST is an index in which these ratings are kept. The rating is in the form of r = (i, j, t, v). Here i and j are the peers that participated in interaction, and v is the rating peer i gave peer j. The range of v is [0, 1], where 0 and 1 means absolutely negative, absolutely positive respectively. t is the time stamp of the interaction. A rating is deleted from the direct trust table after an expiry period D.

From the direct trust table, the direct trust valuation of peer i to peer j at time t is represented as $<D_{ij}^t, \rho_{ij}^t>$, where D_{ij}^t is the direct trust value and ρ_{ij}^t is introduced to express the level of confidence about this direct trust value. Although there are a lot of elements that can be taken into account to calculate the level of confidence, we will focus on two of them: the number of experiences used to calculate the direct trust value and the variability of its rating values. D_{ij}^t is calculated by the following formula:

$$D_{ij}^t = \frac{\sum_{e \in Exp(i,j).EXP\_LIST} e.v * \alpha^{(t-e.t)}}{\sum_{e \in Exp(i,j).EXP\_LIST} \alpha^{(t-e.t)}} \quad (1)$$

Where e.v is the value of the rating e, and α is the decay factor in the range of (0, 1). A malicious node may strategically alter its behavior in a way that benefits itself such as starting to behave maliciously after it attains a high reputation. In order to cope with strategic altering behavior, the effect of an interaction on trust calculation must fade as new interactions happen [10]. This makes a peer to behave consistently. So, a peer with large number of good interactions can not disguise failures in future interactions for a long period of time.

Let CIN_{ij}^t be the level of confidence based on the number of ratings that have been taken into account in computing D_{ij}^t. As the number of these ratings ($Exp(i, j).n$) grows, the level of confidence increases until it reaches a defined threshold (denoted by m).

$$CIN_{ij}^t = \begin{cases} \dfrac{Exp(i, j).n}{m} & if \ \ Exp(i, j).n \le m \\ 1 & otherwise \end{cases} \quad (2)$$

Hence, the level of confidence CIN_{ij}^t increases from 0 to 1 when the number of ratings $Exp(i, j).n$ increases from 0 to m, and stays at 1 when $Exp(i, j).n$ exceeds m.

Let CID_{ij}^t be the level of confidence based on the variability of the rating values. CID_{ij}^t is calculated as the deviation in the ratings' values:

$$CID_{ij}^t = 1 - \frac{1}{2} * \frac{\sum_{e \in Exp(i,j).EXP\_LIST} \alpha^{(t-e.t)} * |e.v - D_{ij}^t|}{\sum_{e \in Exp(i,j).EXP\_LIST} \alpha^{(t-e.t)}} \quad (3)$$

This value goes from 0 to 1. A deviation value near 0 indicates a high variability in the rating values (this is, a low confidence on the direct trust value) while a value close to 1 indicates a low variability (this is, a high confidence on the direct trust value).

Finally, the level of confidence ρ_{ij}^t about the direct trust value D_{ij}^t combines the two reliability measures above:

$$\rho_{ij}^t = CIN_{ij}^t * CID_{ij}^t \tag{4}$$

Indirect trust. After collecting all recommendations about peer j using the rating discovery algorithm proposed by Yu et al [6], peer i can compute the indirect trust about peer j. Let $T_i = \{p_1, p_2, \ldots, p_{ti}\}$ be the set of trustworthy peers which reply the request. If $p_k \in T_i$ had at least one service interaction with p_j, it replies recommendation $< \mathrm{Re}\, c_{kj}^t, CI_{kj}^t >$ based on the local rating records with peer j. For an honest peer p, we have $\mathrm{Re}\, c_{kj}^t = D_{kj}^t$ and $CI_{kj}^t = \rho_{kj}^t$. The inclusion of level of confidence in the recommendation sent to the recommendation requestor allows the recommendation requestor to gauge the how much confidence the peer itself places in the recommendation it has sent. To minimize the negative influence of unreliable information, the recipient of these recommendations weighs them using this attached level of confidence and the credibility of the sender. If the level of confidence has a small value, the recommendation is considered weak and has less effect on the reputation calculation. Credibility is evaluated according to the past behavior of peers and reflects the confidence a peer has in the received recommendation. Credibility computation is presented in the next subsection.

The indirect trust value of peer j according peer i, denoted by R_{ij}^t, is given by the following formula:

$$R_{ij}^t = \frac{\sum_{p_k \in T_i} Cr_{ik}^t * CI_{kj}^t * \mathrm{Re}\, c_{kj}^t}{\sum_{p_k \in T_i} Cr_{ik}^t * CI_{kj}^t} \tag{5}$$

Where Cr_{ik}^t is the credibility of peer k according to peer i, CI_{kj}^t denotes the level of confidence about the recommendation value $\mathrm{Re}\, c_{ij}^t$. So peer i gives more weight to recommendations that are considered to be of a high confidence and that come from peers who are more credible.

Overall Trust. Base on the direct trust value and indirect trust value calculated above, the overall trust value of peer i to peer j's service (denoted by O_{ij}^t) is defined in formula (6).

$$O_{ij}^t = \lambda * D_{ij}^t + (1-\lambda) * R_{ij}^t \tag{6}$$

Where D_{ij}^t denotes the direct trust value of i to j, R_{ij}^t is the indirect trust of peer j according to peer i, the "self-confidence factor" is denoted by λ, which means that how a peer is confident to its evaluation of direct trust value. $\lambda = Exp(i, j).n / m$, $Exp(i, j).n$ is the number of the direct interactions considered, and m is the maximum number to be considered for a peer, and the upper limit for λ is 1.

3.2 Recommendation Credibility

Any peer in our system will also maintain a recommendation credibility table for all the other peers it has got recommendations from. Suppose peer i has got some recommendations with peer k during the last D time units, the entry for peer k is denoted as $REC(i, k) = \langle n, REC\_LIST \rangle$, where n is the number of credibility ratings, and REC_LIST is an index in which these credibility ratings are kept.

In more detail, after having an interaction with peer j, peer i gives its rating about j's service performance as V_{ij}. Now, if peer i received recommendation $<V_{kj}, CI_{kj}>$ from peer k, then the credibility rating value V_w for peer k about this recommendation is given in the following formula:

$$V_w = 1 - \left| V_{kj} - V_{ij} \right| \tag{7}$$

The credibility rating value V_w is set to be inversely proportional to the difference between a witness recommendation value and the actual performance (e.g. higher difference, lower credibility).

The rating about peer k's credibility — r = (i, k, t, V_w, CI_w) — is then appended to peer i's recommendation credibility table. t is the time of peer k providing peer i the recommendations about peer j, $CI_w = CI_{kj}$.

The recommendation credibility of peer i to peer j at time t is denoted by Cr_{ij}^t, it is a [0, 1]-valued function which represents the confidence formed by peer i about the truthfulness of j's recommendations. This function is local and is evaluated on the recent past behavior of both peer i and j. It is locally used to prevent a false credibility from being propagated within the network. The credibility trust value Cr_{ik}^t is calculated as follows:

$$Cr_{ik}^t = \begin{cases} \dfrac{\sum_{b \in Rec(i,k).REC\_LIST} e.V_w * \alpha^{t-e.t} * e.CI_w}{\sum_{b \in Rec(i,k).REC\_LIST} \alpha^{t-e.ts} * e.CI_w} & if \ \ Rec(i,k).REC\_LIST \neq \varnothing \\ c_0 & otherwise \end{cases} \tag{8}$$

Where α is the decay factor in the range of (0, 1) using equation (1), So, it can cope with more complex malicious strategies, for example, peers could try to gain trust from others by telling the truth over a sustained period of time and only then start lying. $e.CI_w$ is the level of confidence about the recommendation value, and

$e . V_w$ is the value of the credibility rating e. If no such ratings has been recorded, we will assign the default credibility trust value, denoted by c_0, to peer j.

Our credibility model considers the level of confidence about the recommendation value. Giving incorrect recommendation can decrease the recommendation credibility of a peer. So, a peer can lower the level of confidence for opinions about which it is not very sure, therefore risking less loss of credibility in case its judgment is incorrect. If a weak recommendation is inaccurate, the recommendation credibility does not diminish quickly. A peer can not be penalized as much for an incorrect opinion that was based on a small number of interactions and/or a large variation in experience. Then, honest peers will not be falsely classified as lying.

3.3   Simple Trust Information Exchange Protocol

The efficiency of the reputation mechanism fully depends on the number of received recommendations and the quality of each of them. In our reputation mechanism, incentive for participation and honest behavior is implemented through a fair differential service mechanism. The goal of service differentiation is not to provide hard guarantees but to create a distinction among the peers based on their contributions to the system. The basic idea is, the more the contribution, the better the relative service. In order to achieve this goal, first, we define two parameters that can be used to create service differentiation in trust information exchange, namely, level of participation, measuring if a peer is active in providing recommendations, and the recommendation credibility defined in section 3.2, assessing if a peer is providing honest recommendations. Second, based on the above two parameters, we propose a simple yet effective trust information exchange protocol using a "tit-for-tat" strategy, to elicit sufficient and honest participation. Based on the rating discovery algorithm proposed in [6], our protocol makes some changes to implement fair service differentiation.

We introduce the level of participation notion as the propensity of a peer for replying to a rating request. It is described by function l_{ij}^t such that l_{ij}^t represents the percentage of times j provided its recommendation to i's queries regarding other peers over the last D time units, with $l_{ij}^0 = 1$. We use a simple approach to calculate l_{ij}^t, which is calculated based on the number of recommendations provided by peer j to i during the last D time units. As the number of these recommendations (retrieved from the recommendation credibility table and denoted by I_{ij}^t) grows, the participation level increases until it reaches a defined threshold (denoted by I_{max}).

$$l_{ij}^t = \begin{cases} \dfrac{I_{ij}^t}{I_{max}} & if \quad I_{ij}^t \leq I_{max} \\ 1 & else \end{cases} \qquad (9)$$

Finally, to elicit sufficient and honest participation, we apply the tit-for-tat strategy during the collect phase, i.e., upon receipt of a rating request from peer j, with probability min(l_{ij}^t, Cr_{ij}^t) peer i provides its recommendation, otherwise it ignores the request. The more details are described in algorithm 1. Consequently, by not participating, requesting peers drive correct witnesses ignoring the request, which clearly makes their reputation mechanism useless. Hence there is a clear incentive for non participating peers to change their behavior. As for participating peers, when peer p receives a request from a requesting peer j then i satisfies j's request with probability Cr_{ij}^t. By doing so, i satisfies j's request if it estimates that j is trustworthy, otherwise it notifies j of its recent faulty behavior by simply ignores the request. As previously, by cheating, a malicious peer penalizes itself by pushing correct witnesses to ignore its request, leading to its effective isolation. We claim that this social exclusion-based strategy motivates j to reliably cooperate.

Algorithm 1: Trust Information Exchange Protocol

1: **upon** (receipt of a rw(j,s,ttl,t) message at peer i) **do**
2:   with (probability min(l_{ij}^t, $C r_{ij}^t$)) **do**
3:     **if** (i has interacted with s in the last D time units)
4:       $$rec_{is}^t \Leftarrow \langle D_{is}^t, \rho_{is}^t \rangle;$$
5:         send rec_{is}^t to j;
6:     **else**
7:         ignore message;
8:     **end if**
9:   **end do**
10: **if**(ttl≠0)
11:     A $\Leftarrow$ getRandomNeighbor(b); // b is branching factor;
12:     **For each** peer k in A **do**
13:         send a rw(j,s,ttl−1,t) message to peer k;
14:         send a witness(s,k,t) to j;
15:     **end do**
16:   **end if**
17: **end do**

---

4 Experimental Evaluation

We will now evaluate the effectiveness of ICRep by means of experiments. Our intention with this section is to confirm that ICRep is robust against the collusion and badmouthing attacks, that it can effectively detect dishonest recommendations in a variety of scenarios where more complex malicious strategies are introduced, and that it is incentive compatible.

4.1 Simulation Setup

In our simulation, we use the topology of the system and the deception models as Bin Yu's reputation mechanism [6]. In order to empirically evaluate our new reputation mechanism against more complex strategies, we make some changes. In our simulation experiment, the quality for a peer to be a SP (service provider) is independent of the quality for a peer to be a rater which provides recommendation. We first define the types of qualities of both SPs and raters used in our evaluation. Three types of behavior patterns of SPs are studied: good peers, fixed malicious peers and dynamic malicious peers. Good peers and fixed malicious peers provide good services and bad services without changing their qualities once the simulation starts respectively. Dynamic malicious peers alter their behavior strategically. The behaviors of peers as raters can be one of the three types: honest peers, fixed dishonest peers and dynamic dishonest peers. Honest and fixed dishonest peers provide correct and incorrect feedback without changing their patterns respectively. Dynamic dishonest peers provide correct feedback strategically, for example, the dynamic dishonest peers which tell the truth over a sustained period of time and only then start lying.

Our initial simulated community consists of N peers, N is set to be 128. The percentage of the bad SPs is denoted by pb, the percentage of the bad raters is denoted by pf. Table 1 summarizes the main parameters related to the community setting and trust computation. The default values for most experiments are listed. In the default setting, 50% malicious peers are fixed malicious service providers, 50% malicious peers are dynamic malicious service providers, with 50% probability giving service maliciously. The dishonest raters are fixed dishonest peers which give complementary rating and the level of confidence is set to 1. We divide the total simulation time into multiple simulation time units. In every time unit, each peer initiates a single request that can be satisfied by any of the potential service providers. Every peer issues one service request per simulation round. When a peer receives a

Table 1. Simulation Parameters

Parameter	Description	Default
N	number of peers in the community	128
pb	percentage of malicious peers in the community	80%
pf	percentage of dishonest raters in the community	80%
res	probability peer responds to a service request	0.1
λ	self-confidence factor	Dynamic
α	the decay factor	0.9
c_0	initial credibility value	0.5
TTL	bound of the referral chain's length	4
B	branching factor in rating discovery algorithm	2
ρ	exaggeration factor	1
D	sliding time window	10
I_{max}	the threshold number of recommendations	20
M	the threshold number of interactions in formula (2)	5

query, it answers it with *res* probability, or refers to other peers. *res* is set to 0.1 in the experiments. Two transaction settings are simulated, namely random setting and trusted setting. In random setting, peers randomly pick a peer from candidate peers who answer the service request to perform transactions. In trusted setting, peers select the reputable peer who has the maximal reputation value. The simulation program has been implemented in Java programming language.

4.2 Effectiveness of the Reputation Mechanism

This simulation evaluates the immunity of ICRep reputation mechanism to the collusion and badmouthing attacks. This set of experiments demonstrates the benefit of reputation mechanism we proposed, peers compare the trustworthiness of peers and choose the peer with the highest trust value to interact with. A transaction is considered successful if both of the participating peers are good peers, otherwise is a failure transaction. We define successful transaction rate as the ratio of the number of successful transactions over the total number of transactions in the community up to a certain time. A community with a higher transactions success rate has a higher productivity and a stronger level of security. The experiment is performed in both non-collusive setting and collusive setting. We show the benefit of our reputation mechanism compared to a community without any trust scheme. We also compare the performance of our scheme against the trust management scheme proposed by Bin Yu in [6].

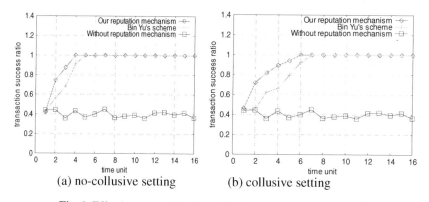

(a) no-collusive setting   (b) collusive setting

Fig. 1. Effectiveness against the collusion and badmouthing attacks

Figure 1 shows the rate of success transactions with respect to the number of time units in collusive and non-collusive setting. We can see an obvious gain of the transaction success rate in communities equipped with a trust mechanism either in non-collusive setting or in collusive setting. Both ICRep and Bin Yu's scheme can help peers avoid having interactions with malicious service providers in both settings, malicious peers are effectively identified even when they launch a collusion attack. This confirms that supporting trust is an important feature in a P2P community as peers are able to avoid untrustworthy peers. While in the collusive setting, dishonest peers' collusive behaviors hardly disturb honest peers' judgment. It needs more interactions to differentiate good peers from bad peers. Moreover, it is observed that Bin Yu's scheme needs more interactions to differentiate good peers from bad peers in both setting, so ICRep outperforms Bin Yu's reputation mechanism.

4.3 Predicting Honesty

We now define a useful metric to evaluate the performance of our proposed recommendation credibility model.

Definition 1. The average recommendation credibility of a witness W_j is

$$Cre_j = \frac{1}{N} \sum_{i=1}^{N} Cr_{ij} \qquad (9)$$

Where Cr_{ij} is the credibility value of witness W_j from peer Pi's acquaintance model [6], and N is the number of peers in whose acquaintance model W_j occurs.

- **Sensitiveness to Strategically Alter Behaviors of Peers**

The goal of this experiment is to show how credibility model we proposed works against strategic dynamic personality of peers. We simulated a community with all good peers but a dynamic malicious rater with dynamic personality. We simulated two changing patterns. First, peer could try to gain trust from others by telling the truth over a sustained period of time and only then start lying. Second, the peer is trying to improve its recommendation trust by telling the truth.

Figure 2 illustrates the changes of recommendation trust of both the peer who is milking its recommendation trust and the peer who is building its recommendation trust in the whole process. The results indicate that our reputation mechanisms is very sensitive to peers' strategically alter behaviors.

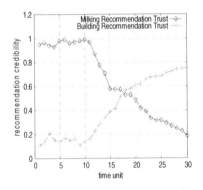
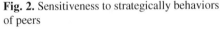
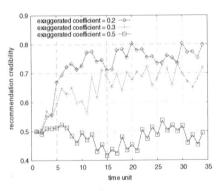

Fig. 2. Sensitiveness to strategically behaviors of peers

Fig. 3. Average recommendation credibility of alter witnesses for different exaggeration coefficients

- **Effects of Exaggeration Coefficient**

The present experiment studies the average recommendation credibility for such witnesses with different exaggeration coefficients [6]. Figure 3 shows the average recommendation credibility for witnesses with exaggerated negative ratings when exaggeration coefficient ρ is set to 0.2, 0.3, and 0.5, respectively. The results indicate that our approach can effectively detect witnesses lying to different degrees. For the witnesses with exaggerated negative ratings, their average recommendation credibility reaches to about 0.8, 0.7, and 0.5, respectively, after 10 time unit. So, the marginal lying cases can be detected.

- **Impact of Level of Confidence**

In the above two experiments, we only considered peers providing service with fixed personality. This experiment considers dynamic attack. An attacker, with x% probability, behaves maliciously by giving malicious service. In the other times, it behaves as a good peer. In this experiment, 80% peers are dynamic attackers with 50% probability giving service maliciously, other peers are good peer, and all the peers provide honest recommendations. The recommendation trust metrics has been observed to understand if honest peers assign fair recommendation trust values to each other.

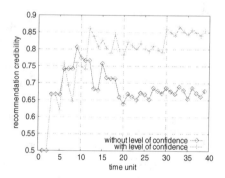

Fig. 4. Impact of level of confidence

Figure 4 shows the recommendation trust of honest peers in this setting, we can conclude that: without level of confidence, a peer may be penalized for an incorrect opinion that was based on a large variation in experience. Our approach allows a peer to determine the level of confidence about its recommendation. Giving incorrect recommendation can decrease the credibility of a peer. So, a peer can lower the level of confidence for opinions about which it is not very sure, therefore risking less loss of credibility in case its judgment is incorrect. If a weak recommendation is inaccurate, the recommendation credibility does not diminish quickly. A peer can not be penalized as much for an incorrect opinion that was based on a small number of interactions and/or a large variation in experience. Then, honest peers will not be falsely classified as lying.

4.4 Effectiveness of Incentive Mechanism

Since we have showed that our credibility model can help peers effectively detect inaccurate recommendations and generate a fair evaluation of recommendation in a variety of scenarios, we focus on the effectiveness of our incentive mechanism in stimulating active and truthful recommendations.

We investigate and compare the performance of the 4 different types of recommenders similar as [20]: active truth-teller, inactive truth-teller, active liar and inactive liar. Each type of entity has the same population, i.e., 32 each. Honest recommenders recommend with their direct trust regarding the trustee, while dishonest recommenders send back lies which are complementary to their direct trust and level of confidence are set to 1. Active recommenders offer recommendations with 90% probability, while inactive ones offer with 10% probability.

An active truth-teller can elicit more honest recommendations, which help him make right trust decisions regarding whether to interact with a peer or not. Therefore, first, we show the number of honest recommendations obtained by the four types of recommenders respectively. Second, we also display the number of wrong trust decisions made by different recommenders. When a peer fails to acquire any helpful recommendation, it has to base its trust decision solely on its direct experiences, which are not significant enough for a sound decision. Namely, the peer is subject to wrong trust decisions, which refer to either false positives (when an honest service provider is identified as an untrustworthy one) or false negatives (when a dishonest service provider is not identified as being so).

- **Elicited Honest Recommendations**

Figure 5 shows the number of elicited honest recommendations for different type of recommenders. We can see that at the beginning, very few recommendations are propagated and the four types of recommenders do not have much difference in the number of obtained honest recommendations. With the accumulation of experiences, the honest peers have enough experiences to recommend. Recommendation credibility is gradually recognized and the order of benefit (AT > IT > IL > AL) starts to be established, from simulation round 5 in Figure 5.

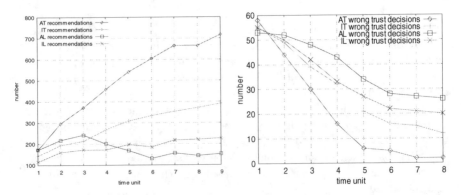

Fig. 5. Number of elicited honest recommendations   **Fig. 6.** Number of wrong trust decisions

- **Wrong Trust Decisions**

Figure 6 presents the number of wrong trust decisions made by the four types of recommenders. It can be seen that, with more accumulated experiences, every type of recommenders make less and less wrong trust decisions. Especially, with the help of honest recommendations, AT peers make the least number of wrong trust decisions and AL peers make the most (the order of AT > IT > IL > AL is enforced). Note that dishonest or inactive recommenders can also tell the honesty and activeness of a recommender using reputation system. However, they have access to less number of truthful recommendations for making the right trust decision.

From these two experiments, we can get a conclusion that ICRep provides peers with the right incentives for truthful reporting of feedback information, as sincere peers receive always more benefit from the peer-to-peer system than liar peers, whose benefit is very low. Thus, the incentive mechanism is effective.

5 Conclusions and Future Work

We present ICRep: an incentive compatible reputation system for P2P systems. Within this system a peer can reason about trustworthiness of other peers based on the available local information which includes past interactions and recommendations received from others. We focus on how to stimulate reputation information sharing and honest recommendation elicitation. Theoretic analysis and simulation show that ICRep can help peers effectively detect dishonest recommendations in a variety of scenarios where more complex malicious strategies are introduced. the precision of inaccuracy detection is improved (e.g. more marginal lying cases can be detected, and honest witnesses will not be falsely classified as lying because of an increased fluctuation in a provider's performance). Moreover, it can also stimulate peers to send sufficiently honest recommendations. The latter is realized by ensuring that active and honest recommenders, compared to inactive or dishonest ones, can receive always more benefit from the peer-to-peer system.

Interactions (service providing and recommendation providing) that occur within a sliding window of width D are considered, therefore, storage requirements for storing trust information are tolerable. The main overhead of our reputation mechanism comes from the reputation queries. In a service session, one provider is selected but reputation values about other providers are deleted. Thus, reputation values about unselected providers can be cached. Since a peer obtains more acquaintances with time, number of cache entries and cache hit ratio increase with time. By this way, we can reduce the overhead of our reputation mechanism comes from the reputation queries.

As a next step, we will be evaluating our reputation mechanism as applied to a peer-to-peer network.

References

1. Oram, A.: Peer to Peer: Harnessing the power of disruptive technologies (2001) ISBN 0-596-00110-X
2. Aberer, K., Despotovic, Z.: Managing Trust in a Peer-2-Peer Information System. In: The Proceedings of Intl. Conf. on Information and Knowledge Management (2001)

3. Kamwar, S.D., Schlosser, M.T., Garcia-Molina, H.: The Eigentrust Algorithm for Reputation Management in P2P Networks. In: The Proceedings of the twelfth international conference on World Wide Web, Budapest, Hungary (2003)

4. Damiani, E., De Capitani di Vimercati, S., Paraboschi, S., Samarati, P.: Managing and sharing servents' reputations in p2p systems. IEEE Transactions on Data and Knowledge Engineering 15(4), 840–854 (2003)

5. Xiong, L., Liu, L.: PeerTrust: Supporting reputation-based trust in peer-to-peer communities. IEEE Transactions on Data and Knowledge Engineering, Special Issue on Peer-to-Peer Based Data Management 16(7), 843–857 (2004)

6. Yu, B., Singh, M.P., Sycara, K.: Developing trust in large-scale peer-to-peer systems. In: Proceedings of First IEEE Symposium on Multi-Agent Security and Survivability (2004)

7. Chang, J., Wang, H., Yin, G.: A Time-Frame Based Trust Model for P2P Systems. In: Proceedings of 9th International Conference on Information Security Cryptology, Seoul, Korea (2006)

8. Jurca, R., Faltings, B.: An Incentive Compatible Reputation Mechanism. In: Proc. of the IEEE Conference on Electronic Commerce, Newport Beach, CA, USA (June 2003)

9. Lam, S.K., Riedl, J.: Shilling recommender systems for fun and profit. In: Proceedings of the 13th World Wide Web Conference (2004)

10. Srivatsa, M., Xiong, L., Liu, L.: TrustGuard: countering vulnerabilities in reputation management for decentralized overlay networks. In: WWW 2005, pp. 422–431 (2005)

11. Withby, A., Jøsang, A., Indulska, J.: Filtering Out Unfair Ratings in Bayesian Reputation Systems. In: Proceedings of the 7th Int. Workshop on Trust in Agent Societies (at AAMAS 2004), ACM, New York (2004)

12. Dellarocas, C.: Immunizing Online Reputation Reporting Systems Against Unfair Ratings and Discriminatory Behavior. In: ACM Conference on Electronic Commerce, pp. 150–157 (2000)

13. Chen, M., Singh, J.: Computing and Using Reputations for Internet Ratings. In: Proceedings of the Third ACM Conference on Electronic Commerce (EC 2001), ACM, New York (2001)

14. Feng, Z.J., Xian, T., Feng, G.J.: An Optimized Collaborative Filtering Recommendation Algorithm. Journal of Computer Research and Development 41(10) (2004) (in Chinese)

15. Dellarocas, C.: Reputation mechanisms. In: Hendershott, T. (ed.) Handbook on Information Systems and Economics, Elsevier, Amsterdam (2006)

16. Fernandes, A., Kotsovinos, E., Ostring, S., Dragovic, B.: Pinocchio: Incentives for honest participation in distributed trust management. In: Jensen, C., Poslad, S., Dimitrakos, T. (eds.) iTrust 2004. LNCS, vol. 2995, Springer, Heidelberg (2004)

17. Papaioannou, T.G., Stamoulis, G.D.: An Incentives' Mechanism Promoting Truthful Feedback in Peer-to-Peer Systems. In: Proceedings of the 5th IEEE/ACM International Symposium in Cluster Computing and the Grid, Cardi, UK (2005)

18. Dellarocas, C.: Reputation mechanisms. In: Hendershott, T. (ed.) Handbook on Information Systems and Economics, Elsevier, Amsterdam (2006)

19. Beth, T., Borcherding, M., Klein, B.: Valuation of Trust in Open Networks. In: Gollmann, D. (ed.) Computer Security - ESORICS 1994. LNCS, vol. 875, Springer, Heidelberg (1994)

20. Liu, J., Issarny, V.: An incentive compatible reputation mechanism for ubiquitous computing environments. In: PST 2006. International Conference on Privacy, Security and Trust, Toronto, Canada (2006)

21. Huynh, T.D., Jennings, N.R., Shadbolt, N.: On handling inaccurate witness reports. In: Proc. 8th International Workshop on Trust in Agent Societies, Utrecht, The Netherlands, pp. 63–77 (2005)

Author Index

Lecture Notes in Computer Science

Sublibrary 4: Security and Cryptology

Vol. 4332: A. Bagchi, V. Atluri (Eds.), Information Systems Security. XV, 382 pages. 2006.

Vol. 4329: R. Barua, T. Lange (Eds.), Progress in Cryptology - INDOCRYPT 2006. X, 454 pages. 2006.

Vol. 4318: H. Lipmaa, M. Yung, D. Lin (Eds.), Information Security and Cryptology. XI, 305 pages. 2006.

Vol. 4307: P. Ning, S. Qing, N. Li (Eds.), Information and Communications Security. XIV, 558 pages. 2006.

Vol. 4301: D. Pointcheval, Y. Mu, K. Chen (Eds.), Cryptology and Network Security. XIII, 381 pages. 2006.

Vol. 4300: Y.Q. Shi (Ed.), Transactions on Data Hiding and Multimedia Security I. IX, 139 pages. 2006.

Vol. 4298: J.K. Lee, O. Yi, M. Yung (Eds.), Information Security Applications. XIV, 406 pages. 2007.

Vol. 4296: M.S. Rhee, B. Lee (Eds.), Information Security and Cryptology – ICISC 2006. XIII, 358 pages. 2006.

Vol. 4284: X. Lai, K. Chen (Eds.), Advances in Cryptology – ASIACRYPT 2006. XIV, 468 pages. 2006.

Vol. 4283: Y.Q. Shi, B. Jeon (Eds.), Digital Watermarking. XII, 474 pages. 2006.

Vol. 4266: H. Yoshiura, K. Sakurai, K. Rannenberg, Y. Murayama, S.-i. Kawamura (Eds.), Advances in Information and Computer Security. XIII, 438 pages. 2006.

Vol. 4258: G. Danezis, P. Golle (Eds.), Privacy Enhancing Technologies. VIII, 431 pages. 2006.

Vol. 4249: L. Goubin, M. Matsui (Eds.), Cryptographic Hardware and Embedded Systems - CHES 2006. XII, 462 pages. 2006.

Vol. 4237: H. Leitold, E.P. Markatos (Eds.), Communications and Multimedia Security. XII, 253 pages. 2006.

Vol. 4236: L. Breveglieri, I. Koren, D. Naccache, J.-P. Seifert (Eds.), Fault Diagnosis and Tolerance in Cryptography. XIII, 253 pages. 2006.

Vol. 4219: D. Zamboni, C. Krügel (Eds.), Recent Advances in Intrusion Detection. XII, 331 pages. 2006.

Vol. 4189: D. Gollmann, J. Meier, A. Sabelfeld (Eds.), Computer Security – ESORICS 2006. XI, 548 pages. 2006.

Vol. 4176: S.K. Katsikas, J. López, M. Backes, S. Gritzalis, B. Preneel (Eds.), Information Security. XIV, 548 pages. 2006.

Vol. 4117: C. Dwork (Ed.), Advances in Cryptology - CRYPTO 2006. XIII, 621 pages. 2006.

Vol. 4116: R. De Prisco, M. Yung (Eds.), Security and Cryptography for Networks. XI, 366 pages. 2006.

Vol. 4107: G. Di Crescenzo, A. Rubin (Eds.), Financial Cryptography and Data Security. XI, 327 pages. 2006.

Vol. 4083: S. Fischer-Hübner, S. Furnell, C. Lambrinoudakis (Eds.), Trust and Privacy in Digital Business. XIII, 243 pages. 2006.

Vol. 4064: R. Büschkes, P. Laskov (Eds.), Detection of Intrusions and Malware & Vulnerability Assessment. X, 195 pages. 2006.

Vol. 4058: L.M. Batten, R. Safavi-Naini (Eds.), Information Security and Privacy. XII, 446 pages. 2006.

Vol. 4047: M.J.B. Robshaw (Ed.), Fast Software Encryption. XI, 434 pages. 2006.

Vol. 4043: A.S. Atzeni, A. Lioy (Eds.), Public Key Infrastructure. XI, 261 pages. 2006.

Vol. 4004: S. Vaudenay (Ed.), Advances in Cryptology - EUROCRYPT 2006. XIV, 613 pages. 2006.

Vol. 3995: G. Müller (Ed.), Emerging Trends in Information and Communication Security. XX, 524 pages. 2006.

Vol. 3989: J. Zhou, M. Yung, F. Bao (Eds.), Applied Cryptography and Network Security. XIV, 488 pages. 2006.

Vol. 3969: Ø. Ytrehus (Ed.), Coding and Cryptography. XI, 443 pages. 2006.

Vol. 3958: M. Yung, Y. Dodis, A. Kiayias, T.G. Malkin (Eds.), Public Key Cryptography - PKC 2006. XIV, 543 pages. 2006.

Vol. 3957: B. Christianson, B. Crispo, J.A. Malcolm, M. Roe (Eds.), Security Protocols. IX, 325 pages. 2006.

Vol. 3956: G. Barthe, B. Grégoire, M. Huisman, J.-L. Lanet (Eds.), Construction and Analysis of Safe, Secure, and Interoperable Smart Devices. IX, 175 pages. 2006.

Vol. 3935: D.H. Won, S. Kim (Eds.), Information Security and Cryptology - ICISC 2005. XIV, 458 pages. 2006.

Vol. 3934: J.A. Clark, R.F. Paige, F.A.C. Polack, P.J. Brooke (Eds.), Security in Pervasive Computing. X, 243 pages. 2006.

Vol. 3928: J. Domingo-Ferrer, J. Posegga, D. Schreckling (Eds.), Smart Card Research and Advanced Applications. XI, 359 pages. 2006.

Vol. 3919: R. Safavi-Naini, M. Yung (Eds.), Digital Rights Management. XI, 357 pages. 2006.

Vol. 3903: K. Chen, R. Deng, X. Lai, J. Zhou (Eds.), Information Security Practice and Experience. XIV, 392 pages. 2006.

Vol. 3897: B. Preneel, S. Tavares (Eds.), Selected Areas in Cryptography. XI, 371 pages. 2006.

Vol. 3876: S. Halevi, T. Rabin (Eds.), Theory of Cryptography. XI, 617 pages. 2006.

Vol. 3866: T. Dimitrakos, F. Martinelli, P.Y.A. Ryan, S. Schneider (Eds.), Formal Aspects in Security and Trust. X, 259 pages. 2006.

Vol. 3860: D. Pointcheval (Ed.), Topics in Cryptology – CT-RSA 2006. XI, 365 pages. 2006.

Vol. 3858: A. Valdes, D. Zamboni (Eds.), Recent Advances in Intrusion Detection. X, 351 pages. 2006.

Vol. 3856: G. Danezis, D. Martin (Eds.), Privacy Enhancing Technologies. VIII, 273 pages. 2006.

Vol. 3786: J.-S. Song, T. Kwon, M. Yung (Eds.), Information Security Applications. XI, 378 pages. 2006.

Vol. 3108: H. Wang, J. Pieprzyk, V. Varadharajan (Eds.), Information Security and Privacy. XII, 494 pages. 2004.

Vol. 2951: M. Naor (Ed.), Theory of Cryptography. XI, 523 pages. 2004.

Vol. 2742: R.N. Wright (Ed.), Financial Cryptography. VIII, 321 pages. 2003.